THE SUP...
CONFRON... ...RTION

THE SUPREME COURT

CONFRONTS

ABORTION

The Briefs, Argument, and
Decision in
Planned Parenthood *v.* Casey

EDITED AND WITH AN INTRODUCTION
BY LEON FRIEDMAN

Farrar, Straus and Giroux
New York

Library of Congress Cataloging-in-Publication Data
Planned Parenthood of Southeastern Pennsylvania.
The Supreme Court confronts abortion : the briefs, argument, and
decision in Planned Parenthood v. Casey / edited and with an
introduction by Leon Friedman.—1st ed.
p.   cm.
Proceedings in the case of Planned Parenthood of Southeastern
Pennsylvania v. Robert P. Casey, decided by the U.S. Supreme Court
in June 1992.
Includes index.
1. Planned Parenthood of Southeastern Pennsylvania—Trials,
litigation, etc.   2. Casey, Robert P. (Robert Patrick)—
Trials, litigations, etc.   3. Trials (Abortion)—Washington (D.C.).
4. Abortion—Law and legislation—United States.   5. Abortion—Law
and legislation—Pennsylvania.   I. Casey, Robert P. (Robert
Patrick).   II. Friedman, Leon.   III. United States.
Supreme Court.   IV. Title.
KF228.P5P5   1993   344.73'04192—dc20 [347.3044192] 93-10947 CIP

CONTENTS

THE SUPREME COURT DECISION, JUNE 29, 1992

APPENDIX

The Supreme Court opinions follow the text in the preliminary version issued by the Court's printer in 1992. Small changes have been made in the transcription of the oral arguments before the Court, and in the briefs, for clarity and for consistency of editorial style. Cross-references to material that this book includes are changed throughout to cite the page numbers here.

THE SUPREME COURT
CONFRONTS ABORTION

INTRODUCTION

This book contains the basic legal documents in one of the most important constitutional confrontations in recent times. On June 29, 1992, the Supreme Court handed down its decision in *Planned Parenthood* v. *Casey*. On its face, the case upheld in part and struck down in part a Pennsylvania law that restricted a woman's right to an abortion. To that extent, the case was merely one of fifteen decisions issued by the Court since *Roe* v. *Wade* was decided in 1973 that dealt with the legal issues surrounding abortion. (A list of the cases and their general subject matter appears at the end of this introduction.) But the case was not only the last decision in this series. It resolved some key issues that had confounded and divided our society since the *Roe* case was decided. Like it or not, the decision fixes the *constitutional* landscape on abortion for years, if not decades, to come.

The case is important for at least three reasons:

1. The decision resolved, for the foreseeable future, one of the most contentious issues in modern American society, namely, whether a woman's right to an abortion would continue to be given any constitutional protection. The Court held that the basic constitutional right to an abortion would continue to be recognized.

2. The decision established the fundamental legal rules on how far the states can go in limiting that right. By holding that only laws that imposed an "undue burden" on the right were unconstitutional and could be struck down, the Court greatly expanded the states' ability to regulate both medical and nonmedical elements of a woman's right to choose whether to terminate her pregnancy.

3. The various opinions issued by the Justices presented a theory of constitutional adjudication that had not previously been articulated by members of the Court—what the Supreme Court's role is in our constitutional scheme, when it should overrule laws passed by a vote of the majority, and when it is appropriate for the Court to change its mind and overrule precedents.

In 1973, the Supreme Court first held, in *Roe* v. *Wade*, 410 U.S. 113 (1973), that the right to "liberty" in the Fourteenth Amendment encompassed certain important rights to privacy, including the right to make personal, autonomous decisions about one's own body. In particular, such liberty and privacy covered a woman's right to make choices about reproduction, including her right to choose to have an abortion. Thus the Court struck down as unconstitutional the laws of over thirty states that made criminal the administering of an abortion (except where the life or health of the mother was in danger) and punished both the woman who requested one and the doctor who performed the operation.

The Supreme Court established a trimester system for examining laws on abortion. It held that the right to an abortion was almost absolute in the first trimester of pregnancy. Only if the state could show a "compelling" reason in that period, could it take any steps to regulate the procedure. In the first three months, the Court said, the "physician in consultation with his [or her] patient, is free to determine, without regulation by the State, that . . . the patient's pregnancy should be terminated." 410 U.S. at 163.

After the first trimester and before viability of the fetus, "a State may regulate the abortion procedure to the extent the regulation reasonably relates to the preservation and protection of maternal health." 410 U.S. at 163. Such restrictions might include establishing medical qualifications for those involved in the operation, insuring that proper medical procedures were followed, and determining the facility where the procedure may be performed. In the third trimester, after the sixth month of pregnancy, the state may prohibit the procedure altogether since it has the right to protect the potential for life in a viable fetus.

On the same day that the Court decided *Roe* v. *Wade*, the Supreme Court also decided *Doe* v. *Bolton*, 410 U.S. 179 (1973). That case struck down three restrictions that the State of Georgia had imposed before a doctor could perform an abortion in that state: (1) abortions could be performed only in an accredited hospital; (2) a hospital abortion committee must approve the procedure; (3) two other doctors must acquiesce in the decision. All three restrictions were found to be improper since they were not *medically* necessary to preserve the health of the patient.

The two cases set the blueprint for the constitutional dispute that would continue for the next nineteen years. Even if the basic right to an abortion was recognized and even though no criminal sanctions could be imposed if a pregnancy was terminated, what steps could the states take to "reasonably" regulate the procedure in order to "preserve" and "protect[] . . . maternal health"? If the states could not place barriers in the way of an abortion, must they affirmatively take steps to facilitate the operation? Did government have to pay for an abortion if it paid for other medical and health care for the poor? Did it have to provide information about an abortion, even if it did not pay for one itself? What rights did other family members have when an abortion was contemplated—in particular, spouses, fathers, or parents? Were there nonmedical aspects of the abortion decision which the state could insist upon—psychological counseling, informed consent, advice about adoption, or a waiting period before the doctor could operate?

The original *Roe v. Wade* decision was adopted by a vote of seven Justices to two. That lopsided vote suggested that the basic constitutional right was firmly fixed and there was little likelihood of any changes in the rule for the foreseeable future. Most observers thought that there might be some tinkering at the edges and some narrow redefining of what state regulations were permissible and which were not. But the definitiveness of the decision in favor of the right seemed to make it unlikely that *Roe v. Wade* could be overruled or restricted in any significant way.

But abortion was not just another question on which the Supreme Court had made a constitutional ruling. Many members of the public considered it the most momentous and pivotal social issue dividing American society, involving the basic question of when life began, what right women had over their own bodies and their own fate, and what power other members of the family had over that choice. Those who considered abortion the taking of human life would not stand by and let matters rest. They would come back again and again to attack *Roe v. Wade* either directly or indirectly—by putting pressure on state legislatures to pass laws that would impose financial and medical obstacles on abortions. Women who considered the right to an abortion part of their basic human destiny would not yield in their insistence that the right be preserved in all respects and that no financial or medical barrier be placed in the way of that choice.

In addition, the composition of the Court would change from 1973 when *Roe* was decided and the political changes would place the Presidency in the hands of those who opposed abortion (Presidents Reagan and Bush) and were therefore in a position to select new Justices who would vote to restrict *Roe*.

The first change in the makeup of the Court occurred when Justice William O. Douglas, a strong supporter of the abortion right, resigned in 1975. He was replaced by Justice John Paul Stevens, who also supported the right. But by the late 1970s Chief Justice Warren Earl Burger had changed his position on certain abortion questions and began to vote in favor of state restrictions. In 1981, Justice Potter Stewart (another pro-choice vote) resigned and was replaced by the first woman Justice, Sandra Day O'Connor. In her first abortion case, she voted (in dissent) in 1983 to uphold a very restrictive abortion law from Akron. Thus, the strong 7 to 2 vote in *Roe* v. *Wade* in 1973 was reduced to a shaky 5 to 4 vote by 1983, with Justices Brennan, Blackmun, Marshall, Powell, and Stevens generally in support of the right and Chief Justice Burger and Justices Rehnquist, White, and O'Connor opposed.

In the context of shifting votes in the Supreme Court, the legal battle continued through the 1970s and early 1980s. State and local governments in states or cities where the anti-abortion movement was strongest—particularly in the States of Missouri and Pennsylvania, where many of the later cases originated—would pass law after law dealing with abortion. Some laws were passed in an effort to deal with the thorny medical and ethical issues surrounding the procedure, others with the avowed purpose of making abortion as difficult as possible.

At first, the Supreme Court rejected almost every effort to inhibit the procedure. Thus, in 1976 the Court decided *Planned Parenthood of Central Missouri* v. *Danforth*, 428 U.S.

52 (1976), in which it struck down most of the provisions of a Missouri law that required spousal and parental consent for an abortion and that prohibited the use of saline amniocentesis after the first twelve weeks of pregnancy. The latter requirement was not medically necessary, according to the Court, but amounted to an "unreasonable or arbitrary regulation designed to inhibit . . . the vast majority of abortions after the first 12 weeks." 428 U.S. at 79. The law also required doctors to use their professional skill and care "to preserve the life and health of a fetus." The Court struck down that provision also, since it did not distinguish between saving a fetus before viability and trying to save its life afterwards. Finally the Court held that it was unconstitutional to give a parent an absolute veto over a minor's decision to have an abortion.

Three years later, in *Colautti v. Franklin*, 439 U.S. 379 (1979), the Court examined a Pennsylvania law (passed in 1974) that once again tried to impose a duty on doctors to preserve the life of a fetus. The law declared that a doctor must take professional care to save a fetus if there is "sufficient reason to believe that the fetus may be viable." This provision did not give the doctor sufficient guidance as to when the law might take effect since it was based not only on his or her best medical judgment, but on what others might believe was the point of viability. The decision was handed down by a 6 to 3 vote, with Chief Justice Burger voting in dissent to sustain the law although he had voted with the majority in the *Roe* case.

The Supreme Court continued to examine the question of parental consent when a minor sought to obtain an abortion. In *Bellotti v. Baird*, 443 U.S. 622 (1979), the Court held that a Massachusetts law that required every child under eighteen years of age to seek her parent's consent before applying to a court for "judicial bypass" (that is, a court order approving the operation) was unconstitutional. The state must provide for an alternative in which she can show a court that she is mature enough to make the decision on her own, or, even if she is not mature enough, that an abortion is in fact in her best interests. But two years later, in *H.L. v. Matheson*, 450 U.S. 398 (1981), the Court upheld a Utah law that required doctors to notify parents of an "unemancipated minor girl living with and dependent on her parents" that the child was seeking an abortion, although the parents could not veto the decision if the child insisted on going forward. (The decision was based upon technical grounds that the child involved simply alleged in her lawsuit that she did not want to notify her parents, without indicating why this would be a burden on her rights.)

Another setback for those defending the abortion right occurred in the area of government funding for abortion. Even if the government could not criminalize or burden the right to an abortion, did it have to facilitate the right by providing funds or facilities for the medical procedure for those who could not afford the operation? In three cases decided in the late 1970s and early 1980s, the Court held that the Constitution did not mandate that government pay for the procedure.

Thus in *Beal* v. *Doe*, 432 U.S. 432 (1977), by a 6 to 3 vote, the Court upheld a Pennsylvania Medicaid regulation that denied funds for nontherapeutic abortions. Similarly, in *Maher* v. *Roe*, 432 U.S. 464 (1977), the Court upheld a Connecticut regulation that denied funds for such abortions, even though the State paid medical expenses incident to childbirth.

Three years later, in *Harris* v. *McRae*, 448 U.S. (1980), the Court upheld the constitutionality of the Hyde Amendment to the federal Medicaid Act (named after its sponsor Representative Henry Hyde) which denied federal Medicaid funds for an abortion except where the life of the mother would be endangered or where a woman was pregnant as a result of rape or incest and the incident had been promptly reported to a law enforcement officer or the public health service.

In 1983, the Court examined—and struck down—an ordinance passed by the City of Akron that placed no less than six unconstitutional restrictions on the right to an abortion (*Akron* v. *Akron Center for Reproductive Health, Inc.*, 462 U.S. 416 (1983)): (1) a requirement that all second-trimester abortions be performed in a hospital; (2) a parental consent requirement affecting girls under fifteen years of age who must obtain parental consent or judicial approval; (3) an informed consent requirement that mandated that doctors tell each woman of the status of her pregnancy, the development of her fetus, the physical and emotional complications that might result from the abortion, and the availability of agencies to help her on adoption; (4) a requirement that the attending physician, as opposed to other nonmedical counseling personnel, must inform the patient of all the medical risks; (5) a twenty-four-hour waiting period before an abortion can be secured; (6) a requirement that the fetus must be disposed of in a "humane" manner. None of these restrictions were upheld.

The *Akron* case was the first abortion case in which Justice Sandra Day O'Connor participated. She had been appointed in 1981 to succeed Justice Potter Stewart, a strong protector of the abortion right. She dissented in the *Akron* case, along with Justices Rehnquist and White. She suggested in her dissenting opinion that only those restrictions on abortion be struck down that "unduly burden" the right to an abortion. She found none of the restrictions sufficiently burdensome to qualify for the test and would have upheld every one.

On the same day that the *Akron* case was decided—June 15, 1983—the Court decided two companion cases, *Planned Parenthood* v. *Ashcroft*, 462 U.S. 476 (1983), and *Simopoulos* v. *Virginia*, 462 U.S. 506 (1983). In both cases, the Court upheld at least some of the state laws involved: in the *Ashcroft* case, the Court upheld by a 5 to 4 vote a Missouri law that required a pathology report after an abortion and also required the presence of a second physician during an abortion after viability. In both cases, Justice Powell, who generally supported the abortion right, voted to uphold the state restrictions. In the *Simopoulos* case, the Court found nothing wrong in a state law that required abortions after twelve weeks to be held in hospitals or outpatient clinics.

By the late 1980s, the political and legal fight over abortion had become even more contentious. The close vote in the Court in the 1983 cases led some states where anti-abortion sentiment was strong to test the waters still further. Pennsylvania had passed a new law tracking many of the restrictions in the Akron law, including the requirement that a woman be informed of seven explicit items of information about the fetus. The law also required that a woman be told about "detrimental physical and psychological effects" and all "particular medical risks" of the procedure, as well as the facts that state assistance would be available to her if she had the child and that the father was responsible for financial assistance. Various reporting requirements were also imposed on the doctors. In addition, a doctor was required to use the abortion technique that would provide the best opportunity for the unborn child to be aborted alive and also required a second physician to be present during an abortion to provide immediate medical care for the child. By a 5 to 4 vote, those restrictions were struck down in *Thornburgh* v. *American College of Obstetricians*, 476 U.S. 747 (1986). (But some of these same restrictions were upheld in the *Casey* case six years later.)

In 1986, Chief Justice Burger resigned and was replaced by Justice Rehnquist in the center position. Justice Antonin Scalia, a respected conservative who was known to oppose abortion, replaced Rehnquist. That change in court personnel did not change the votes on abortion, since Chief Justice Burger had already switched his basic position (he had originally voted in favor of *Roe*) and was voting to uphold the laws restricting abortion.

But a year later, in 1987, Justice Lewis Powell resigned. On the face of the matter, the Court was now split 4 to 4 on upholding the right to an abortion—Justices Blackmun, Brennan, Marshall, and Stevens in favor and Justices Rehnquist, White, O'Connor, and Scalia opposed. It was generally believed that the new Justice would cast the deciding vote.

To replace Justice Powell, President Ronald Reagan then nominated Judge Robert Bork, who was known to oppose any recognition of a right to privacy on which the right to an abortion rested. The bruising confirmation fight before the Senate in the summer and fall of 1987 centered on how the Bork nomination would affect the continued recognition of the right. There is little doubt that Bork's unequivocal opposition to abortion and to any right to privacy generally helped to doom his approval by the Senate.

A new nominee, Judge Douglas Ginsberg, withdrew from consideration when it was learned he had smoked marijuana with his students at parties at the Harvard Law School. Finally, late in 1987 the Senate approved Justice Anthony Kennedy, whose views on abortion were unknown.

The next critical case was decided in 1989, *Webster* v. *Reproductive Health Services*, 492 U.S. 490 (1989), another

5 to 4 vote. The holding was a narrow one, namely, that a Missouri law that prohibited the use of government facilities or hospitals for abortions was valid. But Justice Kennedy, voicing for the first time his views on abortion, voted in favor of the law along with Chief Justice Rehnquist and Justice White. Justice O'Connor also supported the law. More significantly, Justice Scalia explicitly voted to overrule *Roe* v. *Wade*, insisting that the case was wrongly decided and the entire matter should be left to the political process to determine.

In 1990, the Court returned to the issue of parental consent. In *Hodgson* v. *Minnesota*, 497 U.S. 417 (1990), the Court upheld in part and struck down in part a Minnesota law that required a minor to give both parents at least forty-eight hours' notice before she could have an abortion. The Court held that the two-parent notification requirement was unconstitutional, but the condition that the child notify one parent within that period was permissible. In *Ohio* v. *Akron Center for Reproductive Health (Akron II)*, 497 U.S. 502 (1990), it upheld an Ohio law containing a requirement that one parent be notified twenty-four hours before the operation and that also contained a judicial bypass procedure.

For the first time since she was appointed to the Court, Justice O'Connor now voted to strike down a state law on the grounds that it unduly burdened the constitutional right to an abortion, in this instance by the requirement that both parents be notified. On the other hand, Justice Anthony Kennedy voted to uphold all parts of the law and indeed wrote the principal dissenting opinion, joined by Chief Justice Rehnquist and Justices Scalia and White.

In 1990, Justice Brennan resigned and another Supreme Court nomination centered on the candidate's views on abortion. Justice David Souter was questioned closely about his views on abortion but said little that would indicate how he would vote. A year later, in 1991, Justice Thurgood Marshall, another firm vote for abortion, resigned. He was replaced by Justice Clarence Thomas, who claimed that he had never even discussed *Roe* v. *Wade* at any point in his legal career, and therefore had no firm opinion on the issue.

Thus, by the winter of 1991 the outlook for continued

recognition of the abortion right was doubtful. There were only two Justices still on the Court who firmly supported abortion—Justices Blackmun and Stevens. There were three who were firmly opposed to the right—Justices Rehnquist, White (who dissented in *Roe*), and Scalia (who was prepared to overrule the *Roe* decision). Justice O'Connor would vote to strike down a state law only if it "unduly burdened" the right. Justice Kennedy, based on his votes in the *Webster* and *Hodgson* cases, seemed to be in the anti-abortion camp. The new Justices, Souter and Thomas, had not voted on the issue, but neither one seemed likely to have the same pro-choice views as the Justices they replaced.

Indeed, the legal groups supporting the right to an abortion acted as if they expected to lose the next big fight in the Supreme Court. The Pennsylvania law examined in the *Casey* case had been found invalid by the trial court in 1990. On appeal to the Court of Appeals, that court upheld part of the law and struck down other parts in a decision handed down on October 21, 1991. The lawyers could have delayed seeking an appeal to the Supreme Court for ninety days, until late January 1992, so that even if the Supreme Court decided to take the cases for review, it would not hear argument until after the 1992 Presidential elections. (After a petition for review is filed, the opposing party has thirty days to answer and the Court takes another thirty days to consider the matter. Cases accepted for review after the end of January of any given year are generally not heard or decided until the following year.)

But the lawyers attacking the law took extraordinary steps to bring the case to the Court as quickly as they could, filing their petition for review on November 7, 1991, less than three weeks after the Court of Appeals decision was handed down. This would allow the case to be accepted for review in January, which meant it would be argued in April 1992 and decided by June 1992, in time to have an impact on the coming elections.

The lawyers behaved as if they expected the Court to overrule *Roe* v. *Wade*. They thought that such a decision, taking away a woman's basic right to control her reproductive freedom, would energize the women in the country to take their fate into their own hands. They would then use their political power to reestablish their rights by voting for candidates that would protect their control over their bodies.

The Pennsylvania Attorney General went along with this strategy, and he filed his own petition for review in December 1991, also well within the time limits. On January 21, 1992, the Supreme Court accepted the *Casey* case for review, in time for the case to be heard and decided by the summer of 1992.

As occurred in every one of the abortion cases that came before the Supreme Court, a wide variety of interest groups took steps to present their point of view to the Court. These so-called *amici curiae*—"friends of the court"—try to present facts, arguments, or theories that the main parties to the case might not offer. Since the question of whether a woman has the right to an abortion affects virtually every interest group in the country to which women may belong, as well as presenting the most difficult religious and governmental problems, it is no surprise that dozens of groups asked for permission to present their views in the *Casey* case.

We include in this collection the briefs submitted by three *amici* (out of eleven) supporting the right to an abortion and three briefs (out of twenty-three) opposing the right, including the brief submitted by the Solicitor General on behalf of the Bush Administration, which asked the Court to overrule the *Roe* decision. (A list of all the groups submitting briefs is contained in the Appendix to this volume.)

The case was argued before the Supreme Court on April 22, 1992. The lawyers attacking the Pennsylvania law were chiefly concerned with the standard of review that the Court would apply to examine the prohibitions contained in the Pennsylvania law. As Kathryn Kolbert, the Planned Parenthood lawyer, argued: "The central question in the case is what is the standard that this Court uses to evaluate the restrictions that are at issue" [315]. If the right to an abortion is fundamental, part of the liberty contained in the Due Process Clause like the right to free speech, then any restrictions on that right should be subject to what is called "strict scrutiny," that is, they must be closely examined and justified by a compelling governmental reason on the other side.

Two of the restrictions in the Pennsylvania law, the twenty-four-hour waiting period and the counseling requirement, had been examined in previous decisions of the Court, in the *Thornburgh* case decided in 1986 and in the *Akron* case in 1983. If the Court was to change its mind about these types of restrictions, it could do so only if it was prepared to overrule *Roe* or to establish a new, more lenient standard by which these restrictions would be weighed, which would seriously erode the protections of *Roe*. Ms. Kolbert argued: "If this Court were to change the standard of strict scrutiny, which has been the central core of that holding . . . that will undercut the holdings of this Court and effectively overrule *Roe* v. *Wade*" [318]. That is why Ms. Kolbert put her emphasis on the legal standard.

The decision was rendered on June 29, 1992. It is safe to say that the final decision was almost totally unexpected.

The big surprise was the "joint opinion" of Justices O'Connor, Kennedy, and Souter, which decided the outcome of the case. Justices O'Connor and Kennedy had already voted to uphold state restrictions on the abortion right, and the only question raised in their prior opinions was how far the states could go and under what constitutional standard the laws would be tested. Justice Souter was a complete unknown on the subject.

Nevertheless, these three Justices began the joint opinion by unequivocally upholding the basic constitutional right to an abortion as recognized in *Roe* v. *Wade*: "Liberty finds no refuge in a jurisprudence of doubt." To assuage that doubt and insure that the women of the nation can plan their lives in accordance with firmly established constitutional principles, the three moderate Justices felt it important to lay down the bedrock proposition that a woman has a constitutional right to liberty that encompasses the right to have an abortion.

At the outset, the three Justices made clear that they spoke with a single voice. Instead of one Justice claiming credit for writing the opinion, which other Justices may join in, the lead opinion explicitly states that it was the product of all three, a "joint opinion" referred to as such by the other Justices.

The opinion begins by laying out the basic proposition that the right to an abortion is protected by the Constitution, namely, that it is part of the "liberty" right found in the Due

Process Clause of the Fourteenth Amendment. "The Constitution places limits on a State's right to interfere with a person's most basic decisions about family and parenthood," including "personal decisions relating to marriage, procreation, contraception, family relationships, child rearing, and education" [348]. The right to an abortion fits within that general category. The right of a woman to terminate her pregnancy prior to viability of the fetus is vital to her "ultimate control over her destiny and her body" [364].

The three Justices confronted the issue of when the Court should rethink its prior decisions and overrule them. Unlike a legislature which must respond to political pressures and repeal a law when the majority in a particular jurisdiction demands it, the Supreme Court is not supposed to bend with the political winds. Its interpretation of the Constitution is supposed to give guidance to our society for the indefinite future. Certainly it should not change its decisions merely because the composition of the Court has changed. The joint opinion quoted from an earlier opinion of Justice Potter Stewart: "A basic change in the law upon a ground no firmer than a change in our membership invites the popular misconception that this institution is little different from the two political branches of the Government. No misconception could do more lasting injury to this Court and to the system of law which it is our abiding mission to serve" [359–60].

The joint opinion therefore examined whether any change in medical science or the development of the law required a rethinking of the basic premise of the *Roe* decision. The three Justices concluded that no developments in science or the law required a rethinking of the original *Roe* decision. There are times when the basic conditions of society on which a decision is based do change. Thus the Court was correct in reversing the original *Plessy* decision upholding state-enforced segregation. Conditions in twentieth-century America made state-enforced segregation untenable. But no such change justified any reversal of the *Roe* decision.

That does not end the inquiry, of course. Even if *Roe* should not be overruled and the right to reproductive freedom must be recognized, there are considerations which must be weighed on the other side. In this case, the state has an "important and legitimate interest in potential life" that is contained in the fetus. The joint opinion then considered an important part of the *Roe* decision, namely, the trimester test, under which a woman has a virtually unlimited right to terminate her pregnancy during the first three months, regulations designed to protect the woman's health may be imposed during the second three months, and the state may restrict abortions altogether in the last three months.

The joint opinion rejected the trimester test as not affording sufficient recognition to the state's interest in potential life. In place of the trimester test, the three Justices adopted Justice O'Connor's rule, which she first articulated in the *Akron* case. Only those restrictions on the abortion right which impose an "undue burden" are unconstitutional: "The undue burden standard is the appropriate means of reconciling the State's interest with the woman's constitutionally protected liberty" [370].

What that means is that the state cannot impose a "substantial obstacle" in the way of a woman's right to choose. But the state does have the right to take certain measures that might persuade a woman to change her mind and have the child. Thus, the state is allowed to give the woman certain information about the nature of the procedure and the health risks involved, including the probable gestational age of the fetus. The state can also require the woman to be informed about medical assistance for childbirth, about child support from the father, and about adoption—counseling information which the Court had struck down as unnecessary nine years before in the *Akron* case. Furthermore, the state can require a twenty-four-hour waiting period after this information is given before an abortion can be performed.

The parental consent requirement under the Pennsylvania law was similar to those approved two years earlier in the *Hodgson* and *Akron II* cases. Thus, the joint opinion affirmed the validity of that requirement.

The spousal notification prerequisite falls in a different category. In this area, the three Justices found that a serious burden would be imposed on a woman seeking an abortion. The Court recognized that there are "millions of women is the country who are the victims of regular physical and psychological abuse at the hands of their husbands" [384–85]. If they get pregnant "they may have very good reasons for not wishing to inform their husbands of their decision to obtain an abortion" [385]. This requirement will not merely make abortions more difficult or expensive, "it will impose a substantial obstacle." Thus it is unconstitutional even under the "undue burden" standard.

The remaining opinions of the other Justices were more predictable. Justices Stevens and Blackmun applauded the recognition of the central holding of Roe v. Wade, but would have found all of the restrictions in the Pennsylvania law invalid since they did indeed impose a substantial burden on the right to an abortion.

Justice Blackmun, the author of the original Roe decision and the strongest defender of the right to reproductive choice, issued a personal statement reflecting his own anguish on the shift in the law over the past few years. "I fear for the darkness as four Justices anxiously await the single vote necessary to extinguish the light" [413]. He noted that: "I am 83 years old. I cannot remain on this Court forever, and when I do step down, the confirmation process for my successor well may focus on the issue before us today. That, I regret, may be exactly where the choice between the two worlds will be made" [431].

There were four Justices who announced that they would overrule Roe v. Wade altogether. Chief Justice Rehnquist dissented on behalf of Justices White, Scalia, and Thomas: "We believe that Roe was wrongly decided, and that it can and should be overruled" [432]. These four dissenting judges would impose the most lenient standard testing any law restricting abortion. "States may regulate abortion procedures in ways rationally related to a legitimate state interest" [452]. Under well-established constitutional doctrine, the "rational relationship" test requires courts to lean over backwards to rationalize any legislative enactment. As long as the law could conceivably advance any governmental purpose, whether articulated in the law or not, it must be upheld.

Justice Scalia formulated a different reason for upholding the Pennsylvania laws. His plea was that the majority of citizens should decide these questions and not the courts: "The permissibility of abortion, and the limitations upon it, are to be resolved like most important questions in a democracy: by

citizens trying to persuade one another and then voting" [464].
He acknowledged the deep feelings on both sides of the question and the desire of the populace to have the issue resolved by the Court once and for all, as it tried to settle the issue of slavery in the last century. But, said Justice Scalia, "by foreclosing all democratic outlet for the deep passions this issue arouses, by banishing the issue from the political forum that gives all participants, even the losers, the satisfaction of a fair hearing and a honest fight, by continuing the imposition of a rigid national rule instead of allowing for regional differences, the Court merely prolongs and intensifies the anguish" [484].

Thus the Supreme Court told us in the *Casey* case that a woman has a constitutional right to have an abortion and the states could not criminalize or prohibit the procedure altogether, but they could discourage a woman from making that choice, they could make her wait twenty-four hours before undergoing the procedure, thus imposing financial burdens on that choice for women who have long distances to travel, and they can require underage women to notify their parents before an abortion can be performed.

In reaching this result, the Court made us reexamine and rethink the basic system by which our society operates, what rights are so basic that the majority cannot eliminate or restrict them, how our Supreme Court operates to protect those rights, what governmental interests must be considered on the other side, and when and under what circumstances the Court can change its mind. The *Casey* case is important both for the specific holding of the case and for the process by which the decision was reached.

—Leon Friedman

BASIC SUPREME COURT CASES
ON THE RIGHT TO AN ABORTION

Roe v. *Wade*, 410 U.S. 113 (1973), established the basic right to an abortion.

Doe v. *Bolton*, 410 U.S. 179 (1973), struck down medical restrictions on abortion, including a requirement for committee approval before the operation can take place.

Planned Parenthood of Central Missouri v. *Danforth*, 428 U.S. 52 (1976), struck down a Missouri law that required spousal and parental consent before an abortion could take place; also invalidated a law that prohibited the use of saline amniocentesis after the first twelve weeks of pregnancy; also invalidated a provision that required doctors to use their professional skill and care "to preserve the life and health of a fetus."

Beal v. *Doe*, 432 U.S. 432 (1977), upheld a Medicaid regulation that denied funds for nontherapeutic abortions.

Maher v. *Roe*, 432 U.S. 464 (1977), upheld a Medicaid regulation that denied funds for nontherapeutic abortions, even though the state paid medical expenses incident to childbirth.

Colautti v. *Franklin*, 439 U.S. 379 (1979), invalidated a law that imposed a duty on doctors to preserve the life of a fetus.

Bellotti v. *Baird*, 443 U.S. 622 (1979), struck down a law that required parental consent before a minor could choose to have an abortion without providing an adequate "judicial bypass" alternative.

Harris v. *McRae*, 448 U.S. (1980), upheld the Hyde Amendment, which denied Medicaid funds for an abortion except where the life of the mother would be endangered or where a woman was pregnant as the result of rape or incest and the incident had been promptly reported to a law enforcement officer or the public health service.

H.L. v. *Matheson*, 450 U.S. 398 (1981), upheld a law which required doctors to notify the parents of an "unemancipated minor girl living with and dependent on her parents" that the child was seeking an abortion.

Akron v. *Akron Center for Reproductive Health, Inc.*, 462 U.S. 416 (1983), struck down various provisions of a local law that (1) required that all second-trimester abortions be performed in a hospital; (2) required that girls under fifteen years of age obtain parental consent or judicial approval; (3) required informed consent, mandating that doctors tell each woman of the status of her pregnancy, the development of her fetus, the physical and emotional complications that might result from the abortion, and the availability of agencies to help her on adoption; (4) required that the attending physician, as opposed to other nonmedical counseling personnel, inform the patient of all the medical risks; (5) required a twenty-four-hour waiting period before an abortion could be secured; (6) required that the fetus must be disposed of in a "humane" manner.

Planned Parenthood v. *Ashcroft*, 462 U.S. 476 (1983), upheld a law that required a pathology report after an abortion and also required the presence of a second physician during an abortion after viability.

Simopoulos v. *Virginia*, 462 U.S. 506 (1983), upheld a law that required abortions after twelve weeks to be held in hospitals or outpatient clinics.

Thornburgh v. *American College of Obstetricians*, 476 U.S. 747 (1986), struck down a law that required that a woman be given seven explicit items of information about the fetus; required that a woman be told about "detrimental physical and psychological effects" and all "particular medical risks" of the procedure, as well as the facts that state assistance would be available to her if she had the child and that the father was responsible for financial assistance; required a doctor to use the abortion technique that would provide the best opportunity for the unborn child to be aborted alive; and also required a second physician to be present during an abortion to provide immediate medical care for the child.

Webster v. *Reproductive Health Services*, 492 U.S. 490 (1989), held that a Missouri law prohibiting the use of government facilities or hospitals for abortions was valid.

Hodgson v. *Minnesota*, 497 U.S. 417 (1990), struck down a Minnesota law that required a minor to give both parents at least forty-eight hours' notice before she could have an abortion, but upheld an alternative provision that the child must notify one parent within that period.

Ohio v. *Akron Center for Reproductive Health*, 497 U.S. 502 (1990), upheld an Ohio law containing a requirement that one parent be notified twenty-four hours before the operation and that also contained a judicial bypass procedure.

Planned Parenthood of Southeastern Pennsylvania v. *Casey*, 112 S. Ct. 2791 (1992), struck down part of a Pennsylvania law requiring a spouse to be notified before a woman could have an abortion, but upheld other parts of the law that imposed informed consent requirements, a twenty-four-hour waiting period, parental consent, and reporting and record-keeping requirements.

PLANNED PARENTHOOD OF SOUTHEASTERN PENNSYLVANIA, RE-
PRODUCTIVE HEALTH AND COUNSELING CENTER, WOMEN'S
HEALTH SERVICES, INC., WOMEN'S SUBURBAN CLINIC, ALLEN-
TOWN WOMEN'S CENTER, and THOMAS ALLEN, M.D., on behalf of
himself and all others similarly situated,

Petitioners and Cross-Respondents,

v.

ROBERT P. CASEY, ALLAN S. NOONAN, and ERNEST D. PREATE, JR.,
personally and in their official capacities,

Respondents and Cross-Petitioners.

Nos. 91–744 and 91–902
October Term, 1991
Argued April 22, 1992
Decided June 29, 1992

On Writs of Certiorari to the United States Court of Appeals
for the Third Circuit

BRIEFS SUPPORTING THE RIGHT TO AN ABORTION

BRIEF FOR PETITIONERS AND CROSS-RESPONDENTS

STATEMENT OF THE CASE[1]

I. HISTORY OF THE LEGISLATION

In 1988 and again in 1989, following this Court's ruling in *Webster* v. *Reproductive Health Servs.*, 492 U.S. 490 (1989), the Pennsylvania legislature amended the Pennsylvania Abortion Control Act, 18 Pa. Cons. Stat. Ann. §§ 3203–3220 (1983 & Supp. 1991), imposing a series of highly intrusive and burdensome restrictions on women seeking abortion services. In large part, the amendments reenacted the statutory provisions of the 1982 Act, which this Court held unconstitutional in *Thornburgh* v. *American College of Obstetricians & Gynecologists*, 476 U.S. 747 (1986). *See also City of Akron* v. *Akron Center for Reproductive Health, Inc.*, 462 U.S. 416 (1983).[2] Like the provisions of the 1982 Act, the amendments mandate that a physician provide a woman seeking an abortion with a prescribed litany of state-sponsored information dis-

---

1. The opinions and statutes involved are reprinted in the Appendix to the Petition for Certiorari in Case No. 91–744. Citations to this Appendix are made to the page number therein as "_____a." Citations to the Joint Appendix are made to the page number therein as "J.A. _____"

2. Following *Akron*, the Commonwealth of Pennsylvania conceded the invalidity of the 24-hour mandatory delay and physician-only counseling provisions of the Act. *American College of Obstetricians & Gynecologists* v. *Thornburgh*, 737 F.2d 283, 293 (3d Cir. 1984). Thus, the constitutionality of those provisions was not before this Court in *Thornburgh*.

couraging abortion and that the physician delay the procedure for at least 24 hours after she receives this information. 18 Pa. Cons. Stat. Ann. §§ 3205, 3208; 289a–292a, 298a–300a. The amendments also require the collection of detailed, particularized information—some of which must be publicly disclosed—for every abortion performed. 18 Pa. Cons. Stat. Ann. §§ 3207(b), 3214(a) and (f); 298a, 302a–304a.

The amendments also mandate that married women notify their husbands of their abortion decisions, 18 Pa. Cons. Stat. Ann. § 3209; 300a–302a,[3] and that women under the age of eighteen obtain either the "informed consent" of one parent or a court order waiving the requirement. 18 Pa. Cons. Stat. Ann. § 3206; 292a–297a.[4] While compliance with §§ 3205, 3206, and 3209, and other provisions of the Act not before this Court, is exempted where there is a medical emergency, the Act's definition of medical emergency is extremely narrow. 18 Pa. Cons. Stat. Ann. § 3203; 289a.

II. HISTORY OF THE LITIGATION

Six years ago, this Court reaffirmed *Roe v. Wade*, 410 U.S. 113 (1973), and found that provisions of the 1982 Act, nearly identical to the amendments before this Court today, "wholly subordinate[d] constitutional privacy interests . . . in an effort to deter a woman from making a decision that . . . is hers to make." *Thornburgh*, 476 U.S. at 759. Relying principally on this Court's decisions in *Roe*, *Thornburgh*, and *Akron*, and following a three-day bench trial at which ten witnesses testified,[5] the district court issued its opinion and order on

3. The 1974 Abortion Control Act, an earlier version of the 1982 Act, required a married woman to obtain the consent of her husband. It was found unconstitutional in *Planned Parenthood Ass'n v. Fitzpatrick*, 401 F. Supp. 554, 564–66 (E.D. Pa. 1975) (three-judge court), *aff'd mem. sub nom. Franklin v. Fitzpatrick*, 428 U.S. 901 (1976). In 1987, the legislature then passed a "paternal" notification provision. In vetoing this measure, respondent Casey noted that "a state cannot delegate to any third-party—even a husband—a power that the state cannot exercise itself." J.A. 595.

4. The 1974 and 1982 Acts also contained parental consent requirements that were found constitutionally deficient. See *Fitzpatrick*, 401 F. Supp. at 566–68; *American College of Obstetricians & Gynecologists v. Thornburgh*, 656 F. Supp. 879, 887–90 (E.D. Pa. 1987).

5. In addition, the district court reviewed two sets of stipulated facts and the verifications and testimony of four witnesses from the preliminary injunction hearing. J.A. 608–21.

August 24, 1990, enjoining virtually all of the challenged provisions. 104a–288a.

The trial court's detailed findings of fact,[6] which demonstrate that the Act endangers women's lives and health, confirm the findings made by this Court in *Thornburgh* on a more limited factual record. The district court rejected the Commonwealth's argument that *Webster*, 492 U.S. at 517–20, and *Hodgson v. Minnesota*, 110 S. Ct. 2926 (1990), had overruled or modified the strict scrutiny standard of *Roe*, applied in both *Thornburgh* and *Akron*. 231a–233a. It found, however, that this Court's decision in *Bellotti v. Baird*, 443 U.S. 622, 640 (1979) ("*Bellotti II*"), required it to judge the constitutionality of the "informed" parental consent requirement of § 3206 under the less protective "undue burden" standard. 248a. Nevertheless, based on the evidence, the district court found this provision invalid under this more deferential standard. 248a–252a. The Commonwealth appealed.

On October 21, 1991, applying an incorrect interpretation of *Marks v. United States*, 430 U.S. 188 (1977), the Court of Appeals for the Third Circuit reversed in part and affirmed in part the district court's judgment, holding that *Roe*, *Akron*, and *Thornburgh* are no longer the law of the land and that women no longer enjoy a fundamental constitutional right to choose abortion. 30a. Rather, the court of appeals held that *Webster* and *Hodgson* established a new and less protective "undue burden" standard for reviewing the constitutionality of abortion restrictions, a standard first suggested in Justice O'Connor's dissenting opinions in *Akron*, 462 U.S. at 453, 461–64 (O'Connor, J., dissenting) and *Thornburgh*, 476 U.S. at 828–29 (O'Connor, J., dissenting). Rather than remanding the case for application of the new standard by the trier of fact, or for further factual development relevant to this new standard, the court of appeals largely ignored the record and upheld all challenged provisions except the husband notification requirement. These consolidated Petitions for Certiorari followed.

6. The district court carefully documented the record evidence supporting each of its 387 findings of fact, none of which was reversed on appeal. Given the complete absence of "an extraordinary reason" to examine the district court's findings, they must be accepted by this Court. *Goodman v. Lukens Steel Co.*, 482 U.S. 656, 665 (1987).

III. FACTS

A. Husband Notification

Except in extremely limited circumstances, § 3209 of the Act requires every married woman to notify her husband that she is about to undergo an abortion.[7] In the vast majority of marriages, wives discuss their abortion choice with their husbands and reach a decision only after serious dialogue. 193a. In many troubled and dysfunctional marriages, however, the Act forces a woman to involve even an abusive husband in her abortion decision, jeopardizing her own health and safety as well as that of her children.

Marital abuse is surprisingly common in the United States. As the district court found, "one of every two women will be battered at some time in their [sic] life." 195a. In addition to physical battering,[8] which often intensifies during pregnancy, 196a, some husbands resort to sexual abuse, including rape and sexual mutilation; psychological abuse, including verbal insults; and abuse of the children or other family members. 196a, 199a. In an attempt to control all aspects of their wives' lives, some husbands refuse to provide sufficient support to feed, clothe, and shelter the family, 199a; J.A. 213–14; or closely monitor their wives' whereabouts. J.A. 212–13, 229–30. The court of appeals found that "the number of different situations in which women may reasonably fear dire consequences from notifying their husbands is potentially limitless," and includes:

> women who reasonably fear retaliatory psychological abuse; women who reasonably fear retaliatory physical or psychological abuse of their children; women who are separated following a failed marriage relationship and for whom renewal of contact may produce severe emotional distress; women whose husbands

7. The Commonwealth neither requires a husband to notify his wife about any medical procedures affecting his capacity to have children within marriage, nor requires a wife to notify her husband of other surgical procedures, including those that affect her capacity to become a mother. 199a.

8. Bonnie Jean Dillon, a battered woman, testified at trial of "being thrown on the floor in the kitchen and being kicked around with his feet. I remember being drug [sic] from the back room of the office and thrown down the cellar steps while the secretaries were there. I can remember being thrown against the cellar door and smashing my face against the cellar door." J.A. 381.

have serious health problems and who reasonably fear that notification will be health threatening; and women whose marriages are severely troubled and who reasonably fear that notice will precipitate the demise of the marital relationship.

70a. The dangerous and potentially deadly consequences of forced notification cannot be overstated. As Dr. Lenore Walker, a national expert on domestic violence, testified, requiring a battered woman to notify her husband is like "giving him a hammer to just beat her." J.A. 228. See also 201a.

Two of the exceptions to the husband notification requirement purport to relieve women of the devastating consequences of domestic violence caused by the mandatory notification. Section 3209(b)(3) provides that the mandatory notification does not apply where "[t]he pregnancy is a result of spousal sexual assault . . . which has been reported to a law enforcement agency." Section 3209(b)(4) provides for a waiver of notification where the woman reasonably believes that notifying her husband "is likely to result in the infliction of bodily injury upon her." 301a.

Neither of these exceptions provides any meaningful protection for battered women. Section 3209(b)(4)'s exception is expressly limited to situations where the woman fears "bodily injury" to herself. Thus, as the district court found, a married woman must notify her abusive husband of her decision to obtain an abortion even if he psychologically or economically coerces her or her children; punishes her children with physical violence or sexual abuse; threatens to publicize her decision to have an abortion; or threatens to retaliate against her in future child custody or divorce proceedings. 194a, 199a.

Moreover, § 3209(b)(3) applies only in cases where the pregnancy is the "result" of spousal sexual assault that has been reported to a law enforcement official. 18 Pa. Cons. Stat. Ann. § 3128(c). Consequently, the exception provides no assistance when the sexual abuse occurs after the woman becomes pregnant, when the sexual abuse does not result in pregnancy, or when the woman has not or cannot report the abuse. In some cases, rather than exempting the woman, it actually triggers notification, for once officials launch an investigation or file criminal charges, the husband will be notified.

Even where the exceptions apply, they are unlikely to be of any aid. Battering and sexually abusive husbands often threaten their wives with further violence if they break the shroud of secrecy that surrounds the battering. 197a.[9] Similarly, few survivors of marital rape will be able to report the rape to law enforcement officials. 198a. As Dr. Lenore Walker testified at trial, women "will rarely report to a law enforcement agency that they have been sexually abused." J.A. 230.[10] Other battered women deny their abuse as a survival strategy for coping with the pain, and will rarely, if ever, discuss their abuse with anyone. 200a–201a. As the district court found, the realistic fear of retaliation by the abuser, or the psychological condition caused by the abuse, will make battered women "unlikely to avail themselves of the exceptions to § 3209 . . . regardless of whether the section applies to them." 198a.

B. Biased Patient Counseling and Mandatory Delay

Section 3205 of the Act requires that a woman give her voluntary and informed consent to the abortion procedure. 289a. But in a radical departure from accepted medical principles, § 3205 deems consent "informed" only when a physician provides the woman—on pain of criminal penalties and license suspension and revocation[11]—with state-approved information.[12] As the district court found, this information cre-

9. For example, when asked at trial why she had never told anyone about her husband's battering, even after it put her in the hospital five times, Ms. Dillon said, "I was afraid of how he would react if he found out that I was telling people about our secret, about what he was doing to me." J.A. 383.

10. For example, despite years of counseling following the break-up of her marriage, Ms. Dillon had never revealed the fact that she was a survivor of marital rape, until several days before her testimony, and only then after repeated questioning by counsel. J.A. 387.

11. The district court found "no other instance [in which] an informed consent regulation provide[s] for criminal penalties." 180a. The threat of criminal prosecution will deter physicians from performing abortions because medical malpractice insurance contains no coverage for criminal prosecutions. J.A. 144.

12. Included in this information is the nature of the abortion procedure, its risks and alternative treatments, the probable gestational age of the fetus, and the medical risks of carrying the pregnancy to term. Additionally, §§ 3205 and 3208 mandate that physicians or counselors offer the pregnant woman materials that give detailed descriptions and pictures of the fetus at two-week gestational increments from fertilization until full-term, as well as the names of agencies offering alternatives to abortion; and inform the woman of the availability of medical assistance benefits

ates the impression that both the Commonwealth and the physician "disapprove[ ] of the woman's decision," *see* 179a, and is a "poorly veiled attempt[ ] . . . to disguise elements of discouragement of the abortion decision." 180a. By inserting its anti-abortion message into the informed consent dialogue, the Commonwealth has transformed the physician from the impartial counselor mandated by accepted medical standards into a partisan proponent of the state's ideology.

Section 3205 also intrudes heavily on physicians' discretion by requiring them to supply a specified package of information to all patients. This conflicts with the accepted medical practice of giving patients information tailored to their individual needs and circumstances, out of respect for the patient who will be "autonomously making the decision." 177a; J.A. 161.

Much of the required information is not only inflammatory and misleading, but is beyond the expertise of medical professionals. 179a–180a. Physicians or counselors are required to offer women seeking abortions "printed materials which describe the unborn child and list agencies which offer alternatives to abortion." 290a. Some of the listed agencies, however, are ideological anti-abortion groups, notorious for giving women inflammatory and inaccurate information. *See* 169a. Women must also be told that medical assistance benefits may be available if they carry their pregnancies to term, and that the "father of the unborn child is liable to assist in the support of her child . . . ." 290a. But, in truth, most women will be ineligible for medical assistance benefits, or will, in practice, be unable to collect adequate child support payments if they carry their pregnancies to term. *See* 179a–180a. This information will convey the message that the benefits will be adequate to raise a child—a cruel deception for low-income women whose decisions may be based, in part, upon their financial ability to raise additional children.

Before a woman may obtain an abortion, § 3205 also mandates that she delay an additional 24 hours after she is given the state-mandated information.[13] By imposing an inflexible

and of the father's liability for child support payments if she carries her pregnancy to term. 289a–290a, 298a–300a.

13. In no other area of medical decision-making does the Commonwealth require a 24-hour delay after a patient gives informed consent. J.A. 173.

waiting period for all women, the Commonwealth significantly burdens their rights to terminate pregnancy. Because of scheduling complications and a shortage of physicians,[14] the 24-hour mandatory delay will often "result in delays far in excess of 24 hours. For the majority of women in Pennsylvania, delays will range from 48 hours to two weeks." 172a. Moreover, the 24-hour delay will force every woman to make a minimum of two visits to an abortion provider. 171a. Solely because of the Act, the thousands of Pennsylvania women who travel hundreds of miles to obtain an abortion, 172a, must assume the additional costs of transportation, overnight lodging, lost wages, food, and childcare. 172a, 186a. The delay will also twice subject "many women to the harassment and hostility of anti-abortion protestors . . . ." 172a.[15] As the district court found, mandated delay will impose the greatest burdens on low-income women, women who live far from an abortion provider, and women "who have difficulty explaining their whereabouts, such as battered women, school age women, and working women without sick leave." 173a. Indeed, it is likely that many battered women will face additional battering during the mandated delay. 197a–198a; J.A. 227.

C. "Informed" Parental Consent

Creating obstacles far harsher than any prior parental involvement statute reviewed by this Court, § 3206's requirement of "informed" parental consent forces both the parent and the young woman to come to the physician at least 24 hours before the abortion for the biased counseling required by § 3205. 292a–297a. The provision thus necessitates at least

14. In 1987, there were no abortions performed in 40 out of 67 counties in Pennsylvania. In 12 other counties, there were ten or fewer abortions performed. Pennsylvania Induced Abortion Report, January-December, 1987. These figures are consistent with national data finding that 83% of the counties in the United States have no abortion provider. Stanley K. Henshaw and Jennifer Van Vort, *Abortion Services in the United States, 1987 and 1988,* 22 Fam. Plan. Persp. 102, 106 (1990).

15. Section 3205's mandatory delay will also damage the health of women by increasing physical and psychological stress, and the risk of complications. For each week of delay, the risk of complications from abortion increases by approximately 30% and the risk of death increases by approximately 50%. *See* 152a–153a. *See also American Public Health Association Recommended Program Guide for Abortion Services,* 70 Am. Pub. H.J. 652, 654 (1980). Moreover, the forced delay will push some women into the second trimester, substantially increasing both the cost and medical risks of an abortion. 173a.

one visit to the physician by the woman's parent and at least two, and more likely three, visits by the young woman herself, thereby creating "layers of obstacles" that unduly burden a young woman's ability to get an abortion. *See* 172a, 186a.[16]

Moreover, requiring a consenting parent to schedule an appointment with the physician will cause serious delays, even where the young woman's parent is supportive of her decision. For example, many parents will be unable to visit the physician promptly due to work schedules, family obligations, burdensome travel, illness, or lack of financial resources. 183a, 185a; J.A. 617. Where the parent is hostile to the young woman's abortion decision, the provision may result in unnecessary and dangerous delays, or an effective and arbitrary veto of the young woman's abortion choice. J.A. 616.

As the district court found, delays imposed by § 3206 can be "both dangerous and prohibitive" because young women often obtain abortions much later in their pregnancies than older women. 183a.[17] Thus, young women are more likely to be forced into having a second trimester abortion, with its increased health risks, 184a, or may be too late in pregnancy to obtain a safe, legal abortion altogether. Some of these women will resort to desperate measures: they may try to obtain illegal abortions, attempt to self-induce an abortion, or attempt suicide. 185a; J.A. 611, 618.

D. Definition of Medical Emergency

Although §§ 3205, 3206, and 3209 do not apply in medical emergencies, the Act limits this important exception to

16. "Informed" parental consent for young women seeking abortion is a significant departure from state law that recognizes the importance of providing confidential health services to pregnant women under the age of 18. Pennsylvania law allows pregnant young women to consent to medical or health services to treat pregnancy and venereal disease. 35 Pa. Cons. Stat. Ann. § 10103 (1977). Similarly, following a pregnancy, a young woman may consent to medical, dental, and health services for herself, 35 Pa. Cons. Stat. Ann. § 10101 (1977), and her children. 35 Pa. Cons. Stat. Ann. § 10102 (1977). Additionally, a young woman may consent to medical, dental, or health services in cases where a delay in treatment would increase the risk to the young woman's life or health. 35 Pa. Cons. Stat. Ann. § 10104 (1977).

17. For a variety of reasons, young women deny that they are pregnant and postpone decision-making. Some are unaware that they are pregnant because they do not know about their menstrual cycles or because they menstruate irregularly. Other young women delay seeking medical help because of fear, anxiety, and hesitation in divulging to parents sexual activity, pregnancy, or their desire to have an abortion. 183a–184a.

[t]hat condition which, on the basis of the physician's good faith clinical judgment, so complicates the medical condition of a pregnant woman as to necessitate the immediate abortion of her pregnancy to avert her death or for which a delay will create serious risk of substantial and irreversible impairment of a major bodily function.

18 Pa. Cons. Stat. Ann. § 3203; 289a. A far cry from the accepted definition of medical emergency, which gives a physician broad discretion to protect a woman's health,[18] the vague and narrow definition will "interfere[ ] with a physician's ability to act in accordance with his [or her] best medical judgment." 157a.[19] As a result, the Act will cause panic, confusion, and delay in the provision of emergency medical services to pregnant women, and will hinder the physician's ability "to make a rapid response to the detriment of the health of the [ ] patient. . . ." 156a.[20]

The district court identified three medical conditions— inevitable abortion, premature ruptured membrane, and preeclampsia—that exemplify those that would fall outside the Act's definition of "medical emergency." The court found that failure to perform an immediate abortion in these circumstances would pose a threat to the woman's health, but would not pose a "serious risk of substantial and irreversible impairment of major bodily function."

E. Public Disclosure and Reporting Requirements

Sections 3207(b) and 3214(f) require that every abortion facility, including individual physicians, file with the Department of Health a quarterly report listing the name and address of the facility, and the total number of abortions performed

18. Pennsylvania's Emergency Medical Services Act, 35 Pa. Cons. Stat. Ann. § 6923 (Supp. 1991), broadly and clearly defines the term as circumstances "resulting in a need for immediate medical intervention." 155a.

19. Although the Act permits physicians to exercise their "good faith judgment" in applying the medical emergency exception, the district court found that this "does not alter the fact that a 'serious risk of substantial and irreversible impairment of major bodily function' must exist for a situation to constitute a medical emergency under the Act." 157a.

20. Ultimately, some physicians may refuse to offer emergency services out of fear of potential criminal and civil liability. J.A. 188.

by trimester of pregnancy.[21] This information is available for public inspection and copying if the abortion provider receives any State funding, even funding for services wholly unrelated to abortion. 298a, 304a.[22]

Like their counterparts across the nation, Pennsylvania abortion providers and the women seeking care face vicious harassment and violence by opponents of abortion. See NOW v. Operation Rescue, 726 F. Supp. 1483, 1488–90 (E.D. Va. 1989), aff'd, 914 F.2d 582 (4th Cir. 1990), cert. granted sub nom. Bray v. Alexandria Women's Health Clinic, 111 S. Ct. 1070 (1991). Massive blockades, hate mail, bombings, and kidnapping threats against physicians, clinic employees, and family members are commonplace.[23] Public disclosure of their identity will subject abortion providers to increased harassment, discourage new physicians from offering abortion services, and discourage acceptance of State aid, thereby preventing clinics from offering patients a wide range of health care services. 213a–214a.

Section 3214(a) requires a detailed report for each abortion performed, including the names of the referring physician and those physicians concurring in and assisting late-term abortions.[24] Additionally, the report must disclose the basis for the physician's judgment that an abortion performed after the 24th week was authorized by the Act, § 3214(a)(8), and that a medical emergency existed. § 3214(a)(10). Physicians must

21. A nearly identical reporting provision in the 1982 Act was found unconstitutional. American College of Obstetricians & Gynecologists v. Thornburgh, 613 F. Supp. 656, 670 (E.D. Pa. 1985).

22. Most abortion providers in Pennsylvania receive Medicaid payments for abortions provided to survivors of rape and incest and women with life-threatening conditions. State funds are also paid to clinics and physicians for related medical care, as well as building costs, and other purposes unrelated to the provision of abortion services. 210a–211a.

23. David A. Grimes et al., An Epidemic of Anti-Abortion Violence in the United States, 165 Am. J. Obst. and Gyn. 1263 (1991). For example, in September, 1989, five opponents of abortion forced their way into the offices of plaintiff Women's Health Services and dumped buckets of tar onto the main patient care area. 212a. The clinic director's sixteen-year-old daughter was threatened with kidnapping, forcing her family to guard her both at home and at school. J.A. 260–63.

24. This report must include the name of the referring physician, agency, or service, and the names of the concurring physician and second physician for any post–24 week abortion authorized by 18 Pa. Cons. Stat. Ann. § 3211(c)(2), (5)(Supp. 1991). See § 3214(a)(1).

also report the basis for their determination of gestational age. § 3214(a)(11).

The evidence demonstrated that these aspects of § 3214(a) serve no legitimate scientific purpose, will deter physicians from referring women to or assisting abortion providers, or from acting in the patient's best interest. 221a–222a. Referring physicians are "extremely protective of their anonymity" for fear that they will be harassed and that they will lose patients or hospital privileges. 219a; J.A. 31–32. Indeed, testimony at trial revealed that physicians would not refer patients to any abortion provider if their names are required on an abortion report. 220a. Evidence also showed that requiring physicians to report the basis for their medical judgments will make them less willing to act in a pregnant patient's best interests. 222a; J.A. 39.

SUMMARY OF ARGUMENT

Few decisions are more basic to "individual dignity and autonomy" than the right of a woman to choose to terminate or continue a pregnancy. *Thornburgh*, 476 U.S. at 772. So proclaimed this Court only six years ago when it reaffirmed *Roe*, 410 U.S. 113 (1973), and invalidated provisions of a Pennsylvania law virtually identical to those at issue here.

Once again, this Court must reaffirm *Roe* and find unconstitutional Pennsylvania's most recent intrusions on reproductive liberty. Abandoning *Roe* by withdrawing the highest level of constitutional protection would contravene established principles of *stare decisis* and would jeopardize women's dignity and equality. Moreover, history makes clear that overturning *Roe* will not end abortion. Instead, permitting states to criminalize abortion or impose onerous restrictions will tragically and undeniably return thousands of women to back-alley or self-induced abortions. Many will die. Others will be forced by the state to sacrifice their health or to carry unwanted pregnancies to term. *Roe*'s demise will be most devastating for low-income, young, rural, or battered women, who are too vulnerable to overcome state-imposed obstacles.

No legitimate justification supports overturning *Roe*. Fundamental constitutional protection for the abortion right follows logically and necessarily from a century of this Court's decisions recognizing that personal choices affecting bodily integrity, identity, and destiny are largely beyond the reach of government. *Roe*'s trimester framework not only fairly accommodates the interests of the woman and the state, but also serves as a sound guidepost for the courts and state legislatures.

The court of appeals erroneously adopted the vague and unworkable "undue burden" standard of review, which is likely to result in arbitrary and discriminatory applications by lower courts. In contrast to the clarity and equity of *Roe*, both the "undue burden" and "rational basis" standards would sanction and invite intolerable legislative interference with private reproductive decisions. Adopting these lesser standards would ensure an irrational patchwork of state laws and would return to the vicissitudes of local politics what *Roe* properly removed from that forum.

Even under these deferential standards of review, however, this Court must find unconstitutional the Act's challenged provisions. Mandatory husband notification violates rights of privacy and marital integrity by subjecting intimate marital discussions to state surveillance and control, and endangering the lives and health of married women compelled to notify abusive husbands of their abortion choice. By imposing duties only on women and conferring rights solely on men, the Act also perpetuates the pernicious stereotype that women are subordinate within marriage and incapable of making independent moral decisions. The provision thereby violates the Constitution's equal protection guarantees.

Requiring physicians to provide a litany of state-mandated information violates the longstanding medical principle that the informed consent dialogue must be tailored to the needs of each patient, not used to transform the physician into a partisan proponent of the state's ideology. While furthering no legitimate purpose, the Act's 24-hour mandatory delay forces women to travel to their physicians on at least two, and often three, occasions, thereby increasing the expense and medical risks of abortion.

Far more onerous than other parental consent or notification statutes upheld by this Court, the Act's "informed" parental consent requirement presents so insurmountable an obstacle that even parents who have participated in, support, and consent to their daughter's abortion decision may be unable to comply with the law. Rather than furthering communication between parents and their daughters, the Act forces family life to conform to a state-designed ideal.

Furthering no legitimate state interest, the intrusive public disclosure and reporting requirements merely enhance the ability of abortion opponents to intimidate physicians through violence and harassment. Finally, the Act's narrow medical emergency exception is inconsistent with well-established medical standards. By denying pregnant women a waiver of the Act's requirements except in the most dire circumstances, this provision will jeopardize women's lives and health and discourage the provision of emergency services to pregnant women.

In view of the immediate harm that will befall women should these provisions go into effect, this Court must resoundingly reaffirm *Roe*. Without its fundamental protection, women will be unable to maintain the measure of equality they have won so far, and this Court will forsake its historic role as guardian of constitutional liberties.

ARGUMENT

I. THIS COURT MUST REAFFIRM THE CENTRAL HOLDING OF *ROE* V. *WADE* THAT THE RIGHT TO CHOOSE ABORTION IS A FUNDAMENTAL RIGHT PROTECTED BY THE CONSTITUTION.

A. This Court Cannot Uphold the Pennsylvania Statute Without Abandoning the Strict Scrutiny Standard of Review, Thereby Overruling *Roe* v. *Wade*.

This Court's landmark decision in *Roe*, 410 U.S. 113 (1973), holds profound significance for all Americans. In finding a Texas abortion ban unconstitutional, this Court did far more than prohibit the most draconian abortion laws. Rather, this Court held that the right to make private decisions about childbearing is a constitutional liberty of fundamental dimension.

Roe mandates that state laws that intrude upon reproductive choices—whether to carry a pregnancy to term or have an abortion—must be examined with the most exacting scrutiny. Id. at 155. Under this standard, only laws necessary and narrowly tailored to serve the most compelling state interests pass constitutional review. Id.

This Court has consistently applied Roe's strict scrutiny standard to invalidate not only abortion bans, but also laws that encumber the abortion choice with delay, administrative hurdles, or expense, or that disproportionately harm young, low-income, rural, or battered women. See, e.g., Doe v. Bolton, 410 U.S. 179, 193–200 (1973) (accredited hospitalization requirement, hospital review committee approval, and two physician concurrence requirements); Planned Parenthood v. Danforth, 428 U.S. 52, 67–75 (1976) (husband and parental consent); Akron, 462 U.S. at 432–39, 442–51 (24-hour mandatory delay, biased counseling, doctor-only counseling, and second trimester hospitalization requirements); Thornburgh, 476 U.S. at 759–68 (biased patient counseling; reporting and public disclosure requirements). Roe's central premise—that the right to choose abortion is a fundamental right protected by the most exacting scrutiny—thus forbids legislation that places roadblocks before women seeking abortion or that forecloses the abortion option for those women too vulnerable to overcome the state-imposed burdens.[25] The district court found, and the court of appeals acknowledged, that the Pennsylvania law is unconstitutional under the strict scrutiny stan-

25. In this regard, Roe is entirely consistent with this Court's jurisprudence in other areas. Recognizing that constitutionally protected freedoms "are protected not only against heavy-handed frontal attack, but also from being stifled by more subtle governmental interference," Bates v. City of Little Rock, 361 U.S. 516, 523 (1960), this Court has repeatedly invalidated statutes that inhibit the exercise of fundamental rights. See Shapiro v. Thompson, 394 U.S. 618 (1969) (one-year residency requirement as a condition on welfare assistance violates the right to travel); Bates, supra (compulsory disclosure of membership lists violates right of association); Lovell v. City of Griffin, 303 U.S. 444 (1938) (ordinance forbidding distribution of any kind of literature without permission from city manager violates the right of free expression).

dard of *Roe*.[26] In upholding restrictions that this Court already held unconstitutional under *Roe*, the court of appeals found that women no longer enjoy fundamental constitutional protection for the right to choose abortion. Declining to apply strict scrutiny, the court of appeals measured the constitutionality of the Pennsylvania law under the new, far less protective "undue burden" standard.

Because the invalidity of the instant provisions under *Roe* is indisputable, this Court cannot sustain the decision below without overruling *Roe* or so eviscerating its core holding as to render it meaningless. As shown below, *Roe* is eminently sound in principle and workable in practice. Therefore, no valid justification exists for this Court to take the radical and unprecedented step of withdrawing the highest level of constitutional protection from this fundamental right.[27]

B. The Doctrine of *Stare Decisis* Demands Reaffirmation of *Roe*.

This Court has repeatedly held that the doctrine of *stare decisis* "is of fundamental importance to the rule of law." *Hilton* v. *South Carolina Pub. Rys. Comm'n*, 112 S. Ct. 560, 563 (1991) (quoting *Welch* v. *Texas Dep't of Highways & Pub. Transp.*, 483 U.S. 468, 494 (1987)).

> Fidelity to precedent ensure[s] that the law will not merely change erratically, but will develop in a principled and intelligible fashion. [It] permits society to presume that bedrock principles are founded in law rather than in the proclivities of individuals, and thereby contributes to the integrity of our constitutional system of government, both in appearance and fact.

---

26. *See* 30a, 225a. Similarly, the Commonwealth effectively conceded that the Pennsylvania law could not withstand scrutiny under *Roe* when it asked the lower courts to apply a new, less rigorous standard of review. 225a.

27. In addition to the "liberty" guarantee of the Fourteenth Amendment, the right to abortion may be grounded in other constitutional rights: equal protection, freedom of religion, the rights to be free from involuntary servitude and cruel and unusual punishment, and the rights retained by the people under the Ninth Amendment. In the event that this Court abandons *Roe*, it should remand this case for consideration of the other constitutional principles that support the right to choose abortion.

Vasquez v. *Hillery*, 474 U.S. 254, 265–66 (1986).[28]
"[E]ven in constitutional cases, the doctrine carries such persuasive force that . . . departure from precedent [must] be supported by some 'special justification.' " *Payne* v. *Tennessee*, 111 S. Ct. 2597, 2618 (1991) (Souter, J., concurring) (quoting *Arizona* v. *Rumsey*, 467 U.S. 203, 212 (1984)).

By overruling *Roe*, this Court would sanction an abrupt departure from 200 years of American constitutional history. Never before has this Court bestowed, then taken back, a fundamental right that has been a part of the settled rights and expectations of literally millions of Americans for nearly two decades.[29] To regress by permitting states suddenly to impose burdensome regulations or criminalize conduct that a full generation of women has always known to be constitutionally protected would be anathema to any notion of principled constitutional decision-making.[30] Hence, overturning *Roe* would implicate the weightiest of *stare decisis* concerns: as Justice Harlan recognized, *stare decisis* "provides the stability and predictability required for the ordering of human affairs over the course of time . . . ." *Williams* v. *Florida*, 399 U.S. 78, 127 (1970) (Harlan, J., concurring in part and dissenting in part). More recently, this Court emphasized:

> *Stare decisis* has added force when the legislature, in the public sphere, and citizens, in the private realm, have acted in reliance on a previous decision, for in this instance overruling the decision would dislodge settled rights and expectations.

28. *See generally Patterson* v. *McLean Credit Union*, 491 U.S. 164, 172 (1989) ("[S]tare decisis is a basic self-governing principle within the Judicial Branch, which is entrusted with the sensitive and difficult task of fashioning and preserving a jurisprudential system that is not based upon 'an arbitrary discretion.' " (quoting *The Federalist*, No. 78, at 490 (Alexander Hamilton) (H. Lodge ed. 1888)).

29. By 1989, approximately sixteen million women had obtained legal abortions. If current abortion rates continue, nearly half of all women of reproductive age will have had an abortion by the time they reach age forty-five. Rachel B. Gold, *Abortion and Women's Health: A Turning Point for America?* 22 (Alan Guttmacher Institute, 1990) [hereinafter *Abortion and Women's Health*].

30. *Stare decisis* requires adherence to the strict scrutiny standard and trimester framework of *Roe*, as well as its specific holding. *See County of Allegheny* v. *ACLU Greater Pittsburgh Chapter*, 492 U.S. 573, 668 (1989) (Kennedy, J., concurring in part and dissenting in part).

Hilton, 112 S. Ct. at 564.[31] Further, *Roe* does not stand alone. On the contrary, it defines the contours of privacy, which protects individuals from governmental interference in personal decision-making and is the foundation for numerous important freedoms.[32] As Justice Scalia has noted, "the respect accorded prior decisions increases, rather than decreases, with their antiquity, as the society adjusts itself to their existence, and the surrounding law becomes premised on their validity." *South Carolina* v. *Gathers*, 490 U.S. 805, 824 (1989) (Scalia, J., dissenting).

Twice in the past decade, this Court has reconsidered and resoundingly reaffirmed *Roe*. In *Akron*, 462 U.S. 416, this Court rejected the argument that *Roe* "erred in interpreting the Constitution," *id.* at 419, and enumerated the "especially compelling reasons for adhering to *stare decisis* in applying the principles of *Roe* . . . ."

> That case was considered with special care. It was first argued during the 1971 Term, and reargued—with extensive briefing—the following Term. The decision was joined by the Chief Justice and six other Justices. Since *Roe* was decided in January 1973, the Court repeatedly and consistently has accepted and applied the basic principle that a woman has a fundamental right to make the highly personal choice whether or not to terminate her pregnancy.

Id. at 420 n.1.

In *Thornburgh*, this Court held: "[a]gain today, we reaffirm the general principles laid down in *Roe* and in *Akron* . . . . [T]he constitutional principles that led this Court to its de-

---

31. *Cf. Payne*, 111 S. Ct. at 2610 ("Considerations in favor of *stare decisis* are at their acme . . . where reliance interests are involved").

32. For example, courts have relied on *Roe* when recognizing the right to use contraceptives, *Carey* v. *Population Servs. Int'l*, 431 U.S. 678, 684–86 (1977); the right to be free from overly restrictive maternity leave regulations, *Cleveland Bd. of Educ.* v. *La Fleur*, 414 U.S. 632, 639–40 (1974); the right to marry, *Zablocki* v. *Redhail*, 434 U.S. 374, 384–86 (1978); the right to informational privacy, *Whalen* v. *Roe*, 429 U.S. 589, 599–600 (1977); the right to be free from forced sterilization, *Ruby* v. *Massey*, 452 F. Supp. 361, 366 (D. Conn. 1978); the right of bodily integrity, *In re Quinlan*, 355 A.2d 647, 663 (N.J. 1976); *Superintendent of Belchertown State School* v. *Saikewicz*, 370 N.E.2d 417, 424 (Mass. 1977); and the right to be free from court-ordered contraception, *People* v. *Pointer*, 199 Cal. Rptr. 357, 364 (Ct. App. 1984), or court-ordered abortion, *In re Mary P.*, 444 N.Y.S.2d 545, 546–47 (Fam. Ct. 1981).

cisions in 1973 still provide the compelling reason for recognizing the constitutional dimensions of a woman's right to decide whether to end her pregnancy." 476 U.S. at 759.

Given the certainty of disrupting the lives and settled expectations of countless women, overturning *Roe* would be "a rare and grave undertaking," *Webster*, 492 U.S. at 558 (Blackmun, J., concurring in part and dissenting in part), which could be justified only by a strong showing by the Commonwealth that special circumstances demand that result. Only if the precedent is "unsound in principle," "unworkable in practice," or has led to inconsistent, unforeseen, or anomalous results, *see Garcia v. San Antonio Metropolitan Transit Auth.*, 469 U.S. 528, 546–47 (1985); *Vasquez*, 474 U.S. at 266, would this radical step be warranted.[33] None of these justifications is present here.

C. *Roe* Is Soundly Based in the Constitution and Sets Forth a Fair and Workable Standard of Adjudication.

1. The decision to terminate or continue a pregnancy is a fundamental right.

This Court has long recognized rights of privacy and bodily integrity. As early as 1891, it held

> [n]o right is held more sacred, or is more carefully guarded by the common law, than the right of every individual to the possession and control of his own person, free from all restraint or interference of others . . . .

Union Pacific Ry. Co. v. Botsford, 141 U.S. 250, 251–52 (1891). *See also Olmstead v. United States*, 277 U.S. 438, 478 (1928) (Brandeis, J., dissenting) ("The makers of our Con-

---

33. Overruling a decision so recently reaffirmed would seriously undermine public confidence in the integrity of this Court, especially when nothing has changed but the Court's composition. *See* Brief *Amici Curiae* of Certain Members of Congress. *See Florida Dep't of Health v. Florida Nursing Homes Ass'n*, 450 U.S. 147, 154 (1981) (Stevens, J., concurring) (*stare decisis* gives citizens "confidence that the rules on which they rely in ordering their affairs . . . are rules of law and not merely the opinions of a small group of men who temporarily occupy high office"). "[I]t should go without saying that the vitality of . . . constitutional principles cannot be allowed to yield simply because of disagreement with them." *Brown v. Board of Education*, 349 U.S. 294, 300 (1955). *See also Thornburgh*, 476 U.S. at 771–72.

stitution . . . conferred, as against the government, the right to be let alone, the most comprehensive of rights and the right most valued by civilized men"). Throughout the last century, this Court recognized that the fundamental right of privacy protects citizens against governmental intrusion in such intimate family matters as procreation, childrearing, marriage, and contraceptive choice. *Meyer v. Nebraska*, 262 U.S. 390, 399 (1923); *Pierce v. Society of Sisters*, 268 U.S. 510, 534–35 (1925); *Skinner v. Oklahoma ex rel. Williamson*, 316 U.S. 535, 541 (1942); *Griswold v. Connecticut*, 381 U.S. 479, 485–86 (1965); *Loving v. Virginia*, 388 U.S. 1, 12 (1967); *Eisenstadt v. Baird*, 405 U.S. 438, 453 (1972). *See also Stanley v. Georgia*, 394 U.S. 557, 564 (1969). These cases embody the principle that personal decisions that profoundly affect bodily integrity, identity, and destiny should be largely beyond the reach of government. *Eisenstadt*, 405 U.S. at 453; *Thornburgh*, 476 U.S. at 772. *See also Thornburgh*, 476 U.S. at 777 n.5 (Stevens, J., concurring) (concept of privacy embodies the "moral fact that a person belongs to himself and not others nor to society as a whole") (quoting Charles Fried, Correspondence, 6 Phil. & Pub. Aff. 288–89 (1977)).

In *Roe*, this Court correctly applied these principles to a woman's right to choose abortion. The decision to terminate or continue a pregnancy has an impact on a woman's life equal to, if not greater than, decisions about contraception or marriage. 410 U.S. at 153.[34] As this Court held in *Thornburgh*, 476 U.S. at 772, few decisions are more basic to "individual dignity and autonomy," or more appropriate to the "private sphere of individual liberty," than the uniquely personal and self-defining decision of whether to continue a pregnancy. *See also Carey*, 431 U.S. at 684.

State restrictions on abortion violate a woman's privacy in two ways.[35] First, compelled continuation of a pregnancy in-

34. "Indeed, if one decision is more 'fundamental' to the individual's freedom than the other, surely it is the post-conception decision that is the more serious." *Thornburgh*, 476 U.S. at 776 (Stevens, J., concurring). An individual denied the right to use contraception may be able to avoid pregnancy by avoiding sexual intercourse. A pregnant woman has no alternative besides abortion to avoid forced parenthood, *Carey*, 431 U.S. at 713 (Stevens, J., concurring), and pregnancy itself is all too often the result of rape, incest, or contraceptive failure—circumstances outside the woman's control.

35. *See generally* Susan R. Estrich & Kathleen M. Sullivan, *Abortion Politics: Writing for an Audience of One*, 138 U. Pa. L. Rev. 119, 126–30 (1989).

fringes on a woman's right to bodily integrity by imposing substantial physical intrusions and significant risks of physical harm. As Justice O'Connor explained in *Cruzan v. Director, Missouri Dep't of Health*, 110 S. Ct. 2841, 2856 (1990) (O'Connor, J., concurring),

> Because our notions of liberty are inextricably entwined with our idea of physical freedom and self-determination, this Court has often deemed state incursions into the body repugnant to the interests protected by the Due Process Clause.

In addition to the dramatic physical changes that take place during pregnancy,[36] pregnant women also experience a wide range of adverse health consequences. As many as ninety percent of pregnant women develop gastrointestinal problems, including nausea and vomiting.[37] Many women confront potentially more serious problems including gestational diabetes, hypertension,[38] preeclampsia (high blood pressure, water retention, and protein in urine), and eclampsia (a severe form of preeclampsia characterized by headaches and seizures potentially leading to coma).[39]

Labor and delivery pose additional health risks and physical demands. Vaginal delivery entails extreme pain, often lasting up to thirteen hours and in many cases longer,[40] and substantial risk of infection and laceration.[41] The nearly twenty-five

---

36. Pregnancy increases a woman's uterus 500 to 1,000 times its original capacity and her body weight by 25 pounds or more. F. Gary Cunningham, Paul C. MacDonald & Norman F. Gant, *Williams Obstetrics* 129–34, 136–37 (18th ed. 1989) [hereinafter *Williams Obstetrics*].

37. David N. Danforth and James R. Scott, *Obstetrics and Gynecology* 334–35 (5th ed. 1986) [hereinafter *Obstetrics and Gynecology*]. Other common problems include back pain, varicose veins, hemorrhoids, headaches, and water retention. *Williams Obstetrics* at 137, 270–73.

38. Hypertension complicates about six or seven percent of pregnancies. *Williams Obstetrics* at 3. During pregnancy, hypertensive women are at high risk for serious complications, including convulsions and coma. *Id.*

39. *Williams Obstetrics* at 654–72, 818–19. The medical risks of pregnancy are compounded for certain women. Among those facing the greatest risks are teenagers, especially those younger than 15. They suffer high incidences of toxemia, anemia, premature labor, and prolonged labor. *See* Jane Menken, *The Health and Demographic Consequences of Adolescent Pregnancy and Childbearing*, in *Adolescent Pregnancy and Childbearing: Findings from Research* 181, 187 (Catherine S. Chilman ed., 1980).

40. *See* E.J. Quilligan, *Prenatal Care in Gynecology and Obstetrics: The Health Care of Women* 579, 614 (Seymour L. Romney et al. eds., 2d ed. 1981) [hereinafter *Gynecology and Obstetrics*].

41. *Id.* at 626–27, 632–33, 637–38.

percent of women who deliver by cesarean section are exposed to even higher risks of death and adverse health consequences.[42] In sum, as Chief Justice Rehnquist has recognized, pregnancy entails "profound physical, emotional and psychological consequences . . . ." *Michael M.* v. *Sonoma County Superior Court*, 450 U.S. 464, 471 (1981). Indeed, restrictive abortion laws force women to endure physical invasions far more substantial than those this Court has held to violate the constitutional principle of bodily integrity in other contexts. *See, e.g., Botsford,* 141 U.S. at 251–52 (refusing to order physical examination); *Winston* v. *Lee,* 470 U.S. 753 (1985) (invalidating surgical removal of a bullet from a murder suspect); *Rochin* v. *California,* 342 U.S. 165 (1952) (invalidating stomach-pumping).[43] In addition to violating principles of bodily integrity, abortion restrictions also deprive women of the right to make autonomous decisions about reproduction and family planning—critical life choices that this Court has long deemed central to the right of privacy. *Roe,* 410 U.S. at 152–53; *id.* at 211 (Douglas, J., concurring) (Fourteenth Amendment protects "freedom of choice in the basic decisions of . . . life"). Because parenthood has a dramatic impact on a woman's educational prospects,[44] employment opportuni-

---

42. Robert K. Creasy and Robert Resnik, *Maternal–Fetal Medicine: Principles and Practice* 530 (2d ed. 1989). In 25% to 50% of cesarean sections, women face such complications as infection, hemorrhage, aspiration, swelling of the lungs, and pulmonary embolism. *Obstetrics and Gynecology,* at 738. The risk of maternal death is two to four times greater than in vaginal delivery. Carl J. Paverstein, *Clinical Obstetrics* 887 (1987).

43. In contrast, the severity and frequency of death or serious health consequences from abortion is significantly less than with childbirth. A woman is 20 times more likely to die from giving birth than from having an abortion. Katherine Koot, Jacqueline D. Forrest, and Susan Harlap, *Comparing the Health Risks and Benefits of Contraceptive Choices,* 23 Fam. Plan. Persp. 54, 57 (1991). *See also* Scott A. Lebolt, David A. Grimes, and Willard Cates, Jr., *Mortality from Abortion and Childbirth: Are the Populations Comparable?,* 248 J.A.M.A. 188, 191 (1982). Up to the eighth week of pregnancy, abortion is more than 20 times safer than childbirth. *Id.* at 191. Similarly, the nonfatal health risks associated with legal abortion are very limited and substantially lower than the risks of childbirth. *Williams Obstetrics* at 506.

44. Forced parenthood curtails the ability of teenagers to obtain even the most basic education. "[Y]oung women who give birth while they are in junior high school or high school complete on average fewer years of school, are less likely to earn a high school diploma, and are less likely to go on to college and graduate study than those who delay childbearing until their twenties." National Research Council, *Risking the Future: Adolescent Sexuality, Pregnancy, and Childbearing* 126 (Cheryl D. Hayes ed. 1987). Indeed, 56% of women who became mothers at age seventeen or

ties,[45] and self-determination, restrictive abortion laws deprive her of basic control of her life. For these reasons, "the decision whether or not to beget or bear a child" lies at "the very heart of this cluster of constitutionally protected choices." *Carey*, 431 U.S. at 685. Indeed, the right to choose abortion partakes of those constitutional freedoms at the heart of a free society: the freedoms of spirit and self-determination. *See West Virginia State Bd. of Educ. v. Barnette*, 319 U.S. 624, 636–37, 642 (1943); *Wooley v. Maynard*, 430 U.S. 705 (1977).

2. The *Roe* trimester framework is workable and fairly accommodates competing interests.

In *Roe*, this Court identified only two state interests that are sufficiently compelling to override a woman's fundamental right to choose abortion. The state has "an important and legitimate interest in preserving and protecting the health of the pregnant woman"[46] and an "important and legitimate interest in protecting the potentiality of human life." 410 U.S. at 162.

Roe's trimester framework establishes that the latter interest

---

younger do not complete high school. Dawn M. Upchurch and James McCarthy, *Adolescent Childbearing and High School Completion in the 1980s: Have Things Changed?*, 21 Fam. Plan. Persp. 199, 200 (1989). *See also* Laurie Zabin, Marilyn Hirsch and Mark Emerson, *When Urban Adolescents Choose Abortion: Effects on Education, Psychological Status and Subsequent Pregnancy*, 21 Fam. Plan. Persp. 248 (1989).

45. Employment opportunities for women with children are severely limited. *See generally* Reva Siegel, *Reasoning from the Body: A Historical Perspective on Abortion Regulation and Questions of Equal Protection*, 44 Stan. L. Rev. 261, 375–78 (1992); Victor R. Fuchs, *Women's Quest for Economic Equality*, 3 J. Econ. Persp. 25 (1989). Because the workplace typically does not accommodate parental responsibilities, and because child care is often unavailable or unaffordable, women, who bear primary responsibility for young children, are severely disadvantaged in the workplace. Many women are forced to leave their jobs to care for their children. *See Women's Work, Men's Work: Sex Segregation on the Job* 73–74 (Barbara F. Reskin and Heidi I. Hartmann eds. 1986). Others obtain part-time work or move to lower paying, less skilled positions in order to meet parental responsibilities. *Id.* at 74. *See also* Paul Weiler, *The Wages of Sex: The Uses and Limits of Comparable Worth*, 99 Harv. L. Rev. 1728, 1786 (1986) (the "addition of each child enhances the man's earnings by another three percent while depressing that of the woman by fully ten percent"). Where a woman raises a child alone, the economic consequences are even more devastating. U.S. Bureau of the Census, Current Population Reports: Special Studies, Series P–23, No. 162, *Studies in Marriage and the Family*, 18 (approximately half the children in households headed by women live in poverty).

46. Petitioners do not dispute that the state possesses a compelling interest in the protection of women's health. The restrictions at issue here, however, fail to further this interest. *See infra*, Section IV.

is not sufficiently compelling to override a woman's right to choose abortion until the point of viability, *i.e.* that stage in pregnancy when the fetus is capable of independent survival. Even then, the state's interest is paramount only in cases in which the woman's life or health are not endangered by continued pregnancy. *Id.* at 163–64.

The *Roe* trimester framework constitutes a fair and logical means of accommodating the interests of the woman and the state. The compelling state interest in the fetus logically arises at the point of viability:

> The viability line . . . marks that threshold moment prior to which a fetus cannot survive separate from the woman and cannot reasonably and objectively be regarded as a subject of rights or interests distinct from, or paramount to, those of the pregnant woman. At the same time, the viability standard takes account of the undeniable fact that as the fetus evolves into its postnatal form, and as it loses its dependence on the uterine environment, the State's interest in the fetus' potential human life, and in fostering a regard for human life in general, becomes compelling.

Webster, 492 U.S. at 553–54 (Blackmun, J., concurring in part and dissenting in part).[47] Moreover, by placing the compelling point at fetal viability, *Roe* fairly and sensibly "safeguard[s] the constitutional liberties of pregnant women while recognizing and accommodating the State's interest in potential human life."[48] *Id.* at 553.

This Court must reject the view that the state's interest in potential life is compelling throughout pregnancy.[49] That view

47. *Roe* is consistent with the historic legal tradition of assigning greater value to fetal life late in pregnancy. As this Court observed in *Roe*, to the extent that limitations on abortion did exist in ancient and common law, they were imposed after quickening or "viability." *Roe*, 410 U.S. at 132–36. *See generally* Brief *Amici Curiae* of American Historians.

48. The suggestion that the point of viability will recede with advances in medical technology and that *Roe* is therefore on "a collision course with itself," *Akron*, 462 U.S. at 458 (O'Connor, J., dissenting), has no medical foundation. While substantial strides have been made in recent years in saving infants born between 24 and 28 weeks, the earliest point of fetal viability has remained at about 24 weeks gestation—the same as it was at the time *Roe* was decided. *Webster*, 492 U.S. at 554 n.9 (Blackmun, J., concurring in part and dissenting in part). *See generally* Brief *Amici Curiae* of 167 Distinguished Scientists and Physicians, Including 11 Nobel Laureates at 9–13, *Webster*, *supra* (No. 88–605).

49. *See, e.g., Thornburgh*, 476 U.S. at 795 (White, J., dissenting).

would render meaningless this Court's recognition of the abortion choice as a protected liberty interest of fundamental importance.[50] Any restriction, even criminalization of abortion in virtually all circumstances, might be justified by reference to the state's compelling interest in potential life. *Webster*, 492 U.S. at 555–56 (Blackmun, J., concurring in part and dissenting in part). In addition, a compelling interest in potential life throughout pregnancy might justify other extreme intrusions on pregnant women's liberty. For example, would government be free to force pregnant women to act in whatever ways it determined were optimal for the fetus in order to further its compelling interest in fetal life?[51] Could government compel a woman to undergo a cesarean section or fetal surgery to further its interests? Clearly, these profoundly disturbing derailments of personal liberty would be incompatible with this Court's recognizing as "fundamental" those rights necessary to a "free, egalitarian and democratic society." *Thornburgh*, 476 U.S. at 793 (White, J., dissenting). *See also International Union, U.A.W. v. Johnson Controls, Inc.*, 111 S. Ct. 1196, 1207 (1991) ("[d]ecisions about the welfare of future children must be left to the parents who conceive, bear, support, and raise them rather than to the employers who hire those parents").[52] Finally, the *Roe* trimester framework has been a workable guidepost for courts and state legislatures.

---

50. Surely, as the Court of Appeals for the District of Columbia recognized, "a fetus cannot have rights . . . superior to those of a person who has already been born." *In re A.C.*, 573 A.2d 1235, 1244 (D.C. 1990) (en banc). *See also Roe*, 410 U.S. at 158.

51. "Imagine, for example, that a state made the following findings: complete rest in the first three months of pregnancy reduced miscarriages by 9%, and working at video display terminals increased miscarriages by 4%. On these bases the state passed a law prohibiting all pregnant women from working at display terminals or working anywhere more than four hours a day during the first three months of pregnancy. In both of these cases, if the state justified the imposition by asserting its compelling governmental interest in protecting all fetal life, it could contend that there was no less restrictive alternative to this seemingly Draconian measure." Walter Dellinger and Gene B. Sperling, *Abortion and the Supreme Court: The Retreat from Roe v. Wade*, 138 U. Pa. L. Rev. 83, 116 (1989). *See also* Dawn M. Johnsen, Note, *The Creation of Fetal Rights: Conflicts with Women's Constitutional Rights of Liberty, Privacy, and Equal Protection*, 95 Yale L.J. 599 (1986).

52. In other contexts, this Court has refused to allow a state's interest to ride roughshod over a constitutional right. *See, e.g., City of Richmond v. J.A. Croson Co.*, 488 U.S. 469, 498 (1989) (interest in redressing societal discrimination deemed not to be sufficiently compelling to justify raceconscious remedies because it " 'has no logical stopping point' ") (quoting *Wygant v. Jackson Bd. of Educ.*, 476 U.S. 267, 275 (1986) (plurality opinion)).

During the last nineteen years, lower courts, which have cited the decision in over 3,500 cases, have had little difficulty applying *Roe*'s clear mandates. With consistent application and reaffirmation by this Court, questions regarding *Roe*'s meaning were resolved and lower courts were readily able to determine whether state restrictions were constitutional.[53] State legislatures, also understanding *Roe*'s mandates, passed fewer laws restricting abortions for adult women.[54] Even if it could be said, however, that the application of *Roe* has posed difficulties, complexity in application has never provided the basis for abandoning constitutional protection for a fundamental right. *Daniels* v. *Williams*, 474 U.S. 327, 334–35 (1986) (citing *LeRoy Fibre Co.* v. *Chicago, M. & St. P.R. Co.*, 232 U.S. 340, 354 (1914) (Holmes, J., partially concurring)); *see also Webster*, 492 U.S. at 549–50 (Blackmun, J., concurring in part and dissenting in part). A doctrine's legitimacy is not undermined by the challenge of applying constitutional doctrines and making careful differentiations between similar circumstances. 492 U.S. at 549–52 (Blackmun, J., concurring in part and dissenting in part). Rather, "these careful distinctions reflect the process of constitutional adjudication itself" and the discharge of this Court's "duty to do justice carefully, especially when fundamental rights rise or fall with [its] decision." *Id.* at 550, 552.

D. *Roe*'s Guarantee of Safe, Legal Abortion Has Been of Profound Importance to the Lives, Health, and Equality of American Women.

In addition to its soundness and workability as a constitutional doctrine, *Roe* has proven an enormously wise decision

---

53. *See, e.g., Charles* v. *Carey*, 579 F. Supp. 464 (N.D. Ill. 1983), *aff'd in part and rev'd in part sub nom. Charles* v. *Daley*, 749 F.2d 452 (7th Cir. 1984), *appeal dismissed sub nom. Diamond* v. *Charles*, 476 U.S. 54 (1986); *Margaret S.* v. *Treen*, 597 F. Supp. 636, 653–66 (E.D. La. 1984), *aff'd sub nom. Margaret S.* v. *Edwards*, 794 F.2d 994 (5th Cir. 1986); *Ragsdale* v. *Turnock*, 841 F.2d 1358, 1372–73 (7th Cir. 1988), *proceedings deferred*, 493 U.S. 987 (1989).

54. For example, in 1979, the year after the *Akron* ordinance was adopted, 10 states enacted similar laws. In apparent response to lower federal court decisions declaring these laws unconstitutional, the numbers subsequently declined to four laws in 1980, and three in 1981. Patricia Donovan, *Fertility-Related State Laws Enacted in 1981*, 14 Fam. Plan. Persp. 63, 66 (1982). In 1984, the year after *Akron* was decided, only one state legislature enacted a comprehensive anti-abortion statute. The Alan Guttmacher Institute, *Legislative Record, State Legislatures—1984 Bills Enacted* (1984).

of immeasurable benefit to the lives, health, and equality of American women. First, *Roe* has allowed millions of women to escape the dangers of illegal abortion and forced pregnancy. Despite the illegality or highly restricted availability of abortion in the years before *Roe*, women always obtained abortions.[55] Women who could afford the often extraordinary expense traveled to a place where abortion was legal;[56] less affluent women turned to illegal procedures or self-induced abortions. In the 1950s and 1960s, an estimated 200,000 to 1.2 million illegal abortions occurred annually in the United States.[57] As a result of these back-alley and self-induced abortions, as many as 5,000 to 10,000 women died each year,[58] and many other women suffered severe physical and psychological injury. Still other women endured forced pregnancy and its attendant health risks.[59] And history makes clear that, without constitutional protection, low-income women, who are disproportionately women of color, suffered the most.[60] Second, the nationwide legalization of abortion following *Roe* resulted in dramatic advances in the safety of abortion, and, as a consequence, there were substantial decreases in the total number of abortion-related deaths and complications. Between 1973—the year *Roe* was decided—and 1985, the death

55. *See generally* Ellen Messer and Katherine E. May, *Back Rooms: Voices from the Illegal Abortion Era* (1988); *Abortion and Women's Health*, *supra* note 29.

56. Prior to 1970, when abortion was legalized in New York, women traveled to foreign countries to obtain abortions. *Women Flock to London Seeking Abortions Under Liberal Law*, Medical World News Vol. 10, pp. 24–27 (1969). In 1972, 44% of all abortions in the United States were obtained outside a woman's state of residence. *Abortion and Women's Health* at 3. For example, in the two and one-half years preceding *Roe*, nearly 350,000 women traveled to New York State to obtain a legal abortion. *Id.* The need to travel resulted in delayed abortions and, consequently, increased medical risks. *Id.*

57. Christopher Tietze and Stanley K. Henshaw, *Induced Abortion: A World Review* 43 (6th ed. 1986); Willard Cates, Jr. and Roger W. Rochat, *Illegal Abortions in the United States: 1972–1974*, 8 Fam. Plan. Persp. 86, 89 (1976) [hereinafter *Illegal Abortions*].

58. *See* Lawrence Lader, *Abortion* 3 (1966); *Illegal Abortions* at 86–90; Richard H. Schwarz, *Septic Abortion* 7 (1968).

59. *See* Section I.C.1. *supra*. Women with unwanted pregnancies have a higher rate of post-partum infection, hemorrhage, and post-partum depression, and sometimes lasting psychological damage, than women who want to carry their pregnancies to term. Willard Cates, Jr., *Legal Abortion: The Public Health Record*, 215 Sci. 1586, 1587 (1982).

60. Mortality rates from illegal abortions were as much as 12 times higher for women of color than for white women. *Illegal Abortions* at 87–88. "More than two-thirds of the women who died from illegal abortions from 1972 to 1974 were black or from some other minority group." *Abortion and Women's Health* at 5. *See generally* Brief *Amici Curiae* of NAACP Legal Defense Fund et al.

rate for abortion fell more than eight times, from 3.4 deaths per 100,000 in 1973 to 0.4 deaths per 100,000 in 1985.[61] Similarly, abortion-related complications requiring hospitalization fell sharply during the 1970s, with the steepest drop following *Roe* in 1973.[62] Today, at all points in pregnancy, abortion poses a lower risk of death than does childbirth.[63] Experience throughout this country's history amply demonstrates that overturning *Roe* will not end abortion. Instead, permitting states to criminalize abortion or impose burdensome restrictions, either singularly or cumulatively, will tragically and undeniably return women to illegal, back-alley practitioners or self-abortions.[64] As in the days before *Roe*, the number of abortion-related deaths and injuries will soar and women will be forced to continue unwanted pregnancies against their will.

Finally, by affording women greater control over their childbearing, *Roe* has permitted American women to participate more fully and equally in every societal undertaking. The option of safe, legal abortion has enabled great numbers of women to control the timing and size of their families and thus continue their education, enter the workforce, and otherwise make meaningful decisions consistent with their own moral choices. As a result, women have experienced significant economic and social gains since *Roe*.[65] It is simply unconscionable for this Court to allow hostile state legislatures to force women back to the days when "the female [was] destined solely for the home and rearing of the family, and only the male for the marketplace and the world of ideas." *Stanton v. Stanton*, 421 U.S. 7, 14–15 (1975). To do so would wreak havoc on a century of constitutional doctrine and

61. *Abortion and Women's Health* at 28.

62. *Id.* at 32.

63. Tietze & Henshaw, *supra* note 57, at 107–13. Induced abortion is one of the most common and safest surgical procedures performed in this country, with half the risk of death involved in tonsillectomy and one-hundredth the risk of death involved in appendectomy. Warren M. Hern, *Abortion Practice* 23–24 (1984). *See also supra* note 43.

64. For example, because Indiana Public Law 106 required parental consent, 17-year-old Rebecca Bell resorted to an illegal abortion, which resulted in a fatal septic infection. Judy Mann, *Illegal Abortion's Deadly Price*, Washington Post, Aug. 3, 1990, at C3.

65. For example, there has been a substantial increase in women's labor force representation and a diminution in the wage gap between men and women. *See* Fuchs, *supra* note 45, at 36–37; *Women's Work*, *supra* note 45, at 23–24.

"cast[ ] into darkness the hopes and visions of every woman in this country who had come to believe that the Constitution guaranteed her the right to exercise some control over her unique ability to bear children." *Webster*, 492 U.S. at 557 (Blackmun, J., concurring in part and dissenting in part).

II. THE "UNDUE BURDEN" TEST ADOPTED BY THE COURT OF APPEALS IS VAGUE AND UNWORKABLE.

By stretching logic, precedent, and the bounds of its own authority, the court of appeals adopted the less protective "undue burden" standard, which has never commanded a majority or even a plurality of this Court. By so doing, the court of appeals rejected *Roe*, *Akron*, and *Thornburgh* and turned "a single opinion that lacks majority support into national law." *King* v. *Palmer*, 950 F.2d 771, 782 (D.C. Cir. 1991) (en banc) (finding inapplicable *Marks* v. *United States*, 430 U.S. 188 (1977)). *But see Coe* v. *Melahn*, No. 90–1552 (8th Cir. Mar. 2, 1992).

More important, the "undue burden" test is seriously flawed. First, this Court has never applied the "undue burden" analysis to legislation targeting constitutionally protected interests.[66] Unlike strict scrutiny, whose hallmarks are known, and which

66. Relying upon *San Antonio Independent School Dist.* v. *Rodriguez*, 411 U.S. 1 (1973), *Gibson* v. *Florida Legislative Investigation Comm.*, 372 U.S. 539 (1963), and *Bates* v. *City of Little Rock*, 361 U.S. 516 (1960), Justice O'Connor argues in *Akron* that the undue burden standard is not novel to constitutional law. 462 U.S. at 462 (O'Connor, J., dissenting). But none of these cases apply an "undue burden" analysis. In *Rodriguez*, Justice Powell focuses on whether the right to education is a fundamental right, not on whether that right had been substantially infringed. 411 U.S. at 34–37. Moreover, the Court makes clear that strict scrutiny is triggered in cases involving "legislation which 'deprived,' 'infringed,' or 'interfered' with the free exercise of some such fundamental personal right or liberty." *Id.* at 38 (citations omitted). In *Gibson*, although Justice Goldberg occasionally discussed the "substantial" infringement of the right of free association, the Court applied the "strict scrutiny" standard and never examined the degree of interference necessary to trigger this exacting level of review. 372 U.S. at 545–46. Similarly, in *Bates*, the Court held that "where there is a significant encroachment upon personal liberty," the state must demonstrate a compelling purpose. 361 U.S. at 524. But the intent of this discussion was to characterize the interference with petitioner's rights as "neither speculative nor remote." *Id.* Indeed, in *Bates* as in *Gibson*, the Court pointed out that constitutional freedoms are protected against "subtle" governmental interference as well as direct restrictions. *Id.* at 523. *See also Gibson*, 372 U.S. at 544. Moreover, the Court's reliance upon *NAACP* v. *Alabama ex rel. Patterson*, 357 U.S. 449 (1958), makes clear that the traditional strict scrutiny standard was used to invalidate under the First Amendment the state-mandated disclosure of membership lists.

effectively safeguards the right to choose abortion from governmental interference, see Section I.C. supra, the "undue burden" test is a novel concept.

Second, the "undue burden" test provides wholly inadequate protection for women seeking abortions. Although some anti-choice commentators have suggested that the "undue burden" test is an acceptable middle ground between the strict scrutiny and rational basis tests, see James Bopp, Jr. and Richard E. Coleson, What Does Webster Mean?, 130 U. Pa. L. Rev. 157 (1989), all available clues to its application demonstrate that the test provides inadequate protection for the abortion right. Akron, 462 U.S. at 466–67, 470–74 (O'Connor, J., dissenting) (upholding second trimester hospitalization, biased counseling, mandatory delay, and physician-only counseling requirements under "undue burden" test); Thornburgh, 476 U.S. at 827–33 (O'Connor, J., dissenting) (upholding biased counseling, reporting requirements, degree of care for post-viability abortions, and second physician requirement when fetus is possibly viable under "undue burden" test). See also Akron, 462 U.S. at 420 n.1.

Third, if this Court addresses the constitutionality of each state restriction in a piecemeal fashion—as Justice O'Connor did in Akron and Thornburgh—the test is inadequate for yet another reason. Roe mandates that courts ultimately assess

> the degree of burden that the entire regime of abortion regulations places on a woman, . . . [examining] how a given regulation incrementally adds to the cumulative burden on the fundamental right. In contrast, the undue burden standard may allow a state to pile on 'reasonable regulation' after 'reasonable regulation' until a woman seeking an abortion first had to conquer a multi-faceted obstacle course.

Dellinger and Sperling, supra note 51, at 100 (emphasis in original). Cf. Murdock v. Pennsylvania, 319 U.S. 105, 115 (1943) ("cumulative effect" of small license tax could crush religious practice when "exacted town by town").

Fourth, the "undue burden" test is likely to result in arbitrary and discriminatory applications by the lower courts. In Akron and Thornburgh, Justice O'Connor reiterated that heightened judicial scrutiny is reserved for only those instances in which the state has imposed " '*absolute* obstacles or *severe* limitations on the abortion decision,' not whenever a state regulation 'may "inhibit" abortions to some degree.' " *Thornburgh*, 476 U.S. at 828 (O'Connor, J., dissenting) (quoting *Akron*, 462 U.S. at 464 (O'Connor, J., dissenting)) (emphasis added). A burden is not "undue" unless the measure has the effect of " '*substantially* limiting access to the means of effectuating th[e] decision' " to have an abortion. *Akron*, 462 U.S. at 463 (quoting *Carey*, 431 U.S. at 688 (emphasis in original)).[67] Thus lower courts are required to make quantitative and subjective judgments of what constitutes a severe or substantial limitation in order to determine whether the state bears the burden of proving a compelling purpose for the law's enactment.

Even the United States as *amicus curiae* has abandoned the "undue burden" test as flawed. While its *amicus curiae* brief in *Akron*, 462 U.S. 416, urged this Court to adopt the "undue burden" test, its briefs in both *Webster*, 492 U.S. 490, and *Hodgson*, 110 S. Ct. 2926, rejected the standard, finding that the "concept of an undue burden obviously is not self-defining." *See* Brief for the United States as *Amicus Curiae* Supporting Appellants at 22, *Webster*, *supra* (No. 88–605). In *Hodgson*, the United States continued:

Asking whether a particular measure unduly burdens the right provides no meaningful guidelines for assessing the weight of the competing interests, or for determining how much deference to give to legislative judgments. The only measure of constitutionality would be the courts' own subjective assessment of what is "due" or "undue" in any particular context. In these circumstances, the undue burden analysis would offer "no guide but the Court's own discretion," *Baldwin v. Missouri*, 281 U.S. 586, 595 (1930) (Holmes, J., dissenting); *see Webster*, 109 S. Ct. 3066 n.* (Scalia, J., concurring in part and concurring in the judgment), and would serve only to mask judgments made on the basis of assumptions that would remain unarticulated. In our view, great caution should be exercised

---

67. The court of appeals would also examine whether a particular regulation would have a severe or drastic impact upon the time, cost, or number of legal providers of abortions. 33a.

in resolving important constitutional controversies under the "undue burden" mantle.

Brief for the United States as *Amicus Curiae* at 21, *Hodgson, supra* (Nos. 88–1125, 88–1309).

In the several years since this Court decided *Webster*, state legislators have proposed hundreds of restrictions on abortion[68] which, if enacted, would deter, and in many instances prevent, women from obtaining appropriate health care. Because it offers no guidance to lower courts, the "undue burden" standard will require this Court to determine separately whether each and every one of these numerous provisions imposes an undue burden on a right of reproductive privacy and to analyze that question separately for different classes of women.[69] In that event, fears, expressed by some members of this Court, of encouraging unnecessary litigation and sitting as a super-legislature will be magnified tenfold.

Finally, the "undue burden" test will oblige the women already suffering from an act's coercive influence to demonstrate its onerous burdens through costly, time-consuming litigation. Under *Roe*, once plaintiffs prove that a statute will create more than a de minimis impact upon a woman's right to choose abortion, the burden shifts to the state to demonstrate that the law furthers a compelling purpose. This allocation is fair, because the state enjoys substantial resources to make its case, resources that women facing unwanted pregnancies are less able to secure. Placing this extraordinary burden upon women facing unwanted pregnancies will be particularly disadvantageous to low-income women, young women, rural women, and battered women, who also are the very citizens least able to defend their interests in the legislative arena.[70]

---

68. *See* National Abortion Rights Action League, *Who Decides? A State-by-State Review of Abortion Rights,* iii (3d ed. 1992); *Abortion and Women's Health* at 39.

69. Restrictions that appear a mere affront or inconvenience to wealthy, educated women acting with the support of their families may impose prohibitive burdens on women with other life circumstances.

70. As commentators recently noted: "[I]t is simply unfair, and unnecessary, to require that a woman actually sacrifice her constitutional liberty *before* she or anyone else can challenge a restriction on her freedom. The Court should not demand an

III. THE RATIONAL BASIS TEST WILL PROVOKE AND SANCTION EXTREME GOVERNMENTAL INTERFERENCE WITH PRIVATE REPRODUCTIVE DECISIONS.

Unfettered deference to legislative action resulting from the adoption of a rational basis standard will sanction and encourage intolerable legislative interference with women's reproductive choices. In *Webster*, a plurality of this Court abandoned *Roe*'s trimester framework on the assumption that modern legislatures would be unlikely to pass legislation "reminiscent of the dark ages." 492 U.S. at 521. However, the state legislative experience during the last several years has belied any notion of legislative moderation.[71] While courts must give appropriate deference to the legislative process in the economic arena, *see* *Ferguson* v. *Skrupa*, 372 U.S. 726, 727–31 (1963), the framers of the Constitution never intended the political process to resolve questions of individual rights. As this Court has recognized:

The very purpose of a Bill of Rights was to withdraw certain subjects from the vicissitudes of political controversy, to place them beyond the reach of majorities and officials and to establish them as legal principles to be applied by the courts. One's right to life, liberty, and property, to free speech, a free press, freedom of worship and assembly, and other fundamental

---

unwanted child, or a woman maimed by an illegal abortion, as proof that strict scrutiny is warranted." Estrich & Sullivan, *supra* note 36, at 136 (emphasis in original).

71. For example, Utah passed a restrictive abortion law that would have subjected doctors to the death penalty for providing illegal abortion. *See Jane L.* v. *Bangerter*, No. 91–C–345–G (D. Utah filed Apr. 4, 1991). In 1990, Louisiana attempted to revive its pre-*Roe* law subjecting physicians to ten years at hard labor for performing an abortion. *Weeks* v. *Connick*, 733 F. Supp. 1036 (E.D. La. 1990). In 1991, after that attempt failed, the Louisiana legislature passed a law banning abortions and contraceptive methods that operate after conception. 1991 La. Sess. Law Serv. 74 (West). In 1990, the territory of Guam passed a law banning virtually all abortions, as well as counseling, encouraging, or advising a woman to obtain an abortion. *Guam Society of Obstetricians & Gynecologists* v. *Ada*, 766 F. Supp. 1422 (D. Guam 1990), *appeal pending*, No. 90–16706 (9th Cir.). A bill just recently introduced in Rhode Island not only bans abortions except to prevent the immediate death of the pregnant woman, but also prohibits advertisements and referrals about abortion. No. 91–H5310, Rhode Island General Assembly, January Sess. (1991).

rights may not be submitted to vote; they depend on the outcome of no elections.

Barnette, 319 U.S. at 638.

Adoption of a rational basis test will also permit state legislatures to impose numerous restrictions adversely affecting women's lives and health and subjecting women of different states to differing standards. A woman's right to choose abortion will vary solely because she does not live in or cannot afford to travel to a state that is more respectful of her constitutional liberty. The result will be an irrational patchwork of state and local laws that "would not conform to the American legal norm of equality." Laurence H. Tribe, *Abortion: The Clash of Absolutes* 75 (1990); *see also* Brief *Amici Curiae* of Certain State Elected Officials; Brief *Amici Curiae* of the City of New York et al.

Moreover, the rational basis test might sanction a wide variety of other incursions on the personal liberty of pregnant women. To further mere rational state interests, could government dictate the lifestyle or working conditions of pregnant women? Could government compel childbirth to further population expansion?[72] Conversely, could it justify forced contraception, abortion, or sterilization to support its rational interests? *See* cases cited *supra* note 32. These intrusive deprivations of personal liberty and autonomy would conflict with this Court's recognition that "the full scope of the liberty guaranteed by the Due Process Clause . . . includes a freedom from all substantial arbitrary impositions and purposeless restraints . . . [and] that certain interests require particularly careful scrutiny of the state needs asserted to justify their abridgment." *Poe v. Ullman,* 367 U.S. 497, 543 (1961) (Harlan, J., dissenting).

---

72. For example, the pro-natalist policies of the former Ceausescu regime in Romania—including a ban on all forms of contraception and sterilization except in extremely limited circumstances, extra taxation for childless marriages, and monthly birth quotas for factory employees—might be constitutional if rationally related to governmental interests. *See* Charlotte Hord, Henry P. David, France Donnay and Merril Wolf, *Reproductive Health in Romania: Reversing the Ceausescu Legacy,* 22 Stud. in Fam. Plan. 231, 232 (1991).

IV. THE CHALLENGED PROVISIONS ARE INVALID UNDER ANY STANDARD OF REVIEW.

A. Mandatory Husband Notification Violates Rights of Privacy, Marital Integrity, and Equal Protection.

1. In violation of the right of privacy, the Act's husband notification restriction increases the likelihood of violence against women and fails to further any legitimate state interest.

Both the district court and the court of appeals correctly invalidated § 3209's requirement that every married woman first notify her husband that she is about to undergo an abortion. Ever since this Court established that a state may not empower a husband to veto a woman's abortion choice, *Danforth*, 428 U.S. at 67–72, no court has upheld as constitutional a husband notification requirement.[73] As this Court recognized, a notification statute may give the notified person a veto of the woman's decision, by giving that person the opportunity to prevent the abortion or to penalize the woman severely for exercising her choice. *See Hodgson*, 110 S. Ct. at 2939, 2945 n.36; *Bellotti v. Baird*, 443 U.S. 622, 647 (1979) ("*Bellotti II*"). The record in this case amply demonstrates the onerous burden the husband notification requirement would impose. As the court of appeals explained:

> The district court found that § 3209's notification requirement creates a substantial risk that women who would otherwise have an abortion will be prevented from having one. . . . In those situations where a husband is sufficiently opposed to abortion or sufficiently desirous of having a child that the wife will not voluntarily share the fact of her pregnancy and her intention to abort with him, the clinics' experts testified that coerced notification will predictably result in an effort to prevent the abortion.

---

73. *See Planned Parenthood v. Board of Medical Review*, 598 F. Supp. 625, 636 (D.R.I. 1984); *Eubanks v. Brown*, 604 F. Supp. 141, 148 (W.D. Ky. 1984); *Doe v. Deschamps*, 461 F. Supp. 682, 686 (D. Mont. 1976); *Scheinberg v. Smith*, 482 F. Supp. 529 (S.D. Fla. 1979), *aff'd in part, vacated in part, and remanded*, 659 F.2d 476 (5th Cir. Unit B Oct. 1981), *on remand*, 550 F. Supp. 1112 (S.D. Fla. 1982).

66a. Indeed, as the court of appeals observed, the district court found that the number of situations in which "women may reasonably fear dire consequences from notifying their husbands is potentially limitless." 70a; see also 257a n.42. "Even if the woman is not deterred from pursuing an abortion, the same arsenal of physical, economic, and psychological abuse is available to the notified husband to penalize the wife for exercising her constitutionally bestowed right." 68a.

The limited exceptions to the husband notification requirement do not relieve women of these severe burdens. Like the "less than effectual" abuse and neglect exception to Minnesota's two-parent notification statute, Hodgson, 110 S. Ct. at 2950 (O'Connor, J., concurring); see also id. at 2932 n.7, 2939 n.26, the Act's exceptions for sexual assault and bodily injury will leave battered women vulnerable to a range of coercion and abuse. As the district court found and the court of appeals acknowledged, the pattern of random violence inflicted on them ensures that many "battered spouses are psychologically incapacitated from making the assertion required by the statute even when there is ample objective basis for the required fear." 68a–69a; see also 197a–198a, 201a. Survivors of marital rape will also be unable to make the exception's required report to law enforcement officials "[g]iven the devastating effect that a report . . . is likely to have on the marital relationship and the economic support provided the wife by the marriage." 70a; see also 198a.

Moreover, like the inadequate abuse and neglect exception in Hodgson, the spousal sexual assault exception at issue here is, in reality, a means of notifying the husband. Hodgson, 110 S. Ct. at 2950 (O'Connor, J., concurring); see also id. at 2932 n.7. To avail herself of the exception, the woman must report the assault "to a law enforcement agency having the requisite jurisdiction," § 3209(b)(3), within 90 days. 18 Pa. Cons. Stat. Ann. § 3128(c)(Supp. 1991). Her husband will be notified of her action once an investigation begins or criminal charges are filed. Further, once the woman reports the marital rape to the police, the information becomes part of the public record and is therefore no longer confidential. See Scheetz v. The Morning Call, Inc., 946 F.2d 202, 207 (3d Cir. 1991). The "combination of the abused [woman's] reluctance to report sexual or physical abuse, . . . with the likelihood that invoking the . . . exception for the purpose of avoiding notice will result in notice, makes the . . . exception less than effectual." *Hodgson*, 110 S. Ct. at 2950 (O'Connor, J., concurring).

In addition, even though "physical violence is not the only burden reasonably predictable," the harsh exceptions apply only to acts of physical violence against the married woman. 69a. As the district court found, the exceptions would not apply where a husband would if notified,

> threaten to (1) [sic] publicize her intent to have an abortion to family, friends or acquaintances; (b) retaliate against her in future child custody or divorce proceedings; (c) inflict psychological intimidation or emotional harm upon her, her children or other persons; (d) inflict bodily harm on other persons such as children, family members or other loved ones; or (e) use his control over finances to deprive [her] of necessary monies for herself or her children.

194a. A woman protected by a restraining order under the Protection From Abuse Act, 23 Pa. Cons. Stat. Ann. § 6101 *et seq.* (Supp. 1991), also may be unprotected by the exception. 195a; 199a.[74] Moreover, this burdensome provision serves no legitimate state interest whatsoever.[75] The district court found that in the absence of a forced notification provision, "[t]he vast majority of women consult their husbands prior to deciding to terminate their pregnanc[ies]." 193a. As this Court recognized in *Hodgson*, 110 S. Ct. at 2945, "[a] statute requiring . . . notification would not further any state interest in those instances." Where women choose not to notify their husbands, the state interests, to the extent they

74. The exception for a woman unable to locate her husband through "diligent effort" is also of doubtful utility. The district court found that, because the Act does not define "diligent effort," the threat of civil and criminal penalties will compel abortion providers to construe the term in a narrow fashion, imposing another layer of delay before the woman may obtain an abortion. 194a.

75. The statute itself enumerates the interests that it purports to further: "the Commonwealth's interest in promoting the integrity of the marital relationship," and "a spouse's interest in having children within marriage and protecting the prenatal life of that spouse's child." § 3209(a).

are legitimate at all, would actually be disserved by forced notification. As the district court found,

> [t]he record clearly establishes that instead of fostering marital communication and bolstering the state's interest in marital integrity, the exact opposite effect would likely occur. . . . Not only could forced notice hasten the dissolution of a troubled marriage, but it could have potentially disastrous consequences, including subjecting the woman to physical abuse.

262a (citations omitted). *See also* 201a; *Planned Parenthood* v. *Board of Medical Review*, 598 F. Supp. at 640–41.[76] Nor can the Commonwealth's purported interest in protecting the husband's "interests in having children within marriage and in protecting the prenatal life of [his] child," § 3209(a), justify the violation of the woman's right of privacy. Although both men and women have a constitutionally protected interest against state interference in their ability to procreate, *see* Skinner, 316 U.S. at 541, and in their children's welfare, *see, e.g.*, *Michael H.* v. *Gerald D.*, 491 U.S. 110, 123 (1989), neither interest is served by the husband notification requirement. Instead, the statute protects only the husband's "interest" in compelling his wife to bear children for him. That decision, however, must remain with the pregnant woman, "who physically bears the child and who is the more directly and immediately affected by the pregnancy." *Danforth*, 428 U.S. at 71.

2. The Act's husband notification provision unconstitutionally interferes with the protected marital relationship.

This Court has held that the marital relationship is protected by "a right of privacy older than the Bill of Rights" for marriage is regarded as "intimate to the degree of being sacred." *Griswold*, 381 U.S. at 486. It " 'has long recognized that freedom of personal choice in matters of marriage and

---

76. Dr. Walker testified that forced notification would not guarantee discussion among spouses or improve communications in dysfunctional relationships. J.A. 229. Rather than improving marital integrity in any way, forced notification "will make family communication much more difficult and much more dangerous in [battering] relationships." J.A. 233.

family life is one of the liberties protected by the Due Process Clause of the Fourteenth Amendment.' " *Moore v. City of East Cleveland*, 431 U.S. 494, 499 (1977) (plurality opinion) (quoting *La Fleur*, 414 U.S. at 639–40); *see Zablocki*, 434 U.S. at 383–85 (1978); *Prince v. Massachusetts*, 321 U.S. 158, 166 (1944). As Justice Stevens reiterated in *Hodgson*:

> While the State has a legitimate interest in the creation and dissolution of the marriage contract . . . the family has a privacy interest in . . . the intimacies of the marital relationship which is protected by the Constitution against undue state interference . . . . Far more than contraceptives, at issue in *Poe* and *Griswold v. Connecticut*, 381 U.S. 479 (1965), the married couple has a well-recognized interest in protecting the sanctity of their communications from undue interference by the State.

110 S. Ct at 2943, 2944 n.33.

In addition, this Court has "emphasized that the First Amendment protects . . . family relationships, that presuppose 'deep attachments and commitments to the necessarily few other individuals with whom one shares not only a special community of thoughts, experiences, and beliefs but also distinctively personal aspects of one's life.' " *Board of Directors of Rotary Int'l v. Rotary Club*, 481 U.S. 537, 545 (1987) (quoting *Roberts v. United States Jaycees*, 468 U.S. 609, 619–20 (1984)). *See Employment Division, Dep't of Human Resources v. Smith*, 110 S. Ct. 1595, 1601 (1990); *City of Dallas v. Stanglin*, 490 U.S. 19, 24 (1989); *New York State Club Ass'n v. City of New York*, 487 U.S. 1, 18 (1988) (O'Connor, J., concurring).

In the guise of "protecting marital integrity," § 3209 flies in the face of these principles, subjecting marital discussions to state surveillance, censorship, and control. For couples whose relationships do not include discussion of plans regarding childbearing, the state now requires a dialogue which could profoundly alter their most intimate affairs. Even for those who already discuss reproductive choices, an allegation that the wife falsely certified notification would subject the timing, substance, and content of private colloquies to the scrutiny of law enforcement officials who are charged with determining whether the certification is true or whether the couple's discussions are sufficient to meet the vague and undefined level of notification mandated by the Act. This prospect is every bit as intrusive as Connecticut's birth control statute, which "allow[ed] the State to enquire into, prove and punish married people for the private use of their marital intimacy." *Poe v. Ullman*, 367 U.S. at 548 (Harlan, J., dissenting). *See Griswold*, 381 U.S. at 485–86.

In *Hodgson*, this Court observed that while "full communication among all members of a family" may be desirable,

> such communication may not be decreed by the State. The State has no more interest in requiring all family members to talk with one another than it has in requiring certain of them to live together . . . . [A] state interest in . . . making the "private realm of family life" conform to some state-designed ideal, is not a legitimate state interest at all.

Hodgson, 110 S. Ct. at 2946 (citations omitted). *Cf. Gilbert v. Minnesota*, 254 U.S. 325, 335–36 (1920) (Brandeis, J., dissenting).[77]

3. Section 3209 denies women equal protection of the laws.

Although the interests § 3209 purports to advance are framed in gender-neutral terms, the provision imposes duties on women alone, and confers rights solely on men. The district court found that "[m]any medical and surgical procedures, including . . . sterilization, prostate operations and chemotherapy, affect the capacity of males to have children within marriage." 199a. Nevertheless, neither this Act nor any other

---

77. The court of appeals recognized that § 3209 also violates women's rights to informational privacy by forcing them to disclose intimate details of their lives without a guarantee of confidentiality. 67a–68a. *See Whalen v. Roe*, 429 U.S. 589, 599–605 (1977); *Nixon v. Administrator of General Servs.*, 433 U.S. 425, 457–59 (1977); *United States v. Westinghouse Electric Corp.*, 638 F.2d 570, 577 (3d Cir. 1980). Once disclosure of the abortion decision is made, the husband remains free to broadcast this private and intimate information to others. As the court of appeals observed: "When the state forces spousal notification on a wife in a seriously troubled marriage, or even a wife in an untroubled marriage with a husband unalterably opposed to abortion, it compels disclosure of very intimate information with no assurance of confidentiality to someone highly motivated to make a public disclosure." 67a.

Pennsylvania law requires that a married man notify his wife before undergoing a medical procedure that would affect her "interest in having children within marriage." Married men are free to exercise reproductive choices without interference by, or knowledge of, their wives.

The pattern of sex-differentiated roles in marriage implicit in § 3209 is an old one, not unlike the discredited proposition that the husband is the "head and master" of the marital unit;[78] government enforcement of this pattern violates the commands of the Equal Protection Clause. This Court has made clear that, at the very least, a state cannot constitutionally classify on the basis of gender without demonstrating an "exceedingly persuasive justification" for the classification. *Mississippi University for Women v. Hogan*, 458 U.S. 718, 724 (1982) (quoting *Kirchberg*, 450 U.S. at 461); *see also Craig v. Boren*, 429 U.S. 190, 204 (1976). Here, where the offending statute also heavily intrudes on basic interests in autonomy, bodily integrity, and health, this Court must undertake the most exacting review of the statutory objectives to determine whether the Commonwealth has a compelling justification for the gender-based discrimination. *See Zablocki*, 434 U.S. 374 (1978) (applying strict scrutiny under Equal Protection Clause to law forbidding marriage); *Skinner*, 316 U.S. 535 (1942) (applying strict scrutiny under Equal Protection Clause to compulsory sterilization law); cf. *Eisenstadt*, 405 U.S. 452 (1972) (invalidating prohibition on contraception under Equal Protection Clause).[79] Section 3209 must fall by application of these principles. As outlined above, the trial court found and the court of appeals confirmed that § 3209 is a "totally irrational vehicle" with which to further marital in-

---

78. *See Kirchberg v. Feenstra*, 450 U.S. 455 (1981) (striking down Louisiana statute making husband "head and master" of community property upon marriage). At common law, under the doctrine of coverture, a husband had rights to control his wife's person as well as her property. *See Tinker v. Colwell*, 193 U.S. 473, 481 (1904) ("husband has certain personal and exclusive rights with regard to the person of his wife which are interfered with and invaded by criminal conversation with her . . . [and] the wife is in law incapable of giving any consent to affect the husband's rights").

79. Indeed, in *Thornburgh* this Court emphasized that restrictions on abortion also implicate women's equality. The promise of individual liberty "extends to women as well as to men . . . . A woman's right to make that choice freely is fundamental. *Any other result, in our view, would protect inadequately a central part of the sphere of liberty that our law guarantees equally to all.*" 476 U.S. at 772 (emphasis added).

tegrity. 72a, 262a. The Constitution prohibits the state from relying on outdated gender-based stereotypes that perpetuate women's image as the "weaker sex" or "child rearers." *Califano v. Webster*, 430 U.S. 313, 317 (1977); *see also Orr v. Orr*, 440 U.S. 268, 279 (1979). The Commonwealth's attempt to further asymmetrically the husband's "interest in having children within marriage," embodies precisely the prohibited stereotype that wives should bear children. To the extent that the statute may be based on an assumption that women, unlike men, need spousal guidance in their reproductive choices, it transgresses Justice O'Connor's admonition that "if the statutory objective is to exclude or 'protect' . . . one gender because they are presumed to suffer from an inherent handicap or to be innately inferior, the objective itself is illegitimate." *Hogan*, 458 U.S. at 725.

B. The Act's Mandatory Delay Will Jeopardize Women's Health and Furthers No Legitimate State Interest.

In *Akron* this Court held that no

legitimate state interest is furthered by an arbitrary and inflexible waiting period. There is no evidence suggesting that the abortion procedure will be performed more safely. Nor [is] . . . the State's legitimate concern that the woman's decision be informed . . . reasonably served by requiring a 24-hour delay as a matter of course.

Akron, 462 U.S. at 450. Consistent with this holding, the district court confirmed the onerous burdens imposed by the Act's mandatory delay. In particular, the district court found that:

(a) The 24-hour waiting period will force every woman seeking an abortion to make two separate trips to the physician.

(b) Because of scheduling complications, the waiting period will "result in delays far in excess of 24 hours"; for most women, the delay will range from forty-eight hours to two weeks.

(c)   For many women, the 24-hour delay will significantly increase the cost of obtaining an abortion, including the costs of transportation, overnight lodging, and lost wages.

(d)   The requirement of two visits to the provider will subject "many women to the harassment and hostility of anti-abortion protestors . . . ."

(e)   The mandatory delay will be especially burdensome for low-income women, young women, women from rural areas, and women—such as battered women—who may have difficulty explaining their whereabouts.

(f)   A delay of 24 hours or more will adversely affect the physical and psychological health of some patients, and will increase medical complications.

(g)   Where the delay pushes a patient into her second trimester of pregnancy, there will be a substantial increase in the costs of the abortion. Moving the procedure from the early to the middle stages of the second trimester would result in an increased medical risk, including a substantial increase in the risk of death.

171a–174a. In addition, the district court confirmed the lack of any legitimate state interest served by this provision. 174a. Thus, the mandatory delay is unconstitutional under even the least protective standard of review.

The court of appeals did not dispute any of the lower court's factual findings. Indeed it acknowledged both the "adverse consequences" of the mandatory delay, 52a–53a, and the Act's failure to "serve any purpose" for women who have already decided to have an abortion. 55a.[80] Nonetheless, the appeals court concluded that the mandatory delay created no "undue burden" on the right to abortion, because this Court in Hodgson upheld a parental notification provision which caused delays of a week or more. See 53a (quoting Hodgson v. Minnesota, 648 F. Supp. 756, 853 (D. Minn. 1986)).

The flaws in this reasoning are apparent. First, the court of

---

80. "If a physician has concluded that any other type of obstetrical or gynecological procedure is medically necessary and has obtained the informed consent of the patient, there is simply no medical reason to delay performance of the procedure any longer." 174a.

appeals substituted for the record actually developed here a factual finding implicitly adopted in a different case involving completely distinct issues. If undisputed factual findings may be discarded so cavalierly, then the "undue burden" test is truly meaningless. Second, and equally important, in *Hodgson* the state's legitimate interest in allowing parents an opportunity to consult with the young woman was served by the delay. This same interest is not present here. Indeed, in *Hodgson*, Justice O'Connor joined Justice Stevens in expressly distinguishing *Akron* on the ground that no similar interest was served by imposing a 24-hour delay on an adult woman. *See Hodgson*, 110 S. Ct. at 2944–45 n.35.[81]

C. The Act's Biased Counseling Restrictions Violate the Right of Privacy and the First Amendment.

1. Biased patient counseling interferes with the provision of quality medical care and serves no legitimate state interest.

A state may require that a woman give her voluntary and informed consent to the abortion procedure. *Danforth*, 428 U.S. at 67. But precisely because the validity of an informed consent requirement rests on the state's interest in protecting the health of the pregnant woman, the state may not, under the guise of "informed consent," attempt to intimidate women into continuing their pregnancies by forcing physicians to deliver irrelevant, inaccurate, misleading, or inflammatory information. This is true under any standard of review. *Thornburgh*, 476 U.S. at 759–64. This Court has twice invalidated biased patient counseling requirements virtually identical to those at issue here. *Thornburgh*, 476 U.S. at 759–64; *Akron*, 462 U.S. at 442–45. As this Court recently found:

---

81. The court of appeals suggested that the mandatory delay served an interest in ensuring that the woman's decision is "well-considered." 54a. This too, however, is refuted by the undisputed findings of the district court and by this Court in *Akron*, 462 U.S. at 450–51. Only "[a] very small percentage of women are ambivalent concerning whether to have an abortion when they come to a clinic. Arrangements for special counseling sessions are made for women demonstrating any ambivalence about her decision." 171a.

Critical to our decisions in *Akron* and *Thornburg[h]* to invalidate a government intrusion into the patient/doctor dialogue
was the fact that the laws in both cases required *all* doctors
within their respective jurisdictions to provide *all* pregnant
patients contemplating an abortion a litany of information,
regardless of whether the patient sought the information or
whether the doctor thought the information necessary to the
patient's decision.

Rust v. *Sullivan*, 111 S. Ct. 1759, 1777 (1991) (emphasis in
original). Nothing in this record would compel a different
result.

As the district court found, the Act's biased counseling provisions "represent a substantial departure from the ordinary
medical requirements of informed consent." 170a. Because it
requires "the supply of specific information to *all* patients regardless of their specific circumstances, the Act is contrary to
the standard medical practice that informed consent be specifically tailored to the needs of the specific patient." 177a (emphasis added). Far from promoting informed consent, the Act
will undermine this dialogue because it "may actively discourage the free flow of information . . . by relieving any physician
'who complies with the provisions' of Section 3205 from civil
liability for failure to obtain informed consent." 177a.

For many women, some of the specific information mandated by the Act will be irrelevant, misleading, inaccurate,
or inflammatory. For example, the Act requires a disclosure
of medical risks of carrying a pregnancy to term. If a woman
needs an abortion because she is carrying an anencephalic
fetus, no legitimate purpose is served by detailing her risk of
death from preeclampsia or informing her that she may require
a cesarean section at the time of delivery. 178a. Similarly,
"[i]nforming women of the availability of medical assistance
benefits or paternal support for the child has no legitimate
medical justification. The information may mislead or confuse
the patient, and, in the vast majority of the cases, is plainly
inappropriate given the circumstances of the individual patient." 179a.[82] Similarly, requiring physicians to offer to their

82. "Advising a patient of the general availability of such benefits or payments
may cause a woman to rely upon those statements and elect against an abortion only

patients state-prepared materials describing the fetus and listing agencies that provide alternatives to abortion is simply
"an attempt by the Commonwealth to alter a woman's decision
after she has determined that an abortion is in her best interest." 179a. This mandated information "will create the
impression in women that the Commonwealth disapproves of
the woman's decision," and "will create undesirable and unnecessary anxiety, anguish and fear." 178a–179a.

In short, "[u]nder the guise of informed consent, the Act
requires the dissemination of information that is not relevant
to such consent, and thus, *it advances no legitimate state interest.*" *Thornburgh*, 476 U.S. at 763 (emphasis added). The
provisions are therefore unconstitutional under any standard
of review.

Moreover, the Act's requirement that only physicians deliver certain portions of the state-mandated information will
increase the costs of the procedure, require extensive changes
in the operating schedules of physicians and clinics, and ultimately reduce the availability of abortion services. 175a–
176a. Yet, the district court found that non-physician counselors, by virtue of their training and experience, are fully
capable of providing information, discussing the alternatives
to abortion, and securing the patient's informed consent.
175a. Indeed, "[i]n many instances, trained counselors . . .
are more understanding than physicians and have more time
to spend with patients." 175a. Thus, the "state's interest in
ensuring that a woman's consent to an abortion procedure is
informed and unpressured *is in no way furthered* by mandating
the identity of the person that must obtain the informed consent." 176a (emphasis added). As this Court has held, the
"critical factor is whether [the woman] obtains the necessary
information and counseling from a qualified person, not the
identity of the person from whom she obtains it." *Akron*, 462

---

to discover that the benefits or payments were unavailable or insufficient." 179a–
180a. For example, in 1988 only one-quarter of child support payments orders issued
by Pennsylvania state courts were actually enforced. Children's Defense Fund, *The
State of America's Children 1991* 152 (1991). Moreover, child support payments may
be wholly insufficient to allow any meaningful economic support for a woman to
raise a child. Ms. Dillon's case exemplifies this problem. After waiting eighteen
months to obtain a child support order, the order was only $125 per week, clearly
insufficient to provide for her four children. J.A. 386.

U.S. at 448. *See also Ohio* v. *Akron Center for Reproductive Health*, 110 S. Ct. 2972, 2983 (1990).

2. In violation of the First Amendment, the biased counseling provisions force the physician to communicate the state's ideology.

The First Amendment's guarantee "includes both the right to speak freely and the right to refrain from speaking at all"; it protects "the right of individuals . . . to refuse to foster . . . an idea they find morally objectionable." *Wooley*, 430 U.S. at 714, 715 (citations omitted).[83] Even when a speaker is free to disavow the government's message, it is a violation of the First Amendment to "require speakers to affirm in one breath that which they deny in the next." *Pacific Gas & Elec. Co.*, 475 U.S. at 16. When the government compels an individual to be an instrument for the dissemination of "an ideological point of view he finds unacceptable,"[84] *Wooley*, 430 U.S. at 715, the government imposes "a content-based regulation of speech." *Riley*, 487 U.S. at 795. Thus the statute "is subject to exacting First Amendment scrutiny" and may survive only if it is "narrowly tailored" to promote a compelling governmental interest. *Id.* at 798.[85] Section 3205 cannot survive this test. Under duress of law, physicians and counselors must recite a litany of government-mandated information, as well as offer information prepared and provided by the Common-

---

83. *See Barnette*, 319 U.S. at 642 (no official may "prescribe what shall be orthodox" in matters of opinion or "force citizens to confess by word or act their faith therein"); *see also Lehnert* v. *Ferris Faculty Ass'n*, 111 S. Ct. 1950, 1957 (1991); *id.* at 1960 (opinion of Blackmun, J.); *id.* at 1970 (Marshall, J., concurring in part and dissenting in part); *id.* at 1978 (Scalia, J., concurring in part and dissenting in part); *Riley* v. *National Fed'n of the Blind*, 487 U.S. 781, 796–97 (1988); *Pacific Gas & Elec. Co.* v. *Public Utilities Comm'n*, 475 U.S. 1, 10–11 (1986) (plurality opinion).

84. Justice O'Connor recognized that "[e]ven the requirement that women . . . be informed of the availability of those materials, and furnished with them on request, may create some possibility that the physician or counselor is being required to 'communicate [the State's] ideology.' " *Thornburgh*, 476 U.S. at 830 (citing with approval *Akron*, 462 U.S. at 472 n.16, and *Wooley*, 430 U.S. 705).

85. This doctrine is not confined to speech with an ideological viewpoint. *Riley*, 487 U.S. at 797–98. In *Riley*, this Court observed that compelling statements of "fact" regarding the percentage of charitable funds that went to overhead was no more permissible than compelling statements of "opinion": "either form of compulsion burdens protected speech." *Id.* In any case, the compelled speech at issue here clearly conveys an ideological message. *Cf. Bigelow* v. *Virginia*, 421 U.S. 809, 822 (1975).

wealth. These requirements "will undermine the physician's or counselor's ability to counsel a patient according to her individual needs, and will force the physician or counselor to act in a manner inconsistent with their [sic] professional judgment." 179a. Thus, no less than the plaintiffs in *Wooley* and *Riley* and the appellants in *Pacific Gas & Elec. Co.*, the Pennsylvania physicians find themselves forced to convey the state's message at the cost of violating their own conscientious beliefs and professional commitments.[86] The Commonwealth's asserted interest in assuring that the woman's consent is informed and voluntary cannot validate these infringements. As discussed above, although a state may require that a woman "give what is truly a voluntary and informed consent," *Thornburgh*, 476 U.S. at 760, "[i]t remains primarily the responsibility of the physician to ensure that appropriate information is conveyed to his patient, depending on her particular circumstances." *Akron*, 462 U.S. at 443. *See also Thornburgh*, 476 U.S. at 762. The principles of *Wooley* and *Barnette*, which establish the "individual's First Amendment right to avoid becoming the courier for [the government's] message," *Wooley*, 430 U.S. at 717, thus render unconstitutional the biased counseling provisions of § 3205.

D. The Act's "Informed" Parental Consent Restriction Unduly Burdens the Right of Privacy and Forces Family Life to Conform to a State-Designed Ideal.

A state may promote parental involvement in a young woman's abortion decision when necessary to protect its "interest in the welfare of its young citizens, whose immaturity, inexperience, and lack of judgment may sometimes impair their ability to exercise their rights wisely," *Hodgson*, 110 S. Ct. at 2942 (opinion of Stevens, J.), and to "protect[ ] a parent's interest in shaping a child's values and lifestyle . . . ." *Id.* at 2946. However, in promoting parental involvement, the state

---

86. These requirements also violate the First Amendment rights of the woman who must listen to the state's litany in order to obtain an abortion. "While [the government] clearly has a right to express [its] views to those who wish to listen, [it] has no right to force its message upon an audience incapable of declining to receive it." *Lehman* v. *City of Shaker Heights*, 418 U.S. 298, 307 (1974) (Douglas, J., concurring).

is limited by "the constitutional protection against unjustified state intrusion . . . [which] extends to pregnant minors as well as adult women." *Hodgson*, 110 S. Ct. at 2937 (opinion of Stevens, J.). Consequently, the state may not " 'unduly burden' the fundamental right" to abortion. *Id.* at 2949 (O'Connor, J., concurring) (quoting *Akron*, 462 U.S. at 453).[87] Pennsylvania's "informed" parental consent statute goes far beyond the parental notification and consent statutes at issue in *Hodgson*, 110 S. Ct. 2926 (1990), and *Bellotti II*, 443 U.S. 622 (1979). As the district court held, "informed consent" is a term of art,

> and personal contact between the patient and the person rendering the informed consent is essential. The physician's or counselor's observation of the person's demeanor and reactions . . . is essential to permit the physician or counselor to determine whether the patient is competent to give informed consent and whether the patient fully understood the information . . . .

170a. Thus, consistent with the "standard medical principles of informed consent," the district court found that "informed" parental consent under the Act will require in-person consultation with the parent. 182a–183a, 248a.

By mandating face-to-face counseling for parents, the Act undermines, rather than promotes, the state's interests in protecting parental involvement and the well-being of young women. There can be no dispute that by increasing the delay, costs, and medical risks of abortion, the "informed" parental consent requirement will harm young women. As the district court found, the requirement of parental counseling could "cause delays of several days or possibly weeks." 183a; *see also* 182a. Coupled with other requirements of the Act, § 3206 "will create layers of obstacles which could unduly burden a minor woman's ability to get an abortion . . . . In some cases,

---

87. In contrast to the strict scrutiny standard for adult women, the district court correctly recognized that the "undue burden" standard was appropriate to judge restrictions affecting young women. 248a.

the provisions may act in such a way as to deprive her of her right to have an abortion." 186a; *see also* 184a.[88]

The statute's "informed" parental consent requirement will have a particularly irrational and perverse impact on the parents of pregnant young women. As the district court found, even when prepared to consent, some parents will be unable to come to the clinic for several days because of work schedules or family obligations, or because they cannot afford the additional cost of travel, lost wages, and child care expenses. 185a–186a. The requirement presents so insurmountable an obstacle that even parents who have participated in, support, and consent to their daughter's abortion may be unable to comply with the law. 185a. *See also Planned Parenthood Ass'n* v. *Harris*, 670 F. Supp. 971, 987–88 (N.D. Ga. 1987).

Where the parents choose to "shap[e] [their] child's values and lifestyle," *Hodgson*, 110 S. Ct. at 2946, by permitting her to exercise independent judgment, the Pennsylvania statute perversely forces the parents to act contrary to their own beliefs, "slic[ing] deeply into the family itself." *Hodgson*, 110 S. Ct. at 2946 (quoting *Moore*, 431 U.S. at 498). As the district court explained, "The parent may be reluctant to explain his or her absence from work, or may not wish to be seen entering an abortion clinic." 249a. In some cases, "a parent may refuse to accompany their daughter to the facility even though he or she has agreed to consent to the daughter's abortion." 185a. Thus, rather than protect parental rights, the statute merely "substitut[es] its conception of family life for the family's own view." *Hodgson*, 110 S. Ct. at 2946. Such an asserted "state interest in standardizing its children and adults, making the 'private realm of family life' conform to some state-designed ideal, *is not a legitimate state interest at all.*" *Id.* (emphasis added).

---

88. Unlike the regulation of any other medical procedure, the Act requires a physician performing an abortion to evaluate the competency and obtain the informed consent of two separate individuals, with the irrational but inevitable result that if the parent is not competent to give informed consent, the physician cannot perform the abortion, even though a parent has been notified and is involved, and the young woman is fully capable of giving her own informed consent.

E. The Act's Public Disclosure and Reporting Requirements Burden Women's Right of Privacy and Fail to Further Legitimate State Interests.

The Act's reporting and disclosure requirements also burden the right to abortion without serving any legitimate state interest. First, §§ 3207(b) and 3214(f) require every facility that performs abortions to file with the Commonwealth quarterly reports of the total number of abortions performed. The reports of facilities that received state funds within the year prior to filing are available to the public for inspection and copying.

As the district court found, most abortion providers have suffered a wave of extreme anti-abortion violence and harassment. 211a–213a. The public's access to the quarterly reports gives the clinics reasonable basis to fear that this harassment and violence will increase, 213a, and will cause some providers to forego state funds for both abortion and other health services. "The likely result will be that indigent patients who have been the victims of rape or incest or who suffer from a life-threatening condition will find it difficult, if not impossible . . . to obtain abortion services." 213a–214a. Moreover, for physicians who now perform abortions only several times a year, public disclosure and its attendant threat of harassment is enough to deter the performance of abortion altogether.[89] Recognizing that the disclosure provisions further no legitimate or compelling interests in health, the only interest asserted by the Commonwealth to support the requirement is the public's right to know how its funds are spent. 83a. The reports do not, however, accomplish this objective because they include no information about the nature or amount of state funds that trigger public disclosure under the Act.[90] Rather, the requirements merely enhance the ability

---

89. The harassment of physicians is expected to increase in light of the recent strategic announcement by the anti-choice organization Operation Rescue that it plans to drive doctors who perform abortions out of business. Mimi Hall, *Abortion Foes Target Doctors*, USA Today, Feb. 5, 1992, at 3A (quoting Randall Terry) ("We're going to shame [doctors], humiliate them, embarrass them, disgrace them and expose them until they quit"). *See also* Christine Spokar, *Abortion Foes' Mood Defiant*, Washington Post, Jan. 21, 1992, at B1.

90. Records of state appropriations and expenditures are maintained and generally available, however, under Pennsylvania's Right-to-Know Law, 65 Pa. Cons. Stat. Ann. §§ 66.1–66.4 (Supp. 1991). *See* 210a.

of abortion opponents to intimidate abortion providers. The provision must therefore be invalidated. *Thornburgh*, 476 U.S. at 765–66.[91]

In addition to placing an impermissible burden on the right to abortion, the district court also found that the requirement that abortion providers report the name of the referring physician "serves no legitimate scientific purpose." 219a. It "does not add to the pool of scientific knowledge concerning abortion. Nor is it reasonably related to the Commonwealth's interest in promoting maternal health." 272a.[92] Consequently, the provision is invalid.

Even though these reports are to be confidentially maintained, referring physicians "are extremely protective of their anonymity because of fears (often based upon past experience) that any kind of documentation or record-keeping connecting them with any phase of the abortion decision will have adverse effects on their medical practices and patients or their ability to reside peacefully in their communities." 219a.[93] By reducing the number of physicians willing to make referrals for abortion, the Act's reporting requirement unconstitutionally burdens the right to abortion. 272a.[94]

91. By coercing providers into public disclosure as a condition of receiving state aid, the Act also improperly conditions the receipt of a public benefit on the surrender of a constitutionally protected right. This Court has explicitly applied the unconstitutional conditions doctrine to the right to choose abortion. *See Planned Parenthood v. Arizona*, 718 F.2d 938 (9th Cir. 1983), *appeal after remand*, 789 F.2d 1348 (9th Cir.), *aff'd mem. sub nom. Babbitt v. Planned Parenthood*, 479 U.S. 925 (1986) (state funds may not be conditioned on an organization's relinquishment of privately funded abortion-related activities). *See also Harris v. McRae*, 448 U.S. 297, 317 n.19 (1980).

92. As the district court pointed out, although the referring physician may provide some of the state-mandated information, the abortion provider must review the information with the patient, "regardless of what the referring physician may or may not have done . . . . Therefore, the performing physician or abortion facility will have all information the Commonwealth might seek . . . at their disposal." 272a–273a.

93. The district court found specific instances where doctors would stop referring patients for abortions if their names were reported as required by the Act. 220a, 221a.

94. Similarly, the district court found that the Act's requirement that physicians report the basis for their medical judgments concerning viability, the existence of a medical emergency, and the determination of gestational age would "serve no useful scientific purpose," and would interfere with the physician's exercise of medical judgment. 222a, 274a (citation omitted).

F. This Court Must Enjoin Enforcement of the Act's Medical Emergency Exception to the Extent That Compliance Would Pose a Threat to the Life or Health of Women or Must Find the Provision Unconstitutional.

Section 3203 provides an exception to several of the Act's provisions in the case of a "medical emergency." As the district court found, "[w]ithout question, the definition of medical emergency is more restrictive than any other as applied in medical situations." 235a–236a. The Act's definition is "contrary to generally accepted standards of emergency medical care, and interferes with a physician's ability to act in accordance with his best medical judgment." 157a.[95] As a result, compliance with the Act could "ultimately jeopardize the health of the pregnant woman." 162a.

The court of appeals agreed that it was bound by this Court's holding in *Thornburgh*, 476 U.S. at 770–71, that "any abortion regulation which might delay or prevent an abortion must contain a medical emergency exception," 36a, and that a valid medical emergency exception would necessarily include the conditions of inevitable abortion, premature ruptured membrane, and preeclampsia. 37a. Nevertheless, to assure that compliance with Pennsylvania law would "not in any way pose a significant threat to the life or health of a woman," the court of appeals construed the Act to include these conditions within its narrow definition. 40a.

The court of appeals correctly intended to remove the constitutional infirmity in § 3203. Its effort to do so, however, failed for two reasons. First, the court of appeals' holding that the medical emergency definition need only protect women from "significant" threats to their life or health is inconsistent with this Court's holding in *Thornburgh*. It unfortunately fails to ensure that a woman's health remains the physician's paramount consideration. *Thornburgh*, 476 U.S. at 768–69.[96]

95. The district court found that the Act's definition of medical emergency "departs from the normal medical definition of an emergency and is inconsistent with that contained in Pennsylvania's Emergency Medical Services Act." 155a. "No other law infringes so heavily on a physician's discretion to decide when he or she is faced with a medical emergency as the provisions of the Act." 156a.

96. The saving construction also fails to include other complications of pregnancy similar to those recognized by the district court. *See* Brief *Amici Curiae* of American College of Obstetricians & Gynecologists et al.

Second, the interpretation runs afoul of the principle that a federal court may not "rewrite a state law to conform it to constitutional requirements." *Virginia v. American Booksellers Ass'n, Inc.*, 484 U.S. 383, 397 (1988). A federal court's interpretation of state legislation is "not binding on state courts and may be discredited at any time—thus essentially rendering the federal-court decision advisory and the litigation underlying it meaningless." *Moore v. Sims*, 442 U.S. 415, 428 (1979). *See also Lakewood v. Plain Dealer Publishing Co.*, 486 U.S. 750, 770 (1988) (federal courts "will not write nonbinding limits into a silent state statute").[97] Therefore, physicians cannot rely on the court of appeals' narrowing construction to insulate them from criminal prosecution, and must sacrifice their patient's health to avoid the threat of criminal penalties.

To solve these dilemmas, this Court must either find the provision unconstitutional or enjoin enforcement of the definition to the extent that compliance with its requirement would in any way pose a threat to the life or health of a woman. With an injunction in place, a physician could, without risk of criminal prosecution, treat the medical emergency exception as inclusive of those conditions, like inevitable abortion, premature ruptured membrane, and preeclampsia, which threaten a pregnant woman's life or health.

CONCLUSION

For the reasons set forth above, petitioners ask that this Court reaffirm the strict scrutiny standard of *Roe v. Wade*. Any other decision by this Court would forsake the promise of liberty and equality that has safeguarded the lives and health of American women for almost two decades. The judgment of the court of appeals finding unconstitutional the Act's hus-

---

97. The court of appeals cited neither legislative history nor decisional law as an authoritative basis for its construction. Nor could the court of appeals rely on the interpretation offered by the Attorney General. As this Court held in *Virginia v. American Booksellers*, 484 U.S. at 395, because "the Attorney General does not bind the state courts or local law enforcement authorities, we are unable to accept her interpretation of the law as authoritative."

band notification provision in § 3209 must be affirmed and the judgment finding constitutional §§ 3203 (definition of medical emergency), 3205, 3206, 3207(b), 3208, 3214(a) and (f) must be reversed.

Respectfully submitted,

LINDA J. WHARTON
CAROL E. TRACY
Women's Law Project
125 South Ninth Street
Suite 401
Philadelphia, PA 19107
(215) 928-9801

SETH KREIMER
University of Pennsylvania
Law School
3400 Chestnut Street
Philadelphia, PA 19104
(215) 898-7447

ROGER K. EVANS
EVE W. PAUL
DARA KLASSEL
Planned Parenthood Action
Fund, Inc.
810 Seventh Avenue
New York, New York 10019
(212) 541-7800

KATHRYN KOLBERT
(Counsel of Record)
JANET BENSHOOF
LYNN M. PALTROW
RACHAEL N. PINE
ANDREW DWYER
ELLEN K. GOETZ
STEVEN R. SHAPIRO
JOHN A. POWELL
American Civil Liberties
Union Foundation
132 W. 43rd Street
New York, New York 10036
(212) 944-9800

Attorneys for Petitioners
and Cross-Respondents

BRIEF OF THE AMERICAN COLLEGE OF OBSTETRICIANS AND GYNECOLOGISTS, THE AMERICAN MEDICAL WOMEN'S ASSOCIATION, THE AMERICAN PSYCHIATRIC ASSOCIATION, THE AMERICAN PUBLIC HEALTH ASSOCIATION, THE ASSOCIATION OF REPRODUCTIVE HEALTH PROFESSIONALS, THE NATIONAL LEAGUE FOR NURSING, AND THE NATIONAL MEDICAL ASSOCIATION AS *AMICI CURIAE* IN SUPPORT OF THE PETITIONERS

INTEREST OF THE *AMICI CURIAE*

Amici curiae are seven national organizations of physicians and other health care professionals. Each *amicus* is dedicated to promoting public health by maintaining the highest professional standards and providing or ensuring the provision of quality health care.[1]

Amici's interest in this case stems from their concern about the profound impact that recently enacted state abortion laws will have on the lives and health of the female patients that their members serve. As individuals, *amici*'s members hold differing views on the religious and philosophical issues that abortion raises. They agree, however, that when a patient seeks medical care and treatment, such as abortion, state laws should not interfere with a health care provider's ability to exercise his or her best medical judgment in treating that patient. Because the Pennsylvania statute challenged here seriously interferes with a woman's ability, in consultation with her physician, to obtain an abortion, and because the standard of review adopted here will affect the constitutionality of other

---

1. See the Appendix to this brief for a description of each *amicus*.

statutes affecting the lives and health of *amici*'s patients, *amici* wish to present their views.[2]

MEDICAL BACKGROUND

Elective abortion, defined as the termination of a pregnancy before the fetus has reached the stage of viability, is one of the most common medical procedures performed in the United States today.[3] Approximately 1.5 million American women obtain an abortion each year.[4]

When performed correctly by trained and experienced physicians, abortion is a relatively safe procedure. Indeed, it is far safer than childbirth: The risk of dying from an abortion is currently about one-tenth the risk of dying during childbirth.[5] Illegal abortions, however, are substantially riskier than legal abortions. Prior to this Court's decision in *Roe* v. *Wade*, 410 U.S. 113 (1973), complications from illegal abortions constituted a "serious public health problem, especially for the poor and minorities."[6] Although precise data are unavailable, statistics from this era suggest that the overall death rate from illegal abortions was about eight times greater than that for legal abortions,[7] and that the rate was even higher among minority women.[8] The incidence of non-fatal complications from illegal abortions also was extraordinary.[9]

2. Pursuant to Rule 37.3 of the Rules of this Court, the parties have consented to the filing of this brief. The parties' letters of consent have been filed with the Clerk of the Court.

3. *Williams Obstetrics* 501 (F. Cunningham et al., 18th ed. 1989); Binkin, *Trends in Induced Legal Abortion Morbidity and Mortality*, 13 Clin. Obstet. Gynec. 83, 83 (1986). Viability refers to the point at which the fetus would have a reasonable potential for survival if it were removed from the pregnant woman's uterus. *Williams Obstetrics* at 501.

4. R. Gold, *Abortion and Women's Health* 11 (1990).

5. R. Gold at 28–29; Dorfman, *Maternal Mortality in New York City, 1981–1983*, 76 Obstet. & Gynec. 317, 320 (1990).

6. W. Hern, *Abortion Practice* 21 (1984).

7. Cates & Rochat, *Illegal Abortions in the United States: 1972–74*, 8 Fam. Plann. Persp. 86, 91–92 (1976).

8. R. Gold at 5 (minority women twelve times more likely than white women to die from such abortions).

9. In 1962, for example, nearly 1,600 women were admitted to one New York City hospital for treatment of non-fatal complications of abortions. *Id.* at 6.

The high mortality rate for illegal abortions is not surprising given the techniques that many women used—and in some cases, continue to use—to abort their fetuses.[10] These include ingesting Clorox, turpentine, or massive doses of quinine, or inserting such objects as coat hangers, knitting needles, or tree bark into their uteruses.[11]

Because legal abortions are so much safer than illegal ones, abortion-related deaths and other complications dropped sharply after the widespread legalization of abortion.[12] However, such serious medical problems as infection, hemorrhage, perforation of the uterus, or even death, still complicate about 0.5% of all abortions.[13] While the risk of such complications is relatively small, "any delay increases the risk of complications to a pregnant woman who wishes an abortion. Moreover, this risk appears to increase continuously . . . as the length of gestation increases."[14] After eight weeks of gestation, the risk of maternal death doubles with every two weeks of delay,[15] and the risk of other health complications increases at a rate of about 20% per week.[16]

Delays—and the concomitant increase in risk—are of particular concern for women with pre-existing medical conditions that may be exacerbated by pregnancy.[17] Delays are also

10. Even after *Roe* some women continue to seek illegal abortions because legal abortions are either too expensive or not readily available or because of a variety of cultural, religious, or personal reasons. Binkin et al., *Illegal-Abortion Deaths in the United States: Why Are They Still Occurring?*, 14 Fam. Plann. Persp. 163 (1982).

11. Polgar & Fried, *The Bad Old Days: Clandestine Abortions Among the Poor in New York City Before Liberalization of the Abortion Law*, 8 Fam. Plann. Persp. 125, 126 (1976).

12. For example, 39 deaths from unlawful abortions were reported nationwide in the year preceding this Court's decision in *Roe*, while only five deaths were reported in the following year. Cates & Rochat at 87. Similarly, non-fatal complications of abortion also declined after legalization. *See, e.g.*, Bracken et al., *Hospitalization for Medical–Legal and Other Abortions in the United States 1970–1977*, 72 Am. J. Pub. Health 30, 30 (1982) (hospital admissions for septic abortions in California dropped by 68–75% following liberalization of that state's abortion law in 1967).

13. Buehler et al., *The Risk of Serious Complications from Induced Abortion: Do Personal Characteristics Make a Difference?*, 153 Am. J. Obstet. Gynec. 14, 16 (1985).

14. Cates et al., *The Effect of Delay and Method of Choice on the Risk of Abortion Morbidity*, 9 Fam. Plann. Persp. 266, 268 (1977); Buehler et al. at 16.

15. *Williams Obstetrics* at 506.

16. C. Tietze & S. Henshaw, *Induced Abortion: A World Review*, 1986 103 (6th ed. 1986).

17. These conditions include congenital malformations of the heart and its valves, cancer, chronic renal failure, multiple sclerosis, asthma, arthritis, inflammatory bowel

problematic for pregnant adolescents. Unlike older women, many teenagers—because of irregular menses, lack of experience with health care facilities, and difficulty in paying for medical care—wait until late in their pregnancies, often well into their second trimester, before seeking any medical care.[18]

SUMMARY OF ARGUMENT

I

The threshold question in this case concerns the standard of review. In *Roe* v. *Wade*, 410 U.S. 113 (1973), *City of Akron* v. *Akron Center for Reproductive Health, Inc.*, 462 U.S. 416 (1983), and *Thornburgh* v. *American College of Obstetricians & Gynecologists*, 476 U.S. 747 (1986), this Court held that strict scrutiny applies to all statutes that interfere with a woman's right, in consultation with her physician, to choose whether or not to terminate her pregnancy. The court of appeals, however, held that strict scrutiny should apply only to state regulations that severely interfere with or present absolute obstacles to a woman's right to choose an abortion. Pet. App. 14a, 30a.

This Court should put to rest the current confusion over the standard of review by reexamining and then reaffirming its prior holdings that a woman has a fundamental right to decide whether or not to have an abortion. Recognition of this right follows logically and ineluctably from this Court's decades-old recognition that the liberty protected from state interference by the Fourteenth Amendment includes the right to make personal choices regarding family life, marriage, and procreation. This Court should also reaffirm that states may

---

disease, and epilepsy. *See* D. Danforth & J. Scott, *Obstetrics & Gynecology* 494–97 (5th ed. 1986); Rovinsky & Guttmacher's *Medical, Surgical & Gynecological Complications of Pregnancy* 73 (S. Cherry et al., 3d ed. 1985); Williams & Bitran, *Cancer & Pregnancy*, 12 Clin. Perinat. 609 (1985); Noronha, *Neurological Disorders During Pregnancy and the Puerperium*, 12 Clin. Perinat. 695 (1985).

18. Koonin et al., *Abortion Surveillance, United States, 1988*, 40 Morbid. & Mortal. Weekly Rep't 15, 17 (July 1991).

not regulate that right in ways that increase the health risks that pregnant women face.

None of the objections to *Roe* provides a basis for overturning two decades of constitutionally required protection for women's health. The principle that the state may not force a woman to accept increased health risks in order to further the state's interest in preserving fetal life is not arbitrary. To the contrary, that principle is fully supported by basic common law principles respecting the autonomy and bodily integrity of each individual. Nor is there any reason to think that reversing *Roe* will extricate federal courts and this Court from the need to review state abortion legislation. In fact, altering the standard of review will simply initiate another protracted legal battle over which new restrictions are constitutional.

II

By enacting the Abortion Control Act Amendments of 1989, Pennsylvania has again passed a statute that will delay, discourage, and defeat women in their attempt to obtain a medically provided abortion. The specific provisions at issue here place a variety of obstacles—notification, consent, waiting periods, and public disclosure—in the path of a woman seeking an abortion. Each will operate to increase the risks to the health of pregnant women. As was the case with Pennsylvania's previous abortion amendments, "[c]lose analysis . . . shows that they wholly subordinate constitutional privacy interests and concerns with maternal health in an effort to deter a woman from making a decision that, with her physician, is hers to make." *Thornburgh*, 476 U.S. at 759. Indeed, these provisions violate our most basic notions of liberty by subjecting individuals to significant health risks solely to further the state's interest in protecting potential life. Each therefore is unconstitutional.

ARGUMENT

I. THIS COURT SHOULD REAFFIRM THAT A WOMAN'S RIGHT TO CHOOSE WHETHER OR NOT TO CARRY A PREGNANCY TO TERM IS A FUNDAMENTAL RIGHT PROTECTED AGAINST STATE INTERFERENCE BY THE GUARANTEE OF LIBERTY IN THE DUE PROCESS CLAUSE OF THE FOURTEENTH AMENDMENT.

In *Roe* v. *Wade*, 410 U.S. 113, 153 (1973), this Court held that the "Fourteenth Amendment's concept of personal liberty and restrictions upon state action . . . encompass[es] a woman's decision whether or not to terminate her pregnancy." Accordingly, this Court held that state laws that interfere with this right are subject to strict scrutiny. *Id.* at 162–64. In the nearly two decades since *Roe* was decided, this Court has repeatedly reaffirmed this fundamental holding.[19] More recently, however, members of the Court, in separate and plurality opinions, have questioned the trimester-based framework set forth in *Roe* as applied to particular state laws.[20] Relying on these opinions, the court below held that "the strict scrutiny legal standard endorsed by the Court in *Roe*, *Akron*, and *Thornburgh*" is no longer the applicable standard of review. Pet. App. 24a. Instead, the court held, the correct standard is one that applies strict scrutiny only to those state regulations that "impose an undue burden [on a woman's abortion decision] and rational basis review to those which do not." *Id.* at 30a.

This Court should reaffirm that a woman's right to decide whether or not to carry her pregnancy to term is a fundamental right protected against state interference by the guarantee of liberty in the Due Process Clause of the Fourteenth Amendment. This Court also should reaffirm that states may not regulate that right in ways inconsistent with accepted medical practice. Less stringent standards that allow states to interfere

19. *E.g.*, *Thornburgh*, 476 U.S. at 747; *Akron*, 462 U.S. at 416.
20. *See, e.g.*, *Webster* v. *Reproductive Health Servs.*, 492 U.S. 490, 517–21 (1989) (opinion of Rehnquist, C.J.); *id.* at 525–31 (opinion of O'Connor, J.); *id.* at 532–37 (opinion of Scalia, J.).

with this fundamental right are inconsistent with basic constitutional principles and will only provoke a new round of constitutional line-drawing. States have no interest sufficiently compelling to deny pregnant women the personal liberty enjoyed by all other persons to obtain medical treatment and to preserve their health free from state interference.

A. A Woman's Right to Choose Whether or Not to Carry a Pregnancy to Term Is a Fundamental Right.

Prior to *Roe*, the Court had not considered the constitutionality of abortion laws. But like any proper "decision of an apparently novel claim," *Roe* took " 'its place in relation to what went before and further [cut] a channel for what [was] to come.' " *Poe* v. *Ullman*, 367 U.S. 497, 544 (1961) (Harlan, J., dissenting) (citation omitted).

Roe followed, in the first instance, "[t]his Court['s] . . . long recogni[tion] that freedom of personal choice in matters of marriage and family life is one of the liberties protected by the Due Process Clause of the Fourteenth Amendment." *Cleveland Bd. of Educ.* v. *LaFleur*, 414 U.S. 632, 639–40 (1974). By 1923, this Court had recognized that "the liberty thus guaranteed . . . denotes not merely freedom from bodily restraint but also the right . . . to marry, establish a home and bring up children." *Meyer* v. *Nebraska*, 262 U.S. 390, 399 (1923). Over the five decades between *Meyer* and *Roe*, the Court invalidated state laws that infringed the right to choose whether to send one's children to a private school,[21] to marry someone of one's choice,[22] to refuse sterilization,[23] and to obtain and use contraceptives.[24]

At the core of the liberty protected from state interference, then, has been "the right of the individual, married or single, to be free from unwarranted governmental intrusion into mat-

21. *Pierce* v. *Society of Sisters*, 268 U.S. 510, 535 (1925).
22. *Loving* v. *Virginia*, 388 U.S. 1 (1967).
23. *Skinner* v. *Oklahoma*, 316 U.S. 535, 536 (1942) (state law infringes on "the right to have offspring").
24. *Griswold* v. *Connecticut*, 381 U.S. 479 (1965) (married couples); *Eisenstadt* v. *Baird*, 405 U.S. 438 (1972) (any individual); *see also Poe* v. *Ullman*, 367 U.S. 497, 539–55 (1961) (Harlan, J., dissenting).

ters so fundamentally affecting a person as the decision whether to bear or beget a child." *Eisenstadt v. Baird*, 405 U.S. 438, 453 (1972).[25] The right in question in *Roe*, "a woman's decision whether or not to terminate her pregnancy," 410 U.S. at 153, is inextricably part of the web of intensely personal choices in "matters relating to marriage, procreation, contraception, family relationships, and child rearing and education"[26] that the Court had previously protected.

The right recognized in *Roe* also has another important common law and constitutional antecedent. It follows directly from the common law tradition that protects the autonomy of each individual to decide what medical treatments to accept or to refuse. "Before the turn of the century, this Court observed that '[n]o right is held more sacred, or is more carefully guarded, by the common law, than the right of every individual to the possession and control of his own person, free from all restraint or interference of others, unless by clear and unquestionable authority of law.' "[27] This common law "notion of bodily integrity" underlies the requirement of informed consent for medical treatment.[28] Respect for bodily integrity has led state courts to refuse to order individuals to put their own health at risk or otherwise to suffer a bodily invasion (such as an operation) even when such an effort is necessary to save the life of another person.[29] It has also led this Court to invalidate state laws that would have compelled individuals to undergo physically invasive procedures in furtherance of the state's interest in investigating crime.[30] The right to have the state respect each individual's bodily integrity is "so rooted in the traditions and conscience of our people as to be ranked

25. Additional rights encompassed within the liberty protected by the Fourteenth Amendment include, *inter alia*, the right to travel, *Kent v. Dulles*, 357 U.S. 116, 125–27 (1958); *Shapiro v. Thompson*, 394 U.S. 618 (1969); and the right to pursue an occupation, *Schware v. Board of Bar Examiners*, 353 U.S. 232 (1957); *Allgeyer v. Louisiana*, 165 U.S. 578, 589 (1897).

26. *Paul v. Davis*, 424 U.S. 693, 713 (1976).

27. *Cruzan v. Director, Missouri Dep't of Health*, 110 S. Ct. 2841, 2846 (1990) (quoting *Union Pac. R.R. v. Botsford*, 141 U.S. 250, 251 (1891)).

28. *Cruzan*, 110 S. Ct. at 2846–47.

29. *See infra* pp. [90–92] & nn. 37, 40.

30. *See, e.g., Winston v. Lee*, 470 U.S. 753, 763–66 (1985) (state may not compel criminal defendant to undergo minor surgery to remove bullet); *Schmerber v. California*, 384 U.S. 757, 772 (1966); *Rochin v. California*, 342 U.S. 165, 173–74 (1952).

as fundamental,"[31] and therefore provides a second constitutional and common law antecedent to a woman's right to choose not to carry a pregnancy to term.

B. This Court Should Reaffirm That State Abortion Laws That Depart from Accepted Medical Practice and Increase Health Risks to Pregnant Women Are Unconstitutional.

In *Roe*, this Court held that courts should apply strict scrutiny to state laws regulating abortion, and provided an analytical framework based on the trimesters of pregnancy to assist courts in performing that analysis.[32] As the court of appeals explained, a majority of the members of the Court, through separate opinions, has taken the view that the trimester analysis is problematic. Pet. App. 24a–30a. *Amici* believe that the framework provided in *Roe* has proved useful to lower courts and that the Court should not abandon that framework.

Any dispute over the trimester framework, however, should not obscure the fundamental principle that underlies *Roe*. That principle is that states are not free to require individuals, including pregnant women, to subject themselves to increased health risks or significant intrusions of their bodily integrity in order to further the state's interest in the potential or actual life of another person.

This principle—which forbids states to "requir[e] a tradeoff between the woman's health and fetal survival"—is not dependent on trimesters of pregnancy for implementation.[33] It simply looks to the impact of abortion regulation on women's health. Laws that "depart from accepted medical practice" should presumptively be unconstitutional, because such departures likely will pose a risk to the patient's health. *Akron*, 462 U.S. at 431.

---

31. *Snyder v. Massachusetts*, 291 U.S. 97, 105 (1934); *see also Palko v. Connecticut*, 302 U.S. 319, 324 (1937) (rights that are "implicit in the concept of ordered liberty" are immune from state interference).

32. Specifically, the Court held that a state has a compelling interest in protecting maternal health beginning at the second trimester of pregnancy, and a compelling interest in preserving the potential life of the fetus beginning at the time of viability, roughly coincident with the third trimester. 410 U.S. at 162. State laws that are not reasonably related to these interests or that sweep more broadly than necessary to further those interests therefore are unconstitutional. *Id.* at 163–64.

33. *Thornburgh*, 476 U.S. at 768; *see also Colautti v. Franklin*, 439 U.S. 379, 387–401 (1979); *Roe*, 410 U.S. at 164.

This principle is consistent with the cases decided since *Roe*. Thus, this Court has upheld laws that legitimately furthered maternal health[34] or that placed no obstacles in a woman's path to an abortion.[35] The Court, however, has invalidated laws that, "under the guise of protecting maternal health or potential life," have served in fact to increase the risk to maternal health by introducing needless delay into the process or otherwise by interfering with the relationship between patients and their physicians or nurses.[36]

The existence of a competing state interest in preserving fetal life is not sufficient to require departure from this basic principle. Common law principles illustrate the point. The common law imposes no general duty upon individuals to rescue others from life-threatening peril. Restatement (Second) of Torts §§ 314–15 (1965). In particular, states have not required individuals to undergo surgery, or to donate tissue, blood or organs, in order to save the actual life of another person.[37] Certainly this is true of Pennsylvania. In *McFall* v. *Shimp*, 10 Pa. D. & C.3d 90 (County Ct. Allegheny 1978), a Pennsylvania court refused to order the defendant to donate bone marrow needed to save the life of his cousin: "For our law to compel defendant to submit to an intrusion of his body would change every concept and principle upon which our society is founded. To do so would defeat the sanctity of the individual, and would impose a rule which would know no limits, and one could not imagine where the line would be drawn." *Id.* at 91.

The holding in *McFall* is consistent with the respect for individual autonomy that is a traditional element of American

---

34. See, e.g., *Simopoulos* v. *Virginia*, 462 U.S. 506 (1983) (per curiam); *Connecticut* v. *Menillo*, 423 U.S. 9 (1975).

35. *Webster* v. *Reproductive Health Servs.*, 492 U.S. 490 (1989); *Harris* v. *McRae*, 448 U.S. 297 (1980); *Maher* v. *Roe*, 432 U.S. 464 (1977); *Beal* v. *Doe*, 432 U.S. 438 (1977).

36. *Thornburgh*, 476 U.S. at 759; see, e.g., *Akron*, 462 U.S. at 416; *Planned Parenthood* v. *Danforth*, 428 U.S. 52 (1976); *Doe* v. *Bolton*, 410 U.S. 179 (1972).

37. See, e.g., *Bonner* v. *Moran*, 126 F.2d 121 (D.C. Cir. 1941) (surgery upon one person without consent to save the life of another is a battery); *Curran* v. *Bosze*, 566 N.E.2d 1319, 1331 (Ill. 1990) (parent may not give consent on behalf of minor for donation of bone marrow to sibling unless to do so would be in minor's best interest); *Little* v. *Little*, 576 S.W.2d 493 (Tex. Civ. App. 1979) (same); *In re Pescinski*, 226 N.W.2d 180 (Wis. 1975) (same); *In re Richardson*, 284 So.2d 185 (La. Ct. App.) (same), *cert. denied*, 284 So.2d 338 (La. 1973); *Strunk* v. *Strunk*, 445 S.W.2d 145 (Ky. 1969) (same).

common law. The familiar proposition that "[e]very human being of adult years and sound mind has a right to determine what shall be done with his own body"[38] is "fundamental in American jurisprudence . . . ."[39] And as *McFall* and other cases illustrate, this is a "strong right," one that is strictly enforced rather than balanced against competing interests.[40]

At common law, then, the state's interest in preserving actual human lives, weighty though it is, is insufficient to justify forcing persons to endure intrusions of their bodies and concomitant health risks to save those lives. It follows, *a fortiori*, that the state's interest in protecting potential lives, significant though it may be, is not sufficiently compelling to justify forcing a woman to carry her fetus to term or to endure delays and obstacles to abortion that increase her health risks.

C. This Court Should Not Adopt the Undue Burden Analysis Employed by the Court Below.

In adopting what it called "the undue burden standard," the court of appeals held that strict scrutiny applies only to laws that are initially found to impose " 'absolute obstacles or severe limitations' " on the freedom of a woman, in consultation with her physician, to make a decision whether or not to continue her pregnancy. Pet. App. 14a, 24a–25a (quoting *Thornburgh*, 476 U.S. at 828 (O'Connor, J., dissenting)). A

---

38. *Schloendorff* v. *Society of New York Hosp.*, 105 N.E. 92, 93 (N.Y. 1914) (Cardozo, J.).

39. *Canterbury* v. *Spence*, 464 F.2d 772, 780 (D.C. Cir.), *cert. denied*, 409 U.S. 1064 (1972).

40. *Amici* are aware of no state that has required a healthy adult to undergo a medical procedure to protect the health or save the life of another individual; such procedures may be ordered for a minor only if they are in the minor's best interest. *See supra* p. [91] n.37 (citing cases). Some courts have required parents to accept medical treatment where, in contrast to the abortion context, the required intrusion furthers both the state's interest in protecting the life of the parent and the state's interest in the welfare of a minor or viable fetus. Thus, courts have required parents of minor children to accept blood transfusions, *Jehovah's Witnesses* v. *King County Hosp.*, 278 F. Supp. 488 (W.D. Wash. 1967), *aff'd*, 390 U.S. 598 (1968), and pregnant women at term to have cesarean sections where vaginal delivery would endanger the lives of both mother and child, *e.g.*, *Jefferson* v. *Griffin Spalding County Hosp. Auth.*, 274 S.E.2d 457, 458 (Ga. 1981). More recently, however, and correctly in *amici's* view, courts have held that a state cannot require a woman to submit to a life-saving post-partum blood transfusion for the benefit of her minor child or other dependents, *Fosmire* v. *Nicoleau*, 551 N.E.2d 77 (N.Y. 1990); *Public Health Trust* v. *Wons*, 541 So.2d 96 (Fla. 1989), or to undergo a cesarean section if she has not (or would not have) consented to the surgery, *In re A.C.*, 573 A.2d 1235 (D.C. 1990).

majority of this Court has not yet adopted that undue burden standard, and it should not do so here, for three reasons.

First, such a standard is inconsistent with established constitutional principles. This Court has never required a showing of "absolute obstacles" or "severe limitations" on a fundamental right as a threshold for triggering strict scrutiny. Rather, the Court has held that fundamental personal rights and liberties are protected by the Due Process Clause of the Fourteenth Amendment from "infringement" by the states. *Stanley v. Georgia*, 394 U.S. 557, 564, 568 n.11 (1969). *E.g., Carey v. Population Servs. Int'l*, 431 U.S. 678, 686 (1977) (strict scrutiny is required for "regulations *imposing* a burden on" a fundamental right) (emphasis added).[41]

The effect of the undue burden standard, as applied below, is to subject state regulations that significantly burden a fundamental right to review under a mere "rational relationship" standard. Rational-relation review, while appropriate for "legislative Acts adjusting the burdens and benefits of economic life,"[42] has never been accepted as adequate in reviewing legislation affecting "individual decisions in matters of childbearing" or other similarly private matters. *Carey*, 431 U.S. at 687.[43]

In the abortion context, such an approach would lead to a subjective, unpredictable balancing in every case of the degree of health risk and the degree of burden that a particular state law imposes against the weight of the state's interest. Such a balancing approach is squarely rejected in analogous common law cases such as *McFall*, and should be rejected here.

Second, the undue burden test, by weakening protection of women's health and introducing an inherently subjective

41. Even where the Court has used language qualifying the degrees of intrusion necessary, it has not required severe intrusions or absolute obstacles. *E.g., Bates v. Little Rock*, 361 U.S. 516, 524 (1960) ("significant encroachment").

42. *Pension Benefit Guar. Corp. v. R.A. Gray & Co.*, 467 U.S. 717, 729 (1984).

43. Indeed, the very label "undue burden" reflects the confusion this standard—as a threshold test—introduces into constitutional analysis. The threshold question is simply whether a "burden" has in fact been imposed; the question whether that burden is "undue"—*i.e.*, "unwarranted" or "unjustified"—logically should be answered only at the end of the analysis, after the state's interests and any overbreadth have been considered. This Court initially used the phrase "undue burden" to refer not to any threshold standard for triggering strict scrutiny but to the completed analysis. *E.g., Bellotti v. Baird*, 443 U.S. 622, 647 (1979) (plurality).

standard of evaluation, would simply increase the need for this Court's perennial monitoring of state abortion laws.

As the Brief *Amici Curiae* of William J. Guste, Louisiana Attorney General et al. in support of Robert P. Casey's petition for certiorari in this case illustrates, states are now passing legislation that returns state law to the pre-*Roe* era. Thus, a decision to adopt a weaker undue-burden/rational relationship standard of review will require this Court to resolve a host of new and difficult questions. Must states allow abortion when necessary to preserve the health of the mother? Must they do so when necessary to preserve her life? Must abortion be available when the pregnancy results from rape or from incest? Is evidence that pregnancy may render a woman suicidal evidence that it poses a threat to her life? Can a state require clear and convincing objective evidence that an exception is met? Must there be an exception to criminal penalties for women and physicians who act in good faith? Such questions inevitably will arise so long as the abortion issue remains justiciable. The stakes for personal liberty are too high to expect otherwise.

Abandoning the principle that states may not place women's health at risk in regulating abortion therefore will not extricate this Court from the need to draw fine lines between what is permissible legislation and what is not. Reaffirming the basic principle that underlies *Roe*, however, would largely end this Court's oversight role. As discussed below, the Court has already resolved most of the issues that can arise under *Roe*, and has provided the lower courts with ample guidance to deal with any new legislation.

Third, there is no reason not to respect *stare decisis* here, because the principle that underlies *Roe* provides a workable standard that is consistent with constitutional precedent. *Roe* is therefore not a case that has proved "unsound in principle and unworkable in practice." *Garcia v. San Antonio Metro. Transit Auth.*, 469 U.S. 528, 546 (1985). There have been no "changes in society or in the law" since 1973 to require a reversal of *Roe*'s holding—the same concerns raised now were raised at the time *Roe* was argued (and reargued). *Vasquez v. Hillery*, 474 U.S. 254, 266 (1986); *see Akron*, 462 U.S. at 419 n.1. Respect for *stare decisis* is thus compelling here, because it is necessary to demonstrate "that bedrock principles are founded in the law rather than in the proclivities of individuals, and thereby [to] contribut[e] to the integrity of our constitutional system of government, both in appearance and in fact." *Vasquez*, 474 U.S. at 265–66. This Court has never before withdrawn fundamental status from any right previously recognized as fundamental. To depart from that precedent in this or any setting would so undermine accepted notions of "ordered liberty" that it should not be undertaken at all.

In sum, it is not the division of pregnancy into trimesters that determined the standard of review adopted in *Roe*. While the trimester framework was intended to and has provided helpful guidance to lower courts, the essential holding of *Roe* was that strict scrutiny was required where a state law interfered with a woman's right to decide, in consultation with her health care providers, whether or not to continue a pregnancy. That holding is valid today, just as it was two decades ago. This Court therefore should reverse the holding below adopting an "undue burden" standard of review for abortion legislation.

II. PENNSYLVANIA'S HUSBAND NOTIFICATION, INFORMED CONSENT, PARENTAL CONSENT, MEDICAL EMERGENCY, AND DISCLOSURE REQUIREMENTS ARE UNCONSTITUTIONAL.

Each of the challenged provisions of Pennsylvania's Abortion Control Act is unconstitutional. In upholding all but one of these provisions, the court of appeals erroneously required a high threshold showing of an undue burden and ignored uncontroverted factual findings that each provision will cause substantial harm to women's health. The state interest repeatedly asserted in defense of these provisions—preserving the life of the fetus—is inadequate, because this Court's decisions establish that the woman's life and health must always prevail over the fetus' life and health when they conflict. *Thornburgh*, 476 U.S. at 768–69; *see also Colautti* v. *Franklin*, 439 U.S. 379, 400 (1979); *Roe*, 410 U.S. at 163–64.

A. Husband Notification

Section 3209 of the Act makes it a crime for a married woman to obtain an abortion unless she provides her physician a signed statement that she either has notified her husband of her intention to obtain an abortion or has met one of four narrow exceptions to this requirement, and that she understands that a false statement is punishable by law. 18 Pa. Cons. Stat. Ann. § 3209 (1983 & Supp. 1991); Pet. App. 61a n.24, 191a–193a. As the court of appeals concluded, even if a showing of undue burden is required, this husband notification requirement is unconstitutional.[44] This provision severely burdens a woman's fundamental right to choose an abortion without furthering any compelling state interest.

1. Husband notification severely burdens a woman's right to obtain an abortion from her physician.

The district court's extensive factual findings, none of which was or could be found to be clearly erroneous on this record, unambiguously support its conclusion that husband notification imposes "a constitutionally significant burden on the woman's right to an abortion." Pet. App. 193a–201a, 254a. These findings also support the circuit court's finding that the provision imposes an "undue burden" because it "may effectively prevent the abortion or may severely penalize the woman in other ways" for choosing to seek an abortion. Id. at 63a. Indeed, the burden here is comparable to, if not more severe than, the unconstitutional burden imposed upon minors by the notification requirements at issue in Bellotti v. Baird, 443 U.S. 622, 647 (1979), and Hodgson v. Minnesota, 110 S. Ct. 2926, 2945 & n.36 (1990).

a. As both courts below noted, the vast majority of married women seeking an abortion have discussed their plans with their husbands. Pet. App. 66a. Section 3209 is thus targeted at, and will chiefly affect, women who fear that notifying their

---

44. Amici refer here to "husband notification" rather than "spousal notice" because the Act's gender-neutral label is deceptive. It camouflages the fact that Section 3209 applies exclusively to women. Moreover, Section 3209 is unique; no other Commonwealth law imposes any intra-marital notice requirement. Pet. App. 199a.

husbands will lead to physical or psychological intimidation or abuse.

For many women such concerns are all too real. Women in our society are at shockingly high risk for physical and psychological abuse by their husbands. According to one survey, nearly one in eight husbands had physically abused his wife during 1985, and almost one-third of the assaults involved severe aggression.[45] The medical community, recognizing the enormity of this problem, has efforts underway to educate health care professionals about the nature of this problem and its physical and psychological manifestations.[46]

The district court correctly found that requiring pregnant women to notify their husbands of their pregnancy and of their intent to seek an abortion will exacerbate the problem of violence against women because "pregnancy is frequently a flashpoint for battering and violence within the family." Pet. App. 196a. Studies demonstrate, for example, that as many as eight percent of women are physically or sexually abused during pregnancy.[47] In addition, abuse may take the form of actual or threatened violence to the couple's children, dissolution of a marriage, curtailment of financial support, psychological abuse (verbal degradation, food and sleep deprivation, isolation and monitoring), or disclosure of the wife's decision to family, friends, and acquaintances. Id. at 194a, 196a, 199a.[48]

b. The narrow exception for wives who can claim that they fear "the infliction of bodily injury upon [them]" by their husband or someone else is insufficient to eliminate the burden imposed by husband notification. The exception simply does

45. Strauss & Gelles, Societal Change and Change in Family Violence from 1975 to 1985 As Revealed by Two National Surveys, 48 J. Marriage & Family 465, 470 (1986). See also L. Ohlin & M. Tonry, Family Violence 177–80 (1989) (reviewing other empirical studies).

46. See American Medical Association Council on Scientific Affairs, Violence Against Women (1991); American College of Obstetricians & Gynecologists, The Battered Woman (1989).

47. Amaro et al., Violence During Pregnancy and Substance Use, 80 Am. J. Pub. Health 575 (1990); Helton et al., Battered and Pregnant: A Prevalence Study, 77 Am. J. Pub. Health 1337 (1987).

48. In addition to fostering abuse, the requirement that a woman notify her husband will jeopardize the confidential nature of the relationship between the woman and her physician. See Pet. App. 195a. Concerns about confidentiality may cause some women to delay seeking care or perhaps forgo appropriate medical care entirely.

not cover the range of coercive actions that husbands in an abusive situation typically take. Moreover, as the district court found, the "coping strategy" that "most battered women" have developed, *i.e.*, "learned helplessness," leaves them without "the psychological ability to avail themselves of the exceptions of Section 3209." Pet. App. 200a–201a.

Accordingly, such abuse serves both strongly to deter women from seeking an abortion and severely to penalize those who in fact go forward with notification.

c. The dissenting judge below argued that the husband notification provision could not constitute an undue burden because it would affect, at most, only a small "percentage of all women desiring abortions" and "plaintiffs failed to show even roughly how many of the women in this small group would actually be adversely affected by Section 3209." Pet. App. 92a. The dissent's conception of what constitutes a burden on a fundamental right is erroneous as a matter of law.

Because a fundamental right is held by an individual against the state, the abridgment of such a right is significant even if only a small number of individuals are affected. In *Bellotti*, the Court invalidated a Massachusetts statute requiring that parents be notified of any judicial proceeding brought by their daughter to obtain an abortion. Justice Powell, in an opinion joined by then-Chief Justice Burger, then-Justice Rehnquist, and Justice Stewart, acknowledged that there was "no reason to believe" that parents would seek to obstruct their daughter's access to court "in the majority of cases where consent is withheld." 443 U.S. 622, 647 (1979). Nevertheless, the Massachusetts law was declared unconstitutional because "[i]t would be unrealistic . . . to assume that the mere existence of a legal right to seek relief in superior court provides an effective avenue of relief for some of those who need it most." *Id.*

Thus, this Court invalidated the statute in *Bellotti* even though it would burden only a very small proportion of the total number of women seeking abortion, and even though no precise estimate of that percentage was offered.

2. Husband notification does not narrowly serve a compelling state interest.

The Commonwealth asserts an interest in "promoting the integrity of the marital relationship." 18 Pa. Cons. Stat. Ann. § 3209(a); Pet. App. 300a. Undoubtedly, the state has an interest in the integrity of marriages; laws prohibiting bigamy or restricting the availability of divorce, for example, are constitutional. But such laws define and regulate the nature and structure of the institution; they are constitutional precisely because they do not intrude into the marital relationship itself. Marriage "is an association that promotes a way of life, not causes"; thus, state intrusions on marital relations are suspect when they promote a political agenda and particularly suspect when designed to advance the state's agenda on a matter as personal to individuals as procreation. *Griswold v. Connecticut*, 381 U.S. 479, 486 (1965). The state cannot intrude more deeply into a marriage than when it conditions one individual's exercise of constitutional rights on an agreement to engage in state-mandated conversations with his or her spouse.

More critically, regardless of how the state's goal of promoting marital integrity is labeled, that goal is not served by forcing a husband and wife to communicate about a particular topic. As the district court found, "[m]arital accord arises from within the relationship not from the intervention of the state." Pet. App. 262a.[49]

B. Informed Consent Provisions

Section 3205 of the Act makes it a crime for a physician to perform an abortion unless he or she first obtains the "informed consent" of the patient as defined by detailed procedures. 18 Pa. Cons. Stat. Ann. § 3205; Pet. App. 289a. Far from promoting true informed consent, however, Section 3205 will interfere with constructive consultation between physicians and their patients and will undermine patients' health.

---

49. The Commonwealth's other asserted interests, in promoting the husband's interests in "having children within the marriage" and in the "prenatal life" of his child, are not compelling. The interest Pennsylvania seeks to protect is only that of married men, not of biological fathers. The Commonwealth offers no explanation, however, why it is appropriate (let alone compelling) for the state to throw its weight behind one spouse and not the other on the question whether or not the wife will bear a child. In siding with one spouse and against another, the Commonwealth impermissibly intrudes into "the private realm of family life which the state cannot enter." *Prince v. Massachusetts*, 321 U.S. 158, 166 (1944).

1. The requirement that a physician or nurse obtain a patient's informed consent to a medical procedure is fundamental to the common law and medical ethics. The doctrine is rooted in the respect for patient autonomy and the recognition that each patient is an individual with unique beliefs and needs.[50] The point of the consultation is not to inundate a patient with predetermined details on every conceivable facet of all available medical procedures; indeed, a health care provider has an obligation to limit disclosure where necessary to avoid causing the patient anxiety and fear that could jeopardize effective treatment of the patient.[51] Rather, the requirement that a physician or nurse obtain informed consent provides an opportunity for the provider and patient to discuss the risks and benefits of potential therapies germane to that patient, so that the patient can make an informed treatment decision. The information appropriate to each consultation will differ from patient to patient, and providers therefore do and must retain discretion to determine what specific information is relevant.

2. The procedures that Pennsylvania would require under the rubric of "informed consent" are in fact antithetical to informed consent as currently understood and practiced. To begin with, Section 3205 requires that each patient be told that (1) the State Department of Health has prepared "printed materials which describe the unborn child" and that "list agencies that offer alternatives to abortion" which the physician will provide to her "free of charge"; (2) that "medical assistance benefits" may be available to her and that the state's materials contain additional information on such benefits; and (3) that the "father of the unborn child" is liable for child support. 18 Pa. Cons. Stat. Ann. § 3205(a)(2)(i)–(iii); Pet. App. 290a.

As this Court previously held in *Thornburgh*, "[t]he printed

50. *See, e.g., Canterbury v. Spence*, 464 F.2d 772, 780 (D.C. Cir.), *cert. denied*, 409 U.S. 1064 (1972); T. Beauchamp & J. Childress, *Principles of Biomedical Ethics*, 74–75, 91–93 (3d ed. 1989); 1 President's Commission for the Study of Ethical Problems in Medicine and Biomedical and Behavioral Research, *Making Health Care Decisions* 18–39 (1982).

51. *See, e.g., Woolley v. Henderson*, 418 A.2d 1123, 1130 (Me. 1980); *Cobbs v. Grant*, 502 P.2d 1 (Cal. 1972) (en banc); *Roberts v. Wood*, 206 F. Supp. 579, 583 (S.D. Ala. 1962).

materials required by § 3205 . . . [are] nothing less than an outright attempt to wedge the Commonwealth's message discouraging abortion into the privacy of the informed-consent dialogue between the woman and her physician." 476 U.S. at 762–63. Because the Commonwealth's materials "create the impression in women that the Commonwealth disapproves of the woman's decision" to seek an abortion, bringing these materials to the attention of a woman who has already decided with her physician that it is appropriate to obtain an abortion is misleading and can produce needless anxiety and emotional pain. Pet. App. 179a. There is "no legitimate medical justification" to recite such information to each patient, *id.*; indeed, much of the information relates to issues about which physicians or other health professionals have no special knowledge or expertise. Yet "[f]orcing the physician or counselor to present materials and the list [of state agencies] makes him or her in effect an agent of the State in treating the woman and places his or her imprimatur upon both the materials and the list." *Thornburgh*, 476 U.S. at 762–63. The forced disclosures of Section 3205 thus "serve only to confuse and punish [a pregnant woman] and to heighten her anxiety, contrary to accepted medical practice." *Id.* at 762.[52]

3. Section 3205 further intrudes on the physician-patient relationship by criminalizing the performance of any abortion until at least 24 hours have elapsed following the informed consent discussions between the physician or counselor and patient. 18 Pa. Cons. Stat. Ann. § 3205(a)(2); Pet. App. 290a. As the district court found, because of scheduling problems and the scarcity of abortion clinics, this waiting requirement will in fact impose on the majority of women seeking an abortion in Pennsylvania delays of two days to two weeks between the time a woman consents to the procedure and the time her physician is legally entitled to perform it. Pet. App. 172a. This waiting period will significantly increase the risk of death and other complications associated with abortions

---

52. Section 3205(a) also requires the physician, to the exclusion of other qualified counselors, to supply certain information about health risks, including risks that may be irrelevant to a particular woman's situation. This Court in *Akron* held that such a requirement is overbroad, 462 U.S. at 447–49, and the Court should invalidate Section 3205(a) for this reason as well.

which correlate directly with gestational age. *See supra* pp. [84–85].

To be sure, where there is some reason to think that a particular woman needs time to reach a considered judgment, *amici* would agree that additional time for reflection would be appropriate and the individual physician would so advise the patient.[53] But sound medical practice requires the physician to explain to the patient that any benefit of waiting must be weighed against the demonstrated increase in the risks to a woman's health caused by delay. Because the requirements of Section 3205 serve no compelling state interest but will cause harm to women, they are unconstitutional.[54]

C. Parental Informed Consent

Section 3206 forbids physicians from providing abortions to women under the age of 18 unless the physician first obtains the informed consent not only of the woman but also of one of her parents. 18 Pa. Cons. Stat. Ann. § 3206; Pet. App. 292a. The requirement that the parent's consent be "informed" distinguishes this statute from other state statutes restricting the abortion rights of minors reviewed by this Court. Pet. App. 250a–251a. Here, even an approving parent must visit the clinic in person and sit through the mandatory anti-abortion presentation prescribed in Section 3205 before an abortion may be performed.

Section 3206 is unconstitutional because it ensures that minors will face needless and health-threatening delay in obtaining an abortion. Those minors whose parents approve will, in many cases, be delayed because of the difficulties parents face arranging an in-person visit. Pet. App. 249a. Those minors whose parents do not approve must resort to the inherently time-consuming process of obtaining permission from a state court. The adverse effect of this built-in delay is particularly acute for minors, who comprise a high percentage of

53. *See, e.g.*, American College of Obstetricians & Gynecologists, *Standards For Obstetric-Gynecologic Services* 68 (7th ed. 1989) (physician should counsel woman to take time necessary to be certain her abortion decision is the correct one).

54. Indeed, Section 3205's waiting requirement is identical to that invalidated by this Court in *Akron*, 462 U.S. at 450–51, and should be invalidated for this reason alone.

women who obtain an abortion in the second trimester, where the health risks of abortion are greatest. *See supra* pp. [84–85]. Because Section 3206 will impose delays on virtually all minors, and not just on those who elect to use the judicial bypass procedure, it is unconstitutional.

D. Exception for Medical Emergencies

Section 3203 of the Act provides a definition of the term "medical emergency" applicable uniquely to abortions. The Act then incorporates this definition as an exception to the requirements of husband notification, informed consent, and parental informed consent.

As the court below recognized, *Roe* requires a medical emergency exception to any statute that regulates abortion in a way that may cause a health-threatening delay in the performance of an abortion. Pet. App. 36a. On its face, the Commonwealth's exception is inadequate. It makes it a crime for a physician to perform an abortion sooner than 24 hours after initially evaluating a patient unless the physician, in good faith, believes that an abortion is necessary "to avert [the patient's] death" or that "delay will create serious risk of substantial and irreversible impairment of major bodily function." 18 Pa. Cons. Stat. Ann. § 3203; Pet. App. 289a.

The Act's definition is notably narrow when compared to Pennsylvania's general definition of medical emergency and to sound medical practice.[55] The Act precludes physicians from responding in a medically appropriate manner to women for whom pregnancy poses a health risk that, while significant, does not amount to a "serious risk of substantial and irreversible impairment of major bodily function." It therefore requires physicians to place the health of a woman at risk in order to further the state's interest in protecting fetal life, a

---

55. For all procedures besides abortion, Pennsylvania defines a medical emergency as "[a] combination of circumstances resulting in a need for immediate medical intervention." 35 Pa. Cons. Stat. Ann. § 6923 (1977 & Supp. 1991). This is consistent with the definition generally accepted by the health care community. *See, e.g.,* J. Cosgriff & D. Anderson, *The Practice of Emergency Care* 20 (2d ed. 1984) ("An emergency is an unforeseen combination of circumstances creating a condition which in the professional judgment of a physician and surgeon of good standing acting under the same or similar circumstances requires immediate care, treatment, or surgery in order to protect a person's life or health").

"trade-off" this Court has repeatedly disapproved. *Thornburgh*, 476 U.S. at 768–69; *Colautti v. Franklin*, 439 U.S. 379, 400 (1979); *Roe*, 410 U.S. at 163–64.

The court of appeals upheld the definition of emergency by interpreting it liberally to include all circumstances that "in any way pose a *significant* threat to the life or health of a woman." Pet. App. 40a (emphasis added). But it is impossible to reconcile the court of appeals' interpretation with the statute's plain language. Courts, in attempting to save a statute from constitutional attack, may not engage in "judicially rewriting it." *Aptheker v. Secretary of State*, 378 U.S. 500, 515 (1964).

The court of appeals also suggested that the statute was constitutional because the Commonwealth conceded on appeal that three common medical emergencies—inevitable abortions, premature rupture of the membranes, and pre-eclampsia—that do not appear to meet the statute's requirements for an emergency would in fact be considered by the Commonwealth as emergencies. Pet. App. 37a. This concession cannot save the statute.[56] First, the district court found as a matter of fact that no reasonable physician reading the plain language of the statute would believe that these medical conditions would be covered. Pet. App. 162a–163a. Second, the three examples were only illustrative of a broader category of conditions that most physicians would conclude do not meet the plain language of the statute. For example, Section 3203 may prevent physicians from appropriately treating various cardiovascular, renal, pulmonary or neurologic disorders that are exacerbated by pregnancy, *see supra* p. [84] n.17, but that do not necessarily present an immediate and serious risk of irreversible impairment. These points are dispositive, because a criminal statute that is asserted to mean what no reasonable person subject to the statute would interpret it to mean is unconstitutionally vague. *Colautti*, 439 U.S. at 390–97; *Kolender v. Lawson*, 461 U.S. 352, 357 (1983).

56. This concession—and this interpretation of the statutory language—is no more than a "convenient litigating position" which is entitled to no deference. *Bowen v. Georgetown Univ. Hosp.*, 488 U.S. 204, 212–13 (1988). The Commonwealth's position in this case is not binding on the Pennsylvania courts which are free to, and likely will, interpret the statute in exactly the way it is written, *i.e.*, to criminalize the medically appropriate treatment of several of the most common complications of pregnancy.

Finally, the court of appeals erred in holding that the statute was constitutional because a physician can be criminally liable only if he or she "violate[s] his or her own good faith clinical judgment." Pet. App. 42a. The court's reliance on the subjective standard built into the statute simply misses the critical point that the grounds available to the physician for invoking his or her judgment are unduly narrow. Thus, a physician may, in good faith, believe that delay will cause significant risk to the patient, but not a risk of irreversible impairment to a major bodily function. The statute places that physician in an intolerable dilemma: The physician cannot, in good faith, authorize the performance of an abortion under the law, yet the physician cannot, in good conscience, and consistent with the ethical standards of the medical profession, force the woman to wait out the many delays imposed by the statute.

E. Reporting and Public Disclosure Requirements

Physicians, nurses, and counselors who provide abortion services, and women who seek their services, regularly face picketing and verbal harassment both at their offices and their homes, harassment of their families, and periodic threats of death, bombing, and kidnapping. Pet. App. 211a–213a, 267a. The effect of such constant harassment has been to reduce the number of health care providers willing to assist women in obtaining abortions, and to force others to take steps to preserve their anonymity. *Id.* at 219a–221a. By requiring public disclosure of the names and addresses of abortion facilities and affiliated organizations and of the number of abortions performed (total and by trimester) each quarter, and by requiring confidential reports of the names of referring physicians, Sections 3207(b), 3214(f), and 3214(a)(1) will facilitate and exacerbate this harassment, and make it difficult, if not impossible, for "indigent . . . victims of rape or incest or who suffer from a life-threatening condition . . . to obtain abortion services." Pet. App. 213a–214a, 220a–221a; *see id.* at 298a, 302a–304a.

In reversing, the court of appeals simply disagreed with the district court's factual findings. Pet. App. 79a, 82a–83a. The district court's findings are not clearly erroneous, however, and the court of appeals plainly erred in substituting its own assessment of the record for that of the district court.[57] More-over, quite apart from *Roe*, where, as here, it is plain that state-mandated disclosure requirements can only exacerbate private threats, harassment and reprisals, those disclosure requirements cannot stand. *E.g., Brown v. Socialist Workers '74 Campaign Comm.*, 459 U.S. 87, 92–94 (1982); *NAACP v. Alabama ex rel. Patterson*, 357 U.S. 449, 462–63 (1958).

F. Criminal Penalties

The Due Process Clause limits the degree to which states may criminally punish health care providers for assisting individuals in matters of personal choice. *See generally Doe v. Bolton*, 410 U.S. 179, 199–200 (1972); *Carey v. Population Servs. Int'l*, 431 U.S. 678, 686–91 (1977); *Eisenstadt v. Baird*, 405 U.S. 438 (1972). The imposition of criminal penalties upon physicians who perform abortions in circumstances where continued pregnancy poses a significant risk to a woman's health (but not a defined "emergency") is unconstitutional. Uncertainty is an inescapable element of medicine. *Parham v. J.R.*, 442 U.S. 584, 604 (1979); *Addington v. Texas*, 441 U.S. 418, 429 (1979). When physicians are uncertain about the degree of risk that delay may present to a patient, they should choose to err on the side of protecting the health of the patient. Yet, Pennsylvania would make it a crime to do so. Such a law serves no legitimate purpose. The criminal law exists to protect the public safety, health, and welfare; where, as here, its only effect is to subvert public health, the Fourteenth Amendment precludes its enforcement.

* * *

Each of the Pennsylvania Abortion Control Act's challenged provisions, considered individually, unconstitutionally burdens the right of pregnant women to choose whether or not to terminate their pregnancies. Viewed as a whole, however, a clearer picture emerges. This is not a statute designed to protect maternal health. Nor is it a statute intended, through good faith efforts at education and social change, to minimize the need for abortion by getting at the root causes

57. *See Pullman-Standard v. Swint*, 456 U.S. 273, 287 (1982); Fed. R. Civ. P. 52(a).

of unwanted pregnancy. Rather, it is a statute that seeks to discourage, deter, and defeat women in their attempts to obtain abortions by replacing the provider-patient relationship and medical judgment with a procedural obstacle course fraught with criminal and civil penalties.

The most bitter irony for those among *amici*'s members who practiced medicine or nursing prior to 1973 is that restrictive abortion laws in the end will do little to reduce the number of abortions. Rather, they will shift many abortions out of the sterile confines of licensed clinics and into the back rooms of those who are willing, for a price and without regard for patient health, to defy state law. Thus, the health care provider's role in referring or performing an abortion will be replaced by their role in repairing and treating the consequences of illegal abortions. This Court rightly concluded in 1973 that the Fourteenth Amendment protects women from state laws that compel recourse to such desperate and destructive measures, and it should reaffirm that conclusion.

CONCLUSION

The judgment challenged in No. 91–744 should be reversed and the judgment challenged in No. 91–902 should be affirmed.

Respectfully submitted,

ANN E. ALLEN, AMERICAN COLLEGE OF OBSTETRICIANS AND GYNECOLOGISTS, 409 12th Street, S.W., Washington, D.C. 20024, (202) 638–5577

CARTER G. PHILLIPS, *

MARK E. HADDAD,

PAUL E. KALB, SIDLEY & AUSTIN, 1722 Eye Street, N.W., Washington, D.C. 20006, (202) 736–8000

Counsel for *Amici Curiae*

*Counsel of Record

LAURIE R. ROCKETT, HOLLYER, JONES, BRADY, SMITH, TOXELL, BARRETT & CHIRA (Counsel to the American Medical Women's Association, Inc.), 342 Madison Avenue, New York, N.Y. 10173, (212) 818–1110

JOEL I. KLEIN, KLEIN, FARR, SMITH & TARANTO (Counsel to the American Psychiatric Association), 2550 M Street, N.W., Washington, D.C. 20037, (202) 775–0184

NADINE TAUB, Women's Rights Litigation Clinic (Counsel to the American Public Health Association), Rutgers Law School, Newark, N.J. 07102, (201) 648–5637

BETH FOUNTAIN, ASHER & ASSOCIATES (Counsel to the Association of Reproductive Health Professionals), 1819 H Street, N.W., Washington, D.C. 20006, (202) 452–1540

SARAH C. CAREY, STEPTOE & JOHNSON (Counsel to the National Medical Association), 1330 Connecticut Ave., N.W., Washington, D.C. 20036, (202) 429–3000

March 6, 1992

APPENDIX

AMICI CURIAE

Amicus American College of Obstetricians and Gynecologists (ACOG) is a private, voluntary, non-profit organization of physicians who specialize in obstetric and gynecologic care. ACOG is the leading group of professionals providing health care to women; its 25,000 members represent approximately ninety percent of all obstetricians and gynecologists practicing in the United States.

Amicus American Medical Women's Association, Inc. (AMWA) is a non-profit organization of 12,000 women physicians and medical students. One of AMWA's primary missions is to promote quality health care for women. AMWA strongly opposes laws which adversely affect the health of women, or impose constraints on the right of the pregnant patient, in consultation with her physician, to make a personal and medically informed decision whether or not to continue a pregnancy.

Amicus American Psychiatric Association (APA) is the nation's largest professional association specializing in psychiatry, with a membership exceeding 30,000 physicians. APA's purposes include promoting the welfare of patients who require psychiatric services.

Amicus the American Public Health Association (APHA) is a national organization devoted to the promotion and protection of personal and environmental health and to disease prevention. Founded in 1872, APHA is the largest public health organization in the world, with over 50,000 members. It represents all disciplines and specialties in public health, including patients and health professionals such as physicians, nurses, health educators, and family planning specialists.

Amicus Association of Reproductive Health Professionals (ARHP) is an interdisciplinary professional organization comprised of over 1,500 obstetricians/gynecologists and other physicians, researchers, educators, administrators, and other professionals in reproductive health. ARHP's mission is to educate health care professionals and the public on family planning, contraception, and other reproductive health issues including sexually transmitted diseases and urogenital infections, HIV, abortion, menopause, cancer prevention/detection, sexual health, and infertility.

Amicus National League for Nursing is an organization of 12,000 individuals and 2,000 agencies. It represents nurses from all settings of education and practice, as well as other health professionals and health policy makers. The league is the accrediting body for all levels of nursing schools. It works to promote access to affordable, high quality health care.

Amicus National Medical Association (NMA), founded in 1895, is a professional organization representing 16,000 Black physicians and medical students in the United States. The NMA actively addresses all issues affecting the ability of its members to deliver quality health care. It has aggressively sought to ensure equal access and availability to health care services.

BRIEF OF *AMICI CURIAE* OF THE NAACP
LEGAL DEFENSE AND EDUCATIONAL FUND,
INC., ASIAN AMERICAN LEGAL DEFENSE &
EDUCATIONAL FUND, THE CENTER FOR
CONSTITUTIONAL RIGHTS, CENTER FOR
LAW AND SOCIAL JUSTICE AT MEDGAR
EVERS COLLEGE, THE COMMITTEE FOR
HISPANIC CHILDREN AND FAMILIES,
ECO-JUSTICE PROJECT AND NETWORK,
HISPANIC HEALTH COUNCIL, JAPANESE
AMERICAN CITIZENS LEAGUE, THE LATINA
ROUNDTABLE ON HEALTH AND
REPRODUCTIVE RIGHTS, MADRE, MEXICAN
AMERICAN LEGAL DEFENSE AND
EDUCATIONAL FUND, THE NATIONAL
ASSOCIATION OF SOCIAL WORKERS,
NATIONAL BLACK WOMEN'S HEALTH
PROJECT, THE NATIONAL COALITION FOR
BLACK LESBIANS AND GAYS, THE
NATIONAL COUNCIL OF NEGRO WOMEN,
INC., THE NATIONAL EMERGENCY CIVIL
LIBERTIES COMMITTEE, NATIONAL LATINA
HEALTH ORGANIZATION, NATIONAL
MINORITY AIDS COUNCIL, THE NATIVE
AMERICAN WOMEN'S HEALTH EDUCATION
RESOURCE CENTER, THE NEW YORK
WOMEN'S FOUNDATION, THE PUERTO
RICAN LEGAL DEFENSE AND EDUCATION
FUND, THE SOUTHERN POVERTY LAW
CENTER, WOMEN FOR RACIAL &
ECONOMIC EQUALITY, AND THE WOMEN'S
POLICY GROUP

INTEREST OF *AMICI CURIAE*

This brief is filed on behalf of twenty-four organizations that share a deep concern for the health and life chances of poor women, and particularly for poor women of color—*i.e.*, African American, Latina, Asian American and Native American women. Our ranks include attorneys, medical professionals, community educators, and researchers, who fear the devastating effects of greater governmental interference in the reproductive choices of poor women and the provision of abortion services.

Poor women lack access to the quality health care services that more affluent Americans take for granted. Poor communities have few health care providers and poor women are already forced to wait long hours in overcrowded clinics and emergency rooms and to travel at great expense for needed services. As fifteen studies recently reviewed by the Institute of Medicine found, financial barriers, particularly inadequate insurance coverage and limited personal funds, are the most important obstacle to care-seeking among women receiving insufficient care. United States Dept. of Health and Human Services, *Health Status of Minorities and Low-Income Groups: Third Edition* 99 (1991). Indeed, simply paying for the abortion procedure itself entails serious hardship for indigent women who, in order to exercise their right to abortion, must often let bills go unpaid or buy fewer necessities, such as food and clothing. Henshaw & Wallisch, *The Medicaid Cutoff and Abortion Services for the Poor*, 16 Fam. Plan. Persp. 170, 171 (1984). *Amici* are concerned about the adverse impact of statutory provisions that require women to delay treatment, to undertake multiple efforts to obtain care, and to overcome other psychological and procedural obstacles, such as those posed by the need to obtain spousal notification and parental consent.

In 1969, fully seventy-five percent of all the women who died of illegal abortions in the United States were women of color, and from 1972 to 1974, the rate of mortality from illegal abortions for women of color was twelve times greater than that of white women. Gold, *Abortion and Women's Health: A Turning Point for America?* The Alan Guttmacher Institute 5

(1990) (hereinafter cited as *Gold*); Dixon, Ross, Avery & Jenkins, *Reproductive Health of Black Women and Other Women of Color* in *From Abortion to Reproductive Freedom: Transforming a Movement* 157 (Fried ed. 1990). Even after legalization, high numbers of poor women of color were still precluded from obtaining safe and legal abortions. As a result, in 1975 women of color comprised eighty percent of the deaths associated with illegal abortions. Cates & Rochat, *Illegal Abortion in the United States: 1972–1974*, 8 Fam. Plan. Persp. 86, 87 (1986).

If the undue burden standard is to be adopted, it is crucial that the Court seriously consider the impact of statutory restrictions in the real world context in which poor women live. As Justice Marshall admonished nearly two decades ago, "It may be easy for some people to think that weekly savings of less than $2 are no burden. But no one who has had close contact with poor people can fail to understand how close to the margin of survival many of them are." *U.S. v. Kras*, 409 U.S. 434, 460 (1973) (Marshall, J., dissenting). Restrictions on the provision of abortion services and the decision-making process do not fall with equal measure upon rich and poor, and the burdens imposed on poor women should not be ignored.

A complete list of *amici* and their statements of interest are set forth in an Appendix to this brief.

QUESTION PRESENTED

Whether provisions of the Pennsylvania Abortion Control Act that impose a 24-hour waiting period before the performance of an abortion (18 Pa. Cons. Stat. Ann. § 3205(a) (informed consent)), mandate parental consent (18 Pa. Cons. Stat. Ann. § 3206), and require spousal notification (18 Pa. Cons. Stat. Ann. § 3209) unduly burden women's right to privacy.

SUMMARY OF ARGUMENT

Amici, supporting Planned Parenthood of Southeastern Pennsylvania, urge this Court to reaffirm Roe v. Wade, 410 U.S. 113 (1973). If, however, the Court adopts the undue burden test developed by Justice O'Connor, the Court would nevertheless be required to find the provisions of the Pennsylvania Abortion Control Act that define medical emergency, establish reporting requirements, and require informed consent, parental consent, and spousal notification unconstitutional.

The right to privacy is guaranteed to all women, regardless of income, race, or ethnicity. Accordingly, if the Court chooses to adopt the "undue burden" standard articulated by Justice O'Connor, the threshold examination of the statute's "burden" must include the practical impact of the law on the ability of poor women to exercise the protected right. Laws that place obstacles in the path of poor women who have chosen to terminate pregnancy—by imposing delays or procedural obstacles, economic barriers, or other impediments to access—constitute a burden on the privacy rights of poor women.

The Pennsylvania provisions under review would impose enormous burdens on the abortion decisions of poor women. The 24-hour delay, parental consent, and spousal notification requirements, in particular, erect prohibitive barriers in the path of poor women who seek abortions, thereby threatening the health of, and life chances for, many women. These provisions, thus, constitute an undue burden on women's right to reproductive choice.

ARGUMENT

INTRODUCTION

The Court of Appeals erred in upholding the constitutionality of provisions of Pennsylvania's Abortion Control Act that force women to wait 24 hours between the time that a woman's consent for abortion is obtained and the time that the abortion may be performed (18 Pa. Cons. Stat. Ann. § 3205(a) (informed consent)) and that mandate parental consent (18 Pa. Cons. Stat. Ann. § 3206). Through these provisions, as well as the Act's spousal notification requirement (18 Pa. Cons. Stat. Ann. § 3209), the state of Pennsylvania would actively restrict the provision of, and access to, abortion services.[1] The provisions unduly burden the right to privacy, particularly for poor women,[2] and are, therefore, unconstitutional.

In *Roe* v. *Wade*, 410 U.S. at 153, this Court recognized that the right to privacy "is broad enough to encompass a woman's decision whether or not to terminate her pregnancy." This Court has repeatedly affirmed its recognition of "a freedom of personal choice in certain matters of marriage and family life . . . [which] includes the freedom of a woman to decide whether to terminate a pregnancy." *See, e.g., Harris* v. *McRae*, 448 U.S. 297, 312 (1980); *Akron* v. *Akron Ctr. for Reproductive Health*, 462 U.S. 416, 420, n.1 (1983); *Hodgson* v. *Minnesota*, 497 U.S. ____, 111 L. Ed. 2d 344, 360 (1990). As Justice Stevens has reminded us, the Court's abortion cases implicate basic, fundamental values and address "the individual's right to make certain unusually important decisions that will affect [her] own, or [her] family's destiny." *Thornburgh* v. *American College of Obstetricians and Gynecologists*, 476 U.S. 747, 781, n.11 (1986) (quoting *Fitzgerald* v. *Porter Memorial*

1. The issues presently before this Court pertain to five provisions of the Pennsylvania Abortion Control Act, *i.e.* (1) the definition of medical emergency; (2) informed consent; (3) parental consent; (4) reporting requirements; and (5) spousal notification. *Amici* assert that each of these provisions would have a severe and drastic impact upon the cost and timing of abortions, as well as the number of legal providers, and, consequently, would place an undue burden on a woman's abortion decision. The focus of this brief, however, is limited to the three provisions listed in the above text.

2. Laws that restrict the provision of, and access to, abortion services for poor women will necessarily affect a high percentage of women of color. African American women, for example, are five times more likely to live in poverty and three times more likely to be unemployed than white women. United States Commission on Civil Rights, *The Economic Status of Black Women* 1 (1990). Indeed, the percentage of people of color living in poverty in the United States is dramatically high: 29% of Native Americans, United States Dept. of Health and Human Services, 1 *Report of the Secretary's Task Force on Black and Minority Health* 51 (1986), 31% of African Americans, and 26% of Latinos, as compared to 10% of whites. United States Dept. of Commerce, Bureau of Census, *Statistical Abstract of the United States, 1991*, No. 748, 463 (1991) (1989 data).

Hospital, 523 F.2d 716, 719–20 (7th Cir. 1975), *cert. denied*, 425 U.S. 916 (1976)).

For poor women, and particularly for poor African American women, the right to privacy in matters of body and reproduction—a right that was trammeled with state sanction during centuries of slavery—is fundamental to notions of freedom and liberty. For years, governmental protection of the individual's person or her private decision-making was nonexistent. The right to make and carry out reproductive decisions without governmental intrusion or government sanctioned interference was, and continues to be, a valued part of freedom. *See generally* Roberts, *The Future of Reproductive Choice for Poor Women and Women of Color*, 12 Women's Law Reporter 59 (1990) (analysis of the historical significance for poor African American women of reproductive choice and the "struggle against fearful and overwhelming odds . . . to maintain and protect that which woman holds dearer than life . . . to keep hallowed their own persons. . . ."); Bland, *Racial and Ethnic Influences: The Black Woman and Abortion*, in *Psychiatric Aspects of Abortion* 171 (Stotland ed. 1991); Genovese, *Roll, Jordan, Roll: The World The Slaves Made* 497–98 (1st Vintage Books Ed. 1972).[3]

Roe and its progeny established the limits of state authority to regulate the performance of abortions and announced the standards of review by which restrictions on this right are to be adjudged. "Where certain 'fundamental rights' are in-

3. Even today poor women of color are often unable to share in the freedom of personal choice in matters of reproduction guaranteed by *Roe*. Poor women often lack the economic means to avail themselves of health services and are alienated by the inaccessibility of health care. The tragic effects of what is truly a health care crisis for poor women are well known and widely documented. *See, e.g.*, United States Dept. of Health and Human Services, *Health Status of Minorities and Low-Income Groups: Third Edition* 99 (1991); Bland, *Racial and Ethnic Influences: The Black Woman and Abortion*, in *Psychiatric Aspects of Abortion* 171 (Stotland ed. 1991); Zambrana, *Research Issues Affecting Poor and Minority Women: A Model for Understanding Health Needs*, 14 Women and Health 137, 148–50 (1988); American Medical Association, Council on Ethical and Judicial Affairs, *Black-White Disparities in Health Care* 263 J.A.M.A. 2344 (May 2, 1990) ("Underlying the racial disparities in the quality of health among Americans are differences in both need and access. Blacks are more likely to require health care but are less likely to receive health care services."); *see also Harris*, 448 U.S. at 339 (1977) (Marshall, J., dissenting); *Beal v. Doe*, 432 U.S. 438, 455, n.1, 459 (1977) (Marshall, J., dissenting) (taking note of the paucity of abortion providers available to poor women and the lack of a "meaningful opportunity" to obtain an abortion).

volved, the Court has held that regulation limiting these rights may be justified only by a 'compelling state interest' . . . and that legislative enactments must be narrowly drawn to express only the legitimate state interests at stake." *Roe*, 410 U.S. at 155, 164–66; *see Planned Parenthood of Missouri v. Danforth*, 428 U.S. 52, 61 (1976).

Amici join Planned Parenthood of Southeastern Pennsylvania in urging this Court to reaffirm *Roe v. Wade*. If, however, the Court adopts the undue burden test developed by Justice O'Connor, the Court's prior decisions would also require reversal of the Third Circuit, which failed to analyze properly the burden imposed by the Pennsylvania statute.

In *Akron*, Justice O'Connor articulated the conceptual basis for the undue burden standard: "This Court has acknowledged that the right in *Roe v. Wade* can be understood only by considering both the woman's interest and the nature of the State's interference with it. *Roe* did not declare an unqualified 'constitutional right to an abortion'. . . . Rather, the right protects the woman from unduly burdensome interference with her freedom to decide whether to terminate her pregnancy.' " *Akron*, 462 U.S. at 461 (O'Connor, J., dissenting) (quoting *Maher v. Roe*, 432 U.S. 464, 473–74 (1977)). If a statute "places no obstacles—absolute or otherwise—in the pregnant woman's path to an abortion" and imposes "no restriction," then, as this Court found in *Maher*, the "regulation does not impinge upon the fundamental right recognized in *Roe*," and the judicial inquiry has come to closure. *Maher*, 432 U.S. at 474. If, however, a regulation infringes, interferes, or coercively constrains the free exercise of the right, then the statutory burden is established and must be justified.[4] *See Akron*, 462 U.S. at 462, 464 (O'Connor, dissenting). *Accord Maher*,

---

4. The Court's application of a "burden" standard in cases involving First and Fourteenth Amendment protections of free speech and associational rights is instructive: the threshold issue is whether a law burdens the right, not whether there is an undue burden. In *Eu v. San Francisco Democratic Comm.*, 489 U.S. 214, 222 (1989), the Court summarized the standard applied in those cases: To assess the constitutionality of a state election law, we first examine whether it burdens rights protected by the First and Fourteenth Amendments. If the challenged law burdens the rights of political parties and their members, it can survive constitutional scrutiny only if the state shows that it advances a compelling state interest and is narrowly tailored to serve that interest. (citations omitted). *See also Tashjihan v. Republican Party*, 479 U.S. 208, 213–14 (1986).

432 U.S. at 471 ("[T]he central question in this case is whether the regulation 'impinges upon a fundamental right explicitly or implicitly protected by the Constitution.' ").

The application of the undue burden standard involves two steps. First, there is a threshold assessment of the burden imposed by a statute—*i.e.*, an inquiry into whether the regulations restrict, or have a legally significant impact upon, the right to privacy. *See, e.g., Planned Parenthood Ass'n of Kansas City, Missouri v. Ashcroft*, 462 U.S. 476, 490 (1983) (Powell, J.) (regarding the cost of a requirement that pathology reports be conducted); *Akron*, 462 U.S. at 434 ("A primary burden created by the [hospitalization] requirement is additional cost to the woman."); *Danforth*, 428 U.S. at 79 (prohibition of abortion technique after the first twelve weeks of pregnancy would have the effect of inhibiting abortions). To constitute a burden, then, regulations need not impose an absolute bar to obtaining an abortion or create an absolute deprivation. *See, e.g., Akron*, 462 U.S. at 435 (a second-trimester hospitalization requirement held unconstitutional upon finding that the requirement "may force women to travel to find available facilities, resulting in both financial expense and additional health risk").

Second, if a statute is found to be a burden, then courts must determine whether such burden is undue, or lacking in adequate justification.[5] *Hodgson*, 497 U.S. ____, 111 L. Ed. 2d at 361 ("Because the Minnesota statute unquestionably places obstacles in the pregnant minor's path to an abortion, the State has the burden of establishing its constitutionality. Under any analysis, the Minnesota statute cannot be sustained if the obstacles it imposes are not reasonably related to legitimate state interests"). *Compare Webster v. Reproductive Health Services*, 492 U.S. 490, 519 (1989) (viability testing requirement deemed justifiable even though it would raise the cost of abortions) *with Doe v. Bolton*, 410 U.S. 179, 198 (1973)

---

5. The undue burden standard cannot logically be read to require plaintiffs to establish that the burden is undue as a threshold matter. *Cf. Akron*, 462 U.S. at 463 (O'Connor, J., dissenting) ("The 'undue burden' required in the abortion cases represents the required threshold inquiry. . . ."). To require such an expansive assessment as a threshold matter would necessarily encompass a review of the statute's justifications and means—*i.e.*, precisely the same issues considered by the court after the threshold is overcome.

("the interposition of the hospital abortion committee is unduly restrictive of the patient's rights and needs . . ."). As the Court stated in *Jacobson v. Massachusetts*, "[T]he rights of the individual in respect to his liberty may at times, *under the pressure of great dangers*, be subjected to restraint. . . ." 197 U.S. 11, 29 (1905) (emphasis added).

In this brief, *Amici* discuss only the proper analysis for determining whether a protected right is "burdened" by state law. *Amici* refer to the briefs submitted by other *amici* in support of Planned Parenthood of Southeastern Pennsylvania for fuller discussion of how to determine whether the burden is "undue."

In assessing whether a constitutionally protected right is burdened by state law, the Court must consider the practical impact of the law on the ability of the individual to exercise the protected right. In this case, the Pennsylvania Abortion Control Act would so severely restrict the ability of poor women to obtain abortions that it would render illusory the right to make a private, procreative choice without state interference.

A. LAWS THAT OPERATE TO INTERFERE WITH OR IMPAIR ACCESS TO ABORTIONS BURDEN THE PRIVACY RIGHTS OF POOR WOMEN.

Laws that burden women's access to abortion include those laws that deter women from obtaining abortions by interposing procedural obstacles, economic barriers, or other practical impediments to access. *See generally* Siegel, *Reasoning from the Body: A Historical Perspective on Abortion Regulation and Questions of Equal Protection*, 44 Stan. L. Rev. 261, 371, n.431 (1992).[6] To assess whether, and the degree to which, a regulation is burdensome, courts should not and, indeed, must not, ignore the way in which the regulation operates, including its impact on all women.

---

6. The Third Circuit has acknowledged that abortion regulations infringe upon the abortion right in a number of ways, including (1) causing a delay before the abortion is performed; (2) raising the monetary cost of an abortion; and (3) reducing the availability of an abortion by directly or indirectly causing a decrease in the number of legal abortion providers. *Planned Parenthood v. Casey*, 947 F.2d 682, 698 (3d Cir. 1991).

Any analysis of whether a law that regulates or restricts the provision of abortions burdens the right to privacy must include an examination of the law's burden on poor women for the simple reason that they, too, are guaranteed the constitutional right to privacy.[7] Moreover, poor women constitute a significant proportion of the women who utilize abortion services. For example, women with family incomes of under $11,000 are nearly four times more likely to have an abortion than women with family incomes of over $25,000.[8] The greater incidence of unintended pregnancies is a consequence of (1) the greater likelihood of experiencing contraceptive failure; and (2) preferences for having fewer children than nonpoor women.[9] At least one study indicates that for women below the poverty level, six out of ten births are unintended, i.e., unwanted or mistimed, compared to three out of ten births to women above 200% of the poverty level.[10]

In particular, restrictions on the right to abortion fall most heavily on poor women because they are in a worse position to overcome barriers of cost,[11] availability, or delay imposed or generated by the regulation of abortion.

B. PENNSYLVANIA'S ABORTION CONTROL ACT WOULD IMPEDE THE DECISION-MAKING PROCESS AND THE EXERCISE OF THE RIGHT TO REPRODUCTIVE CHOICE FOR POOR WOMEN AND THUS CONSTITUTES A BURDEN ON THE RIGHT TO PRIVACY.

Through its regulations and restrictions, Pennsylvania's Abortion Control Act would actively interfere with the ability of poor women to obtain abortions. And for many poor

---

7. As the Third Circuit correctly concludes, it is unnecessary that the regulations impact upon the entire "universe of pregnant women" in order to constitute a burden. *Planned Parenthood v. Casey*, 947 F.2d at 691.

8. Gold at 16.

9. The Alan Guttmacher Institute, *Abortions and the Poor: Private Morality, Public Responsibility* at 20 (1979).

10. Radecki, *A Racial and Ethnic Comparison of Family Formation and Contraceptive Practices Among Low-Income Women*, 106 Pub. Health Rep. 494, text at nn.32, 33 (Sept./Oct. 1991).

11. *See* O'Hair, *A Brief History of Abortion in the United States*, 262 J.A.M.A. 1875 (1989). Significantly, only 13 states permit the use of state funds for medically necessary abortions. National Abortion Rights Action League Foundation, *Who Decides? A Reproductive Rights Manual* 10 (1990) (hereinafter cited as NARAL).

women, the obstacles caused by the Act would be not merely burdensome, but insurmountable.

1. Section 3205(a) of the Act, which requires a 24-hour delay between the time that a woman's consent for an abortion is obtained and the actual time when the procedure is performed, burdens the right to abortion.

First, the 24-hour delay may significantly increase the costs of abortion for poor women because of the limited availability of abortion services. For poor women, it is already more difficult to find the necessary financial resources, medical information, child care, and time away from work.[12] The additional delay imposed by the 24-hour waiting period—exacerbated by the likelihood of scheduling difficulties at overcrowded facilities at which poor women receive care,[13] as well as barriers of distance and mobility—will actively interfere with the ability of poor women and women of color to obtain abortions.

The need to travel long distances already presents a substantial barrier to care for many women. For example, one of the plaintiff clinics in this case, the Women's Health Services (WHS) in Pittsburgh services an area of 34 counties within Pennsylvania and portions of Ohio, West Virginia, Maryland, and New York. Against this backdrop, patients travel great distances and, according to the testimony of that agency's Executive Director, "it is not unusual for women to travel three, four hours to get to the clinic. Sometimes it's much

12. Lincoln, Doring-Bradley, Lindheim & Cotterill, *The Court, the Congress and the President: Turning Back the Clock on the Pregnant Poor*, 9 Fam. Plan. Persp. 207, 210 (Sept./Oct. 1977); Koonin, Kochanek, Smith & Ramick, *Abortion Surveillance, United States, 1988*, 40 Morbidity & Mortality 17, 18 (July, 1991). Even the informal networks built by women to ensure pregnant women access to abortion are often inaccessible to women of color and the solutions offered unaffordable. Avery, *A Question of Survival/A Conspiracy of Silence: Abortion and Black Women's Health*, in *From Abortion to Reproductive Freedom: Transforming a Movement* 75 (Fried ed. 1990).

13. Overcrowded conditions at public facilities delay and frequently foreclose timely treatment. At Health and Hospitals medical clinics in New York City, for example, patients must wait six to twenty-two weeks to get a first clinic appointment; women must wait four to fifteen weeks for an appointment with a gynecologist. A recent Health and Hospitals Corp. report found that "one patient in eight tires of waiting in city emergency rooms and leaves without treatment." Scott, *HHC Finds Hospitals Hurt by Budget Cuts*, N.Y. Newsday, March 4, 1992, at 21.

longer because they have to take buses to get in." Trial Testimony of Roselle, Vol. II at 80.

In 1985, eighty-two percent of all counties in the United States—in which one-third of all women of reproductive age lived—had no abortion provider.[14] In rural areas the problem is especially acute. Nine out of ten non-metropolitan counties in the United States have no facility that perform abortions.[15]

For example,

—Not a single physician in residence in the state of North Dakota performs abortions.[16]

—In South Dakota there is only one doctor who will perform abortions. As a result, women must travel hundreds of miles to obtain an abortion.[17]

—In northern Minnesota, one clinic must provide all abortions for 24 counties.[18]

In particular, poor Native American women face some of the largest obstacles, since the Indian Health Services, which may be the only familiar provider of health care and the only health service available for hundreds of miles, is prohibited from performing abortions even if women can find the monetary resources to pay for the procedure themselves.[19]

The 24-hour delay may require duplicate journeys, overnight stays away from home, and two or more absences from work, often without pay, as well as added transportation expenses. For many poor women, the additional expense caused by the waiting period will be prohibitive.

Secondly, Section 3205(a) may often result in delays greater than the 24 hours required by statute. The Executive Director of WHS in Pittsburgh testified that her agency would not be able to guarantee that delays would be limited to 24 hours because physicians are not available every day of the week. Trial Testimony of Roselle, Vol. II at 82.

14. Henshaw, Forrest & Van Vort, *Abortion Services in the United States, 1984 & 1985*, 19 Fam. Plan. Persp. 63, 65 (1987).

15. *Id.*

16. See *Leigh v. Olson*, 497 F. Supp. 1340, 1347 (D.N.D. 1980).

17. *Foes Successfully Chip Away at Abortion Rights; Poor, Young Affected Most*, USA Today, June 3, 1991, at 6A.

18. Belkin, *Women in Rural Areas Face Many Barriers to Abortion*, N.Y. Times, July 11, 1989, at A1, col. 3.

19. Nsiah-Jefferson, *Reproductive Laws, Women of Color, and Low Income Women*, in *Reproductive Laws for the 1990's: A Briefing Handbook* 21–22 (1988).

Significant delays in obtaining abortions increase dramatically the health risks associated with abortions. "[A]ny delay increases the risk of complications to a pregnant woman who wishes an abortion. Moreover, this risk appears to increase continuously and linearly as the length of gestation increases."[20] The total morbidity rate rises 20% when abortion is delayed from the eighth to the twelfth week, and the complication rate increases 91% for that same delay.[21] Poor women of color in particular, who disproportionately suffer from illnesses exacerbated by pregnancy,[22] will be most affected by significant delays in obtaining abortion services.

In sum, the 24-hour waiting period places poor women at significant risk of harm and constitutes a burden.

2. Section 3206 of the Act, which requires parental consent before an abortion can be obtained, burdens the rights of low-income young women, creating a virtual bar to abortion.

Although a parental consent requirement with a judicial bypass may be legal in some circumstances, *see Hodgson*, 497 U.S. at ____, 111 L. Ed. 2d at 375; *Bellotti v. Baird*, 443 U.S. 622, 633–39 (1979) (discussion of principles to be applied in parental consent cases), "the constitutional protection against unjustified state intrusion into the process of deciding whether or not to bear a child extends to pregnant minors as well as adult women." *Hodgson*, 497 U.S. at ____, 111 L. Ed. 2d at

---

20. Cates, Schulz, Grimes & Tyler, *The Effect of Delay and Method Choice on the Risk of Abortion Morbidity*, 9 Fam. Plan. Persp. 266, 267 (Nov./Dec. 1977). *See also* Trial Testimony of Allen, Vol. I at 45.

21. *Id.*, at 267.

22. Poor women of color suffer at high rates from a variety of serious health conditions that may be exacerbated by pregnancy. These include high blood pressure, hypertension, diabetes, sickle cell anemia, AIDS, and certain forms of cancer. *See* United States Dept. of Health and Human Services, *Groups: Third Edition* 131–58 (1991); United States Dept. of Health and Human Services, I *Report of the Secretary's Task Force on Black and Minority Health* 74–75 (1985); United States Dept. of Health and Human Services, Office of Minority Health, *Diabetes and Minorities*, in *Closing the Gap* 2 (1988); Drury & Powell, *Prevalence of Known Diabetes Among Black Americans*, in *Advance Data from Vital and Health Statistics*, Pub. No. (PHS) 87–1250; Association for Sickle Cell Education Research and Treatment Inc., *Sickle Cell Anemia: A Family Affair* (1988); Centers for Disease Control, *HIV/AIDS Surveillance: Year-End Edition* 15 (January 1992) (comparison of annual rate of reported AIDS cases for White females, 1.7 per 100,000, with rates for Black and Hispanic females, 24.6 and 12.6, respectively).

360. The judicial inquiry begins with an examination of the burden imposed by the statute. *See, e.g., Hodgson*, 497 U.S. at ___, 111 L. Ed. 2d at 362–66.

As the Executive Director of WHS testified at trial, the combined effect of the 24-hour delay and parental consent provisions will be to create additional obstacles for teenagers who, in many instances, are already in difficult circumstances. "If you talk about a 24-hour period, we're talking about delay and additional costs. If we're talking about parental consent, we're talking about additional delay. If we talk about a judicial bypass, it's still more delay, more expense, more trips to the clinic." Trial Testimony of Roselle, Vol. II at 81–82. In Massachusetts, for example, a parental consent law forced one-third of the state's minors to travel to a neighboring, less restrictive state to obtain an abortion.[23]

Anecdotal evidence points to the horrors of such restrictions: high school student Rebecca Bell died in 1988 of a massive infection after an illegal abortion that she obtained rather than telling her parents that she was pregnant.[24] Thirteen-year-old Spring Adams was shot to death by the father who had impregnated her when he learned that she was going to abort the pregnancy.[25]

Moreover, judicial bypass provisions frequently leave young women and the freedom to exercise their fundamental right to the discretion of hostile judges.[26] One judge, who openly demonstrated the impermissible grounds on which he would base a decision, stated that he did not like the law and that he would only allow a minor to have an abortion without parental consent in cases of incest or the rape of a White girl by a Black man.[27] In some Minnesota counties, judges refuse to hear petitions for judicial bypass, forcing minors to travel 250 miles to receive a hearing. Half of the minors who were able to utilize the bypass procedure of that state's notification

23. O'Keefe & Jones, *Easing Restrictions on Minors' Abortion Rights*, Issues in Sci. & Tech. 74, 78 (Fall 1990).

24. Sharpe, *17 Year Old Died of Fear and Abortion*, Cincinnati Enquirer, Nov. 26, 1989, cited in NARAL at 6.

25. NARAL at 6.

26. *See, e.g.*, Bonavoglia, *Kathy's Day in Court*, in *From Abortion to Reproductive Freedom: Transforming a Movement* 161 (Fried ed. 1990).

27. Wilkerson, *Michigan Judges' Views of Abortion Are Berated*, N.Y. Times, May 3, 1991.

law were not residents of the city in which the hearing was held.[28]

Parental consent provisions exacerbate delay and increase both the cost and the risk to teens: in Minnesota, the parental notification requirement—a far less onerous law than Section 3206 of the Pennsylvania Abortion Control Act—increased the number of minors who obtained second trimester abortions by 26.5%.[29] This change ran counter to the national trend toward earlier term abortions.[30]

The difficulties of obtaining an abortion and the additional obstacles created by statute fall heaviest on young low-income women of color. The proportion of women of color under 15 years of age who have abortions is high—nearly double that for their white counterparts.[31] For these young women, the vast majority of whom had unintended pregnancies,[32] abortion is a necessary health service. Laws that place these services further from reach have a severe, detrimental impact.

The medical dangers of abortion are already particularly acute for adolescents, in part because they often postpone pregnancy confirmation and abortion. See Trial Testimony of Allen, Vol. I at 62–63. As a consequence of the parental consent provision, compounded by the 24-hour delay provision, teenagers will not be able to obtain abortion services until even later, more dangerous stages of pregnancy. The mortality rate for abortion increases fifty percent each week after the eighth week of pregnancy, and the risk of major complications in the procedure increases by approximately thirty percent per week.[33]

---

28. Hodgson, 497 U.S. at _____, 111 L. Ed. 2d at 387 (Marshall, J., dissenting in part).

29. NARAL at 6; Hodgson v. Minnesota, 648 F. Supp. 756 (D. Minn. 1986), aff'd and rev'd in part, 853 F.2d 1452 (8th Cir. 1988), aff'd, 497 U.S. _____, 111 L. Ed. 2d 344 (1990).

30. American Civil Liberties Union Reproductive Freedom Project, Parental Notification Laws: Their Catastrophic Impact on Teenagers' Right to Abortion 15 (1986).

31. Koonin, Kochanek, Smith & Ramick, Abortion Surveillance, United States, 1988, 40 Morbidity & Mortality 17 (July 1991).

32. Among teenagers, 84% of all pregnancies and 92% of premarital pregnancies are unintended. NARAL at 7.

33. Grimes, Second-Trimester Abortions in the United States, 16 Fam. Plan. Persp. 260–65 (Nov./Dec. 1984). See also Cates & Grimes, Morbidity and Mortality of Abortion in the United States, in Abortion and Sterilization: Medical and Social Aspects 155 (Hodson ed. 1981).

3. Section 3209 of the Act, which requires spousal notification before an abortion can be obtained, burdens the right to abortion.

After conducting the requisite legal and factual analyses, the district court concluded that the spousal notification requirement "is constitutionally defective because it impermissibly invades a woman's fundamental right to privacy in the abortion decision." *Planned Parenthood* v. *Casey*, 744 F. Supp. 1323, 1384 (E.D. Pa. 1990). On appeal, the Third Circuit affirmed, holding that the provision imposes an undue burden on a woman's abortion decision and does not serve a compelling state interest. 947 F.2d 682 (3d Cir. 1991). In reaching this conclusion, the Third Circuit looked to this Court's opinion in *Hodgson*, 497 U.S. at ____, 111 L. Ed. 2d at 371, & n.36, and observed,

> The Supreme Court has thus been attuned to the real-world consequences of forced notification in the context of minor child/parent relationships. . . . *In this case, we conclude that the real-world consequences of forced notification in the context of wife/husband relationships impose similar kinds of undue burdens on a woman's right to an abortion.*

947 F.2d at 711 (emphasis added).

Amici fully agree. And just as the courts should be attuned to the real-world consequences of forced notification in the context of familial relationships, so too should they heed the real-world burdens caused by other statutory requirements that would unduly burden a woman's abortion decision.

Roe v. *Wade* and *Doe* v. *Bolton* did not countenance a test of constitutionality that would prohibit only absolute deprivations. *Roe*, 410 U.S. at 164–66 (1973) (specified standards of review); *Doe* v. *Bolton*, 410 U.S. 179 (1973) (procedural requirements held unduly restrictive). Correspondingly, under the undue burden standard, barriers to abortion that are constructed by government and that would impinge upon the ability of poor women to exercise their fundamental right must be recognized as burdensome.

Unlike the line of cases beginning with *Maher* v. *Roe*, 432

U.S. 464 (1977), and evidenced, most recently, in *Webster*, 492 U.S. 490 (1989), and *Rust* v. *Sullivan*, 500 U.S. ____, 114 L. Ed. 2d 233 (1991), this case does not involve the question whether a state may choose not to grant benefits that would further the provision of abortion services. *See also Harris* v. *McRae*, 448 U.S. 297 (1980); *Poelker* v. *Doe*, 432 U.S. 519 (1977); *Beal* v. *Doe*, 432 U.S. 438 (1977). To the contrary, the Pennsylvania laws at issue place discrete and burdensome obstacles in the pregnant woman's path to an abortion. Pennsylvania is not merely encouraging an alternative option, but, instead, actively delaying and otherwise burdening the exercise of a protected activity. *Compare Thornburgh*, 476 U.S. 747 (1986); *Akron*, 462 U.S. 416 (1983); *Danforth*, 428 U.S. 52 (1976); *Doe* v. *Bolton*, 410 U.S. 179 (1973).

"Few decisions are more personal and intimate, more properly private, or more basic to individual dignity and autonomy, than a woman's decision . . . whether to end her pregnancy. A woman's right to make that choice freely is fundamental. Any other result . . . would protect inadequately a central part of the sphere of liberty that our law guarantees equally to all. . . ." *Thornburgh*, 476 U.S. at 772. *Amici* believe that the sphere of liberty guaranteed to all should contain protection for the right of poor women to make reproductive choices free from intrusion by burdensome government restrictions.

We thus ask that the Court consider the burdens of governmental restrictions on the availability of abortions for poor women.

The provisions of the Pennsylvania Abortion Control Act requiring a 24-hour waiting period, parental consent, and spousal notification actively interfere with women's decision-making and the provision of abortion services, and will limit the ability of poor women to obtain needed services. The provisions unduly burden the right to privacy and are unconstitutional.

CONCLUSION

For the foregoing reasons, the judgment of the Third Circuit regarding Sections 3205(a) and 3206 should be reversed, and the judgment regarding Section 3209 affirmed.

Respectfully submitted,

JULIUS L. CHAMBERS,
RONALD L. ELLIS,
MARIANNE L. ENGELMAN
LADO,*
ALICE L. BROWN
99 Hudson St., 16th Floor
New York, NY 10013
(212) 219–1900

PATRICIA WILLIAMS,
SUZANNE SHENDE,
JOAN GIBBS
666 Broadway
New York, NY 10021
(212) 614–6464

Counsel for *Amici Curiae*

*Counsel of Record

APPENDIX

INTEREST OF *AMICI CURIAE*

THE ASIAN AMERICAN LEGAL DEFENSE AND EDUCATIONAL FUND (AALDEF) is a national civil rights organization that addresses the critical problems facing Asian American communities, including the growing trend of anti-Asian violence, immigrant rights, voting rights, labor and employment rights, and redress for Japanese Americans who were incarcerated in camps within the United States during World War II. AALDEF is committed to protecting the right to reproductive choice by women including Asian immigrant women and joins other *amici curiae* in support of reproductive choice as a fundamental right.

THE CENTER FOR CONSTITUTIONAL RIGHTS (CCR), a litigation/education organization headquartered in New York City, was founded in 1966. Born of the civil rights movement and the struggles of Black people in the United States for true equality, CCR has litigated for voting rights, civil rights, and the fundamental and necessary right of each woman to obtain access to safe and legal abortion. CCR decries the disproportionate and potentially devastating effect that the limitation or loss of the right to abortion will have on women of color and low-income and working women, and we urge this Court to protect the right to accessible, safe, and legal abortion in their names.

THE CENTER FOR LAW AND SOCIAL JUSTICE (CLSJ) at Medgar Evers College is a research and advocacy institution created in 1985 by a special appropriation of the New York State Legislature to establish a legally oriented civil rights and social justice institution in New York City. CLSJ conducts litigation and public policy projects on matters involving pressing civil and human rights issues in such areas as employment, health care, and housing.

Discrimination in these areas has historically plagued the African-American communities CLSJ serves, particularly the women in these communities. For that reason, CLSJ joins as *amicus curiae* in this consolidated appeal to the United States Supreme Court.

THE COMMITTEE FOR HISPANIC CHILDREN AND FAMILIES is a not-for-profit organization in New York City dedicated to promoting and strengthening the Hispanic family. In our community education efforts we seek to heighten awareness of issues such as domestic violence, teen pregnancy, and child abuse and neglect. Clearly our goal is to mobilize our community in effective prevention strategies for these and other problems which afflict our community. Key to being able to confront these myriad problems is the need for quality and equitable medical care. We oppose the denial of access to health services including abortion for Hispanic women.

THE ECO-JUSTICE PROJECT AND NETWORK (a project of the Center for Religion, Ethics, and Social Policy at Cornell University) is an organization concerned about both environmental and social justice, and the well-being of all people on a thriving Earth. Our concern in this case focuses on the effect it may have on the lives of poor and socially disenfranchised women. Poor women, already significantly burdened in accessing medical services, will suffer even greater adverse consequences should the Court strip the right to abortion of constitutional protections. We also are concerned about women's rights of privacy, doctors' rights to free speech, and the physician-patient relationship of confidentiality. In a world in which human population may already be exceeding carrying capacity, we wholeheartedly support a woman's right to choose whether or not to give birth to even more human beings.

Founded in 1978, the HISPANIC HEALTH COUNCIL is a community-based research, education, and advocacy organization devoted to the improvement of health, mental health, and general social well-being of Puerto Ricans and other Latino populations in Hartford, Connecticut. Specifically, the Council seeks to empower Latino families for community change through education about health and disease risks, health-related legal rights, and social conditions underlying poverty and illness. The Council also strives to alter existing inadequacies in the quality and quantity of health care available to low-income groups.

We join this case as *amicus curiae* because this kind of legislation has only proven to be discriminatory towards underserved populations and impacts negatively on the lives of the poor because it does not look at other socio-economic factors which influence people's behavior.

THE JAPANESE AMERICAN CITIZENS LEAGUE (JACL) is a national civil and human rights and educational organization concerned with the welfare of Japanese and Asian Americans. It was formed in 1929 and is the oldest and largest Asian American civil rights organization. The JACL is committed to educating the public on the history, experience, contributions, and current concerns of Japanese Americans and Asian Americans in the United States. As a civil rights organization, the JACL has worked to guarantee justice and due process to all persons. To that end, we are firmly committed to a woman's fundamental right of choice and self-determination to exercise her reproductive rights. We believe that abortion— choice—is a fundamental right protected by the United States Constitution.

THE LATINA ROUNDTABLE ON HEALTH AND REPRODUCTIVE RIGHTS (LRHRR) is an organization of Latinas who have come together to examine and address the legislative, judicial, and policy initiatives that affect the health and reproductive freedom of Latinas in New York. The LRHRR is made up of Pro-Choice health care providers, attorneys, educators, policy makers, and community activists who through these efforts defend the rights of Latinas to access abortion services regardless of age, economic, or marital status.

MADRE is a national women's friendship organization that sees the connections between U.S. policy and its effects on women and children in the U.S., Central America, the Caribbean, and the Middle East. MADRE's work includes programs which address health care and child care issues affecting women's daily lives. We support reproductive freedom and quality affordable health care for all. We know that poor women and women of color are most affected by restrictive policies. We therefore sign on to the *amicus* brief in its opposition to any restrictions placed on a woman's reproductive choice.

THE MEXICAN AMERICAN LEGAL DEFENSE AND EDUCATIONAL FUND (MALDEF), established in 1967, is a national civil rights organization headquartered in Los Angeles. Its principal objective is to secure, through litigation and education, the civil and constitutional rights of Hispanics living in the United States. Fundamental among those rights is the right to privacy, which encompasses the right to choose in matters of family planning. MALDEF opposes restrictions on the right to choose, as such restrictions are devastating in their disproportionate effect upon low-income Hispanic women with regard to their family planning rights, choices, and alternatives.

THE NAACP LEGAL DEFENSE & EDUCATIONAL FUND, INC. (LDF) is a non-profit corporation formed to assist African Americans to secure their constitutional and civil rights and liberties. For many years LDF has pursued litigation to secure the basic civil and economic rights of low-income African American families and individuals. Litigation to ensure the non-discriminatory delivery as well as the adequacy of health care services available to African American communities has been a long-standing LDF concern.

Through its Black Women's Employment and Poverty & Justice Programs, LDF is also challenging barriers to economic advancement to help to improve the economic status and living conditions of the many in poverty.

This case implicates the full panoply of these important LDF concerns. Burdensome legislation can severely limit the availability of reproductive health services to poor African American women. This, in turn, will increase the number of unwanted pregnancies and promote continuing cycles of poverty and despair, while creating unnecessary medical risks for poor African American women. LDF feels that it is crucial for the Court to fully consider how statutory restrictions on abortion operate in practice to limit the accessibility of health care for poor women.

THE NATIONAL ASSOCIATION OF SOCIAL WORKERS, INC. (NASW), a non-profit professional association with over 135,000 members, is the largest association of social workers in the United States. The association is devoted to promoting the quality and effectiveness of social work practice, to advancing the knowledge base of the social work profession and to improving the quality of life through utilization of social work knowledge and skills. NASW is deeply committed to the principle of self-determination and to the protection of individual rights and personal privacy. The association has been in the forefront of the struggle for women's equality, and is particularly concerned in the present instance that the state not override a pregnant woman's autonomy nor restrict her right to choose abortion.

THE NATIONAL BLACK WOMEN'S HEALTH PROJECT (NBWHP) is a self-help, health education and advocacy organization which works to improve the health status and quality of life for African American Women and their families. It consists of 150 developing and established chapters in 31 states serving a broad constituency of approximately 2,000 members. The NBWHP is deeply concerned about barriers that impede or prevent access to quality health services, including abortion. The purpose of the NBWHP is the definition, promotion, and maintenance of health for Black women, including full reproductive rights and the essential authority of every woman to choose when, whether, and under what conditions she will bear children.

Because too many single-family households in the United States are headed by Black women living in poverty, possessing fewer educational and job training opportunities, enduring inadequate, often non-existent child care services, subject to substandard housing conditions, and lacking access to appropriate health services of any kind; because more than half of all Black children are poor, born of mothers receiving inferior, if any, prenatal care, suffering the highest rate of infant mortality and neonatal deaths in the Western world; and because we lack fail-safe birth control methods, lack adequate human sexuality education, and suffer also the highest rate of teenage pregnancy in the Western world, we firmly insist upon continued access to safe, legal, and affordable abortion. Restrictive abortion laws exacerbate the low socioeconomic status of women of color, and the passage of such laws will further denigrate the dignity of Black womanhood. The NBWHP joins this brief to voice its opposition to laws which prevent African American women from exercising their rights.

THE NATIONAL COALITION FOR BLACK LESBIANS AND GAYS (NCBLG) is the oldest Black organization in the country working to advocate and promote the empowerment and enhancement of the lesbian and gay community. Formally a chapter organization with branches in Baltimore, Chicago, Detroit, New York, and Oakland/San Francisco, the national office is located in Washington, DC. We have over 500 members nationally and our numbers continue to increase.

Since NCBLG began in 1979, it has been dedicated to equal rights and civil liberties for the entire community regardless of race, gender, or sexual orientation. In spite of the strides that have been accomplished in the last 50 years, injustices continue to be prevalent. NCBLG joins with other concerned organizations in opposing the restrictions on abortion services which threaten the right to reproductive choice and access to health care for low income women and women of color.

THE NATIONAL COUNCIL OF NEGRO WOMEN, INC. (NCNW) is a membership organization of 33 national African American organizations, 250 community based sections in 42 states, and 65,000 individual members. The NCNW has worked for a half century in support of the civil and human rights of African American women and their families. NCNW joins Planned Parenthood in this brief in opposition to the restrictive and burdensome requirements of the Pennsylvania statute, which interferes with the constitutional rights of women.

THE NATIONAL EMERGENCY CIVIL LIBERTIES COMMITTEE is a not-for-profit organization dedicated to the preservation and extension of civil liberties and civil rights. Founded in 1951, it has brought numerous actions in the federal courts to vindicate constitutional rights. Through its educational work, it likewise has sought to preserve our liberties. From time to time NECLC submits *amicus curiae* briefs to the courts when it believes issues of particular import for civil liberties are at stake.

THE NATIONAL LATINA HEALTH ORGANIZATION is committed to work toward the goal of bilingual access to quality health care, reproductive services, and the self-empowerment of Latinas. Our health and reproductive issues have not been addressed. Lack of awareness on the part of the medical profession and the language barrier have had a major impact on our access to quality reproductive services and medical care. Further restrictions and lack of access to safe and legal abortion will jeopardize our health and our lives further. We must have all information and services available to us so we can make knowledgeable, educated, and healthful choices for ourselves.

NATIONAL MINORITY AIDS COUNCIL is a national organization dedicated to creating a greater response among people of color to HIV/AIDS in our communities. The council has as its primary focus leadership. As such we take stands on issues impacting on minority health. Therefore, we recognize the importance of supporting increased access to public health, and a national focus on public health for all women.

THE NATIVE AMERICAN WOMEN'S HEALTH EDUCATION RESOURCE CENTER of Lake Andes, South Dakota (The Resource Center) is a reservation based organization that works with Native women in the empowerment process involving Native women's health, education, and reproductive rights. The Resource Center is currently active in coalition building on the local and national levels with Native women from diverse tribes, in an attempt to move forward policies that promote positive lifestyles and better reproductive health for Native women. As Native women, whose traditions have shown that abortion has always been women's business, determined by women, we must support other women in their fight to have the right to have an abortion, and to make that decision within the personal circles of women's business.

THE NEW YORK WOMEN'S FOUNDATION is a cross-cultural alliance of women helping women and girls. With a membership of approximately 2,000 and a board of forty, The Foundation is committed to address the unmet needs of low-income women in New York City through grants and advocacy. The board of The Foundation believes strongly that every woman has a fundamental right to full information about her reproductive health, a fundamental right to make an informed decision about her reproductive health options, and a fundamental right of access to all reproductive health services.

The Foundation believes that every woman must have access to safe, legal, and affordable abortion and that the disproportionate lack of such access in the African American, Latina, and Asian American communities is particularly deplorable.

THE PUERTO RICAN LEGAL DEFENSE AND EDUCATION FUND is a national organization based in New York City dedicated to protecting and furthering the civil rights of Puerto Ricans and other Latinos. The Fund's litigation efforts focus on the areas of employment, education, housing, and voting rights, with a particular emphasis on safeguarding the rights of Puerto Ricans of low economic status. Puerto Rican women and other women of color are particularly vulnerable to discrimination and therefore the Fund supports efforts to protect their rights. The Fund opposes any efforts to overturn or in any way restrict the rights recognized in *Roe* v. *Wade*.

THE SOUTHERN POVERTY LAW CENTER is dedicated to protecting the legal rights of poor people and minorities. It has served as counsel in numerous cases raising constitutional issues of particular significance for women, including *Frontiero* v. *Richardson*, 411 U.S. 677 (1973).

WOMEN FOR RACIAL AND ECONOMIC EQUALITY is a multi-racial, multi-ethnic national organization founded in 1977. Our members are Black, White, Chicana, Puerto Rican, Caribbean, Asian and Native American Women who are workers, trade unionists, unemployed, welfare recipients, professionals, students, and senior citizens. We are women who may be especially vulnerable to discrimination because of color, national origin, religious beliefs, or sexual preference. We are women whose experiences have shown that racism is the major obstacle to bettering our living conditions in any real or meaningful way. Our program is a 12-point Women's Bill of Rights which includes: the right to reproductive choice; access to federally-funded non-racist, nonsexist sex education and birth control, regardless of age; abortion upon demand; and outlawing of coerced sterilization.

THE WOMEN'S POLICY GROUP (WPG), formed in 1988, is a Georgia-based organization working to improve the lives of women. We study and analyze issues, and work with individuals and other groups on women's concerns. We are interested in a variety of issues affecting women's family, work, and personal lives including insurance coverage for pap smears and mammograms, child custody, child support, child care, family violence, Medicaid coverage for pregnant women and infants, obstetrical malpractice, family medical leave, universal health care coverage, sexual harassment, and reproductive choice.

BRIEF OF 250 AMERICAN HISTORIANS
AS *AMICI CURIAE* IN SUPPORT
OF THE PETITIONERS

INTEREST OF *AMICI CURIAE*

Amici are 250 professional American historians who, with the permission of the parties, here seek to provide the Court a rich and accurate description of our national history and tradition in relation to women's liberty to choose whether to terminate a pregnancy. *Amici* represent a diverse array of historical specialties and approaches. [*] They are united, however, in their conviction that this Court's decision in *Roe* v. *Wade* is supported by American history and the lessons that history imparts.

SUMMARY OF ARGUMENT

This Court has long consulted our nation's history and traditions to determine the contours of fundamental constitutional rights. This brief will demonstrate that for much of our nation's history, abortion was tolerated and not illegal; that for much of the nineteenth century, abortion remained legal prior to quickening; and that when states did enact laws regulating abortion, these statutes did not punish women. A variety of complex factors, and not simply moral or theological impulses, underlay the nineteenth-century laws restricting abortion: concern for women's health, the medical profession's

[*] The names of the *amici* appear in the Appendix to this brief.

desire to control the practice of medicine, openly discriminatory ideas of the appropriate role for women, opposition to
non-procreative sexual activity and to the dissemination of
information concerning birth control, and even concern for
racial and ethnic purity. This brief discusses the prevalence
and visibility of abortion as a common social practice in the
nineteenth century. Above all, this historical account refutes
the erroneous assumption that abortion restrictions enjoyed
broad social support in past eras.

Moreover, this nation's history confirms that abortion restrictions have imposed profound burdens on the liberty and
equality of women. The Court should therefore reaffirm its
commitment to providing strong constitutional protection to
women's fundamental liberty interest in reproductive choice
and control of their own bodies.

ARGUMENT

I. OUR TRADITIONS AND HISTORY HELP DEFINE THE CONTOURS OF FUNDAMENTAL CONSTITUTIONAL RIGHTS, INCLUDING THE RIGHT TO PRIVACY.

Since the beginning of the Republic, no Justice of the Supreme Court has seriously disputed that the meaning of our
Constitution is to be determined by interpreting its words in
light of our nation's history and traditions. "[A]n approach
grounded in history imposes limits on the judiciary that are
more meaningful than any based on [an] abstract formula."
Moore v. East Cleveland, 431 U.S. 494, 503 (1977). Even
when this Court has not specifically identified "history" as a
source of authority, it has frequently taken "judicial notice"
of this country's history and traditions in resolving difficult
constitutional issues.[1] Because an understanding of our na-

---

1. *See, e.g., Munn v. Illinois*, 94 U.S. 113, 125 (1877) ("[I]t has been customary in
England from time immemorial, and in this country from its first colonization, to regulate ferries, common carriers, hackmen, bakers, millers, wharfingers, innkeepers, & c.,
and in so doing to fix a maximum of charge to be made for services rendered,
accommodations furnished, and articles sold"); *Martin v. Struthers*, 319 U.S. 141,

tion's history rightly influences this Court's fundamental constitutional understandings, it is essential to capture that history deeply and accurately. It is no accident that *Scott* v. *Sandford*, 19 How. 1, 19–20 (1857), and *Plessy* v. *Ferguson*, 163 U.S. 537, 544, 550–51 (1896)—two of this Court's most discredited decisions—rested largely on disputed and insupportable readings of history.

The relevance of history to this Court's task often goes beyond exploration of "framers' intent"; not every facet of the Constitution's meaning can be determined by reference to its words or to the apparent intent of its drafters. Justice White has said:

[T]his Court does not subscribe to the simplistic view that constitutional interpretation can possibly be limited to the "plain meaning" of the Constitution's text or to the subjective intention of the Framers. The Constitution is not a deed setting forth the precise metes and bounds of its subject matter; rather it is a document announcing fundamental principles in value-laden terms that leave ample scope for the exercise of normative judgment by those charged with interpreting and applying it.

Thornburgh v. *American College of Obstetricians and Gynecologists*, 476 U.S. 747, 789 (1986) (White, J., dissenting). But if history cannot always pinpoint the views of the framers, the historical perspective can suggest fundamental principles by which to measure the scope of valued constitutional rights. In particular, history and tradition help give content to the open-textured provisions of our Constitution: the prohibition in the Fifth and Fourteenth Amendments of state action that deprives citizens of life, liberty, or property without due process of law; the Fourteenth Amendment's guarantee of equal treatment under the law; and the Ninth Amendment's command that the "enumeration in the Constitution, of certain rights,

---

145 (1943) (door-to-door distribution of literature protected by First Amendment because "in accordance with the best tradition of free discussion"); *McCollum* v. *Board of Education*, 333 U.S. 203, 213 (1948) (Frankfurter, J., concurring) ("released-time" provision unconstitutional in light of the "relevant history of religious education in America" and "the place of 'released-time' in that history").

shall not be construed to deny or disparage others retained by the people."

In 1961, Justice Harlan wrote of the importance of history and tradition in explicating the scope of the due process clause respecting bodily privacy:

> Due process has not been reduced to any formula; its content cannot be determined by reference to any code. The best that can be said is that through the course of this Court's decisions it has represented the balance which our Nation, built upon postulates of respect for the individual, has struck between that liberty and the demands of organized society. . . . The balance of which I speak is the balance struck by this country, having regard to what history teaches are the traditions from which it developed as well as the traditions from which it broke. That tradition is a living thing.

Poe v. *Ullman*, 367 U.S. 497, 542 (1961) (Harlan, J., dissenting). *See also Griswold* v. *Connecticut*, 381 U.S. 479, 501 (1965) (Harlan, J., concurring).

Justice Harlan's words express the Constitution's general protection of the right to privacy, *see Griswold*, 381 U.S. at 483–86, and *Olmstead* v. *United States*, 277 U.S. 438, 474–75 (1928) (Brandeis, J., dissenting), and explain the role of history in illuminating how the autonomy to make fundamental personal decisions is basic to individual liberty. These words are especially relevant to this case. The history of abortion in this country illustrates that this Court was correct in *Roe* v. *Wade* in holding that the right to choose an abortion is fundamental to women's liberty.

This Court's decision in *Roe* v. *Wade*, 410 U.S. 113 (1973), accurately recounted the history of abortion in the United States and at British common law. Since 1973 and *Roe*, ongoing historical research and scholarship have expanded and deepened historians' understanding of abortion in America. In addition to the important legal-historical sources relied on in *Roe* (past statutes, legislative debates, and the decisions of common-law courts), historians in recent decades have begun to document people's actual beliefs and practices throughout history, offering an even deeper and richer understanding of baseline American values and traditions. As scholars familiar with these varied methods of historical inquiry, *amici* believe the Court must consult evidence of daily life as well as official and governmental action to uncover the beliefs and practices of the broad range of American society. It is this inclusive perspective on the past that should inform the Court's investigation of our nation's history and traditions. Such an inquiry does not mean that what has prevailed in the past must govern the present, for that would deny any role for human progress. Rather, consideration of past practices and beliefs offers real lessons about the centrality of those practices and the meaning of attempts to regulate them.

II. AT THE TIME THE FEDERAL CONSTITUTION WAS ADOPTED, ABORTION WAS KNOWN AND NOT ILLEGAL.

As this Court demonstrated in *Roe* v. *Wade*, abortion was not illegal at common law.[2] Through the nineteenth century, American common law decisions uniformly reaffirmed that women committed no offense in seeking abortions.[3] Both common law and popular American understanding drew distinctions depending upon whether the fetus was "quick," *i.e.* whether the woman perceived signs of independent life.[4] There was some dispute whether a common law misdemeanor occurred when a third party destroyed a fetus, after quickening, without the woman's consent. But early common law recognition of this crime against a pregnant woman did not diminish

2. *Roe* v. *Wade*, 410 U.S. 113, 132–36 & n.21 (1973). *See also* J. Mohr, *Abortion in America: The Origins and Evolution of National Policy* 3–19 (1978).

3. For example, in 1845, Chief Judge Shaw of Massachusetts held that abortion, with the woman's consent, was not punishable at common law unless the fetus was quick. *Commonwealth* v. *Parker*, 50 Mass. (9 Met.) 263, 43 Am. Dec. 396 (1845). In 1892, the Massachusetts Supreme Judicial Court held that, despite statutory enactments regulating abortion, the woman having an abortion was not a principal or an accomplice. *Commonwealth* v. *Follansbee*, 155 Mass. 274, 29 N.E. 471 (1892). In *Abrams* v. *Foshee*, 3 Iowa 274, 278, 66 Am. Dec. 77, 80 (1856), the Iowa Supreme Court held that abortion prior to quickening was no crime. *Hatfield* v. *Gano*, 15 Iowa 177 (1863), held that Iowa's statutory enactment did not apply to abortion produced by a woman herself. *See* C. Smith-Rosenberg, *Disorderly Conduct* 219–20 (1985).

4. *See Roe* v. *Wade*, 410 U.S. at 134–36; J. Mohr, *supra* note 2, at 24–26. In the ordinary language of the eighteenth century and much of the nineteenth century, the term "abortion" meant the termination of pregnancy after the point of quickening. *Id.* at 3–5.

the woman's liberty to end a pregnancy herself in its early stages.[5]

Abortion was not a pressing social issue in colonial America, but as a social practice it was far from unknown.[6] Herbal abortifacients were widely known,[7] and cookbooks and women's diaries of the era contained recipes for such medicines.[8] Recent studies of the work of midwives in the 1700s report cases in which the midwives appeared to have provided women abortifacient compounds. Such treatments do not appear to have been regarded as extraordinary or illicit by those administering them.[9]

The absence of legal condemnation of abortion in colonial America is all the more significant because both families and society valued children and population growth in a rural economy, with vast unsettled lands, where diseases of infancy claimed many lives. For these reasons, single women more often sought abortions in the Colonial era than did married women.[10] The absence of legal condemnation is particularly

5. See Roe v. Wade, 410 U.S. at 134–36; J. Mohr, supra note 2, at 24–26. Means, The Phoenix of Abortional Freedom, 17 N.Y.L. Forum 335, 336–53 (1971), demonstrates that commentators who assert that a misdemeanor could be charged against a third party who destroyed a fetus by assaulting a woman late in pregnancy misread the common law precedents upon which they purport to rely. Even in cases involving brutal beatings of women in the late stages of pregnancy, common-law courts refused to recognize abortion as a crime, independent of assault upon the woman. See A. McLaren, Reproductive Rituals 119–121 (1984).

6. Observers in the seventeenth and eighteenth centuries made repeated references to employment of herbal abortifacients by both single and married women, either self-administered or procured by husbands, male partners, or family members. Specific instances are documented in R. Thompson, Sex in Middlesex: Popular Mores in a Massachusetts County, 1649–1699 11, 25–26, 42, 47, 51, 78, 107–08, 182–83 (1986); J. Spruill, Women's Life and Work in the Southern Colonies 325–326 (1972, orig. pub. 1938); L. Koehler, A Search for Power: The "Weaker Sex" in Seventeenth-Century New England 204–205 (1980). See also Dayton, Taking the Trade: Abortion and Gender Relations in an Eighteenth-Century New England Village, 48 Wm. & Mary Q. 19 (1991) (reporting instance of abortion by use of instrument). Compare A. McLaren, supra note 5, at 114 and generally at 113–44, reporting widespread evidence of abortifacient use in England during the same era.

7. The classic work was N. Culpeper, The English Physician (1799). See J. Brodie, Family Limitation in American Culture, Ph.D. dissertation, University of Chicago, 1982, at 224–30.

8. C. Smith-Rosenberg, supra note 3, at 228.

9. One midwife reported, "She is suffering from obstructions and I prescribed the use of particular herbs." Diary of Martha Moore Ballard, Sept. 27, 1789, Maine State Manuscript Library. For a discussion of the possibility that this may refer to an administered abortifacient, see L. Ulrich, A Midwife's Tale: The Life of Martha Ballard, Based on Her Diary, 1785–1812 56 (1990).

10. M. Grossberg, Governing the Hearth 159 (1985). Accord J. D'Emilio & E. Freedman, Intimate Matters 26 (1988) ("Cases of attempted abortion usually involved illicit lovers, not married couples").

striking in the New England culture of tightly-knit, religiously homogeneous communities in which neighbor observed the private behavior of neighbor and did not hesitate to chastise those who violated pervasive moral norms of the community.[11] Further, in an era filled with extensive oral and written moral prescripts from community and religious leaders, it is notable that birth control and abortion were rarely the subject for moralizing. Where abortion is noted, it is not the practice itself that is subject of comment, but rather the violation of other social/sexual norms that led to the pregnancy.[12]

In the late eighteenth century, strictures on sexual behavior loosened considerably. The incidence of premarital pregnancy rose sharply; by the late eighteenth century, one third of all New England brides were pregnant when they married, compared to less than ten percent in the seventeenth century.[13] Falling birth rates in the 1780s suggest that, at the time of the drafting of the Constitution, the use of birth control and abortion was increasing.[14]

11. Adultery, incest, insubordination by children, and even "living alone not subject to the governance of family life," were condemned by the colonial America criminal law—but abortion was not. See Cott, Eighteenth-Century Family and Social Life Revealed in Massachusetts Divorce Records, 10 J. of Soc. Hist. 20, 22–24, 33 (1976); P. Laslett, The World We Have Lost 37–38 (1973); D. Flaherty, Privacy in Colonial New England 42–43, 76 (1972); P. Aries, Centuries of Childhood 405–07 (R. Baldick trans. 1962). For a more popular, fictional treatment, see N. Hawthorne, The Scarlet Letter (1850).

12. J. D'Emilio & E. Freedman, supra note 10, at 12, report the following case from the 1600s: "Captain William Mitchell, an influential Marylander who served on the governor's council, not only impregnated Mrs. Susan Warren and gave her a 'physic' to abort the child, but he also 'lived in fornication' with his pretended wife, Joan Toaste. Even so, the first charge filed against Mitchell by the Maryland attorney was that he professed himself to be an Atheist and openly mocked all Religion."

13. M. Gordon, The American Family 173 (1978). For comprehensive discussions see Smith & Hindus, Premarital Pregnancy in America, 1640–1971, 5 J. Interdisciplinary Hist. 537, 553–57 (1975); Hoff-Wilson, The Illusion of Change: Women and the American Revolution, in The American Revolution 404 (A. Young ed. 1976).

14. Wells, Family Size and Fertility Control in Eighteenth Century America: A Study of Quaker Families, 25 Population Stud. 73 (1971); M. Norton, Liberty's Daughters: The Revolutionary Experience of American Women, 1750–1800 232 (1980).

III. THROUGH THE NINETEENTH CENTURY, ABORTION BECAME EVEN MORE WIDELY ACCEPTED AND HIGHLY VISIBLE.

Through the nineteenth century and well into the twentieth, abortion remained a widely accepted practice, despite growing efforts after 1860 to prohibit it.[15] Changing patterns of abortion practice and attitudes towards it can only be understood against the background of dramatic change in American economic and family life during this period.

During the period between ratification of the Constitution and adoption of the Civil War Amendments, Americans moved to cities and increasingly worked for wages.[16] In 1787, the average white American woman bore seven children; by the late 1870s, the average was down to fewer than five; by 1900 it was 3.56.[17] Carl Degler calls this decline in fertility "the single most important fact about women and the family in American history."[18]

Urban couples limited family size for economic reasons: working-class married women, faced with the material difficulty of managing a family budget on a single male wage, resorted to abortion as the most effective available means of "conscious fertility control."[19] Other economic factors were at work in restricting fertility.[20] Middle-class Americans were

15. C. Degler, At Odds 243–46 (1980). Several studies by physicians in various parts of the U.S. suggest that in the mid-nineteenth century one abortion was performed for every four live births. See J. Mohr, supra note 2, at 76–80. Reports from the late 1870s estimated even greater numbers. Id. at 81–82. The Michigan Board of Health estimated in 1898 that one-third of all pregnancies in that state ended in abortion. Haggard, Abortion: Accidental, Essential, Criminal, Address Before the Nashville Academy of Medicine, Aug. 4, 1898, at 10, discussed in C. Smith-Rosenberg, supra note 3, at 221.

16. See C. Degler, supra note 15.

17. Smith, Family Limitation, Sexual Control, and Domestic Feminism in Victorian America, in A Heritage of Her Own 226 (N. Cott & E. Pleck eds. 1979). For discussion of continual decline in family size in the eighteenth and nineteenth centuries, see R. Petchesky, Abortion and Woman's Choice 73–78 (rev. ed. 1990).

18. C. Degler, supra note 15, at 191.

19. See R. Petchesky, supra note 17, at 53; Rodrique, The Black Community and the Birth Control Movement, in Passion and Power 141–42 (K. Peiss & C. Simmons eds. 1989).

20. The size of rural families also declined sharply during the nineteenth century. Faragher, History from the Inside-Out: Writing the History of Women in Rural America, 33 Am. Q. 536, 549 (1981); R. Petchesky, supra note 17, at 74. James Mohr

influenced by changing definitions of the family and of motherhood. As men's work patterns deviated further from those of women, "wife" and "home" became powerful symbols of men's economic security and social standing.[21] Even as women were regarded as agents of reproduction, the expectation that they turn outward into the larger society served as an incentive to limit the number of children they bore. Nineteenth-century women thus faced sharply conflicting demands: "The True Woman was domestic, docile, and reproductive. The good bourgeois wife was to limit her fertility, symbolize her husband's affluence, and do good within the world."[22]

To limit the number of children they bore, women of all classes adopted a range of strategies, including abortion. Through the 1870s abortion was "common," a "matter of fact" and often "safe and successful."[23] The most common methods of abortion in the nineteenth century involved self-administered herbs and devices available from pharmacists.[24] Nonetheless, women also relied on professional abortionists: in 1871, New York City, with a population of less than one million, supported two hundred full-time abortionists, not including doctors who also sometimes performed abortions.[25]

For most of the nineteenth century, abortion was a visible as well as common practice. "Beginning in the early 1840s abortion became, for all intents and purposes, a business, a service openly traded in the free market. . . . [Pervasive advertising told Americans] not only that many practitioners would provide abortion services, but that some practitioners had made the abortion business their chief livelihood. Indeed, abortions became one of the first specialties in American medical history."[26]

---

observes that by the 1860s abortion "seemed to thrive as well on the prairies as in large urban centers." J. Mohr, supra note 2, at 100.

21. Demos, Images of The American Family, Then and Now, in Changing Images of the Family 51, 52 (V. Tufte and B. Myerhoff eds. 1979).

22. C. Smith-Rosenberg, supra note 3, at 225.

23. L. Gordon, Woman's Body, Woman's Right 51–52 (rev. ed. 1990).

24. See LaSorte, Nineteenth Century Family Planning Practices, 41 J. of Psychohistory 163, 166–70 (1976).

25. New York Times, Aug. 23, 1871, at 6.

26. J. Mohr, supra note 2, at 47. In the 1860s and 1870s both the popular press and medical journals were full of advice about abortion services. Id. at 67–68. See also C. Degler, supra note 15, at 230.

IV. NINETEENTH-CENTURY ABORTION RESTRIC-
TIONS SOUGHT TO PROMOTE OBJECTIVES THAT ARE
TODAY EITHER PLAINLY INAPPLICABLE OR CON-
STITUTIONALLY IMPERMISSIBLE.

Nineteenth-century allopathic physicians enlisted state
power to limit access to abortion for reasons that are, in retrospect, parochial, and have long since been rejected by organized medicine. Indeed, between 1850 and 1880, the newly
formed American Medical Association, through some of its
active members, became the "single most important factor in
altering the legal policies toward abortion in this country."[27]

The doctors found an audience for their effort to restrict
abortion because they appealed to specific social concerns and
anxieties: maternal health, consumer protection, discriminatory ideas about the properly subordinate status of women,
and racist/nativist fears generated by the fact that elite Protestant women often sought abortions. Some of those doctors
also sought to attribute moral status to the fetus.

**A. From 1820 to 1860, Abortion Regulation in the
States Rejected Broader English Restrictions and
Sought to Protect Women from Particularly Dangerous
Forms of Abortion.**

In 1803, English law made all forms of abortion criminal.[28]
Despite this model, for two decades no American state restricted access to abortion. In 1821, when one state, Connecticut, acted, it prohibited only the administration of a
"deadly poison, or other noxious and destructive substance"
as a means of bringing about an abortion.[29] Moreover, the act
applied only after quickening, and punished only the person
who administered the poison, not the woman who consumed

---

27. J. Mohr, *supra* note 2, at 157. *See also* R. Petchesky, *supra* note 17, at 79;
L. Gordon, *supra* note 23, at 59.

28. The law was passed as part of a comprehensive revision of the criminal code,
urged by Lord Ellenborough, broadening the sweep of the criminal law and increasing
penalties. J. Mohr, *supra* note 2, at 23; *Roe v. Wade*, 410 U.S. at 136–38.

29. The Public Statute Laws of the State of Connecticut 152–53 (1821). *See*
J. Mohr, *supra* note 2, at 22. *See also* Quay, *Justifiable Abortion—Medical and Legal
Foundations*, 49 Geo. L.J. 395 (1960–61).

it. In the late 1820s, three other states followed the Connecticut model, prohibiting the use of dangerous poisons after quickening.[30] Most American states did not see abortion as a problem demanding legislative attention.

In 1830, Connecticut became the first state to punish abortion after quickening.[31] In the same year, New York, also animated by a concern for patient safety, considered a law to prohibit any surgery, unless two physicians approved it as essential. Before scientific understanding of germ theory and antisepsis, any surgical intervention was likely to be fatal. The New York act finally adopted applied only to surgical abortion and included the first "therapeutic" exception, approving abortion where two physicians agreed that it was "necessary."[32] As the Court recognized in Roe v. Wade, until the twentieth century, abortion, particularly when done through surgical intervention, remained significantly more dangerous to the woman than childbirth.[33] Because these early abortion laws were drafted and justified to protect women, they did not punish women as parties to an abortion.[34]

None of these early laws, restricting forms of abortion thought to be particularly unsafe, were enforced.[35] That absence itself speaks powerfully, particularly because abortion was a prevalent practice in this era. Despite legislative action and medical opposition, the common and openly tolerated practice suggests that many Americans did not perceive abortion as morally wrong.[36]

---

30. Missouri adopted such a statute in 1825, Illinois in 1827, and New York in 1828. See J. Mohr, supra note 2, at 25–27.

31. 1 Conn. Stat. Tit. 22, § 14 at 152 (1821), reported by Quay, supra note 29, at 453.

32. See N.Y. Rev. Stat., pt. IV, Ch. I, tit. VI, § 21, at 578 (1828–1835), reported by Quay, supra note 29, at 499.

33. See Roe v. Wade, 410 U.S. at 148–50; Means, supra note 5, at 353–54, 358–59, 382–96.

34. Roe v. Wade, 410 U.S. at 151–52; M. Grossberg, supra note 10, at 163–64.

35. J. Mohr, supra note 2, at 39, citing A. Wilder, History of Medicine 499–511 (1901).

36. C. Degler, supra note 15, cites physicians who observe that women who are "otherwise quite intelligent and refined, with a keen sense of their moral and religious obligations to themselves and to others, deem it nothing amiss to destroy the embryo during the first few months of its growth." Id. at 233–34.

B. A Central Purpose of Abortion Regulation in the Nineteenth Century Was to Define Who Should Be Allowed to Control Medical Practice.

Physicians were the principal nineteenth-century proponents of laws to restrict abortion. A core purpose of the
nineteenth-century laws, and of doctors in supporting them,
was to control medical practice in the interest of public
safety.[37] This is not to deny that some doctors had moral
objections to abortion, although their arguments tended to
be framed "from the perspective of medical science."[38] But
the most significant explanation for the drive by medical
doctors to enact statutes regulating abortion is the fact that
these doctors were undergoing the historical process of
professionalization—the effort to attain control over a spe-
cialized body of knowledge.

Medicine was not then the organized, highly regulated
profession we know today. It was an occupation in which
conventional and scientifically authoritative modes of practice
(allopathic medicine) still contended for stature and authority
with other modes, such as botanic medicine, homeopathy,
herbalists, midwives, and abortionists. Allopathic physicians
sought to establish and consolidate professional sovereignty.[39] It was only by mid-century, with the founding of
the American Medical Association, that professional sovereignty was tentatively established for "scientific" medicine.[40]

The nineteenth-century movement to regulate abortions
was one chapter in a campaign by doctors that reflected a
professional conflict between "regulars" (those who ultimately
became the practitioners and proponents of scientific medicine) and "irregulars."[41] As James Mohr explains:

37. J. Mohr, *supra* note 2, at 43.
38. Siegel, *Reasoning from the Body: A Historical Perspective on Abortion Regulation
and Questions of Equal Protection*, 44 Stan. L. Rev. 261, 287 (forthcoming 1992).
39. See P. Starr, *The Social Transformation of American Medicine* (1982).
40. See id.; W. Rothstein, *American Physicians in the Nineteenth Century* (1972).
On professionalization, *see*, for example, G. Geison, ed., *Professions and Professional
Ideologies in America* (1983).
41. Another illustrative chapter is the "medicalization" of childbirth, transforming
what had been an affair of family, friends, and midwives into a procedure associated
with doctors, hospitals, and sophisticated medical interventions. *See* J. Leavitt,

If a *regular* doctor refused to perform an abortion he knew the woman could go to one of several types of *irregulars* and probably receive one. . . . As more and more irregulars began to advertise abortion services openly, especially after 1840, regular physicians grew more and more nervous about losing their practices to healers who would provide a service that more and more American women after 1840 began to want. Yet, if a *regular* gave in to the temptation to perform an occasional discreet abortion, and physicians testified repeatedly that this frequently happened among the *regulars*, he would be compromising his own commitment to an American medical practice that would conform to Hippocratic standards of behavior. The best way out of these dilemmas was to persuade state legislators to make abortion a criminal offense. Anti-abortion laws would weaken the appeal of the competition and take the pressure off the more marginal members of the regulars' own sect.[42]

To be sure, some "regulars" were morally troubled by abortion, and not all "irregulars" performed them. But issues of medical authority and professional sovereignty explain why "regular" physicians became interested in abortion policy from an early date and "repeatedly dragged it into their prolonged struggle to control the practice of medicine in the United States."[43]

C. Enforcement of Sharply Differentiated Concepts of the Roles and Choices of Men and Women Underlay Regulation of Abortion and Contraception in the Nineteenth Century.

The American Medical Association's campaign in the nineteenth century to restrict access to abortion succeeded for many reasons. Concerns over the dangers of surgical abortion to women were well founded. In addition, physicians persuaded political leaders (who were, of course, uniformly male) that "abortion constituted a threat to social order and to male

---

Brought to Bed: Child-Bearing in America, 1750–1950 (1986); R. Wertz & D. Wertz, *Lying-In: A History of Childbirth in America* (1977); B. Ehrenreich & D. English, *For Her Own Good: 150 Years of the Experts' Advice to Women* (1979); C. Smith-Rosenberg, *supra* note 3, at 231.

42. J. Mohr, *supra* note 2, at 37 (citation omitted, emphasis added).
43. *Id.*

authority."[44] Since the 1840s, a growing movement for women's suffrage and equality had generated popular fears that women were departing from a purely maternal role[45]—fears fueled by the decline in family size during the nineteenth century. A central rhetorical focus of the woman's movement was framed by a new perception of women as the rightful possessors of their own bodies.[46]

In 1871, the American Medical Association's Committee on Criminal Abortion described the woman who sought an abortion:

> She becomes unmindful of the course marked out for her by Providence, she overlooks the duties imposed on her by the marriage contract. She yields to the pleasures—but shrinks from the pains and responsibilities of maternity; and, destitute of all delicacy and refinements, resigns herself, body and soul, into the hands of unscrupulous and wicked men. Let not the husband of such a wife flatter himself that he possesses her affection. Nor can she in turn ever merit even the respect of a virtuous husband. She sinks into old age like a withered tree, stripped of its foliage; with the stain of blood upon her soul, she dies without the hand of affection to smooth her pillow.[47]

The nineteenth-century American Medical Association's view of women is strikingly similar to that adopted by Justice Bradley in 1873, when women were denied the right to practice law because "divine ordinance," and "the nature of things," prescribed a "family institution [that] is repugnant to

44. C. Smith-Rosenberg, *supra* note 3, at 235.

45. From the 1840s on, the moral fervor of the abolitionist cause drew Northern women more deeply into public life than ever before in the nation's history. Some of the women who were active in the anti-slavery movement perceived parallels between the subjugation and disenfranchisement of black people and the oppression of women. *See* E. Flexner, *Century of Struggle* ch. 13 (rev. ed. 1975).

46. M. Ryan, *Cradle of the Middle Class* 155–57 (1983); Dubois, *Outgrowing the Compact of the Fathers: Equal Rights, Woman Suffrage, and the United States Constitution, 1820–1878,* 74 J. Am. Hist. 836 (1987).

47. Atlee & O'Donnell, *Report of the Committee on Criminal Abortion,* 22 Transactions of the American Medical Association 241 (1871), quoted in C. Smith-Rosenberg, *supra* note 3, at 236–37. Smith-Rosenberg observes that, although middle-class husbands were undoubtedly active participants in their wives' decisions about abortion, the nineteenth-century AMA "linked doctor and husband as the equally wronged and innocent parties. The aborting wife, in contrast, was unnaturally selfish and ruthless." *Id.* at 236.

the idea of a woman adopting a distinct and independent career from that of her husband."[48] This Court has now come to see this view as part of our "long and unfortunate history of sex discrimination," and as constitutionally illegitimate.[49]

This vision of woman-as-reproductive-vessel was expressed in a range of legal restrictions that enforced a married woman's dependence on her husband. Under the common law, indeed well into this century, a married woman's body and reproductive capacity were subjected to her husband's control.[50] Common law provided the husband a remedy for interference with his right to sole possession of his wife's body and services. The early writ of "ravishment" listed the wife with the husband's chattels. Until recent years, the action for criminal conversation allowed the husband to maintain an action for trespass, not only when his wife was raped, but even when the wife had consented to extramarital sexual relations, "since it was considered that she was not more capable of giving a consent which would prejudice the husband's interests than was his horse."[51] At common law a husband could sue a third party for rendering aid to his wife without his permission—a privilege that strikingly resembles the cause of action conferred upon unconsulted husbands against doctors by the Pennsylvania law at issue in this case.

By the middle of the nineteenth century, such privileges were widely regarded as corrupt and illegitimate impositions of domestic slavery—and not just by women's rights activists. In 1864, for example, the New York Court of Appeals overturned a common-law rule allowing a husband to sue for "enticement" any person who helped his wife to leave him,

48. *Bradwell v. Illinois*, 83 U.S. (16 Wall.) 130, 141 (1873) (Bradley, J., concurring).

49. *Frontiero v. Richardson*, 411 U.S. 677, 684 (1973). In *United Automobile Workers v. Johnson Controls*, 111 S. Ct. 1196 (1991), this Court struck down a sex-specific fetal-protection policy, noting that "[c]oncern for a woman's existing or potential offspring historically has been the excuse for denying women equal economic opportunities." *Id.* at 1210.

50. For the classic statement of the theory of "coverture" followed in the United States, *see* 1 W. Blackstone, *Commentaries* 442. On the legal disabilities associated with coverture, *see* M. Abramowitz, *Regulating the Lives of Women* 54 (1988); Chused, *Married Women's Property Law: 1800–1850*, 71 Geo. L.J. 1359, 1366 (1983); E. Pleck, *Domestic Tyranny* 88 (1987); Note, *To Have and To Hold: The Marital Rape Exemption and the Fourteenth Amendment*, 99 Harv. L. Rev. 1255, 1256 (1986).

51. W. Prosser, *Law of Torts* 877 (3d ed. 1971).

stating: "[A married woman may] invoke and receive aid, shelter and protection from others, even strangers, against the oppression and cruelty of her husband," even if the wife was acting directly contrary to her husband's wishes. "[A stranger] may in such a case treat the wife as a person, an individual entitled to credit, and invested with the rights and claims of, and upon, our common humanity."[52]

Against what they saw as an inequitable vision of gender relations, the women's movement of the nineteenth century affirmed that women—even married women—should have basic rights of self-governance, including the right to decide whether to bear a child. Early feminists sought to enhance women's control of reproduction through a campaign for "voluntary motherhood," ideally to be achieved through periodic abstinence from sexual relations.[53] They attempted, with limited success, to analogize women's control over reproduction to the structure of rights that had overturned chattel slavery. Indeed, it was precisely women's outrage at their sexual subordination that led some feminists to oppose abortion—not on moral grounds, but as an object example of women's victimization at the hands of men.[54] The recently adopted Reconstruction Amendments were a central text in the opposition of women's rights advocates to the social and legal covenants binding women to the marital relation.

Opposition to abortion and contraception were closely linked,[55] and can only be understood as a reaction to the uncertainties generated by changes in family function and anxieties created by women's challenges to their historic roles of silence and subservience. These challenges were critical factors motivating the all-male state legislatures that adopted

52. *Barnes v. Allen*, 1 Keyes 390, 392 (N.Y. 1864) (neighbor who provided wagon ride to wife from her husband's house to her father's house not liable to husband).

53. *See* L. Gordon, *supra* note 23, at 93–113. During this period, much scientific and folk wisdom held a flatly inaccurate view of the cycle of female fertility, which made periodic abstinence an unreliable form of contraception. *Id.* at 99. This inaccurate belief, when viewed in light of hard data on declining birthrates, *see* text at notes 17–19 *supra*, underscores how common abortion must have been.

54. L. Gordon, *supra* note 23, at 108; Siegel, *supra* note 38, at 304–308; Gordon, *Why Nineteenth Century Feminists Did Not Support 'Birth Control' and Twentieth Century Feminists Do*, in *Rethinking the Family* 40, 43 (B. Thorne & M. Yalom eds. 1982).

55. "Anthony Comstock had labeled as abortionists everyone who advocated or dealt in family-limitation materials and services." M. Grossberg, *supra* note 10, at 193.

restraints on women, including restrictions on abortion.[56] In opposition to the feminist demand for control of reproduction, the federal government in 1873 took the lead in banning access to information about both contraception and abortion. The Comstock law[57] restricted not only medical information on abortion and contraception, such as a medical text on physiology written by an eminent Harvard scientist, but also literary depictions, such as Leo Tolstoy's disapproving tale of infidelity, *The Kreutzer Sonata*, and moral literature, including a pamphlet urging total sexual chastity.[58]

D. Nineteenth-Century Contraception and Abortion Regulation Also Reflected Ethnocentric Fears About the Relative Birthrates of Immigrants and White Protestants.

Nativism, notably anti-Catholicism, had been part of American politics and culture as early as the Jacksonian period. The Civil War and Reconstruction Era dramatically raised social fears about national identity and citizenship. Social conservatives in the 1850s articulated an "organicist" ideal in which social unity should predominate over diversity. By the 1870s social thought was turning the insights of Charles Darwin toward racist ends. The political ideology of "free labor," forged in the nascent Republican Party in the years preceding the Civil War,[59] was severely challenged by an influx of foreign labor in the latter part of the nineteenth century.[60] The discriminatory immigration policies and nativist fears of the late nineteenth and early twentieth centuries fanned movements against women's reproductive freedom.

---

56. C. Smith-Rosenberg, *supra* note 3, at 218.

57. The act prohibits mailing, transporting, or importing "obscene, lewd or lascivious" items, specifically including all devices and information pertaining to "preventing conception and producing abortion." *See* Comstock Act, Ch. 258, § 1, 17 Stat. 598 (1873). It was not until 1971 that an amendment was passed deleting the prohibition as to contraception. Pub. L. 91–662, 84 Stat. 1973 (1971). The ban as to information about abortion remains. *See* 18 U.S.C. § 1461 (1988).

58. *See* M. Grossberg, *supra* note 10, at 190; *United States v. Foote*, 25 Feb. Cas. 1140, 1141 (S.D.N.Y. 1876) (rejecting claim that physicians should have right to distribute information concerning contraceptives); L. Gordon, *supra* note 23, at 164–66.

59. E. Foner, *Free Soil, Free Labor, Free Men* (1970).

60. D. Davis, *From Homicide to Slavery* 137–54 (1986). *See also* S. Lipset & E. Raab, *The Politics of Unreason* (1970); G. Frederickson, *The Inner Civil War* (1965); R. Hofstadter, *Social Darwinism in American Thought* (1955); J. Higham, *Strangers in the Land* (1963).

Beginning in the 1890s, and continuing through the first decades of the twentieth century, these nativist fears coalesced into a drive against what was then called "race suicide."[61] The "race suicide" alarmists worried that women of "good stock" —prosperous, white, and Protestant—were not having enough children to maintain the political and social supremacy of their group.[62] Anxiety over the falling birth rates of Protestant whites in comparison with other groups helped shape policy governing both birth control and abortion.[63] As James Mohr points out, "The doctors both used and were influenced by blatant nativism . . . There can be little doubt that Protestants' fears about not keeping up with the reproductive rates of Catholic immigrants played a greater role in the drive for anti-abortion laws in nineteenth-century America than Catholic opposition to abortion did."[64]

V. ENFORCEMENT OF ABORTION RESTRICTIONS IN THE FIRST HALF OF THE TWENTIETH CENTURY FOLLOWED ENTRENCHED ETHNIC AND CLASS DIF-FERENTIATIONS, AFFIRMED TRADITIONAL CON-CERNS ABOUT ENFORCING GENDER ROLES, AND IMPOSED ENORMOUS COSTS UPON WOMEN.

The statutory restrictions on abortion remained virtually unchanged from the early twentieth century until the 1960s.

61. See L. Gordon, supra note 23, at 133–55. On November 20, 1912, 390 federal postal inspectors arrested 173 people for using the mails to disseminate information about abortion and contraception in violation of the Comstock Act. The campaign was called the "federal war on race suicide." Take Chicagoans in Federal War on Race Suicide, Chicago Tribune, Nov. 21, 1912, p. 1.

62. See C. Degler, supra note 15, at 229–30, on the concern of physicians that women of "good stock" were particularly likely to obtain abortions. In Buffalo in 1855, the fertility ratio of Irish women of ages 20–34 was over twice that of native white women, id. at 134, raising concerns about disparities in relative population growth. See also Weisbrod, Birth Control and the Black American: A Matter of Genocide?, 10 Demography 571 (1973).

63. J. Reed, From Private Vice to Public Virtue (1978); D. Kevles, In the Name of Eugenics (1985); D. Kennedy, Birth Control in America (1971).

64. See J. Mohr, supra note 2, at 167. Horatio Robinson Storer, who spearheaded the American Medical Association's mid-nineteenth century anti-abortion campaign, frequently referred to racial themes. Id. at 180–90; H. Storer, Why Not? A Book for Every Woman 85 (1866) ("[S]hall the great territories of the Far West be filled by our children or by those of aliens?"). Carl Degler also documents that physicians of the 1850s and 1860s expressed particular concern that abortion was increasingly sought by married women of "high repute." C. Degler, supra note 15, at 229.

Physicians were allowed to perform abortions only "to preserve the mother's life." Nonetheless, the incidence of abortion remained high, ranging from one pregnancy in seven at the turn of the century, to one in three in 1936.[65] Most abortions were performed illegally.[66] Legal restrictions did not stop abortion, but made it humiliating and dangerous.

The dangers of illegal abortion were exacerbated by law enforcement abuse. Leslie Reagan's study of the regime of criminalized abortion in Chicago in the late nineteenth and early twentieth centuries chronicles the inevitable abuses of police and prosecutorial power that attended efforts to enforce restrictive abortion laws. As Reagan notes, "Popular tolerance of abortion tempered enforcement of the criminal abortion laws. Prosecutors discovered early the difficulty of winning convictions in criminal abortion cases. Juries nullified the law and regularly acquitted abortionists."[67] Faced with these obstacles, prosecutors routinely resorted to enforcement tactics that were at best questionable and at worst grotesque: They extracted "dying declarations" in hospitals from women dying from poorly administered abortions in order to secure evidence needed to prosecute abortionists.

This practice not only subjected dying women to cruel and humiliating interrogations; it also drew reluctant doctors into the web of criminal investigation and encouraged doctors to violate patient confidences in exchange for their own exculpation. A doctor who tried to save the life of a woman dying from an abortion could himself be subjected to harassment or even criminal prosecution as an accessory. But if he managed to secure a "dying declaration" from the woman that named the abortionist, the doctor might hope to perform his medical duties without fear of prosecution. Some doctors, of course, rebelled against a regime that required them to harass sick and

---

65. See F. Taussig, Abortion, Spontaneous and Induced 338, Appendix A, 453–75 (1936). See also Stix, A Study of Pregnancy Wastage, 13 Milbank Memorial Fund Q. 347 (1935); Stix & Wiehl, Abortion and Public Health, 28 Am. J. Pub. Health 622, Table I (1938).

66. See K. Luker, Abortion and the Politics of Motherhood 38–54 (1984).

67. Reagan, "About to Meet Her Maker": Women, Doctors, Dying Declarations, and the State's Investigation of Abortion, Chicago, 1867–1940, 77 J. Am. Hist. 1240, 1247 (1991). See generally L. Reagan, When Abortion Was a Crime, Ph.D. dissertation, University of Wisconsin–Madison, 1991.

dying women. "The business of the doctor is to relieve pain, cure disease and save life, not to act as a bloodhound [for] the state," one Illinois doctor protested in 1933.[68] But such practices seemed inevitable if the laws against abortion were to be enforced in a climate of tolerance for routine violation of those laws.

When advances in medical science in the 1930s and 1940s reduced the number of deaths due to improperly administered abortions, Chicago authorities shifted their enforcement strategy from securing "dying declarations" to more direct but equally coercive means of securing convictions. The 1947 investigation and prosecution of Chicago midwife Helen Stanko, for instance, was replete with instances of forced gynecological examinations and humiliating interrogations of Stanko's patients.[69] The aggressive efforts of Chicago police in the 1940s to enforce criminal statutes that reached into the heart of women's intimate lives and medical relationships led inexorably to law enforcement practices that in retrospect seem medieval.

In the first half of the twentieth century, a two-tiered abortion system emerged in which quality of medical care depended on the class, race, age, and residence of the woman. Poor and rural women obtained illegal abortions performed by people (including some physicians) willing to defy the law out of sympathy for the woman or for the fee. More privileged women pressed private physicians for legal abortions and many obtained them. Some doctors could be persuaded that a delivery would endanger a woman's health. The dilation and curettage procedure effective for abortion was indicated for numerous other gynecological health problems, allowing the word "abortion" to remain unspoken between patient and doctor—even as the procedure went forward.[70]

Shifts in the definition of "therapeutic" abortion responded to larger social forces.[71] Early in the century, "race suicide" fears fueled efforts to suppress both abortion and birth control.

68. L. Reagan, When Abortion Was A crime, *supra* note 67, at 180–81.
69. *Id.* at 277–83. *See People* v. *Stanko,* 402 Ill. 558 (1949); *People* v. *Stanko,* 407 Ill. 624 (1951).
70. *See generally* K. Luker, *supra* note 66.
71. L. Reagan, When Abortion Was a Crime, *supra* note 67, at 284–312.

During the Depression, abortions increased as the medical profession recognized impoverishment as an indication for therapeutic abortion.[72] In the 1940s and 1950s the definition of therapeutic abortion expanded to include psychiatric indications.[73] Physicians were caught in a double bind: abortion was criminal, but the reasons women sought the procedure were so multiple and compelling that doctors found requests for abortion difficult to resist.[74]

In the 1950s, more restrictive attitudes toward both legal and illegal abortions[75] were part of a conservative response to growing female labor-force participation and independence.[76] The movement to legalize abortion in the 1960s arose in response to this rather brief wave of anti-abortion enforcement. Physicians, particularly those who worked in public hospitals and clinics, saw women who needlessly suffered and died as a consequence of illegal abortions.[77] Others were disturbed that most of those women were poor and Black. Many were distressed by the class bias inherent in the psychiatric indications for therapeutic abortions.[78] In the late 1960s, concerned physicians were joined by women who had come to understand that control of reproductive capacity is at the heart of women's self-governance and moral personhood.[79]

As a number of states acted to legalize abortion in the late 1960s and early 1970s, there was pressure for recognition of constitutional protection for the basic right of abortion choice. Class and regional differentiations were accentuated as it be-

72. In 1931 an American Medical Association editorial noted that "poverty . . . does not constitute an indication for abortion, [but] there is no doubt that in the United States many abortions are performed for borderline cases in which there is a strong ethical indication plus a more or less minor medical ailment." *Abortion or Removal of Pregnant Uterus*, 95 J. Am. Med. Ass'n 1169 (1931).

73. K. Luker, *supra* note 66, at 45–47, 54–57.

74. For example, Luker, *id.*, discusses the early 1960s scare over the fertility drug Thalidomide, which caused crippling fetal deformities. The scare underlined the inadequacy of a narrow definition of therapeutic indications for abortion: American women carrying severely deformed fetuses were forced either to carry to term or to travel overseas to find abortion access. *Id.* at 62–65 (case of Sherri Finkbine).

75. L. Lader, *Abortion* 42–51 (1966).

76. M. Ryan, ed., *Womanhood in America* 198–215 (1975); R. Baxandall, L. Gordon & S. Reverby, eds., *America's Working Women* 299–308 (1976).

77. *See, e.g.*, Dudziak, *Just Say No: Birth Control in the Connecticut Supreme Court Before Griswold v. Connecticut*, 75 Ia. L. Rev. 915, 924–927 (1990) (impetus for Connecticut doctors' campaign in 1940s–1960s to legalize birth control in the state was threat to life and health of married women from medically dangerous pregnancies).

78. *See McRae v. Califano*, 491 F. Supp. 630, 668–76 (E.D.N.Y. 1980).

79. K. Luker, *supra* note 66, at 92–125.

came possible for women with resources to travel to states where abortion had been made legal. In its 1973 decision in *Roe* v. *Wade*, this Court responded to these forces in holding that constitutional rights of liberty and privacy protect the right of the woman and her physician to choose abortion.

VI. EMPHASIS ON THE FETUS BECAME CENTRAL TO CULTURAL AND LEGAL DEBATE OVER ABORTION ONLY IN THE LATE TWENTIETH CENTURY, WHEN TRADITIONAL JUSTIFICATIONS FOR RESTRICTING ACCESS TO ABORTION BECAME CULTURALLY ANACHRONISTIC OR CONSTITUTIONALLY IMPERMISSIBLE.

Some of those seeking to enlist the power of the state to deny women's liberty to choose abortion have long articulated a concern for the fetus.[80] Yet until the late twentieth century, this concern was always subsidiary to more mundane social visions and anxieties. The mid-nineteenth century physicians' campaign against abortion was directed at botanic medicine and homeopathy, as well as at abortion. Similarly, those who opposed abortion and birth control as a means of preventing "race suicide" sought to protect the privilege of elite white Protestants, not to protect the racially mixed universe of fetuses.

It is significant that there was virtually no religious support for the nineteenth-century physicians' campaign to bar abortion.[81] Physicians tried hard to enlist moral authority and

---

80. *See* J. Mohr, *supra* note 2, at 165–66.

81. The extensive religious press of the United States, both Catholic and Protestant, "maintained a total blackout on the issue of abortion from the beginning of the nineteenth century through the end of the Civil War." *Id.* at 183. It was not until 1869 that a papal declaration condemned abortion as a violation of the fetus prior to "ensoulment," held to be 40 days gestational age for a male fetus and 80 days for a female. Before that time, Catholic theology condemned early abortion on precisely the same terms as it had condemned masturbation and contraception, *i.e.* a distrust of sexuality and of interference with natural processes. In Catholic doctrine late abortions were always held to be a form of homicide. No American diocesan newspaper reported the Pope's 1869 statement. *Id.* at 187. In that same year, the Bishop of Baltimore issued the only formal nineteenth-century Catholic condemnation of abortion in America, *id.* at 186, and the Old School Presbyterians became the only major Protestant denomination to condemn abortion. *Id.* at 192. No other religious denominations or leaders followed.

organized religion in their campaign to restrict abortion, and "were openly disgusted when the established voices of moral authority refused to speak on their behalf. . . . Medical journals accused the religious journals of valuing abortifacient advertising revenue too highly to risk criticizing the practice."[82]

Further, the limited support offered physicians from Protestant religious leaders appeared to reflect "worr[y] about falling birth-rates among their adherents [more] than . . . the morality of abortion itself."[83] Compared to extensive religious involvement in other nineteenth-century movements for changing social morality, such as temperance, the conspicuous absence of religious support for the physicians' anti-abortion crusade is particularly striking.[84]

Nineteenth-century laws restricting access to abortion did not define the fetus as a human being, nor did courts treat fetuses as legal rights-bearers. To the contrary, New Jersey Chief Justice Green expressed the prevailing judicial opinion in 1849 when he asserted that although it was "true, for certain purposes, [that] the law regards an infant as *in being* from the time of conception, yet it seems nowhere to regard it as *in life*, or to have respect to its preservation as a living being."[85] Michael Grossberg summarizes the nineteenth-century cases, saying, "[A] fetus enjoyed rights only in property law and then only if successfully born. It had no standing in criminal law until quickening, and none at all in tort. The law highly prized children, not fetuses."[86] An important illustration lies in Judith Walzer Leavitt's analysis of turn-of-the-century medical decisions about the procedure of craniotomy (a surgical mutilation of the live fetal head to permit vaginal extraction). Leavitt's research shows that the majority of physicians, confronted with a woman whose pelvis was too small to permit delivery, thought craniotomy (which killed the fully-formed fetus) more appropriate than a Caesarean section (with its

---

82. *Id.* at 184.
83. *Id.* at 195.
84. *Id.* at 182–96; R. Petchesky, *supra* note 17, at 80.
85. *Cooper* v. *State*, 22 N.J.L. (2 Zab.) 52, 56–57 (1849) (emphasis in the original), discussed in M. Grossberg, *supra* note 10, at 165.
86. M. Grossberg, *supra* note 10, at 165.

high risk to the woman)—a revealing comment on the pre-vailing hierarchy of values.[87]

As this Court observed in Roe v. Wade, the pattern of American abortion laws does not support the view that such laws incorporate a view of the fetus as a person. Both the lesser punishment for abortion than for homicide, and the various exceptions allowing the physician to determine when and if abortion is justified, rebut the assumption that laws against abortion reflect simply a belief in fetal personhood.

VII. A PRESUMED INTEREST IN PROTECTING FETAL LIFE DOES NOT JUSTIFY DENYING WOMEN THEIR HISTORIC LIBERTY TO CHOOSE ABORTION.

A culture can, of course, allow growing humanistic impulses to attach greater moral value to fetuses or to potential human life. But this Court should reject state efforts to invoke the protection of fetal life to justify restrictions upon women's access to abortion.

As this brief has demonstrated, the complex historic grounds originally asserted for restricting access to abortion are now either socially irrelevant or recognized as constitu-tionally illegitimate. Both culturally and legally, it is today impossible to defend abortion restrictions as a means of en-forcing an absolutist religious belief that intimate relations must always remain open to the possibility of procreation.[88] Similarly, abortion restrictions cannot be justified by the desire to keep women in traditional roles.[89] Likewise, our social consensus, embodied in principles of legal equality, would not permit the Court to defend restrictions on abortion as a means of encouraging the propagation of white Protestant stock or

---

87. See Leavitt, The Growth of Medical Authority: Technology and Morals in Turn-of-the-Century Obstetrics, 1 Med. Anthropology Q. 230, 233–35 (1987).

88. See Griswold v. Connecticut, supra; Eisenstadt v. Baird, 405 U.S. 438 (1972).

89. Gender-based classifications must be "free of fixed notions concerning the roles and abilities of males and females." Mississippi University for Women v. Hogan, 458 U.S. 718, 724–25 (1982). Accord Orr v. Orr, 440 U.S. 268 (1979); Stanton v. Stanton, 421 U.S. 7 (1975).

of diminishing the population of racial or religious minorities. History should make us skeptical, however, of the notice that basic conflicts underlying these earlier social purposes have disappeared as motive forces for the regulation of abortion, to be entirely displaced by moral concern for the protection of unborn life. Sufficient refutation of this notion lies in the "spousal notification" provision of the Pennsylvania law at issue in this case.[90] In historical terms, the spousal notification requirement rests upon and reanimates the traditional notion that married women's bodies, lives, and will are submerged in their husband's.[91] That "long and unfortunate history" of the subordination of women has now been firmly—and properly —rejected by this Court.[92]

The extensive factual record developed at trial amply demonstrates that the restrictions of the Pennsylvania law impose heavy burdens and costs on women's ability to choose whether to bear a child, and that these burdens fall most heavily on the most vulnerable women. *Planned Parenthood of Southeastern Pennsylvania v. Casey*, 744 F. Supp. 1323, 1329–72 (E.D.Pa. 1990). Similarly, history vividly establishes that the single most obvious and inevitable result of such onerous restrictions is their devastating consequences for the health and autonomy of women.

CONCLUSION

The judgment of the Court of Appeals regarding the spousal notification requirement should be affirmed and the judgment regarding the other provisions of the Pennsylvania act should be reversed. The Court should reaffirm that the Constitution prohibits the state from unduly burdening women's powerful

90. The Circuit Court of Appeals, while concluding that this Court's decision in *Webster v. Reproductive Health Services*, 492 U.S. 490 (1989), compelled it to approve most of the restrictions of the Pennsylvania law, held that the spousal notification requirement constitutes an undue burden on women's ability to choose abortion, not narrowly tailored to serve a compelling state interest. *Planned Parenthood v. Casey*, 947 F.2d 683, 711–715 (3d. Cir. 1991).

91. *Supra* note 50.

92. *Supra* note 49.

liberty and equality interests in controlling their own bodies and lives.

Respectfully submitted,

JANE E. LARSON
Northwestern University
School of Law
357 East Chicago Ave.
Chicago, IL 60611
(312) 503–0321

CLYDE SPILLENGER
University of Wisconsin Law
School
975 Bascom Mall
Madison, WI 53706
(608) 263–2545

SYLVIA A. LAW*
New York University School of
Law
40 Washington Sq. So.
New York, NY 10012
(212) 998–6265

*Counsel of Record

APPENDIX

AMICI CURIAE

Elaine S. Abelson, Garland E. Allen, Kenneth L. Ames, Bonnie S. Anderson, Rima D. Apple, Joyce Appleby, David Arkusch, Stephen Aron, Barbara J. Balliet, Renato Barahona, Marjorie A. Beale, Rudolph M. Bell, Thomas Bender, Judith M. Bennett, Carol Berkin, Constance Berman, Frederick M. Binder, Robert G. Bone, Allan M. Brandt, Barbara Brenzel, Marvin A. Breslow, Renate Bridenthal, Kathleen M. Brown, Mari Jo Buhle, Vern L. Bullough, Jon Butler, Caroline Bynum,

Susan E. Cayleff, Herrick Chapman, Ellen Chesler, Carol Chomsky, Eric Howard Christianson, Paul G. E. Clemens, John Henry Coatsworth, Sherman Cochran, Lizabeth Cohen, Paul A. Cohen, Susan Guettel Cole, James V. Compton, Harold J. Cook, Patricia A. Cooper, Sandi E. Cooper, Nancy F. Cott, Eugene L. Cox, Steve Curry, Jere R. Daniell, Paul David, David Brion Davis, Marc H. Dawson, Philip Dawson, Cornelia Hughes Dayton, Warren Dean, Hannah S. Decker, Jane S. De Hart, Marion Deshmukh, Ileen A.

DeVault, Jane B. Donegan, Ellen Carol DuBois, Arthur P. Dudden, Mary L. Dudziak, Ellen Dwyer,

Arthur M. Eckstein, Sarah Elbert, Sara M. Evans, Mary L. Felstiner, Sidney Fine, Sarah Fishman, Joyce Follet, William E. Forbath, Miriam Formanek-Brunell, Elizabeth Fox-Genovese, Thomas R. Frazier, Estelle B. Freedman, Joshua B. Freeman, Richard M. Fried, Lawrence M. Friedman, Ziva Galili, Vanessa Northington Gamble, Peter Gay, Donald F.M. Gerardi, Pamela Gerardi, Faye Getz, James Gilbert, Janet Golden, Wendy Z. Goldman, Jonathan Goldstein, Linda Gordon, Sarah Barringer Gordon, Victoria de Grazia, Monica H. Green, Cheryl Greenberg, Robert Griffith, Gerald N. Grob, Carol Groneman, Michael Grossberg, Atina Grossman, Gay L. Gullickson,

Jacquelyn Hall, Marilyn Halter, Yukiko Hanawa, Sarah Hanley, Louis R. Harlan, Harry Haroutunian, Barbara J. Harris, John M. Headley, Dorothy O. Helly, Lamar M. Hill, Darlene C. Hine, Joan Hoff, David A. Hollinger, Joel D. Howell, Karl Hufbauer, Isabel V. Hull, Tera Hunter, George Huppert, Paula E. Hyman, Karl Ittmann, Penelope D. Johnson, Peter d'A. Jones, David P. Jordan, Carol F. Karlsen, Stanley N. Katz, Mary Kelley, Linda K. Kerber, Alice Kessler-Harris, Rachel N. Klein, Christine Kleinegger, Claudia Koonz,

Judith Walzer Leavitt, Helen Rodnite Lemay, Darline Gay Levy, Richard S. Levy, Arthur S. Link, Leon F. Litwack, Lawrence D. Longo, Kristin Luker, Elizabeth Lunbeck, Michael A. Lutzker, Phyllis Mack, Frances Malino, Lynn Mally, Elaine Tyler May, Sean D. M. McConville, Stephanie McCurry, Deborah Kuhn McGregor, Sally G. McMillen, Barbara Melosh, Michael Meranze, Walter P. Metzger, Joanne Meyerowitz, Marion Miller, John Modell, Robert Moeller, David Montgomery, Regina Morantz-Sanchez, William Scott Morton, Claire G. Moses, Robyn Muncy, Tetsuo Najita, Guity Nashat, Bruce Nelson, David W. Noble, Mary Nolan, Philip Nord, Mary Beth Norton M.D.,

Mary E. Odem, Annelise Orleck, Michael E. Parrish, K. David Patterson, Kathy Peiss, Martin S. Pernick, Edward Pessen, Rosalind Petchesky, Charles A. Peterson, Marilyn H. Pettit, Walter M. Pintner, Richard Polenberg, Carl E. Prince, Linda C. A. Przybyszewski, David L. Ransel, Leslie Reagan, James Reed, David M. Reimers, Susan M. Reverby, Rebecca Rodgers, Malcolm Rohrbough, Mary Roldan, Ruth Rosen, Emily S. Rosenberg, Norman L. Rosenberg,

David Rosner, Dorothy Ross, Ellen Ross, Guenther Roth, Leslie S. Rowland, Teofilo Ruiz, Mary Ryan,

Kenneth Sacks, Todd L. Savitt, Leo Schelbert, Arthur Schlesinger Jr., Leslie Schwalm, Anne Firor Scott, Joan W. Scott, Jerrold Seigel, Brenda K. Shelton, Barbara Sicherman, Sara Lee Silberman, Miriam Silverberg, David C. Sloane, Daniel Scott Smith, Barbara G. Sniffen, Rayman L. Solomon, Leo Spitzer, Amy Dru Stanley, Christine Stansell, Stephen J. Stearns, Allan Steinberg, Nancy Leys Stepan, David L. Sterling, Deborah A. Stone, Lawrence Stone, Margaret Strobel, Anita Tien, Barbara L. Tischler, Nancy J. Tomes, Christopher L. Tomlins, Randolph Trumbach, Jules Tygiel,

Mary Kay Vaughan, Morris J. Vogel, Rachel Vorspan, Linda J. Waite, Samuel Walker, Daniel J. Walkowitz, Anne Walthall, Patricia Spain Ward, Susan Ware, Susan Cotts Watkins, Sydney Stahl Weinberg, Lynn Y. Weiner, Jonathan Wiener, Barbara Winslow, Peter H. Wood, Gwendolyn Wright, Winthrop R. Wright, Virginia Yans, Madeline C. Zilfi, Judith P. Zinsser, and Michael Zuckerman.

BRIEFS SUPPORTING THE PENNSYLVANIA LAW RESTRICTING ABORTION

BRIEF FOR RESPONDENTS
AND CROSS-PETITIONERS

STATEMENT OF THE CASE

This action challenges the constitutionality of amendments enacted in 1988 and 1989 to Pennsylvania's Abortion Control Act, 18 Pa. Cons. Stat. §§ 3201–3220 (1990). Petitioners, five abortion facilities, and a class of physicians who provide abortions, J.A. 42–43 (order certifying class), sought declaratory and injunctive relief against a wide array of the 1988 and 1989 amendments. The challenged provisions regulate but do not prohibit abortions. The one provision of the Act which does contain an outright prohibition, § 3204(c) (no abortion to be performed solely because of the sex of the unborn child), was not challenged.

I. PROCEDURAL HISTORY

The United States District Court for the Eastern District of Pennsylvania issued a preliminary injunction against certain provisions of the Act before their effective date. J.A. 72–73 (order).

After a bench trial, the District Court issued a permanent injunction granting petitioners virtually all the relief they had requested. The District Court enjoined implementation of provisions of the Act relating to informed consent, parental consent for abortions on minors, spousal notification, public disclosure of certain reports, and the collection of certain other information. 238a–262a, 266a–279a, 285a–287a. In addition, the District Court enjoined implementation of all provisions of the Act that contain an exception for medical emergencies on the ground that that exception was inadequate. 235a–237a, 286a. Respondents appealed.[1]

The Court of Appeals largely reversed the District Court, the three-judge panel unanimously holding most of the challenged provisions of the Act constitutional. 1a–86a. The sole exception was the spousal notice provision, on which the panel divided. The two judges of the majority held this provision unconstitutional, 60a–80a, while the dissenting judge, believing the spousal notice provision to be constitutional, would have reversed the District Court on this point as well. 96a–103a.

To ascertain the correct standard of review, the Court of Appeals turned for guidance to *Marks* v. *United States*, 430 U.S. 188 (1977). 20a–21a. Applying the principles of *Marks* to the Court's fragmented decisions in *Webster* v. *Reproductive Health Services*, 492 U.S. 490 (1989) and *Hodgson* v. *Minnesota*, 110 S. Ct. 2926 (1990), the Court of Appeals identified Justice O'Connor's concurring opinions in *Webster* and *Hodgson* as embodying the controlling standard of those cases. That standard, which the Court of Appeals called the "undue burden" standard, "appl[ies] strict scrutiny review to regulations that impose an undue burden [on the right to abortion] and rational basis review to those which do not." 30a.

Applying this undue burden standard to Pennsylvania's Abortion Control Act, the Court of Appeals held that except for the spousal notice provision, none of the challenged provisions imposed an undue burden and all had some rational basis on their face.[2] 32a–85a.

---

1. Petitioners had asked the District Court to enjoin the collection of virtually all information on abortions, and to enjoin the Act's requirement that the gestational age of the unborn child be ascertained, but the District Court was unwilling to go so far. 263a–266a, 269a–279a. These were the only respects in which the petitioners were unsuccessful in the District Court, and they did not appeal.

2. Because the Act has never been allowed to go into effect, the petitioners' attack on it could only be a facial one.

II. FACTS

Despite what the petitioners say, Br. for Cross-Respondents, No. 91–902, at 3 n.4, the respondents did challenge the District Court's findings of fact on appeal, and continue to do so here.[3] Many of the District Court's errors were of omission. The following discussion therefore relies not only on the District Court's findings, but also upon facts which, although omitted by the District Court, were either admitted by the petitioners or testified to by witnesses whom they called and whom the District Court found "credible in all respects." 115a, 117a–122a.

A. The Definition of Medical Emergency

In cases of medical emergencies, defined in Section 3203 of the Act, compliance with a number of the Act's requirements is excused.[4] A medical emergency is: that condition which, on the basis of the physician's good faith clinical judgment, so complicates the medical condition of a pregnant woman as to necessitate the immediate termination of her pregnancy to avert her death or for which a delay will create serious risk of substantial and irreversible impairment of a major bodily function. *Id.*

The petitioners contended that this definition was too narrow, and the evidence centered around three medical conditions—preeclampsia, inevitable abortion, and premature ruptured membrane—which the petitioners claimed required immediate termination of pregnancy and yet would not fall within the Act's definition of a medical emergency.[5]

---

3. Again despite what the petitioners say, Pet. Br. at [29] n.6, the Court of Appeals held that some of these findings were unsupported by the record, 38a–40a, 79a–80a, 83a, while others were insufficient to establish the statute's unconstitutionality under the more deferential standard of review the Court of Appeals employed. *E.g.*, 46a, 49a, 51a, 53a–54a, 78a.

4. Medical emergencies permit physicians and women to forego the requirements concerning determination of gestational age, § 3204; informed consent, § 3205; parental consent, § 3206; spousal notification, § 3209; and conditions placed on third trimester abortions, § 3211(c).

5. The petitioners' witness Dr. Bolognese, who is certified as a specialist by the American College of Obstetricians and Gynecologists (ACOG), 121a–122a, was asked on cross-examination if there were any other such situations. He could identify only two: a patient with severe and uncontrolled hypertension, or with severe

The expert witnesses called by both sides agreed that pre-eclampsia places the patient at risk of liver and kidney destruction, eclampsia (a seizure disorder of the brain), cerebral hemorrhage, and respiratory distress, all leading to death. J.A. 195–196, 201–202 (testimony of Dr. Bolognese), 332–335 (testimony of Dr. Bowes). Inevitable abortion can cause severe hemorrhaging, leading to shock, infection, and death. J.A. 120–126 (testimony of Dr. Davidson), 331–332 (testimony of Dr. Bowes). Premature ruptured membrane can produce an overwhelming sepsis, loss of the ability to clot blood, hemorrhaging, shock, and death. J.A. 190–195, 200–201 (testimony of Dr. Bolognese), 335–336 (testimony of Dr. Bowes). In fact, these conditions are three of the major causes of maternal death in the United States. J.A. 195 (testimony of Dr. Bolognese).

B. Informed Consent

The Act's informed consent provisions require that, twenty-four hours before an abortion, a physician provide the pregnant woman with medical information on the risks and alternatives to abortion, the gestational age of the unborn child, and the risks of carrying to term. In addition, either a physician or counselor must advise the woman of possible childbirth and paternal support benefits, and the availability of printed materials concerning fetal development and agencies offering alternatives to abortion. 18 Pa. Cons. Stat. §§ 3205(a), 3208.

All of the petitioners currently do inform their patients of the risks and alternatives to abortion, using standardized forms and rote recitations. 134a, 138a; J.A. 398 (counseling guidelines), 410 (consent form), 449, 451–456 (procedure manual), 461–463 (disclosure form), 479–482 (consent form). One of the petitioners processes patients in groups of four, 134a, and two of them use consent forms whose wording is identical to that of § 3205(a)(1)(i). J.A. 464, 469 (consent forms). All

---

and uncontrolled diabetes. He testified that if these pregnancies are not terminated, the hypertensive patient could "stroke out" and suffer permanent paralysis or die, while the diabetic patient faces a diabetic coma or diabetic seizures. J.A. 198–199. The petitioners did not rely on either of these scenarios in the courts below, and indeed it seems obvious that both are medical emergencies within the meaning of Section 3203.

of the petitioners likewise determine the gestational age. J.A. 105 (stipulation); and two of them advise all women, regardless of circumstances, of the risks of carrying to term. J.A. 449, 455–456 (procedure manual), 461 (disclosure form).

To convey this information, the petitioner clinics rely on counselors rather than physicians. These counselors are often part-time employees paid $15,000 or less per year. J.A. 109 (stipulation), 537 (testimony of Sherley Hollas).[6] Most of the petitioners have no minimum educational requirements for these counselors, 149a, J.A. 109–110 (stipulation), 524 (testimony of Sue Roselle), 529 (testimony of Carol Wall),[7] who are not qualified to answer questions on, for example, fetal development. J.A. 266–267 (testimony of Sue Roselle). The petitioners produced no evidence that quantified what the effect would be upon the cost or availability of abortions if this information were to be conveyed by physicians, as § 3205 requires, rather than by counselors.

In addition to conveying the medical information just discussed, most petitioners also require counselors to provide "options counseling" to women about the alternatives to abortion. 49a, 138a, 142a, 146a–147a; J.A. 393, 398, 410, 448, 461, 469, 474 (forms, guidelines, procedure manuals). The clinics either offer, or provide upon request, information and referrals on fetal development (including photographs), financial support, medical assistance benefits, and agencies providing an alternative to abortion. J.A. 153 (testimony of petitioner Allen), 257–258, 267–68 (testimony of Sue Roselle), 401–405, 444–447, 458–459, 474 (forms, guidelines, procedure manuals).

As to the 24-hour waiting period, the evidence showed that a delay as short as this adds no measurable risk to the abortion procedure. J.A. 136 (testimony of petitioner Allen). In the first trimester, which is when 94% of abortions in Pennsylvania are performed, 150a, a delay of even a week results in no additional risk. J.A. 552 (Rule 36 admission by petitioners). Increases in risk are measurable only over spans

---

6. Hollas is executive director of petitioner Women's Suburban Clinic. J.A. 532.

7. Roselle is executive director of petitioner Women's Health Services, 117a; Wall is executive director of petitioner Planned Parenthood of Southeast Pennsylvania. Defendants' Exhibit 56, p. 7.

of two to three weeks, and even then are very small. For example, if an abortion is delayed from the 9–10 week range to the 11–12 week range, the mortality rate rises from 0.8 per 100,000 to 1.1 per 100,000. 153a. Even in the 15th and 16th weeks, abortion is twice as safe as a tonsillectomy and a hundred times safer than an appendectomy. 153a; J.A. 137 (testimony of petitioner Allen).

Some delay is already built into the petitioners' procedures. Most women make two trips to the abortion provider, once for a pregnancy test and once for the actual abortion. The petitioners will not even schedule an abortion until the patient has a positive pregnancy test, and the abortion is then scheduled within one to two weeks thereafter. 133a, 136a, 141a–142a, 146a; J.A. 87, 90–91, 95, 98 (stipulation). The petitioners encourage and sometimes require additional delays when a minor wishes to involve her parents, J.A. 105 (stipulation), when a woman appears ambivalent about her decision, J.A. 93, 96, 98–99, 104–105 (stipulation), and, in one case, when a woman expresses a "politically incorrect" view on abortion. J.A. 486 (consent form), 546 (testimony of Sylvia Stengle).[8]

C. Parental Consent

In 1988, about 12% of the abortions in Pennsylvania were performed on minors under the age of 18. 150a. Section 3206 of the Act requires the informed consent of one parent for a minor who desires an abortion, but provides a judicial bypass option if the minor does not, or cannot, obtain a parent's consent. 18 Pa. Cons. Stat. § 3206.

All of the petitioners encourage minors to discuss their decision with their parents, and encourage parents to accompany their daughter to the abortion clinic. J.A. 105 (stipulation). One petitioner requires that all minors be accompanied by an adult, although not necessarily a parent. 135a. Between 50% and 60% of the minors whom petitioners see are in fact accompanied by one or more parents. 131a, 135a, 139a. In such cases, two of the petitioners require that

---

8. Executive director of petitioner Allentown Women's Center. 118a; J.A. 541.

both the parent and the child sign consent forms. 139a; J.A. 475 (counseling checklist). In addition, the hospital where petitioner Allen practices requires written parental consent before any minor has an abortion. J.A. 104 (stipulation).

D. Spousal Notice

Under Section 3209, a married woman who is about to undergo an abortion must notify her husband of her intention, unless her husband is not the father, or she cannot locate her husband, or the pregnancy is the result of a spousal sexual assault reported to a law enforcement agency, or she fears physical injury. The woman must provide her doctor with a signed statement under penalty of perjury that she has so notified her husband or that she qualifies for one of the exceptions. 18 Pa. Cons. Stat. § 3209.

Section 3209 affects few women. Only 20% of women who obtain abortions are unmarried, 93a; of those, 95% notify their husband. J.A. 243 (testimony of Sue Roselle). The most common reasons for nondisclosure are the husband's illness, the failure of the marriage, or the husband's opposition to abortion. J.A. 244–245 (testimony of Sue Roselle).

Although women who fear physical abuse are exempted from notifying their husbands, petitioners focused on the adequacy of this exception. Petitioners' expert testified that some women who are in a "battering relationship" can suffer from a form of mental disorder called Post-Traumatic Stress Disorder. As a result, some of these women have a psychological inability to avail themselves of Section 3209's exception for fear of physical abuse. 200a–201a; J.A. 219–227, 231–32 (testimony of Lenore Walker).

There was no testimony, however, on how many of the small group of married women seeking abortions without disclosing it to their husbands are battered. 95a; J.A. 235, 239–240 (testimony of Lenore Walker), 392 (testimony of Jean Dillon).[9] Nor was there any testimony on how many of these battered women—who are able to conceal their pregnancies,

9. Dillon is a counselor at the Women's Resource Center of Monroe County and is a member of the Pennsylvania Coalition Against Domestic Violence. 124a–125a, J.A. 387–388.

arrange and have an abortion, and pay for it without their battering husband's knowledge[10]—would be psychologically unable to check a line on a form. 93a–95a & n.6; J.A. 504–505 (spousal notice form). Nor was there evidence on how many women would be unable to invoke Section 3209's other exceptions to notification, or suffer ill effects with disclosure. 93a.

E. Confidential Medical Reports

For the purpose of collecting data for medical and public health knowledge, Section 3214(a) requires each abortion provider to file a confidential report for each abortion performed. 18 Pa. Cons. Stat. § 3214(a). 302a–304a. A variety of information is to be collected, including the basis for a physician's medical judgment concerning the necessity of third-trimester and medical emergency abortions, and the determination of gestational age. Id., § 3214(a)(8), (10), (11). A referring physician's identity, in addition to the performing physician's identity, also is to be collected. Id., § 3214(a)(1). The reports are not open for public inspection, with various safeguards ensuring that the reports are kept confidential.[11] Id., § 3214(b); 75a, 206a–208a, 269a, 277a.

The reporting requirement concerning a physician's medical judgment gathers relevant data relating to maternal health, especially in the area of medically necessary abortions. 78a–79a. Recording the information also ensures compliance with the Act's provisions. 79a.

As to the referring physician's identity, a referring physician may make the required gestational age determination, § 3210(a), and provide informed consent, § 3205(a). 80a. In reviewing reporting forms, the Department of Health occa-

10. Petitioner's expert testified that batterers constantly monitor their wives' activities, thoughts, and feelings—making it difficult for the woman to obtain an abortion. J.A. 212–213, 227, 237 (testimony of Lenore Walker). Yet, any woman must first obtain a pregnancy test to even schedule an appointment. J.A. 95, 98 (stipulations), 263 (testimony of Sue Roselle). Scheduling delays up to two weeks typically occur. J.A. 90–95 (stipulations), 241 (testimony of Sue Roselle).

11. Defendants' Exhibit 47C (J.A. 500–503) is the data collection form the Pennsylvania Department of Health will use to collect the data if petitioners' challenge is rejected. Defendants' Exhibit 47A (J.A. 493–96) is the data collection form presently used.

sionally finds it necessary to contact the performing physician directly, 220a; it may be equally necessary to contact the referring physician for information. 80a.

These reporting requirements increase abortion costs only by "at most a few dollars per abortion." 78a; J.A. 91 (stipulation), 246 (testimony of Sue Roselle). Otherwise, there was no evidence to establish a drastic increase in delays or the reduced availability of abortions.[12] 78a, 80a.

F. Publicly Available Reports

Sections 3207(b) and 3214(f) require every abortion facility to file two reports—one identifying its name, address, and corporate affiliations, and the other showing the total number of abortions performed the preceding year, broken down by trimester. 18 Pa. Cons. Stat. §§ 3207(b), 3214(f) (reporting forms). If a facility receives State-appropriated money for the preceding 12 months, these reports are available for public inspection and copying.[13] Id. Petitioners oppose public availability of these reports due to their fear that such would expose them to harassment and protests.

Presently, petitioners advertise in telephone directories, newspapers, radio broadcasts, and other media. J.A. 111 (stipulation); 441–43, 473, 484–485 (advertisements), 525 (testimony of Sue Roselle). Petitioners also encounter public protests on a regular basis—even though Sections 3207(b) and 3214(f) have never been in effect. 83a, 211a–213a; J.A. 259–260, 270 (testimony of Sue Roselle). The only evidence that the public availability of the facility and statistical reports would somehow increase these ongoing protests was petitioners' fear that it would happen. 82a–83a, 213a.

---

12. In concluding that physicians might stop referring women for abortions if their names are identified in a confidential report, the District Court relied solely upon hearsay over respondents' repeated objections. 220a–221a; J.A. 30–31, 144, 153–54 (testimony of Sue Roselle, petitioner Allen).

13. For the facility registration report, which a facility files only once, the 12 months run from the date of the request to inspect and copy. For the quarterly statistical report, the 12 months run from the date of the report.

SUMMARY OF ARGUMENT

1. *Roe* v. *Wade*, properly understood and applied, permits states to regulate abortions as Pennsylvania has done in its Abortion Control Act. Contrary to what the petitioners say, the Court therefore need not, although it certainly may, use this case as a vehicle for re-examining *Roe*.

Roe does not establish an absolute or unlimited right to abortion on demand, but instead attempts to establish a limited right which also respects the important state interests which exist in protecting fetal life and maternal health, and in other areas. As Justice O'Connor has demonstrated, the Court early formulated the undue burden test to accommodate these important state interests, and that test remains the most appropriate standard for fulfilling *Roe*'s promise that those interests will be respected.

The strict scrutiny of all abortion regulation which petitioners demand is not consistent with *Roe*. This standard's undisguised hostility to any state regulation of the abortion industry would eviscerate *Roe*'s expressed concern for the important state interests at stake, and would instead convert *Roe* into a regime of abortion on demand.

2. None of the provisions of Pennsylvania's law imposes an undue burden on abortion, and all of them further one or more legitimate State interests. The Act contains an adequate exception for medical emergencies, which excuses compliance with many of the Act's requirements. Petitioners failed to show, in any concrete way, that this provision would operate to affect medical care adversely.

The Act's informed consent provisions require the petitioners to provide their patients with accurate, objective, and relevant information at a time and in a manner that encourages well-informed and well-considered decision-making. These provisions are in principle no different from the disclosures which other industries must make to their consumers; and they are consistent with other Pennsylvania law on informed consent, and even with many of the petitioners' own practices. Since the petitioners' scheduling practices require most women to make two trips to an abortion provider in any event, complying with the Act's informed consent provisions will impose little or no burden.

The Act's parental consent provision, with its judicial bypass, complies with this Court's decisions which repeatedly have upheld such requirements. The petitioners' argument that Pennsylvania may require such consent, but may not require that it be "informed," cannot be taken seriously.

To support their facial challenge to the Act's spousal notice provision, the petitioners rely on a worst case scenario that may never happen; there is no evidence that this provision will have the broad practical effect of severely inhibiting access to abortions. The requirement does, however, serve the legitimate purpose of enabling a husband to protect his interests, which the Court has recognized, in the life of the fetus and in his marriage. The petitioners' equal protection claim ignores the Court's repeated admonition that abortion, which involves the purposeful destruction of the fetus, is different from all other medical procedures and may be treated differently. Their claim that the right of privacy in marital communications shields an attempt by one spouse to conceal something from the other is nonsensical.

The Act's reporting requirements serve obvious and legitimate State purposes in protecting maternal health and ensuring compliance with the Act, and they impose no undue burden, either by disclosing confidential information or impeding access to abortion.

As to the disclosure of the identity of abortion facilities which receive tax dollars, the public certainly has a legitimate interest in knowing how its money is being spent. In any event, the petitioners, all of whom advertise their identity and location to the public, can hardly complain that they are harmed by the "disclosure" of information which is already known. All of the Act's provisions are therefore constitutional under *Roe*.

3. Having said all this, it is nevertheless true that *Roe v. Wade* was incorrectly decided, and the Court may wish to take this occasion to review and overrule it. *Roe*'s identification of the abortion right as fundamental finds no support in the Constitution, in history, in a societal consensus, or in the Court's own precedents, and its use of trimesters and viability

to define the contours of that right is at bottom arbitrary. Because of these flaws, *Roe* stands as a source of instability in the law and as a barrier to public understanding of the proper function of the Court in our system of government. *Roe* should share the fate of *Lochner* v. *New York*, its equally ill-conceived forerunner in substantive due process.

ARGUMENT

I. THE COURT NEED NOT REVISIT *ROE* V. *WADE* IN THIS CASE, EXCEPT TO REAFFIRM WHAT IT HAS SAID ABOUT THE LIMITS OF THE RIGHT *ROE* RECOGNIZED.

A. *Roe* Established Only a Limited Right to Abortion, Subject to Reasonable State Regulation to Safeguard Important State Interests.

The linchpin of the petitioners' argument is their assertion that *Roe* v. *Wade*, 410 U.S. 113 (1973), demands "the most exacting scrutiny," Pet. Br. at [41], of all state laws regulating abortion; that Pennsylvania's statute, which they regard as "highly intrusive and burdensome," Pet. Br. at [27], cannot survive such exacting review; and that the Court therefore cannot uphold any part of this statute without overruling *Roe*. Pet. Br. at [40–42]. Petitioners are mistaken. While there are certainly good reasons to overrule *Roe*, and while the Court may well decide that this is an appropriate occasion for reexamining that decision, *see* [204–208] *infra*, there is no necessity for the Court to do so. Pennsylvania's statute comports with *Roe* in all respects; in upholding it, the Court need not address the issue of whether to overrule *Roe*. This is so, partly because the statute is neither burdensome nor intrusive, but mainly because the petitioners seriously misperceive the holding in *Roe*.

The petitioners evidently regard *Roe* as establishing a right to abortion which is absolute, or nearly so, and as holding that virtually all state regulation of abortion is presumptively invalid, sustainable, if at all, only after the most searching—and hostile—judicial scrutiny.[14] Pet. Br. at [58]. In doing so, the petitioners largely ignore what *Roe* actually says, and likewise ignore the way the Court has, for the most part, applied *Roe.*

Roe held that "the Fourteenth Amendment's concept of personal liberty and restrictions upon state action . . . is broad enough to encompass a woman's decision whether or not to terminate her pregnancy." *Id.* at 153. In *Roe* itself, however, the Court emphasized the limited nature of the right it had just recognized:

> [A]ppellant . . . argue[s] that the woman's right is absolute and that she is entitled to terminate her pregnancy at whatever time, in whatever way, and for whatever reason she alone chooses. With this we do not agree. . . . The privacy right involved . . . cannot be said to be absolute. . . . [There is no] unlimited right to do with one's body as one pleases. . . .

Id. at 153–154. *Roe*'s companion case, *Doe* v. *Bolton*, 410 U.S. 179 (1973), underscored this point: "[A] pregnant woman does not have an absolute constitutional right to abortion on her demand." *Id.* at 189. As *Roe*, 410 U.S. at 159, pointed out, "[t]he pregnant woman cannot be isolated in her privacy. She carries an embryo and, later, a fetus," and some measure of state regulation is therefore "reasonable and appropriate."

States have legitimate and important interests in "safeguarding health, in maintaining medical standards, . . . in protecting potential life[,]" *id.* at 154, and in other respects as well, *see, e.g., H.L.* v. *Matheson*, 450 U.S. 398, 411 (1981) (family integrity and protection of minors). In furthering these interests, states may treat abortion, because of its unique nature, differently than other medical procedures. *Matheson*, 450

14. Not content with the traditional formulation of "strict scrutiny"—that, to survive it, laws "may be justified only by compelling state interests, and must be narrowly drawn to express only those interests," *Carey* v. *Population Services International*, 431 U.S. 678, 686 (1977)—petitioners have invented a new "ultra-strict scrutiny," under which "only laws *necessary* and *narrowly tailored* to serve the *most compelling state interests* pass constitutional review." Pet. Br. at [41] (emphases added). There is, of course, no warrant for this novel standard in *Roe* or any other of the Court's abortion-related cases.

U.S. at 412; *Bellotti v. Baird*, 428 U.S. 132, 148–149 (1976) (*Bellotti I*); *Planned Parenthood of Missouri v. Danforth*, 428 U.S. 52, 67 (1976). A state need not "fine-tune its statutes so as to encourage or facilitate abortions[,]" *Matheson*, 450 U.S. at 413. To the contrary, states may adopt policies " 'encouraging childbirth' " over abortion " 'except in the most urgent circumstances.' " *Ibid.*, quoting *Harris v. McRae*, 448 U.S. 297, 325 (1980); *accord, Maher v. Roe*, 432 U.S. 464, 473–474 (1977).

Of all this, there is not the slightest hint in the petitioners' brief. Petitioners' one-sided reading of *Roe* would jettison its carefully limited holding in favor of abortion on demand, and would engraft onto the Constitution their own implacable hostility to any State regulation of their industry.[15] *Roe* recognized not just a right, but necessary and appropriate limits on that right, and this case requires the Court to take seriously, as the petitioners do not, what *Roe* said about those limits.

Regrettably, the Court has not always done so in the past. While this case does not require the Court to repudiate *Roe*, it does require that the Court again repudiate the approach to review of abortion laws of such cases as *Thornburgh v. American College of Obstetricians and Gynecologists*, 476 U.S. 747 (1986), and *Akron v. Akron Center for Reproductive Health*, 462 U.S. 416 (1983), in which the Court seemed eager to seize upon any excuse to strike down any state regulation of abortion. *See, e.g., Thornburgh*, 476 U.S. at 812 (White, J., dissenting) (Court strains to avoid a permissible reading of the statute). Petitioners see this overt hostility to state interests as the essence of *Roe*, but we believe that the dissenting Justices in those cases were correct in asserting that it was the Court's approach, and not the state regulations under attack, which was inconsistent with *Roe*. *See Thornburgh*, 476 U.S. at 783 (Burger, C.J., dissenting) ("The Court has departed from the limitations expressed in *Roe*"); *id.* at 808 (White, J., dissenting) ("The Court's ruling . . . is *not even consistent* with . . . *Roe*") (emphasis in original); *id.* at 829 (O'Connor, J., dissenting) (Court's new test a "dangerous extravagance");

---

15. Petitioners, it bears remembering, are not "women facing unwanted pregnancies," Pet. Br. at [58], but a group of organizations and individuals who are in the business of providing abortions. J.A. 86–87, 89, 91–92, 94, 96–97 (stipulation).

Akron, 462 U.S. at 462–463 (O'Connor, J., dissenting) (Court's analysis inconsistent with previous abortion cases); *see also Colautti* v. *Franklin,* 439 U.S. 379, 401 (1979) (White, J., dissenting) (Court withdrawing from the states some of the power reserved to them in *Roe*). The Court has, we think, already repudiated this approach in *Webster* v. *Reproductive Health Services,* 492 U.S. 490, 521 (1989) (opinion of Rehnquist, C.J.) ("no doubt that our holding today will allow some governmental regulation of abortion that would have been prohibited under the language of such cases as *Colautti* . . . and *Akron.* . . ."), *Hodgson* v. *Minnesota,* 110 S. Ct. 2926 (1990), and *Ohio* v. *Akron Center for Reproductive Health,* 110 S. Ct. 2972 (1990).

In this case, the Court should again reaffirm *Roe's* holding that the right to abortion is not absolute or unlimited, but must accommodate legitimate and important state interests. In our view, that accommodation is best served, short of overruling *Roe*, by employing the "undue burden" standard for reviewing state regulation of abortion.

B. Under *Roe* and Its Progeny, State Regulation of Abortion Is Properly Evaluated Under the "Undue Burden" Standard.

In her dissenting opinion in *Akron,* 462 U.S. at 452, Justice O'Connor, writing for herself and two other Justices, stated her understanding of the correct standard for evaluating state abortion regulations under *Roe* and its progeny:

[N]ot every regulation that the State imposes must be measured against the State's compelling interests and examined with strict scrutiny. This Court has acknowledged that "the right in *Roe* v. *Wade* can be understood only by considering both the woman's interest and the nature of the State's interference with it. *Roe* did not declare an unqualified 'constitutional right to an abortion' . . . Rather, the right protects the woman from unduly burdensome interference with her freedom to decide whether to terminate her pregnancy." . . . If the impact of the regulation does not rise to the level appropriate for our strict scrutiny, then our inquiry is limited to whether the state law bears "some rational relationship to legitimate state purposes."

. . . .

The "undue burden" required in the abortion cases represents the threshold inquiry that must be conducted before this Court can require a State to justify its actions under the exacting "compelling state interest" standard. *Id.* at 461–463; *Thornburgh*, 476 U.S. at 828 (O'Connor, J., dissenting); *Hodgson*, 110 S. Ct. at 2949–2950 (O'Connor, J., concurring in part and concurring in the judgment in part).

This formulation has come to be known as the "undue burden" standard. Petitioners dismiss it as a "novel concept," Pet. Br. at [56], "which has never commanded a majority or even a plurality of this Court," *id.* at [55], but in this they are quite wrong. As Justice O'Connor has demonstrated, "[t]hese principles for evaluating state regulation of abortion were not newly minted" in her *Akron* dissent. *Thornburgh*, 476 U.S. at 828 (O'Connor, J., dissenting). The "undue burden" standard first appeared shortly after *Roe*, in *Bellotti I*, 428 U.S. at 147, and *Danforth*,[16] and was then "articulated and applied with fair consistency . . . in cases such as *Harris* v. *McRae*, 448 U.S. 297, 314 (1980), *Maher* v. *Roe*, 432 U.S. 464, 473 (1977), [and] *Beal* v. *Doe*, 432 U.S. 438, 446 (1977). . . ." *Thornburgh*, 476 U.S. at 828 (O'Connor, J., dissenting). *See Akron*, 462 U.S. at 461–462, n.8 (O'Connor, J., dissenting) (collecting cases). Even in *Akron*, the majority followed this undue burden approach in some respects, *id.* 476 U.S. at 829 (O'Connor, J., dissenting). It was not until *Thornburgh* that the Court made a "clean break with precedent," *id.* at 829 (O'Connor, J., dissenting), discarding any variant of the undue burden standard in favor of the "dangerous extravagance," *ibid.*, of striking down any abortion regulation which "pose[d] an unacceptable danger of deterring the exercise of [the] right." *Id.* at 767–768.

"An undue burden will generally be found in situations involving absolute obstacles or severe limitations on the abor-

---

16. The Court in *Danforth* did not explicitly use the undue burden standard, but in *Bellotti I*, decided the same day, the Court explained that "we held [in *Danforth*] that a requirement of written consent . . . is not unconstitutional unless it unduly burdens the right to seek an abortion." *Bellotti I*, 428 U.S. at 147.

tion decision. . . ." *Id.* at 828 (O'Connor, J., dissenting) (citations and quotations omitted). Thus, in *Roe* itself, the Court struck down a Texas law that prohibited all abortions except those necessary to save the life of the mother. In *Danforth*, the Court invalidated parental consent and spousal consent provisions which allowed third parties to interpose an absolute, and possibly arbitrary, veto on the right to seek an abortion; and likewise invalidated a ban on saline amniocentesis because it had the practical effect of prohibiting most abortions after 12 weeks.

On the other hand, an undue burden does not exist just because a state regulation "may inhibit abortions to some degree." *Thornburgh*, 476 U.S. at 828 (O'Connor, J., dissenting). Thus, in *Planned Parenthood Ass'n v. Ashcroft*, 462 U.S. 476 (1983), five members of the Court joined in upholding a Missouri statute that required a pathology report for all abortions, even though it added about $20 to the cost of each abortion. *Id.* at 490 (opinion of Powell, J.) (extra cost does not "significantly burden" the abortion decision); *id.* at 505 (O'Connor, J., concurring in part and dissenting in part) ("no undue burden"). Similarly, in *Matheson* the Court held "[T]hat the requirement of notice to parents may inhibit some minors from seeking abortions is not a valid basis to void the statute." *Id.* 450 U.S. at 413. See *Akron*, 462 U.S. at 466–467, 472–473 (O'Connor, J., dissenting) (no undue burden imposed by hospitalization for second-trimester abortions and 24-hour waiting period).

The respondents are of course aware of the substantial criticism leveled against the undue burden standard—that it is a standard essentially without content, licensing judges with unchanneled discretion to follow their own subjective leanings.[17] See *Webster*, 492 U.S. at 536 n. * (Scalia, J., concurring

17. The petitioners' other attacks on the undue burden standard, see Pet. Br. at [55–58], require little comment. Their complaint that it is "novel" and therefore unknown, *id.* at [55–56], we have already shown to be unfounded. Their complaint that it is "inadequate" because it would allow forms of regulation that they oppose, *id.* at [56], is pure question-begging. Their final complaint, that the undue burden standard somehow pits "suffering" women against the State in an unequal contest of litigation resources, *id.* at [58], is odd in a brief with the names of fourteen lawyers on its cover; the petitioners at any rate do not lack litigation resources. Nor is this an accident: as a glance at the captions on the Court's abortion cases will confirm, ever since the Court's holding in *Bolton*, 410 U.S. at 188–189, that abortion providers

in part and concurring in the judgment). This criticism is to some degree unfair. The undue burden standard is, after all, not the only test the Court uses that lacks mathematical precision: if the concept of an "undue burden" is not self-defining, neither is that of a "compelling state interest." And, to take an example from another area, when, exactly, does state regulation go "too far" and become a taking of property for which compensation is required? Cf. Pennsylvania Coal Co. v. Mahon, 260 U.S. 393 (1922), with Keystone Bituminous Coal Assn. v. DeBenedictis, 480 U.S. 470 (1987).

Moreover, as Justice O'Connor has pointed out, "[t]he 'unduly burdensome' standard is particularly appropriate in the abortion context because of the *nature* and *scope* of the right that is involved. The privacy right in the abortion context *'cannot be said to be absolute.'* Roe, 410 U.S. at 154." Akron, 462 U.S. at 463–464 (O'Connor, J., dissenting) (emphases in original). Roe is an attempt to establish a limited fundamental right, while at the same time recognizing and accommodating the important interests of the state; and unless the Court is prepared to overrule Roe,[18] the Court should employ a judicial standard which reflects this attempt.

Neither of the obvious alternatives to undue burden analysis accommodates both of the interests which Roe recognized as important. The adoption of rational basis analysis for all abortion regulation is, we believe, simply a way of overruling Roe's attempt to carve out a special constitutional status for the abortion decision. Webster, 492 U.S. at 532 (Scalia, J., concurring in part and concurring in judgment); id. at 556 (Blackmun, J., dissenting); Thornburgh, 476 U.S. at 789–90, 796 (White, J., dissenting); Roe, 410 U.S. at 172–173 (Rehnquist, J., dissenting). Similarly, to decree strict scrutiny for all such regulation does equal violence to Roe, albeit in a very different way, by reducing to "shallow rhetoric" its expressed concern for the important state interests at stake. Thornburgh, 476 U.S. at 784 (Burger, C.J., dissenting). To the extent, then,

---

have standing to assert the rights of pregnant women, the brunt of the litigation against abortion regulation has been borne by the abortion providers who have an economic stake in it.

18. As an alternative argument, we ask the Court to do just that. See [204–208] infra.

that the criticism of undue burden analysis as indeter-
minate and standardless is valid, the fault lies not so much
with the undue burden test as with *Roe* itself. If the undue
burden test is unworkable, it is because *Roe* itself is unworkable.

The respondents are also aware that, however impeccable
its lineage, the undue burden standard apparently does not
now command a majority on the Court, and may indeed retain
the support of only a single Justice. Nevertheless, in the next
part of this brief, we analyze the provisions of Pennsylvania's
law under this standard. We do this, first, because we believe
Justice O'Connor is correct that this is the appropriate standard under *Roe* and its progeny. Second, whether Justice
O'Connor's analysis is historically accurate or not, her opinions in *Webster* and *Hodgson* embody, as the Court of Appeals
pointed out, 18a–30a, the currently governing standard under
the principles of *Marks* v. *United States*, 430 U.S. 188 (1977).
Finally, abortion regulations that pass muster under the undue
burden standard will perforce satisfy any less demanding test.
We turn, then, to the specific provisions of Pennsylvania's
statute.[19]

II. PENNSYLVANIA'S STATUTE IS IN ALL RESPECTS CONSTITUTIONAL UNDER THE UNDUE BURDEN STANDARD.

The petitioners attack the Abortion Control Act's provisions dealing with medical emergencies (§ 3203), informed
consent (§ 3205), parental consent for minors (§ 3206),

---

19. The petitioners suggest that, if their challenge to the statute under *Roe* is
rejected, the Court should remand the case for "consideration of other constitutional
principles that support the right to choose abortion." Pet. Br. at [42], n.27. In some
specific instances, the petitioners have made and preserved alternative challenges to
provisions of the statute; these are discussed in their brief and in ours. In all other
respects, while the petitioners did raise alternative grounds for relief in their complaint, J.A. 67 (complaint), they did not rely on these theories when the case was
submitted to the District Court for decision, or in the Court of Appeals. *See*
Plaintiff's Proposed Findings of Fact and Conclusions of Law, pp. 57–72 (filed June,
1990). They must therefore be considered to have abandoned these claims. *E.g.*,
EEOC v. *Westinghouse Electric Corp.*, 925 F.2d 619, 631 (3d Cir. 1991).

spousal notice (§ 3209), and reporting and disclosure of information (§§ 3207, 3214). We discuss these in turn.[20]

A. Definition of Medical Emergency

Section 3203 of the Act defines a "medical emergency" as "[t]hat condition which, on the basis of the physician's good faith clinical judgment, so complicates the medical condition of a pregnant woman as to necessitate the immediate abortion of her pregnancy to avert her death or for which a delay will create serious risk of substantial and irreversible impairment of a major bodily function."

The existence of a medical emergency, as so defined, excuses compliance with the Act's requirements as to informed consent (§ 3205), parental consent for minors (§ 3206), spousal notice (§ 3209), the determination of gestational age (§ 3210), and procedure in post-viability abortions (§ 3211).

The petitioners attacked the exception for medical emergencies as too narrow and as void for vagueness, and the District Court agreed, 235a–238a, but the Court of Appeals did not.[21] 35a–43a. In this Court, the petitioners claim that the Court of Appeals improperly rewrote the medical emergency provision, broadening it to save it from unconstitutionality, and that even as thus construed it is still too narrow. Pet. Br. at [79–80]. They do not, however, mention their earlier claim that the provision is void for vagueness, and this issue is therefore not before the Court.

Pressed in the courts below to identify concrete medical situations whose urgency would preclude complying with the Act's requirements, but which nevertheless would not constitute medical emergencies within the meaning of Section 3203, petitioners identified three: inevitable abortion, premature ruptured membrane, and preeclampsia. 36a, 237a. The

---

20. As the Court of Appeals said, 74a, n.27, the Act contains a broad severability provision that "the invalidity [of any word, phrase or provision] shall not affect any other word, phrase or provision or application of this Act which can be given effect without the invalid word, phrase, provision or application." *Supra* at [175]. Except for the medical emergency provision, which does implicate several other provisions, see 35a, we believe that all the challenged sections are severable from the Act and from each other; petitioners have not argued otherwise.

21. Technically, the District Court did not reach the petitioners' void-for-vagueness claim, but he did remark that he found it "persuasive." 237a–238a, n.32.

petitioners' own witnesses, as well as the witness for the respondents, agreed that the proper treatment for each of these conditions is to terminate the pregnancy quickly, and that to delay this treatment exposes the patient to the destruction of vital organs, hemorrhaging, shock, infection, and death. *Supra* at [170–71]. There is, we submit, no conceivable reading of Section 3203's definition of medical emergency that does not encompass these life-threatening situations.

The Court of Appeals was thus not engaged in a strained "rewrit[ing] of a state law to conform it to constitutional requirements," Pet. Br. at [80] (quotation marks and citation omitted), but in a straightforward application of the law to an undisputed set of facts. The petitioners were unable to identify any real-life situation in which the operation of the medical emergency provision would adversely affect patient care, and their challenge to that provision is thus without merit.[22]

B. Informed Consent

In their determination to rid themselves of the Act's provisions on informed consent, the petitioners have placed themselves in the odd position of arguing that many of their own practices, now that they are mandated by the Act, "jeopardize women's health," "interfere[] with the provision of quality medical care," and "serve no legitimate . . . interest." Pet. Br. at [68, 70]. Their attack on these provisions is thus best viewed not as the product of a principled disagreement with them, but simply as the knee-jerk reaction of an industry unaccustomed to regulation, to any governmental action that threatens its own prerogatives.

---

22. Despite what they said in the courts below, the petitioners now hint that there may be "other complications of pregnancy" whose proper treatment may be obstructed by the medical emergency provision. Pet. Br. at [79], n.96. They rely on the *amicus* brief submitted by ACOG, which in turn contains a laundry list of "conditions that may be exacerbated by pregnancy." Br. of American College of Obstetricians and Gynecologists et al. at [84] n.17 and [84]. Neither brief explains under what circumstances these conditions may require termination of the pregnancy, what the consequences are to the patient if the abortion is neglected or delayed, or why these situations do not fit within § 3203's definition of a medical emergency. Nor is this the time for such explanations. If these matters were worth exploring, they should have been explored at trial, not in footnotes before this Court. *See supra* at [169], n.[5] (testimony of ACOG-certified specialist).

1. Information Given by Physicians

Section 3205(a)(1) of the Act requires that the operating physician, or the referring physician, inform the woman of "the nature of the proposed procedure . . . and of those risks and alternatives to the procedure . . . that a reasonable patient would consider material to the decision whether or not to undergo the abortion";[23] the probable gestational age of the fetus;[24] and the medical risks of carrying the child to term.

Petitioners make no real effort to show that these provisions impose an undue burden. They do argue that the requirement that physicians personally deliver this information will increase the cost of abortions, but neither they nor the District Court made any effort to quantify this effect, cf. *Ashcroft*, 462 U.S. at 489–90 ($20 increase not a significant burden), or to show that it will limit the availability of abortions significantly, or at all.

Rather, petitioners argue that these provisions do not further any legitimate state interest. As the Court of Appeals said, however, "this type of information clearly is related to maternal health and to the State's legitimate purpose in requiring informed consent." 47a, quoting *Akron*, 462 U.S. at 446. Petitioners do not contend that any of this information is inaccurate, unverifiable, or inflammatory. Indeed, the worst that petitioners can find to say about any of the required information is that one item—the risks of carrying to term—may be irrelevant to those women who are forced to seek an abortion for medical reasons. But a law is not irrational merely because it is overinclusive or underinclusive; laws need not be perfect to be rational. *Vance v. Bradley*, 440 U.S. 93, 108 (1979).[25]

More broadly, the petitioners appear to be arguing for a *per*

---

23. This provision is identical to the general definition of "informed consent" in Pennsylvania law, see Pa. Stat. Ann., tit. 40, § 1301.103 (Purdon 1991 Supp.), and is identical to the recitation on the consent forms used by two of the petitioners. See J.A. 464, 469 (consent forms).

24. All of the petitioners determine probable gestational age before performing an abortion. J.A. 105 (stipulation).

25. In 1986, the five petitioner clinics accounted for about 40% of all the abortions in Pennsylvania. 149a; J.A. 488 (quarterly reports). Of these, only about 0.7% were performed for medical reasons. *Ibid.*

se rule that an informed consent law can never require the provision of any specific piece of information, on the ground that " 'the supply of specific information to all patients regardless of their specific circumstances . . . is contrary to the standard medical practice that informed consent be specifically tailored to the needs of the specific patient.' " Pet. Br. at [71], quoting 177a (District Court opinion). There is no warrant for such a rule: even in *Akron*, the Court said that an informed consent law that required the disclosure of specific information, including gestational age, was "certainly . . . not objectionable." 462 U.S. at 445–446, n.37. Nor do the facts of this case support such a rule. Despite what the District Court said, it is not "standard medical practice" to tailor information to each patient; at least, it is not the petitioners' standard practice. The petitioners themselves uniformly use standardized forms and rote recitations to inform their patients; one of them even takes patients in batches of four. *Supra* at [170].

Nor is it the standard practice in Pennsylvania for other areas of medical practice. Quite apart from the Abortion Control Act, Pennsylvania law on informed consent requires that all patients be given the information that a "reasonable patient" would consider material, Pa. Stat. Ann., tit. 40, § 1301.103 (Purdon 1991 Supp.); *see supra* at [171], an approach which allows the patient to decide what information is relevant to his or her specific circumstances. The approach the petitioners advocate, not surprisingly, would allow the petitioners to decide this question for their patients, on the paternalistic ground that patients must be protected from "anxiety."[26] Pet. Br. at [72]. This approach, simultaneously patronizing and self-serving, *see Canterbury* v. *Spence*, 464 F.2d 772 (D.C.Cir.), *cert. denied*, 409 U.S. 1064 (1972), is certainly not the norm in Pennsylvania.

Finally, the petitioners argue that it is irrational to require physicians personally to deliver this information. Pet. Br. at [72]. As the Court of Appeals said, however, it is "patent that a state may rationally decide that physicians are better qualified

---

26. The Abortion Control Act, like Pennsylvania informed consent law generally, does not allow a physician to omit information if he reasonably believes that providing it will have a "severely adverse effect" on the patient's health. 18 Pa. Cons. Stat. § 3205(c). *Cf.* Pa. Stat. Ann., tit. 40, § 1301.103 (Purdon 1991 Supp.).

than counselors to impart this information and answer questions about the medical aspects of the available alternatives."[27]
47a–48a; *see* J.A. 266–267 (testimony of Sue Roselle) (counselors not qualified to answer questions on fetal development).
The District Court's statements to the contrary, 242a, simply
represent his own disagreement with the considered judgment
of the legislature, and do not show that that judgment is
irrational. Under rational basis analysis, "those challenging
the legislative judgment must convince the court that the
legislative facts on which the classification is apparently based
could not reasonably be conceived to be true . . . . 'The
District Court's responsibility for making findings of fact does
not authorize it to resolve conflicts in the evidence against
the legislature's conclusion or even to reject the legislative
judgment on the basis that [there are no] convincing statistics
in the record to support it.' " *Vance*, 440 U.S. at 111 (citations
and quotation marks omitted).

2. Information Given by Others

Section 3205(a)(2) requires that the pregnant woman also
be informed that the Pennsylvania Department of Health publishes materials which "describe the unborn child and list
agencies which offer alternatives to abortion," and that a free
copy will be provided on request; that medical assistance benefits may be available for prenatal, childbirth, and neonatal
care, with more specific information available in the Department's printed materials; and (except in rape cases) that the
father of the unborn child is liable for child support, even if
he has offered to pay for the abortion. Unlike the medical
information required by Section 3502(a)(1), this information
need not be conveyed by a physician.

Much of what we said in the preceding section applies here
as well. Once again, petitioners rely mainly on the idea that
some of this information will be irrelevant to some patients;
once again, they offer nothing beyond their own conclusory
statements to show that the information required is either

---

27. Counselors are often poorly paid, part-time employees who may have little
formal education. *Supra* at [171].

inaccurate or inflammatory; and once again, Section 3205 will occasion little or no change in their existing practices. As the Court of Appeals noted, 49a, most of the petitioners already offer some form of "options counseling" that explores the alternatives to abortion and the resources that might be available to support the woman's decision not to abort. Among them, the petitioners already offer every item required by Section 3205(a)(2), including pictures describing fetal development. *Supra* at [171], J.A. 153 (testimony of petitioner Allen). Since the petitioners presumably are not in the business of obstructing access to abortions, it seems safe to conclude that these practices do not impose an undue burden, and that they are rationally related to ensuring that the woman's choice is fully informed and not the product of coercion. 49a–50a. If, as the result of receiving this information, a woman decides not to abort her pregnancy, so much the better, for the Commonwealth also has a legitimate interest in preserving the life of the unborn child, and may adopt policies "encouraging childbirth except in the most urgent circumstances." *Matheson*, 450 U.S. at 413, quoting *Harris*, 448 U.S. at 325.

3. First Amendment Issues

The petitioners also argue that the Act's informed consent provisions violate their First Amendment rights, and those of their patients, by forcing them to be unwilling conveyers and recipients of "the state's message, at the cost of violating their own conscientious beliefs and professional commitments." Pet. Br. at [74].[28] The Court of Appeals held, however, that the petitioners were engaged in commercial speech; that the disclosure requirements of Section 3205 are similar to those imposed upon a long list of other industries and professions;

28. As the Court of Appeals said, the information required by Section 3205 is objective, accurate, and relevant. 49a. It would be interesting to know what forbidden "message" the petitioners think is conveyed by telling women about the risks, alternatives, and resources that bear on their decision, and equally interesting to know just what "conscientious beliefs and professional commitments" require that this information be withheld.

and that they are entirely appropriate under the Court's decision in *Zauderer* v. *Office of Disciplinary Counsel*, 471 U.S.
626 (1985). 50a–52a.

We believe that the Court of Appeals' analysis is unan-
swerable, and note that the petitioners have not attempted
to answer it. They do not dispute the Court of Appeals' holding that they are engaged in commercial speech, or even
mention it; nor do they mention, much less try to distinguish,
the holding in *Zauderer*.

4. Waiting Period

Section 3205 requires that the information needed for an
informed consent be provided to the woman at least 24 hours
before the abortion is performed. This Court, as the Court of
Appeals noted, 53a, n.20, has held repeatedly that procedures
which effectively delayed abortions for far longer periods do
not unconstitutionally burden the abortion decision. *Ohio*,
110 S. Ct. at 2980–2981 (judicial bypass of parents that could
consume 14 days), citing *Ashcroft*, 462 U.S. at 477, n.4, 491,
n.16 (same, 17 days). The record in this case supports the
same outcome.

Petitioners and the District Court rely on the arguments
that the 24-hour waiting period necessitates two trips to the
abortion provider, which increases costs, especially for women
who must travel; and that, because abortion clinics do not
perform abortions every day, the waiting period in practice
will produce delays much longer than 24 hours, which in turn
increases the risk of the abortion procedure. Pet. Br. at [68–
69]; 239a–240a. They ignore the facts that most women already make two trips—once for a pregnancy test and once for
the abortion itself—and that there is typically a time lag
between the two. *Supra* at [172]; J.A. 87, 90–91, 95, 98
(stipulation). None of the petitioners will even schedule an
abortion without a positive pregnancy test, and the abortion
is then typically scheduled within one to two weeks thereafter.
Ibid. No reason appears in the record why women could not
be given the information Section 3205 requires at their first

visit, thus obviating any additional delay.[29] Petitioners might have to adjust their procedures somewhat, but they can hardly claim that the Constitution protects their accustomed office routine; "[t]he Constitution does not compel [Pennsylvania] to fine-tune its statutes" for the petitioners' convenience. *Matheson*, 450 U.S. at 413.

As to the idea that a delay in performing an abortion increases the risk to the patient, this is true only in the most general sense, and provides no real support for the petitioners. The record is clear that there is no measurable increase in risk from a delay as short as a day, or even a week. *Supra* at [171–72]. Increases in risk show up only over periods of two to three weeks, and even then the increase is from one very small number to another very small number.[30] *Ibid.; see* 153a. Petitioners themselves entered into a binding admission in this case, *see* Fed. R. Civ. Proc. 36, that "[a] week delay in the first trimester will not likely result in a harm . . .," J.A. 552, and their own practices, which allow, encourage, or even require delay for a variety of reasons, confirm this. *Supra* at [172]. The Court of Appeals thus correctly concluded that the waiting period imposes no undue burden on the abortion decision.

Likewise, the Court of Appeals was correct that the waiting period rationally furthers the Commonwealth's interest "in ensuring that such a decision is *both* informed *and* well-considered[, which is] rationally related to the states' legitimate interest in the life and health of the mother as well as its interest in the potential life of the fetus." 54a (emphases in original).[31] As Justice O'Connor said in *Akron*, "the decision to abort is a stressful one, and the waiting period reasonably relates to the State's interest in ensuring that a woman

29. Of course, not all women get their pregnancy test from an abortion provider, but Section 3205 allows a referring physician, as well as an operating physician, to provide the necessary information for informed consent.

30. For example, from 0.8 to 1.1 deaths per hundred thousand abortions. *Supra* at [172].

31. Such waiting periods are not unique to abortion. *See* 42 C.F.R. § 441.253 (30-day waiting period for Medicaid-funded sterilizations); Pa. Stat. Ann., tit. 73, § 201-7(a) (Purdon 1991 Supp.) (3 business days for consumer to rescind certain sales contracts). "The state's interest in informed and well-considered decisions is surely as weighty in the area of abortion as in the area of consumer sales contracts." *Akron*, 462 U.S. at 474 (O'Connor, J., dissenting) (quotation marks omitted).

does not make this serious decision in undue haste . . . . The waiting period is surely a small cost to impose to ensure that the woman's decision is well considered in light of its certain and irreparable consequences on fetal life, and the possible effects on her own."

C. Parental Consent

Section 3206(a) requires the informed consent of one parent or guardian for an abortion on any unemancipated woman under the age of 18.[32] This section also establishes a judicial bypass to this requirement, both expeditious and anonymous, in which a minor may establish that she is mature and capable of giving informed consent to the abortion, or that an abortion is nevertheless in her best interests. § 3206(c)–(h). The Court has consistently approved parental consent laws, provided that the judicial bypass is adequate. *See Hodgson*, 110 S. Ct. at 2942 (opinion of Stevens, J.) (Court has never challenged state's judgment that the abortion decision be made only after consultation with parent); *Akron*, 462 U.S. at 439–440; *Bellotti II*, 443 U.S. at 639–651 (opinion of Powell, J.)

The petitioners do not quarrel with the desirability of parental involvement when a minor faces so grave a decision; all of the petitioners encourage such involvement and encourage parents to accompany their daughter. *Supra* at [172]. Between 50% and 60% of the minors whom the petitioners now see are accompanied by at least one parent, and one petitioner requires that all minors be accompanied by an adult, if not by a parent. *Supra* at [172–73].[33]

The petitioners concede that Pennsylvania may require parental consent for minors as long as there is an adequate judicial bypass, Pet. Br. at [74], and they do not attack the adequacy of Pennsylvania's judicial bypass. Their only argument is that, while a state may require parental consent, it may not require informed parental consent, *id.* at [75], that is, a state may not require that parents be informed about the

---

32. Where neither a parent nor guardian is available "within a reasonable time . . . and manner," the consent of any adult standing *in loco parentis* is sufficient. § 3206(b).

33. In 1988, about 12% of Pennsylvania abortions were on minors. 150a.

risks, alternatives, and resources that may bear on their own and their daughter's decision.

To call this argument outlandish seems inadequate. The point of requiring parental consent is not to collect a meaningless signature, but to provide the pregnant minor with the benefit of an adult's advice and judgment about the "nature and consequences" of the decision she faces, *Danforth*, 428 U.S. at 67, an objective which is obviously not achievable if the adult is herself not cognizant of these matters. A requirement of informed consent is permissible here for the same reasons it is permissible in all other cases, and for another as well: as the court recognized in both *Matheson*, 450 U.S. at 411, and *Ohio*, 110 S. Ct. at 2983, parents are important sources of medical information on their children, and the informed consent process facilitates this exchange of information. Finally, to the extent that petitioners rely on logistical and other obstacles that may make it burdensome for even a supportive parent to comply with Section 3206, Pet. Br. at [76], the existence of the judicial bypass option obviates any such difficulties.

D. Spousal Notice

Spousal notice is governed by Section 3209 of the Act. Enacted "to further the Commonwealth's interest in promoting the integrity of the marital relationship and to protect a spouse's interests in having children within marriage and in protecting the prenatal life of that child," *ibid.*, Section 3209 requires that a married woman who is about to undergo an abortion notify her husband and provide her doctor with a signed statement that she has done so. *Id.*, § 3209(a).

The spousal notice requirement does not apply in the case of a medical emergency, *id.*, § 3209(c). Nor does it apply where the woman provides a statement that she has not notified her husband because he is not the father of the child or could not, after diligent effort, be located; or because the pregnancy resulted from a reported incident of spousal sexual assault; or because she has reasons to believe that notifying her spouse will likely subject her to bodily injury. *Id.*, § 3209(b).

1. Right to Abortion

The Court of Appeals recognized that in most respects these provisions do not even arguably impose an undue burden on the decision to seek an abortion: they impose no "drastic or severe time delay, increase in costs, or decrease in the number of abortion providers. Nor [do they] give a state-sanctioned veto power over the woman's abortion decision to another person." 63a. The two judges of the majority, however, held that an undue burden inheres in the possible consequences of spousal notification. Relying on *Hodgson*, and on the plurality opinion in *Bellotti* v. *Baird*, 443 U.S. 622 (1979) (*Bellotti II*), they held that spousal notification exposes the woman to the possibility of physical, economic, or emotional pressure from her husband to forego an abortion, or to punish her if she does not, 63a–68a, and that this possibility constitutes a "severe limitation on the woman's abortion decision." 63a. We submit that the Court of Appeals was mistaken, for substantially the reasons advanced by Judge Alito in his dissenting opinion. 87a–96a.

The majority judges, we believe, misapplied the undue burden standard in this instance. To establish that a law imposes an undue burden, it is surely not enough—at least in a facial challenge—to show that it may deter or inhibit some women from getting an abortion. As the Court has said in the related context of parental notice, "[t]hat [a statutory] requirement . . . may inhibit some minors from seeking abortions is not a valid basis to void the statute." *Matheson*, 450 U.S. at 413. Virtually any regulation could be said to deter someone from seeking an abortion, but the Court has not for that reason outlawed all regulation of abortion. Any regulation that increases the cost of an abortion, for example, is likely to make an abortion marginally unaffordable for someone, and yet the Court has refused to strike down regulations on this ground. See *Ashcroft*, 462 U.S. at 489–90 (requirement for pathology report that added $20 to cost not unconstitutional); *Akron*, 462 U.S. at 466–467 (O'Connor, J., dissenting) (no undue burden in hospitalization requirement for second-trimester abortions even though costs more than doubled). Rather, those who would strike down an abortion regulation must show that it will have what Judge Alito called the "broad practical impact," 91a, of severely limiting access to abortions. *See Danforth*, 428 U.S. at 79 (law banning use of saline amniocentesis unconstitutional where it had the practical effect of making abortions unavailable after twelve weeks). Thus properly understood, it is apparent that petitioners failed here to make their case.

First, unlike the record in *Hodgson*, the record in this case shows that the number of women who even theoretically could be affected adversely by spousal notice is very small. In *Hodgson*, which involved a requirement that both parents of a minor be notified before that minor had an abortion, the record showed that about half the children in Minnesota did not live with both parents, *id.*, 110 S. Ct. at 2938, and that the most common reason for not notifying the second parent was fear of physical abuse. *Id.* at 2945, n.36. In this case, the record shows that only about 20% of the women who obtain abortions are married; and of these, about 95% notify their husbands already. *Supra* at [173]. In other words, of all women who obtain abortions, only about 1% are married women who have not notified their husbands.

Of those women who did not notify their husbands and who offered a reason, none cited a fear of abuse. *Ibid.* Moreover, as Judge Alito correctly observed, of these few women, surely some, if Section 3209 were to go into effect, would notify their husbands without adverse consequences, while still others would avail themselves of the statutory exceptions to spousal notice. 93a. The number of women who might actually be deterred from seeking an abortion by the spousal notice provision is thus unknown, and possibly nonexistent, but certainly, at less than one per cent, very small.

Second, the statutory exceptions just referred to further distinguish this case from *Bellotti II* and *Hodgson*. In *Bellotti II*, the statute provided no exception for minors who feared abuse from their parents,[34] while in *Hodgson* the statutory

---

34. Reliance on *Bellotti II* on this issue is problematic in any event, since no opinion in that case commanded a majority of the Court. Four Justices did say that a requirement of parental notice would place an undue burden on minors because some parents might then obstruct the minor's access to an abortion. *Id.* 443 U.S. at 647 (opinion of Powell, J.). The other four Justices who concurred in the judgment, however, noted specifically that the case involved only a requirement for parental consent, and did not decide the constitutionality of notice provisions. *Id.* at 655, n.1 (Stevens, J., concurring in the judgment).

exception turned out to be, in practice, simply an alternative route to parental notification. *Id.*, 110 S. Ct. at 2932, n.7. Pennsylvania's statute, however, does have such an exemption in § 3209(b)(4), and others as well, and unlike the statute in *Hodgson*, the fear-of-physical-injury exemption does not set in motion a series of events that results in the abusive husband being notified.

The petitioners and the majority in the Court of Appeals, however, rely heavily on the District Court's finding that "most battered women do not have the psychological ability to avail themselves" of this exception, 68a–69a, 201a, thus, they believe, making this exception as ineffective as the one in *Hodgson*. Even if this assertion is taken at face value, it does nothing to undermine the point made above, that the spousal notice provision could adversely affect, at most, fewer than 1% of the women who seek abortions. Even this is too generous, however, for there is rather less to the District Court's finding than meets the eye.

The witness upon whom the District Court relied testified about women who are in a "battering relationship." According to this witness, women in such relationships are subjected not only to a recurring cycle of violence, J.A. 219–221, but also to the constant monitoring of their activities and even their thoughts, J.A. 212–213; "most batterers are so sensitive to what the women are behaving and thinking and feeling that he [sic] will pick up something [that] is different. . . ." J.A. 227 (testimony of Lenore Walker). Women in such relationships can suffer from a form of mental disorder called Post-Traumatic Stress Disorder, one manifestation of which is "learned helplessness," the perception by the woman that no action of hers will enable her to escape the violence. 200a. It is women manifesting this "learned helplessness" whom the District Court found would not be able to avail themselves of Section 3209's exception for physical abuse. 201a.

This finding, however, does not address the question of how many of these women would ever seek an abortion without their husband's knowledge in the first place. Battered women who perceive themselves as so helpless that they would never even try such a thing are indeed cruelly burdened, but by their batterers, not by the statute. In real life, the opportunity to

invoke the fear-of-abuse exception will not be encountered
by these battered women, but only by those battered women
who have already mustered the psychological and physical
resources necessary to verify their pregnancies, contact abortion providers, wait for their appointments,[35] arrange for pay-
ment, and physically present themselves at the abortion
sites—all without letting their husbands find out. Neither the
District Court nor the witness—who had no actual experience
with spousal notification provisions, J.A. 239–240 (testimony
of Lenore Walker)—said how many of these women would
find themselves "psychologically incapable" of checking off a
line on a form, which is all that Section 3209 requires. See
J.A. 504–505 (spousal notice form).

The petitioners thus did not show that Section 3209 would
have anything close to the "broad practical effect" of severely
limiting access to abortions. Their challenge is more accurately
characterized as an attempt to rely on a "worst-case analysis"
which may never happen, and which is simply inadequate to
support their facial challenge to the statute. Ohio, 110 S. Ct.
at 2981.

In the absence of any undue burden, the only remaining
question is whether Section 3209 is reasonably related to any
legitimate state interest. Despite what the petitioners say, Pet.
Br. at [61–62], there is no real question that a husband has a
"deep and proper concern" in his wife's pregnancy and in the
fetus she carries, Danforth, 428 U.S. at 69; that the abortion
decision may profoundly affect the marriage, in which he also
has an interest, id. at 70; and that the state legitimately may
act to enable him to protect those interests.[36]

Nor can there be any real question that the law is reasonably
designed to further those ends. The petitioners argue that
wives either tell their husbands about their abortion decisions

---

35. Typically, the woman must have a pregnancy test before her abortion will
even be scheduled, and the abortion itself is typically scheduled within two weeks
thereafter. Supra at [172].

36. The petitioners say that Section 3209, like the law in Danforth, gives a husband
the power to "compel[] his wife to bear children for him." Pet. Br. at [64]. They
ignore the distinction, which the Court has always recognized, between laws requiring
consent and laws requiring mere notice. See, e.g., Matheson, 450 U.S. at 411 n.17;
Hodgson, 110 S. Ct. at 2969. (Kennedy, J., concurring in judgment in part and
dissenting in part).

already, or have good reasons for not telling them. In the first case, they say, the law is unnecessary, in the second case it is harmful, and in either case it is an irrational means of furthering whatever legitimate interests the state may have. Pet. Br. at [61–62]. This argument was well answered in Justice Stevens's concurring opinion in *Matheson*. Speaking in the admittably different context of parental notice, and harking back to his earlier concurrence in *Danforth*, Justice Stevens rejected similar arguments against Utah's statute:

> It is unrealistic, in my judgment, to assume that every parent-child relationship is either (a) so perfect that communication and accord will take place routinely or (b) so imperfect that the absence of communication reflects the child's correct prediction that the parent will . . . [act] arbitrarily to further a selfish interest rather than the child's interest. A state legislature may conclude that most parents will be primarily interested in the welfare of their children. . . .
>
> Utah's interest in its parental-notice statute is not diminished by the fact that there can be no guarantee that meaningful parent-child consultation will actually occur. . . . The possibility that some parents will not react with compassion and understanding . . . does not undercut the legitimacy of the State's attempt to establish a procedure that will enhance the probability that a pregnant young woman exercise as wisely as possible her right to make the abortion decision.

Matheson, 450 U.S. at 423–424 (Stevens, J., concurring in judgment) (footnote and citation omitted, bracketed matter in original), quoting *Danforth*, 428 U.S. at 103–104 (Stevens, J., concurring in part and dissenting in part).

The same is true here.[37] It may well be true that a state cannot simply decree inter-familial communication that conforms to some idealized model of its own. But Section 3209

---

37. We do not suggest that the relationship between spouses equates with the parent-child relationship. Clearly, the interest served by parental notice—making available to the child the advice and support of her parents—is different from the interest served by spousal notice—preserving the possibility for a husband to participate in a decision that profoundly affects his own interest. This, however, does not undercut Justice Stevens's points that notice statutes are a rational way to pursue these interests, and that the possibility that such statutes might not always work out as intended does not destroy their legitimacy.

does nothing of the sort; rather, it seeks only to preserve the husband's interest in the possibility of such communication by making sure that the husband knows of his wife's intentions.

2. Other Issues

The petitioners' remaining arguments require little discussion.[38] First, they claim that Section 3209 interferes with marital privacy. It is not entirely clear, however, what they mean by this, nor is it clear how a right to marital privacy— that is, the right to protect "the sanctity of their [marital] *communications*," Hodgson, 110 S. Ct. at 2944, n.33 (opinion of Stevens, J.) (emphasis added)—can create a privacy interest in one spouse's unilateral decision to conceal important matters from the other. If the woman's own privacy interest is, as argued above, insufficient to justify this concealment, it is hard to see what is added by the invocation of the marital interest.

Lastly, the petitioners claim that Section 3209 violates the Equal Protection Clause. Pet. Br. at [66–68]. Noting that Pennsylvania's law does not require that a husband notify his wife before undergoing a medical procedure that would affect his fertility, they claim that Section 3209 "embodies precisely the prohibited stereotype that wives should bear children." *Id.* at [68]. The short answer to this is that the Court has repeatedly recognized the unique nature of the abortion procedure and has repeatedly held that states are justified, because of its unique nature, in treating it differently from other medical procedures. *Matheson*, 450 U.S. at 412; *Bellotti I*, 428 U.S. at 148–149; *Danforth*, 428 U.S. at 67. Such state laws are based not upon a value judgment that all women should bear children, but upon the biological fact that only women bear children. Petitioners' reliance on the fact that spousal notice is not required in procedures that produce male sterility is thus misplaced. Pet. Br. at [66–67]. The true analog to such procedures is not abortion, but female sterilization procedures. Pennsylvania requires neither wives nor husbands to notify

---

38. The Court of Appeals found it unnecessary to reach these arguments, 103a, n.8, as did the District Court.

their spouses of such procedures, and petitioners' equal protection claim is without merit.

E. Confidential Reports

Section 3214 requires abortion facilities to file with the Department of Health an individual report for each abortion performed. These reports are kept confidential, as the law requires, and there is no evidence that any information from these reports identifying either a patient or a physician has ever been disclosed; in fact, neither this nor any other report even contains patients' names. *Supra* at [174]; 205a–208a. The reports are used to gather a wide variety of information on maternal health, which is then released only in the form of statistical compilations. *See, e.g.*, 149a–152a.

Among the information Section 3214 requires is the name of the referring physician, if any, § 3214(a)(1); and the bases for the following medical judgments: that a third-trimester abortion was necessary to protect the life and health of the mother, § 3214(a)(8);[39] that a medical emergency existed, § 3214(a)(10); and the determination of gestational age, § 3214(a)(11). The petitioners claim that if these matters must be reported, physicians will be reluctant to refer or perform abortions, and that this in turn will reduce the availability of abortions. Pet Br. at [78]. As the Court of Appeals said, however, these fears are at best unfounded, 79a–80a; and, we add, they are at worst self-fulfilling and self-serving. "Laws are not declared unconstitutional because of some general reluctance to follow a statutory scheme the legislature finds necessary to accomplish a legitimate state objective." *Hodgson*, 110 S. Ct. at 2968 (Kennedy, J., concurring in judgment in part and dissenting in part).

These reporting requirements obviously further the Commonwealth's interest in collecting accurate information on maternal health, especially in the area of medically necessary abortions, and in ensuring compliance with the requirements

---

39. Second- and third-trimester abortions together accounted for only 6% of Pennsylvania abortions in 1988. 150a.

of the Act.[40] 78–79a, 80a. They do not impose an undue burden on the abortion decision, and are therefore constitutional.

F. Publicly Available Reports

Section 3209 requires each abortion facility to file a report with the Department of Health disclosing its name and address, and the names and addresses of any parent, subsidiary, or affiliate organizations. Section 3214(f) requires each facility to file with the Department quarterly reports specifying the total number of abortions performed, broken down by trimester. Both of these reports are available for public inspection and copying only in the case of any facility which has received any State-appropriated money within the preceding 12 months. The petitioners claim that the public availability of these reports exposes them and their patients to abuse and harassment from persons and groups who are opposed to abortion.[41] Pet. Br. at [77–78]. This claim, and the District Court's acceptance of it, 267a–268a, simply ignores two facts.

The first is that the identity and location of abortion providers is, and in the nature of things must be, easily accessible to the public. The petitioners could not function otherwise, and in fact all of them advertise in telephone directories, print, or broadcast media. *Supra* at [175]. The second fact, which follows unfortunately but naturally from the first, is that the petitioners are already the targets of substantial public protest, *ibid.*, even though the public disclosure provisions of Sections 3209 and 3214 have never gone into effect. However disruptive and even illegal some of these protests may be, they are obviously not caused by these provisions of the Act. The petitioners, relying solely on their own self-serving specula-

40. Under the Act, a referring physician may make the required determination of gestational age, § 3210(a), and may obtain the patient's informed consent, § 3205(a). In reviewing the reporting forms, the Department of Health sometimes finds it necessary to contact the reporting physician directly. 220a. While it may be true that the Department could rely on abortion clinics to obtain whatever information is needed from the referring physician, 272a–273a, it is not irrational for the legislature to prefer the Department to collect its data from the primary, and therefore most reliable, source.

41. They claim also that the public availability of these reports is an unconstitutional condition on their receipt of public funds, Pet. Br. at [78], n.91. But as the Court of Appeals explained, 83a–85a, this adds nothing to the petitioners' case.

tions, claim that the public disclosure provision will result in an increase in such protests, 211a–213a, but the Court of Appeals correctly rejected their conclusory statements as insufficient to establish that these provisions will unduly burden the right to an abortion. 82a–83a.

On the other hand, the public disclosure provisions do further a legitimate State interest: that the public should know how its money is being spent. Such information is generally available to the public under Pennsylvania law, Pa. Stat. Ann., tit. 65, §§ 66.1 and 66.2 (Purdon 1959 & 1991 Supp.), and it hardly seems necessary to belabor either the legitimacy of the State's interest or the rationality of the means chosen to further it.

III. IN THE ALTERNATIVE, THE COURT SHOULD RE-EXAMINE AND OVERRULE *ROE* V. *WADE* RETURNING THE REGULATION OF ABORTION TO THE STATES' DEMOCRATIC PROCESS.

In the preceding sections, we have argued at length that *Roe* v. *Wade*, properly understood and applied, does not forbid the abortion regulations contained in Pennsylvania's statute, and that this case therefore does not confront the Court with the necessity of reconsidering *Roe*. Nevertheless, it remains true that *Roe* is a deeply flawed decision, and it may be that the time has come to reconsider it.

The reasons for and against taking this step are familiar to the Court and need only be summarized here. On the one hand, the Court is generally reluctant to formulate a rule of law broader than is necessary to decide the case that is actually before the Court. *Webster*, 492 U.S. at 525–526 (O'Connor, J., concurring in part and concurring in the judgment). On the other hand, the Court does overlook this rule fairly frequently, and it would be ironic if *Roe*, which itself decided a question so much more broadly than was necessary, should now be insulated from review by this rule. In addition, the no-broader-than-is-necessary rule, rigidly applied, would mean that many constitutional decisions could never be reconsidered until someone squarely defies them, a process that is unlikely to enhance either the development of the law or respect for the Court's decisions. *Webster*, 492 U.S. at 532–537 (Scalia, J., concurring in part and concurring in the judgment).

If the Court does decide to reach the question of *Roe*'s continuing validity—or, alternatively, if the Court must reach it because the Court holds that Pennsylvania's statute cannot be squared with *Roe*—the respondents have no doubt of the correct outcome. Justice White's formulation of the abortion right, in our view, is the correct one: "a woman's ability to choose an abortion is a species of 'liberty' that is subject to the general protections of the Due Process Clause. I cannot agree, however, that this liberty is so 'fundamental' that restrictions upon it call into play anything more than the most minimal judicial scrutiny." *Thornburgh*, 476 U.S. at 790 (White, J., dissenting); *accord, Roe*, 410 U.S. at 172–173 (Rehnquist, J., dissenting). The Court should overrule anything in *Roe* to the contrary.

The arguments that support this position are, again, well known to the Court from the dissenting opinions in *Thornburgh*, in *Akron*, and in *Roe* itself. *See also* Br. of the United States as *Amicus Curiae*. Again, we do no more than summarize them here.

> First and most importantly, *Roe*'s holding that abortion is a fundamental constitutional right is untenable. The text of the Constitution obviously creates no such right; the text of the Constitution does not even mention abortion. Nor can such a right plausibly be located among the unenumerated, but still fundamental, rights protected by the Due Process Clause. The hallmark of such rights is that they are grounded in some source of constitutional value that reflects not the philosophical predilections of individual judges, but basic choices made by the people themselves in constituting their system of government . . . [Fundamental rights are located] either in the traditions and consensus of our society as a whole or in the logical implications of a system that recognizes both individual liberty and democratic order.

Thornburgh, 476 U.S. at 791 (White, J., dissenting). The holding in *Roe* has no such grounding—not in history and tradition, *Roe*, 410 U.S. at 174–177 (Rehnquist, J., dissenting), not in the necessary implications of a system of ordered liberty, *Thornburgh*, 476 U.S. at 793 (White, J., dissenting), and most certainly not in any consensus of society as a whole.

Nor can *Roe* be defended as the logical extension of the Court's "privacy" decisions. *See Eisenstadt v. Baird*, 405 U.S. 438 (1972); *Stanley v. Georgia*, 394 U.S. 557 (1969); *Loving v. Virginia*, 388 U.S. 1 (1967); *Griswold v. Connecticut*, 381 U.S. 479 (1965); *Skinner v. Oklahoma*, 316 U.S. 535 (1942); *Pierce v. Society of Sisters*, 268 U.S. 510 (1925); *Meyer v. Nebraska*, 262 U.S. 390 (1923). The Court's decision in *Roe* underlined the difference between itself and these earlier privacy cases:

> The pregnant woman cannot be isolated in her privacy. She carries an embryo and, later, a fetus. . . . The situation therefore is inherently different from marital intimacy, or bedroom possession of obscene material, or marriage, or procreation, or education, with which *Eisenstadt* and *Griswold*, *Stanley*, *Loving*, *Skinner*, and *Pierce* and *Meyer* were concerned.

Id., 410 U.S. at 159. The decision in *Roe* was thus in no way preordained by the decisions in *Eisenstadt*, *Griswold* and the rest of the cases cited.[42] *Roe*'s creation of a "fundamental" right which has no sound basis in the Constitution, in history, in a societal consensus, or even in the Court's own precedents, is simply an illegitimate exercise of "raw judicial power," *Doe v. Bolton*, 410 U.S. at 222 (White, J., dissenting), which the Court should disavow for this reason alone.

Second, the key points in *Roe*'s analysis of the abortion right—viability and trimesters—are themselves arbitrary. As Justice White pointed out in his dissenting opinion in *Thornburgh*, the Court has never explained satisfactorily why the state's interest in protecting fetal life is "compelling" at the point of viability but not before. *Id.*, 476 U.S. at 794–795. And as Justice O'Connor pointed out in her dissenting opinion in *Akron*, the trimester approach depends upon medical and technological factors which are of no constitutional significance, and which in turn make the trimester approach so

42. By the same token, *Roe*'s demise would in no way undermine those other decisions.

unreliable that the Court has already been forced to abandon it in part. *Id.*, 462 U.S. at 454–456.

Third, *Roe* has had an "institutionally debilitating effect," *Thornburgh*, 476 U.S. at 814 (O'Connor, J., dissenting), on several levels. *Roe* stands as an anomaly among the Court's cases on fundamental constitutional rights, *Akron*, 462 U.S. at 452 (O'Connor, J., dissenting), working "a major distortion in the Court's constitutional jurisprudence." *Thornburgh*, 476 U.S. at 814 (O'Connor, J., dissenting). Far from being a source of stability in the law, *Roe*'s arbitrariness has forced the Court to return to the issue of abortion time and time again, drawing ever finer lines to govern the states' attempts to regulate in this area. *Webster*, 492 U.S. at 518 (opinion of Rehnquist, C.J.). This arbitrariness at times has infected other areas of the law as well, making it "painfully clear that no legal rule or doctrine is safe from ad hoc nullification by this Court when an occasion for its application arises in a case involving state regulation of abortion." *Thornburgh*, 476 U.S. at 814 (O'Connor, J., dissenting). In addition, by reinforcing the idea that the Court's proper function is to impose its own notions of sound public policy, *Roe* "continuously distorts the public perception of the role of this Court," *Webster*, 492 U.S. at 535 (Scalia, J., concurring in part and concurring in the judgment), in a way that in the long run is bound to damage the Court as an institution.

That damage is not to the Court alone, but also to the very "principles of self-governance" in a democracy. *Id.* at 536 n.*. Abortion is "a field where [the Court] has little proper business since the answers to most of the cruel questions posed are political and not juridical." *Id.* at 532. "Leaving the matter to the political process is not only legally correct, it is pragmatically so. That alone . . . can produce compromises satisfying a sufficient mass of the electorate that this deeply felt issue will cease distorting the remainder of our democratic process." *Ohio*, 110 S. Ct. at 2984 (Scalia, J., concurring). For all these reasons, the Court should overrule *Roe*.

The petitioners protest, however, that "[n]ever before has this Court bestowed, then taken back, a fundamental right that has been part of the settled rights and expectations of literally millions of Americans." Pet. Br. at [43]. This, of course, is not true, and the parallel with the earlier case is instructive. *Lochner v. New York*, 198 U.S. 45 (1905), was, before *Roe*, the Court's last venture into substantive due process.[43] In *Lochner* as in *Roe*, the Court began with an undoubted liberty interest—in *Lochner*, the right of the individual to work as "may seem to him appropriate or necessary for the support of himself and his family," *id.*, 198 U.S. at 56—which the Court then elevated into a fundamental right immune from state regulations which today seem innocuous indeed. In phrases that might have come from *Thornburgh*, the Court struck down New York regulations that allowed bakers to work "only" ten hours per day and "only" sixty hours per week, as "mere meddlesome interferences with the rights of the individual," *Lochner*, 198 U.S. at 61, enacted from "some other motive . . . than the purpose to subserve the public health or welfare." *Id.* at 63. Cf. *Thornburgh*, 476 U.S. at 759 (disparaging the motives presumed to underlie measures regulating abortion).

The Court has long since disavowed *Lochner*—in the petitioners' terms, it "took back" the right it had "bestowed"— *see Ferguson v. Skrupa*, 372 U.S. 726 (1963), and it should do the same with *Roe*. The petitioners' very phraseology betrays their, and *Roe's*, error. In this country, rights are not "bestowed" by this Court, but by the people, through the Constitution which they have ordained. When the Court finds itself usurping this function, as it did in *Lochner* and as we think it did in *Roe*, it is time to change course.

---

43. The suggestion that *Roe* and *Lochner* have much in common is, of course, not a new one. *See Roe*, 410 U.S. at 174 (Rehnquist, J., dissenting).

CONCLUSION

Respondents ask the Court to reverse the Court of Appeals' judgment that the Act's spousal notice provisions are unconstitutional, and in all other respects to affirm the judgment of the Court of Appeals.

Respectfully submitted,

ERNEST D. PREATE, JR.,
Attorney General

BY: JOHN G. KNORR, III,
Chief Deputy Attorney
General, Chief,
Litigation Section,
Counsel of Record

KATE L. MERSHIMER, Senior
Deputy Attorney General
Office of Attorney General
15th Fl.
Strawberry Square
Harrisburg, PA 17120
(717) 783–1471

BRIEF FOR THE UNITED STATES
AS *AMICUS CURIAE*
SUPPORTING RESPONDENTS

INTEREST OF *AMICI CURIAE*

This Court granted review in order to resolve several issues regarding the constitutionality of the 1988 and 1989 amendments to the Pennsylvania Abortion Control Act. In *Webster* v. *Reproductive Health Care Servs.*, 492 U.S. 490 (1989), and *Hodgson* v. *Minnesota*, 110 S. Ct. 2926 (1990), the United States filed briefs as an *amicus curiae* in which we argued that *Roe* v. *Wade*, 410 U.S. 113 (1973), was wrongly decided and should be overruled. Moreover, Congress has enacted laws affecting abortion.[1] The United States therefore has a substantial interest in the outcome of this case.

QUESTIONS PRESENTED

1. Did the court of appeals err in upholding the constitutionality of the following provisions of the Pennsylvania Abortion Control Act: (a) 18 Pa. Cons. Stat. Ann. § 3203 (Purdon 1983 & Supp. 1991) (definition of medical emergency); (b) 18 Pa. Cons. Stat. Ann. § 3205 (Purdon 1983 & Supp. 1991) (informed consent); (c) 18 Pa. Cons. Stat. Ann. § 3206

1. E.g., Act of Sept. 30, 1976, Pub. L. No. 94–439, § 209, 90 Stat. 1434 (the Hyde Amendment); Public Health Service Act (the Adolescent Family Life Act of 1981), 42 U.S.C. 300z *et seq.*

(Purdon 1983 & Supp. 1991) (parental consent); (d) 18 Pa. Cons. Stat. Ann. §§ 3207 and 3214 (Purdon 1983 & Supp. 1991) (reporting requirements)?

2. Did the court of appeals err in holding 18 Pa. Cons. Stat. Ann. § 3209 (Purdon Supp. 1991) (spousal notice) unconstitutional?

STATEMENT

1. In 1988 and 1989, Pennsylvania amended its Abortion Control Act, 18 Pa. Cons. Stat. Ann. §§ 3201–3220 (Purdon 1983 & Supp. 1991). The purpose of the Act is to "protect hereby the life and health of the woman subject to abortion" and "the child subject to abortion," to "foster the development of standards of professional conduct in a critical area of medical practice," to "provide for development of statistical data," and to "protect the right of the minor woman voluntarily to decide to submit to abortion or to carry her child to term." *Id.* § 3203(a) (Purdon 1983); *see also id.* § 3202(b) (Purdon 1983) (legislative findings). The Act outlaws postviability abortions and previability abortions based on the fetus's sex. *Id.* § 3204(c) (Purdon Supp. 1991), § 3211(a) (Purdon 1983 & Supp. 1991). Otherwise, the Act regulates but does not ban abortion. Five such regulations are at issue here: the informed consent, informed parental consent, and spousal notification requirements; the definition of a medical emergency, which is an exception to the first three provisions; and certain reporting requirements.

2. Petitioners, five abortion clinics and one physician, brought this action three days before the 1988 amendments would have taken effect, seeking to have those amendments (and later the 1989 amendments) declared unconstitutional. The district court entered preliminary injunctions against the 1988 and 1989 amendments. After a bench trial, relying on *Roe* v. *Wade, Akron* v. *Akron Center for Reproductive Health,* 462 U.S. 416 (1983) (*Akron I*), and *Thornburgh* v. *American College of Obstetricians & Gynecologists,* 476 U.S. 747 (1986), the court held unconstitutional the five provisions noted above

and permanently enjoined their enforcement. 91–744 Pet. App. (Pet. App.) 104a–287a.

3. The court of appeals, by a divided vote, affirmed in part and reversed in part. Pet. App. 1a–103a. At the outset, the court addressed the correct standard of review for abortion regulations. Relying on *Marks* v. *United States*, 430 U.S. 188 (1977), the court concluded that when this Court issues a judgment without a majority opinion, "the holding of the Court may be viewed as that position taken by those members who concurred in the judgment on the narrowest grounds." Pet. App. 20a, 15a–24a. Applying that approach to this Court's decisions, the court held that the strict scrutiny standard of *Roe, Akron I*, and *Thornburgh* was no longer applicable after *Webster* and *Hodgson*. Instead, the court determined, the undue burden standard adopted by Justice O'Connor now constituted the governing rule. Pet. App. 24a–30a.

The Third Circuit then applied the undue burden standard to the Pennsylvania Act. The court unanimously held that the definition of medical emergency included conditions posing a significant risk of death or serious injury to a woman, and that the informed consent, informed parental consent, and reporting requirements did not unduly burden a woman's right to an abortion. Pet. App. 33a–60a, 75a–85a. By contrast, a majority of the court held that the spousal notification provision was unduly burdensome and that the State lacked a compelling interest in ensuring such notification. Pet. App. 60a–74a. Judge Alito dissented from that portion of the majority's decision. Pet. App. 86a–103a.

SUMMARY OF ARGUMENT

I. Under this Court's decisions, a liberty interest is "fundamental" and thus deserves heightened protection only if our Nation's history and traditions have protected that interest from state restriction. Those sources do not establish a fundamental right to abortion. Abortion after quickening was a crime at common law; the first English abortion statute outlawed abortions throughout pregnancy; state laws condemning or restricting abortion were common when the Fourteenth Amendment was ratified; and 21 of those laws were still in existence in 1973. Thus, strict scrutiny is inappropriate. The correct standard of review is the one endorsed by the *Webster* plurality. In any event, a state has a compelling interest in protecting fetal life throughout pregnancy.

II. The challenged provisions of the Pennsylvania Act are reasonably designed to advance legitimate state interests. The informed consent and waiting period requirements ensure that a woman knows the relevant facts and can reflect on them before making a final decision. The informed parental consent requirement enables parents to make important decisions affecting their child. The spousal notification requirement can help protect the life of a fetus, the integrity of the family unit, and the husband's interests in procreation within marriage and the potential life of his unborn child. The definition of medical emergency includes those conditions that put a woman's life or health at significant risk. The reporting rules help in enforcing the ban on abortion of viable fetuses (except to protect a mother's life or health), in advancing medical knowledge, and in informing the public about the use of State tax dollars.

ARGUMENT

THE PENNSYLVANIA ABORTION CONTROL ACT DOES NOT VIO- LATE THE CONSTITUTION.

In *Roe* v. *Wade*, a divided Court held that a woman has a fundamental right to an abortion; the Court also adopted a complex trimester framework to determine whether and how a state may regulate abortion. Since then, a majority of the Members of this Court has expressed the view that *Roe* and succeeding cases should be limited or overruled. *See Webster*, 492 U.S. at 517–521 (plurality opinion of Rehnquist, C.J., joined by White & Kennedy, JJ.); *id.* at 532 (opinion of Scalia, J.); *Hodgson*, 110 S. Ct. at 2984 (Scalia, J., concurring); *Thornburgh*, 476 U.S. at 786–797 (White, J., dissenting, joined by Rehnquist, J.); *Akron I*, 462 U.S. at 453–459 (O'Connor, J., dissenting, joined by White & Rehnquist, JJ.). At the same time, none of the opinions in recent abortion cases commanded a majority. The result is that considerable uncertainty now prevails with respect to the proper standard of review applicable when legislation affecting abortion is challenged under the Due Process Clause. The Third Circuit's opinion in this case illustrates this uncertainty.

Ascertaining the correct standard of review is not only the threshold issue, but also a critical one. Here, as elsewhere, the question of the correct standard that the courts should employ is not merely "a lawyer's quibble over words," but "establishes whether and when the Court and Constitution allow the Government to" regulate a woman's abortion decision. *Metro Broadcasting, Inc.* v. *FCC*, 110 S. Ct. 2997, 3033 (1990) (O'Connor, J., dissenting). This issue is one in need of clarification if the legislatures, lower courts, and litigants are to have guidance in this difficult area. We believe that the correct standard was the one articulated by the *Webster* plurality: Is a regulation reasonably designed to serve a legitimate state interest? That standard should be applied to the questions in this case and to abortion regulations generally.[2]

I. ABORTION REGULATIONS SHOULD BE UPHELD IF THEY ARE REASONABLY DESIGNED TO SERVE A LEGITIMATE STATE INTEREST.

A. Abortion Regulations Should Be Subject to Heightened Scrutiny Only If They Implicate a Fundamental Right.

The ultimate source for constitutional rights is the text of the Constitution. That text, of course, is silent with respect

---

2. Petitioners note, Pet. Br. [57], that we urged this Court to adopt an "undue burden" analysis in *Akron I*, but criticized and abandoned that standard in *Webster* and *Hodgson*. We adhere to our views as expressed in the latter two cases. In our view, the undue burden standard begs the question at issue (namely, whether there is a fundamental right to abortion) and does not provide a meaningful guide for assessing the weight of the competing interests.

to abortion; the Constitution leaves this matter to the states, since only the states possess a general, regulatory police power. *See Roe*, 410 U.S. at 177 (Rehnquist, J., dissenting) ("the drafters did not intend to have the Fourteenth Amendment withdraw from the States the power to legislate with respect to this matter"); U.S. Const. Amend. X. The "right to an abortion" was judicially recognized in *Roe* as "derived from the Due Process Clause," *Webster*, 492 U.S. at 521 (plurality opinion); *Roe*, 410 U.S. at 153. By its terms, however, the Due Process Clause seeks to ensure that the government affords a person the process she is due before it attempts to deprive her of life, liberty, or property. The text of the Clause therefore focuses on procedure, not substance.

This Court's decisions nevertheless hold that the Clause provides a measure of substantive protection to certain liberty interests. *See, e.g., Moore v. East Cleveland*, 431 U.S. 494 (1977); *Pierce v. Society of Sisters*, 268 U.S. 510 (1925); *Griswold v. Connecticut*, 381 U.S. 479, 501 (1965) (Harlan, J., concurring in the judgment). At the same time, the Court has been cautious in identifying such rights, recognizing that once the courts venture beyond the "core textual meaning" of "liberty" as freedom from bodily restraint, the imputation of substance to that concept is a "treacherous" undertaking. *Michael H. v. Gerald D.*, 491 U.S. 110, 121 (1989) (plurality opinion) (citation omitted). Accordingly, the Court has recognized that it "is most vulnerable and comes nearest to illegitimacy when it deals with judge-made constitutional law having little or no cognizable roots in the language or design of the Constitution." *Bowers v. Hardwick*, 478 U.S. 186, 194 (1986).

The general standard of review in assessing a substantive due process claim is highly deferential to legislative judgments. As a rule, a state or federal law that trenches on an individual's liberty interest will be upheld as long as it is rationally related to a legitimate governmental interest. *See, e.g., Califano v. Aznavorian*, 439 U.S. 170, 176–178 (1978); *Ferguson v. Skrupa*, 372 U.S. 726 (1963); *Williamson v. Lee Optical Co.*, 348 U.S. 483 (1955). In some sensitive areas, however, the Court has gone further and held that certain liberty interests rise to the level of "fundamental rights" and are subject to more exacting scrutiny. *Michael H.*, 491 U.S. at 122 (plurality opinion). Where that is the case, the state may restrict such a liberty interest only through means that are narrowly tailored to serve a compelling state interest. *Roe v. Wade*, 410 U.S. at 155–156 (collecting cases). Accordingly, the applicable standard of review in substantive due process cases is principally a function of the methodology used for identifying what rights are "fundamental."

This Court has held that a liberty interest will be deemed fundamental if it is "implicit in the concept of ordered liberty," *Palko v. Connecticut*, 302 U.S. 319, 325 (1937), is "deeply rooted in this Nation's history and tradition," *Moore*, 431 U.S. at 503 (plurality opinion), or is "so rooted in the traditions and conscience of our people as to be ranked as fundamental," *Michael H.*, 491 U.S. at 122 (plurality opinion) (quoting *Snyder v. Massachusetts*, 291 U.S. 97, 105 (1934)). See *Bowers*, 478 U.S. at 192–194. The precise formulation may vary, but the governing methodology rests on the Nation's history and traditions. *E.g., Burnham v. Superior Court*, 495 U.S. 604, 608–619 (1990) (plurality opinion); *Michael H.*, 491 U.S. at 122–130 (plurality opinion); *Bowers*, 478 U.S. at 192–194; *Moore*, 431 U.S. at 504 n.12 (plurality opinion); *Griswold*, 381 U.S. at 501 (Harlan, J., concurring in the judgment). See *Cruzan v. Director*, 110 S. Ct. 2841, 2846–2851 & n.7 (1990).[3] By so limiting fundamental rights, the Court has sought, in the words of the *Michael H.* plurality, to "prevent future generations from lightly casting aside important traditional values," while assuring that the Due Process Clause does not become a license "to invent new ones." 491 U.S. at 122 n.2. See *Moore*, 431 U.S. at 504 n.12 (plurality opinion).

---

3. That approach is consistent with this Court's procedural due process and Eighth Amendment decisions. In those areas, too, this Court has insisted that, at a minimum, history and tradition must inform the otherwise broad and general constitutional text. See, *e.g., Griffin v. United States*, 112 S. Ct. 466, 469–470 (1991); *Schad v. Arizona*, 111 S. Ct. 2491, 2500–2503 (1991) (plurality opinion); *id.* at 2505–2507 (opinion of Scalia, J.); *Stanford v. Kentucky*, 492 U.S. 361, 368–370 (1989); *Patterson v. New York*, 432 U.S. 197, 202 (1977); *McKeiver v. Pennsylvania*, 403 U.S. 528, 548 (1971) (plurality opinion).

B. The Pennsylvania Abortion Control Act Does Not Implicate a Fundamental Right Under the Due Process Clause.

Petitioners' principal submission is that the Court should reaffirm the fundamental right to abortion identified in *Roe*. As we explained in our briefs in *Akron I*, *Thornburgh*, *Webster*, *Hodgson*, and *Rust v. Sullivan*, 111 S. Ct. 1759 (1991), *Roe v. Wade* was wrongly decided and should be overruled. We strongly adhere to that position in this case.[4] But regardless of whether this case requires reconsideration of *Roe's* actual holding, *see Webster*, 492 U.S. at 521 (plurality opinion), the Court should clarify the standard of review of abortion regulation and, in so doing, make clear that the liberty interest recognized in *Webster* does not rise to the exceptional level of a fundamental right.

1. The Nation's history and traditions do not establish a fundamental right to abortion.

In *Webster*, a plurality of the Court determined that a woman's interest in having an abortion is a form of liberty protected by due process against arbitrary deprivation by the state. 492 U.S. at 520. Under the traditional means used by this Court to identify fundamental rights, however, no credible foundation exists for the claim that a woman enjoys a fundamental right to abortion.[5] That conclusion follows whether the in-

---

4. As we explained in our *Webster* brief (at 9–10), *stare decisis* considerations do not preclude reconsidering and overruling *Roe*. If "neither the length of time a majority has held its convictions nor the passions with which it defends them can withdraw legislation from this Court's scrutiny," *Bowers*, 478 U.S. at 210 (Blackmun, J., dissenting), neither factor should immunize one of this Court's constitutional rulings from re-examination, because in such cases "correction through legislative action is practically impossible." *Burnet v. Coronado Oil & Gas Co.*, 285 U.S. 393, 407 (1932) (Brandeis, J., dissenting).

5. That judgment is shared by a broad spectrum of constitutional scholars. *See, e.g.*, A. Bickel, *The Morality of Consent* 27–29 (1975); Burt, *The Constitution of the Family*, 1979 Sup. Ct. Rev. 329, 371–373; A. Cox, *The Court and the Constitution* 322–338 (1987); J. Ely, *Democracy and Distrust—A Theory of Judicial Review* 2–3, 247–248 n.52 (1980); Epstein, *Substantive Due Process by Any Other Name: The Abortion Cases*, 1973 Sup. Ct. Rev. 159; Gunther, *Some Reflections on the Judicial Role: Distinctions, Roots, and Prospects*, 1979 Wash. U.L.Q. 817, 819; Wellington, *Common Law Rules and Constitutional Double Standards: Some Notes on Adjudication*, 83 Yale L.J. 221, 297–311 (1973).

quiry is framed broadly, in terms of privacy or reproductive choice, or narrowly, in terms of abortion. *Compare Michael H.*, 491 U.S. at 127–128 n.6 (opinion of Scalia, J.), with *id.* at 132 (O'Connor, J., concurring in part). To examine this proposition, we turn to explore the legal history and traditions of the American people to discern the basis and nature of any such right.

a. It is beyond dispute that abortion after "quickening" was an offense at common law.[6] The first English abortion law, Lord Ellenborough's Act, 1803, 43 Geo. 3, ch. 58, outlawed abortion throughout pregnancy; it distinguished pre- from post-quickening abortions only to fix the severity of punishment. Early in our history, this Nation embraced the common law. In 1821, however, states began to enact laws condemning or restricting abortion. By the time the Fourteenth Amendment was ratified, such legislation was commonplace; in 1868, at least 28 of the then-37 States and 8 Territories had statutes banning or limiting abortion. The Reconstruction Era witnessed "the most important burst of anti-abortion legislation in the nation's history." J. Mohr, *Abortion in America* 200 (1978).[7] By the turn of the century, after "the passage of unambiguous anti-abortion laws in most of the states that had not already acted during the previous twenty years," the country had completed the transition from a Nation that followed the common law rule outlawing post-quickening abortion to "a nation where abortion was legally and officially proscribed." *Id.* at 226. "Every state in the Union had an anti-abortion law of some kind on its books by 1900 except Kentucky, where

---

6. The historical materials are discussed in *Roe*, 410 U.S. at 132–141; *id.* at 174–177 & nn.1–2 (Rehnquist, J., dissenting); J. Mohr, *Abortion in America* (1978); Siegel, *Reasoning from the Body: A Historical Perspective on Abortion Regulation and Questions of Equal Protection*, 44 Stan. L. Rev. 261, 281–282 (1992); *Amicus* Br. of the American Academy of Medical Ethics; *Amicus* Br. of Certain American State Legislators.

7. "At least 40 anti-abortion statutes of various kinds were placed on the state and territorial lawbooks during that period [between 1860 and 1880]; over 30 in the years from 1866 through 1877 alone. Some 13 jurisdictions formally outlawed abortion for the first time, and at least 21 states revised their already existing statutes on the subject. More significantly, most of the legislation passed between 1860 and 1880 explicitly accepted the regulars' [i.e., regular physicians'] assertions that the interruption of gestation at any point in a pregnancy should be a crime and that the state itself should try actively to restrict the practice of abortion." J. Mohr, *supra*, at 200.

the state courts outlawed the practice anyway." *Id.* at 229–230. With minor refinements and adjustments, those statutes, which reflected "a basic legislative consensus," remained unchanged until the 1960s. *Id.* at 229. And 21 of those laws were in effect in 1973 when *Roe* was decided, even after a decade of efforts at liberalization.[8]

In view of this historical record, it cannot persuasively be argued that the interest in having an abortion is so deeply rooted in our history as to be deemed "fundamental." The record in favor of the right to an abortion is no stronger than the record in *Michael H.*, where the court found no fundamental right to visitation privileges by adulterous fathers, or in *Bowers*, where the Court found no fundamental right to engage in homosexual sodomy. *Cf. Stanford* v. *Kentucky*, 492 U.S. 361, 370–373 (1989) (no consensus against execution of 16-year-olds when a majority of the states with capital punishment allows them to be executed). In short, this Nation's history rebuts any claim that the right to obtain an abortion is fundamental, since that history does not "exclude . . . a societal tradition of enacting laws denying that interest." *Michael H.*, 491 U.S. at 122 n.2 (opinion of Scalia, J., joined by Rehnquist, C.J., O'Connor & Kennedy, JJ.).[9]

---

8. *Amici* 250 Historians contend that laws banning abortion were originally adopted for various ignoble reasons, not to protect life in the womb. 250 Historians Br. [145–53]. That claim is overstated, J. Mohr, *supra*, 35–36, 165, 200; Siegel, 44 Stan. L. Rev. at 282, but it is irrelevant in any event. "It is a familiar principle of constitutional law that this Court will not strike down an otherwise constitutional statute on the basis of an alleged illicit legislative motive," *United States* v. *O'Brien*, 391 U.S. 367, 383 (1968), and that "the insufficiency of the original motivation does not diminish other interests that the restriction may now serve," *Bolger* v. *Youngs Drug Products Corp.*, 463 U.S. 60, 71 (1983); Epstein, 1973 Sup. Ct. Rev. at 168 n.34. Pennsylvania "places a supreme value upon protecting human life," including prenatal life, 18 Pa. Cons. Stat. Ann. § 3202(b)(4) (Purdon 1983), and the purpose of this Act is to "protect hereby the life and health of the woman subject to abortion" and "the child subject to abortion," *id.* § 3202(a) (Purdon 1983). Just as the widespread use of controlled substances does not render the drug laws unconstitutional, so, too, the prevalence of illegal abortions does not undermine laws outlawing or restricting abortion.

9. The prevalence of bans or restrictions on abortion prior to *Roe* was "not merely an historical accident." *Stanford*, 492 U.S. at 369 n.1 (citation omitted). After studying the abortion laws of 20 Western countries, a leading comparative law scholar reported that "we have less regulation of abortion in the interest of the fetus than any other Western nation," and "to a greater extent than in any other country, our courts have shut down the legislative process of bargaining, education, and persuasion on the abortion issue." M. Glendon, *Abortion and Divorce in Western*

After the publication of Professor Glendon's book, the Canadian Supreme Court struck down its abortion law on grounds similar to those stated in Roe. Morgentaler v. Regina, 1 S.C.R. 30, 44 D.L.R.4th 385 (1988). The West German constitutional court, by contrast, had earlier struck down a law liberalizing access to abortion on the grounds that " 'life developing within the womb' is constitutionally protected." Judgment of Feb. 25, 1975, 39 BVerfGE 1 (quoted in M. Glendon, supra, at 26). See 9 J. Marshall J. Prac. & Proc. 605 (1975) (reprinting decision).

b. Petitioners argue that "compelled continuation of a pregnancy infringes on a woman's right to bodily integrity by imposing substantial physical intrusions and significant risks of physical harm" and that abortion restrictions deny women "the right to make autonomous decisions about reproduction and family planning." Pet. Br. [46–47, 48]. Roe made a similar point. 410 U.S. at 153.[10] We readily agree that pregnancy (like abortion) entails "profound physical, emotional, and psychological consequences." Michael M. v. Superior Court, 450 U.S. 464, 471 (1981) (plurality opinion). But those burdens, albeit substantial, do not themselves give rise to a fundamental right. As this Court has recognized, governmental refusal to

---

Law 2 (1987). Two of those nations (Belgium and Ireland) have blanket prohibitions against abortion in their criminal law, subject only to the defense of necessity. Four countries (Canada, Portugal, Spain, and Switzerland) allow abortion only early in pregnancy and only in restricted instances, such as if there is a serious danger to the pregnant woman's health, a likelihood of serious disease or defect in the fetus, or the pregnancy resulted from rape or incest. Eight countries (Great Britain, Finland, France, West Germany, Iceland, Italy, Luxembourg, and the Netherlands) permit abortion in early pregnancy in a wider variety of circumstances that pose a particular hardship for a pregnant woman. Five nations (Austria, Denmark, Greece, Norway, and Sweden) allow elective abortions early in pregnancy, and strictly limit abortions thereafter. Only the United States permits elective abortion until viability. Id. at 13–15 & Table 1, 145–154. Indeed, Eastern European nations and the former Soviet Union had greater restrictions on abortion than this country does. Id. at 23–24. Thus, the fact that the regime created by Roe is so out of step with these judgments suggests that it is Roe, not the pre-Roe state of our law, that is "an historical accident."

10. Roe did not seek to ground a right to abortion in the text of the Constitution or this Nation's history and tradition. Instead, Roe fashioned the "fundamental right" to abortion by reference to several decisions of this Court. Roe described those decisions as recognizing a "guarantee of personal privacy," which "has some extension to activities relating to marriage, procreation, contraception, family relationships, and child rearing and education." 410 U.S. at 152–153 (citations omitted). "This right to privacy," Roe declared, "is broad enough to encompass a woman's decision whether or not to terminate her pregnancy." Id. at 153.

fund abortions can be quite burdensome, yet the Constitution does not guarantee a woman the right to such funds. And that is so even if the state funds childbirth expenses. *Webster*, 492 U.S. at 507–511. The refusal to supply other forms of government assistance can prove harmful, yet the Constitution does not require a state to intervene to prevent harm from befalling a person. *DeShaney* v. *Winnebago County Dep't of Social Servs.*, 489 U.S. 189 (1989) (police protection); *Lindsey* v. *Normet*, 405 U.S. 56 (1972) (shelter). If risk of physical or psychological harm were sufficient to create a constitutional right, a person would arguably have a right to avoid vaccinations or military service. But there is no such right. *Jacobson* v. *Massachusetts*, 197 U.S. 11 (1905); *Selective Draft Law Cases*, 245 U.S. 366 (1918); *Cox* v. *Wood*, 247 U.S. 3 (1918). In sum, risk of harm, standing alone, does not give rise to a constitutional right.

That line of reasoning, with all respect, is deeply flawed. Even if this Court's pre-*Roe* decisions have a common denominator, it is not a highly abstract right to "privacy," but a recognition of the importance of the family. *Cf. Michael H.*, 491 U.S. at 123 (plurality opinion). Even if those cases have "some extension" to "activities relating to" the family, abortion is "inherently different" from activities such as the use of contraceptives. Abortion, after all, "involves the purposeful termination of potential life." *Harris* v. *McRae*, 448 U.S. 297, 325 (1980); *see generally Thornburgh*, 476 U.S. at 792 n.2 (White, J., dissenting). For that reason, *Roe* itself realized that a "pregnant woman cannot be isolated in her privacy." 410 U.S. at 159. In sum, *Roe* derived a right to abortion from pre-*Roe* cases only by creating an artificial common denominator while denying what makes abortion unique.

By contrast, a law mandating abortions would pose a starkly different issue. At common law, a competent adult had a right to refuse medical care, and involuntary treatment was a battery absent consent or an emergency. *Schloendorff* v. *Society of the New York Hosp.*, 211 N.Y. 125, 129–130, 105 N.E. 92, 93 (1914) (Cardozo, J.); 3 F. Harper, F. James, Jr. & O. Gray, *The Law of Torts* § 17.1 (2d ed. 1986). Relying on that tradition, the Court has held that a competent adult has a liberty interest protected by due process in refusing unwanted, state-administered medical care. *Washington v. Harper*, 494 U.S. 210, 229 (1990); *Vitek v. Jones*, 445 U.S. 480, 494 (1980). Moreover, a compelled intrusion into a person's body is a "search" under the Fourth Amendment, *Schmerber v. California*, 384 U.S. 757, 767–768 (1966), and the Fourth Amendment prohibits as unreasonable certain forcible intrusions into a person's body, *Winston v. Lee*, 470 U.S. 753 (1985).

Nor is this conclusion altered by the fact that abortion is a controversy "of a 'sensitive and emotional nature,' generating heated public debate and controversy, 'with vigorous opposing views' and 'deeply and seemingly absolute convictions.' " New York et al. Br. 11 (quoting *Roe*, 410 U.S. at 116). Other subjects, such as capital punishment, likewise evoke strong emotions and inspire heated debate. Yet the Constitution leaves such questions in the main to the political process to decide.[11] In short, the Due Process Clause does not remove issues from the political process and put them before the judiciary for resolution because they are difficult and divisive.

We believe that the proper inquiry in reviewing an abortion regulation is whether the regulation is reasonably designed to advance a legitimate state interest, as a plurality of this Court articulated in *Webster*. 492 U.S. at 520. That standard of review is deferential, but not toothless. Indeed, this Court has held laws invalid under such a standard. *Compare, e.g., Metropolitan Life Ins. Co. v. Ward*, 470 U.S. 869 (1985); *Zobel v. Williams*, 457 U.S. 55 (1982); *United States Dep't of Agric. v. Moreno*, 413 U.S. 528 (1973). No reason exists to assume that courts will abdicate their responsibility to ensure that abortion regulations pass muster under that standard. Legislatures under that constitutional regime will not be able arbitrarily or unreasonably to constrain a woman's liberty interest.

2. The state has a compelling interest in protecting the fetus throughout pregnancy.

Even if the Court's pre-*Roe* decisions could be said to create a right of "privacy" or to "accomplish or prevent conception,"

---

11. The Court has, of course, established limits in that regard. *See, e.g., Coker v. Georgia*, 433 U.S. 584 (1977). But within those limits, the policy question of using capital punishment is one entrusted to the political processes in a democratic society.

Carey v. *Population Servs. Int'l*, 431 U.S. 678, 685 (1977), that conclusion would not end the inquiry. The Court's decisions make clear that a state can limit or even forbid conduct that is otherwise entitled to constitutional protection if the state acts precisely to vindicate a compelling interest. *See, e.g., Haig* v. *Agee*, 453 U.S. 280, 308–309 (1981) (the government may revoke the passport of a person who wishes to travel in order to disclose intelligence operations and the names of intelligence personnel); *Lee* v. *Washington*, 390 U.S. 333, 334 (1968) (Black, J., concurring) (the government may take threats and tensions from prison racial strife into account for the purpose of maintaining security and order in prison); *Near* v. *Minnesota*, 283 U.S. 697, 716 (1931) (dictum that military needs justify a prior restraint on the disclosure of the sailing date of troop ships). That principle is as applicable in this context as in any other, because, as Justice Harlan once noted, "the right of privacy most manifestly is not an absolute." *Poe* v. *Ullman*, 367 U.S. 497, 552 (1961) (Harlan, J., dissenting). The protection of innocent human life—in or out of the womb—is certainly the most compelling interest that a state can advance. *See Illinois* v. *Gates*, 462 U.S. 213, 237 (1983) ("the most basic function of any government" is "to provide for the security of the individual and of his property") (quoting *Miranda* v. *Arizona*, 384 U.S. 436, 539 (1966) (White, J., dissenting)). In our view, a state's interest in protecting fetal life throughout pregnancy, as a general matter, outweighs a woman's liberty interest in an abortion. The state's interest in prenatal life is a wholly legitimate and entirely adequate basis for restricting the right to abortion derived in *Roe*.

Central to *Roe* was the conclusion that the state lacks a compelling interest in preserving fetal life throughout pregnancy. *Roe* noted that a woman's right to terminate a fetus "is not unqualified and must be considered against important state interests" in "safeguarding health, in maintaining medical standards, and in protecting potential life." 410 U.S. at 154. But *Roe* stated that the weight of those interests is not uniform from conception to birth; instead, they "grow[] in substantiality as the woman approaches term." *Id.* at 162–163. Particularly critical in this regard was *Roe's* conclusion that a state's "important and legitimate interest in potential life" is not "compelling," *i.e.*, sufficiently weighty to overcome the fundamental right to abortion, until the fetus has reached viability, since only then is the fetus capable of "meaningful life outside the mother's womb." *Id.* at 163.

The proposition that a state's interest in protecting life in the womb is compelling only at viability "seems to mistake a definition for a syllogism." Ely, *The Wages of Crying Wolf: A Comment on Roe v. Wade*, 82 Yale L.J. 920, 924 (1973).[12] "The choice of viability as the point at which the state interest in potential life becomes compelling is no less arbitrary than choosing any point before viability or any point afterward." *Akron I*, 462 U.S. at 461 (O'Connor, J., dissenting). Even if the importance of a state's interest in protecting the fetus parallels the fetus's development, it does not follow that the state's interest in this regard is not compelling throughout a pregnancy. An interest may be sufficiently weighty to be "compelling" in the constitutional sense even if it later assumes still greater urgency. Accordingly, since "potential life is no less potential in the first weeks of pregnancy than it is at viability or afterward," *Akron I*, 462 U.S. at 461 (O'Connor, J., dissenting), the state's interest in protecting prenatal life "if compelling after viability, is equally compelling before viability," *Webster*, 492 U.S. at 519 (plurality opinion); *Thornburgh*, 476 U.S. at 828 (O'Connor, J., dissenting).

Roe itself recognized that laws infringing on a fundamental right are not automatically invalid; they survive strict scrutiny if they are "narrowly drawn to express only the legitimate state interests at stake." 410 U.S. at 155. Accordingly, because the state's interest in protecting prenatal life is compelling

12. See J. Mohr, *supra*, at 165 ("Most [19th century] physicians considered abortion a crime because of the inherent difficulties of determining any point at which a steadily developing embryo became somehow more alive than it had been the moment before. Furthermore, they objected strongly to snuffing out life in the making."); see also id. at 35–36, 200; L. Tribe, *American Constitutional Law* 1349 (2d ed. 1988) ("nothing in [Roe] provides a satisfactory explanation of why the fetal interest should not be deemed overriding prior to viability, particularly when a legislative majority chooses to regard the fetus as a human being from the moment of conception and perhaps even when it does not") (footnotes omitted).

throughout pregnancy, we believe that regulations furthering that interest are lawful throughout pregnancy.[13]

Petitioners contend that "the right to abortion may be grounded" in constitutional rights other than due process. Pet. Br. [42] n.27. In our view, those claims are meritless. Indeed, the ceaseless quest for a textual basis for the constitutional right to abortion only underscores the lack of any such support. See, e.g., Harris v. McRae, 448 U.S. at 319–320 (rejecting Establishment Clause challenge to Hyde Amendment); Bowen v. Kendrick, 487 U.S. 589 (1988) (same, Public Health Service Act (the Adolescent Family Life Act of 1981), 42 U.S.C. 300z et seq.); Employment Division, Dep't of Human Resources v. Smith, 494 U.S. 872, 879–890 (1990) (Free Exercise Clause does not invalidate neutral laws directed at secular subjects; rejecting Free Exercise challenge to statute banning drug use); Reynolds v. United States, 98 U.S. 145 (1879) (same, laws banning polygamy); Prince v. Massachusetts, 321 U.S. 158 (1944) (same, law banning child labor, as applied to distribution of religious pamphlets); Jehovah's Witnesses v. King County Hosp., 390 U.S. 598 (1968), aff'd 278 F. Supp. 488 (W.D. Wash. 1967) (upholding life-saving transfusion for a minor child over parents' Free Exercise claim; relying on Prince); United States v. Kozminski, 487 U.S. 931, 944 (1988) (Thirteenth Amendment does not apply to established common law cases, such as parents' right to custody of their children); U.S. Brief in Bray v. Alexandria Women's Health Clinic,

---

13. Petitioners may even agree with us to some extent. The Act prohibits previability abortions based on the sex of the fetus. 18 Pa. Cons. Stat. Ann. § 3204(c) (Purdon Supp. 1991). While petitioners ask the Court to reaffirm Roe, which bars a state from outlawing previability abortions, petitioners did not contend in the courts below, and they do not argue in this Court, that this provision is unconstitutional. It is not difficult to understand why. The prospect that a woman would terminate life in the womb merely because it is a boy or a girl surely should be so utterly odious to every member of "a free, egalitarian, and democratic society" like ours, Thornburgh, 476 U.S. at 793 (White, J., dissenting), that any such abortion would be properly subject to universal condemnation. At the very least, no one could seriously claim that the Constitution offers the remotest protection for such a macabre act. Yet, if a state has a compelling interest in forbidding gender-selection abortions, the Roe trimester framework cannot survive intact. And if the state has a compelling interest in prohibiting abortions for that reason, it may fairly be asked why the state lacks a similar compelling interest in outlawing abortions for other reasons. A state which believes that a child in the womb should not be destroyed simply because it is a boy or a girl should also be free to protect that life if it is the second (or third, etc.) child to be born, or if the pregnancy occurred despite the use of contraceptives.

No. 90–985 (opposition to abortion is not gender discrimination) (a copy has been supplied to the parties' counsel); *see generally* Bopp, *Will There Be a Constitutional Right to Abortion After the Reconsideration of Roe v. Wade?*, 15 J. Contemp. L. 131 (1989).

II. THE PENNSYLVANIA ABORTION CONTROL ACT IS REASONABLY DESIGNED TO ADVANCE LEGITIMATE STATE INTERESTS.

Petitioners claim that the Act is unconstitutional under any standard of review. Pet. Br. [61–80]. In so arguing, petitioners and *amici* (*e.g.*, ACOG Br. [95–98]; American Psychological Ass'n Br.; City of New York et al. Br.; NAACP Legal Defense and Educ. Fund et al. Br.; Pennsylvania Coalition Against Domestic Violence et al. Br.) rely heavily on the burden that could befall some women from provisions such as the spousal notification requirement. Yet, as the court of appeals noted, petitioners brought a facial constitutional challenge to the statute, not an as-applied challenge. Pet. App. 5a, 41a. Thus, the governing legal standard is exacting: Petitioners must prove that the statute *cannot be constitutionally applied to anyone. See, e.g., Ohio v. Akron Center for Reproductive Health*, 110 S. Ct. 2972, 2980–2981 (1990) (*Akron II*); *United States v. Salerno*, 481 U.S. 739, 745 (1987); *Webster*, 492 U.S. at 524 (O'Connor, J., concurring). This they cannot do.[14]

Informed consent. Under the Pennsylvania statute, a woman must be given medical and other information by a physician or his agent, and she must wait 24 hours before consenting to an abortion.[15] Those provisions are valid.

---

14. The majority in *Akron I* and *Thornburgh* struck down statutory requirements similar to those here. The *Webster* plurality, however, explained that many of the rules adopted in *Roe* and later cases would not be of "constitutional import" once *Roe*'s trimester framework is abandoned. 492 U.S. at 518 n.15.

15. A referring or performing physician must inform a woman about (i) the nature of the procedure and risks and alternatives that a reasonable patient would find material; (ii) the fetus's probable gestational age; and (iii) the medical risks involved in carrying a pregnancy to term. 18 Pa. Cons. Stat. Ann. § 3205(a)(1) (Purdon Supp. 1991). A physician or a qualified agent also must tell a woman that (i) medical assistance benefits may be available for prenatal, childbirth, and

The State has a legitimate interest in ensuring that a woman's decision to have an abortion is an informed one. *Thornburgh*, 476 U.S. at 760; *Akron I*, 462 U.S. at 443; *Planned Parenthood v. Danforth*, 428 U.S. 52, 67 (1976).[16] Accurate information about the abortion procedure and its risks and alternatives is related to maternal health and a state's legitimate purpose in requiring informed consent. *Akron I*, 462 U.S. at 446. An accurate description of the gestational age of the fetus and the risks involved in carrying a child to term furthers those interests and the State's concern for potential life. See *Thornburgh*, 476 U.S. at 798–804 (White, J., dissenting); *id.* at 830–831 (O'Connor, J., dissenting).[17] Likewise, the State's interest in preserving potential life is rationally served by informing women that medical assistance benefits and paternal child support may be obtainable, and by making available accurate information about the process of fetal growth and alternatives to abortion. *Id.* at 831 (O'Connor, J., dissenting).

The fact that some information may be of little or no use to some recipients, Pet. App. 177a–180a, does not cast doubt on the validity of the Act. Where, as here, no fundamental right is at stake, government may regulate conduct in an overinclusive manner, as long as it does so rationally. *Vance v. Bradley*, 440 U.S. 93, 108 (1979). A state's belief that its interests are better served with an informed consent provision than without one is, in our view, entirely rational.

It is no argument that the disclosure of accurate information might persuade some women not to have an abortion. Encouraging childbirth is a legitimate governmental objective.

---

neonatal care; (ii) the child's father is liable for child support; and (iii) the state health department publishes free materials describing the fetus at different stages and listing abortion alternatives. *Id.* § 3205(a)(2) (Purdon 1983 & Supp. 1991). A 24-hour waiting period follows.

16. At common law and today, a physician must obtain patients' consent to the contemplated scope of an operation without misleading them about its nature or probable consequences, and must inform patients about the risks posed by available alternative treatments. See, e.g., *Cruzan*, 110 S. Ct. at 2846–2847; *Slater v. Baker*, 2 Wils. 359, 95 Eng. Rep. 860 (K.B. 1767); 3 F. Harper, F. James, Jr. & O. Gray, *supra*, § 17.1.

17. Petitioners' claim that non-physician counselors can provide the same information is beside the point. As the court of appeals observed, it was reasonable for the State to conclude that disclosure by physicians will be more effective than delegation of that task to others. Pet. App. 47a–48a.

Harris v. *McRae*, 448 U.S. 297, 322–323 (1980); *Maher* v. *Roe*, 432 U.S. 464, 478–479 (1977). *Roe* did not purport to impress on the Constitution the proposition that abortion is a public good. *Thornburgh*, 476 U.S. at 797 (White, J., dissenting). Instead, *Roe* professed agnosticism on the question when life begins and declined to debate the morality of abortion. 410 U.S. at 116–117, 159–162. Thus, the fact that the informed consent provision may dissuade some women from having an abortion does not undermine its validity.[18]

Lastly, the Act's 24-hour waiting period readily passes muster. A waiting period provides time for reflection and reconsideration, furthering a state's interests in informed consent and protecting fetal life. A mandatory waiting period burdens women seeking abortions, but the State is constitutionally at liberty to weigh the competing concerns and to strike what it sees as an appropriate balance. The abortion decision, once implemented, is an irrevocable one, and the unique psychological consequences of that singular act will remain with a woman (and her spouse or partner) throughout their lives. Whatever the wisdom of the State's decision, it is clearly a rational one. *See Harris* v. *McRae*, 448 U.S. at 326.

Informed parental consent. An unemancipated or incompetent minor must give her informed consent and obtain that of a parent or guardian before she can obtain an abortion. 18 Pa. Cons. Stat. Ann. § 3206(a) (Purdon 1983 & Supp. 1991).[19] Alternatively, a minor can obtain an abortion if a state court finds that she is mature, is capable of giving informed consent, and gives such consent, or that an abortion

18. Nor do the informed consent provisions violate the First Amendment rights of physicians or counselors. States are free to require professionals to include accurate and reasonably material information in their commercial speech directed toward prospective clients. *Zauderer* v. *Office of Disciplinary Counsel*, 471 U.S. 626, 650–651 (1985). Truthful and relevant information about risks, alternatives, and medical and financial facts is not the kind of "prescribed . . . orthodoxy in politics, nationalism, religion, or other matters of opinion" that violates the First Amendment's protection of commercial speech. *Id.* at 651; *cf. Riley* v. *National Fed'n of the Blind*, 487 U.S. 781, 796 n.9 (1988).

19. Consent of the child's guardian(s) is sufficient if both parents are dead or otherwise unavailable to the physician in a reasonable time and manner. Consent of a custodial parent is sufficient if the child's parents are divorced. Consent of an adult standing *in loco parentis* is sufficient if neither a parent nor a guardian is available to the physician in a reasonable time and manner. 18 Pa. Cons. Stat. Ann. § 3206(b) (Purdon 1983). In the case of pregnancy due to incest by the child's father, the minor need obtain consent only from her mother. 18 Pa. Cons. Stat. Ann. § 3206(a) (Purdon 1983 & Supp. 1991).

is in her best interests. *Id.* § 3206(c) and (d) (Purdon 1983); *see id.* § 3206(e)–(h) (Purdon 1983 & Supp. 1991) (bypass procedures). Those provisions are valid, too.

In our view, a minor has no fundamental right to an abortion without parental consent.[20] In addition, a state has a strong and legitimate interest in involving parents in matters affecting their children's well-being, including abortion. *See, e.g., Hodgson,* 110 S. Ct. at 2948 (opinion of Stevens, J.); *id.* at 2950–2951 (opinion of O'Connor, J.); *id.* at 2970 (opinion of Kennedy, J.). Parental consent laws reasonably advance that interest. Furthermore, if the informed consent provision is valid, the informed parental consent provision is valid, too. A state has a keener interest in protecting minors than adults against their improvement choices.

Spousal notification. The Act adopts a spousal notification requirement in order "to further the Commonwealth's interest in promoting the integrity of the marital relationship," in "protect[ing] a spouse's interests in having children within marriage," and in "protecting the prenatal life of that spouse's child," 18 Pa. Cons. Stat. Ann. § 3209(a) (Purdon Supp. 1991). With certain exceptions, a woman must give the physician a signed statement, under penalty for making a false statement, that she has notified her spouse that she will undergo an abortion. *Ibid.*[21] This notification requirement readily survives facial challenge, because it is reasonably designed to further a number of legitimate state interests.[22]

First, spousal notification is reasonably designed to advance

20. Our position in this regard is set forth in our *amicus* brief in *Hodgson* v. *Minnesota,* Nos. 88–1125 & 88–1309, a copy of which has been provided to the parties' counsel.

21. A woman need not provide the statement if her spouse is not the child's father; if he could not be located after a diligent search; if the pregnancy is the result of a spousal sexual assault that has been reported to the authorities; or if she has reason to believe that notifying her spouse will lead her to suffer bodily injury by him or someone else. *Id.* § 3209(b) (Purdon Supp. 1991).

22. Pennsylvania is not alone in recognizing and protecting the husband's interest in the life of his unborn child. Before and during the 19th century, when abortion was strictly regulated and generally prohibited by state law, there was no need for special protection of the father's interests. *See Poe* v. *Gerstein,* 517 F.2d 787, 795 (5th Cir. 1975), *aff'd,* 428 U.S. 901 (1976). By the time of *Roe,* some states had liberalized their abortion laws, and many of the new laws acknowledged and protected the father's role in the abortion decision. *Doe* v. *Doe,* 365 Mass. 556, 561 & nn.3–5, 314 N.E.2d 128, 131 & nn.3–5 (1974) (citing statutes of 15 states requiring husband's consent for abortions under some or all circumstances). A number of spousal consent and notification laws are currently on the books. *See, e.g.,* Colo. Rev. Stat. Ann. § 18–6–101(1) (West 1986) (spousal consent).

a state's legitimate interest in protecting the fetus. The husband sometimes will oppose a proposed abortion. After being notified, he may persuade his spouse to reconsider her decision, thus achieving the state's interest. Cf. Pet. App. 255a–256a.

Second, a husband's interests in procreation within marriage and in the potential life of his unborn child are unquestionably legitimate and substantial ones.[23] It can hardly be gainsaid that the state acts legitimately in seeking to protect such parental and familial interests. See Michael H., 491 U.S. at 128–129 (opinion of Scalia, J.) (husband's opportunity "to develop a relationship with" the offspring of the marital community may be protected by the state) (quoting Lehr v. Robertson, 463 U.S. 248, 262 (1983)); Labine v. Vincent, 401 U.S. 532, 538 (1971). The spousal notification requirement is certainly a reasonable means of advancing that state interest. By providing that, absent unusual circumstances, a husband will know of his spouse's intent to have an abortion, the notification requirement ensures at least the possibility that the husband will participate in deciding the fate of his unborn child, a possibility that might otherwise have been denied him. The husband's participation, in turn, may lead his spouse to reconsider her options or to rethink a hasty decision.[24] As Judge Alito noted in dissent below, the State legislature "could have rationally believed that some married women are initially inclined to obtain an abortion without their husbands' knowledge because of perceived problems—such as economic constraints, future plans, or the husbands' previously expressed opposition—that may be obviated by discussion prior to the abortion." Pet. App. 102a.

Finally, and for essentially the same reasons, the State's

23. See Danforth, 428 U.S. at 69; id. at 93 (White, J., dissenting in part); Skinner v. Oklahoma, 316 U.S. 535, 541 (1942). Danforth held that a state could not condition a woman's access to an abortion on the consent of her spouse, but that conclusion rested on the flawed premise that "the State cannot regulate or proscribe abortion during the first stage" of pregnancy. 428 U.S. at 69. A spousal notification requirement also impinges far less severely on a woman's ability to have an abortion than does a spousal consent requirement. See Akron II, 110 S. Ct. at 2979.

24. No doubt most wives would consult with their husbands even absent a statutory notice requirement. Pet. App. 193a. Nonetheless, the Act will likely increase the number of such consultations. Many women who otherwise might choose not to tell their spouses of their decision, for reasons of convenience, haste, or concern about disagreement, will be inclined to comply because of the legislative mandate.

interest in "promoting the integrity of the marital relationship," 18 Pa. Cons. Stat. Ann. § 3209(a) (Purdon Supp. 1991), is reasonably furthered by the spousal notice requirement. That interest is legitimate, *Akron I*, 462 U.S. at 443 n.32, and is properly encompassed by the state's traditional power to regulate marriage and strengthen family life, *see Sosna v. Iowa*, 419 U.S. 393, 404 (1975); *Labine*, 401 U.S. at 538. Petitioners' claim, Pet. Br. [61–62], and the district court's ruling, Pet. App. 261a–262a, that the notification requirement does not further the State's interest misses the point. The interest that Pennsylvania has chosen to foster is marital integrity, not "[m]arital accord," Pet. App. 262a. A state may legitimately elect to ensure truthful marital communication concerning a crucial issue such as abortion, despite the possibility that marital discord may result in some instances. *See Scheinberg v. Smith*, 659 F.2d 476, 484–486 & n.4 (5th Cir. 1981).

Petitioners make much of the possibility that some women may be deterred from obtaining an abortion if they must notify their spouses. Pet. Br. [62–64]. But the State could reasonably have concluded that the statutory exceptions for women who reasonably fear bodily injury and for pregnancies resulting from spousal assault would eliminate the principal bases for that concern. The possibility that some women may not take advantage of the exceptions, or may fear other consequences of notification, does not affect the facial validity of the statute. *See Hodgson*, 110 S. Ct. at 2968 (opinion of Kennedy, J.) ("Laws are not declared unconstitutional because of some general reluctance to follow a statutory scheme the legislature finds necessary to accomplish a legitimate state objective."). The State weighed the complex social and moral considerations involved and found such concerns insufficient to overcome the countervailing factors. The wisdom of such a clearly rational decision is not for the courts to judge. *See Harris v. McRae*, 448 U.S. at 326.[25]

25. Petitioners argue that the spousal notification requirement violates the Equal Protection Clause and impermissibly intrudes on "the protected marital relationship." Pet. Br. [66–67]. In our view, neither claim has merit. Women who want an abortion are not a "suspect" or "quasi-suspect" class deserving of heightened scrutiny under the Equal Protection Clause. *See Harris v. McRae*, 448 U.S. at 323; *Maher v. Roe*, 432 U.S. at 470–471; *cf. Geduldig v. Aiello*, 417 U.S. 484, 496–497 n.20 (1974). Likewise no generalized right of marital privacy is infringed by the

Medical emergency. A "medical emergency" is an exception to the above requirements of the Act.[26] Petitioners argued below that the statutory definition of medical emergency was inadequate since it did not include three serious conditions that pregnant women can suffer (preeclampsia, inevitable abortion, and prematurely ruptured membrane). The district court ruled that the definition did not include those conditions, Pet. App. 237a, but the court of appeals disagreed, Pet. App. 41a, relying on the "well-accepted canon[] of statutory interpretation used in the [state] courts," *Webster*, 492 U.S. at 515 (plurality opinion), that a statute should be read to preserve its constitutionality and on the fact that petitioners challenged the Act on its face. Pet. App. 37a, 41a.[27]

Petitioners do not argue that the Act cannot be read that way. Instead, they criticize the Third Circuit for reading the Act too narrowly, as protecting women only from "significant" health risks. Pet. Br. [79–80]. Due process, however, does not require the State to avoid placing insignificant health risks on individuals for the public benefit. This Court in *Jacobson* v. *Massachusetts* upheld a compulsory smallpox vaccination even though the vaccine had a statistical possibility of causing serious illness or death. In this case, the State has a compelling interest in protecting the fetus, which "justif[ies] substantial and ordinarily impermissible impositions on the individual," including "the infliction of some degree of risk of physical harm." *Thornburgh*, 476 U.S. at 808–809 (White, J., dissenting).

Reporting requirements. Facilities performing abortions

---

spousal notification requirement. If the state may—indeed must, *see Kirchberg* v. *Feenstra*, 450 U.S. 455 (1981)—require the participation of both spouses in the disposition of marital property, surely it may require that they both be aware of the far more important decision to terminate a pregnancy.

26. A "medical emergency" is defined as "[t]hat condition which, on the basis of the physician's good faith clinical judgment, so complicates the medical condition of a pregnant woman as to necessitate the immediate abortion of her pregnancy to avert her death or for which a delay will create serious risk of substantial and irreversible impairment of major bodily function." 18 Pa. Cons. Stat. Ann. § 3203 (Purdon Supp. 1991).

27. The State also reads the definition to include all three conditions. *See* Appellants C.A. Br. 5–7, 23–25. A state attorney general's interpretation of a state law is not binding on the state courts, *Virginia* v. *American Booksellers Ass'n*, 484 U.S. 383, 397 (1988), but may be useful in construing state law, *cf. Minnesota* v. *Probate Court*, 309 U.S. 270, 273–274 (1940) (relying on the state attorney general's reading of the state supreme court's opinion).

have various reporting obligations.[28] The requirement that facilities provide confidential reports concerning the identities and medical judgments of physicians involved in abortions is valid given the State's legitimate interests in maternal health and enforcement of the Act. See *Thornburgh*, 476 U.S. at 804 (White, J., dissenting). The other information can be required under *Danforth*, 428 U.S. at 79–81, and furthers the same interests. See *Planned Parenthood Ass'n v. Ashcroft*, 462 U.S. 476, 486–490 (1983) (opinion of Powell, J.); *id.* at 505 (opinion of O'Connor, J.) (upholding compulsory pathology reports). Public disclosure of the number of abortions performed by facilities receiving public funds directly furthers the valid goal of increasing the public's knowledge as to how, and by whom, public money is spent. See *Wyman v. James*, 400 U.S. 309, 319 (1971); Pet. App. 83a.[29]

28. Each facility must file a report with its name and address and that of any affiliated enterprise. Such information is public if a facility received State funds during the past calendar year; otherwise, the information is available only to State law enforcement officials or State medical boards. 18 Pa. Cons. Stat. Ann. § 3207 (Purdon 1983 & Supp. 1991). To "promot[e] . . . maternal health and life by adding to the sum of medical and public health knowledge through the compilation of relevant data, and to promote the Commonwealth's interest in protection of the unborn child," *id.* § 3214(a) (Purdon Supp. 1991), each facility must file a report on each abortion. The reports do not identify patients by name, but they do include other types of information. *Id.* § 3214 (Purdon Supp. 1991). A facility also must file a quarterly report stating the number of abortions performed for each trimester of pregnancy. Here, too, the reports are public only if the facility received State funds during the year prior to the filing of the report. *Id.* § 3214(a) (Purdon Supp. 1991).

29. Petitioners' speculative concerns that these requirements may deter some facilities and physicians from performing abortions and may lead to harassment of abortion clinics, Pet. Br. [78], do not undermine the facial validity of the Act. The State's decision to require the reports was a rational one; the Constitution requires no more.

CONCLUSION

The judgment of the court of appeals in No. 91–744 should be affirmed and in No. 91–902 should be reversed.

Respectfully submitted,

KENNETH W. STARR
Solicitor General

STUART M. GERSON
Assistant Attorney General

PAUL J. LARKIN, JR.
Assistant to the Solicitor
General

THOMAS G. HUNGAR
Assistant to the Solicitor
General

ALFRED R. MOLLIN
Attorney

APRIL 1992

BRIEF OF THE UNITED STATES CATHOLIC CONFERENCE, THE CHRISTIAN LIFE COMMISSION, SOUTHERN BAPTIST CONVENTION, AND THE NATIONAL ASSOCIATION OF EVANGELICALS AS *AMICI CURIAE* IN SUPPORT OF RESPONDENTS AND CROSS-PETITIONERS

INTEREST OF *AMICI CURIAE*

All active Catholic Bishops in the United States are members of the United States Catholic Conference ("Conference"), a nonprofit corporation organized under the laws of the District of Columbia. The Roman Catholic Church, the largest religious denomination in the United States, has over 57 million adherents in 20,000 parishes throughout the country. The Bishops' Conference advocates and promotes the pastoral teachings of the Bishops in such diverse areas as education, family life, health care, social welfare, immigration, civil rights, criminal justice, and the economy. When permitted by court rules and practice, the Conference files briefs as *amicus curiae* in litigation of importance to the Catholic Church and its people throughout the United States. Of the values that the Conference seeks to promote through its participation in litigation, respect for human life is of the highest importance.

The Christian Life Commission ("Commission") is the moral concerns and public policy agency for the Southern Baptist Convention, the nation's largest Protestant denomination, with over 15.2 million members in over 38,000 autonomous local churches. The Christian Life Commission has been charged by the Convention to address public policies affecting the sanctity of human life, the integrity of marriage and the family, and other subjects. Southern Baptists have expressed themselves in repeated resolutions, passed in national conventions over the past two decades, overwhelmingly opposing abortion except to save the life of the mother and calling for the reversal of *Roe* v. *Wade*, 410 U.S. 113 (1973). The Christian Life Commission seeks to advocate positions consistent with these resolutions by filing briefs as *amicus curiae* in important litigation such as this case.

The National Association of Evangelicals ("NAE") is a nonprofit association of evangelical Christian denominations, churches, organizations, institutions, and individuals. It includes some 45,000 churches from 74 denominations and serves a constituency of approximately 15 million people. As its official resolutions attest, NAE is committed to defending the sanctity of human life. The NAE, the Commission, and the Conference believe that the practice of abortion-on-demand in this country undermines respect for all life and jeopardizes other vital interests of individuals, the family, and the community. For this reason, any retreat from the review of abortion jurisprudence begun by this Court in *Webster* v. *Reproductive Health Services*, 492 U.S. 490 (1989), will serve only to confuse the law and derogate other fundamental rights, most especially those of countless unborn children. Because the federal right created in *Roe* v. *Wade* underlies jurisdiction in this case, reconsideration of that case without further delay is appropriate here.

Through their counsel, the parties have consented to the appearance of these *amici*.

SUMMARY OF ARGUMENT

In 1973, this Court held that its privacy jurisprudence "is broad enough to encompass a woman's decision whether or not to terminate her pregnancy." *Roe* v. *Wade*, 410 U.S. at 153. It did so, however, recognizing that this decision involved more than the decisions given constitutional protection in cases from *Meyer* v. *Nebraska*, 262 U.S. 390 (1923), to *Griswold* v. *Connecticut*, 381 U.S. 479 (1965). Abortion involves the termination of a life and the infringement of other personal and community interests. *Roe* v. *Wade*, 410 U.S. at 159. For this reason, the Court held open the possibility that these interests could not only be balanced against, but at times override, the now protected choice of abortion. In nineteen years of legislative efforts and litigation experience, that prospect has never meaningfully materialized. Society, the family, men, women, and millions of unborn children have suffered exceedingly as a result.

In his concurring opinion in *Roe v. Wade* and *Doe v. Bolton*, 410 U.S. 179 (1973), Justice Douglas discussed the nature of "liberty" as including "autonomous control over *the development and expression of one's intellect, interests, tastes, and personality.*" 410 U.S. at 211 (emphasis in original). This right, the Justice said, is "absolute, permitting of no exceptions." *Id.* No other rights encompassed by his notion of liberty, including the right of privacy, were denominated autonomous, and no other Justice spoke of autonomy in relation to personal liberty or privacy in those first abortion cases. 410 U.S. at 113–223. Yet by the time the Court reached its decision in *Thornburgh v. American College of Obstetricians and Gynecologists*, 476 U.S. 747 (1986), a majority had come to employ the concept of autonomy in direct relation to a woman's decision to abort her child. 476 U.S. at 772. By so doing, the Court truly caused the pregnant woman to be "isolated in her privacy" from all other legitimate interests of society, of her community, of her family, and of her unborn child—an outcome that *Roe v. Wade* originally disavowed. 410 U.S. at 159. Having been promised "freedom of choice" by abortion's supporters, pregnant women find themselves poorly served by the abortion industry's contrived "autonomy." The result of isolating expectant mothers from the aid and support they need has been to expose them to victimization by an abortion industry that masquerades as operating in their best interests, while in fact it seeks to avoid legitimate state regulation aimed at protecting health and safety.

When Pennsylvania enacted minimal medical regulations for clinics performing abortions, the United States District Court for the Eastern District of Pennsylvania enjoined them at the request of the abortion providers. This result protected abortion notwithstanding the state's legitimate authority to license and regulate medical practitioners in the interest of protecting all patients. *Barsky v. Board of Regents*, 347 U.S.

442, 449 (1954). The lower court disregarded this Court's teaching that the states have compelling interests in protecting maternal health, preserving prenatal life, and upholding professional standards. Yet the district judge was only applying the hyperextension of *Roe*, especially the sweeping opinion in *Thornburgh*. That decision completed the distortion of the law begun in *Roe*, and its demise as precedent would be a healthy step. For this reason, this Court must complete the process begun in *Webster* v. *Reproductive Health Services*.

The primary problem lies not in *Thornburgh*, whose abandonment is presaged by *Webster*, but in *Roe* v. *Wade* and the collapsing foundation on which it was based. To explain its original extension of the constitutional right of privacy to abortion, this Court had to engage in speculation as to how certain perceived medical, social, or psychological "detriments" to pregnant women might be alleviated by abortion. *Roe* v. *Wade*, 410 U.S. at 153. This nation's experience shows that those predictions were unfounded. Unsafe abortion, maternal and infant mortality, family instability, teenage pregnancy, and similar difficulties continue unabated. Widespread abortion has not solved such problems. Indeed, abortion has created its own list of unexpected and undesirable detriments to our society. The only solution for this Court is not to entrench its decisional law further, but to reconsider its rationale for including abortion within the Due Process Clause of the Fourteenth Amendment. The Court can and should do so because subject matter jurisdiction over this case depends upon abortion remaining a constitutional right. In order for the Court to examine properly its own jurisdiction, as it is bound to do in every case, *Roe* v. *Wade* must be reconsidered and should, on reflection, be abandoned.

ARGUMENT

I. BEFORE ADDRESSING THE MERITS OF THIS CASE, THE COURT SHOULD RECONSIDER *ROE* V. *WADE*.

Since November 7, 1991, when petitioners and their counsel publicly announced their strategy for filing a petition for certiorari in this case, there has been rampant speculation across this nation as to whether *Roe v. Wade* would, could, or should be reconsidered. For the most part, however, prognosticators have ignored the fundamental fact that subject matter jurisdiction is always open to review, and that jurisdiction over this case depends on this Court's decision in *Roe v. Wade*.

Without discussion, the district judge proclaimed, "I have subject matter jurisdiction over this controversy pursuant to 28 U.S.C. § 1331 (1966 and 1990 Supp.), 28 U.S.C. § 1343(a)(3), (4) (1976 and 1990 Supp.), and the Fourteenth Amendment to the United States Constitution." *Planned Parenthood v. Casey*, 744 F. Supp. 1323, 1325 (E.D. Pa. 1990). The court of appeals opinion, on review here, abbreviates but essentially reiterates the district court's jurisdictional proclamation. *Planned Parenthood v. Casey*, 947 F.2d 682, 687 (3rd Cir. 1991), *cert. granted*, 112 S. Ct. 931 (1992). Yet this Court has stated that:

> [E]very federal appellate court has a special obligation to "satisfy itself not only of its own jurisdiction, but also that of the lower courts in a cause under review," even though the parties are prepared to concede it.

Bender v. Williamsport Area School District, 475 U.S. 534, 541 (1986) (quoting *Mitchell v. Maurer*, 293 U.S. 237, 244 (1934)). Every federal court is therefore obliged to examine its subject matter jurisdiction, whether the issue is raised by a party, a witness, an intervenor, an *amicus curiae*, or by the court itself. The question of jurisdiction is so "fundamental" that "the court is bound to ask and answer [it] for itself, even when not otherwise suggested, and without respect to the relation of the parties to it." *Bender*, 475 U.S. at 547 (quoting *Mansfield C. & L.M.R. Co. v. Swan*, 111 U.S. 379, 382 (1884)).

The abortion cases filed in federal courts since the Court's decision in *Roe v. Wade* have relied, as this case does, on 28 U.S.C. §§ 1331 and 1343 for federal jurisdiction. Those statutory provisions require, of course, a "deprivation, under color of any State law, statute, ordinance, regulation, custom or usage, of any right, privilege or immunity secured by the

Constitution of the United States" or a claim "arising under the Constitution, laws, or treaties of the United States." 28 U.S.C. § 1343(a)(3) and 1331. Because of this Court's pivotal holding in *Roe* v. *Wade* that the constitutional "right of privacy . . . is broad enough to encompass a woman's decision whether or not to terminate her pregnancy," federal courts presume that the jurisdictional requirement of a constitutional deprivation or claim is always extant where abortion is involved. In fact, many parties do not even raise the issue, concentrating instead on other jurisdictional issues such as plaintiffs' standing, as the parties in this case did below.[1]

Prior to *Roe* v. *Wade's* elevation of abortion to constitutionally protected status, federal jurisdiction over abortion cases was not at all clear; lower courts cited one another for assurance that they ought even to entertain these complaints. *See, e.g., Doe* v. *Bolton*, 319 F. Supp. 1048, 1052 (N.D. Ga. 1970) and *Doe* v. *Scott*, 310 F. Supp. 688, 689 (N.D. Ill. 1970). This Court has itself assumed jurisdiction in several abortion cases, beginning with *Doe* v. *Bolton*, 410 U.S. 179 (1973), without ever mentioning that subject matter jurisdiction is wholly dependent on the continued efficacy of *Roe* v. *Wade's* central holding.[2] Such silence, however, is decidedly not a binding jurisdictional decision. As this Court noted in another action brought under 28 U.S.C. § 1343:

> Moreover, when questions of jurisdiction have been passed on in prior decisions sub silentio, this Court has never considered itself bound when a subsequent case finally brings the jurisdictional issue before us. We therefore approach the question of the District Court's jurisdiction to entertain this suit as an open one calling for a canvass of the relevant jurisdictional considerations.

Hagans v. *Lavine*, 415 U.S. 528, 533 n.5 (1974) (citations omitted). Similarly, this Court is now faced with a consid-

---

1. *See, e.g.*, Defendants', Robert P. Casey's, et al., Pretrial Memorandum of Law (filed July 20, 1990) at 3–4; *see also Thornburgh* v. *American College of Obstetricians & Gynecologists*, 476 U.S. at 754–55.

2. In both *Thornburgh*, 476 U.S. at 759, and *Akron* v. *Akron Center for Reproductive Health*, 462 U.S. 416, 420 n.1 (1983), this Court reaffirmed *Roe* v. *Wade* without commenting upon the jurisdictional ramification of that holding.

eration of federal jurisdiction under 28 U.S.C. §§ 1331 and 1343; indeed, the obligation to address the issue "is inflexible and without exception," applying "in all cases" and "[o]n every writ of error or appeal." *Bender*, 475 U.S. at 547 (quoting *Mansfield C. & L.M.R. Co. v. Swan*, 111 U.S. at 382). In proceeding then to "canvass all relevant jurisdictional considerations," the Court must begin with studied reconsideration of its decision in *Roe* v. *Wade*, for it is that decision upon which federal jurisdiction rests.

II. THE COURT'S APPLICATION OF PRIVACY PRIN-CIPLES TO ABORTION IN *ROE V. WADE* WAS FUN-DAMENTALLY FLAWED.

In undertaking reconsideration of *Roe* v. *Wade*, this Court should be guided by its line of privacy cases predating this Court's legitimization of abortion-on-demand. Those precedents show proper balance of individual and societal interests—allowance for personal liberty within a framework that protects human life, respects family relationships, promotes the common good, and preserves our free society. Historically, it was always understood that liberty to engage in certain personal actions is not license. In *Jacobson v. Massachusetts*, 197 U.S. 11, 26 (1905), Justice Harlan, writing for the majority, explained:

> [T]he liberty secured by the Constitution of the United States to every person within its jurisdiction does not import an absolute right in each person to be, at all times and in all circumstances, wholly freed from restraint. There are manifold restraints to which every person is necessarily subject for the common good. . . . Real liberty for all could not exist under the operation of a principle which recognizes the right of each individual person to use his own, whether in respect of his person or his property, regardless of the injury that may be done to others.

Although the ability to make certain choices was sometimes given constitutional foundation, often under the Due Process

Clause of the Fourteenth Amendment, this Court has always done so in balance with legitimate, sometimes competing interests rationally related to the choice. *E.g., Allgeyer v. Louisiana*, 165 U.S. 578 (1897).[3] Protection of basic constitutional values has been the Court's dominant adjudicative principle.[4]

The early debate on what became the privacy doctrine in this century occurred during the process of incorporating "federal" rights to the states through the Fourteenth Amendment. In a seminal decision, *Palko v. Connecticut*, 302 U.S. 319 (1937), the Court articulated the necessary standard to distinguish those rights "incorporated" from those "unincorporated." The "incorporated" rights were not necessarily enumerated in the Constitution but were those "fundamental principles of liberty and justice which lie at the base of all our civil and political institutions." *Id.* at 326. Only those liberties "found to be implicit in the concept of ordered liberty" were incorporated.[5] *Id.* at 591.

In his famous dissent in *Poe v. Ullman*, 367 U.S. 497, 542 (1961), Justice Harlan said that the search for fundamental constitutional values was intended to be a "rational process" that must reflect the "traditions of the country, not judges." He found that personal liberty was somewhat of a "continuum which, broadly speaking, includes a freedom from all substantial arbitrary impositions and purposeless restraints. . . ." *Id.* at 543. In that language, endorsed by a plurality in *Moore v.*

3. In *Allgeyer*, the Court found that there was certainly a basic right to engage in business contracts as an element of personal liberty that deserved to be protected. But for purposes of this discussion, it should be noted that the Court did "not intend to hold that in no such case can the State exercise its police power." Indeed the Court found that this fundamental right "may be regulated, and sometimes prohibited, when the contracts or business conflict with the policy of the state as contained in its statutes. . . ." *Allgeyer v. Louisiana*, 165 U.S. at 591.

4. Throughout its cases, the Court has engaged in an effort to apply faithfully those values. Justice Harlan in *Jacobson v. Massachusetts* (197 U.S. at 22) cites approvingly Chief Justice John Marshall in *Sturges v. Crowninshield*, 17 U.S. (4 Wheat.) 122, 202 (1819), for the idea that the spirit of the Constitution "is to be collected chiefly from its words."

5. The Palko Court employed "freedom of thought" as its primary example: "Of that freedom one may say that it is the matrix, the indispensable condition, of nearly every other form of freedom." 302 U.S. at 327. In his concurring opinion in *Roe v. Wade*, Justice Douglas states that such internal matters as thought or belief are integral to one's autonomy and not subject to any infringement by the State. 410 U.S. at 211. Other interests, like the interest in one's health and well-being, are subject to appropriate regulation. *Id.* at 211–14.

City of East Cleveland, Justice Harlan acknowledged that protection of personal liberty often required a balance of different interests.[6] By protecting liberty against "substantial arbitrary" and "purposeless" restrictions, the Court invited express consideration of countervailing interests. In the abortion context, however, the invitation has not, until recently, even been acknowledged, much less accepted.

A. Abortion Is a Threat to the Preservation of a Legitimate Sphere of Protected Privacy.

Until *Webster v. Reproductive Health Services*, a majority had characterized itself as protecting a "promise that a certain private sphere of individual liberty will be kept largely beyond the reach of government." *Thornburgh*, 476 U.S. at 772. In actuality, that (now former) majority separated privacy doctrine from its roots. Although it claimed to the contrary, the Court isolated the pregnant woman in her privacy from all other interests. The Court originally offered a number of rationales—legal, medical, and social—for so doing. Although these rationales when first offered in 1973 were debatable, on further consideration and through actual, lamentable experience, they have been largely unrealized.[7] What is needed now is thorough reconsideration of that illegitimate foundation upon which constitutional abortion in America has rested for the last nineteen years.

Before *Roe*, privacy jurisprudence consisted of a number of discrete cases protecting either certain private places, private relationships, or private spheres of life from unwarranted government intrusion.[8] The shift in privacy jurisprudence that led to *Roe* began with *Griswold v. Connecticut*, when this Court held for the first time that there exists a specific right of privacy formed by "emanations from those [constitutional] guarantees that help give them life and substance."[9] Yet *Griswold* still

6. Moore v. City of East Cleveland, 431 U.S. 494, 501–502 (1977).
7. Chopko, Harris, Alvare, The Price of Abortion Sixteen Years Later, 69 National Forum 18 (Fall 1989).
8. E.g., Terry v. Ohio, 392 U.S. 5 (1968); Loving v. Virginia, 388 U.S. 1 (1967); Prince v. Massachusetts, 321 U.S. 158 (1944); Pierce v. Society of Sisters, 268 U.S. 510 (1925).
9. Griswold v. Connecticut, 381 U.S. 478, 483 (1965).

dealt with marriage, a protected association, and thus did not stray as far from the substance of the Court's earlier conclusions as it implicitly did from the Court's rationale. Where judicial protection of privacy lost any legitimate link with either this Court's precedents or with the Constitution itself was *Eisenstadt v. Baird*, 405 U.S. 438 (1972).[10] *Eisenstadt* abandoned the protectable right of privacy as developed in constitutional litigation by suggesting that personal interests alone—not relational interests such as those at the heart of *Griswold*—are entitled to special protection. 405 U.S. at 453. Having put marriage asunder in *Eisenstadt*, the Court in *Roe* undermined protection for the fruits of marriage—children.

As the majorities in the abortion cases erected a series of "substantial arbitrary impositions and purposeless restraints" on virtually every competing interest, the Court turned legitimate privacy doctrine on its head.[11] *Poe v. Ullman*, 367 U.S. at 542. By stretching privacy doctrine until it was broad enough to cover abortion, the Court introduced a flaw into its jurisprudence that, in subsequent opinions culminating in *Thornburgh*, became a threat to the very constitutional values and legitimate societal interests the right of privacy was originally meant to protect. When a bare majority of this Court used "autonomy" to describe a woman's decision to abort her child,[12] the very principle of liberty under the Fourteenth Amendment was infected with an amorphous concept that threatens the right to privacy itself. "Privacy reduced to its extreme is isolation, one of the conditions conducive to the success of totalitarian movements. It is the intention of free states to recognize and protect an area of privacy for the citizen

10. J. Noonan, *A Private Choice: Abortion in America in the Seventies* 20–22 (1979); see generally M.A. Glendon, *Rights Talk: The Impoverishment of Political Discourse* 56–57 (1991).

11. For example, it is widely recognized that parents have a general right to protect their children from potential adverse consequences of medical decisions. *Parham v. J. R.*, 442 U.S. 584, 604 (1979) (analyzing and rejecting *Planned Parenthood v. Danforth*, 428 U.S. 52 (1976)). Yet, in the abortion area, parents do not have the ability to exercise the same fundamental freedom. Thus has Justice O'Connor observed that, in the area of abortion, different rules come into play and nothing is safe from "ad hoc nullification" at the hands of a majority. *Thornburgh v. American College of Obstetricians and Gynecologists*, 476 U.S. at 814 (O'Connor, J., dissenting). As shown in Argument III, even traditional principles of informed consent have been abrogated in the abortion context. *See id.* at 798–804 (White, J., dissenting).

12. *Thornburgh*, 476 U.S. at 772.

but not to reduce that privacy to isolation."[13] A completely autonomous person becomes a law unto herself; privacy is "reduced to its extreme" and the shared commitment to values necessary to the preservation of a free state is impaired. The results are rifts in the jurisprudence and in the fabric of society.

B. Abortion Is a Threat to the Community Values Necessary to a Free Society.

In perhaps its most candid observation about the nature of the "right" being established in *Roe v. Wade*, the majority specifically recognized that the decisionmaking process it was about to protect differed, in its basic character, from those decisions protected in the line of cases from *Meyer* to *Griswold*. *Roe v. Wade*, 410 U.S. at 159. Even while stating that obvious fact, the Court nonetheless framed the discussion in language that would enable subsequent majorities to run roughshod over other individual, familial, and community interests deserving protection, not derision. *E.g., Thornburgh*, 476 U.S. at 772; *Colautti v. Franklin*, 439 U.S. 379 (1979). The *Roe* Court's promise that maternal health, medical standards, and "potential life" would be considered alongside abortion proved empty. 410 U.S. at 154. Indeed, that Court's statement that the abortion right was not to be absolute has itself been termed disingenuous because, from the beginning, no rights could be asserted on behalf of the unborn child.[14]

Individuals do have truly private choices—decisions that are entirely personal—that do not affect the interests of others or of the state. In other instances, individuals have their choices protected from interference by the state, whether they concern religious preferences,[15] the education of children,[16] the choice of a spouse,[17] or similar interests. It makes sense that the state should have a heavy burden of proof to engage in restriction of individual choices where there are no third-party or societal interests at stake. This may also be true when

---

13. S. Jordan, *Decision Making for Incompetent Persons* 132–33 (1985).
14. M.A. Glendon, *Rights Talk, supra* note 10, at 61.
15. *West Virginia State Board v. Barnette*, 319 U.S. 624 (1943).
16. *Meyer v. Nebraska*, 262 U.S. at 396–403; *Pierce v. Society of Sisters*, 268 U.S. at 529–36.
17. *Loving v. Virginia*, 388 U.S. at 2–13.

the exercise of individual choice falls completely within the context of a protected relationship, like marriage or the family.[18] Yet even in these relationships, the state has regulatory authority, severely circumscribed, but sufficient to ensure that individual choices are worked out in a balance respectful of all members of the protected relationship.[19]

In considering abortion, however, the calculation is never simply one of individual interests competing with interests of the state. The abortion decision is complex and certainly affects the life interests of others: the unborn child, the father, other members of the family, and society itself. The decision implicates the procreative interests of both partners, affects the integrity of the marriage relationship, and ends a life.[20] When a minor becomes pregnant, abortion has other detrimental impacts on family relations, alienating the child from her parents and separating those parents from their unborn grandchild. A constitutional right to abortion subjugates liberties that in other contexts are found to be fundamental, but in this context are considered less worthy of protection.[21]

In *Webster* v. *Reproductive Health Services*, a plurality of the Court suggested that it is not always wise to distinguish between abortion as a "fundamental right" or as a "limited fundamental constitutional right" or as a "liberty interest protected by the Due Process Clause. . . ." 492 U.S. at 520. The plurality made this assertion while discussing "the State's interest in protecting potential human life," where that interest is "compelling" and exists "throughout pregnancy." *Id.* at 519. In that context, where the state's compelling interest would prevail no matter how the right is denominated, such distinctions may be unnecessary to the Court's conclusion. However, it seems unlikely that this Court still seriously seeks to defend its unrestricted abortion decisions. Therefore, using the historical line of privacy cases, this Court must reflect accurately that one person's "liberty" is not "license" to control even one's own body where another's interest could suffer

18. *Griswold* v. *Connecticut*, 382 U.S. at 486; *Prince* v. *Massachusetts*, 321 U.S. at 166.

19. *Prince* v. *Massachusetts*, 321 U.S. at 166–67.

20. Ours has always been a society that "strongly affirms the sanctity of life." *Furman* v. *Georgia*, 408 U.S. 238, 286 (1972) (Brennan, J., concurring).

21. J. Noonan, *A Private Choice, supra* note 10, at 90–95, 190.

or the common good be diminished.[22] *Jacobson v. Massachusetts*, 197 U.S. at 26–27. Because the other vital interest, the unborn child, will suffer death as a result of an exercise of "liberty," the Court must reexamine its basis for making abortion a matter of due process at all.[23]

While debating how to denominate abortion, it is well to remember that the right to life has been recognized as the first right protected by government.[24] The order is not accidental. The right to life is the logical and chronological starting point in any discussion of the fundamental rights of persons. All other rights, interests, and values protected by the state on behalf of its citizens are meaningless if one does not first possess the right simply to exist. The Fourteenth Amendment guarantees this foundational value by denying to the states the power to "deprive any person of life, liberty, or property, without due process of law." Since the addition of those thirteen words to the Constitution, this Court has struggled with the scope and meaning of the word "liberty." *Compare, e.g., Duncan v. Louisiana*, 391 U.S. 145 (1968), with *id.* at 162 (Black, J., concurring), and *id.* at 215 (Harlan, J., dissenting). Yet it is plain that "life" is the necessary prerequisite to the exercise of "liberty" and it is through pregnancy that each of us begins to live.

---

22. Nor is liberty to be equated with autonomy; the illegitimate concept of bodily autonomy must be left out from under the umbrella of the Fourteenth Amendment in order to preserve those rights that are properly within the sphere of constitutional liberty interests. *See* Argument II. A., *supra.*

23. As Professor John Hart Ely noted almost twenty years ago, "What is frightening about *Roe* is that this super-protected right is not inferable from the language of the Constitution, the framers' thinking respecting the specific problem in issue, any general value derivable from the provisions they included, or the nation's governmental structure. . . . At times the inferences the Court has drawn from the values the Constitution marks for special protection have been controversial, even shaky, but never before has its sense of an obligation to draw one been so obviously lacking." Ely, *The Wages of Crying Wolf: A Comment on Roe v. Wade*, 82 Yale L.J. 920, 935–37 (Apr. 1973).

24. The Declaration of Independence places the right to life first in the list of inalienable rights. The Fourteenth Amendment lists the right to life first among those rights of which the states cannot deprive a person, without due process. And Thomas Jefferson's March 31, 1809, letter to the Republican Citizens of Washington County, Maryland, stated that: "The care of human life and happiness, and not their destruction, is the first and only legitimate object of good government." 8 *The Writings of Thomas Jefferson* 165 (H. A. Washington, ed.) (1871).

III. THE MEDICAL REGULATION ISSUES IN THIS CASE EXEMPLIFY THE JURISPRUDENTIAL PROBLEMS EN-GENDERED BY ROE V. WADE.

This Court has developed an abortion jurisprudence which minimizes one salient fact about abortion: regardless of when it is performed, abortion is a surgical procedure that has consequent medical risks and complications. Under *Roe v. Wade*, it was supposedly within a state's authority to regulate abortion because such regulation served legitimate interests in health and safety and in maintaining medical standards. 410 U.S. at 155. That supposition has been largely ignored in the face of consistent efforts by states to assert those interests.

In part, the state's interest in ensuring high standards for the medical profession also advances the protection of maternal health. *See, e.g., Akron v. Akron Center for Reproductive Health*, 462 U.S. at 428–29 (assuming without discussion some relation of the two interests); *Roe v. Wade*, 410 U.S. at 163. The maintenance of medical standards is also related to the state's interest in protecting the unborn child. *See Planned Parenthood Ass'n v. Ashcroft*, 462 U.S. 476, 486 (1983) (upholding second physician requirement). But beyond these aspects, the interest in regulation of the medical profession by itself justifies reasonable supervision of the physician-patient relationship throughout pregnancy under the state's welfare authority.[25] *See, e.g., Connecticut v. Menillo*, 423 U.S. 9, 11 (1975) (per curiam) (upholding physician licensing requirements); *Planned Parenthood v. Danforth*, 428 U.S. at 67 (upholding informed consent requirement); *see also Akron*, 462 U.S. at 460 and nn. 6 & 7 (O'Connor, J., dissenting).

---

25. The authority of a state to license and regulate the practice of medicine is a "vital part of a state's police power." *Barsky v. Board of Regents*, 347 U.S. at 449. *See Bigelow v. Virginia*, 421 U.S. 809, 827 (1975). A licensed physician has no right to practice medicine according to his or her own unfettered judgment but rather is subject to reasonably exercised but extensive authority. *Whalen v. Roe*, 429 U.S. 589, 604 (1977); *see Friedman v. Rogers*, 440 U.S. 1, 9–10 (1979) (Powell, J.) (First Amendment interest in medical service name). *See also Brophy v. New England Sinai Hospital*, 398 Mass. 417, 497 N.E.2d 626 (1986); *In re Guardianship of Grant*, 109 Wash.2d 545, 747 P.2d 445 (1987), and cases cited therein (states' interest in the integrity of the medical profession).

A. The Abortion Industry Has Been Arbitrarily Exempted from Effective State Regulation.

"I had thought it clear," Justice White wrote in *Thornburgh*, "that regulation of the practice of medicine, like regulation of other professions . . ., was a matter peculiarly within the competence of legislatures. . . ." 476 U.S. at 802 (White, J., dissenting); *see also id.* at 783 (Burger, C.J., dissenting). And indeed, before the Court in *Roe v. Wade* threw into doubt constitutional principles it had previously espoused, *id.* at 814 (O'Connor, J., dissenting), regulation of the medical profession in the interest of public welfare was not only a legislative prerogative but a public duty. *See generally Semler v. Board of Dental Examiners*, 294 U.S. 608, 612 (1935). Viewed in this light, Pennsylvania's informed consent, waiting period, and parental and spousal notification requirements are valid exercises of state authority to regulate abortion.[26]

1. Informed Consent

One classic application of the state's regulatory authority over the medical profession has always been the protection of a citizen's right to be informed before consenting to any surgical procedure. In *Dent v. West Virginia*, 129 U.S. 114, 122 (1889), this Court observed:

> The power of the state to provide for the general welfare of its people authorizes it to prescribe all such regulations as, in its judgment, will secure or tend to secure them against the consequences of ignorance and incapacity as well as deception and fraud.

Accord Meffert v. Packer, 66 Kan. 710, 714 (1903), *aff'd mem.*, 195 U.S. 625 (1904). Consistent with this Court's decision in *Virginia Board of Pharmacy v. Virginia Citizens Consumer Council*, state legislatures have not hesitated to act when they

---

26. Pennsylvania Abortion Control Act, 18 Pa. Cons. Stat. Ann. §§ 3205–3206, 3209 (West 1983 & Supp. 1991).

find that the medical community is not providing minimally adequate information to patients.[27]

New York, for example, requires that information be provided to pregnant women about the potential adverse impact of medication used during pregnancy and delivery,[28] and to parents about metabolic disorders in their newborns.[29] Florida has enacted legislation designed to guard against too frequent use of electroconvulsive (shock) therapy by adding new consent requirements.[30] Several states have enacted laws requiring that physicians provide victims of breast cancer oral or written summaries of the various alternative treatments prior to assent to any particular procedure.[31] More recently, a number of jurisdictions have enacted legislation requiring that patients be adequately informed before undergoing testing for the human immunodeficiency virus (HIV).[32] These are examples of measures that directly affect the physician-patient relationship by shaping the content of their dialogue.

It follows that Pennsylvania acted well within the authority traditionally accorded to states in this area when it enacted the informed consent statute.[33] In Akron v. Akron Center for

27. Virginia Board of Pharmacy v. Virginia Citizens Consumer Council, 425 U.S. 748, 750–51, 765 (1976).

28. N.Y. Public Health Law Ann. § 2503 (McKinney 1985). This gives the woman the right to be informed, in advance of delivery, of the drugs that the physician expects to use during pregnancy and at birth.

29. Id. § 2500–a (McKinney 1985 & Supp. 1992).

30. Fl. Stat. Ann. § 458.325 (West 1991).

31. See, e.g., Fl. Stat. Ann. § 458.324(2) (West 1991); see also N.Y. Public Health Law Ann. § 2505 (McKinney 1985) (requiring information about infant nutrition and breast-feeding); Mass. General Laws Ann. c. 123, § 23 (West Supp. 1991) (regarding informed consent by mental patients to shock treatment or lobotomy).

32. Ala. Code § 22–11A–51 (Michie Supp. 1991); Ariz. Rev. Stat. Ann. § 20–448.01 (West Supp. 1991); Colo. Rev. Stat. § 10–3–1104.5 (Supp. 1991); Fl. Stat. Ann. § 381.004 (West Supp. 1992); Hawaii Rev. Stat. Ann. § 325–16 (Michie 1991); Ind. Stat. Ann. §§ 16–8–7–6, 16–8–7.5–14 (Burns 1990); Ky. Rev. Stat. Ann. §§ 214.181, 214.625 (Michie 1991); Md. Health Gen. Code Ann. § 18–336 (Michie 1990); N.H. Rev. Stat. Ann. § 141–F:5 (1990); N.M. Stat. Ann. § 24–2B–2 (1991); N.D. Cent. Code Ann. §§ 23–07.5–02, 23–07.5–03 (Michie 1991); Or. Rev. Stat. § 433.045 (1991); Va. Code Ann. § 32.1–37.2 (Michie Supp. 1991); Wis. Stat. Ann. § 146.025 (West 1989 & Supp. 1991).

33. The parental consent and spousal notification requirements are similarly within the State's authority. Our legal tradition strongly endorses and preserves the mutual support and interdependence of family members—goals served by the Pennsylvania statutes. Society owes much of its stability to the strength of the family and has a vital interest in preserving family integrity. "The intangible fibers that connect parent

Reproductive Health, this Court found unobjectionable certain information relevant to an informed choice, *i.e.*, the status of one's pregnancy, the availability of community and other resources, the existence and efficacy of alternatives to abortion and public assistance, and the particular risks and benefits of options available to the woman. 462 U.S. 416, 445–46 & n.37 (1983). The kind of information Pennsylvania would require be provided to pregnant women seeking an abortion, like the information described in *Akron,* is "the kind of balanced information . . . all could agree is relevant to a woman's informed choice." *Thornburgh* v. *American College of Obstetricians & Gynecologists,* 476 U.S. at 830 (O'Connor, J., dissenting).

2. 24-Hour Waiting Period

The information which Pennsylvania law requires be provided to a pregnant woman seeking an abortion, standing alone, does not ensure that her consent will be truly informed. For this to occur, a woman must have a meaningful opportunity to consider all the information she has been given and make a decision based on it. The Pennsylvania statute preserves that opportunity by requiring that 24 hours lapse from the time information is provided until the abortion is performed. The 24-hour waiting period is an attempt to ensure that the provision of information will not be a merely *pro forma* requirement, but will allow for genuine reflection on the woman's part. Except perhaps in cases of medical emergency,[34] patients contemplating a life-affecting medical pro-

---

and child have infinite value. They are woven throughout the fabric of our society, providing it with strength, beauty, and flexibility. It is self-evident that they are sufficiently vital to merit constitutional protection in appropriate cases." *Lehr* v. *Robertson,* 463 U.S. 248, 256 (1983). Indeed, "the Constitution protects the sanctity of the family precisely because the institution of the family is deeply rooted in this Nation's history and tradition. It is through the family that we inculcate and pass down many of our most cherished values, moral and cultural." *Moore* v. *City of East Cleveland,* 431 U.S. at 503.

34. The 24-hour waiting period does not apply in cases of medical emergency. Pennsylvania Abortion Control Act, 18 Pa. Cons. Stat. Ann. § 3205.

cedure wisely take some period of time to consider their options.[35] Physicians often insist on as much.[36] Even possible "delay[s] of a week or more"[37] did not lead this Court to invalidate a parental notification and judicial bypass statute. Hodgson v. Minnesota, 110 S. Ct. 2926 (1990). The 24-hour waiting period should not be troublesome to this Court in light of its holding that greater delays do not result in a de facto violation of the Constitution. The waiting period furthers a legitimate state interest; it protects patients who otherwise would not be provided, or would not avail themselves of, the opportunity of taking even a brief period of time to weigh information before making a decision.[38] To the extent that some women, after contemplating their options, decide against aborting their children, the waiting period also furthers the state's compelling interest in protecting unborn life.

B. States' Interests in Health and Medical Standards Are Especially Important to the Unborn Child.

Although Roe v. Wade held out the prospect of a compelling state interest in the life of the unborn child,[39] it was the Webster case that finally offered realistic support for that concern. 492 U.S. at 499–522. Throughout other decisions of this and other courts, this compelling interest has been acknowledged, though not always protected, in varying degree

35. Requiring a brief waiting period for major life-affecting medical procedures is not unique to the abortion context. For example, Medicaid regulations for women having sterilization procedures require that "at least 30 days . . . have passed between the date of informed consent and the date of sterilization. . . ." 42 C.F.R. § 441.253(d) (1991). See also 42 C.F.R. §§ 441.257(a), 441.258 (1991); 42 C.F.R. Part 441, Subpt. F, App. (1991) (requisite consent form and physician's statement showing that sterilization was performed 30 days or more after the date of consent).

36. Indeed, petitioners themselves routinely allow some time between a woman's first contact with their clinics and the abortion. See, e.g., 744 F. Supp. at 1335 (options counseling consists of several hours of group sessions); id. at 1336 (abortions usually scheduled within one week); id. at 1337 (options counseling only available on Tuesdays and Thursdays); id. at 1340 (often a one to two week wait to obtain an appointment for an abortion).

37. Hodgson v. Minnesota, 648 F. Supp. 756, 763 (D. Minn. 1986).

38. Chopko, Webster v. Reproductive Health Services: A Path to Constitutional Equilibrium, 12 Campbell L.R. 181, 216 (Spring 1990).

39. Roe v. Wade, 410 U.S. at 163.

and in differing language.[40] In recent years, however, there has been a new term applied to the unborn child—a term that comes from outside the abortion debate and with which none of the advocates can legitimately disagree. That term is patient. *Williams Obstetrics* vii (J. Pritchard & P. MacDonald 16th ed. 1980).

In the 1980s, both the scientific literature[41] and the popular press[42] have heralded the latest medical advances in the field of in utero diagnosis and treatment. The technology that has led the way to many of these advances is ultrasonography. Using ultrasound signals, physicians are able to scan the womb, producing a sonogram or television-like live image of the child in the womb.[43] With ever-increasing refinements in technique and equipment, they can visually diagnose the baby's condition and, if necessary, perform highly delicate surgical and other procedures. Not only are the infant's external features discernible, but internal organs, heartbeat, and blood flow can be examined, and gestational age may be determined.[44]

---

40. The use of different terminology by judges and advocates on all sides of the abortion debate is itself a juridical phenomenon. All engaged in these cases have, consciously or unconsciously, adopted the theory that control of the language determines the outcome of the matter. One of the most misleading labels found in the cases is the adjective "potential" as applied after conception. *See, e.g., Webster,* 492 U.S. at 515–16, 519; *Roe,* 410 U.S. at 150–64. Prior to conception, the phrase "potential human life" might have some logical relevance when referring to the ovum and the sperm. At conception, however, that potential has been realized. Life exists, and it can only be human. The debate may rage over whether to call this life a fetus or a baby, but actual human life, fully capable of further development, clearly exists. No human being exactly like this one has existed before, and none like it will be conceived ever again.

41. *See, e.g.,* Daffos et al., *Prenatal Management of 746 Pregnancies at Risk for Congenital Taxoplasmosis,* 318 New Eng. J. Med. 271 (Feb. 4, 1988); *Neonatal-Perinatal Medicine: Diseases of the Fetus and Infant* (A. Fanaroff & R. Martin 4th ed.) (1987); B. Spirt, L. Gordon & M. Oliphant, *Prenatal Ultrasound: A Color Atlas With Anatomic and Pathologic Correlation* (1987).

42. *See, e.g.,* Henig, *Saving Babies Before Birth,* The New York Times (Feb. 26, 1982) at 18 (Magazine).

43. Chervenak et al., *Current Concepts: Advances in the Diagnosis of Fetal Defects,* 315 New Eng. J. Med. 305–306 (July 31, 1986).

44. One unexpected but welcome by-product of the sonogram is its tendency to promote parental bonding with the prenatal child, even in the earliest stages of pregnancy. Fletcher & Evans, *Sounding Boards: Maternal Bonding in Early Fetal Ultrasound Examinations,* 308 New Eng. J. Med. 392 (Feb. 17, 1983). Once they have seen the living human being inside themselves, some mothers immediately forego thoughts of abortion. *Id.* For this very reason, some abortion supporters openly advise

Innovative treatments now mean that conditions which previously could have proved crippling or fatal to the newborn infant are being treated before birth.[45] Babies delivered prematurely, with extremely low birthweight, are being saved by new high-technology therapy.[46] Maternal behavior and environmental conditions that can affect the development of the unborn child are being studied and treated.[47] Fetal surgery is not only increasing, but can even be accomplished by removing the baby from the womb, operating, and then returning the child until the pregnancy comes full term.[48] Such medical achievements have caused at least one defender of *Roe* to admit that "the same skills that can be used to rescue extremely premature newborns can be brought to bear in these cases [saving aborted fetuses]."[49] Thus medical science has reached a point where the fetus is a patient for all purposes, not only in utero but post-abortion as well. This medical realization should be reflected in proper legal recognition of the unborn child's unique status.

In one oft-quoted passage from *Harris v. McRae*, this Court noted that abortion is "inherently different from other medical procedures" precisely because it terminates a life.[50] And in *Ashcroft*, Missouri's requirement that a second physician be present to try to save the infant victim of a third-trimester

---

against allowing the mother to see the baby's image for fear she will be discouraged from having an abortion. *Warns of Negative Psychological Impact of Sonography in Abortion*, Ob. Gyn. News (Feb. 15–28, 1986). Those who advise this course clearly place a higher priority on maximizing abortions than on informed consent or "freedom of choice."

45. Kolata, *Fetuses Treated Through Umbilical Cords*, The New York Times (Mar. 29, 1988) at C3.

46. Callahan, *How Technology Is Reframing the Abortion Debate*, Hastings Center Report 33–34 (Feb. 1986).

47. *Id.* at 36.

48. Longaker et al., *Maternal Outcome After Open Fetal Surgery*, 265 J.A.M.A. 737 (Feb. 13, 1991); Harrison et al., *Successful Repair in Utero of a Fetal Diaphragmatic Hernia*, 322 New Eng. J. Med. 1582 (May 31, 1990); *Occasional Notes: Fetal Treatment 1982*, 307 New Eng. J. Med. 1651 (Dec. 23, 1982); *Medical Progress: Pediatric Surgery*, 319 New Eng. J. Med. 94 (July 14, 1988). *See also* Blakeslee, *Fetus Returned to Womb Following Surgery*, The New York Times (Oct. 7, 1986) at C1.

49. Callahan, *supra* note 46, at 35. The author then raises the question of whether a woman who chooses to abort is entitled only to the end of pregnancy or to a dead fetus. *See Wynn v. Scott*, 449 F. Supp. 1302, 1321 (N.D. Ill. 1978) ("It never could be argued that she has a constitutionally protected right to kill the fetus."), *appeal dismissed, Carey v. Wynn*, 439 U.S. 8 (1978), *aff'd*, 599 F.2d 193 (7th Cir. 1979).

50. *Harris v. McRae*, 448 U.S. 297, 325 (1980).

abortion was upheld as a legitimate exercise of state regulation. 462 U.S. at 485. In the *Webster* case, the Chief Justice, in abandoning *Roe's* trimester approach, said:

> That framework sought to deal with areas of medical practice traditionally subject to state regulation, and it sought to balance once and for all by reference only to the calendar the claims of the State to protect the fetus as a form of human life against the claims of a woman to decide for herself whether or not to abort a fetus she was carrying.

492 U.S. at 520. Because Pennsylvania's statute falls within the traditional regulation of medical practice, the claim of a right to abort, if any, must be balanced against the unique status of the unborn child as a patient, not against the calendar.

Viewed as a patient, the unborn child is entitled to consideration "of all attendant circumstances—psychological and emotional as well as physical—that might be relevant to the well-being of the patient." *Colautti v. Franklin*, 439 U.S. at 394. The ramifications are obvious and compelling. Prenatal patients cannot protect themselves; cannot be informed or give consent; cannot be made to understand their condition; nor can they choose treatments. Considered from this perspective, the state should be afforded more, not less, latitude to regulate or prevent the surgery known as abortion.

C. States Must Be Allowed to Protect Patients from the Adverse Effects of Abortion.

Another reason that greater state regulation of abortion is called for is to minimize its other known adverse effects. Two of the many tragic ironies of the jurisprudence begun with *Roe v. Wade* are: (1) it predicted great benefits would flow from abortion, yet never subsequently faced the many resulting detriments; and (2) it held that a woman's health was only of interest to the state after she had been pregnant for at least three months. 410 U.S. at 163. The flaw in this latter point was illustrated by Justice O'Connor in *Akron*:

The fallacy inherent in the *Roe* framework is apparent: just because the State has a compelling interest in ensuring maternal safety once an abortion may be more dangerous than childbirth, it simply does not follow that the State has no interest before that point that justifies state regulation to ensure that first-trimester abortions are performed as safely as possible.

462 U.S. at 460. The fallacy identified by Justice O'Connor is remedied by protection of the interest in life throughout pregnancy. *Webster*, 492 U.S. at 520. Indeed, as should have been obvious to the *Roe* majority, protection of women's health is of vital concern at all times. Pregnancy should only heighten, not weaken, this concern. And, as has been demonstrated in the past nineteen years, abortion should raise the level of legitimate state concern even higher.[51]

Despite knowledge of abortion's adverse consequences, persons supporting an "abortion privacy right" often mischaracterize the issue as though it involved only a woman's right to "keep the government out of the bedroom."[52] Some further contend that women's childbearing capacities have been improperly used as a justification for discrimination against them, and that the only effective remedy for this sexism is women's assumption of sole control over every aspect of their reproductive capabilities, including unfettered access to abortion.[53] These assertions are not only misleading, they are detrimental to women's dignity, health, and well-being.[54] What should

51. There is little doubt that the abortion decision is life-affecting. This Court has noted that the "emotional and psychological effects of the pregnancy and abortion experience are markedly more severe in girls under 18 than in adults." *H.L.* v. *Matheson*, 450 U.S. 398, 411 n.20 (1981). The American Psychological Association reported in 1986 that "[c]ompared with adults, adolescents appear to have somewhat more negative responses on average following abortion." *Adolescent Abortion: Psychological and Legal Issues*, Report of the Interdivisional Committee on Adolescent Abortion, American Psychological Association (Univ. of Nebraska Press 1986).

52. Clift, King, Gonzalez, *Taking Issue With NOW*, Newsweek 21–22 (Aug. 14, 1989). In the same article a Planned Parenthood consultant comments: "Framed that way, it becomes the all-American message."

53. *See, e.g.*, Steinem, *A Basic Human Right*, Ms. 39 (Aug. 1989); B. Harrison, *Our Right to Choose* 199 (1983).

54. *See* note 7 and accompanying text, *supra*.

be a paramount concern for the health and welfare of the patients—both mother and child—is lost.

The widespread practice of abortion since *Roe*, premised on a popular misconception that constitutional privacy equals personal autonomy, has increased pressure upon women to abort for a variety of discretionary reasons. Laboring against these pressures are those who willingly explore numerous alternative means for handling difficult pregnancies.[55] The answer to the problems caused by abortion does not lie in making abortion more available but in efforts to ensure that no woman need ever resort to abortion. The process of change will not be easy. Worthwhile solutions never are. This Court can help begin the turn from a society that condones abortion while ignoring its insidious consequences, to one that protects the health of its citizens and respects the lives of their offspring. Restoring the traditional authority of Pennsylvania and other states to regulate the medical profession in order to achieve these goals is an important first step.

CONCLUSION

This Court should reconsider its essential constitutional and jurisdictional holdings concerning abortion. The judgment of the court of appeals finding the Pennsylvania Abortion Control Act, Sections 3203 (definition of medical emergency), 3205 (informed consent), 3206 (parental consent), 3214(a) (reporting requirements) and 3207(b) and 3214(f) (public disclosure of clinics' reports) constitutional should be affirmed.

---

55. These efforts include, *inter alia*, eliciting additional emotional and financial support from the father, family, and friends, additional social welfare support for families, better employer child care policies, and greater adoption services. National Conference of Catholic Bishops, *Pastoral Plan for Pro-Life Activities: A Reaffirmation* (Nov. 1985).

The judgment of the court of appeals finding Section 3209 (spousal notice) unconstitutional should be reversed.

Respectfully submitted,

MARK E. CHOPKO,*
General Counsel
PHILLIP H. HARRIS
Solicitor
UNITED STATES CATHO-
LIC CONFERENCE
3211 Fourth Street, N.E.
Washington, D.C. 20017
(202) 541–3300

*Counsel of Record

MICHAEL K. WHITEHEAD
General Counsel
CHRISTIAN LIFE
COMMISSION,
SOUTHERN BAPTIST
CONVENTION,
400 N. Capitol Street, N.W.
Washington, D.C. 20001
(202) 638–3223

FOREST D. MONTGOMERY
Counsel
NATIONAL ASSOCIATION
OF EVANGELICALS
Office of Public Affairs
1023 15th Street, N.W.
Washington, D.C. 20005
(202) 789–1011

Attorneys for *Amici*

Of Counsel: MICHAEL F. MOSES

BRIEF OF NATIONAL RIGHT TO LIFE, INC. AS *AMICUS CURIAE* IN SUPPORT OF RESPONDENTS AND CROSS-PETITIONERS

INTEREST OF *AMICUS CURIAE*[1]

The National Right to Life Committee, Inc. is a nonprofit organization whose purpose is to promote respect for the worth and dignity of all human life, including the life of the unborn child from the moment of conception. The National Right to Life Committee, Inc. is comprised of a Board of Directors representing 51 state affiliate organizations and about 3,000 local chapters made up of individuals from every race, denomination, ethnic background, and political belief. It engages in various lawful political, legislative, legal, and educational activities to protect and promote the concept of the sanctity of innocent human life.

The members of the National Right to Life Committee, Inc. have been the primary promoters of laws restricting abortion to only those instances in which the mother's life is in danger. Since *Roe* v. *Wade*, 410 U.S. 113 (1973), and *Doe* v. *Bolton*, 410 U.S. 179 (1973), the members of the National Right to Life Committee, Inc. have supported legislation to protect unborn human life within the limits set by those decisions and have sought, through lawful means, those changes in the law which would allow full legal protection for the unborn. The National Right to Life Committee, Inc. seeks to advance its interests by addressing the legal issues herein.

---

1. This brief is filed with permission of all the parties. Letters indicating this permission have been filed with the Clerk of this Court.

STATEMENT OF THE QUESTIONS PRESENTED

1. Did the Court of Appeals err in upholding the constitutionality of the following provisions of the Pennsylvania Abortion Control Act:

(a) 18 Pa. Cons. Stat. Ann. § 3203 (definition of medical emergency)

(b) 18 Pa. Cons. Stat. Ann. § 3205 (informed consent)

(c) 18 Pa. Cons. Stat. Ann. § 3206 (parental consent)

(d) 18 Pa. Cons. Stat. Ann. §§ 3207, 3214 (reporting requirements)?

2. Did the Court of Appeals err in holding 18 Pa. Cons. Stat. Ann. § 3209 (spousal notice) unconstitutional?

QUESTION DEALT WITH HEREIN

1. Does the undue burden test provide a workable and constitutionally sound standard of review for reviewing abortion legislation?

SUMMARY OF THE ARGUMENT

Because *Roe v. Wade* is unworkable and has no proper constitutional foundation, support for it is eroding. In place of *Roe*'s strict scrutiny analysis, the United States Court of Appeals for the Third Circuit in this case employed the undue burden test, which Justice O'Connor previously suggested that this Court has applied to abortion legislation. However, the Third Circuit misunderstood the test and misapplied it with regard to the spousal notice provision which it struck down. As interpreted by the Third Circuit, the undue burden test is unworkable. If this Court should decide to establish an undue burden analysis to govern constitutional abortion jurisprudence, it must set out a clear and workable undue burden analysis. The focus of this analysis is whether the state has compelling interests throughout pregnancy. A majority of the Justices of this Court has recognized (directly or indirectly and in separate opinions) that there are compelling interests in protecting unborn life and maternal health which exist throughout pregnancy. This needs to be clearly established in order to make an undue burden analysis workable. However, the very existence of special constitutional protection for abortion is questionable and has no majority support on this Court. Therefore, it would be preferable to hold that the rational basis test governs constitutional abortion jurisprudence.

ARGUMENT

I. *ROE V. WADE* IS UNWORKABLE.

A. *Roe* Appeared to Give States Some Latitude to Restrict Abortion But Has Not Done So in Practice.

This Court, in *Roe v. Wade*, declared that the right to abortion is not absolute: "The Court has refused to recognize an unlimited right of this kind in the past." *Roe*, 410 U.S. 113, 154 (1973). Rather, the Court stated, "[T]his right . . . must be considered against important state interests in regulation." *Id*. This is so, the Court noted, because the abortion privacy right "is inherently different from marital intimacy, or bedroom possession of obscene material, or marriage, or procreation, or education . . . ." *Id*. at 159. The difference is that "[t]he pregnant woman cannot be isolated in her privacy. She carries an embryo and, later, a fetus, if one accepts the medical definitions of the developing young in the human uterus." *Id*.

The state interests justifying regulation of abortion mentioned by this Court were the interests in protecting maternal health and "the potentiality of human life." *Id*. at 162. Although the *Roe* majority appeared to give some effect to these interests by declaring them compelling at certain points in pregnancy, effectuation of these interests has proven elusive.

The reality has been abortion on demand throughout pregnancy. Even modest attempts to regulate abortion have routinely been struck down. *See, e.g., Thornburgh* v. *American College of Obstetricians and Gynecologists,* 476 U.S. 747, 783 (1986) (Burger, C.J., dissenting) ("[T]oday the Court astonishingly goes so far as to say that the State may not require that a woman contemplating an abortion be provided with accurate medical information concerning the risks inherent in the medical procedure . . . .").

B. The Trimester Framework Is Tied to Advances in Medical Technology, Making Legislative Enactment Virtually Impossible.

Both petitioners and certain *amici* argue that *Roe's* trimester framework "fairly accommodates competing interests," "provides clear guidance to state governments and lower courts," and "provides a workable, predictable framework within which states can regulate abortion and courts can review such regulations."[2] Entirely apart from the arbitrary and essentially legislative nature of *Roe's* trimester regime,[3] the experience of the federal courts in trying to administer the trimester scheme indicates otherwise. *Roe* is "workable," but only in the sense that virtually no regulations designed to safeguard maternal health or protect fetal life are constitutional.

For example, in *Roe,* the Court held that after viability, "the State in promoting its interest in the potentiality of human life may, if it chooses, regulate, and even proscribe, abortion except where it is necessary, in appropriate medical judgment, for the preservation of the life or health of the mother." *Roe,* 410 U.S. at 164–65. In the companion case *Doe* v. *Bolton,* the Court defined the scope of the health exception, relying upon its earlier opinion in *United States* v. *Vuitch,* 402 U.S. 62 (1971): "[T]he medical judgment may be

2. Brief of Petitioners, Cross-Respondents at [49–52]; Brief *Amici Curiae* for Rep. Don Edwards et al. at 24 (herein); Brief *Amici Curiae* of the States of New York et al. at 13–14 (herein).
3. *Roe,* 410 U.S. at 173 (Rehnquist, J., dissenting); *City of Akron* v. *Akron Center for Reproductive Health,* 462 U.S. 416, 460–61 (1983) (O'Connor, J., dissenting); *Thornburgh,* 476 U.S. at 789, 794–95 (White, J., dissenting), 814–15 (O'Connor, J., dissenting) (1986); *Webster* v. *Reproductive Health Services, Inc.,* 492 U.S. 490, 518–19 (plurality opinion by Rehnquist, C.J.) (1989).

exercised in the light of all factors—physical, emotional, psychological, familial, and the woman's age—relevant to the well-being of the patient. All these factors may relate to health." *Doe*, 410 U.S. at 192.

Given this expansive definition of "health," it is doubtful whether any statute attempting to limit post-viability abortions would be constitutional. The authority purportedly conferred upon the states to proscribe abortion after viability has proved to be illusory. In *American College of Obstetricians & Gynecologists v. Thornburgh*, 737 F.2d 283 (3rd Cir. 1984), *aff'd*, 476 U.S. 747 (1986), the Third Circuit, noting that "no Supreme Court case has upheld a criminal statute prohibiting abortion of a viable fetus," stated in dicta that had Pennsylvania attempted to prohibit post-viability abortions performed for psychological or emotional reasons, such a limitation would have violated *Bolton*. 737 F.2d at 298–99. Legislative attempts to restrict post-viability abortions have been uniformly rejected. *See, e.g., Margaret S. v. Edwards*, 488 F. Supp. 181, 191 (E.D. La. 1980) (Louisiana statute prohibiting abortions after viability unless necessary "to prevent permanent impairment to [the woman's] health" held unconstitutional because "[p]reserving maternal health means more than preventing permanent incapacity" and "[a] rape or incest victim may not be able to prove that her mental health will be permanently impaired if she is forced to bear her attacker's child, but she might be able to show that it is necessary to preserve her immediate mental health"); *Schulte v. Douglas*, 567 F. Supp. 522 (D. Neb. 1981), *aff'd per curiam, sub nom. Women's Servs., P.C. v. Douglas*, 710 F.2d 465 (8th Cir. 1983) (statute which prohibited abortion after viability unless "necessary to preserve the woman from imminent peril that substantially endangers her life or health" held unconstitutional); *Rodos v. Michaelson*, 396 F. Supp. 768 (D.R.I. 1975), *vacated for lack of standing of plaintiffs*, 527 F.2d 582 (1st Cir. 1975) (striking down statute prohibiting post-quickening abortions except when "necessary to preserve the life of the mother").

Notwithstanding the Court's recognition of the states' interest in promoting maternal health, reasonable legislative measures intended to make sure that the abortion choice represents an informed decision after consultation with the woman's physician have also been routinely struck down. *See, e.g.*, *Thornburgh*, 476 U.S. at 759–64; *City of Akron* v. *Akron Center for Reproductive Health*, 462 U.S. 416, 442–49 (1983).

The trimester system has proven to be unworkable in other respects, as well. The "bright lines" drawn between the trimesters have become blurred. Attempts to set viability at a definite stage in pregnancy so that enforcement of the laws applicable after viability could be based on objective criteria have been struck down. *See Colautti* v. *Franklin*, 439 U.S. 379, 388–89 (1979).

And, although *Roe* itself indicated that states could require abortions performed after the end of the first trimester to be performed in hospitals, *Roe*, 410 U.S. at 163, this Court retreated from this position in the *Akron* case, striking down a second-trimester hospitalization requirement, *Akron*, 462 U.S. at 433–39. This change in doctrine was attributable to recent medical advances, under which the City of Akron's ordinance requiring second-trimester hospitalization was no longer "reasonable" because it departed from "accepted medical practice." *Id.* at 436–38. The Court's approach to abortion regulation, *i.e.*, making the determination of constitutionality turn upon medical standards in effect at the time the case reaches the Court, is "completely unworkable." *Id.* at 454 (O'Connor, J., dissenting). It requires a state to determine what is "acceptable medical practice" not only for each type of abortion performed, but also for each type of abortion at each week of pregnancy within each trimester. *Id.* at 456. States must not only "continuously and conscientiously study contemporary medical and scientific literature in order to determine whether the effect of a particular regulation is to 'depart from accepted medical practice' insofar as particular procedures and particular periods within the trimester are concerned," *Id.* at 456 (O'Connor, J., dissenting), but must also predict what the "accepted medical practice" will be four or five years in the future when the case may ultimately reach the Supreme Court. Even if the regulation is constitutional when enacted and is upheld by the Court, it could be attacked later based on new medical standards.

As a result of this Court's decisions in *Colautti* and *Akron*, the states have no practical ability to regulate according to the lines established by the trimester system in *Roe*. By tying the states' ability to regulate abortion to ever-shifting medical technology and "accepted medical practice," the Court effectively removed from the states' elected representatives the ability to regulate abortion and placed such decisions within the hands of the medical profession. Instead of engendering stability in the law, this has led to extreme instability in the law. This is additional evidence of the unworkability of the *Roe* trimester framework.

C. *Roe* Did Not End the Abortion Controversy, But Has Distorted the Law in Many Areas.

Roe v. *Wade* was intended to settle the issue of abortion in American law. However, recognizing *Roe*'s weak constitutional foundation, abortion rights advocates continue to assert other constitutional theories. *See, e.g.*, Brief of Petitioners/ Cross-Respondents at [38–39, 42 n.27, 55–56, 66–67] (Equal Protection); Brief *Amicus Curiae* of 178 Organizations in Support of Planned Parenthood of Southeastern Pennsylvania at 8 (Ninth Amendment). *But see* Brief *Amicus Curiae* of Life Issues Institute in Support of Respondents/Cross-Petitioners (herein) (dealing with Equal Protection and Ninth Amendment claims); Bopp, *Will There Be a Constitutional Right to Abortion After the Reconsideration of Roe v. Wade?*, 15 J. Contemp. L. 131 (1989) (discussing and refuting alternative constitutional theories for an abortion right). Because of its weak foundation, *Roe* exacerbated the abortion controversy.

Moreover, *Roe* has proven to be inherently difficult to apply in any consistent and principled manner. Because of this fact, *Roe* has worked a distortion on the normal functioning of the law wherever abortion jurisprudence touches the law. This abortion distortion effect is evident in several areas set forth below.

1. *Roe* Has Confused the Law Protecting the Unborn in Non-Abortion Contexts.

One of the areas in which the abortion distortion effect is most evident is in the law designed to protect preborn human beings in non-abortion contexts. In these areas, *Roe* poses a direct obstacle to the realization of important objectives embodied in laws which recognize and protect unborn human life, in that it has inhibited development of the law in these areas. Examples include the rights of the unborn in tort law, wrongful death actions, in equity, in criminal law, and in laws relating to respect. *See* Bopp & Coleson, *The Right to Abortion: Anomalous, Absolute, and Ripe for Reversal,* 3 B.Y.U.J. Public Law, 181, 246–83 (1989) (discussing the abortion distortion effect of *Roe* on fetal rights in non-abortion contexts).

a. Tort Law—Development of Fetal Rights. The development of the law in the area of torts reveals the dramatic change in the legal protection of the rights of unborn human beings with the progress of scientific knowledge about the fact that each unique, individual human being comes into being at the moment of conception.

The first American case which dealt with fetal injury was the celebrated opinion by Judge Oliver Wendell Holmes, Jr. in *Dietrich v. Northampton,* 138 Mass. 14 (1884). Holmes interpreted the Massachusetts wrongful death act to preclude recovery for the death of a four- to five-month old fetus. He held that "the unborn child was a part of the mother at the time of the injury" and that "any damage to [the fetus] which was not too remote to be recovered for at all was recoverable by her." *Id.* at 17.

Dietrich was followed until 1946, when, in the words of William Prosser, there occurred "the most spectacular [and] abrupt reversal of a well settled rule in the whole history of the law of torts." W. Prosser, *Handbook on the Law of Torts* 336 (4th ed. 1971). In *Bonbrest v. Kotz,* 65 F. Supp. 138 (D.D.C 1946), a federal court allowed the plaintiff infant to recover for injuries sustained when he was negligently taken as a viable fetus, from his mother's womb by the defendant doctor. *Id.* at 143. The *Bonbrest* court reasoned:

> As to the viable child being 'part' of its mother—this argument seems to me to be a contradiction in terms. True, it is in the womb, but it is capable now of extrauterine life—and while dependent for its continued development on sustenance derived from its peculiar relationship to its mother, it is not a 'part' of the mother in the sense of a constituent element—

as that term is generally understood. Modern medicine is replete with cases of living children being taken from dead mothers. Indeed, apart from viability, a nonviable foetus is not a
part of its mother.

Id. at 140.

Since *Bonbrest*, every state has recognized prenatal harm as
a legitimate cause of action for a child subsequently born.
Prosser and Keeton on the Law of Torts 368 (W. Keeton ed.
5th ed. 1984). Some states limit recovery to post-viability
injuries, but the clear trend is toward recovery for all prenatal harm. Prosser and Keeton, *supra*, at 368–69; Note,
*The Law and the Unborn Child: The Legal and Logical
Inconsistencies*, 46 Notre Dame L. Rev. 349, 357 (1970). The
first court to abandon the viability standard declared what
ought to be the guiding principle for all courts: "[L]egal separability should begin where there is biological separability."
Kelly v. Gregory, 282 A.D. 542, 543, 125 N.Y.S.2d 696, 697
(1953). The court noted that it was the knowledge derived
from medical science which powered the engine for change.
Id. at 543–44, 125 N.Y.S.2d at 697–98. Yet despite the recognition of the rights of the unborn in this area, *Roe* has
constrained the full development of tort law, especially inhibiting some courts from providing protection for the preborn
before the point of viability, and as shown in the following
examples.

  b. Wrongful Death. A majority of jurisdictions now recognize a wrongful death cause of action for the death of a
preborn human being—some rejecting the action unless the
child is born alive and then dies and some allowing only post-
viability actions. *Roe* has been cited by courts rejecting wrongful death actions for preborn humans[4] and by courts limiting
the cause of action to viable unborn children.[5] *Roe*'s viability

---

4. *See, e.g., Justus v. Atchison*, 19 Cal. 3d 564, 565 P.2d 122, 139 Cal. Rptr. 97
(1977) (en banc); *Hernandez v. Garwood*, 390 So.2d 357 (Fla. 1980); *Hogan v.
McDaniel*, 204 Tenn. 253, 559 S.W.2d 774 (Tenn. 1977).
5. *See, e.g., Toth v. Goree*, 65 Mich. App. 296, 237 N.W.2d 297 (1975); *Wallace v. Wallace*, 120 N.H. 675, 421 A.2d 134 (1980) ("We remark also in passing
that it would be incongruous for a mother to have a federal constitutional right to
deliberately destroy a nonviable fetus, *Roe v. Wade* [citation omitted], and at the
same time for a third person to be subject to liability to the fetus for his unintended
but merely negligent acts."); *Werling v. Sandy*, 17 Ohio St. 3d 45, 476 N.E.2d 1053
(1985).

line makes no more sense in wrongful death actions than it made in *Roe*, but *Roe*'s pernicious effect on this part of the law is clear.

c. Wrongful Birth. *Roe v. Wade* has even been used by courts recognizing wrongful birth claims, wherein parents seek damages for the birth of a "defective" child whom they would have aborted if they had been apprised of the defect. As of September 1988, seventeen state courts of appeal had recognized a wrongful birth claim. Bopp, Bostrom & McKinney, *The "Rights" and "Wrongs" of Wrongful Birth and Wrongful Life: A Jurisprudential Analysis of Birth Related Torts*, 27 Duq. L. Rev. 461, 462 (1989).

d. Homicide of the Unborn. Following the English statutory and common law pattern, early nineteenth-century American law prohibited feticide by statutes and, in some cases, by common law, which also encompassed abortion. *See* Destro, *Abortion and the Constitution: The Need for a Life-Protective Amendment*, 63 Cal. L. Rev. 1250, 1273–82 (1975). For example, New York in 1828 made it a felony to willfully cause the death of a fetus even before quickening. J. Mohr, *Abortion in America: The Origins and Evolution of National Policy, 1800–1900* 26–27 (1978) (citing N.Y. Rev. Stat. pt. IV, ch. I, tit. II, §§ 8, 9 at 550). When *Roe v. Wade* swept away the state abortion statutes the protection provided the unborn from homicide was also swept away.

Roe has had a detrimental effect on the states' efforts to protect the unborn from homicide outside the abortion context. For example, the California Supreme Court overturned a murder indictment brought against a man for killing an unborn child by kneeing his ex-wife's abdomen, saying, "I'm going to stomp it out of you." *Keeler v. Superior Court*, 2 Cal. 3d 619, 470 P.2d 617, 87 Cal. Rptr. 481 (1970) (en banc), by applying the archaic born-alive rule. When the California legislature promptly redefined the homicide statute to expressly include the killing of a fetus, a California appellate court declared that *Roe* had removed the protection of a nonviable fetus because "as a matter of constitutional law the destruction of a nonviable fetus is not a taking of human life." *People v. Smith*, 59 Cal. App. 3d 751, 755, 129 Cal. Rptr. 498, 502 (1976). Following the California courts and *Roe*, many states have held that *Roe* denies the protection of homicide laws to the unborn.[6] This anomalous result shows *Roe*'s distorting effect on the law.

e. Other Areas. *Roe* has also had a deleterious effect on other areas of the law relating to the rights of the unborn. In *Davis* v. *Davis*, No. E–14496, slip op. (Cir. Ct. for Blount Cty. Tenn. Sep. 21, 1989), a state court listened to exhaustive expert testimony as to whether frozen embryos were children, *i.e.*, individual human beings, or property. Having determined from the scientific evidence that the embryos were children, the judge held that it was in their best interest to be awarded to their natural mother for implantation in her womb. On appeal, the Tennessee Court of Appeals relied in part on the state abortion statute imposed on that state by *Roe* to conclude that the unborn were not legal persons and the constitution protected Mr. Davis from becoming a parent against his will. The Court gave the Davises joint control of the embryos (as property)—dooming them to destruction. *Davis* v. *Davis*, 1990 WL 130807 (Tenn. App. 1990) (now on appeal to the Tennessee Supreme Court). Under the influence of *Roe*, the court ignored the fact that Mr. Davis had already become a parent when he consented to in vitro fertilization with his sperm and the fertilization was accomplished.

2. *Roe* Has Been Used to Argue for an Expansive Interpretation of the Right of Privacy.

Roe has also served as the basis for claims for an expansive interpretation of the right of privacy. For example, it has been argued that there is a privacy right to die, which would encompass assisted suicide, contrary to long-standing public policy, and allow the withdrawal of nutrition and hydration from incompetent but not terminally ill patients. *See, e.g., In re Quinlan*, 70 N.J. 10, 355 A.2d 647, *cert. denied sub nom. Garger* v. *New Jersey*, 429 U.S. 922 (1976) (euthanasia); *Bouvia* v. *Superior Court*, 179 Cal. App. 3d 1127, 225 Cal. Rptr. 297 (Cal. Ct. App. 1986) (suicide); *Cruzan* v. *Director*, 110

---

6. *See, e.g., State* v. *Gyles*, 313 So. 2d 799 (La. 1975); *State* v. *Brown*, 378 So. 2d 916 (La. 1979); *State* v. *Soto*, 378 N.W.2d 625 (Minn. 1985); *Hollis* v. *Commonwealth*, 652 S.W.2d 61 (Ky. 1983).

S. Ct. 2841 (1990). The notion that the right of privacy can be readily extended to encompass whatever someone might desire, springs from the manner in which *Roe* was created without a proper foundation in the Constitution.

3. *Roe* Has Distorted the Law Regarding Rules of General Application.

Roe v. Wade also set procedural precedents for distortion of common rules of adjudication. *See* Bopp & Coleson, *The Right to Abortion, supra,* at 299–350. This was especially evident in *Thornburgh,* 476 U.S. 747, the high-water mark of *Roe's* analysis.

a. Statutory Construction. The abortion distortion factor was at work in the *Thornburgh* decision where this Court ignored the principle that a court should avoid constitutional problems by giving a statute a constitutional construction where fairly possible. The Pennsylvania law at issue in *Thornburgh* required a second physician to be present at post-viability abortions to care for the possibly surviving child. 18 Pa. Cons. Stat. Ann. § 3210(c) (Purdon 1983). For emergency purposes, the law provided that it is "a complete defense to any charge brought against a physician for violating the requirements of this section that he had concluded in good faith, in his best medical judgment, . . . that the abortion was necessary to preserve maternal life or health." *Id.* Although in *Planned Parenthood Association of Kansas City, Missouri v. Ashcroft,* 462 U.S. 476, 482–86 (1983), this Court construed a similar second-physician provision to include an emergency provision for the life or health of the mother—even though none existed—this Court could not bring itself to do so in the Pennsylvania case and struck down the statute. *Thornburgh,* 476 U.S. at 771.

Justice White took the *Thornburgh* majority members to task for their willingness to disregard this principle of statutory construction:

The Court's rejection of a perfectly plausible reading of the statute flies in the face of the principle—which until today I had thought applicable to abortion statutes as well as to other legislative enactments—that '[w]here fairly possible, courts should construe a statute to avoid a danger of unconstitutionality.' *Planned Parenthood Ass'n v. Ashcroft* [citation omitted]. The Court's reading is obviously based on an entirely different principle: that in cases involving abortion, a permissible reading of a statute is to be avoided at all costs.

Id. at 812 (White, J., dissenting). *See* Bopp & Coleson, *The Right to Abortion, supra,* at 315–32 (extended discussion of abuse of the above principle in abortion cases).

b. Evidentiary Standards Applicable to Preliminary Injunction Hearings. Another example of the abortion distortion effect at work is found in *Thornburgh*, where this Court rushed to a judgment on the merits from the appeal of a grant of a preliminary injunction. Shortly before the statute at issue in *Thornburgh* was to go into effect (but four months after the statute had been enacted), the plaintiff abortion providers filed forty affidavits, which became the basis of a court-ordered stipulation, and requested a preliminary injunction. Pennsylvania was not allowed to contest Plaintiffs' facts unless it could give evidence at the hearing on the preliminary injunction. Because of the limited time available, no evidence was submitted by the Commonwealth. Brief for Appellant at 35–49, *Thornburgh*, 476 U.S. 747. The parties were assured that the stipulation would be used solely for the purpose of the hearing. However, on appeal, the appellate court went to the merits and held the Pennsylvania abortion law largely unconstitutional. *Id.* at 8. The *Thornburgh* Court followed suit. In dissent, Justice O'Connor noted the abortion distortion effect at work in these words: "If this case did not involve state regulation of abortion, it may be doubted that the Court would entertain, let alone adopt, such a departure from its precedents." *Thornburgh*, 476 U.S. at 814 (O'Connor, J., dissenting).

With such effects flowing from *Roe*, the erosion of support for *Roe* is unremarkable. The question of what standard will supplant *Roe* remains.

II. IF THE UNDUE BURDEN TEST IS TO BE USED, A WORKABLE STANDARD MUST BE CLEARLY ARTICULATED.

This Court's failure to affirm *Roe* in recent cases suggests that the Court views *Roe's* trimester framework as unworkable. The Court's splintered *Webster* decision led the Third Circuit to adopt Justice O'Connor's undue burden test as the appropriate standard for reviewing abortion legislation. However, as understood and applied by the Third Circuit, that test is also unworkable. Your *amicus* submits that an undue burden standard should not be adopted unless a workable standard is clearly articulated and adopted by this Court.

A. The Undue Burden Test Is Not Workable As Understood and Applied by the Third Circuit.

1. The Third Circuit Failed to Understand That in Determining Whether the Burden Is Undue the Effect on the Class, Not Some Individuals, Must Be Considered.

The Third Circuit held that § 3209, the spousal notice provision, "is likely to dissuade many from seeking an abortion if such notification is required" so that "§ 3209 constitutes an undue burden on a woman's abortion decision." *Planned Parenthood* v. *Casey*, Opinion of Third Circuit, Appendix to Petition for a Writ of Certiorari in No. 91–902 at 70a (1991). However, as dissenting Judge Alito correctly pointed out, "it appears clear that an undue burden may not be established simply by showing that a law will have a heavy impact on a few women but that instead a broader inhibiting effect must be shown." *Id.* at 90a (Alito, J., dissenting). Justice O'Connor has set forth the principle as follows: "the mere possibility that *some* women will be less likely to choose to have an abortion by virtue of the presence of a particular state regulation suffices to invalidate it." *Thornburgh*, 476 U.S. at 829 (O'Connor, J., dissenting) (emphasis in original). Thus, the Third Circuit misunderstood and misapplied the undue burden test with regard to its effect on some women. Clarifying this issue is especially important for upholding parental notice/

consent statutes under the undue burden analysis. Although such requirements may prevent some minors from seeking abortion, that does not make of the requirements an undue burden. *See Thornburgh*, 476 U.S. at 828 (O'Connor, J., dissenting) (finding no undue burden in the parental notice statute upheld in *H.L. v. Matheson*, 450 U.S. 398 (1981)).

2. The Third Circuit Failed to Recognize Compelling State Interests Which It Should Have Recognized.

Where compelling state interests exist, the undue burden test requires only that a statute "bears a rational relationship to legitimate purposes such as the advancement of these compelling interests." *Thornburgh*, 476 U.S. at 828 (O'Connor, J., dissenting). Not only was the Pennsylvania spousal notice provision, § 3209, not an undue burden, as demonstrated *supra*, but the presence of compelling interests meant that— even if the burden had been undue—Pennsylvania had only to show that its statute was rationally related to its legitimate purpose in advancing its compelling state interests. However, the Third Circuit failed to recognize compelling state interests as part of its analysis. Three such compelling interests apply to the review of abortion restrictions.

a. The Court Erred in Failing to Recognize the Father's Compelling Interests. In the case of *Scheinberg v. Smith*, 659 F.2d 476 (1981), the Fifth Circuit considered an abortion spousal notice and consultation statute. In that case, Florida asserted two interests of the father as compelling: "maintaining and promoting the marital relationship; and protecting a husband's interest in the procreative potential of the marriage." *Id.* at 483. The Fifth Circuit telescoped these two interests into one, "a state interest in furthering the integrity of the state-created and regulated institutions of marriage and the family," and held this interest to be "sufficiently weighty to justify the burden on a woman's abortion decision imposed by the spousal notification requirement." *Id.* (citation omitted). The Fifth Circuit concluded that "[t]he state interest sought to be furthered by this legislation . . . [e]ncompasses furthering the institutional integrity of the marital relationship, and of the family. We have held that interest to be, in constitutional terms, compelling, and thus ample justification for establishing spousal notice and consultation requirements." *Id.* at 486.

By ignoring the legitimate and compelling interests a husband has in the integrity of the marriage relationship and in a particular preborn child, as well, *Planned Parenthood of Cent. Mo. v. Danforth*, 428 U.S. 52, 93 (1976) (White, J.) ("[T]he husband has an interest of his own in the life of the fetus which should not be extinguished by the unilateral decision of the wife."), the Third Circuit altered the undue burden analysis in a way fatal to § 3209, the spousal notice provision.

b. The Court Erred in Failing to Recognize the Compelling Interests in Protecting the Unborn Throughout Pregnancy. The Third Circuit also altered the undue burden analysis applicable to the Pennsylvania statute by failing to recognize the interest in protecting unborn life which exists throughout pregnancy. A majority of the Justices of this Court have recognized such an interest. *See Thornburgh*, 476 U.S. at 828 (O'Connor and Rehnquist, JJ., dissenting); *Webster*, 109 S. Ct. at 3055, 3057 (plurality opinion), 3064 (Scalia, J., dissenting) (calling for the plenary reversal of *Roe*, presumably thereby recognizing at least a compelling interest in protecting unborn life).

3. The Third Circuit Erred in Holding That the Spousal Notice Provision Would Have Been Impermissible Even with a Compelling Interest for Not Being Narrowly Drawn.

Finding that § 3209, the spousal notice provision, imposed an undue burden, the Third Circuit said, "[W]e must apply strict scrutiny to determine if § 3209 is narrowly tailored to serve a compelling state interest." *Planned Parenthood v. Casey*, Opinion of Third Circuit, Appendix to Petition for a Writ of Certiorari in No. 91–902 at 71a (1991). This was erroneous, for no narrowly tailored requirement is applicable under the undue burden test. "The Court has never required that state regulation that burdens the abortion decision be 'narrowly drawn' to express only the relevant state interest." *Akron*, 462 U.S. at 467 n.11 (O'Connor, J., dissenting). Rather, abortion restrictions under the undue burden test need only be " 'reasonably related' to the state compelling interest." *Id.*

Therefore, the Third Circuit erred when it declared, "[E]ven if we were to assume that [keeping married individuals together in wedlock] does constitute a compelling state interest, we could not conclude that the Commonwealth has carried its burden of demonstrating that § 3209 is narrowly tailored to promote that interest." Opinion of Third Circuit at 72a.

B. Assuming the Continued Existence of Constitutional Protection for Abortion Above the "Rational Basis" Level, the "Undue Burden" Test Might Be Workable If This Court Sets Forth Clear Standards.

If this Court should choose to employ an undue burden test for abortion jurisprudence, although your *amici* believe a rational basis test to be more workable and constitutionally correct, *see infra,* such a test might be workable if this Court sets forth clear guidelines. These include the following, as articulated in prior opinions by Justice O'Connor and other members of this Court.

1. Any Statute, Regardless of Whether It Imposes an Undue Burden, Will Be Upheld If It Reasonably Furthers a Compelling Interest.

The "undue burden" test is as follows:

Under this Court's fundamental-rights jurisprudence, judicial scrutiny of state regulation of abortion should be limited to whether the state law bears a rational relationship to legitimate purposes such as the advancement of . . . compelling interests, with heightened scrutiny reserved for instances in which the State has imposed an "undue burden" on the abortion decision. . . . An undue burden will generally be found "in situations involving absolute obstacles or severe limitations on the abortion decision," not wherever a state regulation "may 'inhibit' abortions to some degree. . . ." And if a state law does interfere with the abortion decision to an extent that it is unduly burdensome, so that it becomes "necessary to apply an exacting standard of review, . . . the possibility remains that the statute will withstand the stricter scrutiny."

Thornburgh, 476 U.S. at 828 (O'Connor, J., & Rehnquist, C.J., dissenting) (citations omitted). The legitimate purposes to which such regulations might be addressed include "compelling interests in ensuring maternal health and in protecting potential human life, and [those] interests exist 'throughout pregnancy.' " *Id.*

Applying the test involves the following steps:

1. A "threshold inquiry" into whether the nature and degree of the regulatory interference are rationally related to a legitimate governmental objective.

(*a*) If the regulatory burden is not rationally related to a legitimate governmental objective, the regulation fails, *see Hodgson v. Minnesota*, 110 S. Ct. 2926, 2950 (1990) (O'Connor, J., concurring in part, and concurring in the judgment in part) ("broad sweep" and "failure to serve the purposes asserted by the State in too many cases");

(*b*) If the regulatory burden is rationally related to a legitimate governmental interest, and its only impact is to "inhibit abortions to some degree," even a "significant" one, the rational basis finding ends the judicial inquiry, *Akron*, 462 U.S. at 463–64 (O'Connor & Rehnquist, JJ., dissenting);

(*c*) If, however, the nature and degree of the interference may fairly be described as one "involving absolute obstacles or severe limitations on the abortion decision" the burden is "undue" and it becomes "necessary to apply an exacting standard of review."

2. At this stage of the inquiry, the weight of the interests asserted by the state are examined, *Akron*, 462 U.S. at 465 nn. 10 & 11 (O'Connor & Rehnquist, JJ., dissenting);

(*a*) If the state interests are not "compelling" the regulation fails;

(*b*) Because the Court has never actually imposed a requirement that an abortion regulation needs to be " 'narrowly drawn' to express only the relevant state interest" (notwithstanding implications to the contrary in *Roe*), *Akron*, 462 U.S. at 467 n.11 (O'Connor & Rehnquist, JJ., dissenting), the regulation needs only to be rationally related to a compelling state interest in order to "withstand the stricter scrutiny."

Because there is no question, even under *Roe* itself, that the states have both a "legitimate interest in seeing to it that abortion, like any other medical procedure, is performed under circumstances that insure maximum safety for the patient," and "*another* important and legitimate interest in protecting the potentiality of human life," *Roe*, 410 U.S. at 149–150, 162 (emphasis in original), quoted in *Akron*, 462 U.S. at 450 (O'Connor & Rehnquist, JJ., dissenting), the issue for the Court—should it decide to adopt the undue burden analysis —is whether those interests are "compelling" throughout pregnancy.

2. The States Have Compelling Interests, Including the Protection of Unborn Life, Which Exist Throughout Pregnancy.

As noted previously, *see supra* II–A–2–b, a majority of the members of this Court has recognized that states have compelling interests in unborn life and maternal health which exist throughout pregnancy. This needs to be established in a single, majority opinion, if the undue burden test is to be workable. In addition, it should be recognized, as the Fifth Circuit held in *Scheinberg, see supra* II–A–2–a, that husbands have special interests in the integrity of the marital unit and the procreative activity occurring therein which are separate compelling interests. These interests, too, should be recognized by a majority of this Court if the undue burden test is to be employed.

3. Statutes Which Result in Fewer Abortions Would Reasonably Further the State's Interest in Protecting Unborn Life and Would Be Constitutional.

The recognition of a compelling interest in protecting unborn life throughout pregnancy, as a majority of the Justices have done, would not require the states to enact laws restricting abortion. However, it would allow them to do so if they so chose, provided it is done in a reasonable manner. Given the compelling interest in protecting unborn human life, any statute which results in fewer abortions would reasonably further that state interest. This needs to be clearly articulated for an undue burden test to be workable.

4. Failure to Establish the Above Three Elements of the Undue Burden Test Would Result in *Ad Hoc*, Multi-Factor Balancing, Yielding Unclear Guidelines.

The critical legal issue to be determined here is how judges and legislators are to assign a constitutional "weight" to state and paternal interest in the preservation of "the individual fetus." Without such guidance, the "undue burden" test is unworkable.

One of "the fundamental aspiration[s] of judicial decision-making" is to apply "neutral principles 'sufficiently absolute to give them roots throughout the community and continuity over significant periods of time.' " *Akron*, 462 U.S. at 458 (O'Connor & Rehnquist, JJ., dissenting) (citation omitted). *See* Wechsler, *Toward Neutral Principles of Constitutional Law*, 73 Harv. L. Rev. 1, 15–16 (1959) ("[T]he main constituent of the judicial process is that it must be genuinely principled, resting with respect to every step that is involved in reaching judgment on analysis and reasons quite transcending the immediate result that is achieved . . . .").

The alternative is *ad hoc*, multi-factor "balancing" which is, by its very nature, unpredictable and "ill suited to the judicial function," *CTS Corp.* v. *Dynamics Corp. of America*, 481 U.S. 69, 94, (1987) (Scalia, J., concurring in part and concurring in judgment). Multi-factor balancing is inconsistent with the undisputed power of the states to make and effectuate at least some political judgments concerning the balance to be struck between public and private interests in the abortion context. *See Roe*, 410 U.S. at 162–164 (post-viability); *Thornburgh*, 476 U.S. at 785–86 (White and Rehnquist, JJ., dissenting) ("decisions that find in the Constitution principles or values that cannot be fairly read into that document usurp the people's authority"); *Akron*, 462 U.S. at 458 (O'Connor & Rehnquist, JJ., dissenting) ("the Court's framework forces legislatures, as a matter of constitutional law, to speculate").

Moreover, making the weight of the relevant state and private interests depend upon a multi-factor balance was the way in which the Court departed from "evenhanded appli[cation of] uncontroversial legal doctrines," *Thornburgh*, 476 U.S. at 814 (O'Connor, J., & Rehnquist, C.J., dissenting), in *Roe*. Such balancing is the source of the "major distortion in [its] constitutional jurisprudence" wrought by the Court's abortion decisions, *id.*, and the reason that "no legal rule or doctrine [involving regulation of abortion] is safe from ad hoc nullification." *Id.*

By rejecting the trimester analysis of *Roe*, but not addressing the nature of either the rights or the state interests necessarily implicated in abortion, a majority of the members of this Court have rejected multi-factor balancing as the standard of review for abortion cases. In so doing, it has set the stage for a return to evenhanded application of black-letter constitutional law principles.

The Court can reverse the decision of the Third Circuit with respect to § 3209 in either of two ways. First, it can adopt the view that nothing in the Constitution prohibits a finding that the state interest in the preservation of fetal life is "compelling" throughout pregnancy. *See, e.g., Thornburgh*, 476 U.S. at 795 (White, J., dissenting). In the alternative, it can recharacterize the nature of the right recognized in *Roe* as something less than "fundamental."

A decision limited to a discussion of the "compelling" nature of the state's interest would leave intact *Roe*'s holding that there exists some quantum of constitutionally protected interest in the context of abortion (above the minimal protection provided by the rational basis requirement), and, necessarily, this Court's role in deciding what it is. A decision which recharacterizes the nature of the interest recognized in *Roe v. Wade* would effectively overrule the case and return the issue to the states from whence it came.

Justice White has correctly recognized that the difference between abortion and other reproductive decisionmaking "does not go merely to the weight of the state interest in regulating abortion; it affects as well the characterization of the liberty interest itself." *Thornburgh*, 476 U.S. at 792 n.2.

Your *amici* respectfully submit that the second option suggested above—overruling *Roe*—is more consistent with the

Constitution because the weight *Roe* assigns to the interests are, as Professor Gottlieb suggests, "a complex choice, not a clear deduction from constitutional text." Gottlieb, *Compelling Governmental Interests: An Essential But Unanalyzed Term in Constitutional Adjudication*, 68 B.U.L. Rev. 917, 949 (1988). Petitioners make essentially the same point in defense of their argument that the undue burden test should be rejected, Petitioners' Brief at [55–58], but argue the opposite conclusion: that the Court should explicitly reaffirm the balance struck in *Roe*. Petitioners' Brief at [49–52] & nn.47–50. But if the *ad hoc* balancing which has characterized the case law since *Roe* is to be replaced with "black letter" constitutional law in most cases, it is essential that the states be free to act on their view that their legitimate interest in fetal life is "compelling." A single, familiar standard applicable to abortion cases is essential for legislatures, public officials who must interpret and apply the law, and—most importantly—for the courts called upon to engage in a constitutional review of such policy choices.

III. RATIONAL BASIS TEST IS PREFERABLE TO THE UNDUE BURDEN TEST.

Directly or by implication, five Justices have required only a rational basis test in recent abortion litigation, indicating their belief that there is no general, fundamental abortion right. *Ohio v. Akron Center for Reproductive Health*, 110 S. Ct. 2972, 2977, 2983–84 (plurality opinion of Kennedy, J., joined by Rehnquist, C.J., and White and Scalia, JJ.); *Ohio*, 110 S. Ct. at 2981; *Hodgson v. Minnesota*, 110 S. Ct. at 2944 (Stevens, J., joined by O'Connor, J.); *id.* at 2945 (the court); *id.* at 2949 (O'Connor, J., concurring in part and concurring in the judgment in part).

A clear majority ruling on a rational basis would be preferable to employing the undue burden test for several reasons. First, it would not spawn additional litigation as an undue burden test would. Second, the rational basis test has a long pedigree, is well indicated, and is easily applied. Third, the rational basis test squarely addresses the issue of whether there is a fundamental right to choose abortion. This needs to be done to eliminate the presumption of invalidity which automatically attaches to laws interfering with fundamental rights and replace it with the assumption of validity which accompanies rational basis review.

Strict scrutiny is not necessary since there is no fundamental right. While the undue burden test, described *ante*, may provide an adequate test, there is no reason to labor and confuse lower courts with a new test for which exploratory litigation will be necessary when federal jurisprudence already has the fully developed and well understood rational basis test. *Thornburgh*, 476 U.S. at 802 (White, J., joined by Rehnquist, J., dissenting), citing *Williamson v. Lee Optical*, 348 U.S. 483 (1955).

The adoption of the rational basis test for abortion regulation will also permit this Court to avoid the intricate and complex regulation that fundamental rights or undue burden jurisprudence imposes on it. *Webster*, 109 S. Ct. at 3057 (Rehnquist, C.J., joined by White & Kennedy, JJ.) and *Thornburgh*, 476 U.S. at 814 (O'Connor, J., dissenting). The issue remains rightfully with the states.

CONCLUSION

The *Roe* framework is unworkable and has resulted in confused constitutional application and an intricate and complex system of judicially imposed regulation. Provided abortion remains a limited fundamental right, an undue burden analysis would be workable, as a substitute for *Roe*, if the Court finds the state has a compelling interest in potential life.

However, because abortion is not properly a fundamental right, the Court should employ the well-established rational basis test. That test provides clear rules of construction for presumptively valid statutes or regulations. This case offers the opportunity to end the long and distorted constitutional history of the so-called "right to abortion." In any event, this

Court should affirm the decision in No. 91–744 and reverse
the decision in No. 91–902.

Respectfully submitted,

ROBERT A. DESTRO
Columbus School of Law
Catholic Univ. of America
Washington, DC 20064
(202) 319–5140

A. ERIC JOHNSTON
Seier, Johnston & Trippe
2100 Southbridge Parkway
Southbridge Bldg., Ste. 376
Birmingham, AL 35209
(205) 879–9100

Counsel of Record:

JAMES BOPP, JR.
RICHARD E. COLESON
Brames, McCormick, Bopp &
Abel
191 Harding Avenue
P.O. Box 410
Terre Haute, IN 47808–0410
(812) 238–2421

Counsel for *Amicus Curiae*

April 6, 1992

REPLY BRIEF FOR PETITIONERS AND CROSS-RESPONDENTS APRIL 15, 1992

REPLY BRIEF FOR PETITIONERS
AND CROSS-RESPONDENTS

ARGUMENT

I. THIS COURT MUST REJECT THE COMMONWEALTH AND SOLICITOR'S PLEA TO ABANDON *ROE*'S CENTRAL HOLDING.

A. *Roe* Held That the Right to Abortion Is a Fundamental Right Protected by the Strict Scrutiny Standard of Review; This Court Cannot Uphold the Pennsylvania Law Without Abandoning That Standard.

Apparently mindful of the potential negative political repercussions of a decision explicitly overruling *Roe* v. *Wade*, 410 U.S. 113 (1973), the Commonwealth contrives to avoid that result by arguing that the Pennsylvania law "comports with *Roe* in all respects." R.B. [178].[1] In support of this argument, the Commonwealth claims that *Roe* establishes only a "limited" right to abortion, R.B. [178–81], and that Justice O'Connor's undue burden test[2] is the standard of review

1. Petitioners cite the Brief for Respondents as "R.B. ____," the Brief for Petitioners as "P.B. ____," and the Brief of *Amicus* United States as "S.G. ____."
2. *City of Akron* v. *Akron Center for Reproductive Health, Inc.*, 462 U.S. 416, 461–64 (1983) (O'Connor, J., dissenting); *Thornburgh* v. *American College of Obstetricians & Gynecologists*, 476 U.S. 747, 828–29 (1986) (O'Connor, J., dissenting).

mandated by *Roe*. R.B. [182–84].[3] Thus, the Commonwealth claims, this Court need not overrule *Roe* to uphold the Pennsylvania restrictions. R.B. [178].[4]

The Commonwealth's argument misstates *Roe*'s holding and, if accepted, would dismantle this Court's substantive due process jurisprudence. This Court has repeatedly found that once a liberty interest rises to the level of a "fundamental right," restrictions on that right are subject to the strict scrutiny standard of review. *See, e.g., Eu v. San Francisco Democratic Comm.*, 489 U.S. 214, 222 (1989).[5] This Court has also repeatedly acknowledged that *Roe* established the right to choose abortion or childbirth as a fundamental right; state laws that intrude upon these reproductive decisions must therefore be examined with exacting scrutiny. 410 U.S. at 153–55.[6]

The Commonwealth's assertion that this Court can avoid overruling *Roe* by applying the "undue burden" test is disingenuous at best. As the Commonwealth concedes, that test, which presently has "the support of only a single Justice," R.B. [185],[7] provides far less protection for women seeking abor-

---

3. The Commonwealth's argument is inconsistent with that made by all of its supporting *amici*, who concede that *Roe* held that the right to choose abortion is a fundamental right protected by strict scrutiny. *E.g.*, S.G. [212]; Feminists for Life Br. 3.

4. Alternatively, the Commonwealth, joined by the Solicitor, argues that this Court should explicitly overrule *Roe* and replace the strict scrutiny standard of review with the rational basis test. R.B. [204–208]; S.G. [214–16].

5. The Commonwealth confuses fundamental rights with limited state interests. *Roe*'s accommodation of the state's interest in potential human life did not reduce the status of the abortion right to that of a so-called "limited right" and thereby sanction the imposition of a less protective standard of review. *See* R.B. [178]. To the contrary, those concerns relate only to whether a state's interest is sufficient to override a woman's right to choose abortion. 410 U.S. at 163–64.

6. *E.g.*, *Carey v. Population Servs. Int'l*, 431 U.S. 678, 686 (1977); *Thornburgh*, 476 U.S. at 772; *Akron*, 462 U.S. at 419–20 & n.1.

7. Relying on *Marks v. United States*, 430 U.S. 188 (1977), the Commonwealth insists that the undue burden test became the "governing standard" in *Webster v. Reproductive Health Servs.*, 492 U.S. 490 (1989), and *Hodgson v. Minnesota*, 110 S. Ct. 2926 (1990). R.B. [185]. But in *Webster*, Justice O'Connor's decisive opinion found Missouri's viability testing provision consistent with *Roe*'s strict scrutiny standard and expressly declined to reexamine *Roe*'s validity. *Webster*, 492 U.S. at 525–26 (O'Connor, J., concurring). In *Hodgson*, this Court found that the Minnesota restrictions unconstitutionally interfered with "family[] decisionmaking processes," 110 S. Ct. at 2950 (O'Connor, J., concurring), and failed to pass even rational basis review. *Id.* at 2945–47. Even when upholding that portion of the statute with a judicial bypass procedure, this Court carefully reconciled its ruling with past prece-

tion than *Roe's* strict scrutiny standard. *See* P.B. [55–56].[8] Under the undue burden test, heightened judicial scrutiny is reserved for only those instances in which the state imposes " 'absolute obstacles or severe limitations on the abortion decision.' " *Thornburgh*, 476 U.S. at 828 (O'Connor, J., dissenting) (quoting *Akron*, 462 U.S. at 464 (O'Connor, J., dissenting)). By contrast, under *Roe*, any non-*de minimis* interference with the abortion right triggers strict scrutiny.[9] Absent a compelling purpose, both bans on abortion and restrictions—like those at issue here—that encumber the abortion choice with delay, administrative hurdles, or expense are invalid. *See* P.B. [40–42]. In short, upholding the Pennsylvania law under the less protective undue burden standard plainly entails overturning *Roe* by eviscerating its core principle.

Similarly, *Bellotti* v. *Baird*, 428 U.S. 132 (1976), is distinguishable as it involved minors' access to abortion, an area in which this Court has permitted greater state regulation. To conclude from *Bellotti's* casual use of the phrase "undue burden" in describing the holding in *Planned Parenthood* v. *Danforth*, 428 U.S. 52 (1976), that this Court in *Danforth* intended

dents. *Id.* at 2950–51 (O'Connor, J., concurring); *id.* at 2970 (Kennedy, J., concurring in part and dissenting in part) (plurality). Moreover, the Commonwealth's reliance on *Marks* is misplaced. *See* Representative Don Edwards et al. Br. 8–9.

8. Respondents incorrectly cite *Harris* v. *McRae*, 448 U.S. 297 (1980), *Maher* v. *Roe*, 432 U.S. 464 (1977), and *Beal* v. *Doe*, 432 U.S. 438 (1977), to support their claim that the undue burden test has been regularly applied to review abortion regulations. R.B. [180]. In these cases, this Court upheld funding schemes, applying rational basis review because the government's decision to encourage childbirth over abortion "place[d] no governmental obstacle in the path of a woman who chooses to terminate her pregnancy." *Harris*, 448 U.S. at 315. But those cases acknowledged that regulations that interfere with women's rights are subject to exacting scrutiny. *See Maher*, 432 U.S. at 472–73.

9. The right in *Roe*, like other fundamental rights, is not absolute. This Court has upheld numerous "regulations that have no significant impact on the woman's exercise of her right [and are] . . . justified by important state health objectives." *Akron*, 462 U.S. at 430. *See Planned Parenthood Ass'n* v. *Ashcroft*, 462 U.S. 476, 486–90 (1983) (plurality opinion); *id.* at 505 (O'Connor, J., concurring in part and dissenting in part) (requirement that tissue removed following abortion be submitted to pathologist); *Danforth*, 428 U.S. at 65–67, 79–81 (woman's written consent requirement, recordkeeping requirement); *Connecticut* v. *Menillo*, 423 U.S. 9 (1975) (requirement that only physicians perform abortions). Additionally, this Court has upheld state laws regulating the performance of abortions after viability is possible. *Webster*, 492 U.S. at 513–20 (plurality opinion); *id.* at 525–31 (O'Connor, J., concurring) (viability testing requirement); *Ashcroft*, 462 U.S. at 482–86 (plurality opinion); *id.* at 505 (O'Connor, J., concurring in part and dissenting in part) (second physician must be present during postviability abortions).

to replace *Roe's* strict scrutiny standard with a less protective standard of review strains credulity.

B. The Doctrine of *Stare Decisis* Requires Reaffirmation of *Roe.*

This Court has recognized time and time again that the doctrine of *stare decisis* "is of fundamental importance to the rule of law." *Hilton v. South Carolina Pub. Rys. Comm'n,* 112 S. Ct. 560, 563 (1991) (quoting *Welch v. Texas Dep't of Highways & Pub. Transp.,* 483 U.S. 468, 494 (1987)). Here, where there is the potential for disrupting the lives and settled expectations of millions of American women, it is beyond dispute that *stare decisis* applies with special force. P.B. [42–45]. Astonishingly, while boldly advocating *Roe's* demise, the Commonwealth and the Solicitor make only passing reference to this doctrine.

The Solicitor virtually ignores *stare decisis,* arguing in a brief footnote that it has less potency in constitutional cases. S.G. [217] n.4. But "even in constitutional cases, the doctrine carries such persuasive force that . . . departure from precedent [must] be supported by some 'special justification.' " *Payne v. Tennessee,* 111 S. Ct. 2597, 2618 (1991) (Souter, J., concurring) (quoting *Arizona v. Rumsey,* 467 U.S. 203, 212 (1984)). This Court has already concluded that *stare decisis* provides "especially compelling reasons" for continued adherence to *Roe. Akron,* 462 U.S. at 419–20 & n.1; *Thornburgh,* 476 U.S. at 759; *id.* at 780–81 (Stevens, J., concurring).

Similarly, the Commonwealth gives short shrift to *stare decisis,*[10] relying simply on this Court's overturning of *Lochner v. New York,* 198 U.S. 45 (1905), to justify overturning *Roe.* R.B. [208]. However, *Lochner* is not remotely comparable to *Roe.* In overruling *Lochner,* this Court allowed states to regulate the working conditions of employees. While this action upset some expectations of business owners and reduced their profits, it did not withdraw a right central to the ability

---

10. Both approaches to the resolution of this case advocated by the Commonwealth implicate *stare decisis.* As respondents concede, upholding Pennsylvania's biased counseling and 24-hour delay provisions without explicitly rejecting *Roe* would require this Court, at a minimum, to overrule *Akron* and *Thornburgh.* R.B. [207–208].

of countless individuals to order and control their lives and destinies, a result that overruling *Roe* would entail. *See* Jeb Rubenfeld, *The Right of Privacy*, 102 Harv. L. Rev. 737, 806 (1989) (laws upheld following *Lochner* era "did not involve the forced, affirmative occupation and direction of individuals' lives"). Moreover, while *Lochner* frustrated states' ability to protect workers from abusive working conditions, *Roe* protects women from state intervention that endangers their lives and health.[11]

For the past nineteen years, *Roe* has secured fundamental protection for private choices affecting millions of American women. The heavy burden of convincing this Court to destroy those settled expectations falls on those who propose this radical step. Both the Commonwealth and the Solicitor have utterly failed to meet their burden.

C. The Decision to Terminate or Continue a Pregnancy Must Continue to Be Afforded Fundamental Constitutional Protection.

The Commonwealth and the Solicitor premise their argument that the right to abortion must not be accorded fundamental status primarily on two assertions: abortion is not deeply rooted in the nation's history and traditions, R.B. [207], S.G. [221], and abortion is different from other privacy rights previously recognized by this Court. R.B. [207–208], S.G. [220] n. 10. These arguments rest on an incomplete view of history and flawed legal analysis, and fail to distinguish *Roe*'s holding from a century of this Court's privacy decisions.

The Commonwealth and the Solicitor argue that abortion is not rooted in our nation's history and tradition, S.G. [216], R.B. [207], because statutes limiting abortion were common when the Fourteenth Amendment was ratified. The Solicitor's narrow focus on the historical treatment of abortion in the

---

11. In addition, overruling *Lochner* resulted from the changed economic conditions of the 1930s. *See* Laurence H. Tribe, *American Constitutional Law* 578 (2d ed. 1988) ("it was the economic realities of the Depression that graphically undermined *Lochner*'s premises. . . . Positive government intervention came to be more widely accepted as essential to economic survival . . ."). In contrast, no changed social conditions justify overturning *Roe*. P.B. [42–44].

mid-nineteenth century, rather than the general historical protection of the right of privacy, is contrary to the historical analysis traditionally used to identify fundamental rights protected by the Fourteenth Amendment. *See Michael H. v. Gerald D.*, 491 U.S. 110, 132 (1989) (O'Connor, J., concurring) ("the Court has characterized relevant traditions protecting asserted rights at levels of generality that might not be 'the most specific level' available"). *See also id.* at 139 (Brennan, J., dissenting).[12]

Furthermore, in *Roe*, this Court undertook an extensive historical analysis and concluded that there was no longstanding tradition of laws proscribing abortion. 410 U.S. at 129–41. Indeed, as the Solicitor concedes, S.G. [213], at the time of the nation's founding and at common law,[13] abortion was permitted until the time of quickening. *Roe*, 410 U.S. at 140–41; James C. Mohr, *Abortion in America: The Origins and Evolution of National Policy, 1800–1900* 3–19 (1978). The history elucidated by this Court in *Roe* has not changed since 1973.[14]

12. In cases such as *Griswold v. Connecticut*, 381 U.S. 479 (1965), and *Eisenstadt v. Baird*, 405 U.S. 438 (1972), this Court focused on the historic respect for privacy, rather than state laws prohibiting the use of contraceptives. Had this Court adopted the Solicitor's approach, the important rights recognized in these cases might not enjoy constitutional protection at all. *See Michael H.*, 491 U.S. at 139 (Brennan, J., dissenting). For although the first specifically anti-contraception statute was enacted in 1873, Comstock Act, ch. 258, § 1, 17 Stat. 598 (1873) (codified as amended at 18 U.S.C. § 1461 (1988)), anti-obscenity statutes had been used decades earlier to prosecute those who disseminated contraceptive information. J. Reed, *The Birth Control Movement and American Society: From Private Vice to Public Virtue* 9 (1983).

13. *Amicus* American Academy of Medical Ethics purports to demonstrate that abortion was criminal at common law. Their brief fails, however, to cite even one early English common law case in which either a woman or an "abortionist" was criminally prosecuted for a successful, voluntary termination of pregnancy. Rather, the cases cited involved assaults that resulted in injury or death of a pregnant woman and her fetus, *see, e.g., Rex v. Lichefeld*, K.B. 27/974, Rex. m.4 (1505) (defendant charged as accessory to suicide, a felony killing), or the killing of a child born alive, which then, as now, was considered murder. *See, e.g., Regina v. Sims*, 75 Eng. Rep. 1075 (Q.B. 1601) (man who violently beat a pregnant woman indicted for death of child who was born alive and then died due to injuries from the beating).

14. Moreover, historians now condemn as obsolete or illegitimate the major reasons for the adoption of anti-abortion laws in the nineteenth century: nativist fears, the movement to consolidate control over the medical profession, and fears about the rising status of women. Mohr, *supra*, at 37, 166–70. Contrary to the Solicitor's claim, S.G. [219] n.8, the racist and sexist justifications for the criminalization of abortion in the nineteenth century are constitutionally relevant. A legislative enactment motivated by a desire to discriminate on account of race or other constitutionally illegitimate basis is unconstitutional under the Equal Protection Clause,

Finally, the state of the law in 1868 cannot define funda-mental rights for all future generations.[15] As this Court em-phasized in *Harper* v. *Virginia State Bd. of Elections*, 383 U.S. 663, 669 (1966), "we have never been confined to historic notions of equality, any more than we have restricted due process to a fixed catalogue of what was at a given time deemed to be the limits of fundamental rights." *See also Hudson* v. *McMillian*, 112 S. Ct. 995, 1000 (1992) ("the Eighth Amend-ment's prohibition of cruel and unusual punishments 'draw[s] its meaning from the evolving standards of decency that mark the progress of a maturing society' ") (quoting *Rhodes* v. *Chapman*, 452 U.S. 337, 346 (1981)). To choose 1868 as the touchstone by which rights are validated is to state that many of our most unassailable rights are not "fundamental" at all.[16]

The Solicitor makes a second, equally disturbing claim. While conceding that pregnancy entails "profound physical, emotional, and psychological consequences," *Michael M.* v. *Superior Court*, 450 U.S. 464, 471 (1981) (plurality), and that the denial of safe, legal abortion will pose significant burdens

---

unless the state can prove that the law would have been enacted without the ille-gitimate factor. *Hunter* v. *Underwood*, 471 U.S. 222, 228–29 (1985). This is so even where a statute is motivated by permissible as well as impermissible motives. *Id.* at 232. Although the Solicitor tries to downplay the presence of those illegitimate motives by citing the work of certain historians, S.G. [219] n.8, these works support, rather than refute, the argument made by *Amici* 250 American Historians in Support of Petitioners.

15. The Solicitor's use of 1868, rather than 1791 when the Bill of Rights was adopted, as the reference point for determining fundamental rights is not surprising since, in 1791, abortion was legal until quickening. *Roe*, 410 U.S. at 140–41. Were the requirements of due process to depend on the state of the law at the time of the framing of either the Fifth or Fourteenth Amendments, an individual might have fundamental rights guaranteed against interference by the federal government, but not against the states—an "unthinkable" result. *See Bolling* v. *Sharpe*, 347 U.S. 497, 500 (1954).

16. Relying exclusively on what the fifty states have legislated in determining the scope of "liberty" would imperil numerous fundamental freedoms protected by this Court's decisions: the right to be free from racial segregation, *Brown* v. *Board of Educ.*, 347 U.S. 483 (1954), *Bolling*, 347 U.S. 497; the right to marry a person of another race, *Loving* v. *Virginia*, 388 U.S. 1 (1967); the right to live with a person of another race, *McLaughlin* v. *Florida*, 379 U.S. 184 (1964); the right to be free from forced sterilization, *Skinner* v. *Oklahoma ex rel. Williamson*, 316 U.S. 535 (1942); the right of married persons to use contraceptives, *Griswold*, 381 U.S. 479; the right of unmarried persons to use contraceptives, *Eisenstadt*, 405 U.S. 438; the right to travel, *Shapiro* v. *Thompson*, 394 U.S. 618 (1969); the right to court-appointed counsel, *Gideon* v. *Wainwright*, 372 U.S. 335 (1963); the right of women to serve on juries, *Taylor* v. *Louisiana*, 419 U.S. 522 (1975); the right of poor people to vote, *Harper*, 383 U.S. 663; and the right to raise one's natural but illegitimate children, *Stanley* v. *Illinois*, 405 U.S. 645 (1972).

on women, the Solicitor nonetheless urges this Court to turn its back on American women, callously insisting that this Court's constitutional jurisprudence does not protect women from governmentally imposed harms. The cases relied upon to support this preposterous argument, this Court's abortion funding cases, S.G. [24], are totally inapposite. In these cases, this Court upheld the government's refusal to subsidize abortion with public resources. Nothing in those cases suggests that the Constitution would permit the government similar license when it affirmatively prohibits or, as here, places onerous restrictions on the abortion choice.[17] Indeed, just this term, this Court recognized that governmentally imposed harms, less severe than those that forced pregnancy would entail, are unacceptable under our constitutional scheme. *Hudson*, 112 S. Ct. 995.[18]

Both the Solicitor and the Commonwealth further argue that a fundamental right to abortion does not flow logically from the long line of privacy cases relied upon by this Court in *Roe*. S.G. [220] n.10; R.B. [206]. This argument misconstrues the nature of the privacy right in those cases, and fails miserably to distinguish them from *Roe*.

The common denominator of these and subsequent privacy cases is that personal decisions that profoundly affect bodily integrity and destiny are largely beyond the reach of government, and not, as the Solicitor suggests, "a recognition of the importance of the family." S.G. [221]. Indeed, in *Carey*, Justice Brennan rejected precisely this reading of this Court's privacy decisions. Even though the Connecticut statute at issue in *Griswold* intruded into "the sacred precincts of marital bedrooms," 379 U.S. at 485, this Court held that *Griswold*

17. *E.g.*, *Harris v. McRae*, 448 U.S. at 317 n.19. *DeShaney v. Winnebago County Dep't of Social Servs.*, 489 U.S. 189 (1989), and *Lindsey v. Normet*, 405 U.S. 56 (1972), are also cases involving failure to provide governmental assistance and are therefore also inapposite.

18. *Amici* attack plaintiffs for "inflating" the number of women who died from illegal abortions. *See* American Ass'n of Prolife Ob/Gyn et al. Br. [22]. Considering the severe criminal penalties that were attached to abortion, it is not surprising that the figures for reported illegal abortion deaths cited by *amici* are lower than the estimates of actual deaths cited by petitioners. P.B. [48]. But even by *amici*'s figures, almost 2,300 women died from illegal abortion during the 1960s. Surely this demonstrates the catastrophic effects of criminal abortion laws and provides a graphic illustration of the Commonwealth's appalling "rights by numbers" approach, discussed more fully in Section II.B, *infra*.

was "not dependent on that element. . . . *Griswold* may no longer be read as holding only that a State may not prohibit a married couple's use of contraceptives. Read in light of its progeny, the teaching of *Griswold* is that the Constitution protects individual decisions in matters of childbearing from unjustified intrusion by the State." *Carey*, 431 U.S. at 687. Moreover, contrary to the suggestion of *amici, see* U.S. Catholic Conference et al. Br. [244], this Court did not err in *Eisenstadt* by finding that "personal interests alone—not relational interests . . . are entitled to special protection." On the contrary, as this Court explained in *Shelley v. Kraemer*, 334 U.S. 1, 22 (1948), "[t]he rights created by the first section of the Fourteenth Amendment are, by its terms, guaranteed to the individual. The rights established are personal rights."

If accepted, the Solicitor's arbitrary dividing line in this Court's privacy jurisprudence might eliminate privacy protection for millions of Americans who are unmarried, separated, or divorced, or who live in "families" that are not recognized by the state. Not just the abortion right, but all aspects of individual privacy—including the right of bodily integrity, *Union Pacific Ry. Co. v. Botsford*, 141 U.S. 250 (1891), the right to privacy in one's home, *Stanley v. Georgia*, 394 U.S. 557 (1969), the right to use contraceptives, *Eisenstadt*, 405 U.S. 438; *Carey*, 431 U.S. 678, and the right to form alternative families, *Moore v. City of East Cleveland*, 431 U.S. 494 (1977)—might be jeopardized.

Similarly, the Solicitor's attempt to distinguish *Roe* on the ground that a "pregnant woman cannot be isolated in her privacy" misperceives this Court's privacy decisions. S.G. [221]. The privacy right is not dependent on whether an individual is "isolated" in her privacy. Rather, it is a right, "as against the government . . . to be let alone" in making decisions of critical life importance. *Olmstead v. United States*, 277 U.S. 438, 478 (1928) (Brandeis, J., dissenting). The presence of the fetus thus does not change or undercut the "fundamental" nature of the privacy right. *Cf.* note 5 *supra*.[19]

19. This reasoning also ignores the reality that no bright line exists between contraceptives and abortion, *see* Alan Guttmacher Institute et al. Br. 28–45, and might impermissibly sanction a wide variety of incursions on the liberty of pregnant women. P.B. [66].

The weakness of the Solicitor's contention that abortion is not a fundamental right is further evidenced by his wholly unsatisfactory effort to distinguish laws that prohibit abortions from those that compel them. The Solicitor contends "a law *mandating* abortions would pose a starkly different issue" because our nation's legal traditions permit "a competent adult . . . to refuse medical care." S.G. [221] (emphasis in original). As noted by legal scholars, the Solicitor's position not only fails to distinguish compelled abortion from abortion restrictions, but "powerfully supports" *Roe*'s basic holding:

> A competent adult's decision to have an abortion in the early weeks is clearly a decision to "refuse unwanted medical intrusion." Compelled childbirth is a major medical event and far more dangerous than aborting an early pregnancy . . . . By denying women the right to elect early, medically simple abortion, and thereby forcing pregnant women to undergo childbirth, the United States government necessarily violates the principle that it concedes . . .: "competent adult[s] may generally refuse unwanted medical intrusion."

Walter Dellinger and Gene B. Sperling, *Abortion and the Supreme Court: The Retreat from Roe v. Wade*, 138 U. Pa. L. Rev. 83, 96–97 (1989).[20]

---

20. The Commonwealth disputes the propriety of remand should this Court overrule *Roe*. R.B. [186] n.[19]. But upon reversal, courts often remand to allow plaintiffs to pursue alternative claims not reached by the trial court, *see, e.g., Schweiker v. Gray Panthers*, 453 U.S. 34, 50 n.23 (1981), or where there has been a change in the law. *See, e.g., National Railroad Passenger Corp. v. Florida*, 929 F.2d 1532, 1537 (11th Cir. 1991). Where, as here, the trial court's decision was based on fully developed and as yet sound precedent, and "plaintiff[s] had little incentive to insist that the district court's written order also base liability on" their alternative theories, equitable principles demand a remand. *Carter v. Sedgwick County*, 929 F.2d 1501, 1505 (10th Cir. 1991) (remand to consider alternative claims was proper where decision was reversed in light of subsequent Supreme Court decision). Moreover, disputes regarding whether plaintiffs should be allowed to pursue alternative claims on remand are best resolved by the lower courts. *See Nashville Gas Co. v. Satty*, 434 U.S. 136, 146 (1977). Finally, the Solicitor's contention that petitioners opted not to challenge § 3204(c) (prohibiting abortions based on the sex of the fetus) because they believe it is constitutional, S.G. [225] n.13, is simply wrong. While petitioners believe this provision violates *Roe*, it obviously could only be challenged by a plaintiff who could satisfy Article III's standing requirement. Thus, a challenge remains a future possibility.

II. THE PENNSYLVANIA STATUTE IS UNCONSTI-TUTIONAL UNDER ANY STANDARD OF REVIEW.

A. The Factual Findings of the District Court Are Relevant to the Constitutional Issue Before This Court and Are Fully Supported by the Factual Record.

The Commonwealth cannot carry the extraordinary burden of proving that the district court's factual findings are "clearly erroneous" under Federal Rule of Civil Procedure 52(a). This Court has held:

> If the district court's account of the evidence is plausible in light of the record viewed in its entirety, the court of appeals may not reverse it even though convinced that had it been sitting as the trier of fact, it would have weighed the evidence differently. Where there are two permissible views of the evidence, the factfinder's choice between them cannot be clearly erroneous.

Anderson v. City of Bessemer City, 470 U.S. 564, 573–74 (1985) (citations omitted). Here, where the trial court's findings of fact are based heavily on weighing the credibility of witness testimony, "Rule 52(a) demands even greater deference to the trial court's findings . . . ." *Id.* at 575. *See also Hernandez v. New York*, 111 S. Ct. 1859, 1868–70 (1991) (plurality).[21]

The district court carefully documented the record evidence supporting each of its 387 findings of fact. The court of appeals did not reverse any of the district court's factual findings,[22]

---

21. The district court specifically found that the testimony of each of petitioners' nine expert and fact witnesses was "credible in all respects." 115a, 117a–124a. However, the district court made adverse credibility determinations against two of the three witnesses offered by the Commonwealth, and found that the testimony of marriage counselor Vincent Rue was simply "not credible." 127a. Certain of the Commonwealth's *amici* continue to rely on the discredited testimony of the Commonwealth's witnesses, particularly that of Vincent Rue, but the Commonwealth itself does not challenge the district court's credibility determinations in any respect.

22. Both the Commonwealth, R.B. [169] n.[3], and *amici*, *see* Nat'l Legal Found. Br. 27 n.13, claim that the court of appeals overturned some of the district court's factual findings on appeal. However, reference to the cited pages of the court of appeals opinion in fact reveals no instance where the court of appeals declared any finding clearly erroneous. Typically, the cited portions of the court of appeals opinion do not even mention the district court's findings. *See, e.g.*, 38a–40a, 83a.

and the Commonwealth cannot justify challenging a single factual finding under the clearly erroneous standard.[23] Thus, for purposes of this appeal, the district court's findings must be accepted by this Court. P.B. [29] n.6.

Perhaps recognizing the futility of challenging the district court's findings, *amici* argue that facts are irrelevant in a facial constitutional challenge, because plaintiffs "must prove that the statute *cannot be constitutionally applied to anyone.*" S.G. [226] (emphasis in original); *see also* Nat'l Legal Found. Br. 3–5, 27–28. *Cf.* R.B. [196]. For this claim *amici* rely on *Ohio v. Akron Center for Reproductive Health*, 110 S. Ct. 2972, 2980–81 (1990), *United States v. Salerno*, 481 U.S. 739, 745 (1987), and *Webster*, 492 U.S. at 524 (O'Connor, J., concurring). Each of these cases involved speculative challenges to the possible application of statutory provisions in the absence of factual support, and only held that facial challenges cannot succeed "based upon a worst-case analysis that may never occur." *Akron Center*, 110 S. Ct. at 2981. By contrast, far from raising remote or speculative claims based on a worst-case scenario, the record here demonstrates that, if enforced, the Act will severely harm women.

In facial challenges, this Court has always looked beyond the four corners of the statute to consider the facts.[24] In *Hodgson*, for example, the Court relied extensively on the factual findings of the district court in striking down Minnesota's requirement of two-parent notification without a bypass option, a provision that had never been in effect and was chal-

---

23. The Commonwealth insists that it "continue[s]" to challenge the district court's findings of fact, R.B. [169], but its brief reveals no instance where the Commonwealth even attempts to show that any particular finding was clearly erroneous. For example, the district court found that trained counselors are capable of providing to patients the information necessary for obtaining informed consent. 175a. The Commonwealth complains that this finding "simply represent[s] [the district court's] own disagreement with the considered judgment of the legislature," R.B. [190], but does not—and cannot—suggest why this finding is clearly erroneous under Rule 52(a). The Commonwealth also argues that the district court erred in failing to make certain additional findings. But unless the Commonwealth properly challenges the district court's findings, it is immaterial that it might have made other findings as well.

24. *See, e.g.*, *Ashcroft*, 462 U.S. at 483–86 (citing physician testimony); *Akron*, 462 U.S. at 434–37 (multiple references to statistical studies and medical association standards and guidelines); *Colautti v. Franklin*, 439 U.S. 379, 395–96, 398–99 (1979) (citing physician testimony); *Danforth*, 428 U.S. at 75–79 (relying on record evidence).

lenged on its face. *See Hodgson*, 110 S. Ct. at 2938–41, 2945–46; *id.* at 2950 (O'Connor, J., concurring).

Furthermore, adoption of *amici*'s position would effectively preclude all facial challenges and prevent federal courts from scrutinizing legislative findings offered to justify an infringement of constitutional rights.[25] As Justice Thomas recently recognized:

> We know of no support . . . for the proposition that if the constitutionality of a statute depends in part on the existence of certain facts, a court may not review a legislature's judgment that the facts exist. If a legislature could make a statute constitutional simply by "finding" that black is white or freedom, slavery, judicial review would be an elaborate farce. At least since *Marbury* v. *Madison*, 1 Cranch 137 (1803), that has not been the law.

Lamprecht v. *FCC*, No. 88–1395, 1992 U.S. App. LEXIS 1997, at *30 n.2 (D.C. Cir. Feb. 19, 1992).

B. This Court Should Reject the Commonwealth's "Rights by Numbers" Approach and Find Unconstitutional the Husband Notification Provision.

The Commonwealth does not contest the conclusion reached by both lower courts that forced husband notification will impose on some women seeking abortions a wide array of "dire consequences," completely frustrating the abortion decision of some and endangering the lives and health of others.[26] *See* 66a–70a & n.26; 255a–257a &

25. *Sable Communications, Inc.* v. *FCC*, 492 U.S. 115, 129 (1989); *Landmark Communications, Inc.* v. *Virginia*, 435 U.S. 829, 843–44 (1978).

26. Citing Justice Stevens's concurrence in *H.L.* v. *Matheson*, 450 U.S. 398, 423–24 (1981), the Commonwealth contends that the courts below unfairly assumed that either a marriage is so perfect that communication will routinely occur, or it is so imperfect that forced communication will always be harmful. *See* R.B. [200]. But the lower courts, following this Court's decision in *Hodgson*, 110 S. Ct. at 2945, simply made the common-sense observation that the statute serves no purpose for the vast majority of women who voluntarily discuss the abortion decision with their husbands, and therefore must be evaluated based on its impact on women who would otherwise not notify their husbands. *See* 66a, 193a, 261a. As the district court found, in this context, forced husband notification disserves any legitimate state interest. *See* 201a, 262a.

n.42.[27] Nor does it seriously offer a legitimate state interest to support the statute.[28] Instead, the Commonwealth claims that only a "very small" number of women will suffer health consequences and that it is not enough in a facial challenge "to show that [a statute] may deter or inhibit some women from getting an abortion." R.B. [196], (emphasis in original). In the Commonwealth's view, the Constitution only protects American women from legislation that will result in dire consequences to their lives and health, if all, or at least the vast majority of, women are affected.

The Commonwealth's effort to defeat the constitutional rights of entire classes of women surely must fail.[29] This Court has repeatedly recognized that rights under the Fourteenth Amendment are "personal ones" that cannot "depend on the number of persons who may be discriminated against."

---

27. The Commonwealth's asserted distinction between husband notice and consent statutes, R.B. [199] n.36, is conclusively refuted by the holdings of this Court and the record in this case. A notice provision can give the husband effective veto power over the woman's decision, preventing the abortion or penalizing her for exercising her choice. See Hodgson, 110 S. Ct. at 2939, 2945 & n.36; Bellotti v. Baird, 443 U.S. 622, 647 (1979). See also 69a; 256a. That the retaliation comes not from the state but from the husband does not exonerate the state. As Justice Harlan wrote for a unanimous Court in NAACP v. Alabama ex rel. Patterson, 357 U.S. 449, 463 (1958): "The crucial factor is the interplay of governmental and private action, for it is only after the initial exertion of state power . . . that private action takes hold."

28. Raw paternalism informs the arguments of the amici who support husband notification. One brief describes a woman who obtains an abortion without first notifying her husband as one who "considers herself 'liberated,' " or who is a "highly dominant, independent wife who is not in touch with her emotions," or "who makes a hasty, impulsive decision." See Rutherford Inst. Br. 13, 15. The Solicitor argues that husband notification will preserve "marital integrity," albeit not "marital accord." S.G. [231]. The district court's unrefuted findings that forced husband notification could destroy marriages and subject women to physical abuse, see 201a, 262a, make plain that the statute's only purpose is to further the husband's ability to control his wife's behavior.

29. The contention that the numbers of women affected is "very small" is itself highly questionable. The statute affects all married women, who comprise at least twenty percent of the approximately 50,000 women who obtain abortions in Pennsylvania each year. 149a. Even by Judge Alito's calculations, had the notification requirement been in effect in Pennsylvania during the 1980s, 8,500 women could have been affected. See 92a & n.3; 149a. Amicus State of Utah claims that its husband notification requirement has had no ill effects, see Utah Br. 18-19, but this very provision is currently subject to litigation. Jane L. v. Bangerter, No. 91–C–345–G (D. Utah filed Apr. 4, 1991). The self-serving claims of the Attorney General charged with defending this statute are hardly entitled to great weight, especially where, as here, there are declarations to the contrary.

McCabe, *Atchison, T. & S.F. Ry.*, 235 U.S. 151, 161–62 (1914).[30] To accept the Commonwealth's view that a proportionately small class of women may be singled out might justify a wide range of prohibitive restrictions on abortion, including, for example, bans on abortion for Hispanic or Asian women, women under 16 or over 35, or an absolute ban on all second trimester saline abortions.[31] *See Danforth*, 428 U.S. at 75–79. This "rights by numbers" approach is particularly inappropriate here, where the constitutional right to abortion is premised on the right of the individual to make autonomous decisions about critical life issues.[32]

Just as it tries to downplay the number of women harmed by forced husband notification, the Commonwealth attempts to shore up the obviously inadequate statutory exceptions.[33] Ignoring all of the statute's defects save one, *compare* P.B. [61],

30. This Court certainly would not sanction state statutes that prohibit flag burning in protest, *Texas v. Johnson*, 491 U.S. 397 (1989), or advocating the use of violence as a means of accomplishing political reform, *Brandenburg v. Ohio*, 395 U.S. 444 (1969) (per curiam), even though very few people engage in such activities. Nor could a state prohibit from voting any member of the Armed Forces who moves from another state for military duty, *Carrington v. Rash*, 380 U.S. 89 (1965), or disqualify ministers or priests from serving as state legislators, *see McDaniel v. Paty*, 435 U.S. 618 (1978), because only a few would feel the weight of these restrictions. Surely, this Court's holding in *Meyer v. Nebraska*, 262 U.S. 390 (1923), invalidating a state statute prohibiting the teaching of German language in private schools, would not have been different if only a small number of German immigrants lived in Nebraska.

31. Attempting to provide a limit to its argument, the Commonwealth suggests that *Hodgson* presented a case where a sufficiently large percentage of women were affected to raise constitutional concerns. *See* R.B. [197]. But the percentage of women seeking abortions under the age of 18 is only 12%, *see* 150a, far less than the proportion who are married.

32. The Commonwealth ignores altogether the provision's interference with marital integrity and a woman's autonomy. In violation of the right of marital integrity, § 3209 subjects marital discussions to state surveillance and control. P.B. [65–66]. Additionally, by forcing women to obtain counsel from their husbands, the notification requirement strikes at the core of the right of privacy by denying women the ability to make critical life choices independently. As this Court recognized in *Danforth*, 428 U.S. at 69 n.11, "[t]he marital couple is not an independent entity with a mind and heart of its own, but an association of two individuals each with a separate intellectual and emotional makeup. If the right of privacy means anything, it is the right of the *individual*, married or single, to be free from unwarranted governmental interference into matters so fundamentally affecting a person as the decision whether to bear or beget children." *Id.* (quoting *Eisenstadt*, 405 U.S. at 453) (emphasis in original).

33. The Commonwealth tries to distinguish *Hodgson* on the basis that the exceptions there could trigger parental notification, *see* R.B. [198]. However, the spousal sexual assault exception can operate in precisely the same fashion—a point the Commonwealth simply ignores. P.B. [62].

the Commonwealth focuses exclusively on the district court's finding that battered women will be psychologically incapable of availing themselves of the statutory exceptions to forced husband notification. *See* 201a. The Commonwealth concedes, as it must, the validity of this finding, *see* R.B. [197–98], but speculates, without evidence, that women will be too victimized to seek out abortions in the first place. *Id.* at [198]. This Court must reject the Commonwealth's insulting and unacceptable view that women are either too independent to require constitutional protection, or too oppressed to benefit from it.[34]

C. The Biased Counseling Provisions Will Harm Women and Force Physicians to Disseminate Pennsylvania's Anti-Abortion Ideology.

1. The biased counseling provisions interfere with the provision of appropriate medical care.

The Commonwealth argues that the Act's biased counseling provisions must be upheld because the Constitution does not forbid state informed consent laws from requiring the provision of specific information to all patients without regard to their medical needs. R.B. [188]. But this Court has twice rejected this view, finding that nearly identical statutory schemes failed for

34. Citing *Geduldig* v. *Aiello*, 417 U.S. 484 (1974), *amici* contend that § 3209 does not deny women equal protection, because discrimination based on pregnancy is not sex-based. *See, e.g.*, S.G. [231] n.25; Life Issues Inst. Br. 6. Unlike the exclusion of pregnancy from the disability program at issue in *Geduldig*, where the "fiscal and actuarial benefits [of the exclusion] accrue[d] to both sexes," 417 U.S. at 496 n.20, the forced husband notification requirement here gives a right to a class comprised entirely of men. Marriage carries with it for men and only men the right to notification of their wives' reproductive choices. *Cf. International Union, U.A.W.* v. *Johnson Controls, Inc.*, 111 S. Ct. 1196, 1202 (1991) ("Fertile men, but not fertile women, are given a choice as to whether they wish to risk their reproductive health for a particular job"); *Newport News Shipbuilding & Dry Dock Co.* v. *EEOC*, 462 U.S. 669 (1983). Here, where the Commonwealth has refused to impose spousal notification requirements on husbands who obtain surgical procedures altering their reproductive capacity, 199a, the discrimination is particularly invidious. *See Kirchberg* v. *Feenstra*, 450 U.S. 455, 459–61 (1981). Moreover, unlike the program in *Geduldig*, § 3209 does not merely fail to provide benefits in the event of pregnancy, but imposes new and potentially dangerous obligations on pregnant women. *Cf. Satty*, 434 U.S. at 142 (recognizing distinction between refusing to extend to women a benefit that men do not receive and imposing a burden upon women that men need not suffer).

two independent reasons. In conflict with accepted medical practice, the schemes "intrude upon the discretion of the pregnant woman's physician," by requiring that a "specific body of information be given in all cases, irrespective of the particular needs of the patient." *Thornburgh*, 476 U.S. at 762, *see also Akron*, 462 U.S. at 445. They also force physicians to exploit the trust of their patients by disseminating irrelevant, inflammatory, misleading, and inaccurate information that discourages abortion. *Thornburgh*, 476 U.S. at 763. The state's real purpose is to send an ideological message to women,[35] and the Commonwealth concedes that the provisions will have their intended effect. R.B. [191], S.G. [227].[36] The biased counseling provisions will result in disastrous consequences for women's health, P.B. [32, 33, 70, 73], subjecting them to "undesirable and unnecessary anxiety, anguish and fear," 178a; *see also* J.A. 135,[37] and furthering no legitimate state interest. They are therefore invalid.

In a feeble attempt to justify these burdens, the Commonwealth claims that petitioners already provide all of the mandated information. R.B. [189, 190]. But, as evidence amassed at trial shows, absent statutory mandate, abortion providers would not inform all women seeking abortions about the avail-

35. If the state enacted a law requiring a physician to provide all women who decided to continue their pregnancies to term with a list of agencies providing abortion services; information about the availability of medical assistance for abortion; the fact that the woman's male partner may be liable to pay for the abortion; and the complete medical risks of both procedures, even when the woman has already chosen to carry the pregnancy to term, the Act's ideological bias would be obvious. The same is true with the Pennsylvania statute.

36. Although conceding that the Act "may dissuade some women" from their abortion choice, both the Commonwealth and the Solicitor claim that this is constitutionally irrelevant because the statute serves the legitimate interest in encouraging childbirth over abortion. S.G. [227]; R.B. [191[. Unlike the denial of abortion funding, which does "not add any 'restriction on access to abortion that was not already there,' " *Akron*, 462 U.S. at 444 n.33 (quoting *Maher*, 432 U.S. at 474), the state's interest in encouraging childbirth over abortion cannot justify "substituting a state decision for an individual decision that a woman has a right to make for herself. Otherwise, the interest in liberty protected by the Due Process Clause would be a nullity." *Hodgson*, 110 S. Ct. at 2937 (opinion of Stevens, J.).

37. The exemption provided in § 3205(c), where the physician can demonstrate that providing the mandated information would result in a "severely adverse effect on the physical or mental health of the patient," 291a, is wholly inadequate to protect women's health. Women who suffer damage to their health that falls short of a "severely adverse effect" are left totally unprotected.

ability of child support payments and medical assistance benefits if a woman carries to term, nor show them pictures and a description of fetal development. J.A. 252–53, 258. Nor would petitioners provide options counseling or a complete discussion about the many medical risks of carrying a pregnancy to term to those women who have already obtained this counseling or who clearly indicate that their decision to choose abortion is firm. 138a, 142a, 146a, J.A. 140–41.[38]

Although petitioners, consistent with medical standards, offer accurate and appropriate information and referral of the type mandated by the Act to some women, some of the time, J.A. 258, 266–67, this cannot be equated with § 3205's requirement that physicians offer state-prescribed information in all cases, irrespective of the needs of the patient.

2. The biased counseling required by § 3205 is not commercial speech.

The Commonwealth does not dispute that the biased patient counseling provisions compel speech, or that state compulsion of speech is "a content-based regulation of speech," and is therefore "subject to exacting First Amendment scrutiny," *Riley* v. *National Fed'n of the Blind, Inc.*, 487 U.S. 781, 795, 798 (1988). Nor does it dispute that the provision cannot possibly survive this test. Instead, the Commonwealth argues that the physician-patient dialogue falls outside the ambit of the First Amendment because it is "commercial" speech. *See* R.B. [192].

This Court, however, has long eschewed reliance on "mere labels" for determining the level of constitutional protection under the First Amendment. *NAACP* v. *Button*, 371 U.S. 415, 429 (1963). *See also Bigelow* v. *Virginia*, 421 U.S. 809, 826 (1975). In fact, this Court has consistently limited commercial speech to expression that does no more than "propose

---

38. Abortion providers would not refer their patients to many of the crisis pregnancy centers on the state-approved list, since these centers often provide women with inflammatory, misleading, and inaccurate information about abortion. J.A. 256. *See also* 169a.

a commercial transaction." *Board of Trustees v. Fox*, 492 U.S. 469, 473 (1989) (quoting *Virginia State Bd. of Pharmacy v. Virginia Citizens Consumer Council, Inc.*, 425 U.S. 748, 762 (1976)). By contrast, the "right of the doctor to advise his patients according to his best lights seems so obviously within [the] First Amendment . . . as to need no extended discussion." *Poe v. Ullman*, 367 U.S. 497, 513 (1961) (Douglas, J., dissenting).[39] That the physician is paid for her advice "is as immaterial in this connection as is the fact that newspapers and books are sold." *New York Times Co. v. Sullivan*, 376 U.S. 254, 266 (1964). *See also Simon & Schuster, Inc. v. Members of New York State Crime Victims Bd.*, 112 S. Ct. 501 (1991). Like the abortion advertisement in *Bigelow*, the mere "relationship of speech [between a doctor and patient] to the marketplace of products or of services does not make it valueless in the marketplace of ideas." *Bigelow*, 421 U.S. at 826.

Moreover, even if physicians' speech were commercial in part, as the Commonwealth contends, "it is inextricably intertwined with otherwise fully protected speech," namely, the informed consent dialogue that is at the heart of protected professional expression, and therefore no longer "retains its commercial character." *Riley*, 487 U.S. at 796. "[W]e cannot parcel out the speech, applying one test to one phrase and another test to another phrase. Such an endeavor would be both artificial and impractical. Therefore, we apply our test for fully protected expression." *Id.* Thus, *Riley* is controlling here.

Finally, even in cases involving "pure" commercial speech, this Court has recognized that "unjustified or unduly burdensome disclosure requirements" may not be used to " 'prescribe what shall be orthodox in politics, nationalism, religion, or other matters of opinion, or force citizens to confess by word or act their faith therein.' " *Zauderer v. Office of Disciplinary Counsel*, 471 U.S. 626, 651 (1985) (quoting *West Virginia*

---

39. The court of appeals erred in suggesting that petitioners conceded at oral argument that the speech at issue was "commercial." The First Amendment issues were never discussed at oral argument, *see* Appendix A for the full discussion of § 3205, and petitioners' briefs took exactly the contrary position. *See* Brief of Appellees at 33–36, *Casey v. Planned Parenthood*, No. 90–1662.

State Bd. of Educ. v. *Barnette*, 319 U.S. 624, 642 (1943)). In *Zauderer*, the Court upheld a non-criminal reprimand for an attorney who deceived and misled potential clients by failing to disclose in a paid advertisement "purely factual and un-controversial information about the [financial] terms under which [the] services will be available." *Zauderer*, 471 U.S. at 651–53. In this case, by comparison, the Commonwealth, on pain of criminal penalties, forces all abortion providers to disclose often inaccurate and misleading information designed, as the Commonwealth admits, to discourage abortion and encourage childbirth in all but "the most urgent circum-stances." R.B. [191]. By compelling physicians to deliver this anti-abortion message,[40] the statute forces the "individual . . . to be an instrument for fostering public adherence to an ideological point of view he [or she] finds unacceptable." *Wooley* v. *Maynard*, 430 U.S. 705, 715 (1977). Thus, the Act violates the First Amendment.

D. The Judicial Bypass Procedure Does Not Cure the Constitutional Defects of the Act's Informed Parental Consent Provision.

The Commonwealth does not challenge the district court's finding that the Act's "informed" parental consent provision mandates face-to-face counseling for parents,[41] and thereby

40. Imagine, for example, that the state enacted a criminal statute that required an attorney, before agreeing to represent a civil rights plaintiff, to advise the potential client (1) that alternatives to litigation, such as letting the matter drop, ignoring the abuse, or settling the matter for a nominal sum, may be preferable to litigation; (2) that a state-prepared list of agencies able to assist the person in avoiding litigation is available; (3) that the defendant may assume legal fees or that free legal services may be available in the event of settlement; and (4) to ensure proper consideration of the weighty effort the client is about to undertake, that the client must return to the lawyer's office on a second occasion, even if the delay will push the client past the deadline for the statute of limitations on some of his or her claims. There can be little doubt that such a poorly disguised attempt to discourage civil rights suits would interfere with the attorney-client relationship and would violate the First Amendment. Cf. *NAACP* v. *Button*, 371 U.S. at 429–30, 434–37.

41. Contrary to the claims of Nat'l Legal Found. Br. 17–18, the undisputed testimony at trial showed that face-to-face counseling was indeed required. *See* 248a n.38. Petitioners' witnesses, *see* J.A. 133–34, 151, 163–64, as well as the Common-wealth's expert testified that a face-to-face meeting is necessary. *See* J.A. 354; *see also* 170a–171a.

impermissibly burdens privacy rights, nor does it suggest that any legitimate state interest supports this requirement. See also P.B. [74–76]. Instead, relying exclusively on Hodgson, the Commonwealth argues that these defects are cured by the presence of a judicial bypass procedure. See R.B. [195].

Reliance upon Hodgson is misplaced. In Hodgson, this Court held that Minnesota's two-parent notification statute inter-fered with rights of familial integrity.[42] Since only half of the minors in Minnesota reside with both biological parents, this Court recognized that the statute fails to "serve the purposes asserted by the state"—parental involvement—"in too many cases." Hodgson, 110 S. Ct. at 2950 (O'Connor, J., con-curring).

Nevertheless, this Court held that the bypass procedure is the appropriate mechanism to cure the defect in the statute. As Justice Kennedy recognized:

> If one were to attempt to design a statute that would address the Court's concerns, one would do precisely what Minnesota has done . . .: create a judicial mechanism to identify, and exempt from the strictures of the law, those cases in which the minor is mature or in which notification of the minor's parents is not in the minor's best interests.

Id. at 2970 (Kennedy, J., concurring in part and dissenting in part) (plurality opinion).

In contrast, both the purpose of the Pennsylvania law and its constitutional defect are entirely different. Pennsylvania's purpose is not solely to encourage parental involvement and approval—that purpose could be accomplished by a simple parental/judicial consent provision. Rather, Pennsylvania mandates that a parent obtain the information designed to discourage abortion in a face-to-face meeting with the phy-sician. If a parent consents to her daughter's abortion but

---

42. As the evidence in Hodgson demonstrated, where the second parent has no interest in nor relationship with his daughter or where there is a history of abuse between the parents, compelling the involvement of the second parent can have disastrous effects. Hodgson, 110 S. Ct. at 2945.

refuses to accompany her to the doctor's office, or if the parent cannot change work or family commitments to meet the physician in person, P.B. [34, 35, 75, 76], the daughter is forced to obtain judicial authorization for the abortion. But in this instance, the judicial bypass procedure is simply not designed to cure the constitutional defect. The bypass judge cannot ensure that the parent will obtain the information. In most instances, unless subpoenaed, the parent will not even attend the hearing.

Moreover, acceptance of this odious proposition may enable a state to place any restriction on a young woman's right to abortion, however irrational, so long as there was a judicial bypass that could exempt them from the mandate. For example, a state could require young women to obtain consent from complete strangers or require them to have the abortion in a hospital under general anesthesia. If a judicial bypass procedure will cure absolutely anything, then the right to abortion, whether viewed as a "fundamental" right, or as "a component of" the "liberty" guaranteed by the Constitution, *Hodgson*, 110 S. Ct. at 2951 (Marshall, J., concurring in part and dissenting in part); *id.* at 2936 (opinion of Stevens, J.); *id.* at 2949 (O'Connor, J., concurring), would be completely repudiated.

CONCLUSION

In the days before *Roe*, thousands of women lost their lives, and even more were subjected to physical and emotional scars from back-alley and self-induced abortions directly resulting from criminal prohibitions on abortion. Understanding the severe restraints on women imposed by these laws, this Court in *Roe* recognized that the right to make childbearing decisions was a protected liberty of fundamental dimension. Mindful that abandonment on these principles may again subject women to these horrors, petitioners urge this Court to reaffirm *Roe*, *Akron*, and *Thornburgh*, reverse the judgment of the court of appeals in No. 91–744 and affirm the judgment of the court of appeals in No. 91–902.

Respectfully submitted,

LINDA J. WHARTON

CAROL E. TRACY
Women's Law Project
125 South Ninth Street
Suite 401
Philadelphia, PA 19107
(215) 928–9801

SETH KREIMER
University of Pennsylvania Law School
3400 Chestnut Street
Philadelphia, PA 19104
(215) 898–7447

ROGER K. EVANS
EVE W. PAUL
DARA KLASSEL
Planned Parenthood Action Fund, Inc.
810 Seventh Avenue
New York, NY 10019
(212) 541–7800

Counsel of Record:

KATHRYN KOLBERT
JANET BENSHOOF
LYNN M. PALTROW
RACHAEL N. PINE
ANDREW DWYER
ELLEN K. GOETZ
STEVEN R. SHAPIRO
JOHN A. POWELL
American Civil Liberties
Union Foundation
132 W. 43rd Street
New York, NY 10036
(212) 944–9800

Attorneys for Petitioners and Cross-Respondents

APPENDIX

TRANSCRIPT OF ORAL ARGUMENT BEFORE UNITED STATES COURT OF APPEALS FOR THE THIRD CIRCUIT

February 25, 1991
* * *

BY MS. KOLBERT:
* * *

[63] Let me quickly just turn to the 24-hour doctor-only requirements in 3205 and say that our argument is extremely

straightforward. *Akron, Thornburgh* apply, the Court has not changed that standard, and therefore this Court is bound by those precedents.

[64] The Commonwealth has tried a couple of times to distinguish this case from *Thornburgh*. We believe that their efforts are without merit. They argue that *Thornburgh* can't control because the Commonwealth didn't have a chance to put on its facts on *Thornburgh*, but the Supreme Court answered that argument when it rendered its decision and said that facts would make no difference to their ruling.

The second thing they said is, "But the Judge didn't listen to the facts the way we wanted him to listen to it." Again the clearly erroneous standard is what is applicable and the Judge's findings, in our view and I'm hoping yours—whether they were not clearly erroneous.

THE COURT: They also say this was in the era of compelling state interest. The least restrictive means, don't they?

MS. KOLBERT: That's right. But we contend that it is still that era; and therefore, this Court is bound by that precedent.

Lastly, as Judge Stapelton, as you noted, the Court made pains to distinguish in the discussion in *Hodgson* about the 48-hour waiting period, that for the women, the Court sided with the approval and this was an opinion by Justice O'Connor and Justice Stevens, [65] they sided with the approval, the majority opinion in *Akron*, so clearly they had to have viewed that the situation as applied to adult women was still being judged under that more stringent standard.

ORAL ARGUMENT BEFORE THE SUPREME COURT APRIL 22, 1992

IN THE SUPREME COURT OF THE UNITED STATES

PLANNED PARENTHOOD OF SOUTHEASTERN
PENNSYLVANIA, ET AL., PETITIONERS
v.   NO. 91-744
ROBERT P. CASEY, ET AL., ETC.
RESPONDENTS
AND
ROBERT P. CASEY, ET AL., ETC.,
PETITIONERS
v.   NO. 91-902
PLANNED PARENTHOOD OF SOUTHEASTERN
PENNSYLVANIA, ET AL.
RESPONDENTS

Washington, D.C.
Wednesday, April 22, 1992

The above-entitled matter came on for oral argument before
the Supreme Court of the United States at 9:58 a.m.

APPEARANCES:

KATHRYN KOLBERT, ESQ., New York, N.Y.; on behalf of
Planned Parenthood, *et al.*

ERNEST D. PREATE, JR., ESQ., Attorney General of Pennsylvania; on behalf of the Respondent Robert P. Casey, *et al.*

KENNETH W. STARR, ESQ., Solicitor General, Department
of Justice, Washington, D.C.; on behalf of the United States
as *Amicus Curiae*, supporting Casey, *et al.*

PROCEEDINGS
(10:00 a.m.)

CHIEF JUSTICE REHNQUIST: We'll hear argument next in No.
91–744, *Planned Parenthood of Southeastern Pennsylvania v.
Robert P. Casey*; 91–902, *Robert P. Casey v. Planned Parenthood
of Southeastern Pennsylvania*. Ms. Kolbert.

ORAL ARGUMENT OF KATHRYN KOLBERT
ON BEHALF OF THE PETITIONERS

MS. KOLBERT: Mr. Chief Justice and may it please the Court:
Whether our Constitution endows Government with the

power to force a woman to continue or to end a pregnancy against her will is the central question in this case. Since this Court's decision in *Roe* v. *Wade*, a generation of American women have come of age secure in the knowledge that the Constitution provides the highest level of protection for their childbearing decisions.

This landmark decision, which necessarily and logically flows from a century of this Court's jurisprudence, not only protects rights of bodily integrity and autonomy, but has enabled millions of women to participate fully and equally in society.

The genius of *Roe* and the Constitution is that it fully protects rights of fundamental importance. Government may not chip away at fundamental rights, nor make them selectively available only to the most privileged women.

If the right to choose abortion remains fundamental as established in *Roe* v. *Wade*, the strict scrutiny standard is applicable, and as this Court found in *Akron* and in *Thornburgh*, Pennsylvania's onerous restrictions must fall.

Should this Court abandon strict scrutiny, as urged by the Commonwealth and the Solicitor, not only might Pennsylvania's egregious intrusions on privacy stand and a century of this Court's privacy decisions may also be dismantled. Equally disturbing, should this Court remove fundamental protection for the abortion right, women might again be forced to the back alleys for their medical care with grave consequences for their lives and health.

The Commonwealth argues that this Court may overrule *Akron* and *Thornburgh* and abandon strict scrutiny and nevertheless preserve *Roe*'s central meaning. While politically expedient, this view is certainly not based upon this Court's privacy jurisprudence. Every other brief filed in this case agrees that the protection offered by *Roe*'s heightened scrutiny lies at the core of this important decision. To abandon heightened review is to overrule *Roe*.

This Court has repeatedly held that the doctrine of *stare decisis* is of fundamental importance to the rule of law. Fidelity to precedent ensures that our law will develop in a principled and intelligible fashion, and that our guiding rules are founded in law rather than in the proclivities of individuals. Accordingly, this Court has established that departure from precedent must be supported by some special justification, but no special justification exists here.

Only nine years ago in *Akron*, this Court invoked the doctrine of *stare decisis* and expressly reaffirmed *Roe* v. *Wade*. Only three years later, in *Thornburgh*, a case that is virtually identical to that before this Court today, this Court again found especially compelling reasons to reaffirm *Roe* and to find Pennsylvania law unconstitutional under the standard of strict scrutiny.

Nothing has changed since that time. Indeed, millions of women continue to rely on the fundamental rights guaranteed in *Roe* v. *Wade*. The medical conditions that led this Court to create and establish these fundamental rights remain the same. This case, the statute, the parties, are nearly identical to those in *Thornburgh*.

Never before has this Court bestowed and taken back a fundamental right that has been part of the settled rights and expectations of literally millions of Americans for nearly two decades. To regress now by permitting States suddenly to impose burdensome regulations, or to criminalize conduct, would be incompatible with any notion of principled constitutional decision-making.

Roe is both soundly based in the Constitution and sets forth a fair and workable standard of adjudication. From as early as 1891, this Court has recognized that the rights of autonomy, bodily integrity, and equality are central to our notions of ordered liberty. *Roe* lies at the heart of those interests.

While pregnancy may be a blessed act when planned or wanted, forced pregnancy, like any forced bodily invasion, is anathema to American values and traditions. In the same way that it would be unacceptable for Government to force a man or a woman to donate bone marrow, or to compel the contribution of a kidney to another, or to compel women to undergo abortion or forced sterilization, our Constitution protects women against forced pregnancy. If anything, because forced pregnancy will jeopardize a woman's life or health, the constitutional protections ought to be greater.

The Solicitor tries to draw a distinction between constitutional protection against forced abortion, which he agrees is fundamental, and constitutional protection against forced pregnancy, which he maligns, but once this Court removes fundamental status from the abortion right, there is no logical stopping point.

Fundamental status for all reproductive rights, decisions about birth control, pregnancy, sterilization, even high technology around reproduction, may also be jeopardized. Particularly where there is no bright line between abortion and some methods of birth control, the fundamental right both to prevent pregnancy and to end pregnancy may be at stake.

Our Nation's history and tradition also respects the autonomy of individuals to make life choices consistent with their own moral and conscientious beliefs. Our Constitution has long recognized an individual's right to make private and intimate decisions about marriage and family life, the upbringing of children, the ability to use contraception. The decision to terminate a pregnancy or to carry it to term is no different in kind.

Both the Solicitor and some Commonwealth *amici* argue that the Constitution only protects private decision-making within families. It is true that the rights of privacy have been recognized in the familial context. For example, in *Griswold* the Court found unconstitutional the Connecticut statute that prohibited married persons from using birth control and in *Loving* this Court found invalid a Virginia statute that prohibited the marriage of interracial couples.

Nevertheless, this Court has never limited the notions of privacy recognized in these cases as only arising or belonging to married couples. Indeed, in *Eisenstadt* and in *Carey* this Court specifically rejected this view.

Nor can this Court alter its historic recognition of privacy and deny women fundamental freedoms because, as the Solicitor argues, the woman is not isolated in her privacy. Surely if the Government cannot require individuals to sacrifice their lives or health for others or for other compelling purposes, it cannot require women to sacrifice their lives and health to further the State's interest in potential life.

JUSTICE O'CONNOR: Ms. Kolbert, you're arguing the case as though all we have before us is whether to apply *stare decisis* and preserve *Roe* v. *Wade* in all its aspects. Nevertheless, we granted certiorari on some specific questions in this case. Do you plan to address any of those in your argument?

MS. KOLBERT: Your Honor, I do. However, the central question in the case is what is the standard that this Court uses to evaluate the restrictions that are at issue, and therefore one cannot—

JUSTICE O'CONNOR: Well, the standard may affect the outcome or it may not, but at bottom we still have to deal with specific issues, and I wondered if you were going to address them.

MS. KOLBERT: Yes, I am, Your Honor, and I would like in particular to address the husband notification provisions, but the standard that this Court applies will well establish the outcome in this case for a variety of reasons.

This Court has already found that under the principles of *Roe* v. *Wade* the bulk of the Pennsylvania statute is unconstitutional. There is no question that this Court struck down as unconstitutional under strict scrutiny the bias counseling provisions and the 24-hour mandatory delay both in *Thornburgh* and in *Akron*, the case in 1983, and therefore this Court must examine first the question of what's the appropriate standard before determining the constitutionality of those other provisions.

The Court cannot alter its historic recognition of privacy and deny women fundamental freedoms, as I was speaking, because as the Solicitor argues, there is the presence of the fetus.

Surely, if the Government cannot require individuals to sacrifice their lives or health for human beings who are born for other compelling purposes, they cannot do so for purposes of protecting potential fetal life.

And if this Court is to reduce the presence of a constitutional right merely because of the presence of the fetus, other childbearing decisions, whether they be the right to carry the pregnancy to term or make other childbearing decisions will be particularly affected.

Particularly here, as this Court noted in *Roe*, where there is widespread disagreement in both a philosophical and a religious sense about when life begins, this Court cannot sanction one view to the detriment of women's lives and health;

nor can the state of the law in 1868 define or determine constitutional rights for all future generations.

This Court must look generally to whether a right is reflected in our Nation's history and traditions rather than at whether the activity was illegal at the time of the adoption of the Fourteenth Amendment. Relying exclusively on what fifty states have legislated in determining the scope of liberty would imperil numerous freedoms such as rights recognized by this Court in *Brown, Bolling, Griswold,* and *Loving.*

This Court has also recognized as—

JUSTICE SCALIA: Ms. Kolbert, on this last point, I am not sure what you suggest we look to. You say we should not look to what the practice was in 1868. Should we look to what the practice was at the time of *Roe* or what the practice is today? That is, what the States would do, left to their own devices?

MS. KOLBERT: Your Honor, I believe that you have to look very generally at whether the Nation's history and tradition has respected interests of bodily integrity and autonomy and whether there has been a tradition of respect for equality of women. Those are the central and core values—

JUSTICE SCALIA: But not to abortion in particular?

MS. KOLBERT: Well, this Court is— If the Court was only to look at whether abortion was illegal in 1868, that is at the time of the adoption of the Fourteenth Amendment, it would be placed in a very difficult situation because at the time of the founding of the Nation, at the time that the Constitution was adopted, abortion was legal.

JUSTICE SCALIA: Pick 1968, I gather you wouldn't accept 1968 either though.

MS. KOLBERT: Well, we think that the Court ought to look generally at the principles that this decision protects. That while it is important to look—and I would not urge you to ignore the state of the law at different periods of our history, it is only one factor in a variety of factors that this Court has to look to in determining whether or not something is fundamental.

And fundamental status in this instance derives from a history of this Court's acknowledgement and acceptance that private, autonomous decisions made by women in the privacy of their families ought to be respected and accorded fundamental status.

Certainly, the anomalous posture of the fact that abortion was legal at the time of the founding of the Constitution and then illegal at the time of the adoption of the Fourteenth Amendment would place this Court in a very difficult position, that is, rights may be guaranteed under the Fifth Amendment and not the Fourteenth, merely because only the exact state of the law in 1868 is the factor that the Court accepts.

JUSTICE SCALIA: This is not an antiquarian argument you are making. You would have made the same argument in 1868. I think you would have said the mere fact that most States disfavor abortion is no justification for this Court's saying that it is not therefore included within it. You would have made that same argument in 1868.

MS. KOLBERT: I would, and that is the argument that this Court has made in many instances in rejecting exactly the state of the law prior to the granting of fundamental status.

That is, this Court, if we were only to look at whether State legislatures prohibited activity in determining whether or not an activity is fundamental, many of the most precious rights that we now have: rights to travel, rights to vote, rights to be free from racial segregation would not be accorded status because in fact, State legislators have acted to inhibit those rights at the time of the adoption of the Fourteenth Amendment.

JUSTICE SCALIA: Some of those are mentioned in the Constitution like racial segregation.

MS. KOLBERT: Your Honor, this Court has recognized that the rights at issue here, that is, the rights of privacy, the rights of autonomy flow from the liberty clause of the Fourteenth Amendment which is also mentioned in the Constitution.

The debate centers on what is the meaning of that term liberty, and we think that the precedents of this Court that began at the end of the 19th Century and have proceeded from this Court to the very present, would logically and necessarily include fundamental rights to decide whether to carry a pregnancy to term or to terminate that pregnancy.

JUSTICE KENNEDY: I don't question the importance of your arguing that there is a fundamental right, as you have done;

however, there is a fundamental right to speech and we hear any number of arguments in this case on time, place and manner. I don't think our decision on parental notice in the *Akron* case is necessarily inconsistent with a fundamental right.

But one way of our understanding these fundamental rights and their parameters, their dimensions, is to decide on a case-by-case basis, and you have a number of specific provisions here that I think you should address.

MS. KOLBERT: The critical factor is whether, as a result of its fundamental status, this Court will accord the standard of *Roe*, that is, strict scrutiny because under that standard there is no dispute among the parties. Under that standard, the bias counseling provisions, the 24-hour mandatory delay have been found unconstitutional, and significantly, this Court has also gone so far as to say that the husband consent requirements, very similar to the husband notification requirements at issue in this case, have also been found unconstitutional—

JUSTICE KENNEDY: I am suggesting that our sustaining these statutory provisions does not necessarily undercut all of the holding of *Roe* v. *Wade*.

MS. KOLBERT: It is our position, Your Honor, that if this Court were to change the standard of strict scrutiny, which has been the central core of that holding, that in fact, that will undercut the holdings of this Court and effectively over-rule *Roe* v. *Wade*.

To adopt a lesser standard, to abandon strict scrutiny for a less protective standard such as the undue burden test or the rational relationship test, which has been discussed by this Court on many occasions, would be the same as overruling *Roe* for it is the beauty of *Roe*, the protections of *Roe* flow from the fact that this Court gives, upon a proof that particular State regulations interfere with the right.

Roe establishes and creates a burden on Government to come forward with a compelling purpose.

JUSTICE KENNEDY: Well, if you are going to argue that *Roe* can survive only in its most rigid formulation, that is an election you can make as counsel. I am suggesting to you that that is not the only logical possibility in this case.

MS. KOLBERT: Our position is that *Roe*, in establishing a

trimester framework, in establishing strict scrutiny, and in also establishing that the rights of women and the health interests of women always take precedence over the State's interest in potential life.

Those hallmarks of *Roe* are central to this case, and are central to continuing recognition of the right as fundamental. Should the Court abandon that—

JUSTICE O'CONNOR: But did the Court hold that, even after viability of the fetus in *Roe?*

MS. KOLBERT: What the Court—

JUSTICE O'CONNOR: Do you think that was a correct characterization of *Roe*'s holding that you just gave, that the woman's interest always takes precedence? Is that true under *Roe*, in the latter stages of pregnancy?

MS. KOLBERT: Your Honor, under *Roe*, after the point of viability, that is the point when the fetus is capable of survival, the State is free to prohibit abortion but only so long as it is necessary, only so long as the woman's health interests and life interests are not at stake.

That is, potential fetal life is a recognized value, is a recognized State interest after the point of viability; but when in conflict, when the woman's health interest is in conflict with those State interests and potential life, those women's interest, the women's interest in health take precedence.

Now admittedly, the question of viability and the viability line is not as present in this case as it has been in many of the other cases that this Court has seen before here. That is, all of the restrictions that are issue in Pennsylvania attach in pregnancy at the very beginning of pregnancy, and therefore, the State's interest in protection of fetal life really does not come into play.

The real issue is whether or not these health interests, that is, whether or not the State's interest in protecting a compelling interest in health are present. And frankly, this Court need only look to the record, that is, need only look to the findings of the district court to determine that this statute in no way furthers women's health interests.

That in fact, what this statute does is cause a detriment to women's health, submit her to increased dangers as a result of delay, as a result of interference with the doctor/patient relationship, as a result of permitting third parties who would injure individuals who are required to give husband notification, that those interests in health are not furthered in any respect.

The Commonwealth attempts to present the restrictions at issue here as reasonable. For the woman who as a result of mandatory husband notification provisions will be beaten, or will see her children beaten, the restrictions are not reasonable. For the woman who must travel 200 miles on two and three occasions as a result of the act's mandatory delay, the restrictions are not reasonable. For the woman who has become pregnant as a result of marital rape, obtaining information from her doctor that her husband may be liable for child support is both cruel and oppressive. They are not reasonable.

To find these restrictions reasonable, this Court would have to ignore the facts placed in evidence in this case which demonstrate that the restrictions were not enacted to improve women's decision-making or health care.

After listening to the testimony of ten witnesses, including those proffered by the Commonwealth, the district court made 387 findings of fact and repeatedly concluded that the Pennsylvania restrictions will interfere with the ability of physicians to provide quality medical care and will delay and discourage the performance of abortion to further no legitimate State interest.

In particular, the lower court found that the mandatory husband notification provisions will have dangerous and potentially deadly consequences for battered women, likening forced notification in a battering situation to providing the husband with a hammer with which to beat his wife.

CHIEF JUSTICE REHNQUIST: Was the husband notification provision the one that the court of appeals held unconstitutional?

MS. KOLBERT: It was, Your Honor.

CHIEF JUSTICE REHNQUIST: And it upheld the balance of the act, is that correct?

MS. KOLBERT: That's right. The district court found, as well, that bias counseling provisions transform the physician from the impartial counselor mandated by accepted medical standards into a partisan proponent of the State's ideology. And mandatory delay will increase both the expense and medical dangers of abortion, yet furthering no legitimate State purpose.

There is no serious contest about the effect of this law. Nor can there be, for under rule 52 the district court's findings are not clearly erroneous. Nor did the fact that this is a facial challenge require petitioners to prove that the statute cannot be constitutionally applied to any person.

This Court had repeatedly found statutes facially invalid after looking at facts like those present here. For example in *Hodgson*, this Court relied extensively on district court findings to strike down Minnesota's two-parent notification statute with no bypass, despite the fact that that statute had never yet been in effect. The extensive record here demonstrates that the harms are not speculative nor remote, nor is this a worst-case scenario.

The Court should not demand an unwanted child or a woman maimed by an illegal abortion as proof that strict scrutiny is applicable. Pennsylvania women should not be the guinea pigs in the State's experiment with constitutional law. To find otherwise would totally eviscerate the strict scrutiny standard of review, and would prevent Federal courts from scrutinizing legislative findings, a central role in the process of judicial review.

Let me turn now to—specifically to the husband notification provision. There is little doubt that these provisions violate the fundamental right of privacy, marital integrity, and equality. Beginning as early as *Danforth*, this Court recognized that a husband cannot arbitrarily veto the childbearing decisions of his wife.

Like the Missouri law at issue in *Danforth*, State-mandated communication between husbands and wives violates the autonomy of married women to make personal and private decisions, particularly here where a married woman is often the survivor of marital rape and where the penalty for transgressing her husband is likely to be physical violence against her or her family members. Government has the obligation to respect her private decisions, not to involve her husband.

The Solicitor dismisses the import of the State-imposed harm and believes or claims that the Constitution is not intended to remedy them. But this approach seriously ignores that women will be seriously maimed and that harms will be invoked, and it is a callous disregard for their lives and health.

While it may be desirable for husbands and wives to share intimacies in their daily life, the concepts of this Court developed in the principles of marital integrity ensure that the Government cannot decree for those couples how that communication should occur. To decree and direct family life is more destructive of family integrity than permitting families to resolve their differences on their own terms.

The husband notification provisions also violate principles of equality. These are provisions that apply to women and women alone. Imposed notification is— gives a benefit only to men, and as such they violate the dictates of the equal protection clause. The legislative scheme that assumes that husbands are capable and authorized to make all independent decisions but wives are not, reflect an outmoded common law view that women, once married, lost their legal identities to their husbands.

In the days before *Roe*, thousands of women lost their lives and more were subjected to physical and emotional scars from back-alley and self-induced abortions. Recognizing that, this Court established *Roe* and established fundamental protection for women's childbearing decisions. We urge this Court to reaffirm those principles today, to adopt the rulings of this Court in *Akron* and *Thornburgh* that used the *Roe* strict scrutiny standard, and affirm in part and reverse in part, the judgment of the court of appeals.

I would like to reserve three minutes for rebuttal, if there's no further questions from the court.

CHIEF JUSTICE REHNQUIST: Very well, Ms. Kolbert. General Preate, we'll hear from you.

ORAL ARGUMENT OF ERNEST D. PREATE, JR., ESQ. ON BEHALF OF ROBERT P. CASEY, ET AL.

MR. PREATE: Mr. Chief Justice and may it please the Court:
This Court granted certiorari on the question of whether five sections of our Pennsylvania Abortion Control Act are constitutional. It is the position of Pennsylvania that each of

the five provisions is constitutional under the analysis that was applied by this Court in *Webster*; that, further, *Roe v. Wade* need not be revisited by this Court except to reaffirm that *Roe* did not establish an absolute right to abortion on demand, but rather a limited right subject to reasonable State regulations designed to serve important and legitimate State—

JUSTICE BLACKMUN: Mr. Attorney General, I'm not so sure that's so important. *Roe* itself said that—

MR. PREATE: That's correct.

JUSTICE BLACKMUN: That this does not provide for abortion on demand. Have you read *Roe*?

MR. PREATE: Yes, I have.

JUSTICE BLACKMUN: Thank you.

MR. PREATE: In our view the accommodations of the woman's right and the State's legitimate interest in the unborn child is best served, short of overruling *Roe*, by employing the undue burden standard for reviewing State abortion regulations. However, as we argue in part two of our brief, if our statute cannot be upheld under the undue burden standard, *Roe*, being wrongly decided, should be overruled.

I will now address the specific provisions of our statute and start with the requirement of spousal notice, which was the only aspect of our law that the court of appeals found unconstitutional.

It's important to remember, and perhaps more important in this context than any other, that the petitioners brought this action as a facial challenge to the statute. In this kind of a challenge it's enough for the petitioners to show— It's not enough for them to show that the act might be unconstitutional as applied to someone in some hypothetical, worst-case scenario. Rather, the petitioners must show that the statute could not constitutionally be applied to anyone. We asked, have they met that burden, and we submit that they have not met that burden. This is a spousal notice provision, it is not a spousal consent statute.

JUSTICE O'CONNOR: Now, the provision does not require notification to a father who is not the husband, I take it—

MR. PREATE: That's correct, Justice O'Connor.

JUSTICE O'CONNOR: Or notice if the woman is unmarried?

MR. PREATE: It only applies to married women.

JUSTICE O'CONNOR: So what's the interest, to try to preserve the marriage?

MR. PREATE: There are several interests. The interest, of course, in protecting the life of the unborn child.

JUSTICE O'CONNOR: Well then, why not require notice to all fathers? It's a curious sort of a provision, isn't it.

MR. PREATE: It is that, but the legislature has made the judgment that it wanted its statute to apply in this specific instance because it wanted to further the integrity of marriages.

JUSTICE O'CONNOR: Would you say that the State could similarly require a woman to notify anyone with whom she had intercourse that she planned to use some means of birth control after the intercourse that operates, let's say, as an abortifacient? Could the State do that? I mean, it would be the same State interest, I suppose.

MR. PREATE: The State interest would be the same, but I think that would be problematic. I'm not—

JUSTICE O'CONNOR: And why would it be problematic, do you think?

MR. PREATE: I think that with regard to applying a statute to all women, that it might create severe obstacles, an absolute obstacle to their obtaining an abortion.

JUSTICE O'CONNOR: I don't understand.

MR. PREATE: The undue burden standard, as I understand it, is that whether or not the regulation would impose such an absolute obstacle, not whether it would deter or inhibit some women from obtaining an abortion.

JUSTICE O'CONNOR: Well, we're talking about the provision for notification in this case under the statute to the husband, and I'm just asking whether a different type of State regulation would have to be upheld under your standard.

MR. PREATE: Well, if the State had posited its interest as protecting the life of the unborn then utilizing the rational basis standard, then I would submit that it could legitimately require that kind of notification to all people.

In this instance, however, we have a different statute. We have a statute that provides exceptions where exceptions are appropriate, and there are five of them: medical emergency, where the husband is not the father of the child, where the husband cannot be found, where the pregnancy is the result of a reported sexual assault, or where the woman in her judgment believes it's likely that she will be physically abused.

Now, petitioners have produced some testimony and made some argument, essentially through one expert, about battered wives, but the testimony was that some unknown number were rendered so helpless by their battering husbands that they were incapable of checking off a line on the form, the spousal notice form.

We can agree that these women are indeed cruelly burdened, but they're not burdened by the statute, and that's the compelling point. They're not burdened by the statute, but by the circumstance, and the tragic circumstance, of their lives. We're looking at the statute to see if the statute imposes the obstacle. If there is a battering husband that's interposed in there, that's a different story.

JUSTICE O'CONNOR: What's our standard on a facial challenge, whether there's a substantial likelihood of the harm?

MR. PREATE: No, I think you have to ignore what the petitioners have posited, which is a worst-case analysis scenario, and you have to look and see if it could be constitutionally applied and value-tied to anyone, and we submit that in this particular instance the record reflects that right now, in Pennsylvania, 50,000 abortions, 20 percent of those women are married and 95 percent of those women notify their husbands.

Therefore, only one percent of the women are not, in Pennsylvania, notifying their husbands now, and the Act's not even in effect. There is no broad practical effect in the Pennsylvania statute to prohibiting abortion for those women.

If the act goes into effect, some of those one percent of women will then have to notify their husband, and the result will be they will resolve their difficulties amicably. There will be some who will then take the exception, because they don't want to notify their husband. They may be battered, there may be a spousal rape, there may be— They can't find their husband.

So what we're doing is reducing that set of women down to several subsets and the petitioners' burden in a facial challenge is to establish, you see, that there's a broad practical impact. They have not met that burden.

JUSTICE STEVENS: No, but General, may I ask you a question. Is it not true, therefore, that the only people affected by the statute, this very small group, are people who would not otherwise notify their husbands?

MR. PREATE: I'm not sure I got all of that question, Justice Stevens.

JUSTICE STEVENS: Well, you've demonstrated that the public interest is in a very limited group of people, the few women who would not otherwise notify their husbands, and those are the only people affected by the statute.

MR. PREATE: That is correct.

JUSTICE STEVENS: Everyone in that class, should we not assume, would not notify her husband but for the statute.

MR. PREATE: That is correct. Now, in that one percent, not everyone would want to notify, and there are exceptions.

JUSTICE STEVENS: They would not without the statute.

MR. PREATE: They would not without the statute, but there are exceptions, several of them—four.

JUSTICE STEVENS: No, they'd only— You've already taken the exceptions into account in narrowing the group very— To, you know, one percent, or whatever it is.

MR. PREATE: Justice—

JUSTICE STEVENS: You aren't suggesting there's no one whose decision will be affected by the statute.

MR. PREATE: Well, that's the point. On this record, which is what we have to go on, there is nothing established by the petitioners as to how many there are in that category.

JUSTICE STEVENS: Well, if there's no one affected by the statute, what is the State interest in upholding the statute?

MR. PREATE: The State interest in upholding the statute is the protection of the life of the unborn and the protection of the marital integrity, and to ensuring of communication, the possibility— We're not asking—

JUSTICE KENNEDY: But not if the statute has no effect. As a general matter, when we're dealing with rational basis review, we ask whom does the law affect, and so it seems to me that you have to justify the law based on the effect of this one percent who would not otherwise—and you may have an argument.

MR. PREATE: And— And—

JUSTICE KENNEDY: It's a very strange argument to say that the law doesn't affect 90 percent of the people so we're not concerned with the law. I've never heard that argument.

MR. PREATE: We're not in any way advocating that, because we think that the law is rational. If you look at the State interests that are trying to be pursued here—protecting the life of the unborn, protecting the marriage, ensuring the possibility of communication—this statute rationally advances it.

It may not advance it in every single instance, but that is not the test. The test is, does it generally rationally advance the interest that the State is trying to protect? In this instance, it does. But by the sheer numbers that we have demonstrated—

JUSTICE SCALIA: General Preate, I thought we were talking, not rational basis but undue burden. Are they the same thing?

MR. PREATE: No, they are not, Justice Scalia.

JUSTICE SCALIA: How do I go about determining whether it's an undue burden or not? What law books do I look to?

MR. PREATE: This is a quantitative analysis, Justice Scalia. You begin by ascertaining under undue burden the— Whether it is a significant increase in cost such that it broaden the impacts, prohibits women from having abortion or whether it bans abortion.

JUSTICE SCALIA: I suppose it depends on how important I would think it is, that a husband of a wife know before a fetus that he co-generated be destroyed. Would that be part of it?

MR. PREATE: That would be part of the analysis that is done on the weighing side, after you establish whether or not there is in fact— In the first instance, the threshold question is what is the broad practical impact? If there is no broad practical impact, it's minimal, as is in Pennsylvania statute, then you reach the question of the weighing that's involved.

JUSTICE SCALIA: Well, it depends. I mean, if the impact is only minimal, but also the interest involved is only minimal, then I suppose it is an undue burden, and I guess that again leads you to how much weight you place on that kind of an interest.

MR. PREATE: As I understand it, Justice Scalia, what you are talking about is if there is no undue burden, that is, there is no broad practical impact in the initial analysis, then you determine whether or not the statute rationally furthers the State's interest. It's a rational basis test in the second phase of it.

And under the rational basis test, which would be the same rational basis test that some members of this Court have applied in *Webster*, you come to the conclusion that Pennsylvania's spousal notice section does pass undue burden analysis, and it does pass rational basis analysis.

JUSTICE STEVENS: May I ask you a question about your understanding of the undue burden test. Do you think it refers to the number of persons burdened by the law on the one hand or the severity of the burden on a particular individual affected by the law on the other hand? Which is the right analysis?

MR. PREATE: I think, Justice Stevens, in the initial application, it's a quantitative analysis, whether there is a broad practical impact here. The fact that it might—

JUSTICE STEVENS: In other words, it is the number of persons affected is your answer—

MR. PREATE: The number of persons affected—

JUSTICE STEVENS: Regardless of how severe the burden on a particular individual?

MR. PREATE: As the test has been posited, the question of whether or not—

JUSTICE STEVENS: I am just asking you to explain to me what your conception of the test that you are asking us to adopt it.

MR. PREATE: It may be that some women would be deterred to some degree, but that is not sufficient to create an undue burden.

JUSTICE STEVENS: It is the number of women affected?

MR. PREATE: Initially, it is the number of women affected, the broad practical impact of it—

JUSTICE O'CONNOR: How about as applied to a specific woman?

MR. PREATE: As applied to a specific woman? Let's say there is such a woman who has been battered, psychologically battered, and so the exception doesn't work in her instance.

JUSTICE O'CONNOR: Right, let's suppose that.

MR. PREATE: Let's posit that. In that instance, of course, that is a worst-case scenario, that is not the way you test facial challenges, in that instance, the law would work. You would test this statute as applied in the lower courts, and that woman would then be—

JUSTICE O'CONNOR: And you would apply an undue burden test there on the as-applied challenge, do you suppose?

MR. PREATE: No, I would think that—

JUSTICE O'CONNOR: No?

MR. PREATE: No. I would think that you would be asking the court to give full reign to the interests that you have. The woman would have, under rational basis analysis test, a liberty interest protected by the Fourteenth Amendment, or under the undue burden standard, would have a limited right—

JUSTICE O'CONNOR: I would have thought you would look at the burden of the law as applied to the woman.

MR. PREATE: And I think that you would look to that, but you are asking the court, in an as-applied mechanism to give full effect to your right, the statute given. It is a given that it burdens you. So you can't just look at the burden in the as-applied context, but you must look at it in that context, giving full reign to your right, and that is what the woman would be seeking from the district court or for a court of common pleas, in asking the court, in applying this spousal notice section to her particular instance because she didn't have one of the exceptions to check off because she is psychologically or economically pressured.

JUSTICE SCALIA: But in the facial context, I don't understand what you— So there are two undue burden tests. There is one at the facial level in which we consider the statute in gross and decide whether, all things considered in the generality of applications, the burden is undue.

And then we have a second wave of application of the undue burden test case-by-case, so that even though the law facially may be okay, it may be invalid in its particular application because of— Is that what you are saying?

MR. PREATE: In the second instance, as applied it—

JUSTICE SCALIA: I am worried about the first one, not the second one. I thought the—

MR. PREATE: In a facial challenge, Justice Scalia, you are looking at not the worst scenario hypothesis, but whether this act could be applied constitutionally to anyone, and that is—

JUSTICE SCALIA: Any single case, not in gross, to any single case. Isn't that the normal situation? To challenge a statute facially you have to show that it can never be constitutionally applied, isn't that right?

MR. PREATE: That's correct.

JUSTICE SCALIA: That is not looking at it in gross. That is asking whether there is any single case where a woman would not be unduly burdened.

MR. PREATE: In this particular instance, we find that there is no undue burden in our statute, anywhere in our statute, and if the undue burden test is, as applied or understood by this Court, causes our statute to fall, then we ask this Court to adopt rational basis as the appropriate analysis.

JUSTICE O'CONNOR: Do you think that compelling speech requires any kind of First Amendment analysis?

MR. PREATE: Compelling—

JUSTICE O'CONNOR: Speech. The State is compelling a woman to say something to her husband.

MR. PREATE: We are asking that she—

JUSTICE O'CONNOR: Does that invoke any First Amendment concerns?

MR. PREATE: Not in our view, this statute—

JUSTICE O'CONNOR: I would have thought perhaps compelling speech would get us right into a First Amendment area.

MR. PREATE: In this particular instance, this statute, we feel causes notification, but there is a legitimate State interest involved in furthering that interest.

JUSTICE O'CONNOR: In other words, the doctor is to say certain things to the patient, do you think that is really commercial speech there?

MR. PREATE: Yes, I do, Justice O'Connor—

JUSTICE O'CONNOR: Why is that? When the doctor is giving professional advice to the patient, you think that is commercial?

MR. PREATE: That is commercial. The petitioners already do that right now. They already tell their patients, the physicians and the counselors, that there are medical risks associated with this procedure.

JUSTICE O'CONNOR: I wouldn't have thought that was commercial speech. What do you rely on?

MR. PREATE: In *Zauderer*.

JUSTICE O'CONNOR: But that is advertising, that is different.

MR. PREATE: In Pennsylvania's general informed consent law, applying to every single contact between the doctor and a patient, there is the same information that must be presented and that is, the doctor must tell the patient about the medical risks of the procedure and the alternatives to it.

JUSTICE O'CONNOR: Well, it might meet a First Amendment test, but I am wondering how you get to commercial speech on that kind of advice?

MR. PREATE: We think that with the—with the interests involved, the statute furthers those interests and that it can legitimately require the husband to be notified because of the interests involved.

I see that my time is running short, and I wanted to make sure the Solicitor General has some time to respond.

We think that Pennsylvania has developed an intelligent statute that fully comports with the due process clause of the Fourteenth Amendment.

It is a statute that is carefully drafted and it has been amended to reflect the teachings of this Court's jurisprudence since *Roe*. We ask this Court to overturn *Akron* and *Thornburgh*'s strict scrutiny approach as being unwarranted extensions of *Roe*.

On the facial challenge, whereby the petitioners must show that there is no set of circumstances under which these provisions can be valid, the petitioners have utterly failed to do so, done in by no small measure by, as the record demonstrates and as indicated in the Third Circuit Court of Appeals' opinion, but their own rational practices which this statute mirrors.

JUSTICE SOUTER: Mr. Preate, because you have a little time left, there is one point on which I guess I never fully followed your argument, and I wonder if you would go back to it.

You got to the point, you were arguing about the number of instances, the percentage of instances in which the spousal notification would in fact make a difference in the behavior of the parties involved. And as I recall, you got it down to about five percent to begin with who would not otherwise, five percent of the women who would not otherwise give notice to their spouses. Then from that five percent you subtracted some number for those, I guess subject to medical emergencies, those subject to the certification that they would be physically abused, and I think by that process of elimination you got it down to about one percent who would actually be affected by the stricture of the statute, is that right?

MR. PREATE: That is not correct, Justice— You start with the one percent because 95 percent of 20 percent is one percent. You are talking about 500 women that—

JUSTICE SOUTER: You are talking about all women, but the spousal notification applies only to married women.

MR. PREATE: That is correct.

JUSTICE SOUTER: What is the percentage of married women? Well, your time is up.

MR. PREATE: Sorry. Thank you.

CHIEF JUSTICE REHNQUIST: Thank you, Mr. Preate.

ORAL ARGUMENT OF KENNETH W. STARR ON BEHALF OF THE UNITED STATES AS *AMICUS CURIAE* SUPPORTING THE RESPONDENT

GENERAL STARR: Thank you Mr. Chief Justice, and may it please the Court. In view of what has been discussed, let me address very briefly three points.

The first is the standard of review which has been the subject of considerable discussion. In a number of its cases over the last twenty years in the abortion area, the Court has articulated the governing standard of review in different ways. And as a result, there is confusion in the law as to how legislatures, if they choose, can legislate, and how judges are to judge in this extraordinarily sensitive and divisive area.

In our view, the correct articulation of that standard is to be found in the *Webster* plurality opinion. That standard has deep roots. It finds its roots in a long line of due process cases that do not involve liberty interests which, by virtue of the nation's history and its legal traditions, rise to the level of fundamental rights to a free people. This is the process of analysis that is quite familiar to the Court, very lengthily laid out by Justice Harlan in his dissent in *Poe* v. *Ullman*, and then adumbrated in his concurring opinion in *Griswold* v. *Connecticut*.

Second, and relatedly, with all respect, we do not believe

that *stare decisis* considerations weigh against the Court providing that needed clarification as to the standard. This is not an issue—

JUSTICE STEVENS: May I ask you one rather basic question?

GENERAL STARR: Certainly.

JUSTICE STEVENS: It affects the standard of review and everything else. What is the position of the Department of Justice on the question whether a fetus is a person within the meaning of the Fourteenth Amendment?

GENERAL STARR: We do not have a position on that question and this Court has not addressed, or at least there is no Justice at this Court—

JUSTICE STEVENS: It's addressed in *Roe*.

GENERAL STARR: That, that, that is correct. And it does seem to me that ultimately that is an extraordinarily difficult question which this Court need address, and it need not address it in this case.

JUSTICE STEVENS: What is that we need not address? I'm just interested to know—

GENERAL STARR: We do not have a position.

JUSTICE STEVENS: Does the United States have a position on that question?

GENERAL STARR: We do not, because we think it would be an extraordinarily difficult and sensitive issue by virtue of a number of questions that would flow from that, including equal protections and so forth.

JUSTICE O'CONNOR: Well, the Court decided that in *Roe*, did it not?

GENERAL STARR: The Court did, in fact, decide that there is a very keen interest on the part of the State in what the *Roe* Court called potential life, and that's my—

JUSTICE O'CONNOR: Yes, but said the fetus is not a person under the Fourteenth Amendment.

GENERAL STARR: Well I think that that is the necessary consequence of *Roe v. Wade*. But I think that the key point is that a number of the Justices of this Court have said that regardless of that legal question, that constitutional question, that the State does have a compelling interest in the potential life, in fetal life, and that that interest runs throughout pregnancy.

JUSTICE SCALIA: We did not say in *Roe* that a State could

not have a position on whether a fetus is a person, did we?

GENERAL STARR: Certainly the Court—

JUSTICE SCALIA: We said that the Constitution takes no position on whether a fetus is a person, and/or that it does take a position that a fetus is not protected by the Constitution.

GENERAL STARR: The Court seemed to admit of the possibility of State regulation to protect the unborn at all stages.

JUSTICE SCALIA: Including State regulation on the basis of the people's determination within that State that a fetus is a person. There's nothing in *Roe* that says a State may not make that judgment, if it wishes.

GENERAL STARR: That it says, that the State may, if it sees fit, that the State does have— I think *Roe* goes this far. *Roe* says that there is a legitimate interest of the State in the potential life *in utero* throughout pregnancy, and then the nature of that interest changes and becomes stronger over time. But it did, in fact, say that there is a legitimate interest.

And there has been an expression by a number of the Justices of this Court to suggest that that interest is, indeed, a compelling interest on the part of the State.

JUSTICE SOUTER: Is that also not the position of the Government of the United States, that it is a compelling interest throughout pregnancy?

GENERAL STARR: That is our position, that there is a compelling interest.

JUSTICE STEVENS: And what is context. What is the textual basis for that position in the Constitution? Is there any?

GENERAL STARR: Well I think that, if I may, Justice Stevens, it seems to me that it goes to the recognition that we all do, that there is in fact an organism. As, Justice—

JUSTICE STEVENS: I'm asking what is the textual basis in the Constitution? You argue very vigorously there's no textual basis supporting your opponent's position. What is the textual basis for your position that there's a compelling interest in something that is not a person within the meaning of the Fourteenth Amendment?

GENERAL STARR: The State has—

JUSTICE STEVENS: What is the textual basis for it?

GENERAL STARR: The State has an interest in its potential

citizen, it does not have to be granted, have the basis in the Constitution. Justice Stevens, it is my view that the State can look out and say we, historically, regulate and legislate in the interest of those who will come into being, who will be born. It is an interest that every member of this Court has said in potential life.

JUSTICE STEVENS: That's not responsive to my question. My question is what is the textual basis in the Constitution. If you're going to say there is none, fine, that's perfectly all right.

GENERAL STARR: I think it's in the nature of our system. And if nothing else, the Tenth Amendment, Justice Stevens, suggests that the State can order its relationships in ways that reflect the morality of the people, within limits.

JUSTICE SCALIA: General Starr.

GENERAL STARR: There's a determination to— I'm sorry.

JUSTICE SCALIA: Why does there have to be something in the Constitution? There's nothing in the Constitution that requires the State to protect the environment, is there?

GENERAL STARR: Of course not.

JUSTICE SCALIA: And yet that can be a compelling State interest, may it not?

GENERAL STARR: Yes. As I have said, the Constitution does not seek to order and to ordain. There are interests in which the State can have, and our nature of government—

JUSTICE SCALIA: All that *Roe* says is that the Constitution does not protect the fetus under the Fourteenth Amendment. It does not say that a State may not choose to do so.

GENERAL STARR: It doesn't even go so far, it seems to me.

JUSTICE SCALIA: Or that if a State chooses to do so, it is not a compelling state interest. There's nothing in *Roe* that contradicts that.

GENERAL STARR: I think it calibrates it. I think, Justice Stevens, it is, in fact, the nature of our governmental structure. I know no— I do know of prohibitions that the Constitution sets forth. I do not know of particular provisions, other than, indeed, perhaps the Tenth sheds light on this.

That this is a matter that ultimately is, and I think this is quite important in terms of analyzing what Pennsylvania has done here. What Pennsylvania has said, in effect, is that we will not prohibit abortion, save for gender selection abortions.

Our colleagues on the other side believe that *Roe* v. *Wade* forbids that, that it protects that decision. It does not prohibit; it has seen fit to regulate. That is very much in the tradition of the Western democracies.

JUSTICE WHITE: What is the standard? And you started out to tell us what the standard was?

GENERAL STARR: We believe it was articulated, Justice White, by the *Webster* plurality.

JUSTICE WHITE: Well, what is it?

GENERAL STARR: It is the rational basis standard. And that is the standard that has been articulated by this Court in a variety of decisions and by a variety of Justices of this Court, in its abortion jurisprudence.

JUSTICE STEVENS: And under that standard, you would think all of the provisions that are at issue here should be sustained.

GENERAL STARR: Exactly.

JUSTICE SOUTER: And so would complete prohibition, wouldn't it?

GENERAL STARR: Complete prohibition that had no exception for the life of mother, I think could raise very serious questions under—

JUSTICE SOUTER: But subject, subject to that—

GENERAL STARR: The protection of life.

JUSTICE SOUTER: Subject to that exception, it would cover complete pro— It would justify complete prohibition.

GENERAL STARR: I think it best not to answer these in the abstract. We look to the specific interests of the State as it has articulated those interests. For example—

JUSTICE SOUTER: Well, I'll grant you that, but you're asking the Court to adopt a standard and I think we ought to know where the standard would take us.

GENERAL STARR: I think the rational basis standard would, in fact, allow considerable leeway to the States, if it saw fit.

JUSTICE STEVENS: Well, General Starr—

GENERAL STARR: Through the democratic—

JUSTICE STEVENS: It's not really a fair answer. Rational basis under your analysis: there's an interest in preserving fetal life at all times during pregnancy. It's rational, under your view. Ergo it follows that a total prohibition, protected by criminal penalties, would be rational, it would meet your standard.

GENERAL STARR: I don't think so. The common law, the common—

JUSTICE STEVENS: Well why not? In what proviso— What is your rational basis standard if not the traditional one?

GENERAL STARR: Ours is the traditional one. But under that traditional analysis there must, in fact, be a rational connection with a legitimate State interest, and the State cannot proceed in an arbitrary and capricious fashion, in my view. If I may complete this, I think this is an important part of the answer.

It would be arbitrary and capricious. It would, moreover, deprive an individual of her right to life if there were not an emergency exception. And even in *Roe* v. *Wade*, the Texas statute at issue there provided for that exception. It would be quite at war with our traditions, as embodied in the common law, not to provide, at a minimum, for that kind of exception.

JUSTICE STEVENS: No, but what you're saying is the rational basis standard, which normally just requires a reason that is legitimate to support it, can be overcome in some cases by countervailing interest, which is not the normal rational basis standard.

GENERAL STARR: Well, may I respond?

JUSTICE STEVENS: Yes, you may.

GENERAL STARR: I think that the traditional rational basis test does, in fact, analyze the ends. It looks at the ends and the means. And it requires, in fact, that the State not conduct itself in an arbitrary and capricious fashion. That is the ultimate insight of the rational basis test.

I thank the Court.

CHIEF JUSTICE REHNQUIST: Thank you, General Starr. Ms. Kolbert, you have three minutes remaining.

REBUTTAL ARGUMENT OF KATHRYN KOLBERT ON BEHALF OF THE PETITIONERS

MS. KOLBERT: Mr. Chief Justice, I'd like to address two points very quickly. The first is in response to this last dialogue with General Starr. Recognition of a State's interest in fetal life as compelling throughout pregnancy would denigrate and restrict the ability of women at all stages of pregnancy to have an abortion. And certainly in the only exception that Mr. Starr and the Solicitor General have laid out for this Court, is in the very rare instance where only the life of the woman would be excluded from a ban.

Bans of second trimester abortions, bans of certain classes of women having abortions, bans that would prevent women who have serious and long lasting health needs to have abortions, would be significantly approved by this Court if the rational basis standard were adopted, precisely because of a formulation that the State's interest is compelling throughout pregnancy and sufficient to override any liberty interests, any interests of the woman to choose or not choose a pregnancy.

And, in fact, that is why this Court must go back to the hallmark of *Roe*. That is, again reaffirm that the right to choose abortion is fundamental. And only when the Government can show a compelling purpose—as recognized in *Roe* that is, a compelling purpose after the point of viability—should it be able to sustain a statute.

The second point I wanted to raise goes to the question of the rights by numbers approach articulated by the Commonwealth. It is our view that the husband notification statute applies to every single married woman in Pennsylvania. That the rights of autonomy, the rights of communication within the family, are infringed because those communications are subject to criminal prosecution, and subject to independent district attorneys subpoenaing women and probing the communications between husband and wife.

JUSTICE O'CONNOR: Are there First Amendment values at stake there, do you think?

MS. KOLBERT: Your Honor, I do believe there are, not only in this section, but in the bias counseling provisions as well. Clearly, we've set forth in our brief why we believe this is not commercial speech. But in both instances, the Court is forcing the physician to be the proponent of its ideology, and also to communicate information about the abortion decision.

CHIEF JUSTICE REHNQUIST: Thank you, Ms. Kolbert.

MS. KOLBERT: Thank you.

CHIEF JUSTICE REHNQUIST: The case is submitted.

(Whereupon, at 10:56 a.m., the case in the above-entitled matter was submitted.)

THE
SUPREME COURT
DECISION
JUNE 29, 1992

SUPREME COURT OF THE UNITED STATES

Nos. 91–744 and 91–902

PLANNED PARENTHOOD OF SOUTHEASTERN
PENNSYLVANIA, et al., PETITIONERS
v.   91–744
ROBERT P. CASEY, et al., etc.

ROBERT P. CASEY, et al., etc.,
PETITIONERS
v.   91–902
PLANNED PARENTHOOD OF SOUTHEASTERN
PENNSYLVANIA, et al.

ON WRITS OF CERTIORARI TO THE UNITED STATES COURT OF
APPEALS FOR THE THIRD CIRCUIT

[June 29, 1992]

* * *

JUDGMENT OF THE COURT AND JOINT OPINION BY JUSTICES O'CONNOR, KENNEDY, AND SOUTER

Justice O'Connor, Justice Kennedy, and Justice Souter announced the judgment of the Court and delivered the opinion of the Court with respect to Parts I, II, III, V-A, V-C, and VI, an opinion with respect to Part V-E, in which Justice Stevens joins, and an opinion with respect to Parts IV, V-B, and V-D.

I

Liberty finds no refuge in a jurisprudence of doubt. Yet 19 years after our holding that the Constitution protects a woman's right to terminate her pregnancy in its early stages, *Roe v. Wade*, 410 U.S. 113 (1973), that definition of liberty is still questioned. Joining the respondents as *amicus curiae*, the United States, as it has done in five other cases in the last decade, again asks us to overrule *Roe*. See Brief for Respondents [204–208]; Brief for United States as *Amicus Curiae* [217].

At issue in these cases are five provisions of the Pennsylvania Abortion Control Act of 1982 as amended in 1988 and 1989. 18 Pa. Cons. Stat. §§ 3203–3220 (1990). Relevant portions of the Act are set forth in the appendix. *Infra*, at [393]. The Act requires that a woman seeking an abortion give her informed consent prior to the abortion procedure, and specifies that she be provided with certain information at least 24 hours before the abortion is performed. § 3205. For a minor to obtain an abortion, the Act requires the informed consent of one of her parents, but provides for a judicial bypass option if the minor does not wish to or cannot obtain a parent's consent. § 3206. Another provision of the Act requires that, unless certain exceptions apply, a married woman seeking an abortion must sign a statement indicating that she has notified her husband of her intended abortion. § 3209. The Act exempts compliance with these three requirements in the event of a "medical emergency," which is defined in § 3203 of the Act. See §§ 3203, 3205(a), 3206(a), 3209(c). In addition to the above provisions regulating the performance of abortions, the Act imposes certain reporting requirements on facilities that provide abortion services. §§ 3207(b), 3214(a), 3214(f).

Before any of these provisions took effect, the petitioners, who are five abortion clinics and one physician representing himself as well as a class of physicians who provide abortion services, brought this suit seeking declaratory and injunctive relief. Each provision was challenged as unconstitutional on its face. The District Court entered a preliminary injunction against the enforcement of the regulations, and, after a 3-day bench trial, held all the provisions at issue here unconstitutional, entering a permanent injunction against Pennsylvania's enforcement of them. 744 F. Supp. 1323 (ED Pa. 1990). The Court of Appeals for the Third Circuit affirmed in part and reversed in part, upholding all of the regulations except for the husband notification requirement. 947 F. 2d 682 (1991). We granted certiorari. 502 U.S. ___ (1992).

The Court of Appeals found it necessary to follow an elaborate course of reasoning even to identify the first premise to use to determine whether the statute enacted by Pennsylvania meets constitutional standards. See 947 F. 2d, at 687–698. And at oral argument in this Court, the attorney for the parties challenging the statute took the position that none of the enactments can be upheld without overruling *Roe* v. *Wade.* Tr. of Oral Arg. [318]. We disagree with that analysis; but we acknowledge that our decisions after *Roe* cast doubt upon the meaning and reach of its holding. Further, the CHIEF JUSTICE admits that he would overrule the central holding of *Roe* and adopt the rational relationship test as the sole criterion of constitutionality. See *post*, at [432]. State and federal courts as well as legislatures throughout the Union must have guidance as they seek to address this subject in conformance with the Constitution. Given these premises, we find it imperative to review once more the principles that define the rights of the woman and the legitimate authority of the State respecting the termination of pregnancies by abortion procedures.

After considering the fundamental constitutional questions resolved by *Roe*, principles of institutional integrity, and the rule of *stare decisis*, we are led to conclude this: the essential holding of *Roe* v. *Wade* should be retained and once again reaffirmed.

It must be stated at the outset and with clarity that *Roe*'s essential holding, the holding we reaffirm, has three parts. First is a recognition of the right of the woman to choose to have an abortion before viability and to obtain it without undue interference from the State. Before viability, the State's interests are not strong enough to support a prohibition of abortion or the imposition of a substantial obstacle to the woman's effective right to elect the procedure. Second is a confirmation of the State's power to restrict abortions after fetal viability, if the law contains exceptions for pregnancies which endanger a woman's life or health. And third is the principle that the State has legitimate interests from the outset of the pregnancy in protecting the health of the woman and the life of the fetus that may become a child. These principles do not contradict one another; and we adhere to each.

II

Constitutional protection of the woman's decision to terminate her pregnancy derives from the Due Process Clause of the Fourteenth Amendment. It declares that no State shall "deprive any person of life, liberty, or property, without due process of law." The controlling word in the case before us is "liberty." Although a literal reading of the Clause might suggest that it governs only the procedures by which a State may deprive persons of liberty, for at least 105 years, at least since *Mugler* v. *Kansas*, 123 U.S. 623, 660–661 (1887), the Clause has been understood to contain a substantive component as well, one "barring certain government actions regardless of the fairness of the procedures used to implement them." *Daniels* v. *Williams*, 474 U.S. 327, 331 (1986). As Justice Brandeis (joined by Justice Holmes) observed, "[d]espite arguments to the contrary which had seemed to me persuasive, it is settled that the due process clause of the Fourteenth Amendment applies to matters of substantive law as well as to matters of procedure. Thus all fundamental rights comprised within the term liberty are protected by the Federal Constitution from invasion by the States." *Whitney* v. *California*, 274 U.S. 357, 373 (1927) (Brandeis, J., concurring). "[T]he guaranties of due process, though having their roots in Magna Carta's '*per legem terrae*' and considered as procedural safeguards 'against executive usurpation and tyranny,' have in this country 'become bulwarks also against arbitrary legislation.' " *Poe* v. *Ullman*, 367 U.S. 497, 541 (1961) (Harlan, J., dissenting from dismissal on jurisdictional grounds) (quoting *Hurtado* v. *California*, 110 U.S. 516, 532 (1884)).

The most familiar of the substantive liberties protected by the Fourteenth Amendment are those recognized by the Bill of Rights. We have held that the Due Process Clause of the Fourteenth Amendment incorporates most of the Bill of Rights against the States. See, *e.g.*, *Duncan* v. *Louisiana*, 391 U.S. 145, 147–148 (1968). It is tempting, as a means of curbing the discretion of federal judges, to suppose that liberty encompasses no more than those rights already guaranteed to the individual against federal interference by the express provisions of the first eight amendments to the Constitution. See *Adamson* v. *California*, 332 U.S. 46, 68–92 (1947) (Black, J., dissenting). But of course this Court has never accepted that view.

It is also tempting, for the same reason, to suppose that the Due Process Clause protects only those practices, defined at the most specific level, that were protected against government interference by other rules of law when the Fourteenth Amendment was ratified. See *Michael H.* v. *Gerald D.*, 491 U.S. 110, 127–128, n. 6 (1989) (opinion of Scalia, J.). But such a view would be inconsistent with our law. It is a promise of the Constitution that there is a realm of personal liberty which the government may not enter. We have vindicated this principle before. Marriage is mentioned nowhere in the Bill of Rights and interracial marriage was illegal in most States in the 19th century, but the Court was no doubt correct in finding it to be an aspect of liberty protected against state interference by the substantive component of the Due Process Clause in *Loving* v. *Virginia*, 388 U.S. 1, 12 (1967) (relying, in an opinion for eight Justices, on the Due Process Clause). Similar examples may be found in *Turner* v. *Safley*, 482 U.S. 78, 94–99 (1987); in *Carey* v. *Population Services International*, 431 U.S. 678, 684–686 (1977); in *Griswold* v. *Connecticut*, 381 U.S. 479, 481–482 (1965), as well as in the separate opinions of a majority of the Members of the Court in that case, *id.*, at 486–488 (Goldberg, J., joined by Warren, C. J., and Brennan, J., concurring) (expressly relying on due process), *id.*, at 500–502 (Harlan, J., concurring in judgment) (same), *id.*, at 502–507 (White, J., concurring in judgment) (same); in *Pierce* v. *Society of Sisters*, 268 U.S. 510, 534–535 (1925); and in *Meyer* v. *Nebraska*, 262 U.S. 390, 399–403 (1923).

Neither the Bill of Rights nor the specific practices of States at the time of the adoption of the Fourteenth Amendment marks the outer limits of the substantive sphere of liberty which the Fourteenth Amendment protects. See U.S. Const., Amend. 9. As the second Justice Harlan recognized:

"[T]he full scope of the liberty guaranteed by the Due Process Clause cannot be found in or limited by the precise terms of the specific guarantees elsewhere provided in the Constitution. This 'liberty' is not a series of isolated points pricked out in terms of the taking of property; the freedom of speech, press, and religion; the right to keep and bear arms; the freedom from unreasonable searches and seizures; and so on. It is a rational continuum which, broadly speaking, includes a freedom from all substantial arbitrary impositions and purposeless restraints, . . . and which also recognizes, what a reasonable and sensitive judgment must, that certain interests require particularly careful scrutiny of the state needs asserted to justify their abridgment." Poe v. Ullman, supra, at 543 (Harlan, J., dissenting from dismissal on jurisdictional grounds).

Justice Harlan wrote these words in addressing an issue the full Court did not reach in Poe v. Ullman, but the Court adopted his position four Terms later in Griswold v. Connecticut, supra. In Griswold, we held that the Constitution does not permit a State to forbid a married couple to use contraceptives. That same freedom was later guaranteed, under the Equal Protection Clause, for unmarried couples. See Eisenstadt v. Baird, 405 U.S. 438 (1972). Constitutional protection was extended to the sale and distribution of contraceptives in Carey v. Population Services International, supra. It is settled now, as it was when the Court heard arguments in Roe v. Wade, that the Constitution places limits on a State's right to interfere with a person's most basic decisions about family and parenthood, see Carey v. Population Services International, supra; Moore v. East Cleveland, 431 U.S. 494 (1977); Eisenstadt v. Baird, supra; Loving v. Virginia, supra; Griswold v. Connecticut, supra; Skinner v. Oklahoma ex rel. Williamson, 316 U.S. 535 (1942); Pierce v. Society of Sisters, supra; Meyer v. Nebraska, supra, as well as bodily integrity. See, e.g., Washington v. Harper, 494 U.S. 210, 221–222 (1990); Winston v. Lee, 470 U.S. 753 (1985); Rochin v. California, 342 U.S. 165 (1952).

The inescapable fact is that adjudication of substantive due process claims may call upon the Court in interpreting the Constitution to exercise that same capacity which by tradition courts always have exercised: reasoned judgment. Its boundaries are not susceptible of expression as a simple rule. That does not mean we are free to invalidate state policy choices with which we disagree; yet neither does it permit us to shrink from the duties of our office. As Justice Harlan observed:

> "Due process has not been reduced to any formula; its content cannot be determined by reference to any code. The best that can be said is that through the course of this Court's decisions it has represented the balance which our Nation, built upon postulates of respect for the liberty of the individual, has struck between that liberty and the demands of organized society. If the supplying of content to this Constitutional concept has of necessity been a rational process, it certainly has not been one where judges have felt free to roam where unguided speculation might take them. The balance of which I speak is the balance struck by this country, having regard to what history teaches are the traditions from which it developed as well as the traditions from which it broke. That tradition is a living thing. A decision of this Court which radically departs from it could not long survive, while a decision which builds on what has survived is likely to be sound. No formula could serve as a substitute, in this area, for judgment and restraint." *Poe v. Ullman*, 367 U.S., at 542 (Harlan, J., dissenting from dismissal on jurisdictional grounds).

See also *Rochin v. California, supra*, at 171–172 (Frankfurter, J., writing for the Court) ("To believe that this judicial exercise of judgment could be avoided by freezing 'due process of law' at some fixed stage of time or thought is to suggest that the most important aspect of constitutional adjudication is a function for inanimate machines and not for judges").

Men and women of good conscience can disagree, and we suppose some always shall disagree, about the profound moral and spiritual implications of terminating a pregnancy, even in its earliest stage. Some of us as individuals find abortion offensive to our most basic principles of morality, but that cannot control our decision. Our obligation is to define the liberty of all, not to mandate our own moral code. The underlying constitutional issue is whether the State can resolve these philosophic questions in such a definitive way that a woman lacks all choice in the matter, except perhaps in those rare circumstances in which the pregnancy is itself a danger to her own life or health, or is the result of rape or incest.

It is conventional constitutional doctrine that where reasonable people disagree the government can adopt one position or the other. See, *e.g.*, *Ferguson* v. *Skrupa*, 372 U.S. 726 (1963); *Williamson* v. *Lee Optical of Oklahoma, Inc.*, 348 U.S. 483 (1955). That theorem, however, assumes a state of affairs in which the choice does not intrude upon a protected liberty. Thus, while some people might disagree about whether or not the flag should be saluted, or disagree about the proposition that it may not be defiled, we have ruled that a State may not compel or enforce one view or the other. See *West Virginia State Bd. of Education* v. *Barnette*, 319 U.S. 624 (1943); *Texas* v. *Johnson*, 491 U.S. 397 (1989).

Our law affords constitutional protection to personal decisions relating to marriage, procreation, contraception, family relationships, child rearing, and education. *Carey* v. *Population Services International*, 431 U.S., at 685. Our cases recognize "the right of the *individual*, married or single, to be free from unwarranted governmental intrusion into matters so fundamentally affecting a person as the decision whether to bear or beget a child." *Eisenstadt* v. *Baird, supra*, at 453 (emphasis in original). Our precedents "have respected the private realm of family life which the state cannot enter." *Prince* v. *Massachusetts*, 321 U.S. 158, 166 (1944). These matters, involving the most intimate and personal choices a person may make in a lifetime, choices central to personal dignity and autonomy, are *central* to the liberty protected by the Fourteenth Amendment. At the heart of liberty is the right to define one's own concept of existence, of meaning, of the universe, and of the mystery of human life. Beliefs about these matters could not define the attributes of personhood were they formed under compulsion of the State.

These considerations begin our analysis of the woman's interest in terminating her pregnancy but cannot end it, for this reason: though the abortion decision may originate within the zone of conscience and belief, it is more than a philosophic exercise. Abortion is a unique act. It is an act fraught with consequences for others: for the woman who must live with the implications of her decision; for the persons who perform and assist in the procedure; for the spouse, family, and society which must confront the knowledge that these procedures

exist, procedures some deem nothing short of an act of violence against innocent human life; and, depending on one's
beliefs, for the life or potential life that is aborted. Though
abortion is conduct, it does not follow that the State is entitled
to proscribe it in all instances. That is because the liberty of
the woman is at stake in a sense unique to the human condition
and so unique to the law. The mother who carries a child to
full term is subject to anxieties, to physical constraints, to
pain that only she must bear. That these sacrifices have from
the beginning of the human race been endured by woman
with a pride that ennobles her in the eyes of others and gives
to the infant a bond of love cannot alone be grounds for the
State to insist she make the sacrifice. Her suffering is too
intimate and personal for the State to insist, without more,
upon its own vision of the woman's role, however dominant
that vision has been in the course of our history and our
culture. The destiny of the woman must be shaped to a large
extent on her own conception of her spiritual imperatives and
her place in society.

It should be recognized, moreover, that in some critical
respects the abortion decision is of the same character as the
decision to use contraception, to which *Griswold* v. *Connecticut*, *Eisenstadt* v. *Baird*, and *Carey* v. *Population Services International*, afford constitutional protection. We have no doubt
as to the correctness of those decisions. They support the
reasoning in *Roe* relating to the woman's liberty because they
involve personal decisions concerning not only the meaning
of procreation but also human responsibility and respect for
it. As with abortion, reasonable people will have differences
of opinion about these matters. One view is based on such
reverence for the wonder of creation that any pregnancy ought
to be welcomed and carried to full term no matter how difficult
it will be to provide for the child and ensure its well-being.
Another is that the inability to provide for the nurture and
care of the infant is a cruelty to the child and an anguish to
the parent. These are intimate views with infinite variations,
and their deep, personal character underlay our decisions in
Griswold, *Eisenstadt*, and *Carey*. The same concerns are present
when the woman confronts the reality that, perhaps despite
her attempts to avoid it, she has become pregnant.

It was this dimension of personal liberty that *Roe* sought to protect, and its holding invoked the reasoning and the tradition of the precedents we have discussed, granting protection to substantive liberties of the person. *Roe* was, of course, an extension of those cases and, as the decision itself indicated, the separate States could act in some degree to further their own legitimate interests in protecting pre-natal life. The extent to which the legislatures of the States might act to outweigh the interests of the woman in choosing to terminate her pregnancy was a subject of debate both in *Roe* itself and in decisions following it.

While we appreciate the weight of the arguments made on behalf of the State in the case before us, arguments which in their ultimate formulation conclude that *Roe* should be overruled, the reservations any of us may have in reaffirming the central holding of *Roe* are outweighed by the explication of individual liberty we have given combined with the force of *stare decisis*. We turn now to that doctrine.

III

A

The obligation to follow precedent begins with necessity, and a contrary necessity marks its outer limit. With Cardozo, we recognize that no judicial system could do society's work if it eyed each issue afresh in every case that raised it. See B. Cardozo, The Nature of the Judicial Process 149 (1921). Indeed, the very concept of the rule of law underlying our own Constitution requires such continuity over time that a respect for precedent is, by definition, indispensable. See Powell, Stare Decisis and Judicial Restraint, 1991 Journal of Supreme Court History 13, 16. At the other extreme, a different necessity would make itself felt if a prior judicial ruling should come to be seen so clearly as error that its enforcement was for that very reason doomed.

Even when the decision to overrule a prior case is not, as in the rare, latter instance, virtually foreordained, it is common wisdom that the rule of *stare decisis* is not an "inexorable command," and certainly it is not such in every constitutional case, see *Burnet v. Coronado Oil Gas Co.*, 285 U.S. 393, 405–

411 (1932) (Brandeis, J., dissenting). See also *Payne v. Tennessee*, 501 U.S. ____, ____(1991) (slip op., at ____) (SOUTER, J., joined by KENNEDY, J., concurring); *Arizona v. Rumsey*, 467 U.S. 203, 212 (1984). Rather, when this Court reexamines a prior holding, its judgment is customarily informed by a series of prudential and pragmatic considerations designed to test the consistency of overruling a prior decision with the ideal of the rule of law, and to gauge the respective costs of reaffirming and overruling a prior case. Thus, for example, we may ask whether the rule has proved to be intolerable simply in defying practical workability, *Swift & Co. v. Wickham*, 382 U.S. 111, 116 (1965); whether the rule is subject to a kind of reliance that would lend a special hardship to the consequences of overruling and add inequity to the cost of repudiation, *e.g.*, *United States v. Title Ins. & Trust Co.*, 265 U.S. 472, 486 (1924); whether related principles of law have so far developed as to have left the old rule no more than a remnant of abandoned doctrine, see *Patterson v. McLean Credit Union*, 491 U.S. 164, 173–174 (1989); or whether facts have so changed or come to be seen so differently, as to have robbed the old rule of significant application or justification, *e.g.*, *Burnet, supra*, at 412 (Brandeis, J., dissenting).

So in this case we may inquire whether *Roe*'s central rule has been found unworkable; whether the rule's limitation on state power could be removed without serious inequity to those who have relied upon it or significant damage to the stability of the society governed by the rule in question; whether the law's growth in the intervening years has left *Roe*'s central rule a doctrinal anachronism discounted by society; and whether *Roe*'s premises of fact have so far changed in the ensuing two decades as to render its central holding somehow irrelevant or unjustifiable in dealing with the issue it addressed.

1

Although *Roe* has engendered opposition, it has in no sense proven "unworkable," see *Garcia v. San Antonio Metropolitan Transit Authority*, 469 U.S. 528, 546 (1985), representing as it does a simple limitation beyond which a state law is unenforceable. While *Roe* has, of course, required judicial assessment of state laws affecting the exercise of the choice guaranteed against government infringement, and although the need for such review will remain as a consequence of today's decision, the required determinations fall within judicial competence.

2

The inquiry into reliance counts the cost of a rule's repudiation as it would fall on those who have relied reasonably on the rule's continued application. Since the classic case for weighing reliance heavily in favor of following the earlier rule occurs in the commercial context, see *Payne v. Tennessee, supra*, at ____(slip op., at ____), where advance planning of great precision is most obviously a necessity, it is no cause for surprise that some would find no reliance worthy of consideration in support of *Roe*.

While neither respondents nor their *amici* in so many words deny that the abortion right invites some reliance prior to its actual exercise, one can readily imagine an argument stressing the dissimilarity of this case to one involving property or contract. Abortion is customarily chosen as an unplanned response to the consequence of unplanned activity or to the failure of conventional birth control, and except on the assumption that no intercourse would have occurred but for *Roe*'s holding, such behavior may appear to justify no reliance claim. Even if reliance could be claimed on that unrealistic assumption, the argument might run, any reliance interest would be de minimis. This argument would be premised on the hypothesis that reproductive planning could take virtually immediate account of any sudden restoration of state authority to ban abortions.

To eliminate the issue of reliance that easily, however, one would need to limit cognizable reliance to specific instances of sexual activity. But to do this would be simply to refuse to face the fact that for two decades of economic and social developments, people have organized intimate relationships and made choices that define their views of themselves and their places in society, in reliance on the availability of abortion in the event that contraception should fail. The ability of women to participate equally in the economic and social life of the Nation has been facilitated by their ability to control their reproductive lives. See, e.g., R. Petchesky, Abortion and Woman's Choice 109, 133, n. 7 (rev. ed. 1990). The Constitution serves human values, and while the effect of reliance on Roe cannot be exactly measured, neither can the certain cost of overruling Roe for people who have ordered their thinking and living around that case be dismissed.

3

No evolution of legal principle has left Roe's doctrinal footings weaker than they were in 1973. No development of constitutional law since the case was decided has implicitly or explicitly left Roe behind as a mere survivor of obsolete constitutional thinking.

It will be recognized, of course, that Roe stands at an intersection of two lines of decisions, but in whichever doctrinal category one reads the case, the result for present purposes will be the same. The Roe Court itself placed its holding in the succession of cases most prominently exemplified by Griswold v. Connecticut, 381 U.S. 479 (1965), see Roe, 410 U.S., at 152–153. When it is so seen, Roe is clearly in no jeopardy, since subsequent constitutional developments have neither disturbed, nor do they threaten to diminish, the scope of recognized protection accorded to the liberty relating to intimate relationships, the family, and decisions about whether or not to beget or bear a child. See, e.g., Carey v. Population Services International, 431 U.S. 678 (1977); Moore v. East Cleveland, 431 U.S. 678 (1977).

Roe, however, may be seen not only as an exemplar of Griswold liberty but as a rule (whether or not mistaken) of personal autonomy and bodily integrity, with doctrinal affinity to cases recognizing limits on governmental power to mandate medical treatment or to bar its rejection. If so, our cases since Roe accord with Roe's view that a State's interest in the protection of life falls short of justifying any plenary override of individual liberty claims. Cruzan v. Director, Missouri Dept. of Health, 497 U.S. 261, 278 (1990); Cf., e.g., Riggins v. Nevada,

504 U.S. ____, ____(1992) (slip. op., at 7); *Washington* v. *Harper*, 494 U.S.210 (1990); see also, *e.g.*, *Rochin* v. *California*, 342 U.S. 165 (1952); *Jacobson* v. *Massachusetts*, 197 U.S. 11, 24–30 (1905).

Finally, one could classify *Roe* as *sui generis*. If the case is so viewed, then there clearly has been no erosion of its central determination. The original holding resting on the concurrence of seven Members of the Court in 1973 was expressly affirmed by a majority of six in 1983, see *Akron* v. *Akron Center for Reproductive Health, Inc.*, 462 U.S. 416 (1983) (*Akron I*), and by a majority of five in 1986, see *Thornburgh* v. *American College of Obstetricians and Gynecologists*, 476 U.S. 747 (1986), expressing adherence to the constitutional ruling despite legislative efforts in some States to test its limits. More recently, in *Webster* v. *Reproductive Health Services*, 492 U.S. 490 (1989), although two of the present authors questioned the trimester framework in a way consistent with our judgment today, see *id.*, at 518 (REHNQUIST, C. J., joined by WHITE, and KENNEDY, JJ.); *id.*, at 529 (O'CONNOR, J., concurring in part and concurring in judgment), a majority of the Court either decided to reaffirm or declined to address the constitutional validity of the central holding of *Roe*. See *Webster*, 492 U.S., at 521 (REHNQUIST, C. J., joined by WHITE and KENNEDY, JJ.); *id.*, at 525–526 (O'CONNOR, J., concurring in part and concurring in judgment); *id.*, at 537, 553 (BLACK-MUN, J., joined by Brennan and Marshall, JJ., concurring in part and dissenting in part); *id.*, at 561–563 (STEVENS, J., concurring in part and dissenting in part).

Nor will courts building upon *Roe* be likely to hand down erroneous decisions as a consequence. Even on the assumption that the central holding of *Roe* was in error, that error would go only to the strength of the state interest in fetal protection, not to the recognition afforded by the Constitution to the woman's liberty. The latter aspect of the decision fits comfortably within the framework of the Court's prior decisions including *Skinner* v. *Oklahoma ex rel. Williamson*, 316 U.S. 535 (1942), *Griswold*, *supra*, *Loving* v. *Virginia*, 388 U.S. 1 (1967), and *Eisenstadt* v. *Baird*, 405 U.S. 438 (1972), the holdings of which are "not a series of isolated points," but mark a "rational continuum." *Poe* v. *Ullman*, 367 U.S., at 543 (1961) (Harlan, J., dissenting). As we described in *Carey* v.

Population Services International, supra, the liberty which encompasses those decisions

> "includes 'the interest in independence in making certain
> kinds of important decisions.' While the outer limits of this
> aspect of [protected liberty] have not been marked by the
> Court, it is clear that among the decisions that an individual
> may make without unjustified government interference are
> personal decisions 'relating to marriage, procreation, contra-
> ception, family relationships, and child rearing and educa-
> tion.' " *Id.*, at 684–685 (citations omitted).

The soundness of this prong of the *Roe* analysis is apparent
from a consideration of the alternative. If indeed the woman's
interest in deciding whether to bear and beget a child had not
been recognized as in *Roe*, the State might as readily restrict
a woman's right to choose to carry a pregnancy to term as to
terminate it, to further asserted state interests in population
control, or eugenics, for example. Yet *Roe* has been sensibly
relied upon to counter any such suggestions. *E.g.*, *Arnold v.
Board of Education of Escambia County, Ala.*, 880 F. 2d 305,
311 (CA11 1989) (relying upon *Roe* and concluding that
government officials violate the Constitution by coercing a
minor to have an abortion); *Avery v. County of Burke*, 660
F. 2d 111, 115 (CA4 1981) (county agency inducing teenage
girl to undergo unwanted sterilization on the basis of misrep-
resentation that she had sickle cell trait); see also *In re Quinlan*, 70 N.J. 10, 355 A. 2d 647, *cert. denied sub nom. Garger v.
New Jersey*, 429 U.S. 922 (1976) (relying on *Roe* in finding
a right to terminate medical treatment). In any event, because
Roe's scope is confined by the fact of its concern with post-
conception potential life, a concern otherwise likely to be
implicated only by some forms of contraception protected independently under *Griswold* and later cases, any error in *Roe*
is unlikely to have serious ramifications in future cases.

4

We have seen how time has overtaken some of *Roe's* factual
assumptions: advances in maternal health care allow for abortions safe to the mother later in pregnancy than was true in

1973, see *Akron I, supra,* at 429, n. 11, and advances in neonatal care have advanced viability to a point somewhat earlier. Compare *Roe,* 410 U.S., at 160, with *Webster, supra,* at 515–516 (opinion of REHNQUIST, C.J.); see *Akron I, supra,* at 457, and n. 5 (O'CONNOR, J., dissenting). But these facts go only to the scheme of time limits on the realization of competing interests, and the divergences from the factual premises of 1973 have no bearing on the validity of *Roe's* central holding, that viability marks the earliest point at which the State's interest in fetal life is constitutionally adequate to justify a legislative ban on nontherapeutic abortions. The soundness or unsoundness of that constitutional judgment in no sense turns on whether viability occurs at approximately 28 weeks, as was usual at the time of *Roe,* at 23 to 24 weeks, as it sometimes does today, or at some moment even slightly earlier in pregnancy, as it may if fetal respiratory capacity can somehow be enhanced in the future. Whenever it may occur, the attainment of viability may continue to serve as the critical fact, just as it has done since *Roe* was decided; which is to say that no change in *Roe's* factual underpinning has left its central holding obsolete, and none supports an argument for over-ruling it.

5

The sum of the precedential inquiry to this point shows *Roe's* underpinnings unweakened in any way affecting its central holding. While it has engendered disapproval, it has not been unworkable. An entire generation has come of age free to assume *Roe's* concept of liberty in defining the capacity of women to act in society, and to make reproductive decisions; no erosion of principle going to liberty or personal autonomy has left *Roe's* central holding a doctrinal remnant; *Roe* portends no developments at odds with other precedent for the analysis of personal liberty; and no changes of fact have rendered viability more or less appropriate as the point at which the balance of interests tips. Within the bounds of normal *stare decisis* analysis, then, and subject to the considerations on which it customarily turns, the stronger argument is for affirming *Roe's* central holding, with whatever degree of personal reluctance any of us may have, not for overruling it.

B

In a less significant case, *stare decisis* analysis could, and would, stop at the point we have reached. But the sustained and widespread debate *Roe* has provoked calls for some comparison between that case and others of comparable dimension that have responded to national controversies and taken on the impress of the controversies addressed. Only two such decisional lines from the past century present themselves for examination, and in each instance the result reached by the Court accorded with the principles we apply today.

The first example is that line of cases identified with *Lochner* v. *New York*, 198 U.S. 45 (1905), which imposed substantive limitations on legislation limiting economic autonomy in favor of health and welfare regulation, adopting, in Justice Holmes' view, the theory of *laissez-faire*. *Id.*, at 75 (Holmes, J., dissenting). The *Lochner* decisions were exemplified by *Adkins* v. *Children's Hospital of D.C.*, 261 U.S. 525 (1923), in which this Court held it to be an infringement of constitutionally protected liberty of contract to require the employers of adult women to satisfy minimum wage standards. Fourteen years later, *West Coast Hotel Co.* v. *Parrish*, 300 U.S. 379 (1937), signalled the demise of *Lochner* by overruling *Adkins*. In the meantime, the Depression had come and, with it, the lesson that seemed unmistakable to most people by 1937, that the interpretation of contractual freedom protected in *Adkins* rested on fundamentally false factual assumptions about the capacity of a relatively unregulated market to satisfy minimal levels of human welfare. See *West Coast Hotel Co.*, *supra*, at 399. As Justice Jackson wrote of the constitutional crisis of 1937 shortly before he came on the bench, "The older world of *laissez faire* was recognized everywhere outside the Court to be dead." R. Jackson, The Struggle for Judicial Supremacy 85 (1941). The facts upon which the earlier case had premised a constitutional resolution of social controversy had proved to be untrue, and history's demonstration of their untruth not only justified but required the new choice of constitutional principle that *West Coast Hotel* announced. Of course, it was true that the Court lost something by its misperception, or its lack of prescience, and the Court-packing crisis only magnified the loss; but the clear demonstration that the facts of economic life were different from those previously assumed warranted the repudiation of the old law.

The second comparison that 20th century history invites is with the cases employing the separate-but-equal rule for applying the Fourteenth Amendment's equal protection guarantee. They began with *Plessy v. Ferguson*, 163 U.S. 537 (1896), holding that legislatively mandated racial segregation in public transportation works no denial of equal protection, rejecting the argument that racial separation enforced by the legal machinery of American society treats the black race as inferior. The *Plessy* Court considered "the underlying fallacy of the plaintiff's argument to consist in the assumption that the enforced separation of the two races stamps the colored race with a badge of inferiority. If this be so, it is not by reason of anything found in the act, but solely because the colored race chooses to put that construction upon it." *Id.*, at 551. Whether, as a matter of historical fact, the Justices in the *Plessy* majority believed this or not, see *id.*, at 557, 562 (Harlan, J., dissenting), this understanding of the implication of segregation was the stated justification for the Court's opinion. But this understanding of the facts and the rule it was stated to justify were repudiated in *Brown v. Board of Education*, 347 U.S. 483 (1954). As one commentator observed, the question before the Court in Brown was "whether discrimination inheres in that segregation which is imposed by law in the twentieth century in certain specific states in the American Union. And that question has meaning and can find an answer only on the ground of history and of common knowledge about the facts of life in the times and places aforesaid." Black, The Lawfulness of the Segregation Decisions, 69 Yale L. J. 421, 427 (1960).

The Court in *Brown* addressed these facts of life by observing that whatever may have been the understanding in *Plessy*'s time of the power of segregation to stigmatize those who were segregated with a "badge of inferiority," it was clear by 1954 that legally sanctioned segregation had just such an effect, to the point that racially separate public educational facilities were deemed inherently unequal. 374 U.S., at 494–495. Society's understanding of the facts upon which a constitutional ruling was sought in 1954 was thus fundamentally different from the basis claimed for the decision in 1896. While we think *Plessy* was wrong the day it was decided, see *Plessy*, *supra*, at 552–564 (Harlan, J., dissenting), we must also recognize that the *Plessy* Court's explanation for its decision was so clearly at odds with the facts apparent to the Court in 1954 that the decision to reexamine *Plessy* was on this ground alone not only justified but required.

West Coast Hotel and *Brown* each rested on facts, or an understanding of facts, changed from those which furnished the claimed justifications for the earlier constitutional resolutions. Each case was comprehensible as the Court's response to facts that the country could understand, or had come to understand already, but which the Court of an earlier day, as its own declarations disclosed, had not been able to perceive. As the decisions were thus comprehensible they were also defensible, not merely as the victories of one doctrinal school over another by dint of numbers (victories though they were), but as applications of constitutional principle to facts as they had not been seen by the Court before. In constitutional adjudication as elsewhere in life, changed circumstances may impose new obligations, and the thoughtful part of the Nation could accept each decision to overrule a prior case as a response to the Court's constitutional duty.

Because the case before us presents no such occasion it could be seen as no such response. Because neither the factual underpinnings of *Roe*'s central holding nor our understanding of it has changed (and because no other indication of weakened precedent has been shown) the Court could not pretend to be reexamining the prior law with any justification beyond a present doctrinal disposition to come out differently from the Court of 1973. To overrule prior law for no other reason than that would run counter to the view repeated in our cases, that a decision to overrule should rest on some special reason over and above the belief that a prior case was wrongly decided. See, *e.g.*, *Mitchell* v. *W.T. Grant*, 416 U.S. 600, 636 (1974) (Stewart, J., dissenting) ("A basic change in the law upon a ground no firmer than a change in our membership invites the popular misconception that this institution is little different from the two political branches of the Government. No misconception could do more lasting injury to this Court and to the system of law which it is our abiding mission to serve"); *Mapp* v. *Ohio*, 367 U.S. 643, 677 (1961) (Harlan, J., dissenting).

C

The examination of the conditions justifying the repudiation of *Adkins* by *West Coast Hotel* and *Plessy* by *Brown* is enough to suggest the terrible price that would have been paid if the Court had not overruled as it did. In the present case, however, as our analysis to this point makes clear, the terrible price would be paid for overruling. Our analysis would not be complete, however, without explaining why overruling *Roe's* central holding would not only reach an unjustifiable result under principles of *stare decisis*, but would seriously weaken the Court's capacity to exercise the judicial power and to function as the Supreme Court of a Nation dedicated to the rule of law. To understand why this would be so it is necessary to understand the source of this Court's authority, the conditions necessary for its preservation, and its relationship to the country's understanding of itself as a constitutional Republic.

The root of American governmental power is revealed most clearly in the instance of the power conferred by the Constitution upon the Judiciary of the United States and specifically upon this Court. As Americans of each succeeding generation are rightly told, the Court cannot buy support for its decisions by spending money and, except to a minor degree, it cannot independently coerce obedience to its decrees. The Court's power lies, rather, in its legitimacy, a product of substance and perception that shows itself in the people's acceptance of the Judiciary as fit to determine what the Nation's law means and to declare what it demands.

The underlying substance of this legitimacy is of course the warrant for the Court's decisions in the Constitution and the lesser sources of legal principle on which the Court draws.

That substance is expressed in the Court's opinions, and our contemporary understanding is such that a decision without principled justification would be no judicial act at all. But even when justification is furnished by apposite legal principle, something more is required. Because not every conscientious claim of principled justification will be accepted as such, the justification claimed must be beyond dispute. The Court must take care to speak and act in ways that allow people to accept its decisions on the terms the Court claims for them, as grounded truly in principle, not as compromises with social and political pressures having, as such, no bearing on the principled choices that the Court is obliged to make. Thus, the Court's legitimacy depends on making legally principled decisions under circumstances in which their principled character is sufficiently plausible to be accepted by the Nation.

The need for principled action to be perceived as such is implicated to some degree whenever this, or any other appellate court, overrules a prior case. This is not to say, of course, that this Court cannot give a perfectly satisfactory explanation in most cases. People understand that some of the Constitution's language is hard to fathom and that the Court's Justices are sometimes able to perceive significant facts or to understand principles of law that eluded their predecessors and that justify departures from existing decisions. However upsetting it may be to those most directly affected when one judicially derived rule replaces another, the country can accept some correction of error without necessarily questioning the legitimacy of the Court.

In two circumstances, however, the Court would almost certainly fail to receive the benefit of the doubt in overruling prior cases. There is, first, a point beyond which frequent overruling would overtax the country's belief in the Court's good faith. Despite the variety of reasons that may inform and justify a decision to overrule, we cannot forget that such a decision is usually perceived (and perceived correctly) as, at the least, a statement that a prior decision was wrong. There is a limit to the amount of error that can plausibly be imputed to prior courts. If that limit should be exceeded, disturbance of prior rulings would be taken as evidence that justifiable reexamination of principle had given way to drives for particular results in the short term. The legitimacy of the Court would fade with the frequency of its vacillation.

That first circumstance can be described as hypothetical; the second is to the point here and now. Where, in the performance of its judicial duties, the Court decides a case in such a way as to resolve the sort of intensely divisive controversy reflected in *Roe* and those rare, comparable cases, its decision has a dimension that the resolution of the normal case does not carry. It is the dimension present whenever the Court's interpretation of the Constitution calls the contending sides of a national controversy to end their national division by accepting a common mandate rooted in the Constitution.

The Court is not asked to do this very often, having thus addressed the Nation only twice in our lifetime, in the decisions of *Brown* and *Roe*. But when the Court does act in this way, its decision requires an equally rare precedential force to counter the inevitable efforts to overturn it and to thwart its implementation. Some of those efforts may be mere unprincipled emotional reactions; others may proceed from principles worthy of profound respect. But whatever the premises of opposition may be, only the most convincing justification under accepted standards of precedent could suffice to demonstrate that a later decision overruling the first was anything but a surrender to political pressure, and an unjustified repudiation of the principle on which the Court staked its authority in the first instance. So to overrule under fire in the absence of the most compelling reason to reexamine a watershed decision would subvert the Court's legitimacy beyond any serious question. Cf. *Brown* v. *Board of Education*, 349 U.S. 294, 300 (1955) (*Brown II*) ("It should go without saying that the vitality of the constitutional principles [announced in *Brown* v. *Board of Education*, 347 U.S. 483 (1954),] cannot be allowed to yield simply because of disagreement with them").

The country's loss of confidence in the judiciary would be underscored by an equally certain and equally reasonable condemnation for another failing in overruling unnecessarily and under pressure. Some cost will be paid by anyone who approves or implements a constitutional decision where it is unpopular, or who refuses to work to undermine the decision or to force its reversal. The price may be criticism or ostracism, or it may be violence. An extra price will be paid by those who themselves disapprove of the decision's results when viewed outside of constitutional terms, but who nevertheless struggle to accept it, because they respect the rule of law. To all those who will be so tested by following, the Court implicitly undertakes to remain steadfast, lest in the end a price be paid for nothing. The promise of constancy, once given, binds its maker for as long as the power to stand by the decision survives and the understanding of the issue has not changed so fundamentally as to render the commitment obsolete. From the obligation of this promise this Court cannot and should not assume any exemption when duty requires it to decide a case in conformance with the Constitution. A willing breach of it would be nothing less than a breach of faith, and no Court that broke its faith with the people could sensibly expect credit for principle in the decision by which it did that.

It is true that diminished legitimacy may be restored, but only slowly. Unlike the political branches, a Court thus weakened could not seek to regain its position with a new mandate from the voters, and even if the Court could somehow go to the polls, the loss of its principled character could not be retrieved by the casting of so many votes. Like the character of an individual, the legitimacy of the Court must be earned over time. So, indeed, must be the character of a Nation of people who aspire to live according to the rule of law. Their belief in themselves as such a people is not readily separable from their understanding of the Court invested with the authority to decide their constitutional cases and speak before all others for their constitutional ideals. If the Court's legitimacy should be undermined, then, so would the country be in its very ability to see itself through its constitutional ideals. The Court's concern with legitimacy is not for the sake of the Court but for the sake of the Nation to which it is responsible.

The Court's duty in the present case is clear. In 1973, it confronted the already-divisive issue of governmental power to limit personal choice to undergo abortion, for which it provided a new resolution based on the due process guaranteed by the Fourteenth Amendment. Whether or not a new social consensus is developing on that issue, its divisiveness is no less today than in 1973, and pressure to overrule the decision, like pressure to retain it, has grown only more intense. A decision to overrule *Roe*'s essential holding under the existing circumstances would address error, if error there was, at the cost of both profound and unnecessary damage to the Court's legitimacy, and to the Nation's commitment to the rule of law. It is therefore imperative to adhere to the essence of *Roe*'s original decision, and we do so today.

IV

From what we have said so far it follows that it is a constitutional liberty of the woman to have some freedom to terminate her pregnancy. We conclude that the basic decision in *Roe* was based on a constitutional analysis which we cannot now repudiate. The woman's liberty is not so unlimited, however, that from the outset the State cannot show its concern for the life of the unborn, and at a later point in fetal development the State's interest in life has sufficient force so that the right of the woman to terminate the pregnancy can be restricted.

That brings us, of course, to the point where much criticism has been directed at *Roe*, a criticism that always inheres when the Court draws a specific rule from what in the Constitution is but a general standard. We conclude, however, that the urgent claims of the woman to retain the ultimate control over her destiny and her body, claims implicit in the meaning of liberty, require us to perform that function. Liberty must not be extinguished for want of a line that is clear. And it falls to us to give some real substance to the woman's liberty to determine whether to carry her pregnancy to full term.

We conclude the line should be drawn at viability, so that before that time the woman has a right to choose to terminate her pregnancy. We adhere to this principle for two reasons. First, as we have said, is the doctrine of *stare decisis*. Any judicial act of line-drawing may seem somewhat arbitrary, but *Roe* was a reasoned statement, elaborated with great care. We have twice reaffirmed it in the face of great opposition. See *Thornburgh* v. *American College of Obstetricians and Gynecologists*, 476 U.S., at 759; *Akron I*, 462 U.S., at 419–420.

Although we must overrule those parts of *Thornburgh* and *Akron I* which, in our view, are inconsistent with *Roe*'s statement that the State has a legitimate interest in promoting the life or potential life of the unborn, see *infra*, at [375], the central premise of those cases represents an unbroken commitment by this Court to the essential holding of *Roe*. It is that premise which we reaffirm today.

The second reason is that the concept of viability, as we noted in *Roe*, is the time at which there is a realistic possibility of maintaining and nourishing a life outside the womb, so that the independent existence of the second life can in reason and all fairness be the object of state protection that now overrides the rights of the woman. See *Roe v. Wade*, 410 U.S., at 163. Consistent with other constitutional norms, legislatures may draw lines which appear arbitrary without the necessity of offering a justification. But courts may not. We must justify the lines we draw. And there is no line other than viability which is more workable. To be sure, as we have said, there may be some medical developments that affect the precise point of viability, see *supra*, at [356], but this is an imprecision within tolerable limits given that the medical community and all those who must apply its discoveries will continue to explore the matter. The viability line also has, as a practical matter, an element of fairness. In some broad sense it might be said that a woman who fails to act before viability has consented to the State's intervention on behalf of the developing child.

The woman's right to terminate her pregnancy before viability is the most central principle of *Roe v. Wade*. It is a rule of law and a component of liberty we cannot renounce.

On the other side of the equation is the interest of the State in the protection of potential life. The *Roe* Court recognized the State's "important and legitimate interest in protecting the potentiality of human life." *Roe, supra*, at 162. The weight to be given this state interest, not the strength of the woman's interest, was the difficult question faced in *Roe*. We do not need to say whether each of us, had we been Members of the Court when the valuation of the State interest came before it as an original matter, would have concluded, as the *Roe* Court did, that its weight is insufficient to justify a ban on abortions prior to viability even when it is subject to certain exceptions. The matter is not before us in the first instance, and coming as it does after nearly 20 years of litigation in *Roe*'s wake we are satisfied that the immediate question is not the soundness of *Roe*'s resolution of the issue, but the precedential force that must be accorded to its holding. And we have concluded that the essential holding of *Roe* should be reaffirmed.

Yet it must be remembered that *Roe v. Wade* speaks with clarity in establishing not only the woman's liberty but also the State's "important and legitimate interest in potential life." *Roe, supra*, at 163. That portion of the decision in *Roe* has been given too little acknowledgement and implementation by the Court in its subsequent cases. Those cases decided that any regulation touching upon the abortion decision must survive strict scrutiny, to be sustained only if drawn in narrow terms to further a compelling state interest. See, *e.g.*, *Akron I, supra*, at 427. Not all of the cases decided under that formulation can be reconciled with the holding in *Roe* itself that the State has legitimate interests in the health of the woman and in protecting the potential life within her. In resolving this tension, we choose to rely upon *Roe*, as against the later cases.

Roe established a trimester framework to govern abortion regulations. Under this elaborate but rigid construct, almost no regulation at all is permitted during the first trimester of pregnancy; regulations designed to protect the woman's health, but not to further the State's interest in potential life, are permitted during the second trimester; and during the third trimester, when the fetus is viable, prohibitions are permitted provided the life or health of the mother is not at stake. *Roe v. Wade, supra*, at 163–166. Most of our cases since *Roe* have involved the application of rules derived from the trimester framework. See, *e.g.*, *Thornburgh v. American College of Obstetricians and Gynecologists, supra; Akron I, supra*.

The trimester framework no doubt was erected to ensure that the woman's right to choose not become so subordinate to the State's interest in promoting fetal life that her choice exists in theory but not in fact. We do not agree, however, that the trimester approach is necessary to accomplish this objective. A framework of this rigidity was unnecessary and in its later interpretation sometimes contradicted the State's permissible exercise of its powers.

Though the woman has a right to choose to terminate or continue her pregnancy before viability, it does not at all follow that the State is prohibited from taking steps to ensure that this choice is thoughtful and informed. Even in the earliest stages of pregnancy, the State may enact rules and regulations designed to encourage her to know that there are philosophic and social arguments of great weight that can be brought to bear in favor of continuing the pregnancy to full term and that there are procedures and institutions to allow adoption of unwanted children as well as a certain degree of state assistance if the mother chooses to raise the child herself. " '[T]he Constitution does not forbid a State or city, pursuant to democratic processes, from expressing a preference for normal childbirth.' " *Webster* v. *Reproductive Health Services*, 492 U.S., at 511 (opinion of the Court) (quoting *Poelker* v. *Doe*, 432 U.S. 519, 521 (1977)). It follows that States are free to enact laws to provide a reasonable framework for a woman to make a decision that has such profound and lasting meaning. This, too, we find consistent with *Roe*'s central premises, and indeed the inevitable consequence of our holding that the State has an interest in protecting the life of the unborn.

We reject the trimester framework, which we do not consider to be part of the essential holding of *Roe*. See *Webster* v. *Reproductive Health Services, supra*, at 518 (opinion of REHNQUIST, C. J.); *id.*, at 529 (O'CONNOR, J., concurring in part and concurring in judgment) (describing the trimester framework as "problematic"). Measures aimed at ensuring that a woman's choice contemplates the consequences for the fetus do not necessarily interfere with the right recognized in *Roe*, although those measures have been found to be inconsistent with the rigid trimester framework announced in that case. A logical reading of the central holding in *Roe* itself, and a necessary reconciliation of the liberty of the woman and the interest of the State in promoting prenatal life, require, in our view, that we abandon the trimester framework as a rigid prohibition on all previability regulation aimed at the protection of fetal life. The trimester framework suffers from these basic flaws: in its formulation it misconceives the nature of the pregnant woman's interest; and in practice it undervalues the State's interest in potential life, as recognized in *Roe*.

As our jurisprudence relating to all liberties save perhaps abortion has recognized, not every law which makes a right more difficult to exercise is, *ipso facto*, an infringement of that right. An example clarifies the point. We have held that not every ballot access limitation amounts to an infringement of the right to vote. Rather, the States are granted substantial flexibility in establishing the framework within which voters choose the candidates for whom they wish to vote. *Anderson* v. *Celebrezze*, 460 U.S. 780, 788 (1983); *Norman* v. *Reed*, 502 U.S. ____(1992).

The abortion right is similar. Numerous forms of state regulation might have the incidental effect of increasing the cost or decreasing the availability of medical care, whether for abortion or any other medical procedure. The fact that a law which serves a valid purpose, one not designed to strike at the right itself, has the incidental effect of making it more difficult or more expensive to procure an abortion cannot be enough to invalidate it. Only where state regulation imposes an undue burden on a woman's ability to make this decision does the power of the State reach into the heart of the liberty protected by the Due Process Clause. See *Hodgson* v. *Minnesota*, 497 U.S. 417, 458–459 (1990) (O'CONNOR, J., concurring in part and concurring in judgment in part); *Ohio* v. *Akron Center for Reproductive Health*, 497 U.S. 502, (1990) (*Akron II*) (opinion of KENNEDY, J.); *Webster* v. *Reproductive Health Services, supra*, at 530 (O'CONNOR, J., concurring in part and concurring in judgment); *Thornburgh* v. *American College of Obstetricians and Gynecologists*, 476 U.S., at 828 (O'CONNOR, J., dissenting); *Simopoulos* v. *Virginia*, 462 U.S. 506, 520 (1983) (O'CONNOR, J., concurring in part and concurring in judgment); *Planned Parenthood Assn. of Kansas City* v. *Ashcroft*, 462 U.S. 476, 505 (1983) (O'CONNOR, J., concurring in judgment in part and dissenting in part); *Akron I*, 462 U.S., at 464 (O'CONNOR, J., joined by WHITE and REHNQUIST, JJ., dissenting); *Bellotti* v. *Baird*, 428 U.S. 132, 147 (1976) (*Bellotti I*).

For the most part, the Court's early abortion cases adhered to this view. In *Maher* v. *Roe*, 432 U.S. 464, 473–474 (1977), the Court explained: "*Roe* did not declare an unqualified 'constitutional right to an abortion,' as the District Court seemed to think. Rather, the right protects the woman from unduly burdensome interference with her freedom to decide whether to terminate her pregnancy." See also *Doe v. Bolton*, 410 U.S. 179, 198 (1973) ("[T]he interposition of the hospital abortion committee is unduly restrictive of the patient's rights"); *Bellotti I, supra*, at 147 (State may not "impose undue burdens upon a minor capable of giving an informed consent"); *Harris v. McRae*, 448 U.S. 297, 314 (1980) (citing *Maher, supra*). Cf. *Carey v. Population Services International*, 431 U.S., at 688 ("[T]he same test must be applied to state regulations that burden an individual's right to decide to prevent conception or terminate pregnancy by substantially limiting access to the means of effectuating that decision as is applied to state statutes that prohibit the decision entirely").

These considerations of the nature of the abortion right illustrate that it is an overstatement to describe it as a right to decide whether to have an abortion "without interference from the State," *Planned Parenthood of Central Mo. v. Danforth*, 428 U.S. 52, 61 (1976). All abortion regulations interfere to some degree with a woman's ability to decide whether to terminate her pregnancy. It is, as a consequence, not surprising that despite the protestations contained in the original *Roe* opinion to the effect that the Court was not recognizing an absolute right, 410 U.S., at 154–155, the Court's experience applying the trimester framework has led to the striking down of some abortion regulations which in no real sense deprived women of the ultimate decision. Those decisions went too far because the right recognized by *Roe* is a right "to be free from unwarranted governmental intrusion into matters so fundamentally affecting a person as the decision whether to bear or beget a child." *Eisenstadt v. Baird*, 405 U.S., at 453. Not all governmental intrusion is of necessity unwarranted; and that brings us to the other basic flaw in the trimester framework: even in *Roe*'s terms, in practice it undervalues the State's interest in the potential life within the woman.

Roe v. Wade was express in its recognition of the State's "important and legitimate interest[s] in preserving and protecting the health of the pregnant woman [and] in protecting the potentiality of human life." 410 U.S., at 162. The trimester framework, however, does not fulfill *Roe's* own promise that the State has an interest in protecting fetal life or potential life. *Roe* began the contradiction by using the trimester framework to forbid any regulation of abortion designed to advance that interest before viability. *Id.*, at 163. Before viability, *Roe* and subsequent cases treat all governmental attempts to influence a woman's decision on behalf of the potential life within her as unwarranted. This treatment is, in our judgment, incompatible with the recognition that there is a substantial state interest in potential life throughout pregnancy. Cf. *Webster*, 492 U.S., at 519 (opinion of REHNQUIST, C. J.); *Akron I, supra*, at 461 (O'CONNOR, J., dissenting).

The very notion that the State has a substantial interest in potential life leads to the conclusion that not all regulations must be deemed unwarranted. Not all burdens on the right to decide whether to terminate a pregnancy will be undue. In our view, the undue burden standard is the appropriate means of reconciling the State's interest with the woman's constitutionally protected liberty.

The concept of an undue burden has been utilized by the Court as well as individual members of the Court, including two of us, in ways that could be considered inconsistent. See, *e.g.*, *Hodgson* v. *Minnesota*, 497 U.S., at [458] (O'CONNOR, J., concurring in part and concurring in judgment); *Akron II*, 497 U.S., at [480] (opinion of KENNEDY, J.); *Thornburgh* v. *American College of Obstetricians and Gynecologists*, 476 U.S., at 828–829 (O'CONNOR, J., dissenting); *Akron I, supra*, at 461–466 (O'CONNOR, J., dissenting); *Harris* v. *McRae, supra*, at 314; *Maher* v. *Roe, supra*, at 473; *Beal* v. *Doe*, 432 U.S. 438, 446 (1977); *Bellotti I, supra*, at 147. Because we set forth a standard of general application to which we intend to adhere, it is important to clarify what is meant by an undue burden.

A finding of an undue burden is a shorthand for the conclusion that a state regulation has the purpose or effect of placing a substantial obstacle in the path of a woman seeking an abortion of a nonviable fetus. A statute with this purpose is invalid because the means chosen by the State to further the interest in potential life must be calculated to inform the woman's free choice, not hinder it. And a statute which, while furthering the interest in potential life or some other valid state interest, has the effect of placing a substantial obstacle in the path of a woman's choice cannot be considered a permissible means of serving its legitimate ends. To the extent that the opinions of the Court or of individual Justices use the undue burden standard in a manner that is inconsistent with this analysis, we set out what in our view should be the controlling standard. Cf. *McCleskey* v. *Zant*, 499 U.S. ____, 1991) (slip op., at 20) (attempting to "define the doctrine of abuse of the writ with more precision" after acknowledging tension among earlier cases). In our considered judgment, an undue burden is an unconstitutional burden. See *Akron II, supra*, at [506] (opinion of KENNEDY, J.). Understood another way, we answer the question, left open in previous opinions discussing the undue burden formulation, whether a law designed to further the State's interest in fetal life which imposes an undue burden on the woman's decision before fetal viability could be constitutional. See, *e.g.*, *Akron I, supra*, at 462–463 (O'CONNOR, J., dissenting). The answer is no.

Some guiding principles should emerge. What is at stake is the woman's right to make the ultimate decision, not a right to be insulated from all others in doing so. Regulations which do no more than create a structural mechanism by which the State, or the parent or guardian of a minor, may express profound respect for the life of the unborn are permitted, if they are not a substantial obstacle to the woman's exercise of the right to choose. See *infra*, at [390–91] (addressing Pennsylvania's parental consent requirement). Unless it has that effect on her right of choice, a state measure designed to persuade her to choose childbirth over abortion will be upheld if reasonably related to that goal. Regulations designed to foster the health of a woman seeking an abortion are valid if they do not constitute an undue burden.

Even when jurists reason from shared premises, some disagreement is inevitable. Compare *Hodgson*, 497 U.S., at [480–501] (opinion of KENNEDY, J.) with *id.*, at [456]–[461] (O'CONNOR, J., concurring in part and concurring in judgment in part). That is to be expected in the application of any legal standard which must accommodate life's complexity. We do not expect it to be otherwise with respect to the undue burden standard. We give this summary:

(a) To protect the central right recognized by *Roe* v. *Wade* while at the same time accommodating the State's profound interest in potential life, we will employ the undue burden analysis as explained in this opinion. An undue burden exists, and therefore a provision of law is invalid, if its purpose or effect is to place a substantial obstacle in the path of a woman seeking an abortion before the fetus attains viability.

(b) We reject the rigid trimester framework of *Roe* v. *Wade*. To promote the State's profound interest in potential life, throughout pregnancy the State may take measures to ensure that the woman's choice is informed, and measures designed to advance this interest will not be invalidated as long as their purpose is to persuade the woman to choose childbirth over abortion. These measures must not be an undue burden on the right.

(c) As with any medical procedure, the State may enact regulations to further the health or safety of a woman seeking an abortion. Unnecessary health regulations that have the purpose or effect of presenting a substantial obstacle to a woman seeking an abortion impose an undue burden on the right.

(d) Our adoption of the undue burden analysis does not disturb the central holding of *Roe* v. *Wade*, and we reaffirm that holding. Regardless of whether exceptions are made for particular circumstances, a State may not prohibit any woman from making the ultimate decision to terminate her pregnancy before viability.

(e) We also reaffirm *Roe*'s holding that "subsequent to viability, the State in promoting its interest in the potentiality of human life may, if it chooses, regulate, and even proscribe, abortion except where it is necessary, in appropriate medical judgment, for the preservation of the life or health of the mother." *Roe* v. *Wade*, 410 U.S., at 164–165.

These principles control our assessment of the Pennsylvania statute, and we now turn to the issue of the validity of its challenged provisions.

V

The Court of Appeals applied what it believed to be the undue burden standard and upheld each of the provisions except for the husband notification requirement. We agree generally with this conclusion, but refine the undue burden analysis in accordance with the principles articulated above. We now consider the separate statutory sections at issue.

A

Because it is central to the operation of various other requirements, we begin with the statute's definition of medical emergency. Under the statute, a medical emergency is

"[t]hat condition which, on the basis of the physician's good faith clinical judgment, so complicates the medical condition of a pregnant woman as to necessitate the immediate abortion of her pregnancy to avert her death or for which a delay will create serious risk of substantial and irreversible impairment of a major bodily function." 18 Pa. Cons. Stat. (1990). § 3203.

Petitioners argue that the definition is too narrow, contending that it forecloses the possibility of an immediate abortion despite some significant health risks. If the contention were correct, we would be required to invalidate the restrictive operation of the provision, for the essential holding of *Roe* forbids a State from interfering with a woman's choice to undergo an abortion procedure if continuing her pregnancy would constitute a threat to her health. 410 U.S., at 164. See also *Harris v. McRae*, 448 U.S., at 316.

The District Court found that there were three serious conditions which would not be covered by the statute: preeclampsia, inevitable abortion, and premature ruptured membrane. 744 F. Supp., at 1378. Yet, as the Court of Appeals observed, 947 F. 2d, at 700–701, it is undisputed that under some circumstances each of these conditions could lead to an illness with substantial and irreversible consequences. While the definition could be interpreted in an unconstitutional manner, the Court of Appeals construed the phrase "serious risk" to include those circumstances. *Id.*, at 701. It stated: "we read the medical emergency exception as intended by the Pennsylvania legislature to assure that compliance with its abortion regulations would not in any way pose a significant threat to the life or health of a woman." *Ibid.* As we said in *Brockett* v. *Spokane Arcades, Inc.*, 472 U.S. 491, 499–500 (1985): "Normally, . . . we defer to the construction of a state statute given it by the lower federal courts." Indeed, we have said that we will defer to lower court interpretations of state law unless they amount to "plain" error. *Palmer* v. *Hoffman*, 318 U.S. 109, 118 (1943). This " 'reflect[s] our belief that district courts and courts of appeals are better schooled in and more able to interpret the laws of their respective States.' " *Frisby* v. *Schultz*, 487 U.S. 474, 482 (1988) (citation omitted). We adhere to that course today, and conclude that, as construed by the Court of Appeals, the medical emergency definition imposes no undue burden on a woman's abortion right.

B

We next consider the informed consent requirement. 18 Pa. Cons. Stat. Ann. § 3205. Except in a medical emergency, the statute requires that at least 24 hours before performing an abortion a physician inform the woman of the nature of the procedure, the health risks of the abortion and of childbirth, and the "probable gestational age of the unborn child." The physician or a qualified nonphysician must inform the woman of the availability of printed materials published by the State describing the fetus and providing information about medical assistance for childbirth, information about child support from the father, and a list of agencies which provide adoption and other services as alternatives to abortion. An abortion may not be performed unless the woman certifies in writing that she has been informed of the availability of these printed materials and has been provided them if she chooses to view them.

Our prior decisions establish that as with any medical procedure, the State may require a woman to give her written informed consent to an abortion. See *Planned Parenthood of Central Mo.* v. *Danforth*, 428 U.S., at 67. In this respect, the statute is unexceptional. Petitioners challenge the statute's definition of informed consent because it includes the provision of specific information by the doctor and the mandatory

24-hour waiting period. The conclusions reached by a majority of the Justices in the separate opinions filed today and the undue burden standard adopted in this opinion require us to overrule in part some of the Court's past decisions, decisions driven by the trimester framework's prohibition of all pre-viability regulations designed to further the State's interest in fetal life.

In *Akron I*, 462 U.S. 416 (1983), we invalidated an ordi-nance which required that a woman seeking an abortion be provided by her physician with specific information "designed to influence the woman's informed choice between abortion or childbirth." *Id.*, at 444. As we later described the *Akron I* holding in *Thornburgh* v. *American College of Obstetricians and Gynecologists*, 476 U.S., at 762, there were two purported flaws in the Akron ordinance: the information was designed to dissuade the woman from having an abortion and the or-dinance imposed "a rigid requirement that a specific body of information be given in all cases, irrespective of the particular needs of the patient . . . ." *Ibid.*

To the extent *Akron I* and *Thornburgh* find a constitutional violation when the government requires, as it does here, the giving of truthful, nonmisleading information about the nature of the procedure, the attendant health risks and those of child-birth, and the "probable gestational age" of the fetus, those cases go too far, are inconsistent with *Roe's* acknowledgment of an important interest in potential life, and are overruled. This is clear even on the very terms of *Akron I* and *Thornburgh*. Those decisions, along with *Danforth*, recognize a substantial government interest justifying a requirement that a woman be apprised of the health risks of abortion and childbirth. *E.g.*, *Danforth*, *supra*, at 66–67. It cannot be questioned that psy-chological well-being is a facet of health. Nor can it be doubted that most women considering an abortion would deem the impact on the fetus relevant, if not dispositive, to the decision. In attempting to ensure that a woman apprehend the full consequences of her decision, the State furthers the legitimate purpose of reducing the risk that a woman may elect an abor-tion, only to discover later, with devastating psychological consequences, that her decision was not fully informed. If the information the State requires to be made available to the woman is truthful and not misleading, the requirement may be permissible.

We also see no reason why the State may not require doctors to inform a woman seeking an abortion of the availability of materials relating to the consequences to the fetus, even when those consequences have no direct relation to her health. An example illustrates the point. We would think it constitutional for the State to require that in order for there to be informed consent to a kidney transplant operation the recipient must be supplied with information about risks to the donor as well as risks to himself or herself. A requirement that the physician make available information similar to that mandated by the statute here was described in *Thornburgh* as "an outright attempt to wedge the Commonwealth's message discouraging abortion into the privacy of the informed-consent dialogue between the woman and her physician." 476 U.S., at 762. We conclude, however, that informed choice need not be defined in such narrow terms that all considerations of the effect on the fetus are made irrelevant. As we have made clear, we depart from the holdings of *Akron I* and *Thornburgh* to the extent that we permit a State to further its legitimate goal of protecting the life of the unborn by enacting legislation aimed at ensuring a decision that is mature and informed, even when in so doing the State expresses a preference for childbirth over abortion. In short, requiring that the woman be informed of the availability of information relating to fetal development and the assistance available should she decide to carry the pregnancy to full term is a reasonable measure to insure an informed choice, one which might cause the woman to choose childbirth over abortion. This requirement cannot be considered a substantial obstacle to obtaining an abortion, and, it follows, there is no undue burden.

Our prior cases also suggest that the "straitjacket," *Thornburgh, supra,* at 762 (quoting *Danforth, supra,* at 67, n. 8), of particular information which must be given in each case interferes with a constitutional right of privacy between a pregnant woman and her physician. As a preliminary matter, it is worth noting that the statute now before us does not require a physician to comply with the informed consent provisions "if he or she can demonstrate by a preponderance of the evidence, that he or she reasonably believed that furnishing the information would have resulted in a severely adverse effect on the physical or mental health of the patient." 18 Pa. Cons. Stat. § 3205 (1990). In this respect, the statute does not prevent the physician from exercising his or her medical judgment.

Whatever constitutional status the doctor-patient relation may have as a general matter, in the present context it is derivative of the woman's position. The doctor-patient relation does not underlie or override the two more general rights under which the abortion right is justified: the right to make family decisions and the right to physical autonomy. On its own, the doctor-patient relation here is entitled to the same solicitude it receives in other contexts. Thus, a requirement that a doctor give a woman certain information as part of obtaining her consent to an abortion is, for constitutional purposes, no different from a requirement that a doctor give certain specific information about any medical procedure.

All that is left of petitioners' argument is an asserted First Amendment right of a physician not to provide information about the risks of abortion, and childbirth, in a manner mandated by the State. To be sure, the physician's First Amendment rights not to speak are implicated, see *Wooley* v. *Maynard*, 430 U.S. 705 (1977), but only as part of the practice of medicine, subject to reasonable licensing and regulation by the State. Cf. *Whalen* v. *Roe*, 429 U.S. 589, 603 (1977). We see no constitutional infirmity in the requirement that the physician provide the information mandated by the State here.

The Pennsylvania statute also requires us to reconsider the holding in *Akron I* that the State may not require that a physician, as opposed to a qualified assistant, provide information relevant to a woman's informed consent. 462 U.S., at 448. Since there is no evidence on this record that requiring a doctor to give the information as provided by the statute would amount in practical terms to a substantial obstacle to a woman seeking an abortion, we conclude that it is not an undue burden. Our cases reflect the fact that the Constitution gives the States broad latitude to decide that particular functions may be performed only by licensed professionals, even if an objective assessment might suggest that those same tasks could be performed by others. See *Williamson* v. *Lee Optical of Oklahoma, Inc.*, 348 U.S. 483 (1955). Thus, we uphold the provision as a reasonable means to insure that the woman's consent is informed.

Our analysis of Pennsylvania's 24-hour waiting period between the provision of the information deemed necessary to informed consent and the performance of an abortion under the undue burden standard requires us to reconsider the premise behind the decision in *Akron I* invalidating a parallel requirement. In *Akron I* we said: "Nor are we convinced that the State's legitimate concern that the woman's decision be informed is reasonably served by requiring a 24-hour delay as a matter of course." 462 U.S., at 450. We consider that conclusion to be wrong. The idea that important decisions will be more informed and deliberate if they follow some period of reflection does not strike us as unreasonable, particularly where the statute directs that important information become part of the background of the decision. The statute, as construed by the Court of Appeals, permits avoidance of the waiting period in the event of a medical emergency and the record evidence shows that in the vast majority of cases, a 24-hour delay does not create any appreciable health risk. In theory, at least, the waiting period is a reasonable measure to implement the State's interest in protecting the life of the unborn, a measure that does not amount to an undue burden.

Whether the mandatory 24-hour waiting period is nonetheless invalid because in practice it is a substantial obstacle to a woman's choice to terminate her pregnancy is a closer question. The findings of fact by the District Court indicate that because of the distances many women must travel to reach an abortion provider, the practical effect will often be a delay of much more than a day because the waiting period requires that a woman seeking an abortion make at least two visits to the doctor. The District Court also found that in many instances this will increase the exposure of women seeking abortions to "the harassment and hostility of anti-abortion protestors demonstrating outside a clinic." 744 F. Supp., at 1351. As a result, the District Court found that for those women who have the fewest financial resources, those who must travel long distances, and those who have difficulty explaining their whereabouts to husbands, employers, or others, the 24-hour waiting period will be "particularly burdensome." *Id.*, at 1352.

These findings are troubling in some respects, but they do not demonstrate that the waiting period constitutes an undue burden. We do not doubt that, as the District Court held, the waiting period has the effect of "increasing the cost and risk of delay of abortions," *id.*, at 1378, but the District Court did not conclude that the increased costs and potential delays amount to substantial obstacles. Rather, applying the trimester framework's strict prohibition of all regulation designed to promote the State's interest in potential life before viability, see *id.*, at 1374, the District Court concluded that the waiting period does not further the state "interest in maternal health" and "infringes the physician's discretion to exercise sound medical judgment." *Id.*, at 1378. Yet, as we have stated, under the undue burden standard a State is permitted to enact persuasive measures which favor childbirth over abortion, even if those measures do not further a health interest. And while the waiting period does limit a physician's discretion, that is not, standing alone, a reason to invalidate it. In light of the construction given the statute's definition of medical emergency by the Court of Appeals, and the District Court's findings, we cannot say that the waiting period imposes a real health risk.

We also disagree with the District Court's conclusion that the "particularly burdensome" effects of the waiting period on some women require its invalidation. A particular burden is not of necessity a substantial obstacle. Whether a burden falls on a particular group is a distinct inquiry from whether it is a substantial obstacle even as to the women in that group. And the District Court did not conclude that the waiting period is such an obstacle even for the women who are most burdened by it. Hence, on the record before us, and in the context of this facial challenge, we are not convinced that the 24-hour waiting period constitutes an undue burden.

We are left with the argument that the various aspects of the informed consent requirement are unconstitutional because they place barriers in the way of abortion on demand. Even the broadest reading of *Roe*, however, has not suggested that there is a constitutional right to abortion on demand. See, *e.g.*, *Doe* v. *Bolton*, 410 U.S., at 189. Rather, the right protected by *Roe* is a right to decide to terminate a pregnancy free of undue interference by the State. Because the informed consent requirement facilitates the wise exercise of that right it cannot be classified as an interference with the right *Roe* protects. The informed consent requirement is not an undue burden on that right.

C

Section 3209 of Pennsylvania's abortion law provides, except in cases of medical emergency, that no physician shall perform an abortion on a married woman without receiving a signed statement from the woman that she has notified her spouse that she is about to undergo an abortion. The woman has the option of providing an alternative signed statement certifying that her husband is not the man who impregnated her; that her husband could not be located; that the pregnancy is the result of spousal sexual assault which she has reported; or that the woman believes that notifying her husband will cause him or someone else to inflict bodily injury upon her. A physician who performs an abortion on a married woman without receiving the appropriate signed statement will have his or her license revoked, and is liable to the husband for damages.

The District Court heard the testimony of numerous expert witnesses, and made detailed findings of fact regarding the effect of this statute. These included:

> "273. The vast majority of women consult their husbands prior to deciding to terminate their pregnancy. . . .

> · · · · ·

> "279. The 'bodily injury' exception could not be invoked by a married woman whose husband, if notified, would, in her reasonable belief, threaten to (a) publicize her intent to have an abortion to family, friends or acquaintances; (b) retaliate against her in future child custody or divorce proceedings; (c) inflict psychological intimidation or emotional harm upon her, her children or other persons; (d) inflict bodily harm on other

persons such as children, family members or other loved ones; or (e) use his control over finances to deprive of necessary monies for herself or her children. . . .

.   .   .   .   .

"281. Studies reveal that family violence occurs in two million families in the United States. This figure, however, is a conservative one that substantially understates (because battering is usually not reported until it reaches life-threatening proportions) the actual number of families affected by domestic violence. In fact, researchers estimate that one of every two women will be battered at some time in their life. . . .

"282. A wife may not elect to notify her husband of her intention to have an abortion for a variety of reasons, including the husband's illness, concern about her own health, the imminent failure of the marriage, or the husband's absolute opposition to the abortion. . . .

"283. The required filing of the spousal consent form would require plaintiff-clinics to change their counseling procedures and force women to reveal their most intimate decision-making on pain of criminal sanctions. The confidentiality of these revelations could not be guaranteed, since the woman's records are not immune from subpoena. . . .

"284. Women of all class levels, educational backgrounds, and racial, ethnic and religious groups are battered. . . .

"285. Wife-battering or abuse can take on many physical and psychological forms. The nature and scope of the battering can cover a broad range of actions and be gruesome and torturous. . . .

"286. Married women, victims of battering, have been killed in Pennsylvania and throughout the United States. . .

"287. Battering can often involve a substantial amount of sexual abuse, including marital rape and sexual mutilation. . . .

"288. In a domestic abuse situation, it is common for the battering husband to also abuse the children in an attempt to coerce the wife. . . .

"289. Mere notification of pregnancy is frequently a flash-point for battering and violence within the family. The number of battering incidents is high during the pregnancy and often the worst abuse can be associated with pregnancy. . . . The battering husband may deny parentage and use the pregnancy as an excuse for abuse. . . .

"290. Secrecy typically shrouds abusive families. Family members are instructed not to tell anyone, especially police or doctors, about the abuse and violence. Battering husbands often threaten their wives or her children with further abuse if she tells an outsider of the violence and tells her that nobody will believe her. A battered woman, therefore, is highly un-likely to disclose the violence against her for fear of retaliation by the abuser. . . .

"291. Even when confronted directly by medical personnel or other helping professionals, battered women often will not admit to the battering because they have not admitted to themselves that they are battered. . . .

"294. A woman in a shelter or a safe house unknown to her husband is not 'reasonably likely' to have bodily harm inflicted upon her by her batterer, however her attempt to notify her husband pursuant to section 3209 could accidentally disclose her whereabouts to her husband. Her fear of future ramifications would be realistic under the circumstances.

"295. Marital rape is rarely discussed with others or reported to law enforcement authorities, and of those reported only few are prosecuted. . . .

"296. It is common for battered women to have sexual intercourse with their husbands to avoid being battered. While this type of coercive sexual activity would be spousal sexual assault as defined by the Act, many women may not consider it to be so and others would fear disbelief. . . .

"297. The marital rape exception to section 3209 cannot be claimed by women who are victims of coercive sexual be-havior other than penetration. The 90-day reporting require-ment of the spousal sexual assault statute, 18 Pa. Con. Stat. Ann. § 3218(c), further narrows the class of sexually abused wives who can claim the exception, since many of these women may be psychologically unable to discuss or report the rape for several years after the incident. . . .

"298. Because of the nature of the battering relationship, battered women are unlikely to avail themselves of the exceptions to section 3209 of the Act, regardless of whether the section applies to them." 744 F. Supp., at 1360–1362.

These findings are supported by studies of domestic violence. The American Medical Association (AMA) has published a summary of the recent research in this field, which indicates that in an average 12-month period in this country, approximately two million women are the victims of severe assaults by their male partners. In a 1985 survey, women reported that nearly one of every eight husbands had assaulted their wives during the past year. The AMA views these figures as "marked underestimates," because the nature of these incidents discourages women from reporting them, and because surveys typically exclude the very poor, those who do not speak English well, and women who are homeless or in institutions or hospitals when the survey is conducted. According to the AMA, "[r]esearchers on family violence agree that the true incidence of partner violence is probably *double* the above estimates; or four million severely assaulted women per year. Studies suggest that from one-fifth to one-third of all women will be physically assaulted by a partner or ex-partner during their lifetime." AMA Council on Scientific Affairs, Violence Against Women 7 (1991) (emphasis in original). Thus on an average day in the United States, nearly 11,000 women are severely assaulted by their male partners. Many of these incidents involve sexual assault. *Id.*, at 3–4; Shields & Hanneke, Battered Wives' Reactions to Marital Rape, in The Dark Side of Families: Current Family Violence Research 131, 144 (D. Finkelhor, R. Gelles, G. Hataling, & M. Straus eds. 1983). In families where wife-beating takes place, moreover, child abuse is often present as well. Violence Against Women, *supra*, at 12.

Other studies fill in the rest of this troubling picture. Physical violence is only the most visible form of abuse. Psychological abuse, particularly forced social and economic isolation of women, is also common. L. Walker, The Battered Woman Syndrome 27–28 (1984). Many victims of domestic violence remain with their abusers, perhaps because they perceive no superior alternative. Herbert, Silver, & Ellard, Coping with an Abusive Relationship: I. How and Why do Women Stay?, 53 J. Marriage & the Family 311 (1991). Many abused women who find temporary refuge in shelters return to their husbands, in large part because they have no other source of income. Aguirre, Why Do They Return? Abused Wives in Shelters, 30 J. Nat. Assn. of Social Workers 350, 352 (1985). Returning to one's abuser can be dangerous. Recent Federal Bureau of Investigation statistics disclose that 8.8% of all homicide victims in the United States are killed by their spouse. Mercy & Saltzman, Fatal Violence Among Spouses in the United States, 1976–85, 79 Am. J. Public Health 595 (1989). Thirty percent of female homicide victims are killed by their male partners. Domestic Violence: Terrorism in the Home, Hearing before the Subcommittee on Children, Family, Drugs and Alcoholism of the Senate Committee on Labor and Human Resources, 101st Cong., 2d Sess., 3 (1990).

The limited research that has been conducted with respect to notifying one's husband about an abortion, although involving samples too small to be representative, also supports the District Court's findings of fact. The vast majority of women notify their male partners of their decision to obtain an abortion. In many cases in which married women do not notify their husbands, the pregnancy is the result of an extramarital affair. Where the husband is the father, the primary reason women do not notify their husbands is that the husband and wife are experiencing marital difficulties, often accompanied by incidents of violence. Ryan & Plutzer, When Married Women Have Abortions: Spousal Notification and Marital Interaction, 51 J. Marriage & the Family 41, 44 (1989).

This information and the District Court's findings reinforce what common sense would suggest. In well-functioning marriages, spouses discuss important intimate decisions such as whether to bear a child. But there are millions of women in this country who are the victims of regular physical and psychological abuse at the hands of their husbands. Should these women become pregnant, they may have very good reasons for not wishing to inform their husbands of their decision to obtain an abortion. Many may have justifiable fears of physical abuse, but may be no less fearful of the consequences of reporting prior abuse to the Commonwealth of Pennsylvania. Many may have a reasonable fear that notifying their husbands will provoke further instances of child abuse; these women are not exempt from § 3209's notification requirement. Many may fear devastating forms of psychological abuse from their husbands, including verbal harassment, threats of future violence, the destruction of possessions, physical confinement to the home, the withdrawal of financial support, or the disclosure of the abortion to family and friends. These methods of psychological abuse may act as even more of a deterrent to notification than the possibility of physical violence, but women who are the victims of the abuse are not exempt from § 3209's notification requirement. And many women who are pregnant as a result of sexual assaults by their husbands will be unable to avail themselves of the exception for spousal sexual assault, § 3209(b)(3), because the exception requires that the woman have notified law enforcement authorities within 90 days of the assault, and her husband will be notified of her report once an investigation begins. § 3128(c). If anything in this field is certain, it is that victims of spousal sexual assault are extremely reluctant to report the abuse to the government; hence, a great many spousal rape victims will not be exempt from the notification requirement imposed by § 3209.

The spousal notification requirement is thus likely to prevent a significant number of women from obtaining an abortion. It does not merely make abortions a little more difficult or expensive to obtain; for many women, it will impose a substantial obstacle. We must not blind ourselves to the fact that the significant number of women who fear for their safety and the safety of their children are likely to be deterred from procuring an abortion as surely as if the Commonwealth had outlawed abortion in all cases.

Respondents attempt to avoid the conclusion that § 3209 is invalid by pointing out that it imposes almost no burden at all for the vast majority of women seeking abortions. They begin by noting that only about 20 percent of the women who obtain abortions are married. They then note that of these women about 95 percent notify their husbands of their own volition. Thus, respondents argue, the effects of § 3209 are felt by only one percent of the women who obtain abortions. Respondents argue that since some of these women will be able to notify their husbands without adverse consequences or will qualify for one of the exceptions, the statute affects fewer than one percent of women seeking abortions. For this reason, it is asserted, the statute cannot be invalid on its face. See Brief for Respondents [197–201]. We disagree with respondents' basic method of analysis.

The analysis does not end with the one percent of women upon whom the statute operates; it begins there. Legislation is measured for consistency with the Constitution by its impact on those whose conduct it affects. For example, we would not say that a law which requires a newspaper to print a candidate's reply to an unfavorable editorial is valid on its face because most newspapers would adopt the policy even absent the law. See *Miami Herald Publishing Co. v. Tornillo*, 418 U.S. 241 (1974). The proper focus of constitutional inquiry is the group for whom the law is a restriction, not the group for whom the law is irrelevant.

Respondents' argument itself gives implicit recognition to this principle, at one of its critical points. Respondents speak of the one percent of women seeking abortions who are married and would choose not to notify their husbands of their plans. By selecting as the controlling class women who wish to obtain abortions, rather than all women or all pregnant women, respondents in effect concede that § 3209 must be judged by reference to those for whom it is an actual rather than irrelevant restriction. Of course, as we have said, § 3209's real target is narrower even than the class of women seeking abortions identified by the State: it is married women seeking abortions who do not wish to notify their husbands of their intentions and who do not qualify for one of the statutory exceptions to the notice requirement. The unfortunate yet persisting conditions we document above will mean that in a large fraction of the cases in which § 3209 is relevant, it will operate as a substantial obstacle to a woman's choice to undergo an abortion. It is an undue burden, and therefore invalid.

This conclusion is in no way inconsistent with our decisions upholding parental notification or consent requirements. See, e.g., Akron II, 497 U.S., at [510]; Bellotti v. Baird, 443 U.S. 622 (1979) (Bellotti II); Planned Parenthood of Central Mo. v. Danforth, 428 U.S., at 74. Those enactments, and our judgment that they are constitutional, are based on the quite reasonable assumption that minors will benefit from consultation with their parents and that children will often not realize that their parents have their best interests at heart. We cannot adopt a parallel assumption about adult women.

We recognize that a husband has a "deep and proper concern and interest . . . in his wife's pregnancy and in the growth and development of the fetus she is carrying." Danforth, supra, at 69. With regard to the children he has fathered and raised, the Court has recognized his "cognizable and substantial" interest in their custody. Stanley v. Illinois, 405 U.S. 645, 651–652 (1972); see also Quilloin v. Walcott, 434 U.S. 246 (1978); Caban v. Mohammed, 441 U.S. 380 (1979); Lehr v. Robertson, 463 U.S. 248 (1983). If this case concerned a State's ability to require the mother to notify the father before taking some action with respect to a living child raised by both, therefore, it would be reasonable to conclude as a general matter that the father's interest in the welfare of the child and the mother's interest are equal.

Before birth, however, the issue takes on a very different cast. It is an inescapable biological fact that state regulation with respect to the child a woman is carrying will have a far greater impact on the mother's liberty than on the father's. The effect of state regulation on a woman's protected liberty is doubly deserving of scrutiny in such a case, as the State has touched not only upon the private sphere of the family but upon the very bodily integrity of the pregnant woman. Cf. Cruzan v. Director, Missouri Dept. of Health, 497 U.S., at 281. The Court has held that "when the wife and the husband disagree on this decision, the view of only one of the two marriage partners can prevail. Inasmuch as it is the woman who physically bears the child and who is the more directly and immediately affected by the pregnancy, as between the two, the balance weighs in her favor." *Danforth, supra*, at 71. This conclusion rests upon the basic nature of marriage and the nature of our Constitution: "[T]he marital couple is not an independent entity with a mind and heart of its own, but an association of two individuals each with a separate intellectual and emotional makeup. If the right of privacy means anything, it is the right of the *individual*, married or single, to be free from unwarranted governmental intrusion into matters so fundamentally affecting a person as the decision whether to bear or beget a child." *Eisenstadt* v. *Baird*, 405 U.S., at 453 (emphasis in original). The Constitution protects individuals, men and women alike, from unjustified state interference, even when that interference is enacted into law for the benefit of their spouses.

There was a time, not so long ago, when a different understanding of the family and of the Constitution prevailed. In *Bradwell* v. *Illinois*, 16 Wall. 130 (1873), three Members of this Court reaffirmed the common-law principle that "a woman had no legal existence separate from her husband, who was regarded as her head and representative in the social state; and, notwithstanding some recent modifications of this civil status, many of the special rules of law flowing from and dependent upon this cardinal principle still exist in full force in most States." *Id.*, at 141 (Bradley J., joined by Swayne and Field, JJ., concurring in judgment). Only one generation has passed since this Court observed that "woman is still regarded as the center of home and family life," with attendant "special responsibilities" that precluded full and independent legal status under the Constitution. *Hoyt* v. *Florida*, 368 U.S. 57, 62 (1961). These views, of course, are no longer consistent with our understanding of the family, the individual, or the Constitution.

In keeping with our rejection of the common-law understanding of a woman's role within the family, the Court held in *Danforth* that the Constitution does not permit a State to require a married woman to obtain her husband's consent before undergoing an abortion. 428 U.S., at 69. The principles that guided the Court in *Danforth* should be our guides today. For the great many women who are victims of abuse inflicted by their husbands, or whose children are the victims of such abuse, a spousal notice requirement enables the husband to wield an effective veto over his wife's decision. Whether the prospect of notification itself deters such women from seeking abortions, or whether the husband, through physical force or psychological pressure or economic coercion, prevents his wife from obtaining an abortion until it is too late, the notice requirement will often be tantamount to the veto found unconstitutional in *Danforth*. The women most affected by this law—those who most reasonably fear the consequences of notifying their husbands that they are pregnant—are in the gravest danger.

The husband's interest in the life of the child his wife is carrying does not permit the State to empower him with this troubling degree of authority over his wife. The contrary view leads to consequences reminiscent of the common law. A husband has no enforceable right to require a wife to advise him before she exercises her personal choices. If a husband's interest in the potential life of the child outweighs a wife's liberty, the State could require a married woman to notify her husband before she uses a postfertilization contraceptive. Perhaps next in line would be a statute requiring pregnant married women to notify their husbands before engaging in conduct causing risks to the fetus. After all, if the husband's interest in the fetus' safety is a sufficient predicate for state regulation, the State could reasonably conclude that pregnant wives should notify their husbands before drinking alcohol or smoking. Perhaps married women should notify their husbands before using contraceptives or before undergoing any type of surgery that may have complications affecting the husband's interest in his wife's reproductive organs. And if a husband's interest justifies notice in any of these cases, one might reasonably argue that it justifies exactly what the *Danforth* Court held it did not justify—a requirement of the husband's consent as well. A State may not give to a man the kind of dominion over his wife that parents exercise over their children.

Section 3209 embodies a view of marriage consonant with the common-law status of married women but repugnant to our present understanding of marriage and of the nature of the rights secured by the Constitution. Women do not lose their constitutionally protected liberty when they marry. The Constitution protects all individuals, male or female, married or unmarried, from the abuse of governmental power, even where that power is employed for the supposed benefit of a member of the individual's family. These considerations confirm our conclusion that § 3209 is invalid.

D

We next consider the parental consent provision. Except in a medical emergency, an unemancipated young woman under 18 may not obtain an abortion unless she and one of her parents (or guardian) provides informed consent as defined above. If neither a parent nor a guardian provides consent, a court may authorize the performance of an abortion upon a determination that the young woman is mature and capable of giving informed consent and has in fact given her informed consent, or that an abortion would be in her best interests.

We have been over most of this ground before. Our cases establish, and we reaffirm today, that a State may require a minor seeking an abortion to obtain the consent of a parent or guardian, provided that there is an adequate judicial bypass procedure. See, e.g., Akron II, 497 U.S., at [515]; Hodgson, 497 U.S., at [497]; Akron I, supra, at 440; Bellotti II, supra, at 643–644 (plurality opinion). Under these precedents, in our view, the one-parent consent requirement and judicial bypass procedure are constitutional.

The only argument made by petitioners respecting this provision and to which our prior decisions do not speak is the contention that the parental consent requirement is invalid because it requires informed parental consent. For the most part, petitioners' argument is a reprise of their argument with respect to the informed consent requirement in general, and we reject it for the reasons given above. Indeed, some of the provisions regarding informed consent have particular force with respect to minors: the waiting period, for example, may provide the parent or parents of a pregnant young woman the opportunity to consult with her in private, and to discuss the consequences of her decision in the context of the values and moral or religious principles of their family. See *Hodgson, supra,* at [490–96].

E

Under the recordkeeping and reporting requirements of the statute, every facility which performs abortions is required to file a report stating its name and address as well as the name and address of any related entity, such as a controlling or subsidiary organization. In the case of state-funded institutions, the information becomes public.

For each abortion performed, a report must be filed identifying: the physician (and the second physician where required); the facility; the referring physician or agency; the woman's age; the number of prior pregnancies and prior abortions she has had; gestational age; the type of abortion procedure; the date of the abortion; whether there were any pre-existing medical conditions which would complicate pregnancy; medical complications with the abortion; where applicable, the basis for the determination that the abortion was medically necessary; the weight of the aborted fetus; and whether the woman was married, and if so, whether notice was provided or the basis for the failure to give notice. Every abortion facility must also file quarterly reports showing the number of abortions performed broken down by trimester. See 18 Pa. Cons. Stat. §§ 3207, 3214 (1990). In all events, the identity of each woman who has had an abortion remains confidential.

In *Danforth,* 428 U.S., at 80, we held that recordkeeping and reporting provisions "that are reasonably directed to the preservation of maternal health and that properly respect a patient's confidentiality and privacy are permissible." We think that under this standard, all the provisions at issue here except that relating to spousal notice are constitutional. Although they do not relate to the State's interest in informing the woman's choice, they do relate to health. The collection of information with respect to actual patients is a vital element of medical research, and so it cannot be said that the requirements serve no purpose other than to make abortions more difficult. Nor do we find that the requirements impose a substantial obstacle to a woman's choice. At most they might increase the cost of some abortions by a slight amount. While at some point increased cost could become a substantial obstacle, there is no such showing on the record before us.

Subsection (12) of the reporting provision requires the reporting of, among other things, a married woman's "reason for failure to provide notice" to her husband. § 3214(a)(12). This provision in effect requires women, as a condition of obtaining an abortion, to provide the Commonwealth with the precise information we have already recognized that many women have pressing reasons not to reveal. Like the spousal notice requirement itself, this provision places an undue burden on a woman's choice, and must be invalidated for that reason.

VI

Our Constitution is a covenant running from the first generation of Americans to us and then to future generations. It is a coherent succession. Each generation must learn anew that the Constitution's written terms embody ideas and aspirations that must survive more ages than one. We accept our responsibility not to retreat from interpreting the full meaning of the covenant in light of all of our precedents. We invoke it once again to define the freedom guaranteed by the Constitution's own promise, the promise of liberty.

* * *

The judgment in No. 91–902 is affirmed. The judgment in No. 91–744 is affirmed in part and reversed in part, and the case is remanded for proceedings consistent with this opinion, including consideration of the question of severability.

It is so ordered.

APPENDIX TO OPINION

Selected Provisions of the 1988 and 1989 Amendments to the
Pennsylvania Abortion Control Act of 1992

18 PA. CONS. STAT. ANN. (1990)

§ 3203. Definitions.

.   .   .   .

" 'Medical Emergency.' " That condition which, on the
basis of the physician's good faith clinical judgment, so complicates the medical condition of a pregnant woman as to
necessitate the immediate abortion of her pregnancy to avert
her death or for which a delay will create serious risk of substantial and irreversible impairment of major bodily function."

"§ 3205. Informed consent.

"(a) General Rule.— No abortion shall be performed or
induced except with the voluntary and informed consent of
the woman upon whom the abortion is to be performed or
induced. Except in the case of a medical emergency, consent
to an abortion is voluntary and informed if and only if:

"(1) At least 24 hours prior to the abortion, the physician
who is to perform the abortion or the referring physician
has orally informed the woman of:

"(i) The nature of the proposed procedure or treatment
and of those risks and alternatives to the procedure or
treatment that a reasonable patient would consider material to the decision of whether or not to undergo the
abortion.

"(ii) The probable gestational age of the unborn child
at the time the abortion is to be performed.

"(iii) The medical risks associated with carrying her child
to term.

"(2) At least 24 hours prior to the abortion, the physician
who is to perform the abortion or the referring physician,

or a qualified physician assistant, health care practitioner, technician or social worker to whom the responsibility has been delegated by either physician, has informed the pregnant woman that:

"(i) The department publishes printed materials which describe the unborn child and list agencies which offer alternatives to abortion and that she has a right to review the printed materials and that a copy will be provided to her free of charge if she chooses to review it.

"(ii) Medical assistance benefits may be available for prenatal care, childbirth and neonatal care, and that more detailed information on the availability of such assistance is contained in the printed materials published by the department.

"(iii) The father of the unborn child is liable to assist in the support of her child, even in instances where he has offered to pay for the abortion. In the case of rape, this information may be omitted.

"(3) A copy of the printed materials has been provided to the pregnant woman if she chooses to view these materials.

"(4) The pregnant woman certifies in writing, prior to the abortion, that the information required to be provided under paragraphs (1), (2) and (3) has been provided.

"(b) Emergency.— Where a medical emergency compels the performance of an abortion, the physician shall inform the woman, prior to the abortion if possible, of the medical indications supporting his judgment that an abortion is necessary to avert her death or to avert substantial and irreversible impairment of major bodily function.

"(c) Penalty.— Any physician who violates the provisions of this section is guilty of 'unprofessional conduct' and his license for the practice of medicine and surgery shall be subject to suspension or revocation in accordance with procedures provided under the act of October 5, 1978 (P.L. 1109, No. 261), known as the Osteopathic Medical Practice Act, the act of December 20, 1985 (P.L. 457, No. 112), known as the Medical Practice Act of 1985, or their successor acts. Any physician who performs or induces an abortion without first obtaining the certification required by subsection (a)(4) or with knowledge or reason to know that the informed consent of the woman has not been obtained shall for the first offense be guilty of a summary offense and for each subsequent offense be guilty of a misdemeanor of the third degree. No physician shall be guilty of violating this section for failure to furnish the information required by subsection (a) if he or she can demonstrate, by a preponderance of the evidence, that he or she reasonably believed that furnishing the information would have resulted in a severely adverse effect on the physical or mental health of the patient.

"(d) Limitation on Civil Liability.— Any physician who complies with the provisions of this section may not be held civilly liable to his patient for failure to obtain informed consent to the abortion within the meaning of that term as defined by the act of October 15, 1975 (P.L. 390, No.111), known as the Health Care Services Malpractice Act."

"§ 3206. Parental consent.

"(a) General rule.— Except in the case of a medical emergency, or except as provided in this section, if a pregnant woman is less than 18 years of age and not emancipated, or if she has been adjudged an incompetent under 20 Pa.C.S. § 5511 (relating to petition and hearing; examination by court-appointed physician), a physician shall not perform an abortion upon her unless, in the case of a woman who is less than 18 years of age, he first obtains the informed consent both of the pregnant woman and of one of her parents; or, in the case of a woman who is incompetent, he first obtains the informed consent of her guardian. In deciding whether to grant such consent, a pregnant woman's parent or guardian shall consider only their child's or ward's best interests. In the case of a pregnancy that is the result of incest where the father is a party to the incestuous act, the pregnant woman need only obtain the consent of her mother.

"(b) Unavailability of parent or guardian.—If both parents

have died or are otherwise unavailable to the physician within a reasonable time and in a reasonable manner, consent of the pregnant woman's guardian or guardians shall be sufficient. If the pregnant woman's parents are divorced, consent of the parent having custody shall be sufficient. If neither any parent nor a legal guardian is available to the physician within a reasonable time and in a reasonable manner, consent of any adult person standing in loco parentis shall be sufficient.

"(c) Petition to court for consent.—If both of the parents or guardians of the pregnant woman refuse to consent to the performance of an abortion or if she elects not to seek the consent of either of her parents or of her guardian, the court of common pleas of the judicial district in which the applicant resides or in which the abortion is sought shall, upon petition or motion, after an appropriate hearing, authorize a physician to perform the abortion if the court determines that the pregnant woman is mature and capable of giving informed consent to the proposed abortion, and has, in fact, given such consent.

"(d) Court order.—If the court determines that the pregnant woman is not mature and capable of giving informed consent or if the pregnant woman does not claim to be mature and capable of giving informed consent, the court shall determine whether the performance of an abortion upon her would be in her best interests. If the court determines that the performance of an abortion would be in the best interests of the woman, it shall authorize a physician to perform the abortion.

"(e) Representation in proceedings.—The pregnant woman may participate in proceedings in the court on her own behalf and the court may appoint a guardian ad litem to assist her. The court shall, however, advise her that she has a right to court appointed counsel, and shall provide her with such counsel unless she wishes to appear with private counsel or has knowingly and intelligently waived representation by counsel."

"§ 3207. Abortion facilities.

.   .   .   .   .

"(b) Reports.—Within 30 days after the effective date of this chapter, every facility at which abortions are performed shall file, and update immediately upon any change, a report with the department, containing the following information:

"(1) Name and address of the facility.

"(2) Name and address of any parent, subsidiary or affiliated organizations, corporations or associations.

"(3) Name and address of any parent, subsidiary or affiliated organizations, corporations or associations having contemporaneous commonalty of ownership, beneficial interest, directorship or officership with any other facility.

The information contained in those reports which are filed pursuant to this subsection by facilities which receive State appropriated funds during the 12-calendar-month period immediately preceding a request to inspect or copy such reports shall be deemed public information. Reports filed by facilities which do not receive State appropriated funds shall only be available to law enforcement officials, the State Board of Medicine and the State Board of Osteopathic Medicine for use in the performance of their official duties. Any facility failing to comply with the provisions of this subsection shall be assessed by the department a fine of $500 for each day it is in violation hereof."

"§ 3208. Printed information.

"(a) General Rule.—The department shall cause to be published in English, Spanish and Vietnamese, within 60 days after this chapter becomes law, and shall update on an annual basis, the following easily comprehensible printed materials:

"(1) Geographically indexed materials designed to inform the woman of public and private agencies and services available to assist a woman through pregnancy, upon childbirth and while the child is dependent, including adoption agencies, which shall include a comprehensive list of the agencies available, a description of the services they offer and a description of the manner, including telephone numbers, in which they might be contacted, or, at the option of the department, printed materials including a toll-free, 24-hour a day telephone number which may be called to obtain, orally, such a list and description of agencies in the locality of the caller and of the services they offer. The materials shall provide information on the availability of medical assistance benefits for prenatal care, childbirth and neonatal care, and state that it is unlawful for any individual to coerce a woman to undergo abortion, that any physician who performs an abortion upon a woman without obtaining her informed consent or without according her a private medical consultation may be liable to her for damages in a civil action at law, that the father of a child is liable to assist in the support of that child, even in instances where the father has offered to pay for an abortion, and that the law permits adoptive parents to pay costs of prenatal care, childbirth and neonatal care.

"(2) Materials designed to inform the woman of the probable anatomical and physiological characteristics of the unborn child at two-week gestational increments from fertilization to full term, including pictures representing the development of unborn children at two-week gestational increments, and any relevant information on the possibility of the unborn child's survival; provided that any such pictures or drawings must contain the dimensions of the fetus and must be realistic and appropriate for the woman's stage of pregnancy. The materials shall be objective, nonjudgmental and designed to convey only accurate scientific information about the unborn child at the various gestational ages. The material shall also contain objective information describing the methods of abortion procedures commonly employed, the medical risks commonly associated with each such procedure, the possible detrimental psychological effects of abortion and the medical risks commonly associated with each such procedure, and the medical risks commonly associated with carrying a child to term.

(b) Format.—The materials shall be printed in a typeface large enough to be clearly legible.
(c) Free distribution.—The materials required under this

section shall be available at no cost from the department upon request and in appropriate number to any person, facility or hospital."

"§ 3209. Spousal notice.

(a) Spousal notice required.—In order to further the Commonwealth's interest in promoting the integrity of the marital relationship and to protect a spouse's interests in having children within marriage and in protecting the prenatal life of that spouse's child, no physician shall perform an abortion on a married woman, except as provided in subsections (b) and (c), unless he or she has received a signed statement, which need not be notarized, from the woman upon whom the abortion is to be performed, that she has notified her spouse that she is about to undergo an abortion. The statement shall bear a notice that any false statement made therein is punishable by law.

"(b) Exceptions.—The statement certifying that the notice required by subsection (a) has been given need not be furnished where the woman provides the physician a signed statement certifying at least one of the following:

"(1) Her spouse is not the father of the child.

"(2) Her spouse, after diligent effort, could not be located.

"(3) The pregnancy is a result of spousal sexual assault as described in section 3128 (relating to spousal sexual assault), which has been reported to a law enforcement agency having the requisite jurisdiction.

"(4) The woman has reason to believe that the furnishing of notice to her spouse is likely to result in the infliction of bodily injury upon her by her spouse or by another individual.

Such statement need not be notarized, but shall bear a notice that any false statements made therein are punishable by law.

"(c) Medical emergency.—The requirements of subsection (a) shall not apply in case of a medical emergency.

"(d) Forms.—The department shall cause to be published forms which may be utilized for purposes of providing the signed statements required by subsections (a) and (b). The department shall distribute an adequate supply of such forms to all abortion facilities in this Commonwealth.

"(e) Penalty; civil action.—Any physician who violates the provisions of this section is guilty of 'unprofessional conduct,' and his or her license for the practice of medicine and surgery shall be subject to suspension or revocation in accordance with procedures provided under the act of October 5, 1978 (P.L. 1109, No. 261), known as the Osteopathic Medical Practice Act, the act of December 20, 1985 (P.L. 457, No. 112), known as the Medical Practice Act of 1985, or their successor acts. In addition, any physician who knowingly violates the provisions of this section shall be civilly liable to the spouse who is the father of the aborted child for any damages caused thereby and for punitive damages in the amount of $5,000, and the court shall award a prevailing plaintiff a reasonable attorney fee as part of costs."

"§ 3214. Reporting

"(a) General rule.—For the purpose of promotion of maternal health and life by adding to the sum of medical and public health knowledge through the compilation of relevant data, and to promote the Commonwealth's interest in protection of the unborn child, a report of each abortion performed shall be made to the department on forms prescribed by it. The report forms shall not identify the individual patient by name and shall include the following information:

"(1) Identification of the physician who performed the abortion, the concurring physician as required by section 3211(c)(2) (relating to abortion on unborn child of 24 or more weeks gestational age), the second physician as required by section 3211(c)(5) and the facility where the abortion was performed and of the referring physician, agency or service, if any.

"(2) The county and state in which the woman resides.

"(3) The woman's age.

"(4) The number of prior pregnancies and prior abortions of the woman.

"(5) The gestational age of the unborn child at the time of the abortion.

"(6) The type of procedure performed or prescribed and the date of the abortion.

"(7) Pre-existing medical conditions of the woman which would complicate pregnancy, if any, and, if known, any medical complication which resulted from the abortion itself.

"(8) The basis for the medical judgment of the physician who performed the abortion that the abortion was necessary to prevent either the death of the pregnant woman or the substantial and irreversible impairment of a major bodily function of the woman, where an abortion has been performed pursuant to section 3211(b)(1).

"(9) The weight of the aborted child for any abortion performed pursuant to section 3211(b)(1).

"(10) Basis for any medical judgment that a medical emergency existed which excused the physician from compliance with any provision of this chapter.

"(11) The information required to be reported under section 3210(a) (relating to determination of gestational age).

"(12) Whether the abortion was performed upon a married woman and, if so, whether notice to her spouse was given. If no notice to her spouse was given, the report shall also indicate the reason for failure to provide notice.

.   .   .   .   .

"(f) Report by facility.—Every facility in which an abortion is performed within this Commonwealth during any quarter year shall file with the department a report showing the total number of abortions performed within the hospital or other facility during that quarter year. This report shall also show the total abortions performed in each trimester of pregnancy. Any report shall be available for public inspection and copying only if the facility receives State-appropriated funds within the 12-calendar-month period immediately preceding the filing of the report. These reports shall be submitted on a form prescribed by the department which will enable a facility to indicate whether or not it is receiving State-appropriated funds. If the facility indicates on the form that it is not receiving State-appropriated funds, the department shall regard its report as confidential unless it receives other evidence which causes it to conclude that the facility receives State-appropriated funds."

OPINION OF JUSTICE STEVENS

Justice Stevens concurring in part and dissenting in part.

The portions of the Court's opinion that I have joined are more important than those with which I disagree. I shall therefore first comment on significant areas of agreement, and then explain the limited character of my disagreement.

I

The Court is unquestionably correct in concluding that the doctrine of *stare decisis* has controlling significance in a case of this kind, notwithstanding an individual Justice's concerns about the merits.[1] The central holding of *Roe v. Wade*, 410 U.S. 113 (1973), has been a "part of our law" for almost two decades. *Planned Parenthood of Central Mo. v. Danforth*, 428 U.S. 52, 101 (1976) (Stevens, J., concurring in part and dissenting in part). It was a natural sequel to the protection of individual liberty established in *Griswold v. Connecticut*,

---

[1] It is sometimes useful to view the issue of *stare decisis* from a historical perspective. In the last nineteen years, fifteen Justices have confronted the basic issue presented in *Roe*. Of those, eleven have voted as the majority does today: Chief Justice Burger, Justices Douglas, Brennan, Stewart, Marshall, and Powell, and Justices Blackmun, O'Connor, Kennedy, Souter, and myself. Only four—all of whom happen to be on the Court today—have reached the opposite conclusion.

381 U.S. 479 (1965). See also *Carey* v. *Population Services Int'l*, 431 U.S. 678, 687, 702 (1977) (WHITE, J., concurring in part and concurring in result). The societal costs of over-ruling *Roe* at this late date would be enormous. *Roe* is an integral part of a correct understanding of both the concept of liberty and the basic equality of men and women.

Stare decisis also provides a sufficient basis for my agreement with the joint opinion's reaffirmation of *Roe*'s post-viability analysis. Specifically, I accept the proposition that "[i]f the State is interested in protecting fetal life after viability, it may go so far as to proscribe abortion during that period, except when it is necessary to preserve the life or health of the mother." 410 U.S., at 163–164; see *ante*, at [372].

I also accept what is implicit in the Court's analysis, namely, a reaffirmation of *Roe*'s explanation of why the State's obligation to protect the life or health of the mother must take precedence over any duty to the unborn. The Court in *Roe* carefully considered, and rejected, the State's argument "that the fetus is a 'person' within the language and meaning of the Fourteenth Amendment." 410 U.S., at 156. After analyzing the usage of "person" in the Constitution, the Court concluded that that word "has application only postnatally." *Id.*, at 157. Commenting on the contingent property interests of the unborn that are generally represented by guardians ad litem, the Court noted: "Perfection of the interests involved, again, has generally been contingent upon live birth. In short, the unborn have never been recognized in the law as persons in the whole sense." *Id.*, at 162. Accordingly, an abortion is not "the termination of life entitled to Fourteenth Amendment protection." *Id.*, at 159. From this holding, there was no dissent, see *id.*, at 173; indeed, no member of the Court has ever questioned this fundamental proposition. Thus, as a matter of federal constitutional law, a developing organism that is not yet a "person" does not have what is sometimes described as a "right to life."[2] This has been and, by the Court's

---

[2] Professor Dworkin has made this comment on the issue:

"The suggestion that states are free to declare a fetus a person. . . . assumes that a state can curtail some persons' constitutional rights by adding new persons to the constitutional population. The constitutional rights of one citizen are of course very much affected by who or what else also has constitutional rights, because the rights

holding today, remains a fundamental premise of our constitutional law governing reproductive autonomy.

II

My disagreement with the joint opinion begins with its understanding of the trimester framework established in *Roe*. Contrary to the suggestion of the joint opinion, *ante*, at [370], it is not a "contradiction" to recognize that the State may have a legitimate interest in potential human life and, at the same time, to conclude that that interest does not justify the regulation of abortion before viability (although other interests, such as maternal health, may). The fact that the State's interest is legitimate does not tell us when, if ever, that interest outweighs the pregnant woman's interest in personal liberty. It is appropriate, therefore, to consider more carefully the nature of the interests at stake.

First, it is clear that, in order to be legitimate, the State's interest must be secular; consistent with the First Amendment the State may not promote a theological or sectarian interest. See *Thornburgh* v. *American College of Obstetricians and Gynecologists*, 476 U.S. 747, 778 (1986) (STEVENS, J., concurring); see generally *Webster* v. *Reproductive Health Services*, 492 U.S. 490, 563–572 (1989) (STEVENS, J., concurring in part and dissenting in part). Moreover, as discussed above, the state interest in potential human life is not an interest *in loco parentis*, for the fetus is not a person.

Identifying the State's interests—which the States rarely

---

of others may compete or conflict with his. So any power to increase the constitutional population by unilateral decision would be, in effect, a power to decrease rights the national Constitution grants to others.

"If a state could declare trees to be persons with a constitutional right to life, it could prohibit publishing newspapers or books in spite of the First Amendment's guarantee of free speech, which could not be understood as a license to kill. . . .Once we understand that the suggestion we are considering has that implication, we must reject it. If a fetus is not part of the constitutional population, under the national constitutional arrangement, then states have no power to overrule that national arrangement by themselves declaring that fetuses have rights competitive with the constitutional rights of pregnant women."

Dworkin, Unenumerated Rights: Whether and How *Roe* Should be Overruled, 59 U. Chi. L. Rev. 381, 400–401 (1992).

articulate with any precision—makes clear that the interest in protecting potential life is not grounded in the Constitution. It is, instead, an indirect interest supported by both humanitarian and pragmatic concerns. Many of our citizens believe that any abortion reflects an unacceptable disrespect for potential human life and that the performance of more than a million abortions each year is intolerable; many find third-trimester abortions performed when the fetus is approaching personhood particularly offensive. The State has a legitimate interest in minimizing such offense. The State may also have a broader interest in expanding the population,[3] believing society would benefit from the services of additional productive citizens—or that the potential human lives might include the occasional Mozart or Curie. These are the kinds of concerns that comprise the State's interest in potential human life.

In counterpoise is the woman's constitutional interest in liberty. One aspect of this liberty is a right to bodily integrity, a right to control one's person. See, e.g., Rochin v. California, 342 U.S. 165 (1952); Skinner v. Oklahoma, 316 U.S. 535 (1942). This right is neutral on the question of abortion: The Constitution would be equally offended by an absolute requirement that all women undergo abortions as by an absolute prohibition on abortions. "Our whole constitutional heritage rebels at the thought of giving government the power to control men's minds." Stanley v. Georgia, 394 U.S. 557, 565 (1969). The same holds true for the power to control women's bodies.

The woman's constitutional liberty interest also involves her freedom to decide matters of the highest privacy and the most personal nature. Cf. Whalen v. Roe, 409 U.S. 589, 598–

---

[3] The state interest in protecting potential life may be compared to the state interest in protecting those who seek to immigrate to this country. A contemporary example is provided by the Haitians who have risked the perils of the sea in a desperate attempt to become "persons" protected by our laws. Humanitarian and practical concerns would support a state policy allowing those persons unrestricted entry; countervailing interests in population control support a policy of limiting the entry of these potential citizens. While the state interest in population control might be sufficient to justify strict enforcement of the immigration laws, that interest would not be sufficient to overcome a woman's liberty interest. Thus, a state interest in population control could not justify a state-imposed limit on family size or, for that matter, state-mandated abortions.

600 (1977). A woman considering abortion faces "a difficult choice having serious and personal consequences of major importance to her own future—perhaps to the salvation of her own immortal soul." *Thornburgh*, 476 U.S., at 781. The authority to make such traumatic and yet empowering decisions is an element of basic human dignity. As the joint opinion so eloquently demonstrates, a woman's decision to terminate her pregnancy is nothing less than a matter of conscience.

Weighing the State's interest in potential life and the woman's liberty interest, I agree with the joint opinion that the State may " 'expres[s] a preference for normal childbirth,' " that the State may take steps to ensure that a woman's choice "is thoughtful and informed," and that "States are free to enact laws to provide a reasonable framework for a woman to make a decision that has such profound and lasting meaning." *Ante*, at [367]. Serious questions arise, however, when a State attempts to "persuade the woman to choose childbirth over abortion." *Ante*, at [372]. Decisional autonomy must limit the State's power to inject into a woman's most personal deliberations its own views of what is best. The State may promote its preferences by funding childbirth, by creating and maintaining alternatives to abortion, and by espousing the virtues of family; but it must respect the individual's freedom to make such judgments.

This theme runs throughout our decisions concerning reproductive freedom. In general, *Roe*'s requirement that restrictions on abortions before viability be justified by the State's interest in *maternal* health has prevented States from interjecting regulations designed to influence a woman's decision. Thus, we have upheld regulations of abortion that are not efforts to sway or direct a woman's choice but rather are efforts to enhance the deliberative quality of that decision or are neutral regulations on the health aspects of her decision. We have, for example, upheld regulations requiring written informed consent, see *Planned Parenthood of Central Mo. v. Danforth*, 428 U.S. 52 (1976); limited recordkeeping and reporting, see *ibid.*; and pathology reports, see *Planned Parenthood Assn. of Kansas City, Mo., Inc. v. Ashcroft*, 462 U.S. 476 (1983); as well as various licensing and qualification provisions, see, *e.g., Roe*, 410 U.S., at 150; *Simopoulos v. Virginia*, 462 U.S. 506 (1983). Conversely, we have consistently rejected state efforts to prejudice a woman's choice, either by limiting the information available to her, see *Bigelow v. Virginia*, 421 U.S. 809 (1975), or by "requir[ing] the delivery of information designed 'to influence the woman's informed choice between abortion or childbirth.'" *Thornburgh*, 476 U.S., at 760; see also *Akron v. Akron Center for Reproductive Health, Inc.*, 462 U.S. 416, 442–449 (1983).

In my opinion, the principles established in this long line of cases and the wisdom reflected in Justice Powell's opinion for the Court in *Akron* (and followed by the Court just six years ago in *Thornburgh*) should govern our decision today. Under these principles, §§ 3205(a)(2)(i)–(iii) of the Pennsylvania statute are unconstitutional. Those sections require a physician or counselor to provide the woman with a range of materials clearly designed to persuade her to choose not to undergo the abortion. While the State is free, pursuant to § 3208 of the Pennsylvania law, to produce and disseminate such material, the State may not inject such information into the woman's deliberations just as she is weighing such an important choice.

Under this same analysis, §§ 3205(a)(1)(i) and (iii) of the Pennsylvania statute are constitutional. Those sections, which require the physician to inform a woman of the nature and risks of the abortion procedure and the medical risks of carrying to term, are neutral requirements comparable to those imposed in other medical procedures. Those sections indicate no effort by the State to influence the woman's choice in any way. If anything, such requirements *enhance*, rather than skew, the woman's decisionmaking.

III

The 24-hour waiting period required by §§ 3205(a)(1)–(2) of the Pennsylvania statute raises even more serious concerns. Such a requirement arguably furthers the State's interests in two ways, neither of which is constitutionally permissible.

First, it may be argued that the 24-hour delay is justified by the mere fact that it is likely to reduce the number of abortions, thus furthering the State's interest in potential life. But such an argument would justify any form of coercion that placed an obstacle in the woman's path. The State cannot further its interests by simply wearing down the ability of the pregnant woman to exercise her constitutional right.

Second, it can more reasonably be argued that the 24-hour delay furthers the State's interest in ensuring that the woman's decision is informed and thoughtful. But there is no evidence that the mandated delay benefits women or that it is necessary to enable the physician to convey any relevant information to the patient. The mandatory delay thus appears to rest on outmoded and unacceptable assumptions about the decision-making capacity of women. While there are well-established and consistently maintained reasons for the State to view with skepticism the ability of minors to make decisions, see *Hodgson v. Minnesota*, 497 U.S. 417, 449 (1990),[4] none of those reasons applies to an adult woman's decisionmaking ability. Just as we have left behind the belief that a woman must consult her husband before undertaking serious matters, see *ante*, at [387–90], so we must reject the notion that a woman is less capable of deciding matters of gravity. Cf. *Reed v. Reed*, 404 U.S. 71 (1971).

In the alternative, the delay requirement may be premised on the belief that the decision to terminate a pregnancy is presumptively wrong. This premise is illegitimate. Those who disagree vehemently about the legality and morality of abortion agree about one thing: The decision to terminate a pregnancy is profound and difficult. No person undertakes such a decision lightly—and States may not presume that a woman has failed to reflect adequately merely because her conclusion differs from the State's preference. A woman who has, in the privacy of her thoughts and conscience, weighed the options

---

[4] As we noted in that opinion, the State's "legitimate interest in protecting minor women from their own immaturity" distinguished that case from *Akron* which involved "a provision that required mature women, capable of consenting to an abortion, [to] wait 24 hours after giving consent before undergoing an abortion." *Hodgson*, 497 U.S., at 449, n. 35.

and made her decision cannot be forced to reconsider all, simply because the State believes she has come to the wrong conclusion.[5]

Part of the constitutional liberty to choose is the equal dignity to which each of us is entitled. A woman who decides to terminate her pregnancy is entitled to the same respect as a woman who decides to carry the fetus to term. The mandatory waiting period denies women that equal respect.

IV

In my opinion, a correct application of the "undue burden" standard leads to the same conclusion concerning the constitutionality of these requirements. A state-imposed burden on the exercise of a constitutional right is measured both by its effects and by its character: A burden may be "undue" either because the burden is too severe

[5] The joint opinion's reliance on the indirect effects of the regulation of constitutionally protected activity, see ante, [367–69], is misplaced; what matters is not only the effect of a regulation but also the reason for the regulation. As I explained in Hodgson:

"In cases involving abortion, as in cases involving the right to travel or the right to marry, the identification of the constitutionally protected interest is merely the beginning of the analysis. State regulation of travel and of marriage is obviously permissible even though a State may not categorically exclude nonresidents from its borders, Shapiro v. Thompson, 394 U.S. 618, 631 (1969), or deny prisoners the right to marry, Turner v. Safley, 482 U.S. 78, 94–99 (1987). But the regulation of constitutionally protected decisions, such as where a person shall reside or whom he or she shall marry, must be predicated on legitimate state concerns other than disagreement with the choice the individual has made. Cf. Turner v. Safley, supra; Loving v. Virginia, 388 U.S. 1 (1967). In the abortion area, a State may have no obligation to spend its own money, or use its own facilities, to subsidize nontherapeutic abortions for minors or adults. See, e.g., Maher v. Roe, 432 U.S. 464 (1977); cf. Webster v. Reproductive Health Services, 492 U.S. 490, 508–511 (1989) (plurality opinion); id., at 523–524 (O'CONNOR, J., concurring in part and concurring in judgment). A State's value judgment favoring childbirth over abortion may provide adequate support for decisions involving such allocation of public funds, but not for simply substituting a state decision for an individual decision that a woman has a right to make for herself. Otherwise, the interest in liberty protected by the Due Process Clause would be a nullity. A state policy favoring childbirth over abortion is not in itself a sufficient justification for overriding the woman's decision or for placing 'obstacles—absolute or otherwise—in the pregnant woman's path to an abortion.' " Hodgson, 497 U.S., at 435.

or because it lacks a legitimate, rational justification.[6]

The 24-hour delay requirement fails both parts of this test. The findings of the District Court establish the severity of the burden that the 24-hour delay imposes on many pregnant women. Yet even in those cases in which the delay is not especially onerous, it is, in my opinion, "undue" because there is no evidence that such a delay serves a useful and legitimate purpose. As indicated above, there is no legitimate reason to require a woman who has agonized over her decision to leave the clinic or hospital and return again another day. While a general requirement that a physician notify her patients about the risks of a proposed medical procedure is appropriate, a rigid requirement that all patients wait 24 hours or (what is true in practice) much longer to evaluate the significance of information that is either common knowledge or irrelevant is an irrational and, therefore, "undue" burden.

The counseling provisions are similarly infirm. Whenever government commands private citizens to speak or to listen, careful review of the justification for that command is particularly appropriate. In this case, the Pennsylvania statute directs that counselors provide women seeking abortions with information concerning alternatives to abortion, the availability of medical assistance benefits, and the possibility of child-support payments. §§ 3205(a)(2)(i)–(iii). The statute requires that this information be given to all women seeking abortions, including those for whom such information is clearly useless, such as those who are married, those who have undergone the procedure in the past and are fully aware of the options, and those who are fully convinced that abortion is their only reasonable option. Moreover, the statute requires physicians to inform all of their patients of "the probable gestational age of the unborn child." § 3205(a)(1)(ii). This

---

[6] The meaning of any legal standard can only be understood by reviewing the actual cases in which it is applied. For that reason, I discount both JUSTICE SCALIA'S comments on past descriptions of the standard, see post, at [470–71] (opinion of SCALIA, J.), and the attempt to give it crystal clarity in the joint opinion. The several opinions supporting the judgment in Griswold v. Connecticut, 381 U.S. 479 (1965), are less illuminating than the central holding of the case, which appears to have passed the test of time. The future may also demonstrate that a standard that analyzes both the severity of a regulatory burden and the legitimacy of its justification will provide a fully adequate framework for the review of abortion legislation even if the contours of the standard are not authoritatively articulated in any single opinion.

information is of little decisional value in most cases, because 90% of all abortions are performed during the first trimester[7] when fetal age has less relevance than when the fetus nears viability. Nor can the information required by the statute be justified as relevant to any "philosophic" or "social" argument, *ante*, at [367], either favoring or disfavoring the abortion decision in a particular case. In light of all of these facts, I conclude that the information requirements in §§ 3205(a)(1)(ii) and §§ 3205(a)(2)(i)–(iii) do not serve a useful purpose and thus constitute an unnecessary—and therefore undue—burden on the woman's constitutional liberty to decide to terminate her pregnancy.

Accordingly, while I disagree with Parts IV, V-B, and V-D of the joint opinion,[8] I join the remainder of the Court's opinion.

---

[7] U.S. Dept. of Commerce, Bureau of the Census, Statistical Abstract of the United States 71 (111th ed. 1991).

[8] Although I agree that a parental-consent requirement (with the appropriate bypass) is constitutional, I do not join Part V-D of the joint opinion because its approval of Pennsylvania's informed parental-consent requirement is based on the reasons given in Part V-B, with which I disagree.

OPINION OF JUSTICE BLACKMUN

Justice Blackmun, concurring in part, concurring in the judgment in part, and dissenting in part.

I join parts I, II, III, V-A, V-C, and VI of the joint opinion of Justices O'Connor, Kennedy, and Souter, *ante*.

Three years ago, in *Webster* v. *Reproductive Health Serv.*, 492 U.S. 490 (1989), four Members of this Court appeared poised to "cas[t] into darkness the hopes and visions of every woman in this country" who had come to believe that the Constitution guaranteed her the right to reproductive choice. *Id.*, at 557 (Blackmun, J., dissenting). See *id.*, at 499 (opinion of Rehnquist, C.J.); *id.*, at 532 (opinion of Scalia, J.). All that remained between the promise of *Roe* and the darkness of the plurality was a single, flickering flame. Decisions since *Webster* gave little reason to hope that this flame would cast much light. See, *e.g., Ohio* v. *Akron Center for Reproductive Health*, 497 U.S. 502, 524 (1990) (opinion of Blackmun, J.). But now, just when so many expected the darkness to fall, the flame has grown bright.

I do not underestimate the significance of today's joint opinion. Yet I remain steadfast in my belief that the right to reproductive choice is entitled to the full protection afforded by this Court before *Webster*. And I fear for the darkness as four Justices anxiously await the single vote necessary to extinguish the light.

I

Make no mistake, the joint opinion of JUSTICES O'CONNOR, KENNEDY, and SOUTER is an act of personal courage and constitutional principle. In contrast to previous decisions in which JUSTICES O'CONNOR and KENNEDY postponed reconsideration of *Roe* v. *Wade*, 410 U.S. 113 (1973), the authors of the joint opinion today join JUSTICE STEVENS and me in concluding that "the essential holding of *Roe* should be retained and once again reaffirmed." *Ante*, at [343]. In brief, five Members of this Court today recognize that "the Constitution protects a woman's right to terminate her pregnancy in its early stages." *Id.*, at [341].

A fervent view of individual liberty and the force of *stare decisis* have led the Court to this conclusion. *Ante*, at [350]. Today a majority reaffirms that the Due Process Clause of the Fourteenth Amendment establishes "a realm of personal liberty which the government may not enter," *ante*, at [345]— a realm whose outer limits cannot be determined by interpretations of the Constitution that focus only on the specific practices of States at the time the Fourteenth Amendment was adopted. See *ante*, at [346]. Included within this realm of liberty is " 'the right of the *individual*, married or single, to be free from unwarranted governmental intrusion into matters so fundamentally affecting a person as the decision whether to bear or beget a child.' " *Ante*, at [348], quoting *Eisenstadt* v. *Baird*, 405 U.S. 438, 453 (1972) (emphasis in original). "These matters, involving the most intimate and personal choices a person may make in a lifetime, choices central to personal dignity and autonomy, are *central* to the liberty protected by the Fourteenth Amendment." *Ante*, at [348] (emphasis added). Finally, the Court today recognizes that in the case of abortion, "the liberty of the woman is at stake in a sense unique to the human condition and so unique to the law. The mother who carries a child to full term is subject to anxieties, to physical constraints, to pain that only she must bear." *Ante*, at [349].

The Court's reaffirmation of *Roe*'s central holding is also based on the force of *stare decisis*. "[N]o erosion of principle going to liberty or personal autonomy has left *Roe*'s central holding a doctrinal remnant; *Roe* portends no developments at odds with other precedent for the analysis of personal liberty; and no changes of fact have rendered viability more or less appropriate as the point at which the balance of interests tips." *Ante*, at [356]. Indeed, the Court acknowledges that *Roe*'s limitation on state power could not be removed "without serious inequity to those who have relied upon it or significant damage to the stability of the society governed by the rule in question." *Ante*, at [351]. In the 19 years since *Roe* was decided, that case has shaped more than reproductive planning—"an entire generation has come of age free to assume *Roe*'s concept of liberty in defining the capacity of women to act in society and to make reproductive decisions." *Ante*, at [356]. The Court understands that, having "call[ed] the contending sides . . . to end their national division by accepting a common mandate rooted in the Constitution," *ante*, at [362], a decision to overrule *Roe* "would seriously weaken the Court's capacity to exercise the judicial power and to function as the Supreme Court of a Nation dedicated to the rule of law." *Ante*, at [360]. What has happened today should serve as a model for future Justices and a warning to all who have tried to turn this Court into yet another political branch.

In striking down the Pennsylvania statute's spousal notification requirement, the Court has established a framework for evaluating abortion regulations that responds to the social context of women facing issues of reproductive choice.[1] In determining the burden imposed by the challenged regulation, the Court inquires whether the regulation's "*purpose or effect* is to place a substantial obstacle in the path of a woman seeking an abortion before the fetus attains viability." *Ante*, at [372] (emphasis added). The Court reaffirms: "The proper focus of constitutional inquiry is the group for whom the law is a restriction, not the group for whom the law is irrelevant." *Ante*, at [386]. Looking at this group, the Court inquires, based on expert testimony, empirical studies, and common sense, whether "in a large fraction of the cases in which [the restriction] is relevant, it will operate as a substantial obstacle to a woman's choice to undergo an abortion." *Id.*, at [386–87]. "A

---

[1] As I shall explain, the joint opinion and I disagree on the appropriate standard of review for abortion regulations. I do agree, however, that the reasons advanced by the joint opinion suffice to invalidate the spousal notification requirement under a strict scrutiny standard.

statute with this purpose is invalid because the means chosen by the State to further the interest in potential life must be calculated to inform the woman's free choice, not hinder it." *Ante*, at [370]. And in applying its test, the Court remains sensitive to the unique role of women in the decision-making process. Whatever may have been the practice when the Fourteenth Amendment was adopted, the Court observes, "[w]omen do not lose their constitutionally protected liberty when they marry. The Constitution protects all individuals, male or female, married or unmarried, from the abuse of governmental power, even where that power is employed for the supposed benefit of a member of the individual's family." *Ante*, at [389–90].[2]

Lastly, while I believe that the joint opinion errs in failing to invalidate the other regulations, I am pleased that the joint opinion has not ruled out the possibility that these regulations may be shown to impose an unconstitutional burden. The joint opinion makes clear that its specific holdings are based on the insufficiency of the record before it. See, *e. g.*, *id.*, at [375]. I am confident that in the future evidence will be produced to show that "in a large fraction of the cases in which [these regulations are] relevant, [they] will operate as a substantial obstacle to a woman's choice to undergo an abortion." *Ante*, at [386–87].

II

Today, no less than yesterday, the Constitution and decisions of this Court require that a State's abortion restrictions be subjected to the strictest of judicial scrutiny. Our precedents and the joint opinion's principles require us to subject all non-*de minimis* abortion regulations to strict scrutiny. Under this standard, the Pennsylvania statute's provisions requiring content-based counseling, a 24-hour delay, informed parental

[2] I also join the Court's decision to uphold the medical emergency provision. As the Court notes, its interpretation is consistent with the essential holding of *Roe* that "forbids a State from interfering with a woman's choice to undergo an abortion procedure if continuing her pregnancy would constitute a threat to her health." *Ante*, at [375]. As is apparent in my analysis below, however, this exception does not render constitutional the provisions which I conclude do not survive strict scrutiny.

consent, and reporting of abortion-related information must be invalidated.

A

The Court today reaffirms the long recognized rights of privacy and bodily integrity. As early as 1891, the Court held, "no right is held more sacred, or is more carefully guarded by the commonlaw, than the right of every individual to the possession and control of his own person, free from all restraint or interference of others . . . ." *Union Pacific R. Co. v. Botsford*, 141 U.S. 250, 251 (1891). Throughout this century, this Court also has held that the fundamental right of privacy protects citizens against governmental intrusion in such intimate family matters as procreation, childrearing, marriage, and contraceptive choice. See *ante*, at [345]. These cases embody the principle that personal decisions that profoundly affect bodily integrity, identity, and destiny should be largely beyond the reach of government. *Eisenstadt*, 405 U.S., at 453. In *Roe v. Wade*, this Court correctly applied these principles to a woman's right to choose abortion.

State restrictions on abortion violate a woman's right of privacy in two ways. First, compelled continuation of a pregnancy infringes upon a woman's right to bodily integrity by imposing substantial physical intrusions and significant risks of physical harm. During pregnancy, women experience dramatic physical changes and a wide range of health consequences. Labor and delivery pose additional health risks and physical demands. In short, restrictive abortion laws force women to endure physical invasions far more substantial than those this Court has held to violate the constitutional principle of bodily integrity in other contexts. See, *e.g.*, *Winston v. Lee*, 470 U.S. 753 (1985) (invalidating surgical removal of bullet from murder suspect); *Rochin v. California*, 342 U.S. 165 (1952) (invalidating stomach-pumping).[3]

Further, when the State restricts a woman's right to ter-

[3] As the joint opinion acknowledges, *ante*, at [355], this Court has recognized the vital liberty interest of persons in refusing unwanted medical treatment. *Cruzan v. Director, Missouri Dept. of Health*, 497 U.S. 261 (1990). Just as the Due Process Clause protects the deeply personal decision of the individual to *refuse* medical treatment, it also must protect the deeply personal decision to *obtain* medical treatment, including a woman's decision to terminate a pregnancy.

minate her pregnancy, it deprives a woman of the right to make her own decision about reproduction and family planning—critical life choices that this Court long has deemed central to the right to privacy. The decision to terminate or continue a pregnancy has no less an impact on a woman's life than decisions about contraception or marriage. 410 U.S., at 153. Because motherhood has a dramatic impact on a woman's educational prospects, employment opportunities, and self-determination, restrictive abortion laws deprive her of basic control over her life. For these reasons, "the decision whether or not to beget or bear a child" lies at "the very heart of this cluster of constitutionally protected choices." *Carey* v. *Population Services, Int'l*, 431 U.S. 678 (1977).

A State's restrictions on a woman's right to terminate her pregnancy also implicate constitutional guarantees of gender equality. State restrictions on abortion compel women to continue pregnancies they otherwise might terminate. By restricting the right to terminate pregnancies, the State conscripts women's bodies into its service, forcing women to continue their pregnancies, suffer the pains of childbirth, and in most instances, provide years of maternal care. The State does not compensate women for their services; instead, it assumes that they owe this duty as a matter of course. This assumption—that women can simply be forced to accept the "natural" status and incidents of motherhood—appears to rest upon a conception of women's role that has triggered the protection of the Equal Protection Clause. See, *e.g.*, *Mississippi Univ. for Women* v. *Hogan*, 458 U.S. 718, 724–726 (1982); *Craig* v. *Boren*, 429 U.S. 190, 198–199 (1976).[4] The joint opinion recognizes that these assumptions about women's place in society "are no longer consistent with our understanding of the family, the individual, or the Constitution." *Ante*, at [388].

---

[4] A growing number of commentators are recognizing this point. See, *e.g.*, L. Tribe, American Constitutional Law, § 15–10, 1353–1359 (2d ed. 1988); Siegel, Reasoning from the Body: A Historical Perspective on Abortion Regulation and Questions of Equal Protection, 44 Stan. L. Rev. 261, 350–380 (1992); Sunstein, Neutrality in Constitutional Law (With Special Reference to Pornography, Abortion, and Surrogacy), 92 Colum. L. Rev. 1, 31–44 (1992); MacKinnon, Reflections on Sex Equality Under Law, 100 Yale L.J. 1281, 1308–1324 (1991); cf. Rubenfeld, The Right of Privacy, 102 Harv. L. Rev. 737, 788–791 (1989) (similar analysis under the rubric of privacy).

B

The Court has held that limitations on the right of privacy are permissible only if they survive "strict" constitutional scrutiny—that is, only if the governmental entity imposing the restriction can demonstrate that the limitation is both necessary and narrowly tailored to serve a compelling governmental interest. *Griswold* v. *Connecticut*, 381 U.S. 479, 485 (1965). We have applied this principle specifically in the context of abortion regulations. *Roe* v. *Wade*, 410 U.S., at 155.[5]

Roe implemented these principles through a framework that was designed "to insure that the woman's right to choose not become so subordinate to the State's interest in promoting fetal life that her choice exists in theory but not in fact," *ante*, at [366]. *Roe* identified two relevant State interests: "an interest in preserving and protecting the health of the pregnant woman" and an interest in "protecting the potentiality of human life." 410 U.S., at 162. With respect to the State's interest in the health of the mother, "the 'compelling' point . . . is at approximately the end of the first trimester," because it is at that point that the mortality rate in abortion approaches that in childbirth. *Roe*, 410 U.S., at 163. With respect to the State's interest in potential life, "the 'compelling' point is at viability," because it is at that point that the fetus "presumably has the capability of meaningful life outside the mother's womb." *Ibid.* In order to fulfill the requirement of narrow tailoring, "the State is obligated to make a reasonable effort to limit the effect of its regulations to the period in the trimester during which its health interest will be furthered." *Akron*, 462 U.S., at 434.

In my view, application of this analytical framework is no

---

[5] To say that restrictions on a right are subject to strict scrutiny is not to say that the right is absolute. Regulations can be upheld if they have no significant impact on the woman's exercise of her right and are justified by important state health objectives. See, *e.g.*, *Planned Parenthood of Central Mo.* v. *Danforth*, 428 U.S. 52, 65–67, 79–81 (1976) (upholding requirements of a woman's written consent and record keeping). But the Court today reaffirms the essential principle of *Roe* that a woman has the right "to choose to have an abortion before viability and to obtain it without undue interference from the State." *Ante*, at [343]. Under *Roe*, any more than *de minimis* interference is undue.

less warranted than when it was approved by seven Members of this Court in *Roe*. Strict scrutiny of state limitations on reproductive choice still offers the most secure protection of the woman's right to make her own reproductive decisions, free from state coercion. No majority of this Court has ever agreed upon an alternative approach. The factual premises of the trimester framework have not been undermined, see *Webster*, 492 U.S., at 553 (BLACKMUN, J., dissenting), and the *Roe* framework is far more administrable, and far less manipulable, than the "undue burden" standard adopted by the joint opinion.

Nonetheless, three criticisms of the trimester framework continue to be uttered. First, the trimester framework is attacked because its key elements do not appear in the text of the Constitution. My response to this attack remains the same as it was in *Webster*:

> "Were this a true concern, we would have to abandon most of our constitutional jurisprudence. [T]he 'critical elements' of countless constitutional doctrines nowhere appear in the Constitution's text . . . . The Constitution makes no mention, for example, of the First Amendment's 'actual malice' standard for proving certain libels, see *New York Times Co. v. Sullivan*, 376 U.S. 254 (1964). . . . Similarly, the Constitution makes no mention of the rational-basis test, or the specific verbal formulations of intermediate and strict scrutiny by which this Court evaluates claims under the Equal Protection Clause. The reason is simple. Like the *Roe* framework, these tests or standards are not, and do not purport to be, rights protected by the Constitution. Rather, they are judge-made methods for evaluating and measuring the strength and scope of constitutional rights or for balancing the constitutional rights of individuals against the competing interests of government." 492 U.S., at 548.

The second criticism is that the framework more closely resembles a regulatory code than a body of constitutional doctrine. Again, my answer remains the same as in *Webster*.

> "[I]f this were a true and genuine concern, we would have to abandon vast areas of our constitutional jurisprudence. . . .

Are [the distinctions entailed in the trimester framework] any finer, or more 'regulatory,' than the distinctions we have often drawn in our First Amendment jurisprudence, where, for example, we have held that a 'release time' program permitting public-school students to leave school grounds during school hours to receive religious instruction does not violate the Establishment Clause, even though a release-time program permitting religious instruction on school grounds does violate the Clause? Compare *Zorach v. Clauson*, 343 U.S. 306 (1952), with *Illinois ex rel. McCollum v. Board of Education of School Dist. No. 71, Champaign County*, 333 U.S. 203 (1948). . . . Similarly, in a Sixth Amendment case, the Court held that although an overnight ban on attorney-client communication violated the constitutionally guaranteed right to counsel, *Geders v. United States*, 425 U.S. 80 (1976), that right was not violated when a trial judge separated a defendant from his lawyer during a 15-minute recess after the defendant's direct testimony. *Perry v. Leake*, 488 U.S. 272 (1989). That numerous constitutional doctrines result in narrow differentiations between similar circumstances does not mean that this Court has abandoned adjudication in favor of regulation." *Id.*, at 549–550.

The final, and more genuine, criticism of the trimester framework is that it fails to find the State's interest in potential human life compelling throughout pregnancy. No member of this Court—nor for that matter, the Solicitor General, Tr. of Oral Arg. [333]—has ever questioned our holding in *Roe* that an abortion is not "the termination of life entitled to Fourteenth Amendment protection." 410 U.S., at 159. Accordingly, a State's interest in protecting fetal life is not grounded in the Constitution. Nor, consistent with our Establishment Clause, can it be a theological or sectarian interest. See *Thornburgh*, 476 U.S., at 778 (STEVENS, J., concurring). It is, instead, a legitimate interest grounded in humanitarian or pragmatic concerns. See *ante*, at [407] (opinion of STEVENS, J.).

But while a State has "legitimate interests from the outset of the pregnancy in protecting the health of the woman and the life of the fetus that may become a child," *ante*, at [343], legitimate interests are not enough. To overcome the burden of strict scrutiny, the interests must be compelling. The question then is how best to accommodate the State's interest in potential human life with the constitutional liberties of pregnant women. Again, I stand by the views I expressed in *Webster*:

> "I remain convinced, as six other Members of this Court 16 years ago were convinced, that the *Roe* framework, and the viability standard in particular, fairly, sensibly, and effectively functions to safeguard the constitutional liberties of pregnant women while recognizing and accommodating the State's interest in potential human life. The viability line reflects the biological facts and truths of fetal development; it marks that threshold moment prior to which a fetus cannot survive separate from the woman and cannot reasonably and objectively be regarded as a subject of rights or interests distinct from, or paramount to, those of the pregnant woman. At the same time, the viability standard takes account of the undeniable fact that as the fetus evolves into its postnatal form, and as it loses its dependence on the uterine environment, the State's interest in the fetus' potential human life, and in fostering a regard for human life in general, becomes compelling. As a practical matter, because viability follows 'quickening'—the point at which a woman feels movement in her womb—and because viability occurs no earlier than 23 weeks gestational age, it establishes an easily applicable standard for regulating abortion while providing a pregnant woman ample time to exercise her fundamental right with her responsible physician to terminate her pregnancy." 492 U.S., at 553–554.[6]

Roe's trimester framework does not ignore the State's interest in prenatal life. Like JUSTICE STEVENS, I agree that the State may take steps to ensure that a woman's choice "is thoughtful and informed," *ante*, at [367], and that "States are free to enact laws to provide a reasonable framework for a woman to make a decision that has such profound and lasting meaning." *Ante*, at [367]. But

> "[s]erious questions arise when a State attempts to 'persuade the woman to choose childbirth over abortion.' *Ante*, at [409].

---

[6] The joint opinion agrees with *Roe*'s conclusion that viability occurs at 23 or 24 weeks at the earliest. Compare *ante*, at [356], with 410 U.S., at 160.

Decisional autonomy must limit the State's power to inject into a woman's most personal deliberations its own views of what is best. The State may promote its preferences by funding childbirth, by creating and maintaining alternatives to abortion, and by espousing the virtues of family, but it must respect the individual's freedom to make such judgments." *Ante,* at [407] (opinion of STEVENS, J.).

As the joint opinion recognizes, "the means chosen by the State to further the interest in potential life must be calculated to inform the woman's free choice, not hinder it." *Ante,* at [370].

In sum, *Roe's* requirement of strict scrutiny as implemented through a trimester framework should not be disturbed. No other approach has gained a majority, and no other is more protective of the woman's fundamental right. Lastly, no other approach properly accommodates the woman's constitutional right with the State's legitimate interests.

C

Application of the strict scrutiny standard results in the invalidation of all the challenged provisions. Indeed, as this Court has invalidated virtually identical provisions in prior cases, *stare decisis* requires that we again strike them down.

This Court has upheld informed and written consent requirements only where the State has demonstrated that they genuinely further important health-related state concerns. See *Danforth,* 428 U.S., at 65–67. A State may not, under the guise of securing informed consent, "require the delivery of information 'designed to influence the woman's informed choice between abortion or childbirth.' " *Thornburgh v. American College of Obstetricians & Gynecologists,* 476 U.S. 747, 760 (1986), (quoting *Akron,* 462 U.S., at 443–444). Rigid requirements that a specific body of information be imparted to a woman in all cases, regardless of the needs of the patient, improperly intrude upon the discretion of the pregnant woman's physician and thereby impose an " 'undesired and uncomfortable straitjacket.' " *Thornburgh,* 476 U.S., at 762 (quoting *Danforth,* 428 U.S., at 67, n. 8).

Measured against these principles, some aspects of the

Pennsylvania informed-consent scheme are unconstitutional. While it is unobjectionable for the Commonwealth to require that the patient be informed of the nature of the procedure, the health risks of the abortion and of childbirth, and the probable gestational age of the unborn child, compare §§ 3205(a)(i)–(iii) with *Akron*, 462 U.S., at 446, n. 37, I remain unconvinced that there is a vital state need for insisting that the information be provided by a physician rather than a counselor. *Id.*, at 448. The District Court found that the physician-only requirement necessarily would increase costs to the plaintiff-clinics, costs that undoubtedly would be passed on to patients. And because trained women counselors are often more understanding than physicians, and generally have more time to spend with patients, see App. 366a–387a, the physician-only disclosure requirement is not narrowly tailored to serve the Commonwealth's interest in protecting maternal health.

Sections 3205(a)(2)(i)–(iii) of the Act further requires that the physician or a qualified non-physician inform the woman that printed materials are available from the Commonwealth that describe the fetus and provide information about medical assistance for childbirth, information about child support from the father, and a list of agencies offering that provide adoption and other services as alternatives to abortion. *Thornburgh* invalidated biased patient-counseling requirements virtually identical to the one at issue here. What we said of those requirements fully applies in this case:

> "the listing of agencies in the printed Pennsylvania form presents serious problems; it contains names of agencies that well may be out of step with the needs of the particular woman and thus places the physician in an awkward position and infringes upon his or her professional responsibilities. Forcing the physician or counselor to present the materials and the list to the woman makes him or her in effect an agent of the State in treating the woman and places his or her imprimatur upon both the materials and the list. All this is, or comes close to being, state medicine imposed upon the woman, not the professional medical guidance she seeks, and it officially structures—as it obviously was intended to do—the dialogue between the woman and her physician.

"The requirements . . . that the woman be advised that medical assistance benefits may be available, and that the father is responsible for financial assistance in the support of the child similarly are poorly disguised elements of discouragement for the abortion decision. Much of this . . ., for many patients, would be irrelevant and inappropriate. For a patient with a life-threatening pregnancy, the 'information' in its very rendition may be cruel as well as destructive of the physician-patient relationship. As any experienced social worker or other counselor knows, theoretical financial responsibility often does not equate with fulfillment . . . . Under the guise of informed consent, the Act requires the dissemination of information that is not relevant to such consent, and, thus, it advances no legitimate state interest." 476 U.S., at 763.

"This type of compelled information is the antithesis of informed consent," *id.*, at 764, and goes far beyond merely describing the general subject matter relevant to the woman's decision. "That the Commonwealth does not, and surely would not, compel similar disclosure of every possible peril of necessary surgery or of simple vaccination, reveals the anti-abortion character of the statute and its real purpose." *Ibid.*[7]

The 24-hour waiting period following the provision of the foregoing information is also clearly unconstitutional. The District Court found that the mandatory 24-hour delay could lead to delays in excess of 24 hours, thus increasing health risks, and that it would require two visits to the abortion

---

[7] While I do not agree with the joint opinion's conclusion that these provisions should be upheld, the joint opinion has remained faithful to principles this Court previously has announced in examining counseling provisions. For example, the joint opinion concludes that the "information the State requires to be made available to the woman" must be "truthful and not misleading." *Ante*, at [375]. Because the State's information must be "calculated to inform the woman's free choice, not hinder it," *ante*, at [370], the measures must be designed to ensure that a woman's choice is "mature and informed," *id.*, at [376], not intimidated, imposed, or impelled. To this end, when the State requires the provision of certain information, the State may not alter the manner of presentation in order to inflict "psychological abuse," *id.*, at [384–85], designed to shock or unnerve a woman seeking to exercise her liberty right. This, for example, would appear to preclude a State from requiring a woman to view graphic literature or films detailing the performance of an abortion operation. Just as a visual preview of an operation to remove an appendix plays no part in a physician's securing informed consent to an appendectomy, a preview of scenes appurtenant to any major medical intrusion into the human body does not constructively inform the decision of a woman of the State's interest in the preservation of the woman's health or demonstrate the State's "profound respect for the potential life she carries within her." *Id.*, at [370].

provider, thereby increasing travel time, exposure to further harassment, and financial cost. Finally, the District Court found that the requirement would pose especially significant burdens on women living in rural areas and those women that have difficulty explaining their whereabouts. App. to Pet. for Cert. in No. 91–902, pp. 380a–382a (hereinafter App.). In *Akron* this Court invalidated a similarly arbitrary or inflexible waiting period because, as here, it furthered no legitimate state interest.[8]

As JUSTICE STEVENS insightfully concludes, the mandatory delay rests either on outmoded or unacceptable assumptions about the decisionmaking capacity of women or the belief that the decision to terminate the pregnancy is presumptively wrong. *Ante*, at [409]. The requirement that women consider this obvious and slanted information for an additional 24 hours contained in these provisions will only influence the woman's decision in improper ways. The vast majority of women will know this information—of the few that do not, it is less likely that their minds will be changed by this information than it will be either by the realization that the State opposes their choice or the need once again to endure abuse and harassment on return to the clinic.[9]

Except in the case of a medical emergency, § 3206 requires a physician to obtain the informed consent of a parent or guardian before performing an abortion on an unemancipated minor or an incompetent woman. Based on evidence in the record, the District Court concluded that, in order to fulfill the informed-consent requirement, generally accepted medical principles would require an in-person visit by the parent to the facility. App. 399a. Although the Court "has recognized that the State has somewhat broader authority to regulate the

---

[8] The Court's decision in *Hodgson* v. *Minnesota*, 497 U.S. 417 (1990), validating a 48–hour waiting period for minors seeking an abortion to permit parental involvement does not alter this conclusion. Here the 24-hour delay is imposed on an adult woman. See *Hodgson*, 497 U.S., at [449], n. 35 (slip op. 28–29, n. 35); *Ohio* v. *Akron Ctr. for Reproductive Health, Inc.*, 497 U.S. 502, [507] (1990). Moreover, the statute in *Hodgson* did not require any delay once the minor obtained the affirmative consent of either a parent or the court.

[9] Because this information is so widely known, I am confident that a developed record can be made to show that the 24-hour delay, "in a large fraction of the cases in which [the restriction] is relevant, . . . will operate as a substantial obstacle to a woman's choice to undergo an abortion." *Ante*, at [386–87].

activities of children than of adults," the State nevertheless must demonstrate that there is a *"significant state interest* in conditioning an abortion . . . that is not present in the case of an adult." *Danforth*, 428 U.S., at 74–75 (emphasis added). The requirement of an in-person visit would carry with it the risk of a delay of several days or possibly weeks, even where the parent is willing to consent. While the State has an interest in encouraging parental involvement in the minor's abortion decision, § 3206 is not narrowly drawn to serve that interest.[10]

Finally, the Pennsylvania statute requires every facility performing abortions to report its activities to the Commonwealth. Pennsylvania contends that this requirement is valid under *Danforth*, in which this Court held that recordkeeping and reporting requirements that are reasonably directed to the preservation of maternal health and that properly respect a patient's confidentiality are permissible. 428 U.S., at 79–81. The Commonwealth attempts to justify its required reports on the ground that the public has a right to know how its tax dollars are spent. A regulation designed to inform the public about public expenditures does not further the Commonwealth's interest in protecting maternal health. Accordingly, such a regulation cannot justify a legally significant burden on a woman's right to obtain an abortion.

The confidential reports concerning the identities and medical judgment of physicians involved in abortions at first glance may seem valid, given the State's interest in maternal health and enforcement of the Act. The District Court found, however, that, notwithstanding the confidentiality protections, many physicians, particularly those who have previously discontinued performing abortions because of harassment, would refuse to refer patients to abortion clinics if their names were to appear on these reports. App. 447a–448a. The Common-

---

[10] The judicial-bypass provision does not cure this violation. *Hodgson* is distinguishable, since this case involves more than parental involvement or approval—rather, the Pennsylvania law requires that the parent receive information designed to discourage abortion in a face-to-face meeting with the physician. The bypass procedure cannot ensure that the parent would obtain the information, since in many instances, the parent would not even attend the hearing. A State may not place any restriction on a young woman's right to an abortion, however irrational, simply because it has provided a judicial bypass.

wealth has failed to show that the name of the referring physician either adds to the pool of scientific knowledge concerning abortion or is reasonably related to the Commonwealth's interest in maternal health. I therefore agree with the District Court's conclusion that the confidential reporting requirements are unconstitutional insofar as they require the name of the referring physician and the basis for his or her medical judgment.

In sum, I would affirm the judgment in No. 91–902 and reverse the judgment in No. 91–744 and remand the cases for further proceedings.

III

At long last, THE CHIEF JUSTICE admits it. Gone are the contentions that the issue need not be (or has not been) considered. There, on the first page, for all to see, is what was expected: "We believe that *Roe* was wrongly decided, and that it can and should be overruled consistently with our traditional approach to *stare decisis* in constitutional cases." *Post*, at [432]. If there is much reason to applaud the advances made by the joint opinion today, there is far more to fear from THE CHIEF JUSTICE's opinion.

THE CHIEF JUSTICE's criticism of *Roe* follows from his stunted conception of individual liberty. While recognizing that the Due Process Clause protects more than simple physical liberty, he then goes on to construe this Court's personal-liberty cases as establishing only a laundry list of particular rights, rather than a principled account of how these particular rights are grounded in a more general right of privacy. *Post*, at [439]. This constricted view is reinforced by THE CHIEF JUSTICE's exclusive reliance on tradition as a source of fundamental rights. He argues that the record in favor of a right to abortion is no stronger than the record in *Michael H.* v. *Gerald D.*, 491 U.S. 110 (1989), where the plurality found no fundamental right to visitation privileges by an adulterous father, or in *Bowers* v. *Hardwick*, 478 U.S. 186 (1986), where the Court found no fundamental right to engage in homosexual sodomy, or in a case involving the "firing of a gun . . . into another person's body." *Post*, at [440]. In THE CHIEF

JUSTICE's world, a woman considering whether to terminate a pregnancy is entitled to no more protection than adulterers, murderers, and so-called "sexual deviates."[11] Given THE CHIEF JUSTICE's exclusive reliance on tradition, people using contraceptives seem the next likely candidate for his list of outcasts.

Even more shocking than THE CHIEF JUSTICE's cramped notion of individual liberty is his complete omission of any discussion of the effects that compelled childbirth and motherhood have on women's lives. The only expression of concern with women's health is purely instrumental—for THE CHIEF JUSTICE, only women's psychological health is a concern, and only to the extent that he assumes that every woman who decides to have an abortion does so without serious consideration of the moral implications of their decision. *Post*, at [455]. In short, THE CHIEF JUSTICE's view of the State's compelling interest in maternal health has less to do with health than it does with compelling women to be maternal.

Nor does THE CHIEF JUSTICE give any serious consideration to the doctrine of *stare decisis*. For THE CHIEF JUSTICE, the facts that gave rise to *Roe* are surprisingly simple: "women become pregnant, there is a point somewhere, depending on medical technology, where a fetus becomes viable, and women give birth to children." *Post*, at [442]. This characterization of the issue thus allows THE CHIEF JUSTICE quickly to discard the joint opinion's reliance argument by asserting that "reproductive planning could take . . . virtually immediate account of a decision overruling *Roe*." *Id.*, at [443] (internal quotations omitted).

THE CHIEF JUSTICE's narrow conception of individual liberty and *stare decisis* leads him to propose the same standard of review proposed by the plurality in *Webster*. "States may regulate abortion procedures in ways rationally related to a legitimate state interest. *Williamson v. Lee Optical Co.*, 348 U.S. 483, 491 (1955); cf. *Stanley v. Illinois*, 405 U.S. 645, 651–653 (1972)." *Post*, at [452]. THE CHIEF JUSTICE then further weakens the test by providing an insurmountable requirement for facial challenges: petitioners must " 'show that no set of

---

[11] Obviously, I do not share the THE CHIEF JUSTICE's views of homosexuality as sexual deviance. See *Bowers*, 478 U.S., at 202–203, n.2 (BLACKMUN, J., dissenting).

circumstances exists under which the [provision] would be valid.' " *Post*, at [456], quoting *Ohio v. Akron Center for Reproductive Health*, 497 U.S., at 514. In short, in his view, petitioners must prove that the statute cannot constitutionally be applied to *anyone*. Finally, in applying his standard to the spousal-notification provision, THE CHIEF JUSTICE contends that the record lacks any "hard evidence" to support the joint opinion's contention that a "large fraction" of women who prefer not to notify their husbands involve situations of battered women and unreported spousal assault. *Post*, at [458], n. 2. Yet throughout the explication of his standard, THE CHIEF JUSTICE never explains what hard evidence is, how large a fraction is required, or how a battered woman is supposed to pursue an as-applied challenge.

Under his standard, States can ban abortion if that ban is rationally related to a legitimate state interest—a standard which the United States calls "deferential, but not toothless." Yet when pressed at oral argument to describe the teeth, the best protection that the Solicitor General could offer to women was that a prohibition, enforced by criminal penalties, *with no exception for the life of the mother*, "could raise very serious questions." Tr. of Oral Arg. [336]. Perhaps, the Solicitor General offered, the failure to include an exemption for the life of the mother would be "arbitrary and capricious." *Id.*, at [337]. If, as THE CHIEF JUSTICE contends, the undue burden test is made out of whole cloth, the so-called "arbitrary and capricious" limit is the Solicitor General's "new clothes."

Even if it is somehow "irrational" for a State to require a woman to risk her life for her child, what protection is offered for women who become pregnant through rape or incest? Is there anything arbitrary or capricious about a State's prohibiting the sins of the father from being visited upon his offspring?[12]

---

[12] JUSTICE SCALIA urges the Court to "get out of this area" and leave questions regarding abortion entirely to the States. *Post*, at [484]. Putting aside the fact that what he advocates is nothing short of an abdication by the Court of its constitutional responsibilities, JUSTICE SCALIA is uncharacteristically naive if he thinks that overruling *Roe* and holding that restrictions on a woman's right to an abortion are subject only to rational-basis review will enable the Court henceforth to avoid reviewing abortion-related issues. State efforts to regulate and prohibit abortion in a post-*Roe* world undoubtedly would raise a host of distinct and important constitutional questions meriting review by this Court. For example, does the Eighth Amendment impose any limits on the degree or kind of punishment a State can inflict upon physicians

But, we are reassured, there is always the protection of the democratic process. While there is much to be praised about our democracy, our country since its founding has recognized that there are certain fundamental liberties that are not to be left to the whims of an election. A woman's right to reproductive choice is one of those fundamental liberties. Accordingly, that liberty need not seek refuge at the ballot box.

IV

In one sense, the Court's approach is worlds apart from that of THE CHIEF JUSTICE and JUSTICE SCALIA. And yet, in another sense, the distance between the two approaches is short—the distance is but a single vote.

I am 83 years old. I cannot remain on this Court forever, and when I do step down, the confirmation process for my successor well may focus on the issue before us today. That, I regret, may be exactly where the choice between the two worlds will be made.

---

who perform, or women who undergo, abortions? What effect would differences among States in their approaches to abortion have on a woman's right to engage in interstate travel? Does the First Amendment permit States that choose not to criminalize abortion to ban all advertising providing information about where and how to obtain abortions?

OPINION OF CHIEF JUSTICE REHNQUIST, WITH WHOM JUSTICE WHITE, JUSTICE SCALIA, AND JUSTICE THOMAS JOIN

CHIEF JUSTICE REHNQUIST, with whom JUSTICE WHITE, JUSTICE SCALIA, and JUSTICE THOMAS join, concurring in the judgment in part and dissenting in part.

The joint opinion, following its newly-minted variation on *stare decisis*, retains the outer shell of *Roe* v. *Wade*, 410 U.S. 113 (1973), but beats a wholesale retreat from the substance of that case. We believe that *Roe* was wrongly decided, and that it can and should be overruled consistently with our traditional approach to *stare decisis* in constitutional cases. We would adopt the approach of the plurality in *Webster* v. *Reproductive Health Services*, 492 U.S. 490 (1989), and uphold the challenged provisions of the Pennsylvania statute in their entirety.

I

In ruling on this case below, the Court of Appeals for the Third Circuit first observed that "this appeal does not directly implicate *Roe*; this case involves the regulation of abortions rather than their outright prohibition." 947 F.2d 682, 687 (1991). Accordingly, the court directed its attention to the question of the standard of review for abortion regulations. In attempting to settle on the correct standard, however, the court confronted the confused state of this Court's abortion jurisprudence. After considering the several opinions in *Webster* v. *Reproductive Health Services, supra,* and *Hodgson* v. *Minnesota,* 497 U.S. 417 (1990), the Court of Appeals concluded that JUSTICE O'CONNOR's "undue burden" test was controlling, as that was the narrowest ground on which we had upheld recent abortion regulations. 947 F.2d, at 693–697 (" 'When a fragmented court decides a case and no single rationale explaining the result enjoys the assent of five Justices, the holding of the Court may be viewed as that position taken by those Members who concurred in the judgments on the narrowest grounds' " (quoting *Marks* v. *United States,* 430 U.S. 188, 193 (1977) (internal quotation marks omitted)). Applying this standard, the Court of Appeals upheld all of the challenged regulations except the one requiring a woman to notify her spouse of an intended abortion.

In arguing that this Court should invalidate each of the provisions at issue, petitioners insist that we reaffirm our decision in *Roe* v. *Wade, supra,* in which we held unconstitutional a Texas statute making it a crime to procure an abortion except to save the life of the mother.[1] We agree with the Court of Appeals that our decision in *Roe* is not directly implicated by the Pennsylvania statute, which does not prohibit, but simply regulates, abortion. But, as the Court of Appeals found, the state of our post-*Roe* decisional law dealing with the regulation of abortion is confusing and uncertain, indicating that a reexamination of that line of cases is in order. Unfortunately for those who must apply this Court's decisions, the reexamination undertaken today leaves the Court no less divided than beforehand. Although they reject the trimester framework that formed the underpinning of *Roe,* JUSTICES O'CONNOR, KENNEDY, and SOUTER adopt a revised undue burden standard to analyze the challenged regulations. We conclude, however, that such an outcome is an unjustified constitutional compromise, one which leaves the Court in a

---

[1] Two years after *Roe,* the West German constitutional court, by contrast, struck down a law liberalizing access to abortion on the grounds that life developing within the womb is constitutionally protected. *Judgment of February 25, 1975,* 39 BVerfGE 1 (translated in Jonas & Gorby, West German Abortion Decision: A Contrast to *Roe* v. *Wade,* 9 J. Marshall J. Prac. & Proc. 605 (1976)). In 1988, the Canadian Supreme Court followed reasoning similar to that of *Roe* in striking down a law which restricted abortion. *Morgentaler* v. *Queen,* 1 S.C.R. 30, 44 D.L.R. 4th 385 (1988).

position to closely scrutinize all types of abortion regulations despite the fact that it lacks the power to do so under the Constitution.

In *Roe*, the Court opined that the State "does have an important and legitimate interest in preserving and protecting the health of the pregnant woman, . . . and that it has still another important and legitimate interest in protecting the potentiality of human life." 410 U.S., at 162 (emphasis omitted). In the companion case of *Doe* v. *Bolton*, 410 U.S. 179 (1973), the Court referred to its conclusion in *Roe* "that a pregnant woman does not have an absolute constitutional right to an abortion on her demand." 410 U.S., at 189. But while the language and holdings of these cases appeared to leave States free to regulate abortion procedures in a variety of ways, later decisions based on them have found considerably less latitude for such regulations than might have been expected.

For example, after *Roe*, many States have sought to protect their young citizens by requiring that a minor seeking an abortion involve her parents in the decision. Some States have simply required notification of the parents, while others have required a minor to obtain the consent of her parents. In a number of decisions, however, the Court has substantially limited the States in their ability to impose such requirements. With regard to parental *notice* requirements, we initially held that a State could require a minor to notify her parents before proceeding with an abortion. *H. L.* v. *Matheson*, 450 U.S. 398, 407–410 (1981). Recently, however, we indicated that a State's ability to impose a notice requirement actually depends on whether it requires notice of one or both parents. We concluded that although the Constitution might allow a State to demand that notice be given to one parent prior to an abortion, it may not require that similar notice be given to *two* parents, unless the State incorporates a judicial bypass procedure in that two-parent requirement. *Hodgson* v. *Minnesota, supra*.

We have treated parental *consent* provisions even more harshly. Three years after *Roe*, we invalidated a Missouri regulation requiring that an unmarried woman under the age of 18 obtain the consent of one her parents before proceeding with an abortion. We held that our abortion jurisprudence prohibited the State from imposing such a "blanket provision . . . requiring the consent of a parent." *Planned Parenthood of Central Mo. v. Danforth*, 428 U.S. 52, 74 (1976). In *Bellotti v. Baird*, 443 U.S. 622 (1979), the Court struck down a similar Massachusetts parental consent statute. A majority of the Court indicated, however, that a State could constitutionally require parental consent, if it alternatively allowed a pregnant minor to obtain an abortion without parental consent by showing either that she was mature enough to make her own decision, or that the abortion would be in her best interests. See *id.*, at 643–644 (plurality opinion); *id.*, at 656–657 (White, J., dissenting). In light of *Bellotti*, we have upheld one parental consent regulation which incorporated a judicial bypass option we viewed as sufficient, see *Planned Parenthood Assn. of Kansas City, Mo., Inc. v. Ashcroft*, 462 U.S. 476 (1983), but have invalidated another because of our belief that the judicial procedure did not satisfy the dictates of *Bellotti*. See *Akron v. Akron Center for Reproductive Health, Inc.*, 462 U.S. 416, 439–442 (1983). We have never had occasion, as we have in the parental notice context, to further parse our parental consent jurisprudence into one-parent and two-parent components.

In *Roe*, the Court observed that certain States recognized the right of the father to participate in the abortion decision in certain circumstances. Because neither *Roe* nor *Doe* involved the assertion of any paternal right, the Court expressly stated that the case did not disturb the validity of regulations that protected such a right. *Roe v. Wade*, 410 U.S., at 165, n. 67. But three years later, in *Danforth*, the Court extended its abortion jurisprudence and held that a State could not require that a woman obtain the consent of her spouse before proceeding with an abortion. *Planned Parenthood of Central Mo. v. Danforth*, 428 U.S., at 69–71.

States have also regularly tried to ensure that a woman's decision to have an abortion is an informed and well-considered one. In *Danforth*, we upheld a requirement that a woman sign a consent form prior to her abortion, and observed that "it is desirable and imperative that [the decision] be made with full knowledge of its nature and consequences." *Id.*, at 67. Since that case, however, we have twice invalidated state statutes designed to impart such knowledge to a woman seek-ing an abortion. In *Akron*, we held unconstitutional a regu-lation requiring a physician to inform a woman seeking an abortion of the status of her pregnancy, the development of her fetus, the date of possible viability, the complications that could result from an abortion, and the availability of agencies providing assistance and information with respect to adoption and childbirth. *Akron v. Akron Center for Reproductive Health, supra*, at 442–445. More recently, in *Thornburgh v. American College of Obstetricians and Gynecologists*, 476 U.S. 747 (1986), we struck down a more limited Pennsylvania regulation re-quiring that a woman be informed of the risks associated with the abortion procedure and the assistance available to her if she decided to proceed with her pregnancy, because we saw the compelled information as "the antithesis of informed con-sent." *Id.*, at 764. Even when a State has sought only to provide information that, in our view, was consistent with the *Roe* framework, we concluded that the State could not require that a physician furnish the information, but instead had to alternatively allow nonphysician counselors to provide it. *Akron v. Akron Center for Reproductive Health*, 462 U.S., at 448–449. In *Akron* as well, we went further and held that a State may not require a physician to wait 24 hours to perform an abortion after receiving the consent of a woman. Although the State sought to ensure that the woman's decision was carefully considered, the Court concluded that the Consti-tution forbade the State from imposing any sort of delay. *Id.*, at 449–451.

We have not allowed States much leeway to regulate even the actual abortion procedure. Although a State can require that second-trimester abortions be performed in outpatient clinics, see *Simopoulos v. Virginia*, 462 U.S. 506 (1983), we concluded in *Akron* and *Ashcroft* that a State could not require that such abortions be performed only in hospitals. See *Akron v. Akron Center for Reproductive Health, supra*, at 437–439; *Planned Parenthood Assn. of Kansas City, Mo., Inc. v. Ashcroft, supra*, at 481–482. Despite the fact that *Roe* expressly allowed regulation after the first trimester in furtherance of maternal health, " 'present medical knowledge,' " in our view, could not justify such a hospitalization requirement under the trimes-

ter framework. *Akron* v. *Akron Center for Reproductive Health,
supra,* at 437 (quoting *Roe* v. *Wade, supra,* at 163). And in
Danforth, the Court held that Missouri could not outlaw the
saline amniocentesis method of abortion, concluding that the
Missouri Legislature had "failed to appreciate and to consider
several significant facts" in making its decision. 428 U.S.,
at 77.

Although *Roe* allowed state regulation after the point of
viability to protect the potential life of the fetus, the Court
subsequently rejected attempts to regulate in this manner. In
Colautti v. *Franklin,* 439 U.S. 379 (1979), the Court struck
down a statute that governed the determination of viability.
Id., at 390–397. In the process, we made clear that the trimester framework incorporated only one definition of viability—
ours—as we forbade States from deciding that a certain objective indicator—"be it weeks of gestation or fetal weight or
any other single factor"—should govern the definition of viability. *Id.,* at 389. In that same case, we also invalidated a
regulation requiring a physician to use the abortion technique
offering the best chance for fetal survival when performing
postviability abortions. See *id.,* at 397–401; see also *Thornburgh* v. *American College of Obstetricians and Gynecologists,
supra,* at 768–769 (invalidating a similar regulation). In *Thornburgh,* the Court struck down Pennsylvania's requirement that
a second physician be present at postviability abortions to help
preserve the health of the unborn child, on the ground that
it did not incorporate a sufficient medical emergency exception. *Id.,* at 769–771. Regulations governing the treatment of
aborted fetuses have met a similar fate. In *Akron,* we invalidated a provision requiring physicians performing abortions to
"insure that the remains of the unborn child are disposed of
in a humane and sanitary manner." 462 U.S., at 451 (internal
quotation marks omitted).

Dissents in these cases expressed the view that the Court
was expanding upon *Roe* in imposing ever greater restrictions
on the States. See *Thornburgh* v. *American College of Obstetricians and Gynecologists,* 476 U.S., at 783 (Burger, C. J.,
dissenting) ("The extent to which the Court has departed
from the limitations expressed in *Roe* is readily apparent");
id., at 814 (WHITE, J., dissenting) ("[T]he majority indiscrim-

inately strikes down statutory provisions that in no way contravene the right recognized in *Roe*"). And, when confronted with State regulations of this type in past years, the Court has become increasingly more divided: the three most recent abortion cases have not commanded a Court opinion. See *Ohio* v. *Akron Center for Reproductive Health*, 497 U.S. 502 (1990); *Hodgson* v. *Minnesota*, 497 U.S. 417 (1990); *Webster* v. *Reproductive Health Services*, 492 U.S. 490 (1989).

The task of the Court of Appeals in the present case was obviously complicated by this confusion and uncertainty. Following *Marks* v. *United States*, 430 U.S. 188 (1977), it concluded that in light of *Webster* and *Hodgson*, the strict scrutiny standard enunciated in *Roe* was no longer applicable, and that the "undue burden" standard adopted by JUSTICE O'CONNOR was the governing principle. This state of confusion and disagreement warrants reexamination of the "fundamental right" accorded to a woman's decision to abort a fetus in *Roe*, with its concomitant requirement that any state regulation of abortion survive "strict scrutiny." See *Payne* v. *Tennessee*, 501 U.S. ____ – ____ (1991) (slip op., at 17–20) (observing that reexamination of constitutional decisions is appropriate when those decisions have generated uncertainty and failed to provide clear guidance, because "correction through legislative action is practically impossible" (internal quotation marks omitted)); *Garcia* v. *San Antonio Metropolitan Transit Authority*, 469 U.S. 528, 546–547, 557 (1985).

We have held that a liberty interest protected under the Due Process Clause of the Fourteenth Amendment will be deemed fundamental if it is "implicit in the concept of ordered liberty." *Palko* v. *Connecticut*, 302 U.S. 319, 325 (1937). Three years earlier, in *Snyder* v. *Massachusetts*, 291 U.S. 97 (1934), we referred to a "principle of justice so rooted in the traditions and conscience of our people as to be ranked as fundamental." *Id.*, at 105; see also *Michael H.* v. *Gerald D.*, 491 U.S. 110, 122 (1989) (plurality opinion) (citing the language from *Snyder*). These expressions are admittedly not precise, but our decisions implementing this notion of "fundamental" rights do not afford any more elaborate basis on which to base such a classification.

In construing the phrase "liberty" incorporated in the Due

Process Clause of the Fourteenth Amendment, we have recognized that its meaning extends beyond freedom from physical restraint. In *Pierce* v. *Society of Sisters*, 268 U.S. 510 (1925), we held that it included a parent's right to send a child to private school; in *Meyer* v. *Nebraska*, 262 U.S. 390 (1923), we held that it included a right to teach a foreign language in a parochial school. Building on these cases, we have held that that the term "liberty" includes a right to marry, *Loving* v. *Virginia*, 388 U.S. 1 (1967); a right to procreate, *Skinner* v. *Oklahoma ex rel. Williamson*, 316 U.S. 535 (1942); and a right to use contraceptives. *Griswold* v. *Connecticut*, 381 U.S. 479 (1965); *Eisenstadt* v. *Baird*, 405 U.S. 438 (1972). But a reading of these opinions makes clear that they do not endorse any all-encompassing "right of privacy."

In *Roe* v. *Wade*, the Court recognized a "guarantee of personal privacy" which "is broad enough to encompass a woman's decision whether or not to terminate her pregnancy." 410 U.S., at 152–153. We are now of the view that, in terming this right fundamental, the Court in *Roe* read the earlier opinions upon which it based its decision much too broadly. Unlike marriage, procreation and contraception, abortion "involves the purposeful termination of potential life." *Harris* v. *McRae*, 448 U.S. 297, 325 (1980). The abortion decision must therefore "be recognized as *sui generis*, different in kind from the others that the Court has protected under the rubric of personal or family privacy and autonomy." *Thornburgh* v. *American College of Obstetricians and Gynecologists*, supra, at 792 (WHITE, J., dissenting). One cannot ignore the fact that a woman is not isolated in her pregnancy, and that the decision to abort necessarily involves the destruction of a fetus. See *Michael H.* v. *Gerald D.*, supra, at 124, n. 4 (To look "at the act which is assertedly the subject of a liberty interest in isolation from its effect upon other people [is] like inquiring whether there is a liberty interest in firing a gun where the case at hand happens to involve its discharge into another person's body").

Nor do the historical traditions of the American people support the view that the right to terminate one's pregnancy is "fundamental." The common law which we inherited from England made abortion after "quickening" an offense. At the time of the adoption of the Fourteenth Amendment, statutory prohibitions or restrictions on abortion were commonplace; in 1868, at least 28 of the then-37 States and 8 Territories had statutes banning or limiting abortion. J. Mohr, Abortion in America 200 (1978). By the turn of the century virtually every State had a law prohibiting or restricting abortion on its books. By the middle of the present century, a liberalization trend had set in. But 21 of the restrictive abortion laws in effect in 1868 were still in effect in 1973 when *Roe* was decided, and an overwhelming majority of the States prohibited abortion unless necessary to preserve the life or health of the mother. *Roe* v. *Wade*, 410 U.S., at 139–140; *id.*, at 176–177, n. 2 (REHNQUIST, J., dissenting). On this record, it can scarcely be said that any deeply rooted tradition of relatively unrestricted abortion in our history supported the classification of the right to abortion as "fundamental" under the Due Process Clause of the Fourteenth Amendment.

We think, therefore, both in view of this history and of our decided cases dealing with substantive liberty under the Due Process Clause, that the Court was mistaken in *Roe* when it classified a woman's decision to terminate her pregnancy as a "fundamental right" that could be abridged only in a manner which withstood "strict scrutiny." In so concluding, we repeat the observation made in *Bowers* v. *Hardwick*, 478 U.S. 186 (1986):

> "Nor are we inclined to take a more expansive view of our authority to discover new fundamental rights imbedded in the Due Process Clause. The Court is most vulnerable and comes nearest to illegitimacy when it deals with judge-made constitutional law having little or no cognizable roots in the language or design of the Constitution." *Id.*, at 194.

We believe that the sort of constitutionally imposed abortion code of the type illustrated by our decisions following *Roe* is inconsistent "with the notion of a Constitution cast in general terms, as ours is, and usually speaking in general principles, as ours does." *Webster* v. *Reproductive Health Services*, 492 U.S., at 518 (plurality opinion). The Court in *Roe* reached too far when it analogized the right to abort a fetus to the rights involved in *Pierce, Meyer, Loving,* and *Griswold,* and thereby deemed the right to abortion fundamental.

II

The joint opinion of JUSTICES O'CONNOR, KENNEDY, and SOUTER cannot bring itself to say that *Roe* was correct as an original matter, but the authors are of the view that "the immediate question is not the soundness of *Roe's* resolution of the issue, but the precedential force that must be accorded to its holding." *Ante,* at [362]. Instead of claiming that *Roe* was correct as a matter of original constitutional interpretation, the opinion therefore contains an elaborate discussion of *stare decisis.* This discussion of the principle of *stare decisis* appears to be almost entirely dicta, because the joint opinion does not apply that principle in dealing with *Roe. Roe* decided that a woman had a fundamental right to an abortion. The joint opinion rejects that view. *Roe* decided that abortion regulations were to be subjected to "strict scrutiny" and could be justified only in the light of "compelling state interests." The joint opinion rejects that view. *Ante,* at [364]; see *Roe v. Wade, supra,* at 162–164. *Roe* analyzed abortion regulation under a rigid trimester framework, a framework which has guided this Court's decisionmaking for 19 years. The joint opinion rejects that framework. *Ante,* at [364].

Stare decisis is defined in Black's Law Dictionary as meaning "to abide by, or adhere to, decided cases." Black's Law Dictionary 1406 (6th ed. 1990). Whatever the "central holding" of *Roe* that is left after the joint opinion finishes dissecting it is surely not the result of that principle. While purporting to adhere to precedent, the joint opinion instead revises it. *Roe* continues to exist, but only in the way a storefront on a western movie set exists: a mere facade to give the illusion of reality. Decisions following *Roe,* such as *Akron v. Akron Center for Reproductive Health, Inc.,* 462 U.S. 416 (1983), and *Thornburgh v. American College of Obstetricians and Gynecologists,* 476 U.S. 747 (1986), are frankly overruled in part under the "undue burden" standard expounded in the joint opinion. *Ante,* at [370–73].

In our view, authentic principles of *stare decisis* do not require that any portion of the reasoning in *Roe* be kept intact.

"*Stare decisis* is not . . . a universal, inexorable command," especially in cases involving the interpretation of the Federal Constitution. *Burnet* v. *Coronado Oil & Gas Co.*, 285 U.S. 393, 405 (1932) (Brandeis, J., dissenting). Erroneous decisions in such constitutional cases are uniquely durable, because correction through legislative action, save for constitutional amendment, is impossible. It is therefore our duty to reconsider constitutional interpretations that "depar[t] from a proper understanding" of the Constitution. *Garcia* v. *San Antonio Metropolitan Transit Authority*, 469 U.S., at 557; see *United States* v. *Scott*, 437 U.S. 82, 101 (1978) (" '[I]n cases involving the Federal Constitution, . . . [t]he Court bows to the lessons of experience and the force of better reasoning, recognizing that the process of trial and error, so fruitful in the physical sciences, is appropriate also in the judicial function.' " (quoting *Burnet* v. *Coronado Oil & Gas Co.*, *supra*, at 406–408 (Brandeis, J., dissenting))); *Smith* v. *Allwright*, 321 U.S. 649, 665 (1944). Our constitutional watch does not cease merely because we have spoken before on an issue; when it becomes clear that a prior constitutional interpretation is unsound we are obliged to reexamine the question. See, *e.g.*, *West Virginia State Bd. of Education* v. *Barnette*, 319 U.S. 624, 642 (1943); *Erie R. Co.* v. *Tompkins*, 304 U.S. 64, 74–78 (1938).

The joint opinion discusses several *stare decisis* factors which, it asserts, point toward retaining a portion of *Roe*. Two of these factors are that the main "factual underpinning" of *Roe* has remained the same, and that its doctrinal foundation is no weaker now than it was in 1973. *Ante*, at [355–56]. Of course, what might be called the basic facts which gave rise to *Roe* have remained the same—women become pregnant, there is a point somewhere, depending on medical technology, where a fetus becomes viable, and women give birth to children. But this is only to say that the same facts which gave rise to *Roe* will continue to give rise to similar cases. It is not a reason, in and of itself, why those cases must be decided in the same incorrect manner as was the first case to deal with the question. And surely there is no requirement, in considering whether to depart from *stare decisis* in a constitutional case, that a decision be more wrong now than it was at the time it was rendered. If that were true, the most outlandish constitutional decision could survive forever, based simply on the fact that it was no more outlandish later than it was when originally rendered.

Nor does the joint opinion faithfully follow this alleged requirement. The opinion frankly concludes that *Roe* and its progeny were wrong in failing to recognize that the State's interests in maternal health and in the protection of unborn human life exist throughout pregnancy. *Ante*, [370–71]. But there is no indication that these components of *Roe* are any more incorrect at this juncture than they were at its inception.

The joint opinion also points to the reliance interests involved in this context in its effort to explain why precedent must be followed for precedent's sake. Certainly it is true that where reliance is truly at issue, as in the case of judicial decisions that have formed the basis for private decisions, "[c]onsiderations in favor of *stare decisis* are at their acme." *Payne v. Tennessee*, 501 U.S., at ___(slip op., at 18). But, as the joint opinion apparently agrees, *ante*, at [352], any traditional notion of reliance is not applicable here. The Court today cuts back on the protection afforded by *Roe*, and no one claims that this action defeats any reliance interest in the disavowed trimester framework. Similarly, reliance interests would not be diminished were the Court to go further and acknowledge the full error of *Roe*, as "reproductive planning could take virtually immediate account of" this action. *Ante*, at [352].

The joint opinion thus turns to what can only be described as an unconventional—and unconvincing—notion of reliance, a view based on the surmise that the availability of abortion since *Roe* has led to "two decades of economic and social developments" that would be undercut if the error of *Roe* were recognized. [352] The joint opinion's assertion of this fact is undeveloped and totally conclusory. In fact, one can not be sure to what economic and social developments the opinion is referring. Surely it is dubious to suggest that women have reached their "places in society" in reliance upon *Roe*, rather than as a result of their determination to obtain higher education and compete with men in the job market, and of society's increasing recognition of their ability to fill positions that were previously thought to be reserved only for men. [352]

In the end, having failed to put forth any evidence to prove any true reliance, the joint opinion's argument is based solely on generalized assertions about the national psyche, on a belief that the people of this country have grown accustomed to the *Roe* decision over the last 19 years and have "ordered their thinking and living around" it. [352] As an initial matter, one might inquire how the joint opinion can view the "central holding" of *Roe* as so deeply rooted in our constitutional culture, when it so casually uproots and disposes of that same decision's trimester framework. Furthermore, at various points in the past, the same could have been said about this Court's erroneous decisions that the Constitution allowed "separate but equal" treatment of minorities, see *Plessy* v. *Ferguson*, 163 U.S. 537 (1896), or that "liberty" under the Due Process Clause protected "freedom of contract." See *Adkins* v. *Children's Hospital of D. C.*, 261 U.S. 525 (1923); *Lochner* v. *New York*, 198 U.S. 45 (1905). The "separate but equal" doctrine lasted 58 years after *Plessy*, and *Lochner's* protection of contractual freedom lasted 32 years. However, the simple fact that a generation or more had grown used to these major decisions did not prevent the Court from correcting its errors in those cases, nor should it prevent us from correctly interpreting the Constitution here. See *Brown* v. *Board of Education*, 347 U.S. 483 (1954) (rejecting the "separate but equal" doctrine); *West Coast Hotel Co.* v. *Parrish*, 300 U.S. 379 (1937) (overruling *Adkins* v. *Children's Hospital, supra*, in upholding Washington's minimum wage law).

Apparently realizing that conventional *stare decisis* principles do not support its position, the joint opinion advances a belief that retaining a portion of *Roe* is necessary to protect the "legitimacy" of this Court. *Ante*, at [360–68]. Because the Court must take care to render decisions "grounded truly in principle," and not simply as political and social compromises, *ante*, at [361], the joint opinion properly declares it to be this Court's duty to ignore the public criticism and protest that may arise as a result of a decision. Few would quarrel with this statement, although it may be doubted that Members of this Court, holding their tenure as they do during constitutional "good behavior," are at all likely to be intimidated by such public protests.

But the joint opinion goes on to state that when the Court "resolve[s] the sort of intensely divisive controversy reflected in *Roe* and those rare, comparable cases," its decision is exempt from reconsideration under established principles of *stare decisis* in constitutional cases. *Ante*, at [362]. This is so, the joint opinion contends, because in those "intensely divisive" cases the Court has "call[ed] the contending sides of a national controversy to end their national division by accepting a common mandate rooted in the Constitution," and must therefore take special care not to be perceived as "surrender[ing] to political pressure" and continued opposition. *Ante*, at [362]. This is a truly novel principle, one which is contrary to both the Court's historical practice and to the Court's traditional willingness to tolerate criticism of its opinions. Under this principle, when the Court has ruled on a divisive issue, it is apparently prevented from overruling that decision for the sole reason that it was incorrect, *unless opposition to the original decision has died away.*

The first difficulty with this principle lies in its assumption that cases which are "intensely divisive" can be readily distinguished from those that are not. The question of whether a particular issue is "intensely divisive" enough to qualify for special protection is entirely subjective and dependent on the individual assumptions of the members of this Court. In addition, because the Court's duty is to ignore public opinion and criticism on issues that come before it, its members are in perhaps the worst position to judge whether a decision divides the Nation deeply enough to justify such uncommon protection. Although many of the Court's decisions divide the populace to a large degree, we have not previously on that account shied away from applying normal rules of *stare decisis* when urged to reconsider earlier decisions. Over the past 21 years, for example, the Court has overruled in whole or in part 34 of its previous constitutional decisions. See *Payne* v. *Tennessee, supra*, at ____, and n. 1 (slip op., at 18–19, and n. 1) (listing cases).

The joint opinion picks out and discusses two prior Court rulings that it believes are of the "intensely divisive" variety, and concludes that they are of comparable dimension to *Roe*. *Ante*, at [357–62] (discussing *Lochner* v. *New York, supra*, and

Plessy v. Ferguson, supra). It appears to us very odd indeed that the joint opinion chooses as benchmarks two cases in which the Court chose *not* to adhere to erroneous constitutional precedent, but instead enhanced its stature by acknowledging and correcting its error, apparently in violation of the joint opinion's "legitimacy" principle. See *West Coast Hotel Co. v. Parrish, supra; Brown v. Board of Education, supra.* One might also wonder how it is that the joint opinion puts these, and not others, in the "intensely divisive" category, and how it assumes that these are the only two lines of cases of comparable dimension to *Roe*. There is no reason to think that either *Plessy* or *Lochner* produced the sort of public protest when they were decided that *Roe* did. There were undoubtedly large segments of the bench and bar who agreed with the dissenting views in those cases, but surely that cannot be what the Court means when it uses the term "intensely divisive," or many other cases would have to be added to the list. In terms of public protest, however, *Roe*, so far as we know, was unique. But just as the Court should not respond to that sort of protest by retreating from the decision simply to allay the concerns of the protesters, it should likewise not respond by determining to adhere to the decision at all costs lest it *seem* to be retreating under fire. Public protests should not alter the normal application of *stare decisis*, lest perfectly lawful protest activity be penalized by the Court itself.

Taking the joint opinion on its own terms, we doubt that its distinction between *Roe*, on the one hand, and *Plessy* and *Lochner*, on the other, withstands analysis. The joint opinion acknowledges that the Court improved its stature by overruling *Plessy* in *Brown* on a deeply divisive issue. And our decision in *West Coast Hotel*, which overruled *Adkins v. Children's Hospital, supra*, and *Lochner*, was rendered at a time when Congress was considering President Franklin Roosevelt's proposal to "reorganize" this Court and enable him to name six additional Justices in the event that any member of the Court over the age of 70 did not elect to retire. It is difficult to imagine a situation in which the Court would face more intense opposition to a prior ruling than it did at that time, and, under the general principle proclaimed in the joint opinion, the Court seemingly should have responded to this opposition by stubbornly refusing to reexamine the *Lochner* rationale, lest it lose legitimacy by appearing to "overrule under fire." *Ante*, at [362].

The joint opinion agrees that the Court's stature would have been seriously damaged if in *Brown* and *West Coast Hotel* it had dug in its heels and refused to apply normal principles of *stare decisis* to the earlier decisions. But the opinion contends that the Court was entitled to overrule *Plessy* and *Lochner* in those cases, despite the existence of opposition to the original decisions, only because both the Nation and the Court had learned new lessons in the interim. This is at best a feebly supported, *post hoc* rationalization for those decisions.

For example, the opinion asserts that the Court could justifiably overrule its decision in *Lochner* only because the Depression had convinced "most people" that constitutional protection of contractual freedom contributed to an economy that failed to protect the welfare of all. *Ante*, at [357]. Surely the joint opinion does not mean to suggest that people saw this Court's failure to uphold minimum wage statutes as the cause of the Great Depression! In any event, the *Lochner* Court did not base its rule upon the policy judgment that an unregulated market was fundamental to a stable economy; it simply believed, erroneously, that "liberty" under the Due Process Clause protected the "right to make a contract." *Lochner* v. *New York*, 198 U.S., at 53. Nor is it the case that the people of this Nation only discovered the dangers of extreme laissez faire economics because of the Depression. State laws regulating maximum hours and minimum wages were in existence well before that time. A Utah statute of that sort enacted in 1896 was involved in our decision in *Holden* v. *Hardy*, 169 U.S. 366 (1898), and other states followed suit shortly afterwards. See, *e.g.*, *Muller* v. *Oregon*, 208 U.S. 412 (1908); *Bunting* v. *Oregon*, 243 U.S. 426 (1917). These statutes were indeed enacted because of a belief on the part of their sponsors that "freedom of contract" did not protect the welfare of workers, demonstrating that that belief manifested itself more than a generation before the Great Depression. Whether "most people" had come to share it in the hard times of the 1930's is, insofar as anything the joint opinion advances, entirely speculative. The crucial failing at that time was not that workers were not paid a fair wage, but that there was no work available at *any* wage.

When the Court finally recognized its error in *West Coast Hotel*, it did not engage in the *post hoc* rationalization that the joint opinion attributes to it today; it did not state that *Lochner* had been based on an economic view that had fallen into disfavor, and that it therefore should be overruled. Chief Justice Hughes in his opinion for the Court simply recognized what Justice Holmes had previously recognized in his *Lochner* dissent, that "[t]he Constitution does not speak of freedom of contract." *West Coast Hotel Co.* v. *Parrish*, 300 U.S., at 391; *Lochner* v. *New York, supra*, at 75 (Holmes, J., dissenting) ("[A] Constitution is not intended to embody a particular economic theory, whether of paternalism and the organic relation of the citizen to the State or of *laissez faire*"). Although the Court did acknowledge in the last paragraph of its opinion the state of affairs during the then-current Depression, the theme of the opinion is that the Court had been mistaken as a matter of constitutional law when it embraced "freedom of contract" 32 years previously.

The joint opinion also agrees that the Court acted properly in rejecting the doctrine of "separate but equal" in *Brown*. In fact, the opinion lauds *Brown* in comparing it to *Roe*. *Ante*, at [362]. This is strange, in that under the opinion's "legitimacy" principle the Court would seemingly have been forced to adhere to its erroneous decision in *Plessy* because of its "intensely divisive" character. To us, adherence to *Roe* today under the guise of "legitimacy" would seem to resemble more closely adherence to *Plessy* on the same ground. Fortunately, the Court did not choose that option in *Brown*, and instead frankly repudiated *Plessy*. The joint opinion concludes that such repudiation was justified only because of newly discovered evidence that segregation had the effect of treating one race as inferior to another. But it can hardly be argued that this was not urged upon those who decided *Plessy*, as Justice Harlan observed in his dissent that the law at issue "puts the brand of servitude and degradation upon a large class of our fellow-citizens, our equals before the law." *Plessy* v. *Ferguson*, 163 U.S., at 562 (Harlan, J., dissenting). It is clear that the same arguments made before the Court in *Brown* were made in *Plessy* as well. The Court in *Brown* simply recognized, as Justice Harlan had recognized beforehand, that the Fourteenth Amendment does not permit racial segregation. The rule of *Brown* is not tied to popular opinion about the evils of segregation; it is a judgment that the Equal Protection Clause does not permit racial segregation, no matter whether the public might come to believe that it is beneficial. On that ground it stands, and on that ground alone the Court was justified in properly concluding that the *Plessy* Court had erred.

There is also a suggestion in the joint opinion that the propriety of overruling a "divisive" decision depends in part on whether "most people" would now agree that it should be overruled. Either the demise of opposition or its progression to substantial popular agreement apparently is required to allow the Court to reconsider a divisive decision. How such agreement would be ascertained, short of a public opinion poll, the joint opinion does not say. But surely even the suggestion is totally at war with the idea of "legitimacy" in whose name it is invoked. The Judicial Branch derives its legitimacy, not from following public opinion, but from deciding by its best lights whether legislative enactments of the popular branches of Government comport with the Constitution. The doctrine of *stare decisis* is an adjunct of this duty, and should be no more subject to the vagaries of public opinion than is the basic judicial task.

There are other reasons why the joint opinion's discussion of legitimacy is unconvincing as well. In assuming that the Court is perceived as "surrender[ing] to political pressure" when it overrules a controversial decision, *ante*, at [362], the joint opinion forgets that there are two sides to any controversy. The joint opinion asserts that, in order to protect its legitimacy, the Court must refrain from overruling a controversial decision lest it be viewed as favoring those who oppose the decision. But a decision to *adhere* to prior precedent is subject to the same criticism, for in such a case one can easily argue that the Court is responding to those who have demonstrated in favor of the original decision. The decision in *Roe* has engendered large demonstrations, including repeated marches on this Court and on Congress, both in opposition to and in support of that opinion. A decision either way on *Roe* can therefore be perceived as favoring one group or the other. But this perceived dilemma arises only if one assumes, as the joint opinion does, that the Court should make its decisions with a view toward speculative public perceptions. If one assumes instead, as the Court surely did in both *Brown* and *West Coast Hotel*, that the Court's legitimacy is enhanced by faithful interpretation of the Constitution irrespective of public opposition, such self-engendered difficulties may be put to one side.

Roe is not this Court's only decision to generate conflict. Our decisions in some recent capital cases, and in *Bowers v. Hardwick*, 478 U.S. 186 (1986), have also engendered demonstrations in opposition. The joint opinion's message to such protesters appears to be that they must cease their activities in order to serve their cause, because their protests will only cement in place a decision which by normal standards of *stare decisis* should be reconsidered. Nearly a century ago, Justice David J. Brewer of this Court, in an article discussing criticism of its decisions, observed that "many criticisms may be, like their authors, devoid of good taste, but better all sorts of criticism than no criticism at all." Justice Brewer on "The Nation's Anchor," 57 Albany L.J. 166, 169 (1898). This was good advice to the Court then, as it is today. Strong and often misguided criticism of a decision should not render the decision immune from reconsideration, lest a fetish for legitimacy penalize freedom of expression.

The end result of the joint opinion's paeans of praise for legitimacy is the enunciation of a brand new standard for evaluating state regulation of a woman's right to abortion—the "undue burden" standard. As indicated above, *Roe v. Wade* adopted a "fundamental right" standard under which state regulations could survive only if they met the requirement of "strict scrutiny." While we disagree with that standard, it at least had a recognized basis in constitutional law at the time *Roe* was decided. The same cannot be said for the "undue burden" standard, which is created largely out of whole cloth by the authors of the joint opinion. It is a standard which even today does not command the support of a majority of this Court. And it will not, we believe, result in the sort of "simple limitation," easily applied, which the joint opinion anticipates. *Ante*, at [351]. In sum, it is a standard which is not built to last.

In evaluating abortion regulations under that standard, judges will have to decide whether they place a "substantial obstacle" in the path of a woman seeking an abortion. *Ante*, at [370]. In that this standard is based even more on a judge's subjective determinations than was the trimester framework, the standard will do nothing to prevent "judges from roaming at large in the constitutional field" guided only by their personal views. *Griswold v. Connecticut*, 381 U.S., at 502 (Harlan, J., concurring in judgment). Because the undue burden standard is plucked from nowhere, the question of what is a "substantial obstacle" to abortion will undoubtedly engender a variety of conflicting views. For example, in the very matter before us now, the authors of the joint opinion would uphold Pennsylvania's 24-hour waiting period, concluding that a "particular burden" on some women is not a substantial obstacle. *Ante*, at [378]. But the authors would at the same time strike down Pennsylvania's spousal notice provision, after finding that in a "large fraction" of cases the provision will be a substantial obstacle. *Ante*, at [386]. And, while the authors conclude that the informed consent provisions do not constitute an "undue burden," JUSTICE STEVENS would hold that they do. *Ante*, at [410–12].

Furthermore, while striking down the spousal *notice* regulation, the joint opinion would uphold a parental *consent* restriction that certainly places very substantial obstacles in the path of a minor's abortion choice. The joint opinion is forthright in admitting that it draws this distinction based on a policy judgment that parents will have the best interests of their children at heart, while the same is not necessarily true of husbands as to their wives. *Ante*, at [385]. This may or may not be a correct judgment, but it is quintessentially a legislative one. The "undue burden" inquiry does not in any way supply the distinction between parental consent and spousal consent which the joint opinion adopts. Despite the efforts of the joint opinion, the undue burden standard presents nothing more workable than the trimester framework which it discards today. Under the guise of the Constitution, this Court will still impart its own preferences on the States in the form of a complex abortion code.

The sum of the joint opinion's labors in the name of *stare decisis* and "legitimacy" is this: *Roe* v. *Wade* stands as a sort of judicial Potemkin Village, which may be pointed out to passers by as a monument to the importance of adhering to precedent. But behind the facade, an entirely new method of analysis, without any roots in constitutional law, is imported to decide the constitutionality of state laws regulating abortion. Neither *stare decisis* nor "legitimacy" are truly served by such an effort.

We have stated above our belief that the Constitution does not subject state abortion regulations to heightened scrutiny. Accordingly, we think that the correct analysis is that set forth by the plurality opinion in *Webster*. A woman's interest in having an abortion is a form of liberty protected by the Due Process Clause, but States may regulate abortion procedures in ways rationally related to a legitimate state interest. *Williamson* v. *Lee Optical of Okla., Inc.*, 348 U.S. 483, 491 (1955); cf. *Stanley* v. *Illinois*, 405 U.S. 645, 651–653 (1972). With this rule in mind, we examine each of the challenged provisions.

III

A

Section 3205 of the Act imposes certain requirements related to the informed consent of a woman seeking an abortion. 18 Pa. Cons. Stat. § 3205 (1990). Section 3205(a)(1) requires that the referring or performing physician must inform a woman contemplating an abortion of (i) the nature of the procedure, and the risks and alternatives that a reasonable patient would find material; (ii) the fetus' probable gestational age; and (iii) the medical risks involved in carrying her pregnancy to term. Section 3205(a)(2) requires a physician or a nonphysician counselor to inform the woman that (i) the state health department publishes free materials describing the fetus at different stages and listing abortion alternatives; (ii) medical assistance benefits may be available for prenatal, childbirth, and neonatal care; and (iii) the child's father is liable for child support. The Act also imposes a 24-hour waiting period between the time that the woman receives the required information and the time that the physician is allowed to perform the abortion. See Appendix, *ante*, at [393–95].

This Court has held that it is certainly within the province of the States to require a woman's voluntary and informed consent to an abortion. See *Thornburgh v. American College of Obstetricians and Gynecologists*, 476 U.S., at 760. Here, Pennsylvania seeks to further its legitimate interest in obtaining informed consent by ensuring that each woman "is aware not only of the reasons for having an abortion, but also of the risks associated with an abortion and the availability of assistance that might make the alternative of normal childbirth more attractive than it might otherwise appear." *Id.*, at 798–799 (WHITE, J., dissenting).

We conclude that this provision of the statute is rationally related to the State's interest in assuring that a woman's consent to an abortion be a fully informed decision.

Section 3205(a)(1) requires a physician to disclose certain information about the abortion procedure and its risks and alternatives. This requirement is certainly no large burden, as the Court of Appeals found that "the record shows that the clinics, without exception, insist on providing this information to women before an abortion is performed." 947 F.2d, at 703. We are of the view that this information "clearly is related to maternal health and to the State's legitimate purpose in requiring informed consent." *Akron v. Akron Center for Reproductive Health*, 462 U.S., at 446. An accurate description of the gestational age of the fetus and of the risks involved in carrying a child to term helps to further both those interests and the State's legitimate interest in unborn human life. See *id.*, at 445–446, n. 37 (required disclosure of gestational age of the fetus "certainly is not objectionable"). Although petitioners contend that it is unreasonable for the State to require that a physician, as opposed to a nonphysician counselor, disclose this information, we agree with the Court of Appeals that a State "may rationally decide that physicians are better qualified than counselors to impart this information and answer questions about the medical aspects of the available alternatives." 947 F.2d, at 704.

Section 3205(a)(2) compels the disclosure, by a physician or a counselor, of information concerning the availability of paternal child support and state-funded alternatives if the woman decides to proceed with her pregnancy. Here again, the Court of Appeals observed that "the record indicates that most clinics already require that a counselor consult in person with the woman about alternatives to abortion before the abortion is performed." Id., at 704–705. And petitioners do not claim that the information required to be disclosed by statute is in any way false or inaccurate; indeed, the Court of Appeals found it to be "relevant, accurate, and noninflammatory." Id., at 705. We conclude that this required presentation of "balanced information" is rationally related to the State's legitimate interest in ensuring that the woman's consent is truly informed, Thornburgh v. American College of Obstetricians and Gynecologists, 476 U.S., at 830 (O'CONNOR, J., dissenting), and in addition furthers the State's interest in preserving unborn life. That the information might create some uncertainty and persuade some women to forgo abortions does not lead to the conclusion that the Constitution forbids the provision of such information. Indeed, it only demonstrates that this information might very well make a difference, and that it is therefore relevant to a woman's informed choice. Cf. id., at 801 (WHITE, J., dissenting) ("[T]he ostensible objective of Roe v. Wade is not maximizing the number of abortions, but maximizing choice"). We acknowledge that in Thornburgh this Court struck down informed consent requirements similar to the ones at issue here. See id., at 760–764. It is clear, however, that while the detailed framework of Roe led to the Court's invalidation of those informational requirements, they "would have been sustained under any traditional standard of judicial review, . . . or for any other surgical procedure except abortion." Webster v. Reproductive Health Services, 492 U.S., at 517 (plurality opinion) (citing Thornburgh v. American College of Obstetricians and Gynecologists, 476 U.S., at 802 (WHITE, J., dissenting); id., at 783 (Burger, C. J., dissenting)). In light of our rejection of Roe's "fundamental right" approach to this subject, we do not regard Thornburgh as controlling.

For the same reason, we do not feel bound to follow this Court's previous holding that a State's 24-hour mandatory waiting period is unconstitutional. See *Akron v. Akron Center for Reproductive Health*, 462 U.S., at 449–451. Petitioners are correct that such a provision will result in delays for some women that might not otherwise exist, therefore placing a burden on their liberty. But the provision in no way prohibits abortions, and the informed consent and waiting period requirements do not apply in the case of a medical emergency. See 18 Pa. Cons. Stat. §§ 3205(a), (b) (1990). We are of the view that, in providing time for reflection and reconsideration, the waiting period helps ensure that a woman's decision to abort is a well-considered one, and reasonably furthers the State's legitimate interest in maternal health and in the unborn life of the fetus. It "is surely a small cost to impose to ensure that the woman's decision is well considered in light of its certain and irreparable consequences on fetal life, and the possible effects on her own." *Id.*, at 474 (O'CONNOR, J., dissenting).

B

In addition to providing her own informed consent, before an unemancipated woman under the age of 18 may obtain an abortion she must either furnish the consent of one of her parents, or must opt for the judicial procedure that allows her to bypass the consent requirement. Under the judicial bypass option, a minor can obtain an abortion if a state court finds that she is capable of giving her informed consent and has indeed given such consent, *or* determines that an abortion is in her best interests. Records of these court proceedings are kept confidential. The Act directs the state trial court to render a decision within three days of the woman's application, and the entire procedure, including appeal to Pennsylvania Superior Court, is to last no longer than eight business days. The parental consent requirement does not apply in the case of a medical emergency. 18 Pa. Cons. Stat. § 3206 (1990). See Appendix, *ante*, at [395–96].

This provision is entirely consistent with this Court's previous decisions involving parental consent requirements. See *Planned Parenthood Association of Kansas City, Mo., Inc. v.*

Ashcroft, 462 U.S. 476 (1983) (upholding parental consent requirement with a similar judicial bypass option); *Akron v. Akron Center for Reproductive Health, supra*, at 439–440 (approving of parental consent statutes that include a judicial bypass option allowing a pregnant minor to "demonstrate that she is sufficiently mature to make the abortion decision herself or that, despite her immaturity, an abortion would be in her best interests"); *Bellotti v. Baird*, 443 U.S. 622 (1979).

We think it beyond dispute that a State "has a strong and legitimate interest in the welfare of its young citizens, whose immaturity, inexperience, and lack of judgment may sometimes impair their ability to exercise their rights wisely." *Hodgson v. Minnesota*, 497 U.S., at 444 (opinion of STEVENS, J.). A requirement of parental consent to abortion, like myriad other restrictions placed upon minors in other contexts, is reasonably designed to further this important and legitimate state interest. In our view, it is entirely "rational and fair for the State to conclude that, in most instances, the family will strive to give a lonely or even terrified minor advice that is both compassionate and mature." *Ohio v. Akron Center for Reproductive Health*, 497 U.S., at 520 (opinion of KENNEDY, J.); see also *Planned Parenthood of Central Mo. v. Danforth*, 428 U.S., at 91 (Stewart, J., concurring) ("There can be little doubt that the State furthers a constitutionally permissible end by encouraging an unmarried pregnant minor to seek the help and advice of her parents in making the very important decision whether or not to bear a child"). We thus conclude that Pennsylvania's parental consent requirement should be upheld.

C

Section 3209 of the Act contains the spousal notification provision. It requires that, before a physician may perform an abortion on a married woman, the woman must sign a statement indicating that she has notified her husband of her planned abortion. A woman is not required to notify her husband if (1) her husband is not the father, (2) her husband, after diligent effort, cannot be located, (3) the pregnancy is the result of a spousal sexual assault that has been reported to the authorities, or (4) the woman has reason to believe that notifying her husband is likely to result in the infliction of bodily injury upon her by him or by another individual. In addition, a woman is exempted from the notification requirement in the case of a medical emergency. 18 Pa. Cons. Stat. § 3209 (1990). See Appendix, *ante*, at [399–400].

We first emphasize that Pennsylvania has not imposed a spousal *consent* requirement of the type the Court struck down in *Planned Parenthood of Central Mo.* v. *Danforth*, 428 U.S., at 67–72. Missouri's spousal consent provision was invalidated in that case because of the Court's view that it unconstitutionally granted to the husband "a veto power exercisable for any reason whatsoever or for no reason at all." *Id.*, at 71. But this case involves a much less intrusive requirement of spousal *notification*, not consent. Such a law requiring only notice to the husband "does not give any third party the legal right to make the [woman's] decision for her, or to prevent her from obtaining an abortion should she choose to have one performed." *Hodgson* v. *Minnesota, supra*, at 496 (KENNEDY, J., concurring in judgment in part and dissenting in part); see *H. L.* v. *Matheson*, 450 U.S., at 411, n. 17. *Danforth* thus does not control our analysis. Petitioners contend that it should, however; they argue that the real effect of such a notice requirement is to give the power to husbands to veto a woman's abortion choice. The District Court indeed found that the notification provision created a risk that some woman who would otherwise have an abortion will be prevented from having one. 947 F.2d, at 712. For example, petitioners argue, many notified husbands will prevent abortions through physical force, psychological coercion, and other types of threats. But Pennsylvania has incorporated exceptions in the notice provision in an attempt to deal with these problems. For instance, a woman need not notify her husband if the pregnancy is result of a reported sexual assault, or if she has reason to believe that she would suffer bodily injury as a result of the notification. 18 Pa. Cons. Stat. § 3209(b) (1990). Furthermore, because this is a facial challenge to the Act, it is insufficient for petitioners to show that the notification provision "might operate unconstitutionally under some conceivable set of circumstances." *United States* v. *Salerno*, 481 U.S. 739, 745

(1987). Thus, it is not enough for petitioners to show that, in some "worst-case" circumstances, the notice provision will operate as a grant of veto power to husbands. *Ohio v. Akron Center for Reproductive Health*, 497 U.S., at 514. Because they are making a facial challenge to the provision, they must "show that no set of circumstances exists under which the [provision] would be valid." *Ibid.* (internal quotation marks omitted). This they have failed to do.[2]

The question before us is therefore whether the spousal notification requirement rationally furthers any legitimate state interests. We conclude that it does. First, a husband's interests in procreation within marriage and in the potential life of his unborn child are certainly substantial ones. See

[2] The joint opinion of JUSTICES O'CONNOR, KENNEDY, and SOUTER appears to ignore this point in concluding that the spousal notice provision imposes an undue burden on the abortion decision. *Ante*, at [380–90]. In most instances the notification requirement operates without difficulty. As the District Court found, the vast majority of wives seeking abortions notify and consult with their husbands, and thus suffer no burden as a result of the provision. 744 F. Supp. 1323, 1360 (ED Pa. 1990). In other instances where a woman does not want to notify her husband, the Act provides exceptions. For example, notification is not required if the husband is not the father, if the pregnancy is the result of a reported spousal sexual assault, or if the woman fears bodily injury as a result of notifying her husband. Thus, in these instances as well, the notification provision imposes no obstacle to the abortion decision.

The joint opinion puts to one side these situations where the regulation imposes no obstacle at all, and instead focuses on the group of married women who would not otherwise notify their husbands and who do not qualify for one of the exceptions. Having narrowed the focus, the joint opinion concludes that in a "large fraction" of those cases, the notification provision operates as a substantial obstacle, *ante*, at [386], and that the provision is therefore invalid. There are certainly instances where a woman would prefer not to notify her husband, and yet does not qualify for an exception. For example, there are the situations of battered women who fear psychological abuse or injury to their children as a result of notification; because in these situations the women do not fear bodily injury, they do not qualify for an exception. And there are situations where a woman has become pregnant as a result of an unreported spousal sexual assault; when such an assault is unreported, no exception is available. But, as the District Court found, there are also instances where the woman prefers not to notify her husband for a variety of other reasons. See 744 F. Supp., at 1360. For example, a woman might desire to obtain an abortion without her husband's knowledge because of perceived economic constraints or her husband's previously expressed opposition to abortion. The joint opinion concentrates on the situations involving battered women and unreported spousal assault, and assumes, without any support in the record, that these instances constitute a "large fraction" of those cases in which women prefer not to notify their husbands (and do not qualify for an exception). *Ante*, at [386]. This assumption is not based on any hard evidence, however. And were it helpful to an attempt to reach a desired result, one could just as easily assume that the battered women situations form 100 percent of the cases where women desire not to notify, or that they constitute only 20 percent of those cases. But reliance on such speculation is the necessary result of adopting the undue burden standard.

Planned Parenthood of Central Mo. v. *Danforth*, 428 U.S., at 69 ("We are not unaware of the deep and proper concern and interest that a devoted and protective husband has in his wife's pregnancy and in the growth and development of the fetus she is carrying"); *id.*, at 93 (WHITE, J., concurring in part and dissenting in part); *Skinner* v. *Oklahoma ex rel. Williamson*, 316 U.S., at 541. The State itself has legitimate interests both in protecting these interests of the father and in protecting the potential life of the fetus, and the spousal notification requirement is reasonably related to advancing those state interests. By providing that a husband will usually know of his spouse's intent to have an abortion, the provision makes it more likely that the husband will participate in deciding the fate of his unborn child, a possibility that might otherwise have been denied him. This participation might in some cases result in a decision to proceed with the pregnancy. As Judge Alito observed in his dissent below, "[t]he Pennsylvania legislature could have rationally believed that some married women are initially inclined to obtain an abortion without their husbands' knowledge because of perceived problems— such as economic constraints, future plans, or the husbands' previously expressed opposition—that may be obviated by discussion prior to the abortion." 947 F.2d, at 726 (Alito, J., concurring in part and dissenting in part).

The State also has a legitimate interest in promoting "the integrity of the marital relationship." 18 Pa. Cons. Stat. § 3209(a) (1990). This Court has previously recognized "the importance of the marital relationship in our society." *Planned Parenthood of Central Mo.* v. *Danforth, supra*, at 69. In our view, the spousal notice requirement is a rational attempt by the State to improve truthful communication between spouses and encourage collaborative decisionmaking, and thereby fosters marital integrity. See *Labine* v. *Vincent*, 401 U.S. 532, 538 (1971) ("[T]he power to make rules to establish, protect, and strengthen family life" is committed to the state legislatures). Petitioners argue that the notification requirement does not further any such interest; they assert that the majority of wives already notify their husbands of their abortion decisions, and the remainder have excellent reasons for keeping their decisions a secret. In the first case, they argue, the law is unnecessary, and in the second case it will only serve to foster marital discord and threats of harm. Thus, petitioners see the law as a totally irrational means of furthering whatever legitimate interest the State might have. But, in our view, it is unrealistic to assume that every husband-wife relationship is either (1) so perfect that this type of truthful and important communication will take place as a matter of course, or (2) so imperfect that, upon notice, the husband will react selfishly, violently, or contrary to the best interests of his wife. See *Planned Parenthood of Central Mo. v. Danforth, supra*, at 103–104 (STEVENS, J., concurring in part and dissenting in part) (making a similar point in the context of a parental consent statute). The spousal notice provision will admittedly be unnecessary in some circumstances, and possibly harmful in others, but "the existence of particular cases in which a feature of a statute performs no function (or is even counterproductive) ordinarily does not render the statute unconstitutional or even constitutionally suspect." *Thornburgh* v. *American College of Obstetricians and Gynecologists*, 476 U.S., at 800 (WHITE, J., dissenting). The Pennsylvania Legislature was in a position to weigh the likely benefits of the provision against its likely adverse effects, and presumably concluded, on balance, that the provision would be beneficial. Whether this was a wise decision or not, we cannot say that it was irrational. We therefore conclude that the spousal notice provision comports with the Constitution. See *Harris* v. *McRae*, 448 U.S., at 325–326 ("It is not the mission of this Court or any other to decide whether the balance of competing interests . . . is wise social policy").

D

The Act also imposes various reporting requirements. Section 3214(a) requires that abortion facilities file a report on each abortion performed. The reports do not include the identity of the women on whom abortions are performed, but they do contain a variety of information about the abortions. For example, each report must include the identities of the performing and referring physicians, the gestational age of the fetus at the time of abortion, and the basis for any medical judgment that a medical emergency existed. See 18 Pa. Cons. Stat. § 3214(a)(1), (5), (10) (1990). See Appendix, *ante*, at [400–402]. The District Court found that these reports are kept completely confidential. 947 F.2d, at 716. We further conclude that these reporting requirements rationally further the State's legitimate interests in advancing the state of medical knowledge concerning maternal health and prenatal life, in gathering statistical information with respect to patients, and in ensuring compliance with other provisions of the Act.

Section 3207 of the Act requires each abortion facility to file a report with its name and address, as well as the names and addresses of any parent, subsidiary or affiliated organizations. 18 Pa. Cons. Stat. § 3207(b) (1990). Section 3214(f) further requires each facility to file quarterly reports stating the total number of abortions performed, broken down by trimester. Both of these reports are available to the public only if the facility received state funds within the preceding 12 months. See Appendix, *ante*, at [396–97]. Petitioners do not challenge the requirement that facilities provide this information. They contend, however, that the forced public disclosure of the information given by facilities receiving public funds serves no legitimate state interest. We disagree. Records relating to the expenditure of public funds are generally available to the public under Pennsylvania law. See Pa. Stat. Ann., Tit. 65, §§ 66.1, 66.2 (Purdon 1959 and Supp. 1991–1992). As the Court of Appeals observed, "[w]hen a state provides money to a private commercial enterprise, there is a legitimate public interest in informing taxpayers who the funds are benefiting and what services the funds are supporting." 947 F.2d, at 718. These reporting requirements rationally further this legitimate state interest.

E

Finally, petitioners challenge the medical emergency exception provided for by the Act. The existence of a medical emergency exempts compliance with the Act's informed consent, parental consent, and spousal notice requirements. See 18 Pa. Cons. Stat. §§ 3205(a), 3206(a), 3209(c) (1990). The Act defines a "medical emergency" as "that condition which, on the basis of the physician's good faith clinical judgment, so complicates the medical condition of a pregnant woman as to necessitate the immediate abortion of her pregnancy to avert her death or for which a delay will create serious risk of substantial and irreversible impairment of major bodily function." § 3203.

Petitioners argued before the District Court that the statutory definition was inadequate because it did not cover three serious conditions that pregnant women can suffer—pre-eclampsia, inevitable abortion, and prematurely ruptured membrane. The District Court agreed with petitioners that the medical emergency exception was inadequate, but the Court of Appeals reversed this holding. In construing the medical emergency provision, the Court of Appeals first observed that all three conditions do indeed present the risk of serious injury or death when an abortion is not performed, and noted that the medical profession's uniformly prescribed treatment for each of the three conditions is an immediate abortion. See 947 F.2d, at 700–701. Finding that "[t]he Pennsylvania legislature did not choose the wording of its medical emergency exception in a vacuum," the court read the exception as intended "to assure that compliance with its abortion regulations would not in any way pose a significant threat to the life or health of a woman." Id., at 701. It thus concluded that the exception encompassed each of the three dangerous conditions pointed to by petitioners.

We observe that Pennsylvania's present definition of medical emergency is almost an exact copy of that State's definition at the time of this Court's ruling in Thornburgh, one which the Court made reference to with apparent approval. 476 U.S., at 771 ("It is clear that the Pennsylvania Legislature knows how to provide a medical-emergency exception when it chooses to do so").[3] We find that the interpretation of the Court of Appeals in this case is eminently reasonable, and

---

[3] The definition in use at that time provided as follows:
" 'Medical emergency.'—That condition which, on the basis of the physician's best clinical judgment, so complicates a pregnancy as to necessitate the immediate abortion of same to avert the death of the mother or for which a 24–hour delay will create grave peril of immediate and irreversible loss of major bodily function." 18 Pa. Cons. Stat. Ann. § 3203 (Purdon 1983).

that the provision thus should be upheld. When a woman is faced with any condition that poses a "significant threat to [her] life or health," she is exempted from the Act's consent and notice requirements and may proceed immediately with her abortion.

IV

For the reasons stated, we therefore would hold that each of the challenged provisions of the Pennsylvania statute is consistent with the Constitution. It bears emphasis that our conclusion in this regard does not carry with it any necessary approval of these regulations. Our task is, as always, to decide only whether the challenged provisions of a law comport with the United States Constitution. If, as we believe, these do, their wisdom as a matter of public policy is for the people of Pennsylvania to decide.

OPINION OF JUSTICE SCALIA, WITH WHOM THE CHIEF JUSTICE, JUSTICE WHITE, AND JUSTICE THOMAS JOIN

JUSTICE SCALIA, with whom THE CHIEF JUSTICE, JUSTICE WHITE, and JUSTICE THOMAS join, concurring in the judgment in part and dissenting in part.

My views on this matter are unchanged from those I set forth in my separate opinions in *Webster* v. *Reproductive Health Services*, 492 U.S. 490, 532 (1989) (SCALIA, J., concurring in part and concurring in judgment), and *Ohio* v. *Akron Center for Reproductive Health*, 497 U.S. 502, 520 (1990) (*Akron II*) (SCALIA, J., concurring). The States may, if they wish, permit abortion-on-demand, but the Constitution does not *require* them to do so. The permissibility of abortion, and the limitations upon it, are to be resolved like most important questions in our democracy: by citizens trying to persuade one another and then voting. As the Court acknowledges, "where reasonable people disagree the government can adopt one position or the other." *Ante*, at [348]. The Court is correct in adding the qualification that this "assumes a state of affairs in which the choice does not intrude upon a protected liberty," *ante*, at [348]—but the crucial part of that qualification is the penultimate word. A State's choice between two positions on which reasonable people can disagree is constitutional even when (as is often the case) it intrudes upon a "liberty" in the absolute sense. Laws against bigamy, for example—which entire societies of reasonable people disagree with—intrude upon men and women's liberty to marry and live with one another. But bigamy happens not to be a liberty specially "protected" by the Constitution.

That is, quite simply, the issue in this case: not whether the power of a woman to abort her unborn child is a "liberty" in the absolute sense; or even whether it is a liberty of great importance to many women. Of course it is both. The issue is whether it is a liberty protected by the Constitution of the United States. I am sure it is not. I reach that conclusion not because of anything so exalted as my views concerning the "concept of existence, of meaning, of the universe, and of the mystery of human life." *Ibid.* Rather, I reach it for the same reason I reach the conclusion that bigamy is not constitutionally protected—because of two simple facts: (1) the Constitution says absolutely nothing about it, and (2) the longstanding traditions of American society have permitted it to be legally proscribed.[1] *Akron II, supra,* at 520 (SCALIA, J., concurring).

The Court destroys the proposition, evidently meant to represent my position, that "liberty" includes "only those practices, defined at the most specific level, that were protected against government interference by other rules of law when the Fourteenth Amendment was ratified," *ante,* at [345] (citing *Michael H.* v. *Gerald D.*, 491 U.S. 110, 127, n. 6 (1989) (opinion of SCALIA, J.). That is not, however, what *Michael H.* says; it merely observes that, in defining "liberty," we may

---

[1] The Court's suggestion, *ante,* at [345], that adherence to tradition would require us to uphold laws against interracial marriage is entirely wrong. Any tradition in that case was contradicted *by a text*—an Equal Protection Clause that explicitly establishes racial equality as a constitutional value. See *Loving* v. *Virginia,* 388 U.S. 1, 9 (1967) ("In the case at bar, . . . we deal with statutes containing racial classifications, and the fact of equal application does not immunize the statute from the very heavy burden of justification which the Fourteenth Amendment has traditionally required of state statutes drawn according to race"); see also *id.,* at 13 (Stewart, J., concurring in judgment). The enterprise launched in *Roe,* by contrast, sought to *establish*—in the teeth of a clear, contrary tradition—a value found nowhere in the constitutional text.

There is, of course, no comparable tradition barring recognition of a "liberty interest" in carrying one's child to term free from state efforts to kill it. For that reason, it does not follow that the Constitution does not protect childbirth simply because it does not protect abortion. The Court's contention, *ante,* at [355], that the only way to protect childbirth is to protect abortion shows the utter bankruptcy of constitutional analysis deprived of tradition as a validating factor. It drives one to say that the only way to protect the right to eat is to acknowledge the constitutional right to starve oneself to death.

not disregard a specific, "relevant tradition protecting, or denying protection to, the asserted right," 491 U.S., at 127,
n. 6. But the Court does not wish to be fettered by any such
limitations on its preferences. The Court's statement that it
is "tempting" to acknowledge the authoritativeness of tradition in order to "cur[b] the discretion of federal judges," *ante*,
at [344], is of course rhetoric rather than reality; no government official is "tempted" to place restraints upon his own
freedom of action, which is why Lord Acton did not say
"Power tends to purify." The Court's temptation is in the
quite opposite and more natural direction—towards system-
atically eliminating checks upon its own power; and it suc-
cumbs.

Beyond that brief summary of the essence of my position,
I will not swell the United States Reports with repetition of
what I have said before; and applying the rational basis test,
I would uphold the Pennsylvania statute in its entirety. I must,
however, respond to a few of the more outrageous arguments
in today's opinion, which it is beyond human nature to leave
unanswered. I shall discuss each of them under a quotation
from the Court's opinion to which they pertain.

**"The inescapable fact is that adjudication of substantive
due process claims may call upon the Court in interpreting
the Constitution to exercise that same capacity which by
tradition courts always have exercised: reasoned judgment."**

Ante, at [346].

Assuming that the question before us is to be resolved at
such a level of philosophical abstraction, in such isolation
from the traditions of American society, as by simply applying
"reasoned judgment," I do not see how that could possibly
have produced the answer the Court arrived at in *Roe* v. *Wade*,
410 U.S. 113 (1973). Today's opinion describes the methodology of *Roe*, quite accurately, as weighing against the woman's interest the State's " 'important and legitimate interest
in protecting the potentiality of human life.' " *Ante*, at [365]
(quoting *Roe*, *supra*, at 162). But "reasoned judgment" does
not begin by begging the question, as *Roe* and subsequent
cases unquestionably did by assuming that what the State is

protecting is the mere "potentiality of human life." See, *e.g.*, *Roe, supra*, at 162; *Planned Parenthood of Central Mo. v. Danforth*, 428 U.S. 52, 61 (1976); *Colautti v. Franklin*, 439 U.S. 379, 386 (1979); *Akron v. Akron Center for Reproductive Health, Inc.*, 462 U.S. 416, 428 (1983) (*Akron I*); *Planned Parenthood Assn. of Kansas City, Mo., Inc. v. Ashcroft*, 462 U.S. 476, 482 (1983). The whole argument of abortion opponents is that what the Court calls the fetus and what others call the unborn child *is a human life*. Thus, whatever answer *Roe* came up with after conducting its "balancing" is bound to be wrong, unless it is correct that the human fetus is in some critical sense merely potentially human. There is of course no way to determine that as a legal matter; it is in fact a value judgment. Some societies have considered newborn children not yet human, or the incompetent elderly no longer so.

The authors of the joint opinion, of course, do not squarely contend that *Roe v. Wade* was a *correct* application of "reasoned judgment"; merely that it must be followed, because of *stare decisis. Ante*, at [352, 360–61, 371]. But in their exhaustive discussion of all the factors that go into the determination of when *stare decisis* should be observed and when disregarded, they never mention "how wrong was the decision on its face?" Surely, if "[t]he Court's power lies . . . in its legitimacy, a product of substance and perception," *ante*, at [360], the "substance" part of the equation demands that plain error be acknowledged and eliminated. *Roe* was plainly wrong—even on the Court's methodology of "reasoned judgment," and even more so (of course) if the proper criteria of text and tradition are applied.

The emptiness of the "reasoned judgment" that produced *Roe* is displayed in plain view by the fact that, after more than 19 years of effort by some of the brightest (and most determined) legal minds in the country, after more than 10 cases upholding abortion rights in this Court, and after dozens upon dozens of *amicus* briefs submitted in this and other cases, the best the Court can do to explain how it is that the word "liberty" *must* be thought to include the right to destroy human fetuses is to rattle off a collection of adjectives that simply decorate a value judgment and conceal a political choice. The right to abort, we are told, inheres in "liberty" because it is among "a person's most basic decisions," *ante*, at [346]; it involves a "most intimate and personal choic[e]," *ante*, at [348]; it is "central to personal dignity and autonomy," *ibid.*; it "originate[s] within the zone of conscience and belief," *ibid.*; it is "too intimate and personal" for state interference, *ante*, at [349]; it reflects "intimate views" of a "deep, personal character," *ante*, at [350]; it involves "intimate relationships," and notions of "personal autonomy and bodily integrity," *ante*, at [352]; and it concerns a particularly " 'important decisio[n],' " *ante*, at [353] (citation omitted).[2] But it is obvious to anyone applying "reasoned judgment" that the same adjectives can be applied to many forms of conduct that this Court (including one of the Justices in today's majority, see *Bowers* v. *Hardwick*, 478 U.S. 186 (1986)) has held are *not* entitled to constitutional protection—because, like abortion, they are forms of conduct that have long been criminalized in American society. Those adjectives might be applied, for example, to homosexual sodomy, polygamy, adult incest, and suicide, all of which are equally "intimate" and "deep[ly] personal" decisions involving "personal autonomy and bodily integrity," and all of which can constitutionally be proscribed because it is our unquestionable constitutional tradition that they are proscribable. It is not reasoned judgment that supports the Court's decision; only personal predilection. Justice Curtis's warning is as timely today as it was 135 years ago:

> "[W]hen a strict interpretation of the Constitution, according to the fixed rules which govern the interpretation of laws, is abandoned, and the theoretical opinions of individuals are allowed to control its meaning, we have no longer a Constitution; we are under the government of individual men, who for the time being have power to declare what the Constitution is, according to their own views of what it ought to mean."

---

[2] JUSTICE BLACKMUN's parade of adjectives is similarly empty: Abortion is among "the most intimate and personal choices," *ante*, at [414]; it is a matter "central to personal dignity and autonomy," *ibid.*; and it involves "personal decisions that profoundly affect bodily integrity, identity, and destiny," *ante*, at [417]. JUSTICE STEVENS is not much less conclusory: The decision to choose abortion is a matter of "the highest privacy and the most personal nature," *ante*, at [406]; it involves a "difficult choice having serious and personal consequences of major importance to [a woman's] future," *ibid.*; the authority to make this "traumatic and yet empowering decision" is "an element of basic human dignity," *ibid.*; and it is "nothing less than a matter of conscience," *ibid.*

Dred Scott v. Sandford, 19 How. 393, 621 (1857) (Curtis, J., dissenting).

"Liberty finds no refuge in a jurisprudence of doubt."

Ante, at [341].

One might have feared to encounter this august and sonorous phrase in an opinion defending the real *Roe v. Wade*, rather than the revised version fabricated today by the authors of the joint opinion. The shortcomings of *Roe* did not include lack of clarity: Virtually all regulation of abortion before the third trimester was invalid. But to come across this phrase in the joint opinion—which calls upon federal district judges to apply an "undue burden" standard as doubtful in application as it is unprincipled in origin—is really more than one should have to bear.

The joint opinion frankly concedes that the amorphous concept of "undue burden" has been inconsistently applied by the Members of this Court in the few brief years since that "test" was first explicitly propounded by JUSTICE O'CONNOR in her dissent in *Akron I, supra*. See *Ante*, at [370].[3] Because the three Justices now wish to "set forth a standard of general application," the joint opinion announces that "it is important to clarify what is meant by an undue burden," *ibid.* I certainly agree with that, but I do not agree that the joint opinion succeeds in the announced endeavor. To the contrary, its

---

[3] The joint opinion is clearly wrong in asserting, *ante*, at [368], that "the Court's early abortion cases adhered to" the "undue burden" standard. The passing use of that phrase in JUSTICE BLACKMUN's opinion for the Court in *Bellotti v. Baird*, 428 U.S. 132, 147 (1976) (*Bellotti I*), was not by way of setting forth the *standard* of unconstitutionality, as JUSTICE O'CONNOR's later opinions did, but by way of expressing the *conclusion* of unconstitutionality. Justice Powell for a time appeared to employ a variant of "undue burden" analysis in several nonmajority opinions, see, *e.g., Bellotti v. Baird*, 443 U.S. 622, 647 (1979) (plurality opinion of Powell, J.) (*Bellotti II*); *Carey v. Population Services International*, 431 U.S. 678, 705 (1977) (Powell, J., concurring in part and concurring in judgment), but he too ultimately rejected that standard in his opinion for the Court in *Akron v. Akron Center for Reproductive Health*, 462 U.S. 416, 420, n. 1 (1983) (*Akron I*). The joint opinion's reliance on *Maher v. Roe*, 432 U.S. 464, 473 (1977), and *Harris v. McRae*, 448 U.S. 297, 314 (1980), is entirely misplaced, since those cases did not involve regulation of abortion but mere refusal to fund it. In any event, JUSTICE O'CONNOR's earlier formulations have apparently now proved unsatisfactory to the three Justices, who—in the name of *stare decisis* no less—today find it necessary to devise an entirely new version of "undue burden" analysis, see *ante*, at [366].

efforts at clarification make clear only that the standard is inherently manipulable and will prove hopelessly unworkable in practice.

The joint opinion explains that a state regulation imposes an "undue burden" if it "has the purpose or effect of placing a substantial obstacle in the path of a woman seeking an abortion of a nonviable fetus." *Ibid.*; see also *ante*, at [370]. An obstacle is "substantial," we are told, if it is "calculated[,] [not] to inform the woman's free choice, [but to] hinder it." *Ante*, at [370].[4] This latter statement cannot possibly mean what it says. Any regulation of abortion that is intended to advance what the joint opinion concedes is the State's "substantial" interest in protecting unborn life will be "calculated [to] hinder" a decision to have an abortion. It thus seems more accurate to say that the joint opinion would uphold abortion

[4] The joint opinion further asserts that a law imposing an undue burden on abortion decisions is not a "permissible" means of serving "legitimate" state interests. *Ante*, at [371]. This description of the undue burden standard in terms more commonly associated with the rational-basis test will come as a surprise even to those who have followed closely our wanderings in this forsaken wilderness. See, *e.g.*, *Akron I*, *supra*, at 463 (O'CONNOR, J., dissenting) ("The 'undue burden' . . . represents the required threshold inquiry that must be conducted before this Court can require a State to justify its legislative actions under the exacting 'compelling state interest' standard"); see also *Hodgson v. Minnesota*, 497 U.S. 417, [480] (1990) (O'CONNOR, J., concurring in part and concurring in judgment in part); *Thornburgh v. American College of Obstetricians and Gynecologists*, 476 U.S. 747, 828 (1986) (O'CONNOR, J., dissenting). This confusing equation of the two standards is apparently designed to explain how one of the Justices who joined the plurality opinion in *Webster v. Reproductive Health Services*, 492 U.S. 490 (1989), which adopted the rational basis test, could join an opinion expressly adopting the undue burden test. See *id.*, at 520 (rejecting the view that abortion is a "fundamental right," instead inquiring whether a law regulating the woman's "liberty interest" in abortion is "reasonably designed" to further "legitimate" state ends). The same motive also apparently underlies the joint opinion's erroneous citation of the plurality opinion in *Ohio v. Akron Center for Reproductive Health*, 497 U.S. 502, [506] (1990) (*Akron II*) (opinion of KENNEDY, J.), as applying the undue burden test. See *ante*, at [370] (using this citation to support the proposition that "two of us"—*i.e.*, two of the authors of the joint opinion—have previously applied this test). In fact, *Akron II* does not mention the undue burden standard until the conclusion of the opinion, when it states that the statute at issue "does not impose an undue, *or otherwise unconstitutional*, burden." 497 U.S., at 519 (emphasis added). I fail to see how anyone can think that saying a statute does not impose an unconstitutional burden under *any* standard, including the undue burden test, amounts to adopting the undue burden test as the *exclusive* standard. The Court's citation of *Hodgson* as reflecting JUSTICE KENNEDY's and JUSTICE O'CONNOR's "shared premises," *ante*, at [371], is similarly inexplicable, since the word "undue" was never even used in the former's opinion in that case. I joined JUSTICE KENNEDY's opinions in both *Hodgson* and *Akron II*; I should be grateful, I suppose, that the joint opinion does not claim that I, too, have adopted the undue burden test.

regulations only if they do not *unduly* hinder the woman's decision. That, of course, brings us right back to square one: Defining an "undue burden" as an "undue hindrance" (or a "substantial obstacle") hardly "clarifies" the test. Consciously or not, the joint opinion's verbal shell game will conceal raw judicial policy choices concerning what is "appropriate" abortion legislation.

The ultimately standardless nature of the "undue burden" inquiry is a reflection of the underlying fact that the concept has no principled or coherent legal basis. As THE CHIEF JUSTICE points out, *Roe's* strict-scrutiny standard "at least had a recognized basis in constitutional law at the time *Roe* was decided," *ante*, at [450], while "[t]he same cannot be said for the 'undue burden' standard, which is created largely out of whole cloth by the authors of the joint opinion," *ibid.* The joint opinion is flatly wrong in asserting that "our jurisprudence relating to all liberties save perhaps abortion has recognized" the permissibility of laws that do not impose an "undue burden." *Ante*, at [368]. It argues that the abortion right is similar to other rights in that a law "not designed to strike at the right itself, [but which] has the incidental effect of making it more difficult or more expensive to [exercise the right,]" is not invalid. *Ante*, at [368]. I agree, indeed I have forcefully urged, that a law of general applicability which places only an incidental burden on a fundamental right does not infringe that right, see *R. A. V. v. St. Paul*, 505 U.S. ____, ____(1992) (slip op., at 11); *Employment Division, Dept. of Human Resources of Ore. v. Smith*, 494 U.S. 872, 878–882 (1990), but that principle does not establish the quite different (and quite dangerous) proposition that a law which *directly* regulates a fundamental right will not be found to violate the Constitution unless it imposes an "undue burden." It is that, of course, which is at issue here: Pennsylvania has *consciously and directly* regulated conduct that our cases have held is constitutionally protected. The appropriate analogy, therefore, is that of a state law requiring purchasers of religious books to endure a 24-hour waiting period, or to pay a nominal additional tax of 1 cent. The joint opinion cannot possibly be correct in suggesting that we would uphold such legislation on the ground that it does not impose a "substantial obstacle" to the exercise of First Amendment rights. The "undue burden" standard is not at all the generally applicable principle the joint opinion pretends it to be; rather, it is a unique concept created specially for this case, to preserve some judicial foothold in this ill-gotten territory. In claiming otherwise, the three Justices show their willingness to place all constitutional rights at risk in an effort to preserve what they deem the "central holding in *Roe*," *ante*, at [367].

The rootless nature of the "undue burden" standard, a phrase plucked out of context from our earlier abortion decisions, see n. 3, *supra*, is further reflected in the fact that the joint opinion finds it necessary expressly to repudiate the more narrow formulations used in JUSTICE O'CONNOR's earlier opinions. *Ante*, at [371]. Those opinions stated that a statute imposes an "undue burden" if it imposes "*absolute* obstacles or *severe* limitations on the abortion decision," *Akron I*, 462 U.S., at 464 (O'CONNOR, J., dissenting) (emphasis added); see also *Thornburgh* v. *American College of Obstetricians and Gynecologists*, 476 U.S. 747, 828 (1986) (O'CONNOR, J., dissenting). Those strong adjectives are conspicuously missing from the joint opinion, whose authors have for some unexplained reason now determined that a burden is "undue" if it merely imposes a "substantial" obstacle to abortion decisions. See, *e.g.*, *ante*, at [380, 385]. JUSTICE O'CONNOR has also abandoned (again without explanation) the view she expressed in *Planned Parenthood Assn. of Kansas City, Mo., Inc.* v. *Ashcroft*, 462 U.S. 476 (1983) (dissenting opinion), that a medical regulation which imposes an "undue burden" could nevertheless be upheld if it "reasonably relate[s] to the preservation and protection of maternal health," *id.*, at 505 (citation and internal quotation marks omitted). In today's version, even health measures will be upheld only "*if they do not constitute an undue burden*," *ante*, at [368] (emphasis added). Gone too is JUSTICE O'CONNOR's statement that "the State possesses *compelling* interests in the protection of potential human life . . . throughout pregnancy," *Akron I, supra*, at 461 (emphasis added); see also *Ashcroft, supra*, at 505 (O'CONNOR, J., concurring in judgment in part and dissenting in part); *Thornburgh, supra*, at 828 (O'CONNOR, J., dissenting); instead, the State's interest in unborn human life is stealthily downgraded to a merely "substantial" or "profound" interest, *ante*, at [370]. (That had to be done, of course, since designating the interest as "compelling" throughout pregnancy would have been, shall we say, a "substantial obstacle" to the joint opinion's determined effort to reaffirm what it views as the "central holding" of *Roe*. See *Akron I*, 462 U.S., at 420, n. 1.) And "viability" is no longer the "arbitrary" dividing line previously decried by JUSTICE O'CONNOR in *Akron I, id.*, at 461; the Court now announces that "the attainment of viability may continue to serve as the critical fact," *ante*, at [356].[5] It is difficult to maintain the illusion that we are interpreting a Constitution rather than inventing one, when we amend its provisions so breezily.

Because the portion of the joint opinion adopting and describing the undue-burden test provides no more useful guidance than the empty phrases discussed above, one must turn to the 23 pages applying that standard to the present facts for further guidance. In evaluating Pennsylvania's abortion law, the joint opinion relies extensively on the factual findings of the District Court, and repeatedly qualifies its conclusions by noting that they are contingent upon the record developed in this case. Thus, the joint opinion would uphold the 24-hour waiting period contained in the Pennsylvania statute's informed consent provision, 18 Pa. Cons. Stat. § 3205 (1990), because "the record evidence shows that in the vast majority of cases, a 24-hour delay does not create any appreciable health risk," *ante*, at [378]. The three Justices therefore conclude that "on the record before us, . . . we are not convinced that the 24-hour waiting period constitutes an undue burden." *Ante*, at [379]. The requirement that a doctor provide the information pertinent to informed consent would also be upheld because "there is no evidence on this record that [this re-

---

[5] Of course JUSTICE O'CONNOR was correct in her former view. The arbitrariness of the viability line is confirmed by the Court's inability to offer any justification for it beyond the conclusory assertion that it is only at that point that the unborn child's life "can in reason and all fairness" be thought to override the interests of the mother, *ante*, at [365]. Precisely why is it that, at the magical second when machines currently in use (though not necessarily available to the particular woman) are able to keep an unborn child alive apart from its mother, the creature is suddenly able (under our Constitution) to be protected by law, whereas before that magical second it was not? That makes no more sense than according infants legal protection only after the point when they can feed themselves.

quirement] would amount in practical terms to a substantial obstacle to a woman seeking an abortion," *ante*, at [378]. Similarly, the joint opinion would uphold the reporting requirements of the Act, §§ 3207, 3214, because "there is no . . . showing on the record before us" that these requirements constitute a "substantial obstacle" to abortion decisions. *Ante*, at [390]. But at the same time the opinion pointedly observes that these reporting requirements may increase the costs of abortions and that "at some point [that fact] could become a substantial obstacle," *ibid*. Most significantly, the joint opinion's conclusion that the spousal notice requirement of the Act, see § 3209, imposes an "undue burden" is based in large measure on the District Court's "detailed findings of fact," which the joint opinion sets out at great length. *Ante*, at [380–85].

I do not, of course, have any objection to the notion that, in applying legal principles, one should rely only upon the facts that are contained in the record or that are properly subject to judicial notice.[6] But what is remarkable about the joint opinion's fact-intensive analysis is that it does not result in any measurable clarification of the "undue burden" standard. Rather, the approach of the joint opinion is, for the most part, simply to highlight certain facts in the record that apparently strike the three Justices as particularly significant in establishing (or refuting) the existence of an undue burden; after describing these facts, the opinion then simply announces that the provision either does or does not impose a "substantial obstacle" or an "undue burden." See, *e.g.*, *ante*, at [370, 373, 374, 379, 384, 390]. We do not know whether the same conclusions could have been reached on a different record, or in what respects the record would have had to differ before an opposite conclusion would have been appropriate. The

---

[6] The joint opinion is not entirely faithful to this principle, however. In approving the District Court's factual findings with respect to the spousal notice provision, it relies extensively on nonrecord materials, and in reliance upon them adds a number of factual conclusions of its own. *Ante*, at [385–88]. Because this additional factfinding pertains to matters that surely are "subject to reasonable dispute," Fed. Rule Evid. 201(b), the joint opinion must be operating on the premise that these are "legislative" rather than "adjudicative" facts, see Rule 201(a). But if a court can find an undue burden simply by selectively string-citing the right social science articles, I do not see the point of emphasizing or requiring "detailed factual findings" in the District Court.

inherently standardless nature of this inquiry invites the district judge to give effect to his personal preferences about abortion. By finding and relying upon the right facts, he can invalidate, it would seem, almost any abortion restriction that strikes him as "undue"—subject, of course, to the possibility of being reversed by a Circuit Court or Supreme Court that is as unconstrained in reviewing his decision as he was in making it.

To the extent I can discern *any* meaningful content in the "undue burden" standard as applied in the joint opinion, it appears to be that a State may not regulate abortion in such a way as to reduce significantly its incidence. The joint opinion repeatedly emphasizes that an important factor in the "undue burden" analysis is whether the regulation "prevent[s] a significant number of women from obtaining an abortion," *ante,* at [385]; whether a "significant number of women . . . are likely to be deterred from procuring an abortion," *ibid.*; and whether the regulation often "deters" women from seeking abortions, *ante,* at [388]. We are not told, however, what forms of "deterrence" are impermissible or what degree of success in deterrence is too much to be tolerated. If, for example, a State required a woman to read a pamphlet describing, with illustrations, the facts of fetal development before she could obtain an abortion, the effect of such legislation might be to "deter" a "significant number of women" from procuring abortions, thereby seemingly allowing a district judge to invalidate it as an undue burden. Thus, despite flowery rhetoric about the State's "substantial" and "profound" interest in "potential human life," and criticism of *Roe* for undervaluing that interest, the joint opinion permits the State to pursue that interest only so long as it is not too successful. As JUSTICE BLACKMUN recognizes (with evident hope), *ante,* at [418], the "undue burden" standard may ultimately require the invalidation of each provision upheld today if it can be shown, on a better record, that the State is too effectively "express[ing] a preference for childbirth over abortion," *ante,* at [372]. Reason finds no refuge in this jurisprudence of confusion.

"While we appreciate the weight of the arguments . . . that *Roe* should be overruled, the reservations any of us may have in reaffirming the central holding of *Roe* are outweighed

by the explication of individual liberty we have given combined with the force of *stare decisis.*"

Ante, at [350].

The Court's reliance upon *stare decisis* can best be described
as contrived. It insists upon the necessity of adhering not to
all of *Roe,* but only to what it calls the "central holding." It
seems to me that *stare decisis* ought to be applied even to the
doctrine of *stare decisis,* and I confess never to have heard of
this new, keep-what-you-want-and-throw-away-the-rest version. I wonder whether, as applied to *Marbury* v. *Madison,* 1
Cranch 137 (1803), for example, the new version of *stare
decisis* would be satisfied if we allowed courts to review the
constitutionality of only those statutes that (like the one in
Marbury) pertain to the jurisdiction of the courts.

I am certainly not in a good position to dispute that the
Court *has saved* the "central holding" of *Roe,* since to do that
effectively I would have to know what the Court has saved,
which in turn would require me to understand (as I do not)
what the "undue burden" test means. I must confess, however,
that I have always thought, and I think a lot of other people
have always thought, that the arbitrary trimester framework,
which the Court today discards, was quite as central to *Roe*
as the arbitrary viability test, which the Court today retains.
It seems particularly ungrateful to carve the trimester framework out of the core of *Roe,* since its very rigidity (in sharp
contrast to the utter indeterminability of the "undue burden"
test) is probably the only reason the Court is able to say, in
urging *stare decisis,* that *Roe* "has in no sense proven 'unworkable,' " *ante,* at [352]. I suppose the Court is entitled to
call a "central holding" whatever it wants to call a "central
holding"—which is, come to think of it, perhaps one of the
difficulties with this modified version of *stare decisis.* I thought
I might note, however, that the following portions of *Roe*
have not been saved:

• Under *Roe,* requiring that a woman seeking an abortion
be provided truthful information about abortion before giving
informed written consent is unconstitutional, if the information is designed to influence her choice, *Thornburgh,* 476

U.S., at 759–765; *Akron I*, 462 U.S., at 442–445. Under the joint opinion's "undue burden" regime (as applied today, at least) such a requirement is constitutional, *ante*, at [374–78].

• Under *Roe*, requiring that information be provided by a doctor, rather than by nonphysician counselors, is unconstitutional, *Akron I*, *supra*, at 446–449. Under the "undue burden" regime (as applied today, at least) it is not, *ante*, at [378].

• Under *Roe*, requiring a 24-hour waiting period between the time the woman gives her informed consent and the time of the abortion is unconstitutional, *Akron I*, *supra*, at 449–451. Under the "undue burden" regime (as applied today, at least) it is not, *ante*, at [378].

• Under *Roe*, requiring detailed reports that include demographic data about each woman who seeks an abortion and various information about each abortion is unconstitutional, *Thornburgh*, *supra*, at 765–768. Under the "undue burden" regime (as applied today, at least) it generally is not, *ante*, at [390].

"Where, in the performance of its judicial duties, the Court decides a case in such a way as to resolve the sort of intensely divisive controversy reflected in *Roe* . . ., its decision has a dimension that the resolution of the normal case does not carry. It is the dimension present whenever the Court's interpretation of the Constitution calls the contending sides of a national controversy to end their national division by accepting a common mandate rooted in the Constitution."

Ante, at [362].

The Court's description of the place of *Roe* in the social history of the United States is unrecognizable. Not only did *Roe* not, as the Court suggests, *resolve* the deeply divisive issue of abortion; it did more than anything else to nourish it, by elevating it to the national level where it is infinitely more difficult to resolve. National politics were not plagued by abortion protests, national abortion lobbying, or abortion marches on Congress, before *Roe* v. *Wade* was decided. Profound disagreement existed among our citizens over the issue—as it does over other issues, such as the death penalty—but that disagreement was being worked out at the state level. As with many other issues, the division of sentiment within each State was not as closely balanced as it was among the population of the Nation as a whole, meaning not only that more people would be satisfied with the results of state-by-state resolution, but also that those results would be more stable. Pre-*Roe*, moreover, political compromise was possible.

Roe's mandate for abortion-on-demand destroyed the compromises of the past, rendered compromise impossible for the future, and required the entire issue to be resolved uniformly, at the national level. At the same time, *Roe* created a vast new class of abortion consumers and abortion proponents by eliminating the moral opprobrium that had attached to the act. ("If the Constitution *guarantees* abortion, how can it be bad?"—not an accurate line of thought, but a natural one.) Many favor all of those developments, and it is not for me to say that they are wrong. But to portray *Roe* as the statesmanlike "settlement" of a divisive issue, a jurisprudential Peace of Westphalia that is worth preserving, is nothing less than Orwellian. *Roe* fanned into life an issue that has inflamed our national politics in general, and has obscured with its smoke the selection of Justices to this Court in particular, ever since. And by keeping us in the abortion-umpiring business, it is the perpetuation of that disruption, rather than of any *pax Roeana*, that the Court's new majority decrees.

"[T]o overrule under fire . . . would subvert the Court's legitimacy . . . .

"To all those who will be . . . tested by following, the Court implicitly undertakes to remain steadfast . . . . The promise of constancy, once given, binds its maker for as long as the power to stand by the decision survives and . . . the commitment [is not] obsolete. . . .

"[The American people's] belief in themselves as . . . a people [who aspire to live according to the rule of law] is not readily separable from their understanding of the Court invested with the authority to decide their constitutional cases and speak before all others for their constitutional

ideals. If the Court's legitimacy should be undermined, then, so would the country be in its very ability to see itself through its constitutional ideals."

Ante, at [363–64].

The Imperial Judiciary lives. It is instructive to compare this Nietzschean vision of us unelected, life-tenured judges— leading a Volk who will be "tested by following," and whose very "belief in themselves" is mystically bound up in their "understanding" of a Court that "speak[s] before all others for their constitutional ideals"—with the somewhat more modest role envisioned for these lawyers by the Founders.

> "The judiciary . . . has . . . no direction either of the strength or of the wealth of the society, and can take no active resolution whatever. It may truly be said to have neither FORCE nor WILL but merely judgment . . . ." The Federalist No. 78, 393–394 (G. Wills ed. 1982).

Or, again, to compare this ecstasy of a Supreme Court in which there is, especially on controversial matters, no shadow of change or hint of alteration ("There is a limit to the amount of error that can plausibly be imputed to prior courts," *ante,* at [361]), with the more democratic views of a more humble man:

> "[T]he candid citizen must confess that if the policy of the Government upon vital questions affecting the whole people is to be irrevocably fixed by decisions of the Supreme Court, . . . the people will have ceased to be their own rulers, having to that extent practically resigned their Government into the hands of that eminent tribunal." A. Lincoln, First Inaugural Address (Mar. 4, 1861), reprinted in Inaugural Addresses of the Presidents of the United States, S. Doc. No. 101–10, p. 139 (1989).

It is particularly difficult, in the circumstances of the present decision, to sit still for the Court's lengthy lecture upon the virtues of "constancy," *ante,* at [364], of "remain[ing] steadfast," *id.,* at [363], of adhering to "principle," *id., passim.*

Among the five Justices who purportedly adhere to *Roe*, at most three agree upon the principle that constitutes adherence (the joint opinion's "undue burden" standard)—and that principle is inconsistent with *Roe*, see 410 U.S., at 154–156.[7] To make matters worse, two of the three, in order thus to remain steadfast, had to abandon previously stated positions. See n. 4 *supra*; see *supra*, at 11–12. It is beyond me how the Court expects these accommodations to be accepted "as grounded truly in principle, not as compromises with social and political pressures having, as such, no bearing on the principled choices that the Court is obliged to make." *Ante*, at [362]. The only principle the Court "adheres" to, it seems to me, is the principle that the Court must be seen as standing by *Roe*. That is not a principle of law (which is what I thought the Court was talking about), but a principle of *Realpolitik*—and a wrong one at that.

I cannot agree with, indeed I am appalled by, the Court's suggestion that the decision whether to stand by an erroneous constitutional decision must be strongly influenced—against overruling, no less—by the substantial and continuing public opposition the decision has generated. The Court's judgment that any other course would "subvert the Court's legitimacy" must be another consequence of reading the error-filled history book that described the deeply divided country brought together by *Roe*. In my history book, the Court was covered with dishonor and deprived of legitimacy by *Dred Scott* v. *Sandford*, 19 How. 393 (1857), an erroneous (and widely opposed) opinion that it did not abandon, rather than by *West Coast Hotel Co.* v. *Parrish*, 300 U.S. 379 (1937), which produced the famous "switch in time" from the Court's erroneous (and widely opposed) constitutional opposition to the social measures of the New Deal. (Both *Dred Scott* and one line of the cases resisting the New Deal rested upon the concept of "substantive due process" that the Court praises and employs today. Indeed, *Dred Scott* was "very possibly the first appli-

---

[7] JUSTICE BLACKMUN's effort to preserve as much of *Roe* as possible leads him to read the joint opinion as more "constan[t]" and "steadfast" than can be believed. He contends that the joint opinion's "undue burden" standard requires the application of strict scrutiny to "all non-*de minimis*" abortion regulations, *ante*, at [410], but that could only be true if a "substantial obstacle," *ante*, at [370] (joint opinion), were the same thing as a non-*de minimis* obstacle—which it plainly is not.

cation of substantive due process in the Supreme Court, the
original precedent for *Lochner* v. *New York* and *Roe* v. *Wade.*"
D. Currie, The Constitution in the Supreme Court 271 (1985)
(footnotes omitted).)

But whether it would "subvert the Court's legitimacy" or
not, the notion that we would decide a case differently from
the way we otherwise would have in order to show that we
can stand firm against public disapproval is frightening. It is
a bad enough idea, even in the head of someone like me, who
believes that the text of the Constitution, and our traditions,
say what they say and there is no fiddling with them. But
when it is in the mind of a Court that believes the Constitution
has an evolving meaning, see *ante*, at [347]; that the Ninth
Amendment's reference to "othe[r]" rights is not a disclaimer,
but a charter for action, *ibid.*; and that the function of this
Court is to "speak before all others for [the people's] constitutional ideals" unrestrained by meaningful text or tradition
—then the notion that the Court must adhere to a decision
for as long as the decision faces "great opposition" and the
Court is "under fire" acquires a character of almost czarist
arrogance. We are offended by these marchers who descend
upon us, every year on the anniversary of *Roe*, to protest our
saying that the Constitution requires what our society has
never thought the Constitution requires. These people who
refuse to be "tested by following" must be taught a lesson. We
have no Cossacks, but at least we can stubbornly refuse to
abandon an erroneous opinion that we might otherwise
change—to show how little they intimidate us.

Of course, as THE CHIEF JUSTICE points out, we have been
subjected to what the Court calls "political pressure" by *both*
sides of this issue. *Ante*, at [445]. Maybe today's decision not
to overrule *Roe* will be seen as buckling to pressure from *that*
direction. Instead of engaging in the hopeless task of predicting
public perception—a job not for lawyers but for political campaign managers—the Justices should do what is *legally* right
by asking two questions: (1) Was *Roe* correctly decided?
(2) Has *Roe* succeeded in producing a settled body of law? If
the answer to both questions is no, *Roe* should undoubtedly
be overruled.

In truth, I am as distressed as the Court is—and expressed

my distress several years ago, see *Webster*, 492 U.S., at 535
—about the "political pressure" directed to the Court: the
marches, the mail, the protests aimed at inducing us to change
our opinions. How upsetting it is, that so many of our citizens
(good people, not lawless ones, on both sides of this abortion
issue, and on various sides of other issues as well) think that
we Justices should properly take into account their views, as
though we were engaged not in ascertaining an objective law
but in determining some kind of social consensus. The Court
would profit, I think, from giving less attention to the *fact* of
this distressing phenomenon, and more attention to the *cause*
of it. That cause permeates today's opinion: a new mode of
constitutional adjudication that relies not upon text and traditional practice to determine the law, but upon what the
Court calls "reasoned judgment," *ante*, at [346], which turns
out to be nothing but philosophical predilection and moral
intuition. All manner of "liberties," the Court tells us, inhere
in the Constitution and are enforceable by this Court—not
just those mentioned in the text or established in the traditions of our society. *Ante*, at [346]. Why even the Ninth
Amendment—which says only that "[t]he enumeration in the
Constitution of certain rights shall not be construed to deny
or disparage others retained by the people"—is, despite our
contrary understanding for almost 200 years, a literally bound-
less source of additional, unnamed, unhinted at "rights," de-
finable and enforceable by us, through "reasoned judgment."
Ante, at [348].

What makes all this relevant to the bothersome application
of "political pressure" against the Court are the twin facts that
the American people love democracy and the American people are not fools. As long as this Court thought (and the
people thought) that we Justices were doing essentially lawyers'
work up here—reading text and discerning our society's traditional understanding of that text—the public pretty much
left us alone. Texts and traditions are facts to study, not
convictions to demonstrate about. But if in reality our process
of constitutional adjudication consists primarily of making
value judgments; if we can ignore a long and clear tradition
clarifying an ambiguous text, as we did, for example, five days
ago in declaring unconstitutional invocations and benedic-

tions at public-high-school graduation ceremonies, *Lee* v. *Weisman*, 505 U.S. ____(1992); if, as I say, our pronouncement of constitutional law rests primarily on value judgments, then a free and intelligent people's attitude towards us can be expected to be (*ought* to be) quite different. The people know that their value judgments are quite as good as those taught in any law school—maybe better. If, indeed, the "liberties" protected by the Constitution are, as the Court says, undefined and unbounded, then the people *should* demonstrate, to protest that we do not implement *their* values instead of *ours*. Not only that, but confirmation hearings for new Justices *should* deteriorate into question-and-answer sessions in which Senators go through a list of their constituents' most favored and most disfavored alleged constitutional rights, and seek the nominee's commitment to support or oppose them. Value judgments, after all, should be voted on, not dictated; and if our Constitution has somehow accidentally committed them to the Supreme Court, at least we can have a sort of plebiscite each time a new nominee to that body is put forward. JUSTICE BLACKMUN not only regards this prospect with equanimity, he solicits it, *ante*, at [431].

* * *

There is a poignant aspect to today's opinion. Its length, and what might be called its epic tone, suggest that its authors believe they are bringing to an end a troublesome era in the history of our Nation and of our Court. "It is the dimension" of authority, they say, to "cal[l] the contending sides of national controversy to end their national division by accepting a common mandate rooted in the Constitution." *Ante*, at [362].

There comes vividly to mind a portrait by Emanuel Leutze that hangs in the Harvard Law School: Roger Brooke Taney, painted in 1859, the 82d year of his life, the 24th of his Chief Justiceship, the second after his opinion in *Dred Scott*. He is all in black, sitting in a shadowed red armchair, left hand resting upon a pad of paper in his lap, right hand hanging limply, almost lifelessly, beside the inner arm of the chair. He sits facing the viewer, and staring straight out. There seems to be on his face, and in his deep-set eyes, an expression of profound sadness and disillusionment. Perhaps he always looked that way, even when dwelling upon the happiest of thoughts. But those of us who know how the lustre of his great Chief Justiceship came to be eclipsed by *Dred Scott* cannot help believing that he had that case—its already apparent consequences for the Court, and its soon-to-be-played-out consequences for the Nation—burning on his mind. I expect that two years earlier he, too, had thought himself "call[ing] the contending sides of national controversy to end their national division by accepting a common mandate rooted in the Constitution."

It is no more realistic for us in this case, than it was for him in that, to think that an issue of the sort they both involved—an issue involving life and death, freedom and subjugation—can be "speedily and finally settled" by the Supreme Court, as President James Buchanan in his inaugural address said the issue of slavery in the territories would be. See Inaugural Addresses of the Presidents of the United States, S. Doc. No. 101–10, p. 126 (1989). Quite to the contrary, by foreclosing all democratic outlet for the deep passions this issue arouses, by banishing the issue from the political forum that gives all participants, even the losers, the satisfaction of a fair hearing and an honest fight, by continuing the imposition of a rigid national rule instead of allowing for regional differences, the Court merely prolongs and intensifies the anguish.

We should get out of this area, where we have no right to be, and where we do neither ourselves nor the country any good by remaining.

APPENDIX
THE AMICUS BRIEFS

THE *AMICUS* BRIEFS

(Those starred are included in this volume.)

Amicus Briefs Supporting Petitioners and Attacking Pennsylvania Law

Brief of 167 Distinguished Scientists and Physicians, Including 11 Nobel Laureates

Brief of 178 Organizations in Support of Planned Parenthood

*Brief of 250 American Historians

Brief of the Alan Guttmacher Institute et al.

*Brief of the American College of Obstetricians and Gynecologists, the American Medical Women's Association, the American Psychiatric Association, the American Public Health Association, the Association of Reproductive Health Professionals, the National League for Nursing, and the National Medical Association

Brief for the American Psychological Association

Brief of the City of New York, the Association of the Bar of the City of New York, Committees on Sex and Law, Civil Rights and Medicine and Law, and the New York City Health and Hospitals Corporation

*Brief of the NAACP Legal Defense and Educational Fund, Inc., Asian American Legal Defense & Educational Fund, the Center for Constitutional Rights, Center for Law and Social Justice at Medgar

Evers College, the Committee For Hispanic Children and Families, Eco-Justice Project and Network, Hispanic Health Council, Japanese American Citizens League, the Latina Roundtable on Health and Reproductive Rights, Madre, Mexican American Legal Defense and Educational Fund, the National Association of Social Workers, National Black Women's Health Project, the National Coalition for Black Lesbians and Gays, the National Council of Negro Women, Inc., the National Emergency Civil Liberties Committee, National Latina Health Organization, National Minority Aids Council, the Native American Women's Health Education Resource Center, the New York Women's Foundation, the Puerto Rican Legal Defense and Education Fund, the Southern Poverty Law Center, Women for Racial & Economic Equality, and the Women's Policy Group

Brief of the Pennsylvania Coalition Against Domestic Violence, the American Association of University Women, Alle-Kiski Area Hope Center, Inc., Battered Women's Program, Capital Area Family Violence Center, Inc., Berks Women in Crisis, Bradford County Coalition for Choice, Caring Unlimited, Inc., Cleveland Rape Crisis Center, Clinton County Women's Center, Colorado Domestic Violence Coalition, Connecticut Coalition Against Domestic Violence, Domestic Violence Research and Resources, Families in Transition Center, Family Service of Philadelphia, Florida Coalition Against Domestic Violence, Gwinnett Citizens for Choice, Hospitality House Services for Women, Inc., Houston Area Women's Center, Illinois Coalition Against Sexual Assault, Laurel House Lutheran Social Services, South Region, Marin Abused Women's Services, Men Stopping Violence, Inc., My Sister's Place, National Coalition Against Domestic Violence, National Coalition Against Sexual Assault, National Women Abuse Prevention Center, New Jersey Coalition for Battered Women, New York State Coalition Against Domestic Violence, Oregon Coalition Against Domestic and Sexual Violence, Pennsylvania Campaign for Choice, Pennsylvania Coalition Against Rape, Psychology Society Survivors, Inc., Tioga County Women's Coalition, Turning Point of Lehigh Valley, Inc., Vermont Network Against Domestic Violence and Sexual Assault, Volunteers Against Abuse Center of Butler County, Inc., Washington Coalition of Sexual Assault Programs, A Woman's Place, Women Against Abuse, Inc., and Women Against Abuse

Legal Center, Inc., Women's Center & Shelter of Greater Pittsburgh, Women's Center of Montgomery County, Women's Center of Warren and Forest Counties, Inc., Women's Coalition of St. Croix, Virgin Islands, Women's Help Center, Inc., Women's Resources of Monroe County, Inc.

Brief for Representatives Don Edwards, Patricia Schroeder, Les Aucoin, Vic Fazio, Bill Green, and Constance A. Morella; Senators Alan Cranston, Bob Packwood, Howard Metzenbaum, John Chafee, Timothy E. Wirth, William S. Cohen, Brock Adams, and Barbara Mikulski; and Certain Other Members of the Congress of the United States

Brief of the States of New York, Connecticut, Delaware, Hawaii, Illinois, Iowa, Maine, Maryland, Massachusetts, Nevada, New Jersey, New Mexico, North Carolina, Rhode Island, Texas and Vermont and the District of Columbia, Joined by 13 Governors, 12 Lieutenant Governors and 995 State Legislators from Fifty States

Amicus Briefs Supporting Respondents and Defending Pennsylvania Law

Brief of Agudath Israel of America

Brief of "America 21," Family Values for the Twenty-First Century

Brief of the American Academy of Medical Ethics

Brief of the American Association of Prolife Obstetricians and Gynecologists (AAPLOG) and the American Association of Prolife Pediatricians (AAPLP)

Brief of Catholics United for Life, Orthodox Christians for Life, National Organization of Episcopalians for Life, Presbyterians Pro-Life, American Baptist Friends of Life, Baptists for Life, Lutherans for Life, Wels Lutherans for Life, United Church of Christ Friends for Life, Disciples for Life, Nazarenes for Life, Task Force of United Methodists on Abortion and Sexuality, Concerned Women for America, the American Center for Law and Justice, the Catholic League for Religious and Civil Rights, and the Christian Action Council

Brief of Certain American State Legislators

Brief of Feminists for Life of America, Professional Women's Network, Birthright, Inc., and Legal Action for Women

Brief for Focus on the Family, Family Research Council, the Lutheran Church–Missouri Synod, and American Family Association Law Center

Brief of Hon. Henry J. Hyde, Hon. Christopher H. Smith, Hon. Alan B. Mollohan, Hon. Harold L. Volkmer, Hon. Robert G. Smith and other United States Senators and Members of Congress

Brief of James J. Crook

Brief of the Knights of Columbus

Brief of Life Issues Institute

Brief of the National Legal Foundation

*Brief of National Right to Life, Inc.

Brief of Nineteen Arizona Legislators

Brief of the Rutherford Institute and the Rutherford Institutes of Alabama, Arizona, Arkansas, California, Colorado, Connecticut, Delaware, Florida, Georgia, Hawaii, Illinois, Kansas, Kentucky, Louisiana, Maryland, Michigan, Minnesota, Nebraska, New York, North Carolina, Ohio, Oklahoma, Oregon, Pennsylvania, South Carolina, Tennessee, Texas, Virginia, Washington, West Virginia and Wisconsin

Brief for the Southern Center for Law & Ethics

Brief for the State of Utah

Brief of Texas Black Americans for Life

*Brief for the United States

*Brief of the United States Catholic Conference, the Christian Life Commission, Southern Baptist Convention, and the National Association of Evangelicals

Brief of University Faculty for Life

Brief of William J. Guste, Louisiana Attorney General, et al.

Amicus Brief Supporting Neither Party

Brief by Legal Defense for Unborn Children

INDEX

INDEX OF CASES